Silesia and Central European Nationalisms

D1607896

Central European Studies

Charles W. Ingrao, senior editor

Gary B. Cohen, editor

Silesia and Central European Nationalisms

The Emergence of National and Ethnic Groups in Prussian Silesia and Austrian Silesia, 1848–1918

Tomasz Kamusella

Purdue University Press

West Lafayette, Indiana

ISBN 978-1-55753-371-5

Library of Congress Cataloging-in-Publication Data

Kamusella, Tomasz.
   Silesia and Central European nationalisms : the emergence of
national and ethnic groups in Silesia, 1848-1918 / Tomasz Kamusella.
      p. cm. -- (Central European studies)
   Includes bibliographical references and index.
   ISBN-13: 978-1-55753-371-5 (alk. paper)
   1. Nationalism--Silesia. 2. Nationalism--Europe, Central.
3. Silesians--Ethnic identity. 4. Language policy--Silesia. 5. Silesia
--Politics and government. 6. Europe, Central--Politics and government.   I. Title.
DK4600.S4275K36 2006
320.5409438'509034--dc22

                              2006018368

*To my Parents
and
Parents-in-law*

Rodzicom
i
Teściom

Contents

Acknowledgments

The inception of this book dates back to my master's thesis on the dynamics of ethnic cleansing in Silesia during the nineteenth and twentieth centuries, which I wrote in 1994 under the supervision of Ferdinand Kinsky at the Central European University in Prague. With his and Ernest Gellner's support I received a grant from the Research Support Scheme of Prague, which allowed me to develop this thesis into a full-fledged research work between 1995 and 1997. During the intervening years I made part of the work into a Ph.D. dissertation under the supervision of Janusz Sawczuk at Opole University. Finally, in 2001, I defended it in the Institute of Western Affairs in Poznań, with the support of the Institute's director, Maria Wolff-Powęska, and the assistance of Wojciech Józef Burszta, Krzysztof Frysztacki, and Andrzej Sakson.

I was gratified when Charles Ingrao encouraged me to submit the manuscript to the Purdue University Press. Upon receiving detailed replies from two anonymous reviewers he urged me to overhaul the text in line with their suggestions, which I undertook during my 2003/2004 sojourn in Washington, D.C., where I was a fellow at the John W. Kluge Center, Library of Congress. At this stage Kurt Bassuener, Karen Oslund, and John Cox generously read and commented on parts of this work.

I am also grateful to William Cremer and Mark Vander Hart, who read through and commented on the whole of the manuscript. Daniel Pinkerton provided editorial assistance. Parts of the book were also corrected by Anthony Dutton, William Harwood, Lori Ann Lahlum, and Hunt Tooley. At the Purdue University Press Margaret Hunt saw the book through all the production stages.

I thank all the persons without whose help the publication of this book would not have been possible, as well as my wife Beata and daughter Ania for their patience and understanding. Obviously, I alone remain responsible for all infelicities and errors.

Maps

**Ethno-linguistic map of Upper Silesia,
Austrian Silesia and northern Moravia 1850-1918**

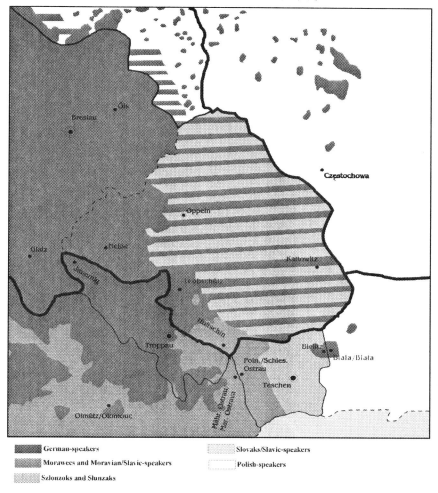

German-speakers

Morawecs and Moravian/Slavic-speakers

Szlouzoks and Slunzaks

Slovaks/Slavic-speakers

Polish-speakers

Prussian Silesia 1815/1825-1918 and Austrian

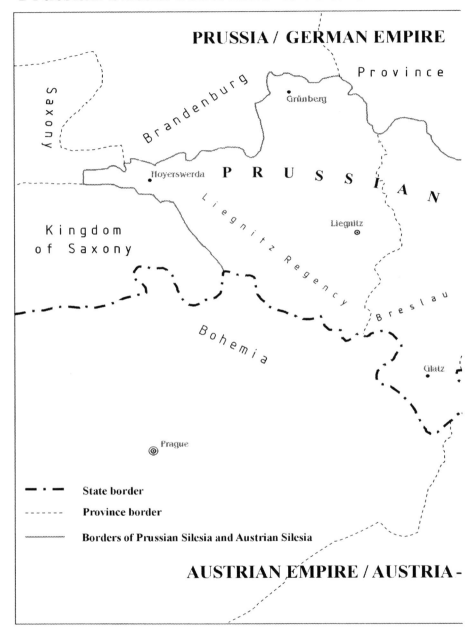

PRUSSIA / GERMAN EMPIRE

Province

Saxony

Brandenburg

Grünberg

Hoyerswerda

P R U S S I A N

Liegnitz

Liegnitz Regency

Kingdom
of Saxony

Breslau

Bohemia

Glatz

Prague

— · —   State border

- - - - - -   Province border

~~~~~~~~   Borders of Prussian Silesia and Austrian Silesia

AUSTRIAN EMPIRE / AUSTRIA-

Silesia 1849-1918

of Posen

Gubernia of Kalisz

RUSSIAN EMPIRE

Gubernia of Piotrków

Breslau

• Öls

SILESIA

Regency

Częstochowa

Gubernia of Kielce

Oppeln

Oppeln Regency

• Neiße

Kattowitz

Jauernig

AUSTRIAN

Leobschütz

• Ratibor

Cracow

Galicia

Hultschin

Troppau

Bielitz

Poln./Schles.

• Ostrau

Biała/Biała

Moravia

Teschen

• Olmütz/Olomouc

Mähr. Ostrau/
Mor. Ostrava

SILESIA

HUNGARY

Kingdom of Hungary

Roman Catholic Breslau Diocese 1821-1922

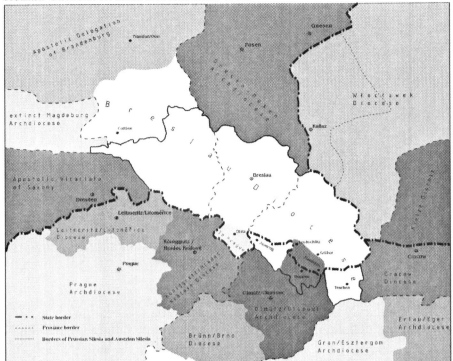

Foreword

Tomasz Kamusella is certainly not the only non-native English speaker to have published a book in the Central European Studies book series. But he is surely the first among them who could not have published it in his native language. This volume represents, after all, an unusual case of a central European scholar who has dared to deviate from the orthodox narrative that unites citizens of his nation-state at the expense of dividing them from their neighbors. Adding insult to injury, he has dared to research thoroughly the equally contentious scholarship of Czech and German partisans in the three-way struggle for control of Silesia's history and destiny. His account offers a fresh alternative to these national narratives in its representation of the cultural development of the historic duchy's Slavic speakers. It is also a far more sophisticated and nuanced account of a single, yet polyglot society that nurtured a common regional *mentalité* amid multiple identities defined by class, confession, geography and other environmental influences. With this book, it will no longer be possible to identify Silesians merely as Czechs, Germans, and Poles, but as a single society, many of whose citizens considered themselves to be members of two of more of the duchy's multiple national and heretofore largely anonymous ethnic groups.

Of course, the existence of mutually exclusive, proprietary narratives is hardly unique to Silesia. Rather, it is an all-too-common feature across central Europe as the intelligentsia of each successor state has sought to justify its existence by systematically eradicating all evidence of a harmonious, multicultural past. This reader certainly appreciates the parallels with the half-dozen newly independent states of the western Balkans, each of which articulates its own account of the multiethnic Habsburg, Ottoman and Yugoslav worlds from which it evolved. Over the past decade, the unwillingness to acknowledge a common history has even bred the affectation of distinctive languages for Bosnia, Croatia, Serbia, and, most recently, Montenegro. Today it is impossible for a publisher to market a single edition of a classic work like A.J.P. Taylor's *Habsburg Monarchy, 1809–1918* without carefully reconstructing the prose and changing the imprint to persuade prospective buyers that it has been published in their national language.

Hence the multiple justifications for publishing this volume in English, which represents not only the broadest possible platform for scholars and educated laypeople, but a neutral one that does not impugn the impartiality of either the author or his readers. Whatever the idiom, this volume will reinforce the view of most contemporary western scholars who reject the notion of primordial national markers, while stressing the notion famously posited by Benedict Anderson of "imagined communities" that were fashioned by generations of supposedly progressive cultural elites. At the same time, however, it will broaden the discussion in several ways. Whereas western scholars have long lamented the fate of national minorities within newly created or reconfigured nation-states, we have heretofore paid scant attention to the parallel experience of ethnic minorities like the Szlonzoks, Slunzaks and Morawecs examined here. Not only does this study apply Miroslav Hroch's incremental model of national development to Silesia's ethnic Slavs, but it also underscores their greater vulnerability at the hands of Austro-German census takers and postwar peacemakers, whose preconceived notions of language and identity ignored the very existence of discrete ethnic groups. Indeed, unlike the national minorities of the interwar period, Silesia's Slavic-speaking ethnic groups could not even appeal or emigrate to national homelands. Despite their enforced anonymity, there remain perhaps a quarter million people in contemporary Poland who identify themselves—and are belatedly recognized in this book—as Szlonzoks and Slunzaks. As such they constitute the largest remaining minority in what was once a multiethnic space that overwhelmed the finite classifications of today's ethnographers.

—*Charles Ingrao*

Introduction

The rhetoric of nationalism, being mainly emotive, does not mix well with scholarship and its paramount goal of objectivity. However, the practice of rational scholarship began to flourish on a massive scale in the nineteenth century, when the ideology of nationalism blossomed. Not surprisingly, through their research, many scholars contributed to the spread and development of nationalism (cf. Deletant, 1988). Successful nation-states with sufficient economic resources eagerly supported the scholars in this task. This was because academics and their expertise proved indispensable for the technological and economic advancement of their nation-states, the development of popular education (in recently standardized national languages) and the creation of social services. Without attaining these modernizing goals, it would have been impossible to achieve social cohesion, economic robustness and military strength—the very preconditions for the successful process of nation- and nation-state-building.

This bond between nationalism and scholarship continued unabated until the mid-twentieth century (Miles, 1989: 42–50). For instance, in the nineteenth century biology was employed to support racist theories, which politicians utilized in the processes of nation- and nation-state-building. They presupposed the innate "inferiority" and "uncivilizedness" of some groups and starkly contrasted them with the allegedly superior qualities of their own so as to justify their group's nation- and nation-state-building efforts, while denying the same right to the former (cf. Dmowski, 1996: 92). At the beginning of the twentieth century, this tendency led to the rise of "racial science" (*Rassenkunde*) and eugenics, the tenets of which were applied to populations in order to improve the "health" and "strength" of nations[1] (Quine, 1996). Such instruments were most thoroughly applied in the Third Reich, where racial science became one of the most popular and ideologically correct "sciences" (cf. Petry, 1989: 100–101).

In Adolf Hitler's Germany, science became strongly ennationalized.[2] For instance, Berlin denigrated Albert Einstein's theories as "Jewish physics." But the United States' "Jewish" A-bomb project was successful, unlike the Reich's, and the bombs dropped on Hiroshima and Nagasaki brought about the unconditional capitulation of Germany's Asian ally, Japan. Unfortunately, it has remained a popular usage to speak of "national (for instance, Polish, German, French) science." This popular label denotes the collectivity of scholars and their research in a given nation-state. Even after 1945, some continued to believe in the national or ideological specificity of science, as clearly exemplified by the rise of "communist biology," which Trofim Denisovich Lysenko (1898–1976) developed and Joseph Stalin institutionalized as a part of Soviet scientific orthodoxy.

On the other hand, some eugenic practices, such as sterilization of the mentally ill and minorities, survived in a few western and central European states until the 1980s (as in Sweden and Czechoslovakia). With the principles of racial science politicians "scientifically" justified racial segregation in the United States into the 1960s and in South Africa until the 1990s.

Today the idea of any causal connection between ethnicity and science has been thoroughly discredited. However, the link of nationalism with the humanities and arts forged during the age of Romanticism continues in a more or less conscious manner to this day. The coterminousness of culture and state remains *the* basis for construction and maintenance of the ethnic nation-state—the very model of this nation-state in central Europe (Gellner, 1983: 1).

The author realizes that attaining absolute objectivity is impossible, because the very "stuff" whereby humans think—language—is based on relative metaphors specific to various cultures. One perceives the world through the lens of one's culture, and only via this medium decides for himself and his group what is "real," "true," "unreal" and "untrue" (Lakoff, 1980: 156–225; Whorf, 1956: 252). Despite this epistemological hurdle, the quest for objectivity should continue. That is why the author decided to avoid using the pronoun "I" so as not to fall into the trap of believing in his convictions rather than facts.

Pronouns, the very deictic element of language, do not convey any inherent meaning but serve as the hinge between the speaker, the hearer and reality. Without them communication would be impossible. Although a crucial constituent of language, deixes are, on the other hand, empty shells and very susceptible to manipulation. In the twentieth century nationalism became the only truly global ideology that underlies and justifies the division of the world's whole land surface (with the tentative exception of the Antarctic) among the nation-states. This ideology forms the very foundation of the political organization of the globe (cf. Kohn, 1962). And at the level of verbal and written communication, proponents of nationalism have most effectively used deixes to achieve this ideology's goals (cf. Kamusella, 2003).

The pronoun "we" is used to build cohesive and clearly delineated human groups through its main function of simultaneous exclusion and inclusion. Understandably, nationalists have employed this function to build nations and have made the pronoun into one of the main metaphors of nation construed as an extended family, *Gemeinschaft*. Hence, should the author succumb to using the pronoun "we" in this work, he would quite imperceptibly suggest to the reader that, presumably belonging to the same nation as the author, he should share the author's views and opinions. And such an invitation to the false community of common opinion ought to be precluded.

Therefore the author hopes that despite all the difficulties that the avoidance of the pronouns "I" and "we" creates in the flow of the narrative, the reader will accept (if not appreciate) the unusual usages put to work in this book.

Another aspect which requires explanation is why the author wrote this work in English though it is not his mother tongue. Silesia has been contested by German, Czech and Polish nationalisms since the second half of the nineteenth century.[3] These nationalisms, like any other in central and eastern Europe, are steeped in language and culture as their basis, unlike those in western Europe and the Americas, where civic values formed the foundation of the nation- and nation-state-building endeavors. The German language, along with officially espoused Protestantism, underlay the official national ideology of the German Empire. The Czech language was standardized and championed so that it was granted an official status in Bohemia during the 1880s, in response to Vienna's *Großdeutsch* (Greater German)[4] nationalism. In the years 1795–1918, when the Polish state did not exist, the Polish language functioned as a kind of cultural nation-state in lieu of a political one. The Poles also managed to obtain for their mother tongue the status of the leading official language in the Austrian Crownland of Galicia (1869). As Jeremy King (2002: 58, 134, 164) points out, by the turn of the twentieth century the possibility of other than language-based national identification had been banned.

This typically central European grounding of nationalism in language led to its extensive use in ennationalizing endeavors directed at Silesia. This process in the region's various areas, controlled by Poland, Czechoslovakia and Germany, was carried out mainly with the help of language and language policies. Monolingualism and the corresponding monistic national identity (as opposed to multilingualism and the composite multiple identity) were the aims, the achievement of which was to ensure coterminousness of political and ethnic borders. Without that the striven-for nation-states would remain imperfect. But such a success was not in the cards for any of these three nation-states and their nationalisms. The three states' mutually opposed ennationalizing efforts, to varying degrees, neutralized one another in Silesia.

Ethnic nationalisms involved in the strife over the national ownership of Silesia have traditionally harnessed to their ends the humanities, arts, social sciences, and even sciences. Although this tendency came to an end in West Germany during the 1980s, and in Poland and Czecho(slovakia) after 1989, most of the available literature on Silesia was written in a more or less nationalist manner. Putting historiography to the task of "proving" and "justifying" Polish, German or Czech ownership of this land even spawned specific national vocabularies and concepts connected to Silesia and its history, whole customized terminologies geared to specific national claims. This is most obvious in the variegated territorial base employed for conducting research on Silesia. German scholars usually limit themselves to Prussian and West Austrian Silesia because East Austrian Silesia was too Slavic to credibly claim it for Germandom. Polish scholars focus on Prussian Silesia east of the Oder-Neisse line and on East Austrian Silesia, because the westernmost tip of the former Prussian province lying west of the Oder-Neisse line remained in Germany after 1945. As such it was not accessible to Polishdom, limited in this respect by the postwar Polish-German border. Regarding Austrian Silesia, even prior to 1918 Polish nationalists accepted that its western half constituted an integral part of emerging Czechdom. Czech scholars concentrate their research on the territory of former Austrian Silesia and the southernmost reaches of Lower and Upper Silesia, which they can claim as Czech from the ethnic and historical point of view (cf. Gawrecki 2003; Popiołek 1972).

The author chose to write this study in English so as to avoid unreflective espousal of the respective tunnel visions of these three national historiographies and of their Silesianist terminologies. In this manner, having to explicate in English the specific Polish, German and Czech concepts connected to Silesia, he stood a better chance of noting and sifting away various nationalist biases and presuppositions that escape easy notice when one writes in one's mother tongue. On the other hand, the English language, not having been involved in the nationalist strife over Silesia (unlike German, Polish or Czech), provided the author with a potentially more objective instrument of expression and research.

What is more, when the Iron Curtain divided Europe and the world, there was little exchange between intellectuals living on the opposite sides of this barrier. Scholars doing research on Silesia were often unfamiliar with Silesianist literature from neighboring states. The monolingual policies of ennationalization made this phenomenon acute. Many (if not most) scholars employed at Polish and Czech(oslovak) specialist institutes devoted to Silesian studies did not speak or read German. Although Czech and Polish are largely mutually intelligible, Polish scholars hardly ever made an effort to read in Czech. Czech Silesianists more eagerly acquainted themselves with Polish works on Silesia. No meaningful research on the *deutsche Ostgebiete*[5] was allowed in East Germany. Many West German scholars were expellees from postwar Poland or Czechoslovakia, with a good working command of Polish and Czech. This allowed German scholars of this background to use Polish and Czech literature on Silesia. But because many of them were connected to the expellee organizations, they often focused on criticizing Polish and Czech researchers' studies devoted to Silesia and on "proving" Germany's inherent "right" to this region. Also, Polish and Czech researchers participated in similar activities aimed against the West German "revanchists."

The author hopes this study has not fallen prey to solipsistic forgetfulness of any of the three national historiographies entrenched in their respective national languages and myths. He trusts that having written it in English, this work will be of more immediate access to Polish, German and Czech scholars (at least to those of younger generations) so as to foster dialogue and scholarly exchange in the field of Silesian studies. Moreover, the language of this work should make this study available to scholars worldwide, especially those involved in the study of nationalism and ethnicity. A broader choice of variegated case studies is needed so as not to remain, in their theoretical generalizations, confined to western Europe only.

In 1999 the Czech Republic, Hungary and Poland joined NATO and, five years later, the European Union (EU). Silesia's history and ethnolinguistic issues will now have to be taken into consideration when developing EU policies and laws. The author trusts that this study will contribute to a better understanding of this region as well as of its inhabitants' past and current needs.

Beyond this utilitarian value, the work analyzes the rise of nationalism in Silesia and its influence in shaping the national and ethnic groups living in the territory. Contrary to the popular nationalist belief that nationality is something "natural," "primordial" and "unchanging," this study illustrates that the first inklings of nationalism reached Silesia with the Napoleonic onslaught in 1806 (Schulze, 1998: 101–110). Napoleonic France's political and military success, achieved thanks to this ideology, prompted emulation of this new French model of the nation-state in Prussia. Simultaneously, the abrupt intrusion of the French Other gave inhabitants of the various states and statelets emerging from the breakup of the Holy Roman Empire a feeling of difference. This was the first step they took toward defining themselves as "Germans." This forging of German nationalism accelerated with the War of Liberation (1813–1815), which commenced in Breslau (Wrocław).[6]

The beginning of German nationalism is unambiguously associated with Silesia. But after the Congress of Vienna, when the neo-absolutist order was established in Prussia and the Austrian Empire, the center of this emergent nationalism shifted to the German-speaking states on the western flank of the erstwhile Holy Roman Empire. In this area, directly influenced by France, these more democratic and liberal governments were more eager to espouse and implement new political ideas.

Polish nationalism in its ethnic form (which continues to this day) emerged after the failed uprisings of 1830–1831 and 1863–1864. The repeated defeats at the hands of the Russian imperial armies indicated that even the relatively numerous (by European standards) Polish *natio*[7] and intelligentsia were not able to re-establish erstwhile Poland-Lithuania as a Polish nation-state of their own. This realization necessitated broadening the concept of the Polish nation so as to embrace the Polish-speaking *populus*.[8] Czech and German nationalisms eventually entered the mainstream of politics during the revolutionary year of 1848.

Significantly, none of these three nationalisms developed a center in Silesia. The geographically most proximate centers of German nationalism sprang up in Berlin and Vienna, of Polish nationalism in Cracow and Posen (Poznań), and of Czech nationalism in Prague. But after the founding of the university in Breslau in 1811, German nationalist ideas began to spread among the *Bildungsbürgertum*[9] in Lower Silesia. Following the founding of the German Empire in 1871, Lower Silesia fit into the new political organism very well. The fact that, like the empire's heartlands, the region was almost homogenously Protestant and German-speaking facilitated Lower Silesia's integration into this new nation-state. On the other hand, multilingual and overwhelmingly Catholic Upper Silesia still had to be ennationalized into the *Kleindeutsch*[10] pattern of nationhood.

In the second half of the nineteenth century, German nationalism clashed repeatedly with its Polish counterpart in the Province of Posen. At the same time, Polish nationalists operated relatively free of obstruction in Galicia after the introduction of autonomy in 1867, and Czech nationalism grew steadily in Bohemia, radiating its influence into Moravia and Austrian Silesia. Initially, the development of nationalisms was stalled in the Austrian Empire because Vienna rightly perceived the national movements as a possible threat to the Danubian monarchy. However, the Austrian emperor had to offer some concessions to this novel political-social-economic force in the wake of the defeat at the hands of Prussia in 1866. The Seven Weeks' War destroyed the German Confederation, buried the alternative of building a *Großdeutsch* nation-state, and forced Vienna to acknowledge Hungarian nationalism by overhauling, in 1867, the empire into the Dual Monarchy of the Austrian Empire and the Kingdom of Hungary. The subsequent rise of various nationalisms in Austria-Hungary caused their German counterpart to emerge strongly in the 1890s. By then the days of traditional loyalty to the emperor, the dynasty and the empire (*Kaisertreue*) were numbered.

One of the main theses of this study maintains that nationalisms did not develop in Silesia due chiefly to the region's peripheral location in Prussia and the Austrian Empire. Nationalisms started infiltrating Silesia during the last three decades of the nineteenth century and, subsequently, precipitated the nationalist tensions at the beginning of the twentieth century. These centrifugal forces led to the carving-up of Silesia, first in line with the national principle after the Great War and after 1945 on the basis of the communist-nationalist logic.

Central European nationalisms are deeply steeped in ethnicity, because in this part of the continent nationalists accepted language as the indicator of nationality (Kamusella, 2001; Kamusella, 2004). Consequently, this work focuses on Upper Silesia and East Austrian Silesia, with their overwhelmingly West Slavic-speaking populaces. West Austrian Silesia and the Breslau Regency fall into this analysis's purview due to their sizeable shares of West Slavic-speakers. But the Liegnitz (Legnica) Regency is hardly mentioned, though it contained quite a few Slavic-speaking Sorbs. However, the Sorbian ethnic group historically split among Silesia, Brandenburg and Saxony (without too much respect for their homeland of Lusatia), and the author decided not to include their problematic in this study. Dealing with Sorbian matters would require a closer look at Brandenburg and Saxony, thereby weakening the focus on Silesia.

This study does not devote much space to Silesia's Jews and Roma. On the latter little is known, as prior to the 1990s they were popularly considered to be "people without history" and paragons of "uncivilizedness" who were to be assimilated and forgotten rather than constituting a legitimate subject of research. The Jews of Silesia, like those in other German-speaking states, were emancipated by the mid-nineteenth century. Under the influence of the Haskalah or Jewish Enlightenment (unlike the Jews living on the territory of former Poland-Lithuania), they became an almost indistinguishable part of the German nation, unless one took the effort to probe into their genealogies or into religious practices. This, however, happened on a large scale only after 1933, though the revival of *Großdeutsch* nationalism and the emergence of Pan-Germanism hinged on rabid anti-Semitism already in the 1890s.

Another important thesis of this work points out that before the rise and spread of the monistic national identities in Silesia, the region's inhabitants also possessed their specific identities, though clearly *non-national* ones. The national historiographies lead one to believe that since the dawn of history the population of Silesia has consisted of clear-cut Germans, Poles and Czechs. And even if the inhabitants did not explicitly express their national identities, they were indubitable Czechs, Poles and Germans, though perhaps unaware of their nationality. The role of nationalisms was to "reawaken" their "dormant nationalities." The Czech, German and Polish national historiographies have devoted most space to the process of presupposed "national awakening," while conveniently gliding over the "nationally dormant" section of the Silesian population with the gnomic and supposedly self-explicating labels of the "nationally labile" and the *"Zwischenschicht"* or *"warstwa pośrednia"* (in-between people). Some scholars also spoke of people with "uncrystallized national identity."

The last phrase is quite illustrative of this mindset. Nationality is something "crystalline," aspired to, the "pinnacle of civilizedness," which one can reach only having done one's best to leave the "mud" of everything that is *not* national. But looking closely at the historical evidence, it is clear that before arrival of nationalisms in Silesia, the region's population enjoyed their own specific identities, as was the case elsewhere before nationalism came to the fore. The most significant constituents of one's identity before ennationalization were religion, loyalty to the monarch and the bond with one's village or parish, which usually was one's place of birth and life-long residence. Modernization added to these loci of identification also the distinctive region and the state where one lived. More often than not these constituents were of equal value and together composed one's multiple identity, which the process of ennationalization sought to replace with the monistic national identity, ideally consisting of one element only—a specific nationality. Other identificational constituents were to be obliterated or subjugated to the national identity.

The process of ennationalization into Germandom in Lower Silesia was largely swift and painless, as the populace was overwhelmingly Protestant and German-speaking. As a consequence, turning these people into Germans did not demand of them too much sacrifice. This was made easier because *Kleindeutsch* nationalists did not oppose cherishing one's regional identity and civic Prussian identity. They found it congruent with Germandom until Hitler, who set out on the course of forced centralization and homogenization (*Gleichschaltung*) of the German nation-state.

The situation differed in Upper Silesia, where *Kleindeutsch* nationalism threatened the traditional way of life, instead of incorporating it, as in Lower Silesia. The Catholic and Slavic-speaking character of Upper Silesia was too different to be easily incorporated into *Kleindeutsch* Germandom. Berlin's ennationalizing efforts, together with modernization and the growth of regional identification, caused most of Upper Silesia's Slavic-speaking Catholics to develop their specific *Szlonzokian*[11] ethnic identity. Similar though less intensive processes, coupled with the infiltration of Polish and Czech nationalisms, brought about the emergence of the *Slunzakian*[12] ethnic group in East Austrian Silesia, and of the *Morawec*[13] ethnic group in the northern reaches of the Olmütz (Olomouc) Archdiocese. The Morawecs' homeland contained the Moravian salient between East and West Austrian Silesia, the eastern part of West Austrian Silesia, and the southern sliver of Upper Silesia.

These ethnic identities, besides remaining multiple, also let the member of an ethnic group incorporate a national identity as one of the multiple identity's constituents. In this way one could preserve one's old way of life without running afoul of the authorities bent on pursuing their pet ennationalizing programs.

Taking into consideration the Szlonzokian ethnic group makes it possible to account for the following:

— why more Upper Silesians supported the project of establishing an independent Upper Silesian nation-state than fought on either the Polish or German side in the Silesian Uprisings (or Rebellions, as German commentators called them) that preceded the division of Upper Silesia between Germany and Poland (1922);

— why the population of Germany's interwar Oppeln (Opole) Regency, considered homogenously Polish by Warsaw, could dissolve into Germandom by the 1930s;

— why a similar process repeated itself at an even quicker pace during World War II in the territory of Poland's erstwhile Silesian Voivodeship, incorporated into Germany's wartime Province of Upper Silesia;

— why, after 1945, the Upper Silesian population retained as Poles by Warsaw chose to emigrate to West Germany and to became Germans. Or, if they remained in postwar Poland, they mostly did *not* become Poles;

— why Szlonzokian nationalism tended to emerge periodically in the past, and, most significantly, in the second half of the 1990s.

A similar set of questions cannot be satisfactorily answered in the case of Austrian Silesia and the south of Upper Silesia without remembering the existence of the Slunzaks and the Morawecs. One also has to bear in mind that in the course of the nationalist struggle that commenced in Silesia at the turn of the nineteenth and twentieth centuries, the ennationalizing efforts of German, Czech and Polish nationalisms tended to cancel one another out. This process became more visible after 1918, when frequent border changes shuffled and reshuffled people from one nation-state to another, thereby convincing them to remain entrenched in their ethnic groups. Such identification, besides allowing them to go on with their traditional way of life, also allowed them to express each of the required national identities without too much of a strain.

This study describes and analyzes the process of the emergence of the national and ethnic groups in Silesia. Due to its temporal framework, this work falls short of applying these findings to the interpretation of the Silesian past after 1918. This task remains to be carried out by other researchers (Kamusella, 2001a).

The author chose to divide the subject matter of this book into two parts, one devoted to the period of 1848–1871 and the other to the years 1871–1918. The former, bounded by the revolutionary year of 1848 and the founding of the German Empire, focuses on the rise of nationalisms. The other part, delimited by the foundation of the same *Kleindeutsch* nation-state and the end of the Great War, analyzes the incorporation of the tenets of nationalism into Silesia's political, social and economic life. Obviously central Europe provides the broad cultural and geographic context because similar processes took place not only in Silesia but in other central European regions. Like Silesia, many of them were subjected to thorough ennationalization after 1918 when the national principle was elevated to the basis of political organization in Europe. During World War II not much changed when Hitler strove to actualize the dream of the Pan-German empire in central Europe. In the wake of the 1945 defeat of the Third Reich, Stalin established his own Pan-Slavic empire in the form of the Soviet bloc. The territorially overhauled and ethnically cleansed nation-states, isolated from one another and subjected to Moscow's overlordship, were tightly controlled under the imperial principle of *divida et impera*.

In part 1, chapter 1 presents a general overview of nationalism in central Europe together with an outline of the 1848 events. Chapters 2 and 3 concentrate on the rise of German and Polish nationalist ideas and the place of Silesia in the plans and actions of the corresponding national movements. Chapter 4 analyzes the way in which the Polish, Czech and German nationalisms infiltrated Austrian Silesia, while chapter 5 gives an overview devoted to the emergence of the national and ethnic groups in Silesia following the model developed by the Czech scholar Miroslav Hroch (1985).

Part 2 opens with an outline of nationalism in central Europe and Silesia, presented in chapter 6. The narrative of the consolidation of the German Empire (that is, the German nation-state) continues in chapter 7. Chapter 8 analyzes the gradual incursion of Polish nationalism into Prussian Silesia, and the growing nationalist tension in Austrian Silesia is presented in chapter 9. Chapter 10 traces the development of the national question in Silesia during the years of World War I, and chapter 11 closes part 2 with a reflection on the ethnic and national groups in Silesia.

Chapters 5 and 11, where the narrative of the work's two parts is summarized, had to include some analytical framework that would allow for presenting the findings in a synthetic manner. The author believes that in order to clothe the spread of various nationalisms in Silesia in an analytic garment, it is useful to accept the model that Miroslav Hroch worked out on the basis of his meticulous research into development of nationalisms in central Europe. He distinguishes the following phases in the growth of national movements:

> Phase A: a small group of intellectuals devoted themselves to scholarly enquiry into the language, history, traditional culture and so on, of the . . . ethnic group;

> Phase B: a new range of activists emerged, who now began to agitate for their compatriots to join the project of creating a fully-fledged nation;

> Phase C: where a majority of the population responded to the patriotic call and formed a mass movement; during Phase C, the full social structure of the nation would come into being, and political differentiation begin to emerge. (Hroch, 1994: 5)

Another eminent scholar of nationalism, the British historian E. J. Hobsbawm, commenting on the last phase, adds that the transition from phase B to phase C occurs more often after the creation of a nation-state than before (Hobsbawm, 1990: 12).

Considering theoretical matters, it is necessary to remark that the work employs Ernest Gellner's seminal definition of nationalism, which says that this ideology is "primarily a political principle, which holds that the political and the national unit should be congruent" (1983: 1). From this perspective the term "national movement" denotes a group of people who work out and espouse the idea of a given nation. The group's intention is to popularize the national idea among the prospective members of the nation so that they indeed decide to become members of it. As is clear from Hroch's scheme, the nation comes into being when the membership of the national movement largely overlaps with the demographic extent of the postulated nation.

The vision of nation as employed here is a modern concept that denotes a modern sociopolitical phenomenon. According to the U.S. scholar Liah Greenfeld, England was the first nation to emerge by pure chance and coincidence, as early as the sixteenth century (1992). However, only the American and French Revolutions provided the models of nation-states, which initially were emulated in western Europe, and in the Caribbean and in Latin America during the first half of the nineteenth century. So despite the legitimizing claims to antiquity often voiced by national histories and leaders, the overwhelming majority of the extant nation-states are not older than two centuries (Anderson, 1994). In one of the simplest typologies of nationalism, ethnic nations are opposed to civic ones. It is not a clear-cut binary opposition, however, as all nation-states are based upon a bureaucratic-ideological framework that contains varying degrees of ethnicity.

The difference lies in which element is dominant in such a mixture. In civic nation-states citizenship equals nationality understood, as one's membership in a nation. The conferring of citizenship on a person renders his original ethnic background irrelevant. In consequence, the citizenry of a nation-state equals the nation, and no civic nation can exist prior to the founding of its state. In this case the state precedes and forges its own nation.

This dynamics of sociopolitical ties varies in ethnic nation-states. By its very nature the ethnic nation comes into being earlier than its nation-state. Actually an ethnic nation suffers the acute condition of statelessness before gaining a nation-state of its own. Nationality equals a specific ethnicity, that is, an appropriate mixture of cultural elements (language, way of life, religion, etc.) that one has to possess and display as a badge that entitles him to commonality with a nation. When the ethnic nation wins its nation-state, this nationality gives one the right to citizenship. Citizenship is secondary to ethnically construed nationality (Brubaker, 1992).

Because of the nature of human relations, groups of "ethnically foreign" persons have always lived in the territories of nation-states. It is easy to homogenize a population in civic nation-states, where citizenship is the national common denominator. Changing one passport for another requires some paperwork and meeting several legal requirements. This is not so in the case of ethnic nationality. Renouncing one so as to acquire another requires an enormous effort on the part of an individual. First he has to unlearn and forget a language or a religion and the whole socially sensitive paradigm of behavior. Then he must internalize parallel ethnic markers that would clearly announce that he is an accepted member of another ethnic nation. This is a difficult feat, more often than not achieved only by children and grandchildren of a person who set out on the way to change his ethnic nationality.

Finding oneself between two different nationalities makes one into a person who, because of his half-membership in both the ethnic nations, does not rightfully belong to either of them. At the level of nation-states such people are marginalized and treated as second-class citizens. Even worse, when living in the territory not belonging to "their" nation-states, they do not wish to assimilate and choose the status of a national minority. Going against the ideal of ethnic purity of the nation-state is the worst crime in the eyes of ethnic nationalists. As the twentieth century amply showed, approaches to national minorities range from cold-shouldered tolerance to expulsion and outright extermination (Altermatt, 1996).

Significantly, stateless national movements and nations, by definition, must be overwhelmingly ethnic, as there are no states that would clothe their national aspirations in the garb of civic values. "De-ethnicization" or "civicization" of an ethnic nation-state may take place only after it has gained its own nation-state. Unlike in western Europe, in central Europe not a single prenational state managed to transform itself into a nation-state. But the influence of national ideas was felt in this part of Europe immediately after the creation of the French nation-state. Imperial France's invading armies and occupation administrations started spreading the gospel of nationalism already at the very beginning of the nineteenth century.

With the absence of polities that would be in position to oppose the French onslaught as well as eager to reinvent themselves as nation-states, the answer to this challenge was ethnic nationalism. An ideology developed on the basis of Herderian thought and initially was applied to the construction of German nationalism (cf. Buse, 1985: 35–58; Kedourie, 1960). The founding of the German nation-states in the form of the German Empire required the amalgamation of a multitude of northern German-speaking polities as well as the destruction of the German Confederation. This process was largely completed in 1918, when new nation-states of Czechoslovakia and Poland, among others, emerged after the dissolution of Austria-Hungary and the severe territorial losses suffered in this region by the German and Russian empires. Unlike in western Europe, where the prenational states reinvented themselves as nation-states, the construction of the new national order in central Europe required the thorough destruction or overhauling of the prenational polities (Chlebowczyk, 1980 and 1983; Gellner, 1997).

From this outline it is clear that Hroch's model describes the emergence of ethnic nations. This scheme is especially useful for analyzing nation-building in central Europe, where all the existing nations and nation-states emerged in this manner. This work's author believes that this model may also be used to probe the rise of ethnic nations elsewhere in the world, but there is a problem with such a proposition. Namely, ethnic nation-states are concentrated mainly in central and eastern Europe as well as in some parts of Asia. Elsewhere in the world the civic model of nation-state predominates. However, irrespective of a geographical area, wherever a stateless national movement comes into being, it has to confront some nation-state, because the whole globe has been divided among the nation-states since the break-up of the Soviet Union. Such a stateless nation-in-making has no choice but to discredit the legitimacy of an established nation-state on ethnic grounds.

Thus, ethnic national movements are prevalent globally regardless of the model of nation-states that dominates there (Minahan, 2002). It seems that Hroch's model can be fruitfully applied to the analysis of successful and failed creations of all these postulated ethnic nations, the majority of which will never pop up on the political map of the world that schoolchildren glance at in their geography and history classrooms.

In this work, Hroch's explanatory framework is applied in an analysis of the unsuccessful emergence of the Szlonzoks, the Slunzaks and the Morawecs as ethnic nations. The Slunzaks and the Morawecs disappeared from the political and social arena of central Europe, having assimilated into the Polish, Czech and German nations. The Szlonzoks persist to this day, and as of 1997, their national movement is gaining strength. In the 2002 Polish census they emerged as Poland's largest *national* minority. This emphasizes all the more the topical significance of this study, to which Polish and European Union decision-makers may refer so as to better comprehend the social, historical and political roots of Szlonzokian nationalism in the broader context of central Europe.

This book is devoted to the ethnic groups of the Szlonzoks, the Slunzaks and the Morawecs, as well as to the three local national groups. The last term denotes the Silesian branches of the Czech, German and Polish national movements and nations. Hroch's model allows such an application as outlined in his own examples of the Czech national movement in the Austrian Crownland of Bohemia, and of the Danish national movement in Germany's Schleswig (1985: 44–61, 117–124). The intended treatment of the Silesian sections of the Czech, German and Polish national movements or nations as "national groups" permits singling them out so as to compare these national groups with the smaller and more localized ethnic and sometimes national movements of the Szlonzoks, the Slunzaks and the Morawecs.

The main goal of this work is to reintroduce into scholarly discourse these human groups, which national historiographies have traditionally disregarded and written out of history. This happened because proponents of successful ethnic nationalisms portrayed ethnic groups and unsuccessful ethnic national movements as mere "ethnographic mass" that, with time, should assimilate with the ethnic nations that secured their own nation-states. But studied neglect and marginalization does not always lead to disappearance through assimilation. Sometimes such policies backfire, strengthening, revitalizing or even helping reinvent ethnic identities that were long thought dead. Thanks to such a process the nations of Spain's Galicians, the United Kingdom's Welsh and ex-Yugoslavia's Bosnians appeared on the political map of Europe.

◆   ◆   ◆

Before launching into the narrative it is necessary to briefly sketch the political, administrative and ecclesiastical divisions of Silesia. These divisions form the indispensable canvas on which the picture is painted of the aforementioned national and ethnic groups and their growth.

Prussian Silesia came into being between 1740 and 1742, when Frederick the Great wrestled the land away from Maria Theresa. It existed until 1923, with Breslau as its capital. In that year the region was divided into the provinces of Lower and Upper Silesia.

The southernmost fragment of Upper Silesia, which remained with the Habsburgs, was reconstituted by Vienna as a separate crownland. Although in the official nomenclature it was the Duchy of Lower and Upper Silesia, it came to be more commonly known as Austrian Silesia. It was combined with Moravia into the Moravian-Silesian Gubernium in 1782, but in 1849 Austrian Silesia was detached from Moravia. As a separate crownland, Austrian Silesia survived until the dissolution of Austria-Hungary in 1918. This crownland consisted of the two territories, separated by the Moravian wedge and known as West Silesia and East Silesia. The crownland's capital—Troppau (Opava)—was located in West Silesia, while Teschen (Cieszyn, Těšín) served as the main administrative center of East Silesia.

This territorial separation of West and East Silesia provided the basis for the more or less official division of Austrian Silesia into two administrative areas centered on Troppau and Teschen. Beginning in 1819 the province of Prussian Silesia consisted of the three regencies of Liegnitz, Breslau and Oppeln. All three regencies had come into being in 1815, along with a fourth, the Reichenbach (Dzierżoniów) Regency, which was abolished four years later. Its territory was apportioned to the Liegnitz and Breslau Regencies. Significantly, the Oppeln Regency was the first Prussian administrative division that overlapped with the historical region of Upper Silesia. Lower Silesia was split between the Liegnitz and Breslau Regencies.

The ecclesiastical organization of Silesia dated back to the late Middle Ages and persisted largely unaltered well into the 1970s. The Holy See chose not to take notice of the changes in political borders made either under the pressure of Protestant Prussia or of the "ungodly" Soviet Union (in 1945). The Breslau Diocese contained most of historical Silesia. In Lower Silesia the exception was the Glatz (Kłodzko) Margravate, which was included within the borders of the Prague Archdiocese. In Upper Silesia the situation was even more complicated. The southernmost strip of Prussia's Oppeln Regency, along with the eastern half of West Austrian Silesia and with Troppau, belonged to the Olmütz Archdiocese. The Breslau Diocese comprised the rest of Austrian Silesia, that is, the whole of East Silesia and the western half of West Silesia.

On top of that, in 1821 a papal bull terminated the largely formal subjugation of the Breslau Diocese to the Polish Primate, who had his seat in Gnesen (Gniezno) in the Province of Posen. Subsequently, the Holy See directly administered the Breslau Diocese. In the same year the easternmost counties of Pleß (Pszczyna) and Beuthen (Bytom) in Prussia's Upper Silesia were transferred from the ecclesiastical jurisdiction of the Cracow archbishop to the Breslau Diocese.

This administrative and ecclesiastical organization of Prussian and Austrian Silesia continued unchanged until the end of the Great War, which also closes this work's temporal framework. However, the post-1918 creation of the Polish and Czechoslovak nation-states, of such importance for the inhabitants of both the Silesias, justifies the short sketch of the later history of political, administrative and ecclesiastical divisions in these regions. The dramatic changes illustrate the sheer force of Czech, German and Polish nationalisms that coalesced in the course of the nineteenth century. Prior to 1918 the imperial order in central Europe allowed for the effective containment of conflicts simmering between the proponents of these three national ideologies. But when this order collapsed in the wake of World War I, the ground was cleared for national movements that then emerged as the paramount force of central European politics.

Obviously, the decisions taken or fought for by Czech, German and Polish nationalists were in the interest of their respective nations and nation-states. Those human groups who fell in between these national projects and could not fashion equally successful nationalisms of their own had to be crushed, that is, assimilated to one of these three mentioned nations or marginalized, made into second-class citizens. This was to be the fate of the Szlonzoks, the Slunzaks and the Morawecs in Upper and Austrian Silesias.

In 1920, following the decisions reached in the Treaty of Versailles, small border fragments in northern Upper Silesia were transferred to Poland. Czechoslovakia received a similar amount of land from southern Upper Silesia, but in one piece centered around the town of Hultschin (Hlučín). Following the breakup of Austria-Hungary, Prague took control of West Austrian Silesia, while Poland and Czechoslovakia contested East Austrian Silesia until 1920, when the Allies split it between both the states. In the same year the joint allied administration organized by France, Italy and the United Kingdom took over central and eastern Upper Silesia so as to prepare a plebiscite in order to determine what the Allies should do about this region, where the Polish-German nationalist conflict triggered three military conflicts in 1919, 1920 and 1921. The plebiscite took place in 1921, and in the following year this Upper Silesian Plebiscite Area was divided between Poland and Germany.

Obviously, neither the Allies nor Warsaw or Berlin took seriously the Szlonzoks' aspirations for some form of administrative and cultural autonomy, if not outright independence, complete with their own nation-state. Such attempts had failed earlier in the context of Austrian Silesia, where the local politicians had hoped to maintain the unity of this crownland or to transform East Austrian Silesia into a Slunzakian nation-state. In Upper Silesia this blatant disregard for the interests and needs of the inhabitants stood fast despite the fact that it was Szlonzoks who organized Upper Silesia's largest and most influential political movement of that time. The bilingual Bund der Oberschlesier or Związek Górnoślązaków (Union of the Upper Silesians) boasted a membership of 300,000 to half a million, almost the entire Slavophone adult male population in the region. Because women did not receive the right to vote until 1919, men were the only voters eligible to decide the political future of their region.

Further changes in the administrative and political borders of the fragments of Silesia allocated to Czechoslovakia, Germany and Poland were extremely numerous in the years 1922–1945. A decisive alteration occurred at the end of World War II when the Allies agreed to the incorporation of almost all the *deutsche Ostgebiete* into postwar Poland, including the vast majority of German Silesia. Interestingly, the Catholic Church decided to adjust the ecclesiastical borders accordingly only in the case of the internationally sanctioned division of Upper Silesia. This took place in 1925. Czechoslovakia's conflict with the Catholic Church and the atheistic character of the Soviet bloc established in 1945 prevented the Vatican from making any further concessions in this hostile climate. Thanks to its principled stance, to a certain degree the Catholic Church functioned as "ersatz fatherland," especially to the Szlonzoks, but also to the Slunzaks and the Morawecs.

The Holy See allowed for the eventual overlapping of the ecclesiastical borders with the political ones as late as 1972 and 1978 in the respective cases of Poland and Czechoslovakia. The pope's decisions followed the treaties of 1970 and 1973 signed by West Germany with Warsaw and Prague. In these documents the three states recognized their mutual borders and the Cold War division of central Europe as introduced in 1945.

PART I

1848–1871

CHAPTER 1

Nationalism and the Revolutionary Year of 1848

The uneasy calm that followed the turbulence of the French Revolution (whose ideas were disseminated throughout Europe by Napoleonic troops) was kept through the mutual endeavors of the main European powers united in the Holy Alliance. Tentative attempts to improve the lot of the peasantry and to spread popular education to wider strata of society took place as discord grew among the states and empires through which Prince Klemens Metternich (1773–1859) wished to maintain the balance of power on the continent. The subsequent spread of liberal and national ideas in the increasingly socially and spatially mobile populations heightened political tensions and resulted in the deterioration and the final dismantling of the Vienna-led "Concert of Europe" in 1848.

In central Europe the gradual termination of serfdom and the onset of industrialization underlay these social and political changes. They were also possible thanks to the growing role of the state, whose influence on the life of the individual became dominant after the introduction of conscript armies and popular education. State bureaucracy grew to support and organize the expanding system of schools and the modernizing military. The individual was expelled from the post-medieval "paradise" of stability where one's place under the sun was guaranteed by tradition or, in the eye of the beholder, by divine right. Awaiting him was modernity's completely man-made world of constant flux. One has to find or construct one's own niche in this brave new world, and the niche tends to escape one's grasp, as its shape must be continually modified to adapt it to incessant change.

These cataclysmic alterations overhauled the political system of Europe, dismantling and transforming old states as well as giving birth to new ones. It too reorganized the manner in which states were governed. The new dimensions of governance that appeared in the process of modernization proved to be decision-intensive. Old government structures concentrated in the hands of the monarch and his coterie were not sufficient to cope with the plethora of issues which flooded royal palaces. Willy-nilly, state power (gradually separated from the Church) was strictly divided into the three branches of the executive, legislative and judiciary. Simultaneously, in order to ensure that the state would not be outdistanced or absorbed by its neighbors, power had to be devolved, first to the bureaucratic apparatus, and subsequently to wider societal strata. The latter development took place in accordance with the principles of liberalism. This ideology paved the way for the electoral democracy as practiced today. Concomitantly, the growing ranks of educated people (the intelligentsia), who used reading and writing to function in the newly complicated and interactive society, aspired to participate in governance and politics because they had espoused some liberal tenets. They also became aware of their place in state and society vis-à-vis the Other with whom they were often confronted. They met the Other in the course of mass migrations brought about by emancipation of serfs, industrialization and the Napoleonic Wars. These encounters with otherness appeared decisive for the shaping of one's identity, since they did not take place in the safe confines of one's own place in the premodern world.

Previously, when a Jewish merchant, Armenian tradesman, Scottish peddler, Italian itinerary craftsman, or a group of Roma had entered a village, they had not posed a challenge to one's identity. The villagers interpreted the visitors as being "different" but also possessing their own established place in the society. Conversely, it had not been so significant for the peasant that his neighbor spoke a Germanic dialect and he himself a Slavic one, whereas their lord spoke the Hungarian language. Although the peasant had not been unaware of speech differences, he had not differentiated among people on a linguistic basis. Instead, he had used religion and the pyramid structure of social organization (Billig, 1995: 25). This collapsed with modernization. Swifter communication among and control over the bureaucracy, conscript army, industrial workers, as well as the popular educational system, was practical only with the conscious choice and imposition of some more widely spoken idiom. Subsequently, it would be standardized and made into a literary language complete with normative dictionaries and grammars. The growth of written literature in this tongue and the state-ensured status guaranteed such a language's hegemony over other idioms that one could hear on the territory of a given polity (Edwards, 1994: 125–136; Schulze, 1991: 35–42).

To illustrate the process of constructing standard languages (later called "national languages") from local idioms, it is worthwhile remembering that in 1789, 50 percent of the inhabitants of France did not speak French at all, and only 12 to 13 percent spoke it "correctly." At the time of Italy's unification in 1860, a mere 2.5 percent of the population used Italian for everyday purposes. The administration of the multitude of German-speaking principalities and states before their unification in 1871 required few civil servants. Together with their families and academics they constituted, at most, 300 to 500 thousand readers of works in the literary vernacular, and almost certainly a much smaller number of them spoke *Hochdeutsch* (standard German) in everyday situations (Hobsbawm, 1990: 60–61).

The rather arbitrary choice of local dialects for standardization conducted by various power centers keen on homogenizing their states (e.g., the United Kingdom and France) or on constructing new homogenous states (e.g., Italy and Germany) was easy to accept for those segments of population who spoke related dialects. It posed, however, a difficult problem for those who used completely different languages. Usually, everyone who graduated from a secondary school or became a civil servant tacitly agreed to accommodate his speech to the standard language. But uneducated people, who usually remained entrenched in a local idiom that was often starkly different from standard speech, were confronted with the growing linguistic otherness of their environment at school, in offices, and in industrial centers. This function of linguistic homogenization was accepted and supported by the state at the cost of the non-standard-language-speakers. The latter, without an appropriate command of the official language, increasingly felt left out, discriminated against and made into second-class citizens. Their inability to access the mainstream of society in a nation-state-under-construction often led to the establishment of nationalist movements. They sought to upgrade the social status of the linguistically disadvantaged groups through standardizing their specific idioms. In central Europe this amounted to constructing new nations that, presumably, would be better off in their own ethnolinguistic nation-states (cf. Anderson, 1991: 67–82).

Other elements can also be used as a springboard for national movements. In central Europe, however, language has been consistently equated with nationality. This justifies the narrow language-based approach in the case of Silesia (cf. Kopeć, 1980: 7–8, 25–26).

The general pattern of modernization in Europe during the first half of the nineteenth century coalesced around three cores: the political one associated with democratization, liberalization and emancipation; the economic one of industrialization and capitalism; and the sociopolitical one of nationalism. They are singled out above for the purpose of analysis, but in reality they are closely intertwined (Greenfeld, 2001). That is why, though this study concentrates mainly on nationalism, it is indispensable to present all the three cores and their manifestations in a general overview of modernization in this period. Only a background of this scope allows comprehension of the changes that swept Silesia after 1848.

In 1830, in agreement with the absolutist principles of the Holy Alliance, France, Great Britain and Russia issued the London Protocol, which negated the Greek constitution and declared Greece an autonomous kingdom under their united protection. Due to the Austro-Russian conflict for spheres of influence in southeastern Europe, the Alliance ceased to have any real significance after

1830. The elaborate international system established at the Congress of Vienna (1815) started to unravel, with the emergence of new states and the risk of discord among the neighbors Austria, Russia and Prussia. The growing weakness of the traditionalistic Ottoman Empire, faced with the modernizing West, opened its Mediterranean and Black Sea regions as well as the Middle East to European penetration. These events relaxed social control exerted by states and let liberal forces manifest themselves in the French Revolution of 1830. It broke out in late July in reply to Charles X's (ruled 1824–1830) attempts to limit the prerogatives of the Chamber of Deputies and the civic freedoms promulgated by the French Revolution. He was deposed and the restoration monarchy replaced his neo-absolutist regime, though without concessions for the propertied bourgeoisie, such as the broadening of the suffrage. Under the influence of the July Revolution, the United Kingdom of the Netherlands split into Belgium and Holland. On October 4, 1830 the former declared its independence, which amounted to a major breach of decisions reached at the Congress of Vienna. In the face of this fait accompli, Austria, Prussia, Russia and Great Britain decided to recognize the new nation-state instead of trying to reestablish the status quo of the Congress system. The July Revolution also stirred unrest in several German-speaking states. As a result, during 1830 and 1831 constitutions became the basis of legitimate governance in Saxony, Hanover, Brunswick and Hesse-Kassel. In 1832 these liberalizing developments inspired the Genovese Giuseppe Mazzini (1805–1872) to establish the secret society Giovane Italia (Young Italy). It sought to bring about unification of Italy. In turn liberal and national elements in Austria and Prussia received a renewed impetus after the period of neo-absolutism of 1815 through 1830.

The French events of 1830 also affected Russia's Congress Kingdom of Poland. There the Polish nobility staged the November Uprising (1830–1831) against Russian dominance. St. Petersburg suppressed it, and Pope Gregory XVI (1831–1846) explicitly condemned this insurrection in his encyclical *Cum primum* of 1832. The Holy Alliance gained a new lease on life. In 1833 Russian and Austrian negotiators attended a conference in Münchengrätz (Mnichovo Hradiště) in Bohemia to make common provisions for the mutual suppression of any future Polish troubles. The Prussians were not slow to join them (Morley, 1952). However, popular support for this uprising was widespread, particularly in the less absolutist western German-speaking states (Kinder, 1978: II 44; Lang, 1989). This expression of German sympathy for the plight of the Poles reflected the Germans' hopes for the eventual creation of a German nation-state, hopes that had arisen during the War of Liberation. Consequently, the beginning of the 1830s marks the onset of the *Vormärz*,[1] which preceded the 1848 revolutions in the German Confederation (Deutscher Bund).

In Silesia, the years from the end of the Napoleonic Wars to 1842 were relatively uneventful. Article 13 of the Viennese Act (1815) established the

German Confederation, but it did not provide for common representation in the Confederation. It only stipulated establishment of representative organs for lands and provinces, not the Confederation as a whole. The first provincial diet (Provinziallandtag) of Silesia convened in the autumn of 1825. The body assembled every two to four years and was effectively powerless. During the second diet of 1828 a deputy presented a motion to discuss the gradual suppression of the progressive reforms at the hands of Frederick William III (ruled 1797–1840) and his administration. Thanks only to the efforts of *Oberpräsident*[2] (Senior President) Theodor von Merckel[3] this attack against the king had no further repercussions, but it necessitated censoring all motions before they reached the diet. Thus the deputies were effectively silenced. The enthronement of the new king, Frederick William IV (ruled 1840–1861), stirred some hopes for change among Silesian liberals. The city of Breslau proposed to the sixth provincial diet (1841) that the king should be reminded of the royal promise of 1815. At that time Frederick William III in his *Verfassungsversprechen* (Constitutional Speech) had pledged to grant his subjects a constitution. Predictably this motion was turned down, but word of this occurrence did reach the new king. He decided to placate these anti-royal tendencies in the province by visiting Breslau in 1841, the centenary of Prussia's annexation of Silesia from Vienna in 1740–1742. The inhabitants warmly welcomed the monarch, but he never came to the Silesian capital again, deeming it insufficiently loyal. This came as no surprise. Some of the Silesian nobility still harbored pro-Austrian inclinations, whereas Silesia and Breslau had been a source of democratic impulses in Prussia before the *Vormärz* (Neubach, 1995: 153–154).

The unrealized expectations for the democratic reorganization of Prussia and unification of Germany found explicit expression among the liberals. The lack of any systemic or political reform in this period of accelerating industrialization and agricultural revolution led to the rapid deterioration of the social and economic situation in Silesia in the early 1840s, a condition mirrored in many other areas of the German Confederation. Since the end of the eighteenth century, reforms initially aimed at limiting and abolishing serfdom had gradually produced the stratification of the Silesian peasantry, since the structure of land ownership remained largely feudal.[4] In 1840, half of the Silesian peasants were poor or landless (Michalkiewicz, 1970: 163, 171, 178). Seasonal agricultural workers were paid subsistence wages. Their earnings did not keep pace with the rising cost of living brought about by mass production. Factories offered a range of previously luxurious (or unheard of) goods at affordable prices. This entailed an improvement in the quality of life, but these commodities could be enjoyed only by reasonably well-off peasants and the growing middle class of clerks, teachers and qualified workers. Their standard of living substantially improved, while that of the agricultural and industrial workers stayed the same or, depending on one's perspective, rapidly worsened in comparison to that of the better-off layers of Silesian society.

The relative impoverishment of the Silesian countryside and industrial workers worsened as mechanization made numerous farm and factory hands redundant. Crop failures aggravated the tense social situation as many people were left destitute and penniless, which led to sudden hikes in the price of staples in 1842 (Michalkiewicz, 1970: 341–342). In 1844 the early socialist Wilhelm Wolf from the county of Frankenstein (Ząbkowice Śląskie) described, in a series of uncensored articles published in the *Schlesische Zeitung*, the fate of thousands of poor workers. They succumbed to living in unused casemates of the fortifications surrounding the Silesian capital. Under the influence of these articles, new charitable societies were established in Breslau to alleviate the tragic poverty (Neubach, 1995: 157). However, similar situations prevailed throughout the German Confederation. It became clear that the widespread social problems overwhelmed any grassroots initiatives and demanded systemic reforms on the part of the state. This was especially true if one took into consideration the fact that analogous circumstances, which had earlier developed in more advanced areas of Europe, had incited repeated worker and agricultural unrest in England, France and Bohemia (Michalkiewicz, 1970: 343).

Faced with this dramatic situation, Frederick William IV trusted too much in the stability of post-1815 Europe and in the divine right of a monarch to rule as he pleased. This same approach to governance, common to central and eastern European rulers and elites, contributed to the revolutionary outbreaks of 1848. An early warning came from Silesia in the form of the Weaver Uprising (1844). It took place in June in the foothills of the Sudeten mountains in the two Lower Silesian villages of Peterswaldau (Pieszyce) and Langenbielau (Bielawa).[5] This revolt was sparked by the increasingly lavish lifestyle of factory owners, which contrasted sharply with the miserable poverty of their suppliers and workers, the local weavers. The uprising broke out on June 3 and was suppressed on June 5, leaving 11 dead and about 200 wounded weavers, and only 3 wounded soldiers. Out of the 150 arrested insurrectionists, 87 were sentenced to terms of imprisonment up to nine years, and almost all of them were flogged. Even though this uprising lasted just three days and did not spread widely, its repercussions were felt throughout Europe.[6] It became a model for later worker and peasant movements in Silesia and the Germanophone states. It started a tradition of dissent different from that of the British Luddites in Great Britain, as not the machines but rather the factory owners were the target of protest (Czapliński, 1990: 463; Herzig, 1994: 506; Michalkiewicz, 1970: 341–344).

The difficult economic situation worsened by the inflexible stance of the absolutist governance culminated in worker strikes and turbulences in Glogau (Głogów) (1845), Breslau (1846, 1847), Neurode (Nowa Ruda) (1847) and Königshütte (Królewska Huta) (1847) (Michalkiewicz, 1970: 347–350). In the mid-1840s a few pro-worker and early socialist organizations were founded in

Silesia (Michalkiewicz, 1970: 351–353). This trend influenced Ferdinand Lassalle (1825–1864), who attended a gymnasium in his native city of Breslau before moving to Berlin. In 1863 he established and provided the theoretical framework for the Allgemeiner Deutscher Arbeitsverein (Universal German Workingmen's Association—a forerunner of the later SPD (Sozialdemokratische Partei Deutschlands, Social Democratic Party of Germany) (Scheuermann, 1994: 1:910; Thorne, 1975: 765). The intellectual basis for Lassalle's writings and thought was prepared in Silesia in 1842–1844 by such "revolutionary" journalists as Johannes Ronge, Hoffmann von Fallersleben, Wilhelm Wolff, Heinrich Simon and Karl Friedrich Wilhelm Wander. They vehemently criticized the dearth of intellectual, political, social and confessional freedoms in Prussia (Neubach, 1995: 158). The growing political and social tensions of Lower Silesia were not so pronounced in the backward and predominantly Slavophone Upper Silesia. The tragic poverty of the region's agricultural population became known to the outside world only when deepened by famines and epidemics recurring in 1843, 1846 and 1847–1848 (Herzig, 1994: 494; Michalkiewicz, 1970: 391–393). The last of these famines culminated in a hunger-induced typhus epidemic that ravaged the counties of Pleß (Pszczyna) and about 80,000 people contracted the disease and 16,000 died. Mortality was highest in the Pleß region, reaching 20 percent (Neubach, 1995: 159; Snoch, 1991: 61).

News of the Cracow Uprising (February 20–March 4, 1846) probably added a new degree of radicalization to the dissatisfaction among Upper Silesian peasants living under difficult conditions. This insurrection, restricted to the Republic of Cracow and neighboring areas of Galicia, was a paler version of a general Polish uprising due to poor planning and preventive arrests. The insurrectionists, drawn exclusively from the nobility, wished to show the three partitioning powers[7] that their aim to re-establish the Polish state would be widely supported by the peasantry. To the contrary, their armed efforts were thwarted by a popular jacquerie as peasants rose against their lords. The Austrian authorities chose not to intervene. In the relatively small area of the counties of Tarnow (Tarnów), Neu Sandez (Nowy Sącz), Bochnia and Sanok peasants killed 1,100 noblemen and their attendants, as well as six clergymen. They robbed 470 manors and 52 presbyteries. Blood was shed in more than 200 localities. The peasantry, suffering poverty comparable to that in Upper Silesia and East Silesia, turned against their own lords, hoping that the emperor, rather than their own direct oppressors, would abolish serfdom. Some insurrectionists fled to Prussian Silesia but did not receive so warm welcome as their compatriots following the November Uprising. German intellectuals increasingly perceived that the possible re-emergence of a Polish state could hamper their efforts to create a unified Germany. Fortunately (for the latter), the last independent piece of Poland-Lithuania bordering directly on Prussia's Upper Silesia, the urban Republic of Cracow, was abolished by the

Austro-Russian treaty of November 16, 1846. The borders of Prussia, Austria and Russia converged in the vicinity of the Upper Silesian town of Myslowitz (Mysłowice). This point[8] remained the symbol of central European stability (and oppression in the eyes of Polish thinkers) until World War I (Davies, 1991: II 336–338; Kracik, 1996: 8; Michalkiewicz, 1970: 389).

Economic, social and political problems similar to those in Prussian Silesia also beset Austrian Silesia. The social, economic and political reforms begun by Joseph II continued on a limited scale during the reign of his brother, Leopold II. But the son and successor to the latter, Francis II, who had seen the destructive effects of the French Revolution and the Napoleonic Wars, strove to maintain the unity of his empire. To this end he reestablished and reaffirmed the feudal character of land ownership and absolutist governance. The Holy Alliance was to guard this traditional order internationally. The failure to dismantle the serfdom system bred discontent, especially in East Austrian Silesia (Michalkiewicz, 1970: 159–160). For instance, even after 1848, 44 percent of land remained in the hands of 55 great landowners (Grobelný, 1992: 68).

As a pragmatic measure, in 1781 Joseph II united Austrian Silesia and Moravia into one crownland with the capital at Brünn (Brno). This displeased the political elites of Austrian Silesia, although some autonomous prerogatives were still preserved separately for East and West Silesia. The political pressure on Vienna to separate Austrian Silesia from Moravia and create a crownland on its own (Bein, 1995: 140) became stronger with Austrian Silesia's economic and political growth. East Silesia was strongly Protestant (one-third of the population) and the established Austrian Protestant Church originated in the local parish of Teschen. This process led to the establishment of the Department of Protestant Theology at the University of Vienna in 1821 (Bein, 1995: 140). Industrialization began in the northwestern corner of East Silesia, where the Ostrau (Ostrava)-Karwin (Karviná) industrial basin was starting to bloom, with its numerous mine shafts and steel works. In the second half of the nineteenth century it became the largest industrial complex of the Dual Monarchy. The tradition of Silesian weaving and linen production gave rise to the largest Austrian center of textile production, in Bielitz (Bielsko) adjacent to Galicia (Bein, 1995: 144; Pitronova, 1992: 57–58).

Due to industrialization and technological advancement in agriculture the Austrian Silesian population grew from 295,436 in 1798 to 443,912 in 1857 (Bein, 1995: 141). Such a steep increase led to sharp economic stratification and deprivation of the peasantry. Many peasants were made landless, and a worker class began to emerge, not unlike in Prussian Silesia (Michalkiewicz, 1970: 173). Poverty was somewhat mitigated in West Silesia, which was largely German-speaking and better socially developed than Slavic-speaking East Silesia. The contrast between these two parts of Austrian Silesia can be likened to that between Lower and Upper Silesia in Prussia. Hence it is not surprising that following the onset of the 1845–1848 economic crisis (Prinz, 1995: 311) West Silesia fared better than especially the southeastern mountainous and impoverished regions of East Silesia. Beginning in the mid-1830s, recurrent potato blight repeatedly deprived the Austrian Silesians of their staple. Moreover, from 1844 onwards frequent total crop failures and rinderpest joined the blight. Outside food supplies could not relieve ensuing hunger and typhus because of the economic crisis and the lack of quick means of transportation. The railroad from Vienna to Oderberg (Bohumín) was completed only in 1847. Mortality was highest and brought about visible depopulation in the west and south of East Silesia (Pitronova, 1992: 58).

The similar concoction of social, economic and political problems developed in Prussian and Austrian Silesia, though in the latter region on a smaller scale and without the presence of early socialist or worker movements. However, the ignition which released the pent-up tension in the revolutionary disturbances of 1848 was to come from outside, that is, from Berlin and Vienna, respectively. The speed with which the revolution spread to the two Silesias was made possible only due to the construction of the above-mentioned Vienna-Oderberg line, and to the railway line which between 1842 and 1848 connected Berlin with Myslowitz on the Russian border in Upper Silesia via Görlitz (Zgorzelec), Liegnitz and Breslau in Lower Silesia, and Oppeln, Gleiwitz (Gliwice) and Kattowitz (Katowice) in Upper Silesia (Koziarski, 1993: 194).[9] The latter rail line became the economic backbone of Prussian Silesia as the Oder (Odra) River had previously been. Consequently, most of the subsequent economic initiatives were connected directly to this transportation route.

The impulse to stage uprisings and social unrest throughout central Europe came from Paris. The banning of a banquet by supporters of liberal reforms unleashed the February Revolution (February 22–24, 1848). On February 24 King Louis Philippe (ruled 1830–1848) abdicated and a group of republican leaders proclaimed the Second French Republic. The constitution adopted in November established a presidential republic with a single assembly. Both the president and assembly were to be elected by universal male suffrage. Although the creation of the Second Empire in 1852 partially reversed these democratic changes, their influence on central Europe, dominated by a thinly concealed absolutism, was immediate. The Habsburg Empire also received another democratizing stimulus from the Apennine Peninsula. In January 1848 the people of Palermo rose and drove out the forces of Ferdinand II (ruled 1830–1859), the King of the Two Sicilies, who thereupon granted his Italian subjects a constitution and summoned a separate parliament for Sicily. At the same time, Leopold II (ruled 1824–1859), Grand Duke of Tuscany, issued a constitution for his duchy, and Pope Pius IX (1846–1878) consented to a constitution for the Papal States. Uprisings also broke out in Milan, Venice and Naples.

In the German-speaking states the first sign of coming changes could be seen in Switzerland. Here the civil war of 1847 resolved the deepening conflict between autocratic and democratic elements, as well as between the Protestant and Catholic areas. This event persuaded the republic to adopt a new constitution based on the American model in 1848. The first state of the German Confederation to espouse democratic ideals was Baden. Already on February 12, 1848 Friedrich Basserman (1811–1855) spoke in the Baden parliament on unifying Germany in the form of a federal state similar to the United States. There followed demands for a common German parliament, freedom of speech and press, and a reorganized judicial system. This sudden outburst in support of liberal changes culminated in a mass rally in Mannheim (February 27). The grand duke and his government vacillated and the Austrian envoy advised concessions that in turn encouraged the subjects. The revolution facilitated by the railway network spread swiftly throughout south and western "Germany,"[10] predominantly made up of constitutional monarchies like Baden. There and in Württemberg, Hesse-Darmstadt, Hesse-Nassau, Hesse-Kassel, Bavaria and Saxony, liberals joined local governments thanks to the unwavering support of peasants, artisans and workers. Newly formed national guards protected the freedoms of press, speech and assembly. The judicial systems were overhauled and the liberal leaders promised universal male suffrage and the unification of Germany, the unfulfilled dream born in the War of Liberation. The first phase of the March Revolution was crowned with a meeting in Heidelberg (March 5), where southern German liberals resolved to convene the Constituent National Assembly in Frankfurt am Main.

The radicals (*petite bourgeoisie* and peasants along the Rhine, in Baden, Saxony and Silesia) and the propertied liberal bourgeoisie disagreed on their demands. The former aspired to a democratic republic, whereas the latter limited their more moderate aims to petitions. Yet they all shared the wish for national unification. The ad hoc assembly of the German Confederation abolished censorship, but its plans for reform came too late. Still, the revolution spread to the larger states of Prussia and the Austrian Empire.

On March 13, 1848, students unleashed the first rising in Vienna. Metternich was forced out of office and fled to England. Nothing could save his Concert of Europe any longer. His last success—the suppression of the Cracow Uprising—had proved to be a harbinger of his undoing. The Habsburg court expected that the aged Metternich's resignation would facilitate a quick restoration of the old order, but quite to the contrary, the revolution spread across the empire (Ehrich, 1992: 522). On the same day, the first revolutionary rally took place in Berlin. On March 17 Frederick William IV promised concessions, but on the next day the demonstrators were fired upon in front of the royal palace. Under public pressure the king withdrew the troops from the capital and paid tribute to the 230 "victims of March." He also promised a national assembly that would debate a draft for a constitution and a solution to the national question that would allow Prussia to become part of Greater Germany (*Großdeutschland*) (Czapliński, 1990: 474; Kinder, 1978: II 57). On March 20 the revolutionaries unexpectedly freed political prisoners from the notorious Moabit fortress in Berlin, including 254 Polish conspirators.

The latter, in 1845–1846, under the leadership of Ludwik Mierosławski (1814–1878), had prepared an insurrection in Prussia's partition zone of the erstwhile Poland-Lithuania. It was meant to be part of an unrealized Polish general uprising to encompass all the lands of former Poland-Lithuania.[11] They were condemned to harsh sentences after a drawn-out trial that lasted from August to December 1847. Berliners greeted their liberation with enthusiasm, even though there was a danger that Russia—not affected by the revolutionary developments—might decide to intervene. Mierosławski then came to the fore, proposing a restored Poland to ensure the security of a united Germany by acting as an *antemurale* against the "expansionist pressure from Asia." He returned to the Grand Duchy of Posen to organize a voluntary force of 10,000 Polish troops.

Two decrees of the Prussian monarch issued in April divided the duchy into two parts, one of which was to enjoy Polish self-government. This part was rather small and unfortunately did not contain the duchy's capital of Posen. On top of that, it would be included in the German Confederation, contrary to the expectations of Mierosławski and his supporters. This led to the outbreak of the Wielkopolska Uprising of 1848. The insurrectionists signed the capitulation on May 9 when they had failed to incite the duchy's peasantry to rebellion (Anon., 1985: 717; Czapliński, 1990: 474–475, 478; Dralle, 1991: 188–189; Jakóbczyk, 1989: 15; Neubach, 1995: 217).

In May 1848 the Constituent National Assembly convened in St. Paul's Cathedral in Frankfurt am Main,[12] as did Prussia's National Assembly in Berlin. Both bodies had been elected under universal male suffrage. The former was to work out the framework and a constitution for a united Germany, and the latter to reorganize Prussia in accordance with liberal principles.

The Habsburg Empire's problems extended from the revolutionary and nationalist unrest in its Italian provinces, Croatia, Bohemia and Hungary to renewed turbulence in Vienna (May). So the court decided to convene the first elected Reichstag (Imperial Diet) the same month. Under the leadership of the youngest deputy, Hans Kudlich (1823–1917),[13] the Reichstag definitively emancipated the peasantry. This was of crucial importance for the underdeveloped (or rather unevenly developed) and largely agricultural Habsburg Empire to keep pace with the development of Prussia, and to struggle for hegemony in "Germany." The effective solution of the peasant question lessened the peasantry's support for revolution and gave the Austrian government some desperately needed breathing space. Now Vienna could deal with the uprisings throughout its far-flung empire. All were suppressed by the end of 1848, with the exception of the Hungarian insurrection, which lasted until August 1849. Russian troops helped crush it. On October 3, 1848, mutinous imperial units meant to fight in Hungary instigated the outbreak of the third uprising in Vienna. The court fled to Olmütz (Olomouc) in Moravia, but Prince Alfred Windischgrätz broke the resistance of the national guard fielded by revolutionaries. In November the Reichstag was transferred to the provincial town of Kremsier (Kroměříž) in southern Moravia. On December 2, chances for the monarchy improved when the mentally unbalanced Ferdinand I abdicated in favor of his nephew Francis Joseph I (ruled 1848–1916). On March 7, 1849, Austrian troops dispersed the Reichstag and in the same month a new constitution (imposed by the monarch)[14] was decreed. This opened the way for creating a semblance of the prerevolutionary status quo.

In a similar, but less violent, manner the revolutionary movement was extinguished in Prussia. The liberal March cabinet fell in June and was replaced by a moderate one. Finally, in September the conservative cabinet of General Ernst von Pfuel (1779–1866) took over. The storming of Vienna reinforced reactionary attitudes, and this last government moved the National Assembly from Berlin to the town of Brandenburg on November 9. The next day General Friedrich von Wrangel (1784–1877) quelled the revolutionary mood by stationing his 13,000 troops in Berlin. The National Assembly was dissolved on December 5. The king imposed a constitution by decree the same month, setting the framework of the political system that, with a few minor changes, lasted in Prussia until 1918. Prussia received a two-chamber parliament (1854). The First, or Upper, Chamber, officially named the Herrenhaus (House of Lords), was composed of representatives of the great landed proprietors (*Junkers*) and large towns, as well as of life and hereditary peers. The Second, or Lower, Chamber, elected by all taxpayers, was divided into the three classes according to the taxes paid. Unlike Austria's Reichstag, Prussia's National Assembly did not abolish serfdom until March 2, 1850, when the Prussian Parliament (Landtag) issued an act to this end (Anon., 1992: 753; Czapliński, 1990: 486–487; Kinder, 1978: II 58–59; Lis, 1993: 83; Macartney, 1992: 706; Plaček, 1996: 19).

The revolution focused on social (mainly peasant), democratic, liberal, and national issues. In the Habsburg Empire and Prussia the elites recognized that maintaining the institution of serfdom came at the cost of depriving newly emerging, labor-hungry industrial centers of workers. Solutions to the second question varied. In Prussia, a semblance of parliamentary democracy was introduced, whereas the Habsburg Empire opted for neo-absolutism, which actually weakened the state by merely postponing necessary political reforms until 1867. The empire was then transformed into the Dual Monarchy and parliamentary democracy integrated into its political framework. The explosive national issue, raised by academics and intellectuals advocating the ideology of nationalism as the main state-organizing principle, remained largely unresolved.

The idea of establishing a united German state and forging a German nation from the multitude of the Silesians, Prussians, Hessians, Austrians, Badenians, Württembergers, Saxons and so on (cf. Bunsen, 1858: vii; Czapliński, 1990: 462; Kedourie, 1960: 63) was instigated by the general experience of otherness. This perception took hold during the War of the Second Coalition (1799–1802), when French troops marched eastward and subdued a majority of the German-speaking states of the Holy Roman Empire. German nationalism, with clearly formulated goals, emerged during the War of Liberation when the unity of the Germanophone polities facilitated the defeat of Napoleon and political reorganization of the continent at the Congress of Vienna. The concept of a united German state was promoted even then, but the idea was barely realized in the form of the loose German Confederation. In a rather a-national manner Metternich transformed it into an instrument for maintaining the peaceful status quo as agreed upon at the Congress of Vienna. He was not interested in forging a German nation that would necessarily undermine the legitimacy of the Habsburg Monarchy. However, from the 1830s onwards, under the influence of the nationalist ideals propagated by the secret society Giovane Italia (Young Italy), the poets of the Young Germany movement (such as Heinrich Heine and Karl Gutzkow) appealed for the creation of a common German state to house the entirety of the German nation. The Frankfurt Parliament recognized the urgency of the problem, and after its commencement on May 18, 1848, started working toward establishing common bodies for the whole of the German Confederation. Already on June 29, Archduke Johannes Habsburg was chosen to the post of the *Reichsverweser* (Imperial Administrator). He appointed the common German government, which started sending out its ambassadors. However, these were accepted only by less significant states (for example, the United States). The largest Germanophone states did not support the government, clearly indicating its political insignificance. On July 16, 1848, Prussia, Austria, Hanover and Bavaria refused to place their armies under the Frankfurt government's control (Czapliński, 1990: 482; Kinder, 1978: II 51, 57; Ehrich, 1992: 526).

The German-speaking states were not prepared to relinquish their separate sovereignties to some federal body. There were also other obstacles as well. First of all, the Hungarian part of the Danubian monarchy was not included in the German Confederation at all, and the Grand Duchy of Posen, along with East and West Prussia, were accepted into its fold only in 1848, and excluded again in 1851 (Jähnig, 1991: 121). Also an unusually high percentage of professors and professionals acted as deputies in the Frankfurt Parliament. Among its 586 deputies were 223 members of the legal profession, 106 professors, 46 industrialists, 3 craftsmen and only one peasant, interestingly, a Christian Minkus from the Upper Silesian county of Rosenberg (Olesno). This statistic shows that the idea of German unification and of building a German nation was intelligible and appealing only to a narrow stratum of the educated (*Bildungsbürgertum*). Only they espoused the ideals of nationalism propounded by the "Young" movements throughout the Apennine Peninsula and central Europe. These attempts to construct a German state in accordance with the tenets of ethnic nationalism conveniently overlooked large non-Germanic minorities in Prussia and the Habsburg Empire. The German-speakers in the latter were a numerical minority, as were all other language groups. The ethnic composition of both states was reflected in the diverse ethnolinguistic backgrounds of the members of Prussia's National Assembly and Austria's Reichstag.

Not surprisingly, a bitter dispute ensued. The supporters of the *Großdeutsch* (Great German) movement favored a federation to include the whole Habsburg Empire under the leadership of a Catholic Habsburg dynasty, or a unitary-democratic state (republic) to include only Germanophone Austria. Those of the *Kleindeutsch* (Little German) leanings wanted a nation-state (with the exclusion of Austria) under a Protestant Prussian dynasty. Had the projects of the *Großdeutsch* faction been implemented, the result would have been a multiethnic state, because even the Austrian part of the empire contained a sizeable Italian minority, along with entire ethnic groups of Czechs and Slovenes. The *Kleindeutsch* vision of a unified German state to more closely comply with the tenets of ethnic nationalism began to prevail at the end of 1848.

On March 28, 1849, the Parliament ratified the constitution. It organized the would-be German nation-state as an empire, and offered the imperial crown to Frederick William IV. The *Kleindeutsch* solution seemed to have won the day. The Prussian king declined this offer on April 21. Among other considerations he feared such a decision might legitimize the revolution and pit Prussia against Austria's Francis Joseph I. Subsequently, Prussia and Austria recalled their deputies from the parliament, which had moved to Stuttgart (May 30), where it was dispersed on June 18. Riots in defense of the constitution flared up in several Germanophone cities in May 1849. The confrontation between prorevolutionary and conservative forces lasted the longest in Bavaria's Palatinate and Baden before Prussian troops tipped the balance in favor of the conservatives at the end of July. The negative outcome of 1848 for the liberal forces triggered off a massive emigration to America, France, Switzerland and England (Czapliński, 1990: 483, 489, 487–488; Ehrich, 1992: 522; Kinder, 1978: II 57, 59; Neubach, 1995: 160; Snoch, 1991: 92; Turner, 1992: 107).

Besides making it clear how a unified German state would look, the Frankfurt Parliament also spawned the ideals of Pan-Germanism in its two basic forms. One strove for a multinational German state with central Europe and perhaps the Balkans with Constantinople. The other hoped to build Germany as a state to embrace all the Germanic peoples, namely, apart from the German-speaking states of the German Confederation, to include Scandinavia, the Netherlands and Switzerland (Anon., 1992a: 103; Czapliński, 1990: 483). All these ethnically defined trends of Pan-Germanism and German nationalism brought about a negative reaction of the Czechs to a potential German nation-state. Living in the compact areas of Bohemia and Moravia-Silesia, the two most developed crownlands of the Danubian monarchy, the Czechs were well-suited to build a nation of their own. They advocated a reorganization of the empire that would recognize the "unity of the historical provinces of the Czech Crown: Bohemia, Moravia and Silesia" (Waldenberg, 1992: 40). Czech intellectuals also hoped to make the ideal of equality of all the nationalities the organizing principle of the empire. In 1848 the Czech provinces were treated as an integral part of the German Confederation. Czech nationalists disagreed, arguing that this confederation was a German proto-nation-state, of which the Czech nation could not be part. Vienna's unwillingness to come to terms with the Czech postulates and Prussia's decision to incorporate the Grand Duchy of Posen into this confederation (May 1848) appeared to the Czech nationalist leaders as an attack on Slavdom. They were confirmed in their opinion when it had become clear that the Frankfurt Parliament would seek to establish a German nation-state or a German-dominated state. The historian František Palacký (1798–1876) rejected the participation of Czech representatives in the parliament, and as a counterforce he organized the Slav Congress[15] (Ehrich, 1992: 522; Kinder, 1978: II 59).

In order to comprehend the significance of this congress, it is necessary to observe the unfolding of the Czech national movement. The decline in the use of Bohemian (Czech) as a written language after the defeat of the Czech nobility at the Battle of White Mountain (Bíla Hora, 1620) was reversed in the second half of the eighteenth century. At that time efforts were undertaken to reestablish this language as a medium of polite discourse, equal to German (Waldenberg, 1992: 40). The mainly literary endeavors underwent transformation after 1790, when the Königlich-Böhmische Gesellschaft der Wissenschaften (Royal Bohemian Society of Sciences) was established. The society spread the ideals of Herder, Goethe, Leibniz and Rousseau, and prepared Bohemia for accepting the romantic mode of writing and thinking. This intellectual ferment served as the springboard for the nascent Czech nationalist movement. The scholar Josef Dobrovský[16] (1753–1829) published his *Geschichte der Böhmischen Sprache und Literatur* (History of the Czech Language and History) in 1792, and eight years later the *Deutsch-böhmisches Wörterbuch* (German-Czech Dictionary, 1802–1821). Josef Jungmann (1773–1829) is credited with the creation of the Czech literary language thanks to his five-volume *Slownjk česko-německý* (The Czech-German Dictionary, 1835–1839) and numerous translations from the western European languages. In his theoretical writings he declared the Czech language as the foundation for building the Czech nation. He also propagated the necessity of a common Slavic language to transform the vague ideas of Pan-Slavism into a real movement. Jan Kollár (1793–1852), a Slovak writing in Czech, composed original poetry, collected peasant songs, and, most importantly, advocated the union of all Slavic peoples. He illustrated this idea with an allegory. Russia was presented as the union's head, Poland served as the body, Bohemia as the arms, and other Slavic peoples as the limbs.[17] Pavel Josef Šafařík (1795–1861), another Slovak writing in Czech, published his *Geschichte der slawischen Sprache und Literatur nach allen Mundarten* (A History of the Slavic Language and Literature Created in All the Dialects) in Buda in 1826, and *Slovanske starožitnosti* (Slavonic Antiquities, the first historical study of all the Slavic peoples) in Prague in 1836–1837. These works provided the theoretical framework of Pan-Slavism.

František Palacký is hailed the "father of the Czech nation" because his contribution to the Czech national movement was of crucial significance. The Royal Bohemian Museum (which emulated the Johanneum in Graz) was founded in Prague in 1818. In 1827 Palacký and Jungmann successfully advocated for a Czech-language version of the *Monatsschrift der Gesellschaft des vaterländischen Museums in Böhmen* (Monthly of the Association of the Regional Museum in Bohemia). Its Czech-language variant *Časopis společnosti vlastneského Museum v Čechách* started appearing in the same year. Not any longer could academics dismiss the Czech language as a mere peasant dialect. On January 1, 1831, Palacký established the Matice česká (Czech Cultural Society) as a scholarly institution of the Association of the Regional Museum in Bohemia, parallel to a similar institution in Serbia (Matice srpska, 1826). He propagated the Czech language and culture through numerous books and textbooks, and the society became the principal force in creating Czech national feeling. It thereby became a model for similar institutions in the Slavic northern parts of the Habsburg Empire after 1848. Thanks to its existence Jungmann could publish his groundbreaking Czech-German dictionary in 1835–1839, and Palacký his monumental *Geschichte von Böhmen* (History of Bohemia)[18] in 1836–1867. Palacký's work became the bible of Czech nationalism, an ideological weapon in nationalist strife, which some Czech, Slavic, and German historians-turned-ideologues have waged to this day (Alter, 1994: 44; Černý, 1995: 6–20; Polišenský, 1991: 91; Schenk, 1993: 62–63; Szyjkowski, 1948: 38–39, 50, 55, 58, 60, 63–64).

Bearing in mind how the Czech national and Pan-Slavic movements developed under the influence of Pan-Germanism and German nationalism, it is no surprise that a united German nation-state or a centralized Habsburg Empire did not attract the Czech nationalists. Inclusion of the Czechs in any of these polities would preclude the possibility of their own nation-state. In a letter of April 11, 1848, Palacký rejected the idea of Slavic deputies from the Habsburg Empire being elected to the Frankfurt Parliament, as well as the idea that the Danubian monarchy could become part of a united German nation-state. Rather he wanted Vienna to act as the protector of Slavic peoples against Pan-Germanism and the westward expansion of Russia. When Eberhard von Wächte-Spittler and Ignaz Kuranda met Palacký on April 28 in order to convince him that deputies of Slavic origin should also participate in the Frankfurt Parliament, he explained that Bohemia, Moravia and (Austrian) Silesia, as the historical lands of the Czech Crown, were not German and should not belong to the German Confederation.

The negative attitude of the Czech national movement, which could endanger appropriate representation from the crownlands in Frankfurt, convinced the medical doctor Ludwig von Löhner to establish the Verein der Deutschen aus Böhmen, Mähren und Schlesien zur Aufrechterhaltung ihrer Nationalität (Society of the Germans from Bohemia, Moravia and Silesia for the Maintenance of Their Nationality) in Vienna. This organization, thanks to the grassroots support, managed to secure representation from Bohemia, Moravia and Silesia to the Frankfurt Parliament. On the other hand it coaxed many German-speaking Bohemians, Moravians and Austrian Silesians to accept the view that they were Germans and as such inherently different from the Slavic-speaking inhabitants living in these crownlands. This feeling directly contributed to exacerbating the nationalist cleavage after 1848 (Carter, 1992: 922; Ehrich, 1992: 522; Schenk, 1993: 65–66).

Palacký organized the Slav Congress with the assistance of Karel Havlíček (1821–1856) and František Rieger (1818–1903). It commenced on June 2, 1848, in Prague, and was attended by representatives of all the Slavic peoples living in the Danubian monarchy as well as by some Poles, Serbs, Bulgarians, and the Russian anarchist Mikhail Bakunin (1814–1876). In sum, the congress gathered 340 participants. Two-thirds came from Bohemia and Moravia. Due to widely disparate interests, Palacký could not persuade the congress to adopt his moderate program of supporting the empire as the guarantor of the historical rights of its Slavic peoples. The majority passed a romantic appeal to the rulers to convene an all-people congress to solve the international questions. They also said that the Slavs of the Danubian monarchy should enjoy equal rights in a reorganized empire. The congress had not reached any final resolution when its debates were disturbed by the outbreak of the Pentecost uprising in Prague (June 12). The insurrectionists fought in support of the ideals, supported by the congress but against the wishes of its leaders, who preferred to attain their goals by legal means.

This disturbance played into the hands of the Germans and the Magyars who viewed this congress as a danger to their own nation-building efforts. Therefore they welcomed the speedy suppression of the rising by Prince Alfred Windischgrätz (1787–1862). The capitulation of June 17 also ended the congress. At that time its political significance was not clear, but soon, in the second half of the nineteenth century, it became obvious that diverse Slavic national movements and Pan-Slavism (turned into a tool of St. Petersburg as Pan-Russianism) constituted a distinct force that could disrupt the Danubian monarchy. For the time being, Pan-Slavism was considered an unrealistic utopia. Critics pointed out that the congress's official language was German, which indicated that the Slavic languages were not so close to one another as popularly believed. Others noticed that Slavic leaders often spoke better German than their respective vernaculars. It was ironic, as it made them "false" Slavic nationalists, at least in the eyes of the German proponents of the national idea.

Palacký firmly opposed any illegal steps to alter the status of the Czechs within the empire. He wanted it to last and wrote accordingly: "If the Austrian state had never existed, we should, in the interest of Europe and even of Humankind, try to create it." In 1865, just before transforming the empire into a bipartite Austria-Hungary two years later (without granting any concessions to the Czechs), Palacký remained convinced that the Slavs would calmly accept the proclamation of Austro-Hungarian dualism with regret, but without fright. He believed that the Czechs and other Slavic peoples or nations of the Habsburg Empire would be finally granted an appropriate place in the polity's framework, and that the Danubian monarchy, whatever its numerous flaws, was a safer place for Slavs than a world without it. Palacký's ideas in this regard formed the intellectual basis of Austroslavism (Anon., 1908: 735; Carter, 1992: 922; Černý, 1995: passim; Czapliński, 1990: 484; Ehrich, 1992: 522; Kinder, 1978: II 59; Schenk, 1993: 66–67).

In 1849, with the final suppression of the remnants of the revolutionary movements of the previous year, the intra-German conflict between Austria and Prussia came to the fore. Frederick William IV strove to marginalize the Habsburg Empire in the German-speaking world. He proposed establishing a looser confederation with Austria on the basis of a central European customs union, within which a *Kleindeutsch* state would guarantee Prussia's supremacy. In May 1849, at the Potsdam conference, Bavaria rejected this project, but Prussia, together with Saxony and Hanover, formed the "alliance of the three kings" to pursue this political solution. By the end of the summer, a majority of the Germanophone states (with the exception of Württemberg and Baden) joined this alliance. With Austria engaged in the suppression of the Hungarian rebellion, Prussia could implement its project of the union. However, after the meeting of the emperors in Warsaw in May 1849, Tsar Nicholas I (ruled 1825–1855) promised aid to Francis Joseph I in crushing the Hungarian Uprising. And on July 10, 1849, under the combined pressure of Russia, Great Britain and France, Prussia had to conclude an armistice with Denmark in its seemingly victorious war to conquer Schleswig-Holstein. After the suppression of the Hungarian Uprising in August 1849, the Habsburg Empire was free to oppose Prussia more actively. However, on March 20, 1850, the latter state managed to convene the Erfurt Union parliament, which deliberated a draft constitution for a Northern German Union proposed by Prussia. Prince Felix Schwarzenberg (1800–1852), representing the Danubian monarch, counteracted and won over many delegates of the German-speaking states to the counter-project of reestablishing the German Confederation. In May they assembled in Frankfurt. The open Austro-Prussian conflict pushed the Germanophone states and the Austrian Empire to the brink of a war, but following the arbitration of the tsar, who favored Austria, Prussia had to accept the Olmütz (Olomouc) Punctation (November 29). Under its terms Berlin agreed to the restitution of the German Confederation with the Habsburg emperor at its helm (Czapliński, 1990: 490–491; Ehrich, 1992: 523; Kinder, 1978: II 59–61; Turner, 1992: 108).

Seemingly the continent returned to the times of Metternich, and his "Concert of Europe" would prevail again to guarantee peace and stability. This point of view overlooked the unprecedented political mobilization of large numbers of peoples who, after 1848, started defining themselves as "nations." This translated into severe cleavages that deepened when the underlying ethnic lines were increasingly politicized by national movements. Last but not least, after the abolishment of serfdom, peasants started streaming to towns. This demographic phenomenon gave a decisive boost to industrialization. Production grew rapidly during the next two decades.

Nothing could remain in central Europe as it had been.

◆   ◆   ◆

The preceding broad discussion of the 1848 events in relation to the social and political (re-)organization of the German-speaking states is indispensable, as these polities constituted the reality of central Europe up to 1914–1918. Prussian Silesia and Austrian Silesia were an inseparable part of the region. The author believes that without this background, it would have been necessary to mention general German national developments, while explicating some fine points connected to the various nascent nationalist movements in Silesia. This would unnecessarily impede the narrative in the course of focusing the work on Silesia.

Likewise, this concern also made it indispensable to present the rise of the Czech national movement, as this nationalism rose to the rank of a significant political and social force through its steadfast opposition to and emulation of German nationalism during the second half of the nineteenth century. In this role, Czech nationalism strongly contributed to setting the stage on which further central European and Silesian social and political movements unfolded.

The picture would not be complete without sketching a course of change in the Polish national thought. All the main anti-Russian uprisings led by the Polish nobility, and the minor ones directed against Prussia and Austria, ended in defeat. A change in tactics was necessary to allow the Polish idea to survive in the age of mass politics. The decision to ground it in ethnic nationalism permitted the inclusion of the Polish-speaking peasants in the new national movement, but precluded the chance of rebuilding Poland-Lithuania as a civic nation-state that, apart from the Poles, would also include Lithuanians, Ukrainians and Belarusians (Porter, 2000; Snyder, 2003).

CHAPTER 2

The Rise of German Nationalism in Prussian Silesia to the Founding of the German Empire (1871)

An analysis of the effects of the 1848 revolutions on Silesia requires a brief overview of the ideological and historical roots of the German, Polish and Czech nationalist movements in this region prior to the mid-nineteenth century. Accordingly, this chapter focuses on the problem of German nationalism, while similar introductions on the origins of Polish and Czech nationalisms commence chapters 3 and 4, respectively.

German nationalism in Silesia arrived there in the form of its initial concepts before Prussia's annexation of this province. The first ideas that defined the German nation in terms of common (peasant) culture and language started seeping into Silesia from the central and western areas of the Holy Roman Empire. Gotthold Ephraim Lessing (1729–1781) was one of the first to delimit, through his writings, the ethnic border between the Germans and their western neighbors. With his pen he fought against the French influence on German literature of that period. Lessing perceived French literary models as "foreign," "un-German," and as "polluting" German culture. Justus Möser (1720–1794) celebrated the "ancient roots" of German tradition, and pitted it against alien cultures that, according to him, endangered Germanness. Friedrich Gottlieb Klopstock (1724–1803) spoke about the necessity of "love for one's fatherland." These three representatives of the *Bildungsbürgertum*, among others, and their followers co-invented and espoused the vague concept of the German nation. At that time they saw this tentative nation's fatherland in the Holy Roman Empire of the German Nation. Obviously the term "nation" in this name is the modern translation of the Latin *natio*. The empire's *nationes* were the Franks or, later, Teutons (future Germans and Dutchmen), the Lombards and the Burgundians (would-be Italians in the north of the Apennine Peninsula and Frenchmen in the west of France), together referred to as "Romans." The empire's territorial losses in the west and in the south made the Teutons in their kingdom of *Teutschland* (future Germany) into the dominant *natio*, and as of the sixteenth century the unofficial qualification of "Teutonic *natio*" crept into the empire's name (Bryce, 1919: 189–190, 364; Noël, 1998: 104–106).

During the second half of the eighteenth century the German-speaking *Bildungsbürgertum* became painfully aware of the ennationalizing policies pursued in France and the United Kingdom. Underwritten by industrialization and the economic power of both the states, their growing influence was felt in the empire, especially in the prestigious position of all things French, with the French language at the fore. Worst of all, the German-speaking aristocracy and rulers tended to be contemptuous of the German language and literature and chose to speak and write in French. The Prussian King Frederick the Great clearly presented this stance in his *De la Littérature allemande* (On German Literature, 1780, in Snyder, 1958: 118–119).

The nationally minded *Bildungsbürgertum*'s most tangible success was the founding of German-language theaters in emulation of the Théâtre-Français (1680), one of the most potent symbols of early French nationalism. The earliest German theaters came into being in Hamburg (1767), Vienna (1776), Mannheim (1779) and Berlin (1796–1814) (Anon., 1889f: 4). Johann Gottfried Herder (1744–1803), in his *Ideen zur Philosophie der Geschichte der Menschheit* (Outlines of a Philosophy of the History of Man, 1784–1791), unwittingly provided the nascent German national movement with its preliminary theoretical framework. Herder introduced the notion of *Volksgeist* (spirit of the people, national character), which he defined as an unconsciously creative entity manifested in vernaculars (unwritten languages) and folk songs. These ideas gave birth to the strain of nationalism[1] that elevates language into the foundation of nation.

In agreement with Herder's postulates, the first collections of German folk songs already began appearing during the last decades of the eighteenth century. In this manner the oral tradition was translated into the literary one as the nation's idealized past. Herder, however, praised the value of all the vernaculars and various oral traditions connected to them. Many German-speaking scholars brought out folk song collections in languages other than German and thus created the ethnolinguistic bases for other central European national movements. In 1863 Julius Roger (1819–1865) had his collection *Pieśni Ludu Polskiego w Górnym Szląsku z muzyką* (The Songs of the Polish People in Upper Silesia, with Tunes) published in Breslau. Not surprisingly, at the end of the nineteenth century, this book became one of the "proofs" that the Slavophone population of this region was Polish (Roger, 1991).

In the second half of the eighteenth century the creators and consumers of literature in German were nurtured on the blossoming diet of the press and popular education. The literate stratum, indispensable for the spread of the nationalist ideology, grew (Greenfeld, 1992: 293–310; Struve, 1997: 29). The *Bildungsbürgertum* constituted the readership of the works by Johann Wolfgang von Goethe (1749–1832) and Friedrich Schiller (1759–1805). German national literature came into being thanks to the increasing number of readers and the rise in the production of printed texts. This phenomenon also spawned and brought about necessary standardization of the literary—or, in other words, national—language of the Germans. Future writers and readers of German books were educated in the use of this standard in school. Thus, codified German evolved into *the* proper medium of oral and written communication among the Germans.

The writings of the philosophers Johann Gottlieb Fichte (1762–1814) and Friedrich Wilhelm Schelling (1775–1854) were a formative influence on German romantic poets. These two turned their attention to folk culture, which was thought to be authentically rooted in historical uniqueness, from which Germanness sprang up. The romantic principles of discourse on the German nation gradually seeped into music, art, literature, history, legal studies and political theory. This romanticism of German nationalism also contributed to the rise of such novel disciplines as philology, ethnography and religious studies. Almost to this day, academics working in these fields have contributed as much to their respective nationalisms as to scholarship (Gellner, 1983: 35–38; Kinder, 1978: II 32; Schulze, 1991: 43–47).

The idea of nation internalized by, and enshrined in, the general intellectual framework of the *Bildungsbürgertum* at the turn of the eighteenth and nineteenth centuries began to appear as "natural." German thinkers, striving to express this received meaning, clung to the familiar-sounding term "Volk" rather than "Nation." The latter, derived from Latin *natio,* was more at home in French than German, and appeared inappropriate as a description of the German nation that formed in opposition to the expansionist policies of the French nation-state.

Prior to the Napoleonic onslaught, the biggest Germanophone states strove to emulate the political and economic success of France and the United Kingdom. Industrialization caused the speedy growth of bureaucracy. The state, faced with this novel challenge, expanded popular education so as to sustain the industrial development with the required numbers of clerks, civil servants and qualified literate workers. This involvement of the state in the matters of the individual and local communities had to be measured. Statistics proved the most convenient tool to this end. This discipline entered the service of states in 1796 when the first statistical office was established in France. After initial failure, it was firmly refounded four years later. Having been espoused by France—the "archetypal" nation-state—statistics became another national symbol along with the national anthem, the national flag and the national coat-of-arms.

These symbols evoked the idea of a unity whose nebulous center started to attract an increasing number of individuals. Schools and compulsory military service for men taught them the standardized form of a vernacular now elevated to the rank of the national language. They formed ennationalized populaces who, through mass migration from the countryside to cities, made possible the rise of straggling urban centers of industrialization. In turn, growing cities accelerated the homogenization of inhabitants in the nationally approved paradigm of culture and social behavior.

National statistical offices, besides fulfilling a symbolical role, proved deft instruments of mass control as well as of development planning. Rulers aspiring to build nation-states obtained a flexible yardstick with which to measure the "ethnic purity" of their nations-under-construction and to delimit (that is, to clip and expand) their ethnic borders so that they would converge with the frontiers of the nation-states postulated as being of these nations. Bavaria created its own statistical office in 1801, the Kingdom of Sardinia (the kernel of future Italy) in 1803, Prussia in 1805, and Austria in 1810. Other European states then followed suit in the 1830s. The first modern censuses were conducted in Sweden (1749), the United States (since 1790), and, in 1801, in the United Kingdom and France. Prussia joined this club of statistical modernity in 1816. Since the establishment of the German Customs Union (Deutscher Zollverein) in 1834, censuses had been regularly organized in the territory of this future *Kleindeutschland* (Anon., 1889a: 243; Anon., 1890a: 275; Anon., 1908a: 61; Anon., 1908b: 696).

The attack of Napoleonic France forced further modernizing changes on the German-speaking polities. The dissolution of the Holy Roman Empire in 1806 reduced the number of the Germanophone polities from roughly 300 to about 50. The two largest of these states—the Habsburg Empire and Prussia—suffered crushing defeats, which led to sweeping reforms within their borders. The direct clash with the national forces of the French nation-state tangibly proved that the German-speaking polities remained a bundle of inefficient post-feudal organisms. Without modernizing their administrations and armies, these polities could not hope to escape absorption into the French Empire.

The shock was felt most acutely in Prussia, which Napoleon almost erased from the political map of Europe in 1806. The ensuing reforms introduced by Karl vom Stein (1757–1831) and his successor Karl von Hardenberg (1750–1822), as well as vigorous diplomacy, spared Prussia the sad fate of Poland-Lithuania. One of the most important changes was applied to the Prussian army. From a multiethnic mercenary force it was transformed into a national conscript army in which only Prussian male citizens served (Anon., 1992: 752; Anon., 1992b: 552). Another element of nation-state-building was added to Prussia's German national repertoire.

At the level of ideas, various concepts of liberty were voiced as a solution to the predicament of the Germans suffering under French dominance. Friedrich Schiller wrote *Die Jungfrau von Orleans* (1801) and *Wilhelm Tell* (1804). Friedrich

Hölderlin (1770–1834) glorified the "free people of Greece" and their struggle against the Ottoman Empire. Johann Gottlieb Fichte demanded freedom of thought for the sake of political renewal in his series of lectures entitled *Addresses to the German Nation* (1807–1808). In a nationalist exaggeration, he equated Germanness with genuine morality and culture (or rather *Kultur*[2]). Patriotic sermons preached by the Silesian Protestant theologian Friedrich Schleiermacher (1768–1834) roused feelings of national community, and Heinrich von Kleist (1777–1811) gave way to his hatred of the French occupiers of Prussia in *Die Hermannsschlacht* (1808). This play provided the model for a national (or, in the German case, nation-creating) uprising.[3] In the *Rheinischer Merkur,* Joseph Görres (1776–1848) established the most aggressive anti-Napoleonic journal, indicating the way in which the German press could contribute to expelling French troops from the German-speaking states. The poet Ernst Moritz Arndt (1769–1860) translated the vague aims of the coalescing German national movement into the popular and direct language of national action. For instance, he wrote, "to be one people is the religion of our day."

Moreover, Arndt popularized the idea of the German nation as a community of the German language. He predicted that the borders of the would-be German nation-state should converge with the territorial extent of this language community. He expressed this idea in his fiery song "Was ist des deutschen Vaterland?" (What is the German Fatherland?):

> What is the German fatherland?
> So name me thus my land!
> *Wherever rings the German tongue*
> And God in Heaven sings,
> So shall it be, so shall it be,
> It shall be all Germany.
> (Arndt, in Fishman, 1996: 166; my emphasis)

Other national songs appealing to German-speakers and urging unity against Napoleon were composed by Max von Schenkendorf (1783–1817) and Karl Theodor Körner (1791–1813).

All these diverse ideas produced three different notions of the German nation. First, under the influence of the Enlightenment, it was seen as a community of culture. Second, some conceived the German nation as a preordained national union in line with the romantic concept of the German *Volk*, with its fatherland in the shape of the medieval Holy Roman Empire. Thirdly, the example of the French nation-state convinced some thinkers that the German nation could rise as a political community of free male citizens. The confusing array of often conflicting lines of thought was very difficult to overcome in the interest of German unity, and it has not produced a satisfying definition of the German nation to this day (Greenfeld, 1992: 360–371; Hargreaves-Mawdsley, 1968: 23, 188, 263, 296, 484, 481, 487; Kinder, 1978: II 32; Thorne, 1975: 54, 745).

The disdain for the French Other on the part of the *Bildungsbürgertum* spread to other strata of the population with the abolishment of serfdom and the rise of conscription. The educational system of Prussia, reformed in agreement with Wilhelm Humboldt's (1767–1835) proposals, modernized universities and schools and also contributed to the spread of the German national idea. On the other hand, the organizational source of massive German national movements came from associations of riflemen,[4] singers[5] and gymnasts. They became especially active in the national field after 1811. Of these three different kinds of associations, the gymnastic movement embraced the gospel of nationalism in the most committed manner.

Jean-Jacques Rousseau's (1712–1778) ideas presented in his *Émile* (1762) and supported by other educators in the second half of the eighteenth century who considered physical education an indispensable complement of intellectual growth proved a seminal influence on Friedrich Ludwig Jahn (1778–1852). He established the first gymnasium in Berlin (1811) and, later, many others elsewhere. The most famous ones included those at the universities in Halle, Jena and Breslau. Through the growing network of these gymnasia Jahn inculcated the youth with the ideas of German unity and struggle for freedom—that is, against the French—besides helping them improve their brawn. Strategic and tactical games educated physically skillful and highly motivated would-be soldiers for the War of Liberation. Students who participated in this war also contributed to the development of the German national movement through their *Burschenschaften* (fraternities).[6] Unlike *Landsmannschaften* (associations of students from the same regions), they gathered students from all the Germanophone states, irrespective of their social and geographic origin (Anon., 1888: 133; Anon., 1889b: 943–944; Alter, 1994: 47; Czapliński, 1990: 453; Kinder, 1978: II 33; Thorne, 1975: 692).

The War of Liberation commenced in Silesia or, more exactly, in Breslau and Lower Silesia. The largely rural and Slavic-speaking population of Upper Silesia[7] with their strong local identities remained indifferent to the conflict. They expressed a similar attitude toward the Polish uprisings that would take place across the border in the Russian and Austrian empires. So the brunt of national enthusiasm was most felt in the west of Silesia. This province, together with its capital, became the center of renewed Prussian statehood and the German national movement. It was not important that only 65 years had elapsed from the Prussian takeover and that the Catholic Silesian nobility were traditionally more at home in Vienna than in Protestant Berlin. Prussia and Austria had been parts of the Holy Roman Empire, and the Napoleonic onslaught was not against one of them but against *all* the German-speaking states. The common enemy united erstwhile foes, ensuring loyalty of the nobility to the national cause along with the majority of the Silesians.

The idea of German unity was popular among Silesia's *Bildungsbürgertum* already at the end of the eighteenth century and at the beginning of the nineteenth century. This led to the establishment of the Gesellschaft zur Beförderung der Naturkunde und Industrie (Society for the Advancement of Natural Sciences and Industry) in Breslau in 1803. Initially, it adhered more to the universal ideas of the Enlightenment, but a change came with French expansionism. The society, under the new telltale name of the Schlesische Gesellschaft für Vaterländische Kultur (Silesian Society of Fatherland Culture), emulated the so-called "patriotic societies" ("patriotische Gesellschaften") active in other Germanophone cities (Herzig, 1994: 523–524; Scheuermann, 1994 I 408). This process rapidly accelerated in 1811 when Breslau's Catholic Jesuit College of Leopoldina was reestablished as a modern, that is, national university in 1811 (Herzig, 1995: 124). Students from all the German-speaking states arrived at the Silesian capital and founded numerous *Burschenschaften*. The gymnastic movement reinforced their efforts to foster German unity. Jahn's supporters appeared in Breslau much earlier than the first gymnasium, which opened there in 1815.

Already in 1813 Ludwig von Lützow (1782–1834) came to Silesia to organize the renowned corps of volunteers, later known as the Black or Lützowsche Jäger. Jahn was the first of important figures to leave Berlin in answer to the king's appeal *An mein Volk* (To my People) delivered in Breslau. Gymnasts under Jahn's leadership joined the corps. The volunteer force embraced many other renowned activists of the nascent German national movement as well as numerous students moved to action by Jahn's *Turnidee* (the patriotic idea of the gymnastic movement) and the *Burschenschaften*.

However, it is worthwhile illustrating the ideological vagueness of the German national movement at that time with the person of the German romantic poet from Silesia, Joseph von Eichendorff (1788–1857). After attending the University of Vienna he and his older brother Wilhelm joined the Lützowsche Jäger. Like his fellow soldiers, Joseph never participated in battle. Prussian officers did not deem this corps a dependable force. Although Eichendorff's poetry and his person were used for boosting German nationalism, in reality he was a singer of nature and Catholicism, not of German unity or the German nation. The concepts of a German fatherland (that is, a nation-state) did not evoke in him any lyrical emotion, unlike his regional homeland as emphasized in the poem "Heimat" (Homeland). Interestingly, Eichendorff did not even identify with Silesia but with the locality of the Lubowitz (Łubowice) palace and the surrounding forests where he had spent his childhood.

Thus the composition of Eichendorff's identity was similar to that of the non-German-speaking Upper Silesians at that time and, probably, of the majority of the uneducated Silesians. The difference, though, lies in the fact that, having received extensive schooling, the poet also identified with the totality of European culture. He knew Latin, translated from Spanish and read in French. Moreover, Eichendorff was proficient in the southern version of Upper Silesia's Slavic dialect, which the Lubowitz peasants spoke. So for Eichendorff it was quite impossible to espouse Arndt's idea that the German nation-state should converge with the area inhabited by German-speakers only. When in the Prussian civil service in 1841, Eichendorff wrote a memorandum. He stressed the need for allowing the use of Polish as the medium of instruction in the secondary and tertiary educational institutions in the Grand Duchy of Posen, a part of defunct Poland-Lithuania. Obviously, he did not foresee any use of standard Polish in Slavophone Upper Silesia, because Polish had never been used in the capacity of an administrative language in Silesia.

Eichendorff's brother, who entered the Habsburg civil service, must also have shared similar ideas about his personal identity. When the first language censuses were conducted in the Danubian monarchy, Wilhelm indicated Polish as his "home language" in spite of the fact that by that time, having had few occasions to practice his Polish, he spoke German much better. It was not important, because he saw the local Slavic dialect of his Lubowitz homeland as close to Polish. He had no other "home language," since only his family and the staff spoke German in the palace (Anon., 1888: 133; Anon., 1888b: 1031; Kinder, 1978: II 32; Koprowski, 1995; Pawlicki, 1995; Scheuermann, 1994: I 245, II 1781, 1785; Stein, 1993: 43, 98; Thorne, 1975: 818).

In 1815 the anti-French feeling was still high. For instance, in 1815 during the second anniversary of the Battle of Leipzig, which had sealed the fate of Napoleon, a person remarked, "If you want to teach your daughter French, equally well you can educate her as a tart" (Czapliński, 1990: 452–453). The poet and ideologue of German nationalism, Arndt, agreed by saying, "I hate all Frenchmen without distinction in the name of God and of my people, I teach this hatred to my son, I teach it to the sons of my people . . . I shall work all my life that the contempt and hatred for [the Frenchmen] strike the deepest roots in German hearts" (Arndt, in Greenfeld 1992: 276). It took time before this hatred of all things French could subside after the Congress of Vienna had reorganized a Europe ravaged during the course of the Napoleonic Wars. With the Union Act of June 8, 1815, this Congress also founded the German Confederation, which, under Austrian hegemony, supplanted the erstwhile Holy Roman Empire. Seemingly, this solution should have satisfied everybody, but the activists of the German national movement perceived it as a direct contradiction of the ideals for which they had fought in the War of Liberation. In unison with the German princes they stood for a united Germany, a real nation-state. What was offered to them was a loose confederation of more than 40 sovereign states (Jähnig, 1991: 125).

Metternich recreated a semblance of the pre-Napoleonic order in central Europe, so princes perceived active political involvement on the part of their subjects as redundant in a time of peace, or even as a usurpation and direct threat to the monarchs' absolutist power. The Wartburg Festival (1817) gathered the academic youth from all the Germanophone states and celebrated the tercentenary of the Reformation. It worried the princes deeply as a grassroots event (Ehrich, 1992: 522). In 1818–1819, in Breslau, the gymnastic movement was accused of encouraging immature behavior in its members as well as a high rate of school absenteeism. The altercation between supporters and adversaries of gymnastics continued until 1819. Then, in Mannheim, a radical student murdered the journalist and poet August von Kotzebue (1761–1819), widely known as a staunch opponent of the gymnastic movement and *Burschenschaften*. As to his motive, the student alleged that Kotzebue was a Russian spy.

This crime provided the conservative powers with the opportunity they had been waiting for. The 80 Prussian gymnasia were closed immediately, and the Carlsbad (Karlsbad, Karlovy Vary) Decrees were passed in August 1819. These put the German and Austrian universities under strict government control. *Burschenschaften* and other student organizations (that is, the gymnastic movement) were prohibited, and censorship became stricter. An investigation commission was established in Mainz, and students suspected of liberal or nationalist inclinations were blacklisted throughout the German-speaking states. At Metternich's behest, the German Confederation introduced new oppressive measures on an even larger scale to counter the wave of grassroots demonstrations staged in support of German unity and liberal reforms. These took place in Hambach, the Palatinate in 1832 and in the following year, in Frankfurt am Main (Ehrich, 1992: 522; Scheuermann, 1994: II 1782–1783).

To avoid retribution, supporters of German unity had to express their views in a less direct manner, as politics remained the prerogative of the sovereigns. From 1819, Karl vom Stein published the multivolume *Monumenta Germaniae Historica* (Monuments of German History), the first authoritative collection of medieval sources of German history, so as to inspire popular interest in the past. He was right in hoping that this work would facilitate absorption of the multifaceted and multiethnic past of the Holy Roman Empire and central Europe into the national history of the German nation-under-construction. Significantly, each volume bore the motto *Sanctus amor patriae dat animum* (holy love of the fatherland inspires us) (Alter, 1994: 45; cf. Hobsbawm, 1992).

In 1822 the first congress of German natural scientists and medical doctors convened, in 1828 the first congress of German natural scientists, in 1838 the first congress of German classicists, in 1845 the first congress of German writers, and in 1846 the first congress of German writers and philologists. Participants from all the Germanophone states attended the quatercentenary of printing, celebrated in Leipzig (1840), and they flocked to the first German industrial exhibition, in Mainz (1842), and many other "all-German" events (Czapliński, 1990: 464). In the absence of any political Germany, these events functioned as a spiritual or *Kultur* nation-state.

In 1842, one of the first great national monuments of the would-be German nation was erected in Regensburg, Bavaria. The Valhalla[8] built on the Danube is a pseudo-Germanic temple, complete with the monumental feminine figure of Germania. This Germania resembles the Frenchmen's popular symbolical representation of their own nation-state that drew on Jeanne d'Arc. Sculptures of the most renowned Teutonic chiefs, together with 163 busts of distinguished Germans[9] as beloved sons, surround their mother—Germania (Anon., 1890b: 360).

By the time of the 1848 revolutions, the new generation of *national* historians came into being. They were members of *Burschenschaften* and the gymnastic movement who supported the project of German nation-building. To this end they appropriated various histories of different German-speaking states as the presumed past of the German nation, which the German national movement still had to deliver. Other scholars, in emulation of their French and British colleagues, started speaking about German *national* art, German *national* literature, German *national* music, German *national* theater and so on. Nobody split hairs about the difference in the meaning of the western European "nation" and the German "*Nation*." In the former case this term alluded more to the state, while in the latter, to ethnic nation, the *Volk*.

This ennationalization of elements associated with so-called "high culture," irrespective of the territorial divisions separating the German-speaking states, provided the German national movement's activists with more ideological blocks from which to construct the German nation, and with which to delimit the nation's ethnic border. The Verein für Geschichte Schlesiens (Association for the Study of Silesian History),[10] established in Breslau in 1846, remodeled the Silesian past accordingly, so that it would nicely fit into the new German national history (Herzig, 1994: 524).

In the meantime, the rivalry between Prussia and Austria to dominate the German Confederation considerably weakened this political organization and unexpectedly transferred the process of German unification to the sphere of economy. The postmedieval organization of the Germanophone states did not correspond to the needs of the modern economy. In the year following the 1815 crisis, all internal customs tariffs were abolished in Prussia east of the Elbe. In 1818, this measure was extended to the state's entire territory. However, the remaining 38 customs borders and dozens of incommensurable coins seriously hindered trade and industry within the German Confederation, putting it at a clear disadvantage in relation to France and England.

Reflecting on this plight, Friedrich List[11] (1789–1846) translated the idea of German unity into the sphere of economics. He introduced the concept of national economy and presented his views on this subject in his *National System of Political Economy* (1841). In 1819 List founded the Deutscher Handels- und Gewerbeverein (German Commerce and Craft Union). In 1828 the Prussian-Hessian, Central German and South German customs unions came into being. In 1834 Prussia outbid all the contenders for the title of Germany's economic center. Berlin established the German Customs Union. Almost all the German-speaking polities that were to join the *Kleindeutsch* nation-state of 1871 had acceded to this union by 1867.

In addition, the 1838 monetary convention regulated the currency system in the German Confederation and gave a further boost to the economic unity within the borders of the German Customs Union. Austria still retained political control over the Germanophone states within the framework of the German Confederation. But the actual significance of Prussia grew at an ever-increasing pace. Not being able to compete with Vienna at the level of central European politics, Berlin found the field of economy more promising. At that time, the Austrian decision-makers perceived economic activity as a matter of course regulated by centuries of tradition, and as such not worth worrying about, and so concentrated on politics. In this way, Prussia was free to develop a modern unified and quickly industrializing economy. Progressively it integrated with the economies of other members of the German Customs Union. Consequently, the Kingdom of Prussia turned into an economic juggernaut. The absolutist and unevenly developed Habsburg Empire, which stuck to premodern (postmedieval, postfeudal) forms of economic organization never caught up with Berlin. And soon after the mid-nineteenth century it was obvious that Vienna would not be able to effectively compete with Prussia and its German Customs Union (Czapliński, 1990: 450; Kinder, 1978: II 47; Szporluk, 1988: 79–166; Thorne, 1975: 797).

The economic rise of Prussia weakened Austria's hold over central Europe and facilitated the half-hearted rebirth of liberal ideas that appeared in this part of the continent after the July Revolution in France (1830). The Rhein crisis accelerated both these processes. In 1840, the French Prime Minister Louis Thiers (1797–1877) sought to gain prestige with advances in Egypt and through pushing the French border to the Rhein. French expansionist policies fired nationalist fervor throughout the middle class in the German-speaking states, or, more exactly, among senior civil servants (many of whom had belonged to *Burschenschaften*), the commercial and propertied bourgeoisie (especially active in the singers' movement), academics and artisans. The anti-French feeling showed most in the newly composed nationalist songs, such as "Die Wacht am Rhein" (The Guard on the Rhein), "Deutschlandlied" (German Song), and Arndt's "Der Rhein, Deutschlands Strom" (The Rhine, Germany's River). These lyrics and German national politics made the Rhein into another potent symbol of national unity.

The support for German nationalism, previously limited to the *Bildungsbürgertum*, became a widespread phenomenon with a massive social basis. The ascension of Frederick William IV to the Prussian throne in the year of this crisis also reawakened hopes for liberal reforms and the speedy unification of Germany. In 1842 the king was the first Prussian monarch to participate in a Catholic mass. The mass celebrated the resumption of construction of the Cologne cathedral (completed shortly afterwards). In this manner, Frederick William indicated that he was a prospective ruler of all the Germans, irrespective of their confessional adherence. He successfully bridged the postmedieval cleavage between the Catholic and Protestant German-speaking states. This symbolic union above confessional differences elevated this cathedral to another national symbol of would-be German unity.

Also in 1842, the royal edict of June 6 legalized the gymnastic and *Burschenschaft* movements and granted amnesties to "demagogues" (that is, liberal activists) who, in the wake of the July Revolution, had been incarcerated or had emigrated. Singers', riflemen's and gymnasts' associations, along with societies supporting the cathedral project, lent a broad popular base to the German national movement. A year later, the Prussian monarch consolidated it with the celebration of the millennium of the "German" Empire.

This rekindled German national movement began to achieve successes already in 1848. A guard of honor composed of gymnasts greeted the National Assembly (Frankfurt Parliament) when the delegates entered the Paulskirche (St. Paul's Church) in Frankfurt am Main. In numerous German-speaking states national guards were formed in emulation of similar forces created in revolutionary France. The *Burschenschaften's* black, red and gold tricolor was widely accepted as the German national flag. Despite the failure to unify Germany in the years 1848–1849, the activists of the German national movement resolved to lend their support to the *Kleindeutsch* solution as worked out by the Frankfurt Parliament.

The German national movement failed to win solid backing from either the lower classes or the peasants, who remained firmly attached to local dynasties and their narrow parish, town or village environs. But the definitive abolishment of serfdom during the *Völkerfrühling* (Spring of Nations or Springtime of the Peoples)[12] and industrialization increased mobility of all the social strata. The general level of literacy also grew, thanks to popular education and compulsory military service. The Prussian schools and the army spread the national idea. By the end of the 1840s, the movement for German unity began to attract massive adherence from all layers of society (Alter, 1994: 51–52; Anon., 1889:c: 3; Hargreaves-Mawdsley, 1968: 23; Kinder, 1978: II 47, 49; Scheuermann, 1994: 2:1783; Schulze, 1991: 69–79; Thorne, 1975: 1264).

The post-1848 reaction severely dashed the expectations of those who hoped for liberalization of absolutist regimes in the Germanophone states and for the unity of Germany. The rejuvenated Danubian monarchy once again won the contest for hegemony over these states and reestablished the German Confederation.

One of the first acts of this new German Confederation was to do away with the nation- and nation-state-building decisions reached at the Frankfurt Parliament. In 1851 the all-German black, red and gold banner was lowered from the Thurn und Taxis palace in Frankfurt am Main, which was intended to become the seat of the all-German government. Four years later the fleet of a would-be German nation-state was sold at auction.

But Prussia, supportive of a *Kleindeutsch* nation-state, regained the lost ground during the next two decades. As a major economic power in the making, Berlin scored a significant political success in 1853. After the expiration of the founding treaties of the German Customs Union, contracted for 20 years, Vienna attempted to dominate the union or supplant it with its own vision of economic order in central Europe. A majority of the German-speaking states, already in a tight economic connection with Prussia, swiftly renewed these treaties without changes. Furthermore, even more states joined, so that the Customs Union gained direct access to the North Sea.

Russia, Vienna's ally for over a century, abandoned Austria after the Crimean War (1853–1856) and moved into the camp of the Danubian monarchy's enemies. St. Petersburg supported the cause of Italian unification. In 1859 Austria, weakened by the 1857 economic crisis, lost the confrontation with the Franco-Sardinian forces in the Italian War of Unification. As a consequence, Francis Joseph II ceded Lombardia to Sardinia, which became the kernel of a united Italy when the Sardinian King Victor Emanuel II (ruled 1849–1878) ascended the throne of the Italian kingdom in March 1861 (Czapliński, 1990: 492, 497; Ehrich, 1992: 524–525; Kinder, 1978: II 61, 72–73).

The political stagnation brought on in Prussia by Frederick William IV's mental illness worsened in 1857. The next year, the king's brother, Prince William, assumed the regency. Prussia's steady rise to the rank of a new major powerhouse of the world bolstered the economies of the German Customs Union's members, and entailed tightening of direct links with the more liberal economies of western Europe. This brought about liberalization in the economic policies of the Kingdom of Prussia. The relaxation spilled over into the sphere of politics when the Prussian government did not suppress the liberal opposition during the 1858 elections.

This meant more space for the activities of the German national movement that continued promoting the *Kleindeutsch* solution. More national organizations sprang up: the Kongress deutscher Volkswirte (Congress of German Economists, 1858), the Deutscher Handelstag (German Economic Organization, 1861) and the Deutsche Abgeordnete-Tage (Organization of German Parliamentarians, 1862), among others. Popular support for German unity was expressed during the gymnastic festivals organized by the growing Vereinsturnwesen (Gymnastic Association).[13] These festivals took place in Koburg in 1860, in Berlin in 1861, and in Leipzig in 1863. The riflemen's and gymnasts' festival in Gotha (1861) led to the establishment of the all-German Bundesschießen (Union of Riflemen's Associations). A saying from the early 1860s aptly summed up these events: "Die Turner und die Schützen sind des Reiches Stützen" (Gymnasts and riflemen hold the Reich steady) (In Alter, 1994: 52).

In 1863 the German nation-in-construction obtained another national symbol—the Hall of Liberation in Kelheim near Ratisbona (Regensburg). It glorified the War of Liberation, during which the idea of German unity had been forged. The general growth of the German national movement and its activities at the turn of the 1850s and 1860s crystallized in the founding of the Deutscher Nationalverein (German National Society) in 1859 in Frankfurt am Main—the symbolic seat of the 1848 German National Assembly. This organization emulated the Italian Società Nazionale (1857) and gathered middle and upper bourgeoisie, intelligentsia, smaller factory owners and several significant captains of industry.

From the last group, Count Guido Henckel von Donnersmarck (1830–1916) merits mention. His capital and property were concentrated in Upper Silesia. The German National Society's membership soared to 25,000 in 1862. The society collected money for the construction of an all-German fleet and openly appealed for a *Kleindeutsch* nation-state under Prussia's leadership. Berlin did not wish to isolate Austria, so in 1865 the Prussian government declared that the goals of the society had never been those of Prussia's, since the proposed unification would mean subjugation of Prussia to some all-German institutions (Alter, 1994: 47, 51; Anon., 1889: 671; Anon., 1889b: 945; Anon., 1889d: 4; Czapliński, 1990: 499–501).

The dissolution of the Deutscher Nationalverein took place in 1867, but its *Kleindeutsch* program, supported by many German historians and academics in their academic writings, was not discarded. They claimed that Germany could not be united by any popular mass movement but only by Prussia through systematic enlargement of its territory. Regent William (king 1861–1888, German emperor from 1871) and his prime minister, Otto von Bismarck (1815–1898), readily, though tacitly, espoused this theory. In 1862 Bismarck deftly solved the budget crisis in defiance of the constitution and the Prussian Landtag, and forestalled abdication of the king. Having stabilized the monarchy and reinforced the army,[14] Bismarck could devote more attention to foreign policy with the invaluable aid of Prussia's economic clout.

His long-term goal was to snatch hegemony in the German Confederation from the Habsburg Empire. Prussia supported Russia in the suppression of the Polish January Uprising (1863–1864), and in this manner gained a powerful ally. Simultaneously, the Polish national movement was weakened, so that it could not endanger the territorial integrity of Prussia. At that point no European politician took seriously Polish wishes for a Polish nation-state to be established, let alone that the Prussian province of Posen ought to be united with such a state.

In 1863, urged on by Bismarck, William I stayed away from the Fürstentag

(Assembly of the Princes), the supervising body of the German Confederation. In the same year the Danish King Christian IX (ruled 1863–1906) approved the Danish November Constitution, which sanctioned annexation of Schleswig (Slesvig) and its separation from Holstein. The German national movement demanded from Denmark independence for both the duchies. Bismarck pointed to the violation of the London Protocol (1852), which had settled the previous German (Prusso)-Danish conflict over the status of the two duchies (1848–1850). This treaty had declared the duchies autonomous entities in a personal union with Denmark. At the end of 1863, in the context of growing Franco-Austrian enmity, Bismarck offered the Danubian monarchy a chance of improving its position in Europe through a joint Prusso-Austrian intervention in Schleswig-Holstein.

The common German victory over Denmark galvanized German national enthusiasm, although it also created problems regarding the joint administration of the condominium. The Convention of Gastein (1865) temporarily settled the differences between Berlin and Vienna. It granted the Danubian monarchy the administration of Holstein and Prussia that of Schleswig. The defeat of Denmark contributed to the consolidation of the German national movement in Silesia, as elsewhere in Prussia and other Germanophone states. At railway stations, the local population welcomed the Austrian troops on their way north to Schleswig-Holstein. Those trains also crossed Silesia, and members of various organizations arranged aid for front soldiers. After the war, in April 1864, the first transports with Danish POWs arrived in Silesia. Most of them (386) were interned at the Glogau (Głogów) fortress (Anon., 1889d: 4; Biały, 1990: 265; Czapliński, 1990: 501–502, 504; Kinder, 1978: II 75).

The stalemate over the control and status of Schleswig-Holstein incited Prussia to propose the reform of the German Confederation by adding an elected parliament. This offended the Austrians, who appealed to the Assembly of the Confederation to decide the Schleswig-Holstein question. Prussia responded to this violation of the Convention of Gastein by invading Holstein and leaving the German Confederation altogether. The confederation, under Austrian leadership, mobilized against Prussia. A majority of the German-speaking states stood firmly in support of the Danubian monarchy, but the Thuringian states (with the exception of Solingen), Oldenburg, both Mecklenburg-Schwerin and Mecklenburg-Strelitz, Anhalt and the Hanseatic cities, sided with Prussia.

The Seven Weeks' War, the final war for supremacy in Germany, commenced on June 16, 1866. Four days later Italy joined in the hostilities as Prussia's ally, forcing Vienna to fight on two fronts. The Prussian forces, in accordance with the superior strategy of the chief of staff, Helmuth von Moltke (1800–1891), launched a three-pronged attack on Bohemia from Lower Silesia and from Dresden after having defeated Saxony, an Austrian ally. The Austrian armies were defeated on July 3 at Sadowa (Sadová) near Königgrätz (Hradec Králové), and the rapid advance of the technologically and numerically superior Prussian force could have easily reached Vienna. But Bismarck refused to be dazzled by the brilliance of the victory and concluded the preliminary Peace of Nikolsburg (Mikulov) (July 26) in order to forestall possible French intervention. The Treaty of Prague (August 23) confirmed the terms of capitulation. Austria would have to recognize the dissolution of the German Confederation and the reorganiza-tion of "Germany" without Vienna's participation. The Habsburgs transferred their rights in Schleswig-Holstein to Prussia. Yet no territorial cessions were demanded, and Vienna assured the preservation of the territorial integrity of its most faithful allies, Saxony and Hesse Darmstadt. Prussia annexed all the other belligerent states north of the Main River. In the Italian-speaking dominions of the Habsburgs, the Italians suffered a defeat at Custozza in Lombardy as well as in the naval Battle of Lissa (Vis). However, thanks to the Prusso-Italian alliance, the Danubian monarchy had to cede Venetia to Italy.

Since the 1st and 2nd Prussian armies congregated in Lower Silesia before the attack, and the majority of the military operations during the Seven Weeks' War took place just south of the Silesian border in Bohemia, money and other donations were collected throughout Silesia for the sake of Prussian soldiers and their families. Civic guards were formed in Silesian localities near the border, and later field hospitals were organized for the wounded. The news of the Prussian victory at Sadowa electrified the Silesians. On their own initiative, local self-governments and various associations organized patriotic rallies, and Prussian flags were hung at public buildings. The demonstration of support and joy at the victory was overwhelming. Subsequently, thousands of Austrian POWs were transported to Silesia, and the majority of them (5,400) interned in the Glogau fortress. Last but not least, the Catholic Church in Silesia and the pro-Austrian Silesian nobility realized that there was no hope for Silesia's return to Habsburg rule. They had to work out a better consensus with the Prussian government that would guarantee them an acceptable form of coexistence with Berlin (Biały, 1990: 266; Czapliński, 1990: 514; Ehrich, 1992: 525; Kinder, 1978: II 73, 75; Klaußmann, 1996: 70–74; Turner, 1992: 110).

The victorious war of 1866 gave Prussia absolute dominance in northern Ger-many. Following the break-up of the German Confederation, Prussia overhauled the economic organization of the German Customs Union into the political one of the North German Confederation (Norddeutscher Bund). This confederation came into being on the basis of the Federal Treaty of August 18, 1866, signed by 22 states. Importantly, the majority of the south German-speaking states, which had sided with Austria, remained outside the new confederation, namely, the Palatinate, Baden, Hesse, Württemberg and Bavaria. Berlin effectively con-trolled the North German Confederation, as Prussia constituted four-fifths of the confederation's territory and population. The Prussian monarch held the executive authority vested in the confederation's presidency. The Prussian chancellor helped him in this task and was accountable only to the king.

There was no absolute majority of Prussian deputies in the legislature (composed of the Bundesrat and the lower chamber, the Reichstag), but the relative majority and the dominant stance of Prussia always allowed Bismarck to piece together a workable majority in support of his policies. The federal constitution of the North German Confederation provided no bill of rights, no ministerial responsibility, and no civilian supervision over military affairs. It did introduce, however, uniformity in currency, weights, measures, commercial practices, industrial laws, and financial regulations. In short, it created the economic unity the middle class long had demanded. This homogenous economic space was expected to be the necessary prelude to the creation of a German nation-state in the *Kleindeutsch* form.

Bismarck could seek this solution only after September 3, 1866, when the Prussian Landtag voted in favor of the indemnity proposal. Thereby, the legislature retroactively approved of Bismarck's erstwhile unconstitutional measures. Now, acquitted of the accusations of illegal decision-making and with the comfortable control of Prussia and the North German Confederation executed via democratic procedures, the chancellor was in a position to proceed with the project of German unification in a more decisive manner (Czapliński, 1990: 519; Kinder, 1978: II 75–76; Turner, 1992: 111).

On February 12, 1867, the first elections to the parliament of the North German Confederation took place, and on April 16 the parliament passed the constitution by an absolute majority of votes (230 to 53). This was the first all-German constitution that was to be used in practice, unlike the one passed by the Frankfurt Parliament in 1849. Among those deputies who voted against the new symbol[15] of the nascent German nation-state were 13 Poles from the province of Posen, 3 Danes from Schleswig, 18 clericalists, and 1 socialist. This opposition vote clearly indicated that the national minorities[16] perceived the confederation as a preliminary form of a German nation-state where their rights would be limited unless they assimilated, or joined, or established their own nation-states.

Bismarck displeased liberals with his autocratic style of governance, so a sizeable group of them formed the National Liberal Party (Nationalliberale Partei) in February 1867. But they believed the aim of establishing a united German nation-state to be liberal in and of itself. At the end of 1866 and the beginning of 1867 the conservative camp split on the issue of German unity as the east German landed gentry—*Junkers*—considered it a possible threat to their prominent social and political status in Prussia. However, a majority of conservatives dismissed these fears and established the Free Conservative Party (Freiekonservative Partei), which stood by Bismarck's unifying policies. Subsequently, it became *the* governing party (Anon., 1889i: 650; Biały, 1990: 266; Czapliński, 1990: 519; Turner, 1992: 111).

The brief Seven Weeks' War of 1866 produced the most far-reaching effect in the Habsburg Monarchy. Having been banished from the rank of the genuine first-rate powers, the Austrian Empire abandoned its ambitions to dominate "Germany." The *Großdeutsch* solution was definitively passé. On top of that, the introduction of the ideas of nation and nation-state into central Europe with the unification of Italy and Germany seriously jeopardized the existence of this multiethnic empire. Its composition from territorially and legally heterogeneous parts stood in stark opposition to the homogenizing juggernaut of national ideology. Hence, from 1866 onwards, the Habsburgs necessarily devoted the majority of their efforts to the preservation of the Austrian Empire, which did not allow them to extend its influence abroad with the exception of the Balkans.

The constitutional reorganization of the Habsburg Monarchy, discussed since 1859, was brought to an early conclusion. On February 17, 1867, Francis Joseph I restored the Hungarian constitution of 1848, and in May 1867 the parliament approved Law XII, which legalized the *Ausgleich* (Compromise). This act turned the empire into a dual Austria-Hungary, where Germans and Hungarians attained the dominant status in their respective parts of the bipartite monarchy. The ensuing stabilization of the domestic political scene, previously disrupted by obstructionist measures applied by the deputies of non-German ethnicity, allowed the adoption of the Fundamental Laws in December 1867. Under the name of the "December Constitution" they remained the legal basis of Austria-Hungary until 1918. This constitution granted the population, importantly construed as citizens, equality before law, and freedom of the press, speech, and assembly. It also protected the interests of the various ethnic groups, which were then turning into proto-nations. To this end the document read:

> all nationalities[17] in the state enjoy equal rights and each one has an inalienable right to the preservation and cultivation of its nationality and language. The equal rights of all languages in local use are guaranteed by the state in schools, administration, and public life. (in Ehrich, 1992: 526)

But these stipulations did not guarantee the same level of privileges for all ethnic and national groups in the empire as that enjoyed by the Germans and the Hungarians.

The Czechs were especially angered, as all their lands were included in the Austrian part of Austria-Hungary without any respect for the tradition of the Czech Crown as composed of Bohemia, Moravia and Silesia. Consequently, in 1868 they demanded a compromise similar to that which had been granted to the Hungarians. Acceptance of their demands would have altered the monarchy into a tripartite empire. Vienna was afraid that such multiethnic federalism would incite similar demands from other national and ethnic groups. German-speaking

Austrians and the Magyars would lose their privileged position in the empire. So the Czech petition was disregarded. The Magyars attacked the possibility of this concession more decidedly than Vienna, as they had not even had time to enjoy their recently granted privileges.

In 1868, the Poles of Galicia issued a declaration similar to the Czech one. There was a difference, though. The Poles asked for autonomy and not for recognition of their nation-state within the framework of the Habsburg Empire. They did not share this option with the Czechs because most territory of the prepartition Poland-Lithuania lay beyond the borders of the Danubian monarchy. The Austrian government never fully recognized the Polish demands but nevertheless instituted important concessions, as it badly needed Polish votes in the Reichstag. Otherwise, the Czech deputies would have brought this legislative body to a standstill, especially in the years 1869–1873. In 1869, Vienna granted Galicia use of Polish as the official medium of administration, the police and courts. Gradually, it became the language of instruction in schools as well as at the universities and in other tertiary educational institutions in Cracow and Lemberg (Lviv, Lwów, Lvov). In 1871, the Ministry of Galicia, headed by a Pole, came into being, as did the Akademia Umiejętności ([Polish] Academy of Sciences in Galicia).[18] However, the Austrians checked the political clout of the Polish politicians by promoting the development of the rival Ruthenian (later known as Ukrainian) national movement in eastern Galicia (Buszko, 1989: 1–6; Ehrich, 1992: 526–527; Polišenský, 1991: 98–99).

The internal political and economic weakness of Austria-Hungary compelled the southern Germanophone states to establish tighter links with Prussia. They, however, stayed away from the North German Confederation, bent on preserving their sovereignty. A clear opportunity to amend this state of affairs was offered by Napoleon III's (ruled 1852–1870) political blunders. He sought to regain, both in France and abroad, the prestige lost as a result of numerous diplomatic reverses, particularly those brought about by the Seven Weeks' War. Contrary to Paris's expectations, this conflict did not lead to the weakening of Austria and Prussia, but it gave a definitive boost to the idea of German unity under Berlin's leadership. The political advance of Prussia, coupled with its steeply increasing military might, posed a threat to French dominance in Europe. Napoleon III resolved to mitigate this discomfiture by seeking compensation in the Rhineland, Luxembourg, or Belgium. But Prussia succeeded in frustrating these plans, and in this manner Bismarck expressed his government's dislike for France's influence in the southern and western German-speaking states.

In this situation, Berlin and Paris had reasons to seek a test of strength. The immediate occasion came in the spring of 1870. Under Bismarck's pressure Prince Leopold von Hohenzollern-Sigmaringen accepted the candidacy for the Spanish throne, which was rendered vacant by the Spanish revolution in 1868.

The French government, alarmed at the possibility of a Prusso-Spanish alliance that would flank France from the west and the east, demanded that William IV order Leopold to withdraw his candidacy, which he did. But for reasons of prestige, Napoleon III asked for an official guarantee that the candidacy would not be renewed. In an interview with the French ambassador at Ems, William IV rejected this demand. The same day, Bismarck obtained William IV's authorization to publish the French demands and the Prussian rejection contained in the Ems Dispatch. Bismarck edited this document in a way calculated to aggravate the tension and reinforce national enthusiasm for a war against France (Czapliński, 1990: 522–529; Kinder, 1978: II 75; Turner, 1992: 111).

France declared war on Prussia on July 19, 1870. The southern Germano-phone states, in fulfillment of their treaties with Prussia, immediately joined William IV in a common front against France. France, with its army of 238,000 men, was outmatched by a German force of 535,000 troops. The Prussian army, which constituted the core of the German troops, was better organized and equipped with superior artillery. One of the most experienced European strategists, Helmuth von Moltke (1800–1891), commanded it, and the French soldiers could not hold out for long even with their state-of-the-art rifles and quick-firing guns. As a result, the French lost one battle after another, and the military engagements were unusually bloody.

The turning point of the Franco-Prussian War was marked by France's defeat in the Battle of Sedan (September 2). The victory, in the eyes of the Germans, became a symbolic redress for France's expansion in the Rhineland and all the German defeats suffered at French hands, especially in Jena in 1806. Throughout the existence of the German Empire (1871–1918) the date was celebrated as a significant national holiday consciously and explicitly basing German unity and identity on enmity towards France. The French defeat at Sedan brought about an explosion of national enthusiasm throughout Germany, which contrasted with the sadness of Poles in Posen, who did not cheer or illuminate their windows.

In Polish national thought Napoleon Bonaparte was a great Polish national hero, since he had reconstituted the Polish state in the form of the Duchy of War-saw (1807–1813/1815). Not surprisingly, many Polish national activists expected Napoleon III to do the same had he defeated Prussia. But the outcome of the war seemed to lead to the establishment of a closely knit homogenous German nation-state in which there would be no place for the Polish language or culture. The indifference of the Poles towards the common German victory at Sedan ignited some anti-Polish excesses in Posen (Biały, 1990: 267; Czapliński, 1990: 525; Kinder, 1978: II 81).

After the defeat in Sedan, German soldiers captured Napoleon III together with 83,000 troops. Paris rose in rebellion. The French emperor was deposed and the Third Republic was proclaimed. At the end of September 1870, German forces surrounded the French capital. After a long and bitter siege, Paris capitulated on January 28, 1871, and on May 10 the Treaty of Frankfurt officially brought the war to a close. The Third Republic had to cede Alsace-Lorraine (Elsaß-Lothringen), pay an indemnity of five billion francs, and accept an army of occupation. It was a Carthaginian peace designed to crush a dangerous rival for influence in Europe. Both the German and French national movements mythologized the Franco-Prussian (German) War, reinforcing mutual enmity incited by this conflict.

The enthusiasm the victory over France aroused in the German-speaking states was overwhelming. Following the success of the unification treaties contracted at the end of 1870, with the parliaments of the North German Confederation members and with the four southern Germanophone states, Bismarck saw to the completion of his and the German national movement's dream. On the symbolic date of January 18, 1871 (the 170th anniversary of the coronation of the first king of Prussia, Frederick I), the Second German Empire was founded in the Hall of Mirrors at the Palace of Versailles. William IV became the German emperor (deutscher Kaiser), bearing the name of William I. At last a unified German state came into being. In time, it would forge the German nation from the multitude of disparate Prussians, Silesians, Bavarians, Hessians and other regional groups.

The cherished hope was that this empire could swiftly turn into a German nation-state. But this did not happen, as the new polity left outside its borders the German-speaking territories in Austria-Hungary but included Danish-speaking and Slavophone minorities with their own national aspirations. William I readily recognized this nuance, because he did not become an emperor "of the Germans" or "of Germany." The title of the German emperor sufficed. So it was just the beginning of nation-state-building that would reach its logical completion in the years 1938–1939 with the *Anschluß* of Austria and the annexations of Bohemia, Moravia and the German territories, which Berlin had ceded to Poland after World War I (Czapliński, 1990: 527–529; Kinder, 1978: 2:75; Turner, 1992: 111).

In Silesia, the Prusso-German[19] (and more rarely purely German) national feeling and enthusiasm rose during the Franco-Prussian War. In all the localities of the province aid was organized for the families of the mobilized and professional soldiers. Emergency hospitals were prepared for the wounded, and medicines and medical equipment were collected. The press appealed for a popular war loan. In the town of Glogau alone the army raised 22,000 thalars. Profits from numerous artistic performances and exhibitions of captured French military equipment were transferred to the army. Every Prusso-German victory produced outbursts of national joy all over Silesia. It reached its apex with the news of the French defeat at Sedan and of the proclamation of the Second German Empire (Biały, 1990: 267; Klaußmann, 1996: 172–173).

Vast economic improvements since 1848 contributed to this ardor. Silesia was Prussia's "poor man" no longer. In 1860, Silesia, with its 10 percent share of Prussia's total production, secured a respectable place among the provinces. Only three surpassed Silesia in economic performance: the Rhineland with a 13 percent share, Brandenburg-Saxony with 12 percent and Westphalia with 11 percent. The gap between the developed western and the previously backward eastern provinces of Prussia had been bridged at last (Herzig, 1994: 552). In the German Empire, Silesia retained its significance, and not only due to its geographical proximity to the imperial seat in Berlin. Before the Ruhr industrial basin Upper Silesia was known as "the black diamond in the crown of Prussia." The Upper Silesian princes von Fürstenberg, Henckel von Donnersmarck, von Hochberg of Pleß and Von Hohenlohe were not satisfied with playing the usual aristocratic roles at the royal or imperial courts. They also acted as veritable captains of industry, forging large industrial groups (Fuchs, 1994: 554).

From the point of view of the Silesian everyman, the overall situation also looked much better in 1871 than it had 30 years earlier. Rapid economic development triggered general civilizational advance, facilitated by improved popular education, increased standards of hygiene, the spread of railways and the shift of population from the countryside to towns. Epidemics and famines no longer decimated the Silesian population. More children grew to adulthood and fewer women died in childbirth. The change in the standard of living was most dramatic in Upper Silesia, which had been the most backward part of the province of Silesia. The general framework for these improvements unfolded with the special acts of 1769, 1811 and 1854. They guaranteed old age and disability pensions for miners and metallurgical workers in Silesia as well as widow pensions for their families (Michalkiewicz, 1976: 405–408). The state was also concerned with the physical fitness of recruits. At the behest of the military authorities, which had advocated protective legislation since 1828, child labor under the age of 9 was prohibited in 1839, and children younger than 12 were banned from the labor market in 1854. After 1871 Germany became the global leader in social politics, for the cause of which the influential Verein für Sozialpolitik (Association for Social Policy, established in 1872) actively canvassed (Kinder, 1978: II 67).

From an economic perspective, there was no reason why the Silesians should not remain firmly loyal and supportive of Prussia and the German Empire. But the logic of nation- and nation-state-building was to dictate otherwise, at least in the case of some non-German-speaking Silesians. The Herderian vision that conflated the spirit of *Volk* with its language arrived in Silesia along with Prussian civil servants who graduated from German universities in the first two decades of the nineteenth century. They strove to translate the philosophical ideas into the language of bureaucracy and state practice and decided that statistics would be the most appropriate tool for this purpose. Consequently, in the 1830s and 1840s, the first trial linguistic surveys were conducted in Prussia (Martuszewski, 1974: 8–9). The German philologist Richard Böckh (1824–1907) argued that language was the *only* adequate indicator of nationality in his article "Die statistische Bedeutung der Volkssprache als Kennzeichen der Nationalität" (The Statistical Importance of Vernacular as the Indicator of Nationality, 1866). Three years later he published his full-fledged academic work entitled *Der Deutschen Volkszahl und Sprachgebiete in den europäischen Staaten* (The Number of Germans and the Areas Where Their Language Is Used in the European States). The equation of language with nationality became the standard approach to the national problem all over Europe.

Not surprisingly, the principle of measuring nationality with language was endorsed at the International Statistical Congress in St. Petersburg in 1872. This congress recommended using language for assessing the demographic size of national groups in censuses. According to the congress's participants, language was the only aspect of nationality that could be objectively inquired about and tabulated. Until today this conclusion, which conflated nationality with language, has remained the standard approach to defining nations and national minorities in central and eastern Europe (Kamusella, 2001).

In western Europe there was no clear intention to espouse this point of view. The civic dimension of nationalism still prevailed. For instance, France, the first state in Europe that allowed emancipation of Jews (1791), contained Sephardic and Ashkenazic Jews, who spoke Ladino ("medieval Spanish") and Yiddish (a Germanic language), respectively. Should one take language as the indicator of their identity, they could have been considered Spanish and German. However, in the light of the French law stemming from the time of the French Revolution, both the linguistic groups of Jews were equally French once they accepted the conditions of French citizenship. Obviously, one of these conditions was to speak French, but it was not paramount. So while Paris employed language policy as one of the nation-building instruments, in central Europe this policy became the sole tool of building nations.

This suited the German national movement well, since German-speakers were widely scattered all over central and eastern Europe. What is more, the language-based definition of nationality also allowed inclusion of the Ashkenazic Jews in the boundaries of the postulated German nation. They spoke Yiddish, a German dialect or a Germanic language not much more different from standard German than the Allemanic dialect spoken in Bavaria and Austria. Thanks to this line of thinking, German politicians and decision-makers could justify the annexations of Holstein and Elsaß (Alsace), whose inhabitants spoke various Germanic idioms (Anon., 1889a: 243; Hobsbawm, 1990: 21–22, 98–99; Kinder, 1978: II 62; Michalkiewicz, 1976: 44).

After having settled on language as the measurable emanation of the ever-elusive nationality, there was no agreement what exactly censuses were to measure.

As a scholar, the Austrian statistician Julius von Ficker (1826–1902) rejected the choice of the language of public life, which the state may impose on individuals. His view was entirely acceptable to his French and Hungarian colleagues. For the same reason Ficker rejected the language of church and school. The Habsburg statisticians also tried to make room for reflecting the flux and change in language. As a result they did not ask citizens about their mother tongues (that is, the very first language one acquires in the earliest childhood), but settled on "family tongue" (*Umgangsprache*), that is, the language usually spoken at home. Obviously one's mother tongue could differ from one's family tongue. Eventually, central and eastern European governments ended up using various aspects of linguistic reality in their censuses. They usually made their choices with an eye to arriving at results that would most please the national movement that dominated the state.

Vienna rightly perceived this principle of equating language with nationality as a delicate issue that could disrupt the Danubian monarchy. Cautiously, the Habsburgs put off the language question until the census of 1880.[20] What nobody quite appreciated at that time was that asking such a question would in fact generate linguistically based ethnic nationalism. Each census became a battlefield between national movements, and asking the language question for the first time *forced* everyone to choose not only a nationality but a linguistically defined nationality. This state-ordained groundbreaking event pushed central and eastern European ethnic groups into the age of nationalism and nationalist conflicts. They necessarily arose from numerous demographic and territorial claims and counterclaims which accompanied the processes of nation- and nation-state-building (Hobsbawm, 1990: 99–100; Michalkiewicz, 1976: 45).

The limited trial language censuses took place in Prussian Silesia between 1828 and 1858. The first full-fledged comprehensive census in the course of which the Silesians were asked the language question was held in 1861 (Michalkiewicz, 1976: 44; cf. Triest, 1984). Due to the aforementioned disinclination on the part of the Habsburg authorities to measure nationality, this question was asked in Austrian Silesia at the same time as elsewhere in Austria-Hungary, that is, in 1880 (Zahradnik, 1992: 160). In consequence, well before the end of the nineteenth century, the principle of nationality as officially accepted by Prussia/Germany and Austro-Hungary did enter Silesia's political and social life in the form of language planning.[21] It strongly contributed to dismantling prenational multiple identities that were based on region and locality. National language policies predictably favored monistic national identities founded on language. This process of language-oriented nation-building was shortly to destroy the still-prenational social cohesion of Prussian Silesia and Austrian Silesia, which were multiethnic lands *par excellence*.

Not much attention was given to Silesia as a separate political and administrative entity in the above analysis of German nationalism prior to 1871. One may consider this approach as contradictory to the subject of this work, but at that time most of Silesia was subsumed into the Prussian kingdom. Understandably, its German national movement was intrinsically linked with the overall German national movement. It is impossible, then, coherently to describe the movement from the regional viewpoint, unlike the Polish and Czech ones that coalesced in Silesia after 1848. However, the author realizes that the two latter national movements, to a certain degree, also developed due to outside material and ideological aid flowing from Posen and Cracow, and Prague, respectively. Also the influence of the German national movement spread to Silesia from the universities in central and western Germany as well as from those in Berlin and Königsberg (Kaliningrad).

This statement is quite valid in the case of Austrian Silesia but must be qualified regarding Prussian Silesia. In the latter province the War of Liberation commenced. This event shaped German nationalism, giving it its first martyrs and its initial royalist form. It should not be forgotten that both Slavic national movements came into being predominantly as a reaction to the assimilating policies of German nationalism. After 1871, it was the German state that actively pursued such policies in Prussian Silesia.

The focus of this chapter, however, is mainly on the period 1848 to 1871. So now it is time to turn the readers' attention to the intellectual and organizational roots of the Polish and Czech national movements in Prussian and Austrian Silesia. These movements had no choice but to formulate their goals and policies in reply to German nationalism. Not surprisingly, they replicated this nationalism's ethnic paradigm.

CHAPTER 3

The Role of Silesia in Polish National Thought and the Beginnings of Polish Nationalism in Prussian Silesia

The beginnings of the Polish national movement in Silesia are associated with bilingual education. It was gradually introduced in the second half of the eighteenth century in areas with Polish/Slavic-speaking populations in Upper Silesia and northeastern Lower Silesia.[1] The goal of this school subsystem was to improve the general education of the inhabitants in these usually backward areas and, hopefully, to prepare them to attend secondary schools and universities. Obviously, at this level, education was provided there exclusively in German and Latin (Kosler, 1929: 223–225).

Bilingual schools were organized and run by the Catholic and Protestant Churches, which controlled popular education in Prussia until the establishment of the German Empire (1871). Due to this confessional influence, the non-German-language section of the curricula drew on the earlier tradition of publishing religious and prayer books in Polish, which still flourished. The crowning moment for these two trends, directed at bettering the comprehension of matters religious and the general education of the inhabitants in the Polish/Slavic-speaking areas of Silesia, came with the publication of the Polish-language monthly *Gazety Szląskie dla Ludu Pospolitego*[2] (Silesian Newspaper for the Common Folk, 1789–1806). The Korn publishing house[3] issued it in Breslau with a tremendous circulation for the time—10,000. Copies of this newspaper were distributed free of charge in the predominantly Polish/Slavic-speaking counties of Prussian Silesia (Gröschel, 1993: 317; Snoch, 1991: 35).

The presence of the Polish language and culture began to be felt quite directly in Lower and Upper Silesia after the two last partitions of the Polish-Lithuanian Commonwealth (1792 and 1795). The state border disappeared between Silesia, and the Grand Duchy of Posen and New Silesia (the area concentrated around the towns of Sosnowiec and Będzin). These two erstwhile Polish territories, among others, became part of Prussia. This transformed Prussia into a virtually bilingual state until 1806, when Napoleon deprived the Prussian Monarchy of the majority of its Polish gains, including New Silesia and the Grand Duchy of Posen. In the former case it was a permanent change, as in accordance with the decisions of the Congress of Vienna, New Silesia remained part of the Congress Kingdom of Poland under Russian supervision. At the same time, the Grand Duchy of Posen was reincorporated into Prussia.

Activists from this grand duchy continued to exert increasing Polish-language influence on Silesia, especially after 1848. This fact was readily recognized by the Korn Verlag, which established its branches in Posen, Warsaw, Lemberg, Vilna (Vilnius) and St. Petersburg to cater to the Polish-speaking market. Since the mid-eighteenth century Korn had brought out works on Polish culture and literature in German and Latin, as well as Polish originals and German translations of renowned Polish writers. Korn also produced brochures, textbooks and various books in Polish, especially prior to the mid-nineteenth century. This climate, which encouraged publication of books in Polish and on matters Polish in Silesia, was possible thanks to the general Prussian interest in the situation of dismembered Poland-Lithuania (cf. Johann Josef Kausch, *Nachrichten über Polen* [News on Poland], 1793). In this respect one should not underestimate a certain acknowledgment of the culture and language of the Polish/Slavic-speaking Silesians that stemmed from the espousal of Herder's philosophy (cf. Johann Gottlieb Schummel's *Reise durch Schlesien* [A Travel through Silesia], 1792).

In 1802 Korn published *Historisch-kritische Analecten zur Erläuterung der Geschichte des Ostens von Europa* (The Historical-Critical Analects Explaining the History of the East of Europe), the first work of the young Polish scholar Jerzy Samuel Bandtke (or Bandtkie, 1768–1835), who studied and worked in Breslau. It included a groundbreaking treatise, "Über die polnische Sprache in Schlesien" (On the Polish Language in Silesia). The following year his Polish-German dictionary[4] appeared and was followed by the *Polnische Grammatik für Deutsche* (Polish Grammar for Germans, 1808) and the *Handbuch der gebräuchlisten Wörter in deutscher, französischer und polnischer Sprache* (Handbook of the Most Useful Words in the German, French and Polish Languages, 1809) (Lubos, 1974: 496–499; Scheuermann, 1994: 838–839; Sosnowski, 1948: I 2, 35).

In the second half of the eighteenth century and in the first half of the nineteenth, Polish travelers boosted interest in Silesia and its Polish/Slavic-speaking population with their travelogues. Following the final elimination of the Polish-Lithuanian Commonwealth from the political map of Europe in 1795, first Polish national thinkers and then activists strove to formulate the notions of the Polish nation and state in emulation of the national postulates forwarded by the French Revolution. Thanks to Napoleon's defeat of Prussia (1806), the Grand Duchy of

Warsaw came into being in the following year. In 1807 and 1808, respectively, Stanisław Staszic (1755–1826) and Hugo Kołłątaj (1750–1812) defined the Polish state in historic and ethnic terms. As a consequence, they demanded for it the territories extending between the Black and Baltic Seas, including Silesia, and the western border on the Oder River (Kulak, 1990: 41–42). Napoleon's defeat in 1815 frustrated the nascent Polish national movement's plans for an extensive nation-state. The Grand Duchy of Warsaw, less the Grand Duchy of Posen, was transformed into the Congress Kingdom of Poland with the Russian tsar crowned as the Polish king (Davies, 1996: 1264).

In 1821 a new national voice was heard. The writer Julian Ursyn Niemcewicz (1758–1841) pointed to the medieval rule of the House of Piast in Silesia as *the* "proof" that Silesia was Polish and should belong to a would-be Polish state (Niemcewicz, 1990: 49). In this manner the so-called Piast myth of Silesia was born. The Polish national activists chose to overlook the fact that language was of no significance for medieval rulers. To these monarchs the only "true" language was Latin, and others appeared to be mere vernaculars unworthy of committing to expensive parchment. Moreover, it was the Piast princes who invited Germanic settlers, without whom Silesia would not have become a Germanic/German-speaking land. In 1830 Tomasz Ujazdowski defined the Polish/Slavic-speaking Silesians as brethren of the Poles through the "same speech, custom and garb," but he shied away from calling them "Poles." He settled on describing them as a "nation [that is, *gens, natio*], which is most favorably disposed to the Poles from all the Slavic nations" (Ujazdowski, 1990: 51). In the first half of the nineteenth century the term "Polish nation" still meant "Polish *natio*," or the multiethnic and multilingual nobility of former Poland-Lithuania. When one referred to "a Pole" it meant a member of this nobility (cf. Pufendorff, in Orłowski, 1998: 81). At the same time, the efforts to extend and limit the meaning of the concept of "Polish nation" so that it would denote all the Polish-speakers, irrespective of social status, were already undertaken in the period between the November and January Uprisings (1831–1864). But this idea of an ethnically defined Polish nation gained currency only at the end of the nineteenth century.

The Towarzystwo Demokratyczne Polskie (Polish Democratic Society, 1832–1862), established in France by Polish émigrés after the failure of the anti-Russian November Uprising, published its manifesto in 1836. It appealed for a greater Polish nation-state extending from the Oder and the Carpathians beyond the Dnieper and the Dvina Rivers, and from the Baltic to the Black Sea (Kulak, 1990: 54). This meant that the whole of Silesia would be included in such a Polish state, similar in territorial extent to that claimed earlier by Staszic and Kołłątaj. In 1837 an analogous postulate appeared in the periodical *Polak* (Pole) in Paris (Kulak, 1990: 55). In 1846 Ludwik Mierosławski planned to involve the Polish/Slavic-speaking Silesians in an all-Polish uprising, which was to take place in the

Prussian, Russian and Austrian partitions of erstwhile Poland-Lithuania,[5] but the insurrection was suppressed before it could actually break out. The 1846 Cracow Uprising constituted a modest branch of this effort. The organizers of the insurrection even reserved a seat for an Upper Silesian representative in their provisional national government but, tellingly, it remained unclaimed (Lis, 1993: 78).

Thus the fringes of the Polish national movement began to visualize Silesia as a vaguely possible addition to a would-be Polish nation-state. The above-presented views of early Polish nationalists never reached the Polish/Slavic-speaking Silesians, though these ideas must have influenced Polish national activists in the Grand Duchy of Posen and Galicia. Consequently, they began to perceive Upper Silesia and East Austrian Silesia, respectively, as potential directions toward which the Polish national propaganda should be directed. At that time no political border would bar it from infiltrating Silesia.

On the other hand, bilingual education and use of Polish in Catholic churches in Upper Silesia and Protestant churches in northeastern Lower Silesia generated a sizeable number of bilingual priests and trained teachers. Some of them came under the influence of Herderian thought and were impressed by German nationalist activists. Together with Polish students from various regions of the then defunct Polish-Lithuanian Commonwealth, they also belonged to the Polish student fraternity Polonia (1817). As a member of the Allgemeine deutschen Burschenschaften (Association of German Student Fraternities) this fraternity was abolished in 1819. Since 1798 the Polish language had been taught at Leopoldina in Breslau and afterward at the Friedrich Wilhelm University, into which the former had been transformed. This led to the establishment of the Towarzystwo Literacko-Słowiańskie (Association of Slavic Literary Research, 1836–1850) under the leadership of the renowned Bohemian physiologist and Pan-Slavist Jan Evangelista Purkyně (1787–1869). Due to his efforts, the Slavistisches Institut (Institute of Slavonic Studies) came into being at the university in 1841 (Lubos, 1974: 500–501; Snoch, 1991: 118; Zielonka 1994: 317).

At the same time, modernization of Prussia brought about homogenization of the state after the Congress of Vienna and prior to the revolutionary events of 1848. This homogenization was also expressed in the growing dominance of the German language as the official medium of communication. In 1817 the Prussian authorities prohibited pilgrimages to the Catholic shrine of Jasna Góra at the nearby town of Częstochowa in Congress Poland. This severed links between the Upper Silesian Catholic Church and the Congress Polish Catholic Church. This move predated the papal bull of 1821 that pushed eastward the western reaches of the Cracow diocese so that they would coincide with the Silesian-Galician (Prussian-Austrian) border.

In the 1820s and 1830s, the Catholic and Protestant Churches limited the number of masses and celebrations conducted in Polish and other Slavic languages at the behest of the Prussian government. In this manner Berlin aimed at transforming bilingual schools into German monolingual ones, and making Polish monolingual schools bilingual. This effort constituted an example of the conscious use of language planning for advancing ethnolinguistic homogeneity in Silesia. The Prussian administration needed the collaboration of both Catholic and Protestant churches, as they controlled and staffed the educational system. This policy of language shift toward German was especially successful with respect to the Silesian Protestants. In 1840 Polish-language celebrations took place in 2 (0.2 percent) churches, German and Polish in 59 (4.3 percent), Czech in 3 (0.3 percent), Czech and German in 2 (0.2 percent), Sorbian and German in 28 (2.5 percent) and German in 1,094 (92.5 churches), though German-speaking Protestants constituted 89 to 90 percent of Silesia's Protestant population, while the Polish/Slavic-speaking Protestants accounted for between 5 and 7 percent.

Unlike church services, the number of Protestant schools with different languages as the medium of instruction duly reflected this proportion between Germanic/German-speakers and Slavic/Polish-speakers. In Catholic schools, which dominated in the Oppeln Regency, 49 percent of the total of 647 schools were bilingual, 31 percent Germanophone and 20 percent Polonophone at the end of the 1830s (Michalkiewicz, 1970: 412–416). In 1819 German became a compulsory subject in Upper Silesian schools, which forced bilingualism on some of the schools where teachers and parents had steered the system in the direction of Polish monolingualism. The supplanting of the bilingual primary educational system with its monolingual German version started in 1839. At that time German (due to its official status and the role of the unifying factor of the Prussian state) was introduced as the medium of instruction in all the elementary schools of the Oppeln Regency (Lis, 1993: 78; Michalkiewicz, 1970: 416).

Moreover, in 1838 Polish was banned from the bilingual weekly *Amts-Blatt der Königlichen Oppelnschen Regierung* (Government Gazette of the Oppeln Regency), which since its inception in 1816, had also reached out to the Polish/Slavic-speaking Upper Silesians thanks to its considerable run of 6,000 copies (Gröschel, 1993: 192). The changes that followed in accordance with the logic of homogenization and language planning favored the German language as the unifying element of the postulated German nation and nation-state, to the obvious detriment of linguistic minorities. In Upper Silesia this attitude brought about a decline in the level of education as German-medium education proved unintelligible to Polish/Slavic-speaking pupils. Hence, comprehension of religious issues among the younger faithful lessened to the great displeasure of the then still-universalistic Catholic Church. However, no overt opposition against this trend emerged in the period when the European powers excelled in suppressing any dissent that would endanger the absolutist prerogatives of the central and eastern European monarchs. But the language policy generated some unexpected consequences. For instance, the supply of bilingual teachers decreased. These were required to educate successfully the Polish/Slavic-speaking students so that by the last years of elementary school, pupils would have attained fluency in German. This immediate need caused the introduction of Polish to the Oberglogau (Głogówek) Catholic teachers' seminary in 1844 (Michalkiewicz, 1970: 417).

The official limitation of the use of Polish created a dearth of publications in this language. The Catholic and Protestant Churches, responsible for bilingual education, readily recognized this predicament, as did private entrepreneurs who perceived it as a potentially profitable market niche. In 1834 the Korn publishing house issued the only volume of *Marzanna*[6]—the "literary and genealogical yearbook for the fair sex" (Gröschel, 1993: 318). From the 1840s onwards, Korn did not publish as many Polish publications and translations from Polish originals as previously, increasingly limiting its interest in Polish books to importing them from Congress Poland and Galicia. Korn's role as a Polish-language publisher was taken over by the Schletter publishing house. It published 135 Polish titles in the years 1835–1855. Polish books (although few in number) also appeared in Oppeln, where in 1833 Edmund Baron established the only Polish bookshop in Silesia (Zielonka, 1994: 201, 310–311).

Publication of Protestant religious books and sermons in Polish (but, importantly, printed in the German Gothic type) continued in Breslau, Oels (Oleśnica), Groß Wartenberg (Syców) and Brieg (Brzeg). The last renowned Protestant author who wrote in Polish was Rev. Robert Fiedler (1810–1877). In the period 1839–1872 he put forth in Polish his sermons and Polish language textbooks. He also published articles and treatises both in Polish and German on the Silesian dialect of the Polish language as well as on customs and traditions of the Polish/Slavic-speaking population in Lower and Upper Silesia (Gajda, 1987: 48–53; Snoch, 1991: 32; Zielonka, 1994: 19–20).

Father Jan Ficek (Fietzek) (1790–1862) was active at the pilgrimage center of Piekar (Piekary). In 1842 he issued the Silesian editions of Piotr Skarga's *Żywoty świętych* (Hagiographies) and Florian Jaroszewicz's *Matka świętych Polski* (Mother of Poland's Saints). Notably, the latter book, with hagiographies of Polish Catholic saints, commenced with the biographies of the first two historical rulers of the Polanian state (that is, Mieszko I and Bolesław Chrobry). This might indicate an early attempt at transplanting Polish nationalism cloaked in the Catholic faith into Upper Silesia. Between 1844 and 1847 Ficek as a charismatic priest organized the widespread temperance movement in eastern Upper Silesia. It was so effective that it led to the emptying of taverns and, thanks to pastoral advice delivered in Polish, considerably fortified the Catholic Church's influence in Upper Silesia. It was the first genuine grassroots movement in the region, involving up to 300,000 people, and was a harbinger of mass politics in the coming age of nationalism.

Epidemics and famines that set in before the outbreak of the revolutionary events of 1848 undid the temperance movement. But as the first mass movement of Upper Silesia, it clearly indicated the potential degree of authority the Catholic Church could muster among the Polish/Slavic-speaking Upper Silesians should it choose to employ a language close to their spoken idiom rather than the official German (1992: 63; Snoch, 1991: 32; Zielonka, 1994: 66). The Church, however, was responsible for implementing the Prussian homogenizing policies at schools and it had to follow the official line. Thus in 1849, out of 354 priests catering for the Polish/Slavic-speaking Upper Silesians, 59 (16.6 percent) spoke German only. The rest were largely bilingual in the spirit of the earlier prenational policies of the Prussian state, which were designed to integrate all inhabitants irrespective of their vernacular (Surman, 1992: 70).

Józef Lompa (1797–1863) was one of the earliest and most significant laymen who invented and implemented the notions of the Polish national movement in Silesia. He came from the Upper Silesian county of Rosenberg (Olesno), which bordered directly on the Congress Kingdom of Poland. He wrote in Polish and German and published about 50 of his books and brochures (among them novels and collections of poetry) as well as 250 articles. Lompa predominantly used Polish, and in 1843 he put forth his *Krótki rys jeografii Szląska* (A Short Outline of Silesian Geography), which emphasized "primordial" links of the land with Polishdom. Beginning in 1844 he joined various cultural and scholarly societies operating in the territories of the ex-Polish-Lithuanian Commonwealth and closely cooperated with the opposition weekly *Rosenberger-Creutzburger Telegraph* (1844–1850).

This periodical published official announcements in Polish and, in this role, partly took over the aforementioned *Amts-Blatt der Königlichen Oppelnschen Regierung,* which had been published exclusively in German since 1838. Thanks to this connection Lompa became the deputy editor of the Polish version of the *Rosenberger-Creutzburger Telegraph.* This version appeared only during the revolutionary period (1848–1849) as *Telegraf Górno-Szląski* (Upper Silesian Telegraph). Notably, the Polish language used in this weekly was strongly influenced by the Slavic dialect of Upper Silesia and the Upper Silesian Slavic-Germanic creole (Anon., 1984: 763; Gröschel, 1993: 246; Snoch, 1991: 83; Zielonka, 1994: 196–197).

In 1844 the first Polish-language calendar, *Kalendarz Postny* (Lent Calendar), appeared in Beuthen (Kossakowska-Jarosz, 1994: 23–24) and was followed by the *Kalendarz Katolicki* (Catholic Calendar, 1846–1850, Gleiwitz and Beuthen), published by Father Antoni Stabik (1807–1887). He worked at Michalkowitz (Michałkowice, today part of Siemianowice [Siemianowitz]), just a few kilometers from the border of Congress Poland. His *Opis Ziemi Świętej* (A Description of the Holy Land, 1847) was the first of its kind published in Polish in Silesia. He also issued a collection of his poetry in 1848 (Snoch, 1991: 133). Another Catholic priest who furthered knowledge of the Polish language among the faithful was

Father Józef Szafranek (Josef Schaffranek) (1807–1874). Since 1839 he had been active in Beuthen, then the very center of the Upper Silesian industrial basin under the direct ecclesiastical jurisdiction of the Cracow Diocese until 1821. He appealed for the wider use of Polish in Upper Silesian schools and in 1848 entered the political arena as a deputy to the Prussian National Assembly in Berlin (Lubos, 1974: 515; Snoch, 1991: 135; Zielonka, 1994: 83).

The Pleß county, with arguably the largest percentage of Polish/Slavic-speakers in its population compared to other counties in Upper Silesia, was served by *Tygodnik Polski* (Polish Weekly, 1845–1847). The local publisher, Christian Schemmel, had established it and also owned the weekly *Plesser Kreisblatt* (Pleß County Newspaper, 1841–1922), where Polish articles had begun to appear in 1844. Another Polish periodical, *Gwiazdka dla Ludu Górnoszlązkiego* (Small Star for the Upper Silesian Folk, 1846–1848), was published in Beuthen (Gröschel, 1993: 35, 224; Zielonka, 1994: 29).

These cultural-commercial and religious initiatives championed some limited reintroduction of the Polish language to public life in Upper Silesia, contributing to the idea that Polish could also serve as a medium of instruction, at least in elementary schools. This trend culminated in the unexpected developments of 1848, when production of Polish-language books and periodicals increased considerably.

The difficult and sometimes tragic economic and social situation prior to 1848 manifested itself in worker and peasant riots. These prepared the ground for the spread of popular dissent. The revolution broke out in Berlin on March 18, 1848. Thanks to the direct railway link, the news incited the inhabitants of Breslau (the second largest Prussian city [Herzig, 1994: 542]) to begin building barricades and demanding liberal reforms the very next day. Elsewhere in Silesia, unrest appeared for the first time in Hirschberg (Jelenia Góra) on March 20, and at the end of March 1848 disturbances spread to other towns in southwestern Lower Silesia, that is, to Schmiedeberg (Kowary), Lauban (Lubań) and Greiffenberg in Schlesien (Gryfów Śląski). The local authorities successfully contained these riots as well as concomitant widespread plunder and disturbances in the countryside, where peasants demanded scrapping of the remnants of serfdom.

The same revolutionary pattern of events repeated itself in Upper Silesia. Initially, peasants demanded freedom from serfdom's obligations, which continued there in a more oppressive form than in Lower Silesia. Eventually, the situation forced the lords to grant them this concession. On March 22, 1848, workers and artisans demonstrated at Ratibor, and unrest spread to the counties of Ratibor, Kreuzburg (Kluczbork), Rosenberg, Rybnik (Rybnik), Grottkau (Grodków) and Neisse (Nysa). Due to the separatist strife in the Grand Duchy of Posen, where local Poles rose against the Prussian authorities, and because of the danger of a conflict with Russia, Berlin suppressed the revolutionary disturbances with military force. This was accomplished first in Lower Silesia and later in Upper Silesia.

The convening of the Frankfurt *Vorparlament* (Preliminary Parliament, March 30–April 4, 1848) channeled popular dissent into the sphere of politics. Parties representing all sides of the social conflict were busy preparing themselves for the elections to the German National Assembly in Frankfurt, scheduled for May 1. At the beginning of May the elections to the Prussian National Assembly at Berlin took place, inciting further political agitation in Prussian Silesia. The democratizing developments were not enough to prevent demonstrations of unemployed miners and metallurgical workers in Gleiwitz, Beuthen and Nikolau (Mikołów), and general unrest in Oppeln and Cosel (Koźle), which continued throughout May. The promise of liberal reforms (including full abolishment of serfdom) and of broader suffrage, as well as field works, delayed any further riots until autumn (Czapliński, 1990: 477; Kinder, 1978: II 54; Lis, 1993: 79–80; Michalkiewicz, 1970: 488–500; Snoch, 1991: 120).

Participation in the first free elections[7] to the assemblies at Frankfurt and Berlin provoked considerable interest, as 30 to 50 percent of the eligible voters took part. As a result, for the first time the political voice and concerns of the Polish/Slavic-speaking Silesians were heard directly at the power centers. Twenty-four deputies from Upper Silesia were elected to the Prussian Assembly. Perhaps nine of them were bilingual, mainly peasants, but also one industrial worker and the Beuthen vicar Józef Szafranek. On the other hand, the Frankfurt Parliament's national goal of forging German unity was of no immediate concern to the rural Polish/Slavic-speaking population of Upper Silesia. Their first priority was to do away with the last remnants of serfdom in order to improve their lot. Hence, the national ideals of the Frankfurt Parliament seemed to them insignificant, if not completely unintelligible. A similar attitude prevailed among peasants throughout the German-speaking states. The national message spread among professors, lawyers, industrialists, professionals and craftsmen—that is, the upper middle class that dominated the parliament. It is worth mentioning that the only peasant deputy to this assembly was Krystian Minkus, from the Upper Silesian village of Marienfeld (Oś) in Lompa's home county of Rosenberg (Lis, 1993: 80–81).

The political and social unrest, coupled with the rapid development of the German national movement, caused repeated demands for the use of the Polish language in Upper Silesian schools. This also incited the first propagators of the Polish language in Silesia to put forward some Polish national theses. German public opinion and Polish activists in the Grand Duchy of Posen were shocked by Szafranek's petition, lodged with the Prussian Assembly on August 24, 1848. Among other things, he demanded bilingual German-Polish courts and administration for Upper Silesia, that Polish be the sole medium of instruction in elementary schools and that it be equal to German in secondary schools and the Breslau University. Furthermore, he asked for the proceedings of the assembly to be translated into and published in Polish[8] (Szafranek, 1990: 65–66).

His demands were rejected as impractical, but this petition marked the tentative beginning of the Polish national movement in Silesia. Remarkably, the *Liga Polska* (Polish League, 1848–1850), established in Berlin by activists from the Grand Duchy of Posen, supported Szafranek's position. This nationalist society organized local branches in Upper Silesia and its theoretician Karol Libelt (1807–1875) included Upper Silesia, within the postulated boundaries of a Polish nation and nation-state. On the basis of Arndt's famous thesis, which defined Germany in linguistic terms, Libelt thought that the territorial extent of spoken Polish should coincide with the borders of a reconstituted Polish state.

In 1848 some Polish nationalists noticed that there was potential for the spread of the Polish national idea in Upper Silesia, which encouraged the flow of Polish periodicals from the Grand Duchy of Posen to Silesia. One of them, *Gazeta Polska* (Polish Newspaper), emphasized that Polish national activists from the grand duchy and Galicia should support development of the Polish national movement in Upper Silesia (Wanatowicz, 1992: 24–25). The preliminary intellectual and cadre base of such a movement coalesced around the following Polish Upper Silesian Polish-language periodicals: *Dziennik Górno Szląski* (Upper Silesian Daily, 1848–1849), *Telegraf Górno-Szląski* (Upper Silesian Telegraph, 1848–1849), *Tygodnik Górnoszląski* (Upper Silesian Weekly, 1848–1852), *Tygodnik Katolicki* (Catholic Weekly, 1848–1850), and *Gazeta Wiejska dla Górnego Szląska* (Village Newspaper for Upper Silesia, 1849–1850).

The first of these periodicals, *Dziennik Górno Szląski*, was openly nationalist. The Liga Polska financed this publication, which was edited by Aleksander Mierowski (1823–?), Józef Łepkowski (1826–1896) and Emanuel Smołka (Smolka) (1820–1854) with Lompa's active cooperation. Łepkowski came from Cracow and later became rector of the Jagiellonian University. Two other periodicals, *Telegraf Górno-Szląski* and *Tygodnik Górnoszląski*, catered to the commercial and everyday needs of the Polish/Slavic-speaking population, not unlike the two last ones, *Tygodnik Katolicki* and *Gazeta Wiejska dla Górnego Szląska*. Being initiatives of the Catholic Church, obviously, they would be focused on matters religious. But even in these four periodicals, relatively free from nationalist agitation, Ficek represented a pro-Polish stance in *Tygodnik Katolicki*, whereas *Telegraf Górno-Szląski* and *Gazeta Wiejska dla Górnego Szląska* were pro-German (Glensk, 1995: 89; Gröschel, 1993: 65–66 195, 225, 247; Lis, 1993: 89).

In 1848–1849 Polish language and Polish national life was concentrated in Beuthen and the town's vicinity (Michalkiewicz, 1970: 517–518; Zielonka, 1994: 29). The number of people involved in it was considerable. In 1848, Lompa clothed it with his Towarzystwo Pracujących dla Oświaty Ludu Górnośląskiego (Society for Education of the Upper Silesian Folk), later renamed the Towarzystwo Nauczycieli Polaków (Society of Teachers who are Poles). The Klub Narodowy (National Club), established in Beuthen on October 28, was chaired by the

Upper Silesian Polonophile Carl von Koschützki (Karol Kosicki)[9] (1788–1863). This club mainly consisted of the intellectuals involved in publishing *Dziennik Górno-Szląski* (Brożek, 1995: 55; Snoch, 1991: 61, 67–68, 83). Three days before founding the Klub Narodowy, this radical newspaper published an article that, on a linguistic basis, exhorted the Upper Silesian Polish/Slavic-speakers not to identify themselves as Germans or Prussians because they were Poles and ought to serve their Polish fatherland.

This appeal suggested that Upper Silesia was part of Polishdom and, as such, should be included in a future Polish nation-state (Kulak, 1990: 66–67; Michalkiewicz, 1970: 513). Another institution worth mentioning is the Klub Niedzielny (Sunday Club) (1848–1849), which Jan Gajda and Józef Lompa founded in Lubetzko (Lubecko). This club supported an amateur theater troupe, which commenced the tradition of using the theater as a tool of nationalism in Upper Silesia. Performances produced to this end mushroomed in Upper Silesia at the beginning of the 1870s (Mykita-Glensk, 1988: 5). Most importantly, funded from Posen, Polish reading rooms were established in Beuthen, Lublinitz (Lubliniec), Woischnik, Rybnik and Myslowitz (Łepkowski, 1990: 70) between 1848 and 1849. They disappeared in the 1850s, but beginning in the 1880s, the institution of the reading room became the mainstay of the early Polish national movement in Upper Silesia (Snoch, 1991: 148–149).

The revolutionary movement peaked dramatically, and then quickly declined. The unprovoked massacre of liberal protesters at Schweidnitz (Świdnica) on July 31, 1848, triggered a renewed wave of unrest all over Silesia that peaked in the autumn. Thereafter the absolutist rulers of the German-speaking states gradually regained control. The radical strain of the Silesian revolutionary movement was squelched by the end of 1848. The abolishment of serfdom and granting of the constitution calmed the situation. Repression came with the complete extinguishing of the revolutionary flame in 1849 (Michalkiewicz, 1970: 524, 532–535).

All the Polish-language Upper Silesian periodicals previously mentioned went defunct shortly thereafter, and Polish activists who were not Prussian citizens (for example, Łepkowski) were expelled from Silesia. Many German national politicians active throughout the German Confederation emigrated from Europe. Those who remained kept a low profile. Interestingly, these political émigrés established the routes of emigration to the New World, which were later followed by Prussian and Silesian peasants.

Peasants decided to emigrate due to the excessive individual cost of the abolishment of serfdom. They were burdened with indemnifications paid to erstwhile lords for lost labor. The economy, shaken by systemic reforms, remained poor. These factors did not allow any immediate improvement in the lot of the Silesian peasantry, and their fate was especially difficult in Upper Silesia. Other reasons for emigration were more personal, for instance, evasion of conscription. In 1850, emigration to the United States, and especially to Texas (incorporated into the United States in 1845), became popular in Lower Silesia.

The first Upper Silesian group, under the leadership of their vicar, Father Leopold Moczygemba, arrived in Texas in 1854. They established their own town, Panna Maria (Holy Virgin Mary), hailed as the first Polish settlement in the United States. It survives to this day with a considerable percentage of inhabitants speaking the Slavic Silesian dialect interlaced with numerous Anglicisms (Brożek, 1972: 13, 232–237). In the 1860s, a considerable number of Prussian citizens emigrated to Brazil, and the first Upper Silesians joined this trend in 1867. By the 1880s overseas emigration decreased due to the rapid development of the German Empire. Instead of emigrating, Silesians chose to migrate to the western German industrial centers. To illustrate this fact, one can glance at the statistics. In 1845 Silesians constituted 5 percent (19,000) of Berlin's total population and 7.1 percent (142,215) in 1907. This migration even engendered a saying: "Jeder zweite Berliner stammt aus Schlesien" (Every second Berliner comes from Silesia) (Düspohl, 1995: 190, 193–194). In 1907, in all approximately 730,000 Silesians lived outside their homeland but still within the borders of the German Empire (Brożek, 1969; Brożek, 1988: 21; Miś, 1969; Wrzesiński, 1995: 181).

In the years following the 1848 revolution, there were attempts to revive some Polish-language periodicals. They had to stay away from politics so as not to face the danger of immediate closure. Carl von Koschützki supported the publication of the weekly *Poradnik Górno-Szląski* (Upper Silesian Magazine of Advice, 1851–1853/1854) and in the years 1848–1851 and 1857–1859 some Polish texts appeared in *Amts-Blatt der Königlichen Oppelnschen Regierung*. Poles and Polish-speaking students at the Breslau University established the weekly *Marchołt* (Markolf,[10] 1851) and the yearly *Znicz* (Eternal Flame, 1851–1852), but the periodicals quickly went defunct. The very use of the Polish language became a political issue in the eyes of the authorities, and no significant Polish-language periodicals were allowed in Silesia until the 1860s. Only *Penelope: Nowy Żurnal Deseniowy Robót i Mód Damskich* (Penelope: A New Journal of Knitting and Female Fashion, 1853–1862), devoted to a politically neutral subject and directed mainly at the Polish female readership in the Province of Posen, could be published, in Glogau, Lower Silesia. This was safely far away from Upper Silesia (Gröschel, 1993: 66–67, 192, 318–319, 393).

In the period of the dynamic development of the German press in Silesia there was no Polish/Slavic-language parallel in multiethnic and multilingual Upper Silesia. Polish nationalists from Posen, who a priori appropriated the Polish/Slavic-speaking Silesians for their movement, openly considered this population to be Polish (Kulak, 1990: 71). Posen Poles strove to ameliorate this dearth of Polish-language publications by facilitating Silesian subscriptions to Polish-language periodicals from their province. The most popular of them were *Wielkopolanin* (The Inhabitant of Wielkopolska) and, during the 1860s, the weekly *Przyjaciel Ludu* (The Friend of the People), published in Culmhof (Chełmno) near Bromberg (Bydgoszcz). In 1867 the latter periodical's 249 copies arrived in 35 Upper Silesian localities (Glensk, 1992: 17). In this period, however, Paweł Stalmach's *Gwiazdka Cieszyńska* (The Cieszyn Small Star, 1851–1920), from East Austrian Silesia, held sway among Polish national activists in Prussian Silesia. Between 1848 and 1851 it had appeared under the title *Tygodnik Cieszyński* (Cieszyn Weekly) and had been overtly pro-Polish. In conjunction with Stalmach's national activities this weekly had helped to create the Polish national movement in East Austrian Silesia (Michalkiewicz, 1976: 278; Pater, 1991: 204; Snoch, 1991: 45; Zahradnik, 1989: 85, 200).

After 1848, language policies qualitatively changed. The Catholic and Protestant Churches, while remaining fully loyal to Prussia, demanded wider use of Polish and other Slavic vernaculars in order to spread the Gospel in a manner that would best suit their faithful. This universalistic goal clashed with the homogenizing policies of Berlin, but at that time Prussia could ill afford rejecting cooperation with these institutions. Their strong positive influence on the wide strata of unhappy peasantry and industrial workers helped create a modicum of stability in the post-1848 period. As a consequence, no protests took place to oppose the reintroduction of enlightened absolutism with few elements of parliamentarian democracy.

Moreover, in the eyes of Prussian decision-makers and intellectuals, the Upper Silesian was the epitome of the "noble savage" who had to be civilized so as not to degenerate and imperil the task of nation-building in this far-flung corner of the Prussia (Ring, in Lüer, 1995: 82). From this perspective, it seemed unrealistic to enforce the use of German without prior bilingual education to prepare this "backwater" population for receiving the German language and culture. The significance of this task can be well illustrated by the sheer numbers of Polish/Slavic-speakers. In 1861, there were between 416,000 and 666,000 Polish-speakers[11] in Upper Silesia, and 54,000 in Lower Silesia. The lower number in the case of Upper Silesia is the official German figure, and the higher one is a modern Polish estimate that includes bilingual persons whom Prussian statisticians considered to be Germans (Pater, 1991: 119). From the confessional point of view, the majority of Polish/Slavic-speaking Protestants were concentrated in northeastern Lower Silesia. Their number, including Polish/Slavic-speaking Protestants from Upper Silesia, amounted to 120,000 in 1857 (Kokot, 1973: 20; Pater, 1991: 119–120).

The subsequent reform that reintroduced bilingual education in Prussian Silesia is connected to Father Bernhard Bogedain (1810–1860), who was born in the village of Fröbel (Wróblin) near Glogau, close to the border of the Grand

Duchy of Posen. Knowledge of Polish was not unusual in this Lower Silesian area. His uncle served as a vicar in Wielkopolska, and thanks to his backing, Bogedain was ordained by the Gnesen-Posen (Gniezno-Poznań) Archbishop (and Polish Primate, though not recognized by the Prussian authorities) Marcin Slugustowski-Dunin (in office 1831–1842). Bogedain also found employment in this archdiocese. Having noticed the poor quality of Polish-language primers and prayer books in the grand duchy, Bogedain compiled the popular hymnal *Pieśni nabożne dla użytku katolików w archidiecezji gnieźnieńskiej* (Church Songs for the Use of Catholics in the Gniezno Archdiocese).

On May 15, 1848, he was nominated for the position of Oppeln Regency School Councilor, and on February 5, 1849, in a by-election, he was elected to the National Assembly in Berlin. At this assembly he supported Father Szafranek's stance on the use of Polish in Upper Silesia (Świerc, 1990: 3–7). Bogedain argued that fluency in German was necessary for improving the standard of living but added that Upper Silesians should be allowed to praise God in their mother tongue, Polish, and use this language in elementary school. He reasoned that without formal knowledge of Polish they would not be able to learn German properly (Herzig, 1994: 498).

In his capacity as the Oppeln Regency School Councilor, Bogedain advocated the use of standard Polish in the Slavophonic areas of Upper Silesia. Apparently he came to the conclusion that as German children were taught *Hochdeutsch* (standard German) and not the local dialects spoken at home, Upper Silesian schoolchildren should not use their specific Polish/Slavic dialects or creoles at school. Inadvertently, this decision improved Upper Silesians' comprehension of publications imported from Posen and created a linguistic difference vis-à-vis East Austrian Silesia. In this Austrian province, initially a majority of "Polish" publications were printed in the local Slavic dialect(s) precisely for the sake of better comprehension among the readership, which was ignorant of standard Polish.

At first, Bogedain carried out his policy by publishing the conservative weekly *Gazeta Wiejska dla Górnego Szląska,* sponsored by the government of the Oppeln Regency (Gröschel, 1993: 15). Obviously, the Breslau Bishop Melchior von Dipenbrock (1845–1853) and the Prussian government favored Bogedain's efforts (Pater, 1991: 122). By the beginning of the 1850s standard Polish was the medium of instruction and Polish-language textbooks were introduced to elementary schools in the predominantly Polish/Slavic-speaking areas of Upper Silesia. In 1857, there were 491 bilingual and 182 Polish-language schools in the Oppeln Regency (Michalkiewicz, 1976: 467). This decision entailed reforming the teachers' seminaries in Peiskretscham (Pyskowice), Oberglogau and Pilchowtz (Pilchowice) to produce competent specialist teachers to work in bilingual elementary schools. However, knowledge of standard Polish among Upper Silesian priests remained unsatisfactory. After finishing elementary education, future priests continued learning at secondary schools where Polish was merely an elective subject (Kraszewski, 1990: 85; Lis, 1993: 89; Surman, 1992: 73; Świerc, 1990: 8).

The state authorities wholeheartedly supported the reformatory ideas of Bogedain. They extended Bogedain's changes, targeted toward Catholic schools, to the Protestant educational system, which catered to the Protestant Polish/Slavic-speaking population in the Breslau Regency. Standard Polish was introduced as a medium of instruction to Protestant schools in 1850. For instance, in the county of Groß Wartenberg there were 34 Polish-language schools, 2 Czech and 14 Polish-German (Pater, 1991: 122–123, 195). At the end of the 1850s, a Protestant teachers' seminary was built in Kreuzburg (Kluczbork) to turn out Polish language teachers for this Protestant bilingual educational system. Silesia's elementary education catered to 128,288 Polish-speaking pupils in 1864 and 159,441 in 1871; 11,662 Czech-speaking ones in 1864 and 10,396 in 1871; and 5,103 Sorbian-speaking ones in 1864 and 5,376 in 1871. Bilingual pupils included 22,333 Polish-and-German-speakers, 2,516 Czech-and-German-speakers and 1,322 Sorb-and-German-speakers in 1864. In 1871 the figures for these three categories were 22,074, 1,026 and 1,452, respectively (Brożek, 1995: 56; Michalkiewicz, 1976: 484–485).

Similarly, the Prussian government, eager to improve agricultural productivity in Upper Silesia with its rich soils, established the Agricultural Academy (1847–1880) in Proskau (Prószków) near Oppeln. During its existence, many local and Polish students (407, mainly from Wielkopolska) attended, and spread interest in the Polish language and culture. Polish students subscribed to Posen periodicals. With pecuniary aid flowing from Polish national circles in Posen, they organized the school's Polish-language library in 1856 and made it open to the local population. The students also established the Towarzystwo Literacko-Rolnicze (Literary-Agricultural Society) within whose framework the Komisja Ludowa (People's Commission) was incorporated. The commission's goal was to spread education and Polish national feeling among the locals (Pater, 1991: 211).

Simultaneously, some Polish students from Congress Poland and the province of Posen were active at the Breslau University. They were developing cultural and national initiatives under the organizational roof of the Towarzystwo Literacko-Słowiańskie (1836–1886), which the authorities, at last, ceased to molest. Thanks to their efforts, the Towarzystwo Przemysłowców Polskich (Society of Polish Industrialists) came into being in 1866, and two years later the students managed to legalize their social academic club and its provident fund.

Interestingly, Polish/Slavic-speaking Upper Silesian students declined any invitations to join these bodies and grouped themselves in their own academic club, Towarzystwo Akademików Górnoślązaków (Society of Upper Silesian Students), which was established in the academic year 1862–1863. About forty of them attended the Breslau University at the end of the 1860s (Kraszewski,

1990: 86–87). There were, however, exceptions to this unspoken rule that Upper Silesian students did not join the organizations of Polish students from Posen. For instance, Father Konstanty Damrot (Damroth) (1841–1895) belonged to the Upper Silesian academic club and to the Towarzystwo-Literacko Słowiańskie. He is considered the most outstanding Polish lyricist of nineteenth-century Upper Silesia. Although he wrote equally well in Polish and German, he chose to consider himself a Pole, and this conviction caused him to steer the Towarzystwo Akademików Górnoślązaków toward the Polish national tendency in 1866–1867. Unofficially, its members called it the Towarzystwo Polskich Górnoślązaków (Society of Polish Upper Silesian) (Michalkiewicz, 1976: 351; Snoch, 1991: 25).

But most Upper Silesian Slavic/Polish-speaking students stayed away from the Polish national movement. They mainly read Catholic theology to become priests. In accordance with the universalistic line of the Church, they did not dabble in nationalism. They aimed at becoming dexterous shepherds of the faithful in Upper Silesia's bilingual and Polish/Slavic-speaking parishes, and not at becoming Poles. Obviously, the Catholic Church authorities carefully encouraged this traditional, prenational stance among the Polish/Slavic-speaking Silesians. For instance, in 1852, the Breslau Bishop von Diepenbrock asked the Silesian clergy, in an official letter, to limit the inflow of periodicals from the Province of Posen. He rightly opined that they could attract some Silesian Polish/Slavic-speakers into the fold of the Polish national movement (Michalkiewicz, 1976: 291).

At the level of national declarations, Upper Silesian priests and students of theology remained loyal bilingual Polish/Slavic- and German-speaking subjects of the Prussian king. With the development of the officially espoused German national movement, some of them began to feel themselves to be Germans too. In short, their prenational multiple identity can be adequately described with the medieval-like Latin label: *gente poloni natione Pruteni et/vel Germani*[12] (Surman, 1992: 72–73). Lompa decried their attitude as neutral to the laudable ethos of the Polish national movement. He believed that their stance played into the hands of the Prussian state and the German national movement (Lompa, in Surman, 1992: 72). As a convinced Pole and Polish national activist,[13] Lompa could not support the universalistic stance of the Silesian clergy and their belief that language and national identity were secondary phenomena not worth greater veneration than the Gospels.

Traditionally, the Breslau bishop nominated a Polish/Slavic-speaking bishop suffragan to look after multilingual Upper Silesia (Świerc, 1990: 13), but he did not facilitate the spread of Polish national feeling there in the period 1850–1871. This was because the Polish/Slavic-speaking Upper and Lower Silesians preferred to identify themselves with the Prussian kingdom and "Germany" (Malinowski, 1990: 93), at that time equated with the North German Confederation.

The relative strength of this multiple regional-state identity is illustrated by the fact that many of the Polish/Slavic-speaking Upper Silesian settlers in Texas and their descendants identified themselves as Prussians as late as 1874. It was the main reason they were not interested in establishing any Polish organizations in their locality of Panna Maria. However, this did not preclude a feeling of animosity toward German-speakers as well as toward English-speaking neighbors, who labeled them "Silesian Poles" (Borek, 1979: 57–58; Brożek, 1995: 57). Here it is worth noting that at the end of the 1860s not only these Texan Upper Silesians but Upper Silesia's Polish/Slavic-speaking population at large considered the word "Pole" a slur (not unlike the English "Polack"). In their eyes Polishdom was associated with poor vagabonds from Congress Poland. In Silesia they were perceived as potential criminals and, on the whole, did not constitute a good advertisement for Polish nationalism (Malinowski, 1990: 94).

The traditional multiple identity of the Polish/Slavic-speaking Upper Silesians, steeped in patriotism to Prussia, Germany and the Hohenzollerns, persisted due to radical improvements in the economy, standard of living and agriculture. The rapidly elevated political position of Prussia in Europe and in the world instilled patriotic pride in Upper Silesians no less than in other Prussians. In such a situation, why should they have identified with the Polish-speakers and their elusive nonexistent state? Upper Silesians living next to the border with Russia's Congress Poland and Vienna's Galicia were appalled by the low standard of living and economic conditions suffered by the Polish-speaking populations across the frontier. Upper Silesians did not aspire to common identification with this poverty and "Asiatic uncivilizedness" (Kulak, 1993: 107).

Importantly, the authorities did not press the Upper Silesians to abandon their own Polish/Slavic heritage and dialects. On the linguistic plane the Upper Silesians preserved their prenational multiple identity, speaking Polish/Slavic dialects to family members and neighbors, German[14] to strangers and officers, and standard Polish to teachers and priests. On the whole, they took pride in the Prussian military victories of 1864, 1866 and 1870–1871, and remained staunchly loyal to the Hohenzollern monarch in his capacity as Prussian king and German emperor. Polish national agitation emanating from Posen and Galicia fell on deaf ears in Upper Silesia, despite fears of the Prussian officialdom to the contrary. The Upper Silesian Polish/Slavic-speakers did not express any interest in the Polish January Uprising (1863–1864) that played out in Congress Poland, or in the endeavors to unite Germany, for that matter. All these national efforts seemed to take place "far away" from their homeland (Pater, 1991: 210, 221–222, 226–227). Upper Silesians still felt secure in their region, entrenched in a prenational cocoon of multilingual and multicultural tradition, shielded as well from the outside world with their Catholic and Protestant religiosity. Nationalism—German or Polish—held no allure. Nonetheless, Lompa and his successors strove to break this status quo.

The starting point for the Polish national movement was the traditional ecclesiastical link between east Upper Silesia and Cracow. It continued despite the severance of this area from the Cracow Diocese in 1821, and became quite strong by the 1840s. At that time, Galician clergy successfully initiated the temperance movement in Upper Silesia, the first grassroots mass movement in this region. It involved 300,000 people. After 1848, the Silesian-Galician borderland unfolded into a kind of "common market" integrated by the transportation infrastructure, economic interests and mobile labor. Prussia and Austria closely guarded their borders with Russia, but not their common border.

Some Upper Silesians participated in pilgrimages to Catholic shrines in Cracow and, more rarely, to Częstochowa (Congress Poland). Moreover, religious books printed in Posen and Teschen often found their way to Upper Silesia. In addition to locally produced Polish-language religious-themed publications, Polish/Slavic-speaking Upper Silesians also perused popular books containing fantastic tales and doggerel poetry. They acquired the habit of reading for pleasure at bilingual elementary school. Literacy, one of the preconditions of developing a national movement, was quite widespread in Upper Silesia, in contrast to the territories of former Poland-Lithuania (with the exception of Wielkopolska), where illiteracy persisted up into the 1950s (Pater, 1991: 202, 210; Wanatowicz, 1992: 30–31).

Stalmach's *Gwiazdka Cieszyńska* added a degree of political turbulence to this prenational Upper Silesian calm, but the leading role in this respect was reserved for Polish national activists from the Province of Posen. Being part of Prussia, no international border separated this province from Silesia. Thanks to the economic development of the Prussian kingdom, the Posen Polish national movement had at its disposal enough wealth to project Polish nationalism into Upper Silesia. This ideology grew in the Grand Duchy of Posen between 1827[15] and 1848. Thereafter the local Polish national movement fortified itself in reaction to the liquidation of the grand duchy's autonomy. The Grand Duchy of Posen became a regular Prussian province and was included within the borders of the German Confederation (until 1851). In the 1850s the ongoing modernization of the province's economic system allowed the Polish national movement to adopt an organizational framework similar to its German counterpart in order to compete successfully with the latter (Jakóbczyk, 1989: 1–23).

By the 1840s Mierosławski had already commenced the Posen Polish national movement's contacts with the Polish/Slavic-speaking population of Upper Silesia. In the 1850s, this trend continued with the flow of Polish periodicals and books into the region from Posen and because of the activities of the Polish students at the Agricultural Academy in Proskau. The leaders of these students usually hailed from the Province of Posen. In the 1860s, the Polish movement in Wielkopolska was strong enough actively to proselytize Polish nationalism in Upper Silesia. Posen Polish activists foresaw Silesia as part of a reconstituted Poland and pointed to the necessity of attracting the Polish/Slavic-speaking Silesian everyman to the cause of the "Polish struggle against the partition power of Prussia."

It was a typically ideological message spread by such renowned national agitators from Wielkopolska as Józef Chociszewski[16] (1837–1914), Ignacy Danilewski[17] and Father Franciszek Bażyński[18] (1801–1876) (Wanatowicz, 1992: 31, 32). From a historical point of view, only the Province of Posen had constituted a part of prepartition Poland-Lithuania, thus the Polish-speaking inhabitants of Wielkopolska could consider Prussia a partition power. However, this was not the case for the Silesians, whose land left the territorial composition of the Kingdom of Poland as early as the beginning of the fourteenth century, that is, before the rise of Poland-Lithuania. However, since the 1860s, many Polish national activists had begun to consider Upper Silesia part of the Prussian partition of Poland-Lithuania. It was the Polish national writer Józef Ignacy Kraszewski (1812–1887) who introduced this novel way of thinking about Silesia in the terms of "invented history" (Wanatowicz, 1992: 36).

The early 1860s was an opportune time for Polish national agitators from Posen to step into Upper Silesia. At that time some Polish/Slavic-speaking Silesians were unhappy with decisions that limited the role of standard Polish as the medium of instruction in elementary schools. In 1859, the Oppeln Regency authorities obliged teachers actively to support knowledge of German among their students. As of 1863, Polish was used as a medium of instruction only in the first grade of elementary school. In higher grades, German took over, with the exception of religious instruction. Polish could function only as an auxiliary language. Initially, the limitations were not staunchly enforced and teachers often lapsed into the old ways. They often spoke in standard Polish while striving to foster comprehension of difficult topics among their Polish/Slavic-speaking students (Michalkiewicz, 1976: 468–469). Instruction in Polish in secondary schools was reduced throughout Silesia, and it was completely phased out by 1874 (Pater, 1978: 239).

Lompa's ideological successors, a new generation of Polish activists in Upper Silesia, capitalized on the situation. The sudden dearth of education in Polish and of Polish-language periodicals created a sociopolitical vacuum that would be gradually filled by the Polish national message (Brożek, 1995: 55). Initially, the success of the Prussian reforms discouraged Polish national identification in Silesia, and the universalism of the Catholic Church hindered any national identification. The regionally based identity of Silesians was enriched with a new element of attachment to Prussia. This was due to modernization, which increased the level of their social and spatial mobility.

The teacher Karol Miarka (1825–1882) met Bogedain in 1853 and accepted the need for Polish to be the medium of instruction at elementary schools (Świerc, 1990: 5), though he continued to identify himself as a German until 1862. Only under the influence of Paweł Stalmach, who serialized Miarka's novel in *Gwiazdka Ciezyńska*, did Miarka become a convinced Pole. In 1862, he appealed to the Prussian Home Ministry to allow publication of a Polish-language periodical that would be loyal to Prussia, but to no avail (Michalkiewicz, 1976: 282–283). In 1863, *Gwiazdka Cieszyńska* published his article, which criticized limitations imposed on the use of Polish at Prussian Silesian schools. Significantly, Miarka bluntly stated that "We [that is, Polish/Slavic-speaking Upper Silesians] are Poles" (Brożek, 1995: 59). During his academic studies at Breslau University in the first half of the 1860s, a similar epiphany of Polish identity descended on the aforementioned Konstanty Damrot (Michalkiewicz, 1976: 352).

However, Miarka, Damrot and some other of their Polish/Slavic-speaking Upper Silesian followers who decided to identify themselves as Poles largely remained loyal subjects of the Prussian monarch. Their number in comparison to the total Polish/Slavic-speaking population of Silesia was slight, as was their political clout. For instance, in 1867 Ignacy Danilewski, the editor of *Przyjaciel Ludu*, decided to stand in Upper Silesia for an election to the Parliament of the North German Confederation. He advertised his candidacy in his paper but lost, receiving only 350 votes. This is a representative measure of the strength of the Polish national movement in Silesia at that time (Michalkiewicz, 1976: 278–279).

The Polish-language press in Upper Silesia remained ephemeral until the late 1860s. A qualitative change came at the end of the 1860s. In 1868 the first full-fledged Polish-language periodical (since the time of the short-lived ones that had appeared in the wake of the 1848 events), the weekly *Zwiastun Górnoszląski* (Upper Silesian Announcer, 1868–1872), appeared in Piekar. In 1869 there was a failed attempt to publish *Gazeta Mikołowska* (Mikołów Newspaper) in Nikolai (Mikołów). In 1864, Miarka established contact with Chociszewski and other Polish activists from the Province of Posen. In 1869, with Chociszewski's help Miarka purchased the weekly *Katolik* (Catholic, 1868–1931). Subsequently, he transplanted it from Culm to Upper Silesia. This weekly made a difference. Its 1869 the usual run of 1,000 copies increased to 2,500 in 1871, and to over 4,000 in 1872. These numbers contrasted sharply with the run of several hundred copies in the case of *Zwiastun Górnoszląski,* and with a similarly low number of Silesian subscriptions to Posen Polish-language periodicals.

In 1870 Miarka also began to publish the popular yearly *Katolik. Kalendarz Górno-Szląski* (Catholic: An Upper Silesian Calendar, 1870–1932). In 1870 the Towarzystwo Polskich Górnoślązaków (Society of Polish Upper Silesians) at Breslau University published one issue of *Gazeta Piwna* (Beer Newspaper) and, together with the academic club of Polish students, launched the pro-Polish *Poczwary* (Monsters, 1870–1886) in a few hand-written copies. In 1869 some Upper Silesian representatives, along with Polish participants from all the three partitions, took part in a national rally,[19] held in Schwibitz (Svibice, Sibica) near Teschen. This was possible because the Poles of Galicia had enjoyed cultural autonomy since 1867 and were active in East Silesia too.

Drawing on their Posen experiences, Miarka and Juliusz Ligoń (1823–1889) organized the Kasyno Katolickie (Catholic Club) in Königshütte (Królewska Huta) in 1869. This club spread culture and education in Polish, though in the overall framework of the Catholic faith. Similar clubs sprang up in Beuthen, Myslowitz, Pleß, Siemianowitz and Sohrau (Żory). The tireless Miarka also opened a Polish-language bookshop in Königshütte in 1869 and the next year commenced the Polish-language amateur theater in Upper Silesia. A Polish artisan association in Myslowitz staged one Polish-language play in 1868, and a Cracow troupe of professional actors did three further productions in Polish in one day the following year. But these events did not lead to the creation of a sustained tradition of Polish-language theater performances yet. Polish-language amateur theater became quite popular in the following decades. Provident funds had rapidly developed in Upper Silesia since 1861, and these were ultimately harnessed for the needs of the Polish national movement as well. Utilizing this grassroots economic tradition, in 1869, Juliusz Szaflik (1844–1918) and Juliusz Ligoń[20] founded the Towarzystwo Pożyczkowe dla Zawadzkiego i Okolic (Loan Society for Zawadzkie [Zawadzki] and Its Vicinity). The Polish cooperative movement from Posen and Pomerania aided Ligoń in this undertaking.

These Posen and Pomeranian Polish national and economic organizations closely cooperated with Miarka, who had already become *the* leader of the Polish-language movement in Upper Silesia. To this end the Towarzystwo ku Wspieraniu Moralnych Interesów Ludności Polskiej pod Panowaniem Pruskim (Society of Support for the Moral Interests of the Polish Population under Prussian Rule) was founded in Thorn (Toruń), West Prussia in 1869. This society established several Polish reading rooms in Upper Silesia during the same year. Some Polish peasant circles (*kółka włościańskie*) also were established in Upper Silesia at that time.

This kind of peasant organization originated in the Province of Posen at the beginning of the 1860s. These circles formed loose decentralized structures that drew the peasantry to the Polish national movement by means of cultivating traditional customs and songs, as well as through disseminating some information on scientific and technological issues pertaining to agriculture. Members of these circles met on Sundays after mass, and in the case of conflicts between neighbors they often aligned along Polish-German ethnic lines. This social demarcation was aided by the homogenizing Prussian law that limited the use of the Polish language (Jakóbczyk, 1989: 31–34). The circles helped Polish national activists turn some of the peasants into self-conscious Poles who identified and supported the goals of the Polish national movement. The fact that the movement did not distance itself from the Catholic Church also facilitated such an identification on the part of the peasants. However, the efficacy of these circles in ennationalizing Upper Silesian peasants to Polishdom was much lower than in the Province of Posen (Brożek, 1995: 59–60; Gröschel, 1993: 67; 143–144,

226, 321–322; Kossakowska-Jarosz, 1994: 24; Lis, 1993: 91; Mykita-Glensk, 1988: 5–7; Pater, 1991: 205; Rajman, 1990: 32–33; Wanatowicz, 1992:30).

One might wonder why the Polish national movement erupted so suddenly in Upper Silesia at the end of the 1860s after almost two decades of inactivity following 1848. It happened due to energetic canvassing for Polish nationalism emanating from Posen, as well as from East Austrian Silesia and Galicia. This canvassing targeted the Polish/Slavic-speaking Upper Silesian population through the portal of perceived commonality, provided by the Polish language and Catholicism. Polish/Slavic-speaking Upper Silesians achieved a reasonable grasp of standard Polish by the 1850s thanks to Bogedain's school reforms, so some of them were prepared to espouse Polish nationalism, especially after the establishment of the North German Confederation in 1866. This was even more pronounced for educated Polish/Slavic-speaking Upper Silesians. If they did not accept the German language as the medium of "polite discourse" and an instrument of social and career advancement (which was often the case), they felt that their Polish/Slavic language and tradition were endangered due to the homogenizing policies of the Prussian state. The project of German unification in its *Kleindeutsch* form clashed with their Catholic and linguistic identity. This meant confining the use of Polish to elementary schools and progressive assimilation through the German-language administration and military conscription.

Such policies might have been uncomfortable for the Upper Silesian Polish/Slavic-speaking everyman, but they were not unbearable. His educated counterpart who espoused Polish nationalism would find it so. The divide separating educated Upper Silesians from the uneducated Polish/Slavic-speaking masses who identified themselves as Catholics and Prussians would have remained if Berlin's policies of homogenization had not extended to the sphere of the Catholic religion. The Catholic Church during the reign of Pius IX (1846–1878) was the most universalistic in its modern history. The pope continued his policy of intransigence toward modern secular and liberal culture and showed clearly that he was unable to adapt the Church to the profound social and political transformations that unfolded around it. He centralized and fortified the structures of the Catholic Church throughout the world, which culminated in the dogma on papal infallibility (1870). In the German-speaking states, the Catholic Church disliked the *Kleindeutsch* solution, which would give supremacy to Protestantism and secularism. Not surprisingly, the Catholic hierarchy campaigned for the *Großdeutsch* option under Vienna's leadership.

However, the *Großdeutsch* solution was clearly out of question after the Battle of Sadowa (1866). In Silesia, which was more than 50 percent Catholic, the struggle generated a gaping cleavage, especially in overwhelmingly (90 percent) Catholic Upper Silesia. The universalistic Catholic movement established its Silesian organ *Schlesische Volkszeitung* (Silesian People's Newspaper) in 1869, one year before the founding of the all-German Zentrumspartei (Center Party).[21] This party agitated against the *Kleindeutsch* nationalism and the *Kleindeutsch* nation-state, which coalesced during the time of the Franco-Prussian War (1870–1871). Its natural bastion was Upper Silesia. But in order to win and retain the support of the local population, the Center Party had to accept the cultural and linguistic distinctiveness of the populace. From the universalistic and non-national point of view, it was easily done. Miarka, with his *Katolik* and, torn between loyalty to the Prussian state and Catholicism, entered into an alliance with the Zentrum. The conflict festered. The state supported the emergent Old Catholic movement, which did not accept the dogma of papal infallibility. As a result, a majority of the teaching staff at Upper Silesian secondary schools were Old Catholics.

The growing role of Old Catholicism played into Bismarck's hands. He wanted to weaken the Catholic Church so as to integrate the German Empire around civic values to the exclusion of any papal or Austrian influences. The breach with the papacy forced the Old Catholic Church into the embrace of the state and made it into a state church. The movement reached Silesia quite early. In April 1870 Father Jeltsch from Liegnitz criticized the new dogma of infallibility in the *Schlesische Zeitung* (Silesian Newspaper). In 1878 there were 122 Old Catholic parishes in Germany with over 52,000 faithful. Eight of these parishes were located in Silesia: Breslau, Kattowitz, Gleiwitz, Groß Strehlitz (Strzelce Opolskie), Neisse, Hirschberg, Sagan (Żagań) and Gottesberg (Boguszów). These catered to 1,100 faithful in Silesia, one-third of which lived in Upper Silesia.

Interestingly, one of the supporters of this movement was Miarka's collaborator, Father Paweł Kamiński. He even published the Polish-language weekly *Prawda* (Truth, 1871–1877) in Kattowitz. This periodical achieved a considerable degree of popularity with its run of 2,500 copies in 1871. But the staunchly Catholic Upper Silesians sided with the universalistic position of the Catholic Church. What is more, Miarka's *Katolik* was against Kamiński and Old Catholicism. In 1872, Kamiński's Kattowitz parish of 1,500 faithful consisted mainly of German liberal Catholic intelligentsia, as well as French and Italian workers employed in Upper Silesia, a congregation that steadily dwindled to 300–400 members in 1895. It was politically and socially insignificant only by the 1880s (Gröschel, 1993: 115; Michalkiewicz, 1976: 293–298; Piątek, 1993: 17–19).

In an 1870 article in *Katolik*, Miarka expressed his sympathy with Catholic France, which did not sit well with Bismarck. During the first Reichstag elections in 1871, Miarka supported a Zentrum candidate in Upper Silesia who defeated a conservative one. This success was soon overshadowed by the onset of the *Kulturkampf*. This term, "war of cultures," denoted the increasing conflict between the homogenizing ideology of *Kleindeutsch* nationalism and the universalism of the Catholic Church. The struggle played out in the fields of education, publishing and state administration (Fischer-Wollpert, 1990: 299). Bismarck hoped that this attempt at subordinating the Catholic Church to the state would allow for improved social and political integration of the German Empire. At the grassroots level, German citizens who confessed Catholicism would have to choose between allegiance to German national identification or the Catholic faith.

This ideological conflict provided credibility and strong political voice to Miarka's movement for the sake of the Polish language and culture. In a legalistic vein, Miarka remained loyal to the monarchy and the Prussian/German state, while he continued collaborating closely with the Zentrum. Thanks to this alliance and his catering to the cultural and religious needs of the Polish/Slavic-speaking Upper Silesians, Miarka's movement was destined to grow into a force which the government of the German Empire would not be able to overlook (Bokenkotter, 1977: 308; Brożek, 1995: 60; Fischer-Wollpert, 1990: 181–182; Fuchs, 1994: 597–598; Kopiec, 1991: 85; Lis, 1993: 91–92).

CHAPTER 4

Nationalisms in Austrian Silesia

In the previous chapters the author sketched the origins of the Polish national movement in Upper Silesia, as well as the beginning of national polarization triggered by the homogenizing policies of German nationalism and its Polish counterpart. German nationalism was the main political force of Prussian (and later German) politics since the mid-nineteenth century, while Polish nationalists penetrated Upper Silesia from their bases in Posen, Galicia and East Austrian Silesia.

Now it is necessary to observe how the processes of ennationalization unfolded in Austrian Silesia. In the Habsburg Monarchy nationalism was not accepted as a state ideology until its demise in 1918, due to the multiethnic character of its population, with perhaps the exception of the *Ausgleich* (Compromise) (1867). As a result of this document, signed by Vienna and Magyar politicians, Austria-Hungary came into being. Consequently, Magyar (Hungarian) nationalism held sway in the Hungarian part of the Dual Monarchy. But German nationalism never achieved such a privileged status in the Austrian part of the empire, as Vienna had to accommodate aspirations of the various Slavic nationalisms. In this context ethnic difference, which was subordinated to the overall land (regional) identity[1] prior to 1848, later gave way to the rise of various national identities in Austrian Silesia.

The Czech language had been quite popular among all the educated Slavic-speaking inhabitants of Silesia and of the Kingdom of Poland since the fifteenth century because Polish had not developed as a written language of the royal and princely chancelleries until the sixteenth century. Subsequently, when Silesia became a land of the Czech Crown, the position of Czech there was solidified with its introduction as an official language of Upper Silesia along with Latin and German[2] in the sixteenth century. With the advance of German after the Prussian annexation of Silesia (1740–1742), the use of Czech was limited to Austrian Silesia and southern Upper Silesia, especially in the counties of Ratibor and Leobschütz (Głubczyce), whose southern areas remained part of the Olmütz Archdiocese.

Czech national activists used these facts to "justify" their attempts at building a Czech national movement in Silesia with the aid of the usual method of the anachronistic appropriation of the past for contemporary goals. The Polish national movement acted in a similar vein, and made those Silesian authors who had happened to write something in Polish into the movement's own precursors. German and Czech national activists followed this path too. Czech historians promoted Mikuláš z Kozlí (1385–1431/1432) as the "father of Czech literature in Silesia." In the monk-writer's time, however, national differentiation based on language made no sense, since people identified themselves by their immediate environs, regions, kingdoms as subjects of respective rulers, and a church. Language was of no importance. Everybody knew that Latin was the real language and all the rest were but vernaculars unworthy of being committed to expensive parchment.

Mikuláš was one of the intellectually enterprising persons who jotted down some songs in local vernaculars and placed them in his linguistically variegated manuscript, which contains short pieces in various genres. Here the nationalist researcher should stop, because looking deeper into the author's writings could endanger the researcher's a priori conclusions. The Polish nationalist knows Mikuláš as "Mikołaj z Koźla" and considers this Franciscan friar to be the "father of Polish literature in Silesia" because Mikołaj also included in his manuscript some pieces in chancery Polish. By the same token, the German nationalist immediately recognizes this monk under the name of Nikolaus aus Kosel and may consider him one of the early German Silesian authors (Lubos, 1974: 588; Zielonka, 1994: 137).

The problem arises then how this Nikolaus/Mikołaj/Mikuláš identified himself. As emphasized above, before the age of nationalism language was not a part of the core of one's identity, as it often is in contemporary central and eastern Europe. Multilingualism was taken for granted in the multiethnic, premodern states of medieval Europe. Consequently, this Franciscan friar, being a clergyman, most probably would swear his allegiance to the Catholic Church and the pope. Another of his obvious identificational choices would be Wenceslas IV, who ruled the lands of the Czech Crown (including Silesia) and the Holy Roman Empire at that time. Last but not least, Nikolaus could have a soft spot in his heart for his own homeland, Silesia, as well as for his place of birth, the town of Cosel. If a nationalist wished to continue this line of questioning, he would ask Nikolaus which language was of greatest import to him. Nikolaus would reply that it was Latin, and the nationalist interviewer would have to classify his interlocutor as a citizen of the former Roman Empire. It is important to note that the friar never spelled his name in the manner nationalist historians do. He signed documents as Nicolaus di Cosel.[3]

This absurd treatment of the past at the hands of various national movements was extremely intensive in the case of Austrian Silesia, since the Polish, German and Czech national movements vied for ownership of this land and its inhabitants despite the fact that a significant section of Austrian Silesians endeavored to maintain this region as Silesian rather than national. Moreover, some Slovak and Hungarian influences were felt there too, especially in East Silesia, which bordered on Upper Hungary (today's Slovakia). Nowadays it often happens that Polish works on Silesia stress "imagined Polishness" of some Silesian historical figures, German ones their "Germanness" and Czech ones their "Czechness," without the authors' realizing that they commit the basic error of anachronism.

Bearing this warning in mind it is now safe to present early Silesian authors who left some significant pieces in chancery Czech, usually besides their main corpus of writings in Latin and chancery German. Kundrát of Benešov (Beneschau) (born in 1350) translated seventy-three hymns into Czech. Rev. Martinus Philadelphus Zámrský (1550–1592, born in Zamrsk [Zámrsk]), wrote a collection of sermons and religious songs in Czech in order to serve the religious needs of his Slavic-speaking parishioners in a more efficient way. Mikuláš Albrecht of Kamitz (Kaménka) (died in 1617) participated in the translation of the Bible into Czech. Georg Tarnoscius (Jiří Tařnovský in Czech, Juraj Tranovsky in Slovak, and Jerzy Trzanowski in Polish, 1592–1637, born in Trzanowitz [Třanovice]), contributed to the spread of Protestantism among the Slovak-speakers, and translated Latin and German religious texts and songs into Czech. Jan Liberda (1701–1742, born in Trzytiesch [Strítez]) edited the Czech translation of the New Testament, which had been carried out by the Bohemian (Czech) Brethren. Joseph Nowak (born in Groß-Pohlom [Velká Polom] in 1766) wrote a German textbook for "Czech-, Moravian- and Slovak-speakers." Father Leopold Johann Sherschnik[4] (Scherschnick in German, Szersznik in Polish, Šeršník in Czech, 1747–1814, born in Teschen) organized the biggest Austrian Silesian library in Teschen. In 1802 it was transformed into the oldest museum located in the lands of the Czech Crown (Lubos, 1974: 589–601; Myška, 1993: 92–93).

After the Prussian annexation of Silesia, German replaced Czech and Latin as the official language of Prussian Upper Silesia. The non-administrative use of Czech was limited to the southern part of this region, inhabited by Silesian Czech-speaking or, more correctly, Moravian-speaking people who called themselves "Moravians," that is, *Moravce* in Czech, or *Morawzen* in German.[5] Although some claim the dialect of the Moravians to have been Czech, it is a questionable statement, especially in the period before the spread of standard Czech in the second half of the nineteenth century. Thus, this dialect of southern Upper Silesia and Austrian Silesia, not unlike other (sub)dialects of Moravia, obtained its name from the Crownland of Moravia. Similarly, dialects used in Bohemia were referred to as the Bohemian language rather than Czech. In the same manner, the inhabitants of Moravia and the Austrian and Prussian Silesian territories included within the borders of the Olmütz Archdiocese continued to call their speech and written idiom the Moravian language until 1918 (cf. Triest, 1984 [1864]: 34).

The Prussian imposition of official German on the social and cultural life of the Morawecs caused a decrease in their number by one-third, to 45,500 in 1840.

This phenomenon took place mainly in the Leobschütz county (Kokot, 1973: 74). The official role of Czech steadily declined in Austrian Silesia in the second half of the eighteenth century, and especially after 1782, when Austrian Silesia was merged with Moravia in order to rationalize regional administration. After 1790 German dominated in this region, though for practical reasons official announcements were often published in both languages (Gawrecka, 1993: 65; Gawrecki, 1992: 58; Knop, 1992: 112).

Joseph II tried to imitate Frederick II's policy of infusing less populated regions with settlers in order to boost development, and encouraged a similar population action in Austrian Silesia. By the beginning of the nineteenth century, 103 new settlements had been created in this manner, mainly in West Silesia. Undoubtedly, this contributed to the fortification of the dominant role of German in this region of Austrian Silesia (Bein, 1995: 141). The linguistic situation was more complicated in East Silesia, where Protestantism spread in the sixteenth century and at the beginning of the seventeenth, mainly thanks to Czech-speaking pastors and preachers. However, later in the first half of the seventeenth century, when the Teschen Prince Adam Wenzel (Wacław) converted to Catholicism, the balance was tipped by the arrival of Polish-speaking Catholic priests from the Cracow Diocese.

Since West Silesia was part of the Habsburg Monarchy and not of the disintegrating Polish-Lithuanian Commonwealth, Czech-language prayer books and hymnals dominated, and for the sake of convenience the state and church authorities used Czech as the means of communication with all the Slavic-speaking subjects in the northern segment of the empire. With the Habsburgs' tacit acceptance of Protestantism in Silesia, strong links developed between the Protestant parish of Teschen (which, at that time, served all of Upper Silesia) and the northeastern Lower Silesian Protestant parishes with the Polish/Slavic-speaking faithful. After 1742, when Teschen remained the only Protestant parish in the monarchy, the local Protestants inevitably maintained contacts with their coreligionists in Prussian Silesia. In Prussia their religion occupied a somewhat privileged position vis-à-vis Catholicism, in stark opposition to the indignities Protestants still suffered at the hands of the Austrian authorities in East Silesia.

Therefore, pastors (often German-speaking) shuttled between East Silesia and northeastern Lower Silesia, frequently bringing to East Silesia Polish-language religious prints from Brieg, Kreuzburg, Wohlau (Wołów) and Groß Wartenberg. With the decline of the northeastern Lower Silesian center of Polish-language Protestantism, due to the increasing dominance of German, and with the increasing acceptance of Protestantism in the Habsburg Empire, Teschen took over the role of the former Polish-language stronghold of Protestantism in Lower Silesia. This town became the main center of Polish-language Protestant publishing. Between 1716 and 1848, seventy-one Polish-language books appeared in East Silesia, slowly contributing to the later differentiation of its Slavic-speaking population into Polish-speakers and Czech-speakers.

In reality the Silesian transitory dialects between Polish and Czech that the Slavic-speaking East Silesians spoke were so close to one another that no communication problems arose. Difficulties started with the spread of popular education in the second half of the eighteenth century. Initially, church teachers used the languages of their parishes, that is, German or Slavic dialects, in elementary schools (any further education was conducted in Latin and German). Soon, however, textbooks began to be produced in order to augment the process of education. For practical reasons, the Austrian authorities promoted the use of German and Czech textbooks in East Silesia. When, in 1807, the school inspector Sherschnik appealed also for the introduction of Polish textbooks, the answer of the Brünn (Brno) administration was that it would be unfeasible to produce Polish textbooks for only a handful of schoolchildren.

However, teachers started to use a German-Polish dictionary published in Brieg and the Polish translation of the Protestant New Testament in some Protestant elementary schools in East Silesia. Eventually the Brünn authorities permitted the use of a Polish-language Protestant religious textbook in 1817. In 1828 a Polish-German dictionary was introduced, and two further Protestant religious textbooks followed in 1823 and 1833 (Zahradnik, 1992a: 18–21). It is estimated that in 1846, the population of Austrian Silesia was made up of 222,000 (47.7 percent) German-speakers, 147,000 (31.5 percent) Polish/Slavic-speakers and 94,000 (20 percent) Czech/Slavic-speakers. On the basis of the fragmentary school statistics on the medium of instruction, 54.4 percent of the schools in Austrian Silesia were Slavic-speaking, 36.5 percent German-speaking and 9.2 percent bilingual (Gawrecka, 1993: 62; Prinz, 1995: 309).

It is enlightening to observe that the German-speaking Austrian Silesians had 10 percent fewer schools than they "should have" had according to their share of the crownland's population. It clearly indicates that at that time nationalism could not have been a guideline for the policies of the Habsburg authorities, because the situation would have been the other way around. Moreover, the broad description of the non-German-speaking Austrian Silesians as "Slavic-speakers" shows that language had not yet become an issue worth official attention. The authorities continued to invest the religious rather than the linguistic cleavage with political significance.

The question now arises as to what the identity of the inhabitants of Austrian Silesia was. Before 1740 the Silesians in the whole of the yet undivided province felt an essentially medieval attachment to the localities in which they lived. The provincial all-Silesian ties were quite loose because religious differences predominated, pitting larger confessionally variegated groups against one another. Only with the modernization of Austrian and Prussian Silesias after the 1740–1742 division, two specific regional identities emerged. So at the end of the eighteenth century one can speak of the Prussian Silesians and the Austrian Silesians. However, the memory of a united Silesia lasted, and attachment to religious convictions continued. Many Catholic noblemen from Prussian Silesia entered the civil service of the Habsburg Empire, distrustful of Protestant Prussia. On the other hand, numerous Protestant civil servants in the East Silesian town of Oderberg (Bohumín), on the border with Prussian Silesia, sympathized with the Protestant monarch of Prussia, as they were weary of the injustices suffered at the hands of the Habsburg Catholic authorities.

The regional or provincial identity arose or strengthened in Austrian Silesia, partially as a reaction to the centralistic policies of the Habsburgs. It is proved by the fact that in the period 1782–1849, when Austrian Silesia was merged with Moravia, the Austrian Silesian estate diet (*Landtag*) continued to assemble and regularly protested against the subjection of Austrian Silesia to Brünn. At the beginning of the nineteenth century this identity received its outward symbols, which the later national movements would appropriate. These symbols included the public museum in Teschen (1802) and the crownland theater in Troppau (1805), where the crownland museum[6] opened in 1814. Consequently, prior to the 1840s, provincial identity dominated in Austrian Silesia, and some educated authors even chose to describe the inhabitants of the Austrian and Prussian Silesias as one Silesian nation (that is, *natio*) that the Habsburgs and the Hohenzollerns had unjustly torn apart between 1740 and 1742 (Gawrecki, 1992: 56; Gawrecki, 1993: 50–53).

The influence of Herderian philosophy and the ideals of the French Revolution entered Austrian Silesia by virtue of locals who studied at Germanophone universities as well as by invading French troops. The latter also confronted the Austrian Silesians with the Other, thereby forcing them to perceive their own distinctiveness more clearly. This socio-ideological preparation was necessary so that nationalism could start timidly seeping into Austrian Silesia during the 1840s. Because German was the official language of Austrian Silesia and the discussion on unifying Germany continued in Austrian Silesia, as it did elsewhere in the German-speaking states, the first tenets of German nationalism were present in this land even before 1848 (Gawrecki, 1992: 59; Gawrecka, 1993: 67).

In the case of the Czech national movement, its beginnings in Austrian Silesia are associated with Father Jan Alois Zabranský (died in 1842) from Jaktar (Jaktař). He and Father Cyprian Lelek (1812–1883) promoted knowledge of Czech/Moravian among the Czech/Slavic-speaking schoolchildren. The latter priest was active among the Czech/Slavic-speakers living in the region of Hultschin (Hlučín), that is, on the border of Austrian Silesia in the south of the Ratibor county, in Prussian Upper Silesia. During his studies in Breslau, Lelek came under the Pan-Slav influence of the Czech lecturer Jan Evangelista Purkyně, who had established the Literary-Slavic Society at the Breslau University. When the development of Slavic-language classes became less restrained in Prussian Silesia after 1842, Lelek published his Czech/Moravian-language primer in 1844 and *Opis Slézka* (Description of Silesia) in 1846. In the same year he established the Czech monthly *Holubice* (The Dove), but only one issue appeared.

In this early period Lelek's role for the future Czech national movement in Austrian Silesia (and, to a lesser extent, in Prussian Silesia) was similar to Lompa's in relation to the later Polish national movement in Upper Silesia. Both of them wrote descriptions of Silesia for schools in Polish and Czech/Moravian, respectively. In this manner they appropriated this land for the Czech and Polish national movements that were to be attached to these languages. Through their activities they also influenced the educational system, emphasizing Polish and Czech as media of instruction (Gröschel, 1993: 235; Lubos, 1974: 606–607; Myška, 1994: 74–75; Plaček, 1996a: 6–7). Prior to 1848 only small groups of Austrian Silesians dedicated their efforts to the ideals of Polish and Czech nationalisms. In Katharein (Kateřinky), near Opava, the rich peasant Filípek organized a Czech library, and there were two Czech reading circles in Krawarn (Kravař) (1825–1839) and Troppau (1845). Another Czech reading circle was organized in the 1840s at the Protestant gymnasium in Teschen.

At the same gymnasium Paweł Stalmach (1824–1891) and Andrzej Cinciała (1825–1898) established two Polish reading circles, which existed until 1842/1843 and 1847–1850, respectively. Also in the 1840s the gymnasium teacher Jan Winkler (1794–1874), who had good contacts with young František Palacký, organized another reading circle. Through it Winkler promoted the ideas of "Slavic reciprocity" (*slovanská vzájemnost*), which was an ideological forerunner of Pan-Slavism (Fazan, 1991: 44–45; Gawrecki, 1992: 59; Myška, 1994: 137).

The social and economic situation in Austrian Silesia was as difficult in the 1840s as in Prussian Silesia. Repeated crop failures brought about by potato blight between 1844 and 1849 caused hunger and the deaths of 5,000 people in 1847 and 16,000 in 1848 in East Silesia alone. This period was aptly described as the "hunger years." Also the Weavers' Uprising in Lower Silesia, as well as worker and social unrest in Prussian Silesia, resounded in Austrian Silesia, leading to similar turmoil. Of those, the 1845 and 1846 disturbances in Wagstadt (Bílovec) merit mention.

Remnants of serfdom and the unbalanced land structure contributed to the increased social tension, especially in East Silesia, where fifty landowners possessed 44 percent of all the arable land. When the 1848 revolutions broke out in Berlin and Vienna, the news traveled quickly among Austrian Silesian students. In order to support the goals of the revolutionary movement they immediately formed the Association of Austrian Silesians in Vienna and, traveling by train, quickly brought this news home. The Demokratische Gesellschaft (Democratic Society) came into being in the largest Habsburg textile center, Bielitz (Bielsko), and peasants demanded abolishment of remaining obligations of the serfdom system throughout Austrian Silesia. Thanks to this grassroots support the "peas-

ant liberator" Hans Kudlich could force through the Reichstag legislation to this
end, which was passed on September 7, 1848.

Unfortunately, this legislation placed the costs of phasing out serfdom on
the backs of the peasantry. Protests against this decision erupted in the countryside during the autumn of 1848. In the western part of West Silesia regular
riots were staged, and hungry people hunted game in the forests belonging to
large landowners. Only with the help of the military were the disturbances suppressed. West Silesian weavers who worked in their houses also protested against
the exploitative conditions of their work. The general commotion was additionally influenced by the dramatic events just across the Prussian border, where in
the Hultschin region local peasants had attacked two palaces (Gawrecki, 1992:
57–58; Grobelný, 1992: 68–69; Lis, 1993: 83–84).

The emergence of the Association of Austrian Silesians indicated that regional identity had developed and was quite strong, especially among the educated
inhabitants of Austrian Silesia, who felt themselves to be Austrian Silesians or
Silesian Austrians (Gawrecki, 1993: 54; Grobelný, 1992: 61). The popular support for detaching Austrian Silesia from Moravia solidified such that on June
19, 1848, the Austrian Silesian estate diet was transformed into the provisional
diet (*Landtag*) of Austrian Silesia. Immediately, this body started campaigning
for the establishment of a separate crownland under the name of the Herzogtum
Ober- und Niederschlesien (Duchy of Upper and Lower Silesia).[7] At last, their
wish was fulfilled on December 30, 1849, legalized with the appropriate imperial
patent (Bein, 1995: 142).

The national (that is "of the Austrian Silesian *natio*") revolutionary guards
attracted many volunteers: 780 in Bielitz and 800 in Troppau. However, it was
already a swan song of the prenational multiple identities tied to localities. Austrian Silesia sent out seven deputies to the Frankfurt Parliament, which aimed
at establishing a united German nation-state in fulfillment of the German national movement's goals. None of them championed the causes of the Czech or
Polish national movements. Although these deputies felt most bound to their
homeland, in the long run they contributed to the development of the German
national movement in Austrian Silesia. The very fact that they attended the German National Assembly in Frankfurt was enough to foster the rise of German
nationalism in Austrian Silesia.

Father Cyprian Lelek maintained a position different from that of these
deputies. In 1849 he entered the Frankfurt Parliament thanks to the 1849 by-
election in the Ratibor county in Prussian Silesia. In the universalistic manner,
not unlike Szafranek (Schaffranek) and Bogedain in the Prussian National Assembly in Berlin in regard to Polish, Lelek appealed for the wider use of Czech
in teaching and in the religious life of his Moravian faithful in the Hultschin
region. Obviously, his stance made an impression across the border in Austrian

Silesia but could not directly reinforce the incipient Czech national movement. Lelek remained loyal to the Prussian state and to the Catholic Church, which was clearly stated in his newspaper *Holubice*. As neither Bogedain nor Szafranek attempted to create a Polish national movement in Prussian Upper Silesia, neither did Lelek wish to encourage Czech nationalism in this region (Gawrecki, 1992: 59; Gröschel, 1993: 235).

Palacký and his circle in Bohemia developed the concept of the unity of the "historical lands" of the Czech Crown. They hoped that these lands could function as a separate entity within the Habsburg Empire, reconstituted as a federal state. This concept grew into the political basis of the Czech national movement. But the political and intellectual elites of Moravia, albeit of Slavic origin, did not espouse this goal. The Austrian Silesian elites were even less enthusiastic. They thought this idea to be specific to Bohemia and resented the crownland's attempts to dominate Moravia and Austrian Silesia. Regional identity still prevailed, and nationalism could not sway it.

This program of unification of the Czech lands reached Austrian Silesia with the few copies of the Czech papers *Národne noviný* (National News) from Prague and *Moravské noviný* (Moravian News, 1848–1852) from Moravia. The Moravian lawyer Jan Kozánek (1819–1890) regularly contributed to these periodicals and supported the idea of unification of the historical lands of the Czech Crown. He also belonged to the Troppau (Opava) Czech reading circle and maintained contacts with Lelek. This facilitated his agitation for the goals of the Czech national movement in West Silesia and the south of Prussian Upper Silesia. Kozánek also distributed a leaflet with an article from *Národne noviný* entitled "Bratři Moravané a Slezané" (To Brothers Moravians and Silesians). It incited some Moravian students from Olmütz to help him promote Czech nationalism in Troppau (Gawrecki, 1992: 60; Myška, 1993: 67).

When the Slav Congress convened in Prague in reaction to the Frankfurt Parliament, no one represented West Silesia. Actually many Czech/Slavic-speaking Austrian Silesians (for instance, J. Filípek, who supported knowledge of the Czech language and culture with his Czech library open to the public) agitated against this congress. They considered it a dangerous event whose somewhat anti-state Pan-Slav ideology could, in the future, submerge Austrian Silesia in an all-Czech autonomous state. These Czech/Slavic-speaking Austrian Silesians, not unlike their German-speaking countrymen, preferred to advocate the cause of the Frankfurt Parliament because this body did not foresee doing away with distinctive regions. As a consequence, Austrian Silesia's Czech/Slavic-speaking elites supported the activities of the Verein der Deutschen aus Böhmen, Mähren und Schlesien zur Aufrechterhaltung ihrer Nationalität (Union of the Germans from Bohemia, Moravia and Silesia for the Maintenance of Their Nationality). This organization strove to offset the Czech national propaganda that advocated electing no representatives to the German National Assembly from the historical lands of the Czech Crown (Gawrecki, 1992: 60; Gawrecki, 1993: 54; Schenk, 1993: 66).

The universalistic East Silesian Polish-language weekly *Nowiny dla Ludu Wiejskiego* (News for the Rural Folk, 1848–1849) also espoused this line of thinking. Because of its pronounced loyalty toward the Danubian monarchy and the Catholic Church, this periodical spoke against the Polish national movement. This movement's mouthpiece, *Tygodnik Cieszyński* (Cieszyn Weekly, 1848–1851), established by Paweł Stalmach with Andrzej Cieńciała's cooperation, came into being thanks to the aid offered by the Polish Prince Jan Lubomirski (1826–1908) from Congress Poland and by the Czech-speaking East Silesian lawyer Ludvík Kludsky (Ludwik Klucki in Polish). The latter was the mayor of Teschen at that time. Initially, this weekly was an organ of the group of East Silesia's Slavic-speaking intellectuals that coalesced around Jan Winkler.

They emphasized the need for cooperation and reciprocity among all the Slavic inhabitants of the Habsburg Empire in order to unite their lands into a separate political entity within the framework of the monarchy. On this basis they sympathized with the emergence of the Polish national movement in East Silesia and did not readily espouse the idea of the unification of the historical lands of the Czech Crown. They found it too particularistic. Over time though, the Polish activists Stalmach and Cieńciała began to dominate the newspaper (Fazan, 1991: 38, 170–171; Gawrecki, 1992: 60; Grobelný, 1992: 71; Snoch, 1991: 151; Zahradnik, 1989: 122, 200).

Stalmach and Andrzej Kotula, another Polish activist from East Silesia, were the only official delegates to the Slav Congress from Austrian Silesia—or, more precisely, from East Silesia. The program they represented in Prague was clearly pro-Polish and openly directed against the ideals of Pan-Slavism, as well as against the Czech and German national movements. They also opposed the continued unity of Austrian Silesia as a separate crownland (Gawrecki, 1992: 60). In a memorial submitted to this congress on June 8, 1848, Stalmach described all the Slavic-speaking Silesians as "Poles." He justified his stance with the fact that in the Middle Ages Silesia had been part of the Kingdom of Poland. On this basis he demanded that Austrian Silesia be merged with Galicia and Prussian Silesia with the Grand Duchy of Posen. Stalmach required, too, the introduction of the Polish language into schools and offices in the Polish-speaking areas of Prussian and Austrian Silesia. And he concluded that "the Silesians expect to receive all the constitutional freedoms of faith, press, speech, the right of equality before law, and abolishment of serfdom" through "linking the lot of [all] Silesia with the lot of Poland" (Stalmach, 1990: 63–64).

Stalmach unambiguously demonstrated his identification with Polishness. At the commencement of the Slav Congress he said: "We Silesians as Poles can belong only to the Polish section." It was one of the first declarations of the Polish/Slavic-speaking East Silesians in which they identified themselves as Poles. Stalmach's declaration was similar to statements made in 1848 by Lompa and his collaborators in Prussian Silesia, and later by Miarka and Damrot. After Stalmach's intervention all the delegates from East Silesia worked at the congress in the joint Polish-Ruthenian[8] section. The Czech representatives did not oppose this arrangement, stipulating that Czech nationalists did not or were not prepared to lay an explicit claim to East Silesia yet (Michalkiewicz, 1970: 544).

The sudden emergence of the Polish national movement in East Silesia came as a shock to the Galician Polish-language press and intelligentsia. They rather expected such developments more in the eastern territories of erstwhile Poland-Lithuania than in the regions that had stretched beyond the partitioned commonwealth's western border (Fras, 1992: 24–25). Only later would researchers associate the roots of this movement with Vienna's annexation of the Republic of Cracow in 1846. It removed the political frontier between East Silesia and Cracow and attracted casual train travelers to this city, a former capital of the Kingdom of Poland and still a significant center of Polish culture. Some Polish/Slavic-speaking students of the Teschen Protestant gymnasium undertook such train trips in search of Polish-language books as well as of moral and financial support (Fazan, 1991: 46).

The 1851 onslaught of absolutist reaction caused a certain ideological reunification of the Czech and Polish movements on the common ground of Austroslavism. Although more in words than in deeds, numerous Polish activists supported the program of unification of the historical lands of the Czech Crown, at least until the 1860s, but only partially and with reservations. The symbiosis of the Polish and Czech national movements was over in the 1870s, but various forms of cooperation between these movements continued until 1914. It happened on the platform of their opposition toward the German national movement (Grobelný, 1992: 72). The possible unity of the Czech lands gradually became a more distant prospect due to the Habsburg policy of liquidating administrative ties among the crownlands in favor of binding them directly to the imperial hub in Vienna (Gawrecki, 1993: 55).

Moreover, a majority of the Slavophone Austrian Silesians spoke against the Slavic national movements and the ideology of Pan-Slavism, with which they associated the former. The authorities perceived this ideology as anti-state and playing into Russia's hands. The Austrian Silesian everyman shared this opinion and sided somewhat with the German national movement, attracted to it by the social reforms worked out in Frankfurt and Vienna. These were the real issues for them, rather than the vague prospect of building a Czech or Polish nation-state. Such social considerations were absent from the Czech national program. Some inkling of this was included in Stalmach's memorial, which obviously could not be actualized without the Habsburg administration's agreement and help (Gawrecka, 1993: 67).

After 1848 the Polish national movement managed to maintain continuity, unlike its Czech counterpart. Stalmach and the circle of Polish activists centered around him successfully transformed the politically tarnished *Tygodnik Cieszyński* (1848–1851) into the apolitical *Gwiazdka Cieszyńska* (1851–1920). It represented the universalistic stance in accordance with Vienna's official *Großdeutsch* line. This Polish-language weekly, besides serving the gradually formalized Polish national movement in East Silesia, also catered to the Polish activists in Prussian Silesia, where no Polish periodical worth mentioning appeared in the period 1853–1869. Later, this success allowed *Gwiazdka Cieszyńska* to reach Polish readership in all the lands of partitioned Poland-Lithuania (Zahradnik, 1989: 85–87).

Czech activists did not maintain a similar continuity of cultural life in Austrian Silesia. The goals of the Czech national movement, meandering among Pan-Slavism, Austroslavism and unification of the historical lands of the Czech Crown, were unfocused and often mutually exclusive. In the prenational so-called "complicated ethnic situation" of Austrian Silesia, where the Czech/Slavic-speaking population[9] constituted just one-quarter of the population, this ideological discord preserved the regional identity and symbiosis with the Polish national movement. Obviously, some Czech-language periodicals from Moravia and Bohemia reached Austrian Silesia, but this was of no national significance until the 1860s. Only then Young Czechs partly renounced Austroslavism and Pan-Slavism, previously championed by Old Czechs under the leadership of Palacký. Young Czechs emphasized the significance of unification of the Czech lands and, in this manner, clearly delineated the goal of the Czech national movement. Clarity breeds comprehension and support. Not surprisingly, at that time this movement won some popularity among the Czech/Slavic-speaking Austrian Silesians (Bělina, 1993: 99; Gawrecki, 1993: 55; Jakubíková, 1994: 143).

The 1848 revolution engendered some low key, grassroots linguistic traditions that survived the period of reactionary absolutism. Subsequently, they formed the springboard for the later dynamic development of the Polish and Czech national movements in Austrian Silesia. In 1848 Polish was introduced as the medium of instruction in elementary schools in the Polish/Slavic-speaking areas of East Silesia (Michalkiewicz, 1970: 545), which fortified the position of Czech and Polish vis-à-vis German. Article 21 in the imposed 1849 constitution established the principle of equality of all the peoples living in the Habsburg Empire (Prinz, 1995: 327). Consequently, Polish and Czech were accepted as crownland languages in Austrian Silesia, increasingly on par with German.

This legal equality of Czech and Polish with the German language proved illusory, as German remained the sole medium of instruction in secondary schools. Moreover, the official status of Czech and Polish was scrapped in 1851, which left German as the sole official language of Austrian Silesia (Gawrecka, 1993: 68; Michalkiewicz, 1970: 545). It was one of the first steps taken in this crownland in order to institutionalize reactionary absolutism after the successful suppression of the revolution in the Habsburg lands. This caused political emigration of Kudlich and Kolatschek and brought about the persecution of Paweł Oszelda. In the eyes of the authorities they were guilty of having mobilized the national guards of Austrian Silesia so that they would go to Vienna in order to bolster a revolution endangered by the reactionary forces. Oszelda even delivered a speech to this end at a revolutionary rally (Gawrecki, 1992: 60; Lis, 1993: 84).

In 1848 the Czytelnia Polska (Polish Reading Circle) was founded and, two years later, the Biblioteka Polska dla Ludu Kraju Cieszyńskiego (Polish Library for the Folk of the Cieszyn Country). Their boards were composed of members of Polish, Czech and German provenances (Fazan, 1991: 54). Ethnic difference did not create an insurmountable cleavage at that time. The fact that some of them were Protestants and others Catholics did not pit them against one another either. What united the members of these two boards was their shared regional Austrian Silesian identity and their liberal opposition to absolutism. In 1854 the authorities dissolved both these organizations,[10] which were portrayed as an example of the dangerous institutionalization of Pan-Slavism. This decision also marked the end of the activities of the Polish-language amateur theater, which had produced ten plays between 1852 and 1854 (Fazan, 1991: 47, 54, 63, 65).

Stalmach tried to deflect this blow to the Polish movement by accepting the rules of the political game played within the ideological confines of neo-absolutism. Having managed to preserve *Gwiazdka Cieszyńska*, in 1856 he founded the apolitical cultural organization of Kasyno (Casino) in Teschen, which local Polish/Slavic-speaking and German-speaking inhabitants frequented. In 1859 together with Kludsky he founded the Kasa Oszczędności (Savings Society) (Myška, 1993: 101). This channeling of radical revolutionary and national movements into the fold of cultural and economic activity was in line with the situation in education. In 1848 German-Polish elementary schools appeared in addition to German, Czech and German-Czech schools of this kind. Polish textbooks were imported from Galicia in the case of Catholic schools of East Austrian Silesia, whereas for Protestant schools Jan Śliwka published his Polish primer (1852), geography textbook (1863) and collection of Polish reading texts for higher grades (1870) (Fazan, 1991: 29–30; Michalkiewicz, 1976: 357).

Not unlike Polish, the Czech language also remained a medium of instruction in elementary schools. In addition, in the 1850s and 1860s, it was taught as an elective subject in Austrian Silesian secondary schools (Jakubíková, 1994: 143). Czech and Polish were also used in church and in everyday contacts between pastors, priests and their faithful. Both these languages differed considerably from standard Czech and standard Polish. They were often heavily interlaced with influences stemming from local Slavic dialects, or these dialects simply went under the name of "Czech" and "Polish" (Grobelný, 1992: 60).

A comparable situation developed across the border in the region of Hultschin located in the south of the Ratibor county in Prussian Silesia, directly on the border with Austrian Silesia. The official Prussian statistics referred to the medium of instruction employed in the Hultschin schools as the Moravian language (Kokot, 1973: 74). The inhabitants of this area spoke a Slavic subdialect (akin to the Slavic subdialects of northern Moravian) as well as a Slavic-German creole. This linguistic situation did influence language use in school despite Bogedain's stance that standard Polish and Czech should be used as media of education instead of local dialects or creoles (cf. Kamusella, 1998). The local Hultschin priest Cyprian Lelek introduced the Moravian language (today incorrectly interpreted as Czech) into elementary schools. His strongly dialectal primer remained in use at these schools from 1849 to 1863 and 1873. The two latter dates mark the times when the use of Moravian was seriously limited in favor of German (Plaček, 1996: 7).

Prior to the 1860s the Czech/Slavic-speaking (dialectal) life of Austrian Silesia was also concentrated in parish churches and voluntary fire-fighting organizations (Jakubíková, 1994: 143). The rapid industrialization in the Ostrau-Karwin industrial basin constituted another impulse for changes in the sphere of language use. In 1822 its mining industry produced a mere 6,700 tons of coal, in 1842 62,000, in 1852 168,000 (that is, one-quarter of the entire coal output in the Habsburg Empire at that time), 1,100,000 tons in the 1870s and 2,600,000 in 1882. After 1848 this progress in mining was accompanied by the swift development of the metallurgical, coking and textile industries in the northwestern and northeastern parts of East Silesia. The rise of an increasingly extensive railway network accompanied this economic boom.

Industrial activity in Austrian Silesia was concentrated in East Silesia and in the adjacent wedge of northern Moravia around Ostrau. Since the mid-nineteenth century it started attracting labor from outside the region. Engineers and managers were recruited from the Czech-speaking and German-speaking areas of Bohemia and Moravia, whereas workers usually originated from the Polish-speaking and, later, even from the Ruthenian-speaking areas of Galicia. Industrialization and modernization caused a steady growth in the Austrian Silesian population—from 154,782 in 1754 to 237,340 in 1790; 337,224 in 1815; 466,002 in 1846; and 511,581 in 1869, with a single drop after 1848 to 438,586 in 1851.

The educated strata employed in the industrial basin were predominantly German- and Czech-speaking. On top of that at least 80 percent of the Polish/Slavic-speaking graduates of Austrian Silesian secondary schools preferred to identify themselves as Germans. Not surprisingly the industrialized areas of East Silesia acquired the same linguistic characteristic. The uneducated Polish-speaking migrant workers from Galicia more often than not became Germanized or Czechized through school, church and cultural organizations. This was true especially in the early period, at which time no Polish nationalist propaganda could stop this process of peaceful assimilation of Galician peasants. Having no national identification, they assimilated either to Germandom or Czechdom (Gawrecki, 1992: 56, 61; Grobelný, 1992: 64–65; Lis, 1993: 86; Michalkiewicz, 1976: 357; Myška, 1993: 99; Zahradnik, 1992a: 41).

The end of absolutism came with the collapse of the Habsburg hegemony over the Italian-speaking states in 1859. The subsequent constitutional reforms gave more rights to the citizen and various peoples (this is, nations-*in-statu-nascendi*) of the empire. Liberalization was inevitable, though the government consciously procrastinated until 1866. In that year the Danubian monarchy definitively lost hegemony over the German-speaking states, and Prussia emerged as the clear winner as well as the leader of the *Kleindeutsch* national project (Kinder, 1978: II 61).

In 1861 Czechs won a vast majority of 75 to 15 in the Prague self-government (Kořalka, 1995: 17). In the same year the first issue of the Czech national movement's mouthpiece *Národní listý* (National Newspaper) appeared. The Sokol (Falcon) gymnastic association, established in 1863, proved a useful instrument for transforming the Czech national movement. The appeal of gymnastics to the youth was considerable. The patriotic (national) message the Sokol spread allowed the broadening of this national movement's social base from the narrow strata of Czech intellectuals and politicians to Czech-speaking masses. The Sokol members gathered in great numbers at large meetings called *tabors*. They later evolved into political rallies—the basic manifestation of the Czech national struggle (Prinz, 1995: 339).

Further concessions to Czech national activists included promotion of the Czech language and culture. In 1864 Bohemian secondary schools were divided into Czech, German and bilingual. In the case of Bohemia's technical schools the process was even clearer. In 1869 they were split into Czech- and German-language schools but without the compromise solution of bilingual schools (Bělina, 1993: 98). The process of dividing the Bohemian educational system along the linguistic cleavage continued to its logical conclusion in 1882, when the Prague University split into the two separate Czechophone and Germanophone universities (Hemmerle, 1992: 197).

The *Ausgleich* of 1867 dashed the hopes of uniting the historical Czech lands within the framework of the Habsburg Empire. It transformed the Danubian monarchy into dual Austria-Hungary with complete disregard for the Czech national interest. Czech patriots protested this decision by paying an ostentatious visit to the Moscow Exhibition (1867). They even conducted some discussions with the French Emperor Napoleon III, but this was more a protest against Vienna's shortsighted policies than pursuit of separation of the Czech lands from the Dual Monarchy. Above all, neither the tsar nor Napoleon displayed any particular interest in the Czechs and their national aspirations (Polišenský, 1991: 98–99).

Old Czechs continued to petition Francis Joseph I, asking him to apply the Hungarian formula to their lands so that the dual empire would consist instead of three parts. But the monarch repeatedly declined the invitations to come to Prague so as to be crowned with the ancient crown of St. Vaclav. Moreover, the Hungarians would have opposed such a move in order not to lose their privileged position in the empire. The German-speakers living in the Czech lands would have readily supported Budapest, as the fulfillment of the Czech national aspirations would have turned them into an underprivileged national minority in the Czech lands. In addition, in 1871 the German Empire came into being and the Habsburgs could not disregard the wishes of German nationalists anymore. This would have posed a threat to Vienna, in that the Germanophone Bohemians, Moravians and Austrian Silesians would become disloyal and turn for support to Emperor William I.

Afterward Czech nationalists were faced with the dilemma of whether to boycott the Reichstag and the crownland diets (*Landtagen*) or to join the government majority in return for further concessions in education and economic life. It drove the wedge deeper between the conservative Old Czechs and the Young Czechs, leading to a definitive split in 1874 (Carter, 1992: 923). The former faction, led by František Rieger, stood fast by Palacký's federal idea of Austroslavism. Like Palacký (his father-in-law) Rieger strongly contributed to standardization of the Czech language and culture with the first Czech encyclopedia (1859–1874), which he edited (Anon., 1985a: 889). But the time when they had headed the Czech national movement unrivaled had passed, and the Young Czechs, under the leadership of Karl Kramař (1860–1937), with their program of an independent Czech nation-state, began to win more votes than their predecessors.

These changes in Bohemia's Czech national politics influenced Austrian Silesia. The local Czech national movement, centered on the concept of unification of the Czech lands, arrived in this crownland only at the beginning of the 1860s. The key figure of this movement was the Troppau gymnasium teacher Antonín Vašek (1829–1880). When Rieger founded *Národní listý* (1861), Vašek commenced the publication of the first Czech-language newspaper in Austrian Silesia, *Opavský besedník* (Opava Entertaining Newspaper, 1861–1865). After this weekly went defunct, Vašek, together with Father Antonín Gruda (1844–1903) and the historian Jan Zacpal (1844–1888), established *Opavský týdenník* (Opava Weekly, 1870–1913). In this early period both periodicals gathered the first group of Czech intellectuals who forged the Czech national movement in Austrian Silesia. Among others, they included Jan Lepař (1827–1902), Vincenc Prasek (1843–1912) and Josef Zukal (1841–1929).

In 1864 the Spolek čtenářů a zpěváků (Society of Readers and Singers) emerged in the framework of the Katharein parish. In 1870 Father Gruda transformed it into the Katolicko-politicka beseda (Catholic-Political Club), and similar clubs had been earlier established in Stiebrowitz (Stěbořice), Jaktar (Jaktař) and Tiefengrund (Hlubočec). More such clubs opened in other localities as well. In 1865, when Vašek had to close down his *Opavský besedník* due to financial problems, he tried to establish a reading society in the Austrian Silesian capital of Troppau. The authorities allowed it in February of the following year, but Germanophone activists and citizenry of the town opposed this project so much that Vašek had to abandon the effort.

It was a *signum temporis*. At the beginning of the 1860s the Austrian Silesian diet and the German newspaper *Silesia* advocated equality for all the peoples of the Habsburg Empire. The official press organ of the crownland, *Troppauer Zeitung* (Troppau Paper), warmly welcomed the appearance of the first Czech-language newspaper in Austrian Silesia, *Opavský besedník*. The situation changed dramatically in the second half of the 1860s. For instance, in 1868 *Silesia* wrote that Vienna's accommodation of the rights of *other* Austrian peoples was too thorough and caused the German *nation* to lose ground each day. Under the influence of German nationalism and Pan-Slavism, non-German peoples (usually referred to as "nationalities" in Austria-Hungary) wanted to become recognized nations—not unlike the Germans, who had already attained this status.

In the case of the Czech national movement the culmination came with *tabors* (open-air political rallies, organized as popular picnics) in support of unity of the Czech lands. These events with mass attendance took place between 1868 and 1871. The most famous of all was the *tabor* organized in 1868 in Ostrá Hůrka, near Chabitschau (Chabičov). According to the presumably inflated Czech figures, between 1868 and 1871, 25,000 people participated in the *tabors* in Austrian Silesia, whereas 1.5 million in Bohemia participated along with 450,000 in Moravia (Waldenberg, 1992: 41).

Germans opposed these events with their own anti-*tabor* staged in Schelenburg (Šelenburk) near Jägerndorf (Krnov). In return the Czech-speaking Austrian Silesians protested the project of moving Lemberg University[11] to Troppau, as they were afraid that it would fortify Austrian Silesian Germandom. In 1871 the crownland authorities were handed a petition in which 1,500 people who signed it asked for the establishment of a Czech-language gymnasium and a Czech-language teachers' seminary in Troppau. Their effort amounted to nothing, as the crownland authorities declined this petition. It was at that time that the Czech and German national movements began to delineate their positions in Austrian Silesia through a continuous conflict played out in the arenas of politics, education and culture.

The regional identity that encompassed all the Austrian Silesians had been displaced. The nascent German-Czech national conflict spilled across the border to Prussian Upper Silesia's region of Hultschin. Father Lelek advocated the reading of *Národní listy* along with *Opavský besedník* and *Opavský tydenník*. He regularly contributed articles to the two latter Moravian periodicals (Gawrecka, 1993: 68, 70; Gawrecki, 1992: 63; Jakubíková, 1994: 143–144; Lubos, 1974: 608–609; Myška, 1994: 75).

Similar developments were observed in the rise of the Polish national movement. Initially, unlike their Czech counterparts, the Polish national activists had managed to maintain the continuity of their movement in the difficult 1850s, mainly thanks to *Gwiazdka Cieszyńska* and the Kasyno. After the end of absolutism Stalmach organized the Czytelnia Ludowa (Folk Reading Room), which was founded and frequented by Polish-, Czech- and German-speaking members of the East Silesian elite. Although this reading room was intended to spread knowledge of the Polish language and culture among the Polish/Slavic-speaking East Silesians, it was not a strictly national organization. In a very universalistic manner promoted by the Catholic Church, Stalmach's Czytelnia attracted members across ethnic lines, not unlike his *Gwiazdka Cieszyńska*.

In 1863 Stalmach established the Teatr Polski Amatorski (Polish Amateur Theater) in the framework of the Czytelnia Ludowa. By 1881 it had staged 118 productions (Fazan, 1991: 67–68, 77). In the same year Stalmach led the consolidation of the economic life of the Polish/Slavic-speaking East Silesians in the Towarzystwo Solnicze (Salt Society) (Myška, 1993: 101), and in 1869 he contributed to the establishment of the Towarzystwo Rolnicze (Agricultural Society). Stalmach also supported the founding of Polish reading rooms throughout East Silesia. Reading rooms that came into being during this early period were located in Jablunkau (Jablunkov), Skotschau (Skoczów), Obersuchau (Horní Suchá) and Zabrzeg (Zabrzeg) (Grobelný, 1992: 72; Zahradnik, 1992a: 40).

In 1861, 1866 and 1870 rich Polish/Slavic-speaking peasants from East Silesia who hailed from at least sixty different localities sent three petitions to Francis Joseph I. They requested more official use of Polish, or even elevating this language to the status of a crownland language, but to no avail. Nothing was achieved in this respect, even after the common delegation of these peasants and East Silesian Polish national activists was received in 1870 by the President of Imperial and Royal Ministers, Count Adam Potocki (1822–1872), a Polish politician and aristocrat from Galicia. The first political successes came in 1867 when Józef Dostal became the first Polish/Slavic-speaker to be elected to the Austrian Silesian Landtag. Four Polish-speaking representatives entered this body in 1871, and in 1873 the rich Polish-speaking peasant Jerzy Cienciała from Mistrzowitz (Mistřovice) was elected to the imperial Reichsrat (Michalkiewicz, 1976: 359).

Thanks to the continued existence of the Polish-language press in Austrian East Silesia since 1848, the local Polish national movement influenced the development of its counterpart in Prussian Upper Silesia. East Silesia's Polish activists also established numerous ties with the Polish national centers in Congress Poland and Galicia. Their contacts with Cracow were especially fruitful due to the lack of an international border that would obstruct them. In turn, the Cracow Polish national elite became quite receptive to the needs of the Polish national movement in East Silesia, especially after 1867–1873, when Galicia obtained full cultural autonomy. In line with its autonomous status, Polish became Galicia's official language (1869). Administration and education were Polonized,[12] together with universities and higher education institutions in Cracow and Lemberg.

In 1871 the Polish scientific society Akademia Umiejętności (Academy of Knowledge) came into being in Cracow (Buszko, 1989: 6). Hence, East Silesia obtained easy access to the mainstream of Polish national and cultural life in Cracow. East Silesian delegates duly attended various Polish national events that took place in Cracow and Lwów (Lemberg, Lviv) in 1870 and 1871 in the wake of the introduction of autonomy (Grobelný, 1992: 72). Even earlier such links with Polishdom had been forged by the sojourn of January Uprising refugees from Congress Poland in East Silesia during 1863 (Michalkiewicz, 1976: 358), and thanks to the Polish national festivals in Schwibitz (Svibice) and Roppitz (Ropice) in 1869 and 1871, respectively. These events were attended by Polish delegates from all the lands of partitioned Poland-Lithuania and Upper Silesia.

These festivals mimicked the Czech *tabors* and were a visible example of cooperation between Polish and Czech national movements. Polish activists attended Czech national events and vice versa. Polish nationalists also participated in the symbolic events of significance for the entire Czech national movement. For instance, they attended the celebrations accompanying the moving of the Czech coronation jewels from Vienna to Prague in 1867, and transportation of the body of the Czech poet Boleslav Jablonský (pseudonym of Karl Eugen Tupy, 1813–1881) from Cracow to the Bohemian capital. Due to the routes of the Habsburg railway network, which avoided venturing into the Kingdom of Hungary, both the trains with their nationally significant contents had to cross East Silesia.

In these formative years for the Polish and Czech national movements, their adherents chose to cooperate with one another, defining these movements against their already firmly established German counterpart. German national activists also encouraged cooperation between the Polish and Czech national movements by lumping them together as an instance of "dangerous anti-state Pan-Slavism." However, the first conflicts between the two Slavic national movements cropped up at the close of the 1850s and in the 1860s, especially at the level of the communes (*Gemeinde*). These initial altercations were connected to the attempts to delineate a clear linguistic border between the western part and eastern part of East Silesia. The former was believed to be Czechophone, whereas the latter was considered to be Polonophone. Certainly, employing language for this task was of no help as East Silesia's Slavic-speaking population used the whole spectrum of Silesia's transitory Slavic subdialects. These subdialects changed gradually from village to village, and nowhere was there any point where the area of Polish-speakers would stop and that of the Czech-speakers would commence. Interlacing of the local Slavic subdialects with various linguistic influences from German and the Slavic-Germanic creole made this mission even more difficult.

The Polish-Czech national dispute in East Silesia evolved into an open conflict with the Polish activists' demands that the Polish language should be introduced into elementary schools in this linguistically transitory area—for instance, in the parishes of Tierlitzko (Terličko) and Deutschleuten (Německí Lutyně). Predictably Czech nationalists protested and demanded the introduction of Czech as the medium of instruction (Grobelný, 1992: 71). Czech and Polish nationalists clearly realized, though they did not openly articulate this knowledge, that the Slavic-speaking East Silesians, with their prenational multiple identities, were the "game" the national movements intended to "hunt" for their respective nations-in-making. The mechanism for claiming a group of inhabitants for one nation or another was quite simple. Everything hinged on the decision as to which language was introduced into elementary education in a given parish or commune (*Gemeinde*). Irrespective of whether it was Czech, German or Polish, success came after one generation. If the schoolchildren completed their education in a Czech-medium school, 80 percent of them could be expected to become Czechs. And the same phenomenon took place in those localities where Polish or German was introduced into schools and maintained its presence in the educational system for at least two decades. The schoolchildren educated in one of these three national languages felt closer to the nation defined by the language in which they received their education. Then, already being conscious members of a given nation, the children in turn superseded their parents, who usually stuck to their prenational identities. As time progressed the ennationalization of social reality unfolded.

This ideological competition that played out among the German, Czech and Polish national movements for the "souls" of the Slavic-speaking East Silesians caused many an East Silesian to recoil from the unfolding brave new world of nationalisms. This happened especially in the rural Catholic parishes, which were entrenched in the universalistic tradition and still undisturbed by industrialization. The Catholic Church strove to encourage such an anational attitude in the time of the *Völkerfrühling* when it published to this end the weekly *Nowiny dla Ludu Wiejskiego* (1848–1849). This initial universalistic impetus in the 1860s and 1870s emphasized the difference between the still-prenational Slavic-speaking East Silesian population and the swelling ranks of the nationally defined Germans, Poles and Czechs.

The Protestant Church also championed this anational trend. In 1877 it established the successor to *Nowiny dla Ludu Wiejskiego*, the political weekly *Nowy Czas* (New Time, 1877–1920). With German aid, both the Catholic and Protestant Churches had campaigned for the establishment of the Silesian nation since the 1870s, hoping to curb the influence of Polish and Czech nationalisms in East Silesia. Initially, they thought that this initiative would preserve the unity of their faithful on the ground of the common Austrian Silesian crownland (regional) identity. The East Silesian Slavic-speakers, at whom this propaganda was directed, were quite receptive to it. It was easier for them to accept the promise of preserving their prenational world in the tolerant fold of politically and economically successful German nationalism than to identify with Czech or Polish nationalisms. The economic success of the German nation-state was readily visible across the border in Prussian Silesia, while Czech and Polish patriots advocated the cause of still-nonexistent Czech and Polish nation-states. For the peasant, with his social and political experience limited to the confines of his parish, it is more acceptable to believe in things that are than in those claimed to be coming in some unspecified future.

Moreover, the seminal stereotypes of Galician poverty and *polnische Wirtschaft* (that is, "typically Polish inability to organize anything") also deterred them from becoming Poles. In the second half of the nineteenth century anything of Slavic provenance somehow smacked of "civilizational inferiority." On top of that, the specter of the "Russian danger" was frequently evoked in the context of various Slavic nationalisms that emerged in Austria-Hungary. According to Vienna's pundits this phenomenon, coupled with Russian expansionism, threatened the very existence of the Danubian monarchy. Pan-Slavists did their best to aggravate these fears in order to gain more political influence, even though St. Petersburg remained rather uninterested in their services. The discourse about presumed ties with Pan-Slavism concerned more the Czech national movement than its staunchly anti-Russian Polish counterpart, and as such was the most potent argument that prevented Slavophone East Silesians from turning into Czechs. The situation was somewhat similar in Prussian Upper Silesia, where aforementioned arguments caused the Polish/Slavic-speaking Upper Silesians to shy away from Polish nationalism and the Czech/Slavic-speaking Morawecs from Czech nationalism (Černý, 1995: 45–84; Gawrecka, 1993: 71; Nowak, 1995: 27; Wanatowicz, 1986; Zahradnik, 1989: 122).

From the geographical point of view the German national movement of Austrian Silesia concentrated in the west, center and southeast of West Silesia and around Bielitz (Bielsko) and other industrial centers of East Silesia. This was so because the Austrian Silesian German-speakers living in these areas enjoyed German-language schools and church services. The Czech/Slavic-speaking population dominated in the northeast of West Silesia and across the border in the Hultschin region, as well as in the Moravian wedge between East and West Silesia and in the eastern sliver of East Silesia. Across the blurry ethnic line in the center, the east of East Silesia was populated by Polish/Slavic-speakers. The Polish and Czech national activists predominantly operated in their "own" ethnic areas. In cities and industrial regions the situation got more entangled, as well as in the transitory region, whose population was to become the electorate of the Silesian (national) movement (cf. Nabert, 1994: map).

Language policies as applied in schools, churches and local county governments became the basis for opening the radical ethnic and national cleavages in Austrian Silesia. The linguistic definition of such cleavages came to the fore after the fateful year 1880, when the "national question about one's language" was included for the first time in the Austro-Hungarian census. It made people with prenational multiple identities choose one and only one national identity. The census-taker had to disregard the phenomenon of bi- or even multilingualism and subsume local dialects under the larger rubrics of defined and standardized national languages. Declarations that one spoke the "Silesian language" or one's "own idiom" were brushed aside as evidence of ignorance. The authorities knew better. The same approach was applied to Austro-Hungarian Jews, who were forbidden to declare Yiddish as their "Jewish language." According to Vienna it was German, even though it was "kitchen German," hardly worth this name.

Thus, the "objective instrument" of statistics, harnessed for the needs of Austro-Hungarian politics, gave birth to clearly delineated nations. This development, which the Austro-Hungarian authorities dreaded so much, took place precisely because of their decisions. The populace of Austrian Silesia, like the entire population of Austria-Hungary, was split into separate nations, which would eventually prove to be the unmaking of the Dual Monarchy. Jeremy King (2002: 57–59, 225) has analyzed the process in detail in the case of the southern Bohemian town of Budweis (České Budějovice), whose previously non-national population was split between the linguistically defined nations of Czechs and Germans in the course of the 1880s.

As mentioned above, such a decisive, nation-making census had taken place in Prussia (including Prussian Silesia) already in 1861.

CHAPTER 5

National and Ethnic Groups in Silesia Prior to 1871

Part 1 of this work traced the elevation of the previously unimportant ethnic difference to the very basis of the ideology of nationalism in central Europe as exemplified by the case of Silesia. In conclusion it seems justifiable to state that German, Polish and Czech nationalisms arrived in Silesia from outside with the partial exception of Lower Silesia, one of the areas of the Holy Roman Empire where German nationalism was initially forged. This part of Prussian Silesia had easy access to western Germanophone universities, where the Herderian philosophy of *Völkergeist* bloomed. Lower Silesian intellectuals actively participated in the subsequent discussion on the German nation and state from an early date. Lower Silesia also formed the stage on which the first, most formative event of German nationalism unfolded, the War of Liberation (1813–1815). Later the center of gravity of German nationalism moved to Frankfurt, the seat of the German National Assembly in 1848–1849, and to Berlin, which was elevated to the rank of the German imperial capital in 1871.

As mentioned in the Introduction, the model of the Czech historian Miroslav Hroch is employed here to analyze the emergence of the national and ethnic groups in Silesia during the period 1848–1871, discussed in part 1 of this work. In his classic book he applied his model to stateless ethnic nations (for instance, the Czechs or the Norwegians) as well as to parts of larger ethnic nations (for instance, Danes in Germany's Schleswig-Holstein or the Flemish, which seem to form a broader Netherlandish nation together with the Dutch). In a nutshell, in phase A, a few scholars describe the ethnic specificity of a human group, namely, customs, religion, language and economy. In this manner the ethnic boundary of such a group is delimited and prepared for possible politicization in the future. More often than not these scholars are elite researchers with ethnic backgrounds different from those of the groups they studied. For example, usually Germanophone philologists set themselves the task of describing the Estonians or the Latvians.

In phases B and C the politicization of such a delimited group commences. In the former phase an early and narrow educated elite stemming from this group makes its people into a national project. This elite endows its postulated nation with a standardized national language, national history and the goal of attaining a nation-state. In phase C a majority of the people earmarked for the new nation accept this vision proposed by the national activists. They consciously choose to become members of this nation. The nationalist movement has grown into a massive political force. Another qualitative jump occurs when this national force wins its own nation-state.

The German national movement of Prussian Silesia was mainly concentrated in Lower Silesia. Its development cannot be separated from the emergence of German nationalism in Prussia and other German-speaking states. Hence, phase A of cultural, literary and folkloric pursuits opened during the second half of the eighteenth century. The ideas of Herder and of the French Revolution provided an ideological basis for the transition to phase B. This transitional period, in the case of Prussian Silesia, lasted from the crushing defeat of 1806 to the War of Liberation. During the 1848 revolution the transformation of German nationalism into a mass movement commenced. The national question asked in the 1861 Prussian census formalized the ideological foundation of the German-speaking "Prussian nation," which was forged into a "*Kleindeutsch* nation" in the course of the successful wars of 1864, 1866 and 1870–1871.

The transition to phase C was complete with the creation of the *Kleindeutsch* nation-state in the form of the German Empire in 1871. However, a specific problem arose. This German nation-state excluded Germans of Austro-Hungary and contained large Slavic-speaking minorities. Silesia shared the same patterns of ideological problems. First, Upper Silesia was largely Slavophone. Second, part of historical Silesia—Austrian Silesia, with its German-speaking population—found itself outside the borders of the German Empire.

The Polish national movement was concentrated mainly in eastern Upper Silesia. It entered phase A shortly before 1848 when Lompa published his books that linked the Slavic-speaking Upper Silesians with the Polish nation. But this phase opened in earnest only after the mid-nineteenth century. The politics of the Catholic Church (and less so of the Protestant Church, which was bound more closely to the state) aimed at keeping the Slavic-speaking Silesian faithful within the universalistic ideas of Christianity. The message of the Catholic hierarchy transcended state borders and the logic of nationalism. On top of that the church still had not come to terms with the non-divine legitimization of power and instilled in its faithful loyalty to the Prussian monarch as one of God's anointed representatives on the earth.

The Prussian state facilitated the church's task by allowing the church-controlled educational system to cater to the children of the Slavic-speaking faithful in standard Polish or Moravian.[1] The state also urged the Protestant Church to adopt a similar position. Both the churches and the Prussian government hoped that in this manner they would win the Polish/Slavic-speaking Silesians for the cause of Germandom or manage to keep them in phase A indefinitely. These goals were largely achieved in the case of the Protestant Polish/Slavic-speakers of northeastern Lower Silesia. Later many of them assimilated with their German-speaking neighbors, despite the fact that their villages and towns directly bordered on the Polish-speaking areas in the Province of Posen and in Congress Poland. From the latter the Polish/Slavic-speaking Protestants were isolated by the state border, but nothing hindered their access to Posen and Wielkopolska. What mattered was the religious difference—their Polish-speaking neighbors were Catholics. That was enough for the Protestants to overcome the language barrier and become Germans.

The Polish national movement in the Province of Posen entered phase B after the failed uprising of 1848. Unexpectedly, in the wake of the defeat of the January Uprising (1863–1864), Polish nationalists from Posen began campaigning among the pro-Polish Upper Silesian activists of phase A for more support. Posen's nationally minded intellectuals hoped to involve such Upper Silesians in the cause of the all-Polish national movement, which strove for the reestablishment of the Polish-Lithuanian state as a Polish nation-state. This message was fortified by the continued influence of East Silesia's Polish national movement in Upper Silesia. This movement on the Austrian side of the border had already entered the transitional period between phases A and B. The steady support of Galicia's phase-B Polish national movement was crucial for this development in East Silesia. That was because the Galician Poles suddenly jumped into the transitional period between phases B and C when their crownland was granted full Polish-language cultural and political autonomy between 1867 and 1873. However, Upper Silesia's Polish national movement shifted into the transitional period between phases A and B only after 1871, primarily due to the impact of the anti-Catholic *Kulturkampf*.

The achievements of Prussian Silesia's German national movement echoed across the frontier in Austrian Silesia. Phase A of the German national movement in the German-speaking Habsburg lands largely coincided with the phase A pattern of this movement elsewhere in the Holy Roman Empire with the notable exception of language politics. Latin remained the official language of the Habsburg lands up to the 1784, when German superseded it. In Austrian Silesia German also replaced chancery Czech, which had been the traditional language of the Upper Silesian administration until the Prussian takeover of Silesia in the 1740s. Czech had still continued to function in this capacity in the territory of Austrian Silesia that had remained with the Habsburgs. As in the case of Latin, the official use of chancery Czech lingered there until the turn of the nineteenth century.

The wars of the Habsburgs with Napoleonic France and their participation in the War of Liberation did not sway the German national movement into phase B but only into the protracted transitional zone between phases A and B. After the Congress of Vienna (1815), when the German Confederation came into being, the Habsburgs were not ready to encourage emergence of the German national movements in the Austrian Empire. Vienna was well aware that such official support would inevitably trigger various non-German national movements, thus endangering the existence of the empire. The Habsburg court could not espouse the idea of a German nation-state either, as it hoped to incorporate non-Germanophone lands of the Danubian monarchy into the German Confederation.

The sudden appearance of Slavic national movements in 1848 quickened the transition of the German national movement into phase B. But the reactionary policies of the 1850s hindered the completion of this transition until the 1860s, at which time constitutional reforms were introduced, and Austro-Hungarian statisticians accepted the principle of nationality, though its practical implementation had to wait until the 1880 census. The decisive shock of the Austro-Prussian War of 1866 terminated the existence of the German Confederation. The hopes for actualization of some *Großdeutsch* nation-state were shattered and Austria-Hungary's German-speakers were excluded from the "safe national haven" of the *Kleindeutsch* nation-state when it came into being five years later. Hence this date is the watershed that marks the beginning of phase B for the German-speakers of Austrian Silesia. They had started renouncing their regional identity only after 1848.

The Polish movement of East Silesia entered phase A just prior to 1848 but in earnest only afterwards. Its continuity was maintained during the very anti-national 1850s, and the movement bloomed in the liberal 1860s. It gradually shifted toward phase B thanks to influence from Galicia, where in the 1860s and 1870s the Polish national movement decisively entered phase C.

Bohemia's Czech national movement moved into phase A at the turn of the nineteenth century and reached phase B in 1848. This situation lasted until 1867, when Czech activists, not content with minor cultural and linguistic concessions, repeatedly demanded from Vienna partner-level treatment, as had been granted to the Hungarians in the 1867 *Ausgleich*. Afterward, the Young Czechs tabled more radical demands and eventually obtained even more concessions, the most important of which was the equalization of the status of the Czech language with German in Bohemia during the second half of the 1880s. This steered Bohemia's Czech national movement into phase C in the 1890s after the Old Czechs had lost elections and their influence on this movement to the Young Czech radicals (Carter, 1992: 923).

However, the development of the Czech national movement in Moravia and especially in Austrian Silesia was much slower. Phase A of Austrian Silesia's Czech national movement lasted from 1848 to 1861, when *Opavský besedník* was founded.

This newspaper promoted the idea of unity of the Czech lands and initiated the transition to phase B. It was largely complete at the turn of the 1860s and 1870s, when the firm ties emerged linking Austrian Silesia's Czech national movement to its counterparts in Bohemia and Moravia.

The Czech national movement of Prussian Silesia's Hultschin region remained in phase A until the beginning of the 1890s due to the policies of the *Kulturkampf,* which fortified the Catholic dimension of the Slavophone inhabitants' identity. On top of that they had no direct organizational connections with the centers of the Czech national movement in Bohemia, Moravia or Austrian Silesia. The situation changed in 1893 when the weekly *Katolické Nowiny, pro lid moravský v Pruském Slezsku* (Catholic News for the Moravian People in Prussian Silesia, 1893–1920) started to appear. This periodical commenced the transitional period to phase B. Not unlike the case of the Silesian national movement in East Silesia, the Hultschin region's Czech national movement was transformed into a pro-German Morawec national movement steeped in the local written Slavic dialect or the Moravian language (Gröschel, 1993: 240).

East Silesia's locally oriented Silesian (Slunzakian) national movement entered phase A in 1848 with the publication of the weekly *Nowiny dla ludu Wiejskiego.* This periodical aimed at countering the pro-Polish influence of *Tygodnik Cieszyński* until the latter was overhauled and became the neutral Catholic *Gwiazdka Cieszyńska* in 1851 (Kwaśniewski, 1997: 142). The Slunzakian movement emerged again in the 1860s after a period of discontinuity in the 1850s. Slunzakian national proponents—mainly priests and pastors of German provenance—drew on folkloric, cultural and linguistic material worked out during the specific phase-A periods of Austrian Silesia's German, Polish and Czech national movements. The Slunzakian national movement's transition toward phase B started with the founding of its press organ, *Nowy Czas,* in 1877.

A parallel Upper Silesian national movement could have evolved around Father Bogedain's *Gazeta Wiejska dla Górnego Śląska,* but it was a short-lived periodical. What is more, this weekly promoted standard Polish rather than the local Slavic dialect. After the revolutionary events of 1848, the relative absence of publishing in standard Polish or the local Slavic dialect, combined with lukewarm interest in Upper Silesia on the part of the mainstream Polish national movement, translated into the weakness of the fledgling local Polish national movement in this region. Thus, because such a Polish national movement did not exist, it did not have to be countered. At the same time Berlin did not actively support German nationalism until the 1860s because of Vienna's adverse view of anything that smacked of nationalist ideology. The Prussian government had to bow to this attitude, as the Habsburgs dominated the German Confederation. Consequently, the use of standard Polish was limited to church life and primary schools, and the use of German to offices, education and the army, so there were no immediate ennationalizing endeavors influencing the Upper Silesian population (cf. Reiter, 1989: 122). The Slavic-speakers, with their multiple identities, were left alone, as were the inhabitants of the rapidly industrializing cities of eastern Upper Silesia, where the Slavic-Germanic creole emerged.

This situation changed after the establishment of the *Kleindeutsch* nation-state and with the commencement of the *Kulturkampf*. In effect, the Polish national movement received a boost through anti-Catholic policies that, by extension, attacked the use of standard Polish in churches and elementary schools. In Upper Silesia this development transformed the state's conflict with Catholicism into the German-Polish politicized linguistic conflict, increasingly defined in national terms. This development gradually exerted ennationalizing pressure on all the Upper Silesians with non-national multiple identities. Supported by the Catholic Church, they resisted this pressure, and the Szlonzokian national movement entered phase B with the publication of the bilingual weekly *Schlesier-Szlązak* (The Silesian, 1872–1879). After the end of the *Kulturkampf* in the mid-1880s, Berlin rightly hoped that this movement, in combination with the universalistically minded Catholic clergy, would limit the attraction of the Polish national movement in Upper Silesia.

Usually, in Polish sources Józef Lompa and Karol Miarka are portrayed as the fathers of the Polish national movement in Upper Silesia. To a certain extent, their deeds and statements substantiate this opinion, especially in relation to Lompa's writings and organizational efforts during the revolutionary period of 1848, and after 1871 in the case of Miarka's journalism and his activities as a publisher of Polish-language periodicals and books. It is, however, too easily overlooked that Lompa referred to himself as a (Polish-speaking) Silesian and wrote for the (Polish-speaking) Silesians (Lompa, 1996: 1), whereas Miarka felt himself to be a German. Only in the late 1860s did he declare himself a (Polish-speaking) Upper Silesian and began publishing in Polish for the (Polish-speaking) Upper Silesian people/nation (Miarka, 1984: 25, 55).

Having surveyed the development of the national movements in Prussian and Austrian Silesia prior to 1871, it is necessary to see how they related to the national and ethnic groups that inhabited these two provinces.

As mentioned earlier, multiple identity was the norm before the ideology of nationalism introduced its monistic counterpart, usually founded on a single constituent of the former identity. Prior to the age of nationalism, there was only the German *natio*, or more correctly, the *Bildungsbürgertum* of the standard German language and culture in Prussian and Austrian Silesias. Members of the Czech-speaking *natio* of the Czech Crown disappeared after the Battle of White Mountain (1620). The extent of the Polish *natio* was limited to Wielkopolska in Prussia and to Galicia in the Habsburg Empire. Both regions had been wrenched from Warsaw in the course of the partitions of Poland-Lithuania. This was not so in the case of Silesia, as it had become part of the Kingdom of Bohemia and the Holy Roman Empire as early as the fourteenth century. This entailed the transition of the members of the Silesian *gens*[2] (local nobility) into the German or Bohemian *nationes* of the Holy Roman Empire. After the Battle of White Mountain the difference between both these *nationes* lessened as the members of the latter began to speak German too.

Obviously, members of some foreign *nationes* settled in Silesia. They were not pressed to enter the fold of the locally extant German or Bohemian *nationes* because the fixation of homogeneity was then limited to faith only. With time, however, descendants of these noble immigrants became members of the local *nationes,* not being able to maintain any practical link with the original *nationes* of their forefathers.

After the Peace of Westphalia (1648), the increasingly German-speaking *natio* of Silesia (Reiter, 1989: 119) was purged of non-Catholic elements, though some limited privileges were granted to Protestant burghers and noblemen in western Lower Silesia, which remained predominantly Protestant. Following the division of Silesia between Prussia and the Habsburgs, Protestants gained equal rights in Prussian Silesia. This did not entail oppression of the local Catholics, although they did not enjoy the privileged status they had under the Habsburgs. The Hohenzollerns welcomed loyal Protestant nobility to Silesia and promoted local Protestant burghers and civil servants through ennoblement. As a result the Germanophone *natio* in Prussian Silesia had a dual Protestant-Catholic character. The authorities based their rule on the Protestant segment of this *natio,* while its Catholic members were torn between loyalty to the Habsburgs and to the new rulers. This vacillation in the loyalty of the Catholic nobility continued in a decreasing manner until the establishment of the *Kleindeutsch* nation-state.

The Catholic character of the German-speaking *natio* was maintained in Austrian Silesia, though an increasing number of rights were granted to Protestant burghers in East Silesia. Consequently, when in the course of modernization the *Bildungsbürgertum* emerged, it was of mixed Catholic-Protestant character in East Silesia.

The split of historic Silesia also translated into a gradual overhaul of the constituents of the multiple identity of the members of the German-speaking *natio* or *Bildungsbürgertum* in Prussian Silesia and Austrian Silesia. Regional loyalties to both Silesias and the respective monarchs who controlled them developed. This process accelerated after the demise of the Holy Roman Empire (1806). Following this event, the *Bildungsbürgertum* of both Silesias could no longer refer to the ultimate suzerain in the person of the emperor. Thus, the tentative link between these two Silesias, in the form of the Holy Roman Emperor of the German Nation, was gone.

From the turn of the nineteenth century to the mid-nineteenth century, urbanization, industrialization, and growth of the transportation and communication networks were accompanied by the gradual phasing out of serfdom. It had a tremendous effect on the peasantry, which, prior to that time, had been immobile and, consequently, existed in laterally insulated communities. Their identities were largely based on their localities and on religion (cf. Gellner, 1983: 9). It had been the *natio/Bildungsbürgertum* that had mediated between them and the wider world. What is more, the persons of the monarch and the emperor had served as the instrument of cohesion between the peasantry and this *natio/Bildungsbürgertum*, and constituted the locus of common loyalty.

The end of serfdom endowed the peasantry with a degree of mobility, and the processes of modernization began to draw them into the German nation, which was emerging from the *Bildungsbürgertum*. Instruments used to this end were popular education, compulsory military service and the gradual abolishment of the estate structure, thanks to the democratization of political life. Initially, suffrage was extended to all adult males, and next the varying weights of their votes were made equal. Hence, male inhabitants were gradually transformed from subjects into citizens.

Democratization proceeded at a quicker pace in Prussia/Germany than in Austria/Austria-Hungary (Davies, 1996: 1295). Modernization varied in intensity and geographical extent in different areas of Prussian and Austrian Silesia. As a result, the variegated pace and the varying degree of completeness in the transition of peasants into the fold of the *Bildungsbürgertum*/German nation, as well as of the members of the *Bildungsbürgertum* into the German nation, brought about different rates of success in ennationalization.

First of all, after the dissolution of the Holy Roman Empire, all the inhabitants of Prussian Silesia developed an attachment to their region as well as to Prussia (cf. Fiedler, 1987: 148). A similar development took place with respect to the inhabitants of Austrian Silesia, though it was delayed a bit by the administrative merger of this crownland with Moravia. What is more, the usually less mobile peasants tended to identify either with West or East Silesia, Austrian Silesia being territorially discontinuous. On the other hand, the Austrian Empire was not such a unitary state as Prussia (especially after the establishment of Austria-Hungary). Hence, at the level of the state, the inhabitants of Austrian Silesia first tended to express their loyalty to the emperor before they developed a tentative identification with Cisleithania[3] as Austrians.

Bearing in mind what has been said concerning the development of the national movements in Prussian and Austrian Silesia prior to 1871, it seems that the overwhelming number of the inhabitants of Lower Silesia became Germans[4] during that period. It was more questionable in the case of Catholic Lower Silesians, but with the end of the alienating policies of the *Kulturkampf* nothing hindered them from becoming Germans anymore. In the case of Upper Silesia, only those who were Protestants, spoke German and did not speak the local Slavic dialect or Slavic-Germanic creole readily chose to become Germans.

German-speakers of Austrian Silesia could not easily identify themselves as Germans because the only effective strain of German nationalism (that is, *Kleindeutsch* nationalism), which resulted in the establishment of the *Kleindeutsch* nation-state, hinged on Protestantism. Only after the end of the *Kulturkampf* in Germany, and with the rise of various non-German nationalisms in the Danubian monarchy, did Vienna and Berlin inch toward cooperation, as did the respective groups of German nationalists from both these states. At the turn of the twentieth century they would eventually find a unifying ideological plane in the form of Pan-Germanism, anti-Semitism and racial superiority vis-à-vis the Slavs. Consequently, prior to 1871 the majority of the German-speakers in Austrian Silesia retained their multiple identity, but some broadened it with an element of German nationality.

The nascent Polish and Czech national movements did not produce more than several hundred people who began to feel themselves to be Poles or Czechs. But they still did not renounce their multiple identities, which also allowed them to identify themselves as Silesians, Prussians and Catholics in Upper Silesia or Austrian/West/East Silesians, Austrians, Catholics/Protestants in Austrian Silesia. In the case of Polish nationalism in Prussian Silesia such multiple identity did not merge with Protestantism.

The Slavic-speaking Protestants of northeastern Lower Silesia and of the County of Pleß in Upper Silesia were as repelled by Polish nationalism as they were attracted to Prussia/Germany. This was because Polish nationalism hinged on Catholicism, whereas Prussia espoused Protestantism as the religion of the state. As mentioned above, Slavic-speaking Protestants of northeastern Lower Silesia became Germans by the end of the nineteenth century. This was not the case with the Pleß group, who lived in a very backward and rural corner of Upper Silesia, so that the influence of the German ennationalizing efforts was not felt as deeply as in Lower Silesia or in the industrialized areas of Upper Silesia. But the Slavophone Protestants of Pleß did not become Poles either. Similarly, in Austrian Silesia all the combinations of the available constituents in the local multiple identities did not merge as well with the Polish or Czech national identity. Those with Czech national leanings were overwhelmingly Catholic, while those with Polish leanings were Catholic and Protestant.

The rise of German, Polish and Czech nationalisms gradually forced those of non-national multiple identities into a corner. However, in the future, the ennationalizing efforts of these competing national ideologies would somewhat cancel one another out, and the Catholic Church as a matter of principle continued to oppose the advance of nationalism, considering it contrary to Catholicism's universalistic message. The danger of having to abandon the old way of life under pressure from these three nationalisms, together with a modicum of protection from ennation-alization offered by the Catholic Church, created niches in which specific ethnic groups emerged. This development was also facilitated by the fact that Upper Silesia and Austrian Silesia were located on the peripheries of Prussia/Germany and the Austrian Empire/Austria-Hungary, as well as in the multicultural and multilingual borderland. As a consequence, ennationalizing policies, even if supported by the state, could not be as effective as in the centers of these states.

Ethnic groups drew on the local non-national multiple identities, but the increasing ennationalizing pressure made the rather straightforward dynamics of these identities more complex. These groups began to coalesce as more distinctive entities so as to protect their established ways of prenational life from the outside world of ongoing homogenization in the name of one or another nation. Multiple identities changed accordingly. The local identification, based on a parish or village, was pushed aside, and the idea of belonging to an ethnic group and a region emerged as the core of identification. But the core remained visible only to fellow members of an ethnic group, while other constituents of the multiple identity were emphasized when one met Germans, Poles or Czechs.

Thus, for instance, this new multiple ethnic identity allowed a Slavic-speaking Upper Silesian to be perceived ideally as a Szlonzok[5] among other Szlonzoks, a Pole among Poles, a German among Germans, and a Czech among Czechs. From the Czech, Polish or German national point of view, such a Szlonzok seemed to have a monistic national identity, while only other Szlonzoks understood it as merely one of the constituents of the Szlonzokian multiple ethnic identity. Such an identity protected the Szlonzok from encroachments on the part of national administrations and, ideally, reinforced the cohesion of the Szlonzokian ethnic group.

The emergence of an ethnic group is a gradual process. The Szlonzoks did not spring up suddenly out of nowhere when the effects of modernization had already been well entrenched in the societal reality. Usually larger ethnic groups are welded from smaller ones, often labeled as "ethnographic groups" (Magocsi, 1978: 2). These micro-groups tend to be intricately connected to their few localities that are spatially close to one another.[6] Hence, such small groups preceded the emergence of the Szlonzoks, as they did the rise of other ethnic groups extant in Prussian and Austrian Silesia. Information on the existence and ethnonyms of such groups may be obtained from nineteenth-century ethnographic and linguistic works. For instance, two of the many small groups which became the basis for the emergence of the Szlonzoks were known as the Kobylorze and the Golocy[7] (Bąk, in Cząstka-Szymon, 1996: I, map between pp. 10 and 11).

Szlonzoks referred to themselves as "Szlonzoki" or "Schlonsoki," which, pho-nemically, is the same word in Polish and German spellings, respectively. In German sources the Szlonzoks were referred to as "Wasserpolen," and their vernacular as "Wasserpolnisch," "Oder-Wendisch" or "Böhmisch-Polnisch." Prior to the first efforts undertaken to ennationalize the Szlonzoks as part of the German nation in the mid-nineteenth century and, later, to the Polish nation, they had inhabited most of Upper Silesia contained within the borders of the Breslau Diocese. They spoke a West Slavic dialect. Due to the development of popular elementary education they were subjected first to the influence of standard German, and also between 1848 and 1873 to the influence of standard Polish. In the second half of the nineteenth century, in the industrial towns of eastern Upper Silesia, a Slavic-Germanic creole emerged. It became one of the markers of the Szlonzokian identity (Kamusella, 1998). From the confessional viewpoint, the Szlonzoks were Catholics, with the exception of a several-thousand-strong group of Protestants in the border county of Pleß (Triest, 1984: 564, 569), more akin to the Slunzaks of East Silesia than to the Szlonzoks. The Szlonzokian way of life was initially limited to agriculture, but in the process of industrialization many Szlonzoks became workers in mines and metallurgical works that sprang up in eastern Upper Silesia. Although many did become industrial workers, after the shift they often toiled on their own small plots of land or in gardens at their houses (Pallas, 1970: 9–35).

The Slunzaks refer to themselves as "Ślunzoki" or "Szlunzoki" in Polish spelling as well as "Schlonsaken" and "Šlunzoky" in German and Czech orthographies (Bahlcke, 1996: 114; Pallas, 1970: 44). They lived in East Austrian Silesia, which was included within the borders of the Breslau Diocese. But in 1851, about 50,000 of them were Protestants (along with 8,000 German-speakers of the same confession). This amounted to over 40 percent of the inhabitants in this part of Austrian Silesia. The rest of the populace (including most Slunzaks) was Catholic (Grobelný, 1992: 68–69; Seidl, 1996: 146). This Catholic-Protestant character of the Slunzaks constituted the basic core of their ethnic specificity (Nowak, 1995: 27), which to a degree was shared by the Slavic-speaking Protestants from Pleß County, which lay across the border in Prussian Silesia.

The Slunzaks spoke a West Slavic dialect referred to as "Wasserpolnisch" in German sources (Wurbs, 1982: 33). It differed, however, from Upper Silesia's Slavic dialect of the Szlonzoks. This was because Slunzakian speech was less influenced by German or Germanic dialects. In 1880 only 14 percent of East Silesia's population were classified as German-speakers (Anon., 1992c: 61). Unlike its Szlonzokian counterpart, the Slunzakian dialect enjoyed stronger links with the Slavic dialects of northern Moravia, northwestern Upper Hungary (Slovakia) and western Galicia. What is more, standard Polish and standard Czech had influenced the Slunzakian dialect earlier and for a longer time than German, through Polish- and Czech-language publications flowing from Cracow and Moravia, respectively. However, this influence was less intensive than that of standard Polish on the Szlonzokian dialect between 1849 and 1872, when this language was the medium of instruction in Prussian Silesia's elementary schools (Knop, 1967: maps between pp. 48–49; Wronicz, 1995). Due to the relatively small German-speaking population concentrated around Bielitz and in the Ostrau-Karwin industrial basin, unlike in Upper Silesia, no Slavic-Germanic creole developed in East Silesia. Only ephemeral Slavic-Germanic pidgins arose, as they were useful for communication in retail commerce and in plants staffed with linguistically variegated labor. Another factor that hindered the emergence of a Slavic-Germanic creole was the prevalence of agriculture in most of East Silesia.

The next ethnic group of interest to this work is the "Mährer" or "Morawzen," as they were called in German. In Czech one spoke of the "Moravce," while they themselves wrote down their ethnonym as the "Morawce" (Pallas, 1970: 36–38). The ethnonym's meaning is that of the "Moravians." This frequently led to the confusion of the Morawecs with the Moravians (Mährer in German, Moravané in Czech). The Moravians, unlike the Morawecs, were the inhabitants of Moravia who identified themselves with their crownland or Moravia's Slavic-speakers (cf. Žáček, 1995). The Morawecs lived mainly in the south of Prussian Upper Silesia, the northeast of West Austrian Silesia, the Moravian salient between West and East Austrian Silesia, and the western sliver of East Austrian Silesia. They constituted a territorially compact group, though they were separated by the Prussian/German-Austrian and crownland borders. But even the international Austrian-German border was quite porous until 1918.

In the north the Morawecs bordered on the Szlonzoks of Prussian Upper Silesia, in the northwest and in the west on the German-speaking Austrian Silesians, and in the east on the Slunzaks of East Austrian Silesia. The south was open to direct influence from the Slavic-speaking Moravians. Initially, however, the pastoral Vlachs inhabited these areas (Nabert, 1994: map). These Vlachs (*Walachen* in German, *Valaši* in Czech, *Wałachowie* in Polish) should not be confused with the Vlachs of the Balkans, with whom they shared the transhumant way of life but not a language. Moravia's Vlachs spoke in Slavic, while those of the Balkans were the predecessors of the Romanians. The Moravian Vlachs inhabited the westernmost ranges of the Carpathians crisscrossing the Moravian-Upper Hungarian and Moravian-East Silesian borders. By the close of the nineteenth century they were assimilated into the locally extant neighbor nations and ethnic groups, and could not isolate the Morawecs from the Moravians any more (Nabert, 1994: map; Šatava, 1994: 60).

The societal cohesion of the Morawecs was ensured by Catholicism, their agricultural way of life and the inclusion of the areas of their settlement in the Olmütz Archdiocese, with the exception of the western sliver of East Austrian Silesia. On top of that and quite significantly for that matter, they enjoyed the continuous tradition of the Moravian language (*mährische Schriftsprache*). This written language of the Morawecs was close to the written "Moravian," "Slavic-Moravian" or "Slavic" language employed in Moravia proper. But the written language of the Moravians was based on different dialects. The Morawecs drew on their own speech, that is, the Silesian-northern Moravian Slavic dialect (Knop, 1967: map 1). Moravian—the Morawecs' written language—was employed in elementary education, textbooks and predominantly religious publications, as well as in church and public life. The Moravian language retained the sixteenth-century spelling of chancery Czech, which in the case of modern standard Czech was dropped in the mid-nineteenth century. This process was quicker in Bohemia than in Moravia and never took hold in the areas inhabited by the Morawecs before the end of World War I. What is more, Moravian texts were consistently written and printed in Gothic letters until 1918, while the Czech language shifted to regular Roman lettering already in the 1830s.

The development of the Ostrau-Karwin industrial basin located on the border of East Silesia and Moravia brought about, especially beginning in the second half of the nineteenth century, an increase in the contacts of the *Morawecs* (those from the Moravian salient between West and East Austrian Silesia) with the Slavic-speaking Moravians from Moravia proper. As a result, the former began to identify themselves with Moravia and the Slavic-speaking Moravians, which facilitated the infiltration of this salient by the Czech national movement. This took place especially in the 1870s, when the movement's activists successfully propagated the idea that the Slavic-speakers of Bohemia and Moravia were one nation of the Czechs (Pallas, 1970: 36–37). During the last two decades of the nineteenth century the Czech national idea also penetrated West and East Austrian Silesia. On the other hand, the Morawecs who lived in Prussian Silesia were not influenced by Czech nationalism until 1920, when the Allies transferred part of their area of settlement concentrated around the town of Hultschin to newly established Czechoslovakia.

Prior to this the Morawecs had been shielded from Czech nationalism by the policies of the Moravian Catholic Church and the Prussian/German administration, which promoted the Morawec ethnic identity. Additionally, any other possible identification changes were prevented by the Morawecs' traditionally agricultural way of life and their continuing low spatial mobility. Understandably no significant labor was derived from among them either in the Upper Silesian or Ostrau-Karwin industrial basins before 1919.

The contents of these three ethnic groups' identification loci were described above. Now one wonders what constituted the ethnic border that separated these ethnic groups from one another and also from the neighboring national groups.

The Szlonzoks were separated from the Morawecs by the inclusion of the former in the Breslau Diocese and the latter in the Olmütz Archdiocese (Pallas, 1970: 38). Catholicism shielded the Szlonzoks from the Slunzaks, as many of the latter were Protestants too. As in the case of the Szlonzoks, homogenous Catholicism separated the Morawecs from the Slunzaks, as well as the fact that the Slunzaks belonged to the Breslau Diocese.

From the linguistic viewpoint, Upper Silesia's Slavic-Germanic creole, especially widespread in the Upper Silesian industrial basin, constituted a strong marker of the Szlonzokian identity vis-à-vis the Morawecs and the Slunzaks. In addition, Slavic-German bilingualism began to play this role after it had spread in the urbanized and industrialized areas of Upper Silesia. The Morawecs differed from the Szlonzoks because, to a large degree, their religious, educational and public life was based on the Moravian written language. In these social contexts, since 1848, the Szlonzoks had used standard Polish and the Slunzaks their own written dialect, which gradually inched toward standard Polish. This was because of the Polonizing influence that flowed from neighboring Galicia, where Polish gained the status of an official crownland language in 1869. Moreover, the three ethnic groups were separated from one another by their own specific West Slavic dialects, which, nevertheless, were quite similar. Although members of these groups referred to their language as speaking "po naszymu" ("in our own way"), with time the dialect of the Morawecs (especially of those who lived outside Upper Silesia) borrowed increasingly from standard Czech. The Slunzakian dialect borrowed from standard Polish, and that of the Szlonzoks mostly from standard German and the Upper Silesian creole, but also from standard Polish.

Taking into consideration the "way of life," the distinctive feature of the Szlonzoks was their increasing employment in industry. This was also true only with regard to a decidedly smaller group of the Slunzaks (and to very few Morawecs), who obtained jobs in the Ostrau-Karwin industrial basin. The Morawecs, both in Upper Silesia and outside of it, generally continued to work as peasants, while the Slunzaks had better opportunities of finding employment in the Ostrau-Karwin industrial basin as well as in one of the largest Austro-Hungarian centers of the textile industry at Bielitz (Kuhn, 1977a: 29). The relatively lesser mobility of the Morawecs was caused by the slower and later development of the railway network in the regions of their residence than in the much more economically attractive areas of east Prussian Upper Silesia and of East Austrian Silesia. There, since the mid-nineteenth century, the phenomenon of mass commuting had begun to emerge. With no railway in their villages potential Morawec workers had no possibility to commute to the nearby industrial basins.

Another factor deepening differentiation among these three ethnic groups was international and administrative divisions, which had emerged since the split of Silesia in 1740–1742. The Szlonzoks identified themselves with Upper Silesia and Prussia. They were also loyal to their Prussian king. Due to the territorial discontinuity of Austrian Silesia, the Slunzaks tended to identify themselves with East Silesia (Kożdoń, in Kaciř, 1997: 54). They also felt special affinity with the whole Danubian monarchy by virtue of their loyalty to the emperor. On the other hand, the group cohesion of the Morawecs was limited by geographic divisions. Living in Prussia/Germany and the Austrian Empire/Austria-Hungary, as well as in West and

Austrian East Silesia and in Moravia, the Morawecs developed variegated loyalties to different states, rulers and administratively delineated regions.

During more or less intensive social interactions among members of these three ethnic groups, certain stereotypes emerged among them. These increasingly reaffirmed the ethnic borders separating the groups from one another. In their mutual interactions the Morawecs and the Slunzaks employed the most distinctive of these stereotypes. This was because the administrative, ecclesiastical or linguistic divisions between the two ethnic groups did not delineate them clearly. The Morawecs referred to the Slunzaks pejoratively as "Lachy" (sg. "Lach") or "Lachamani" (sg. "Lachman") In the Slavic dialects of Austrian Silesia and northern Moravia these words denote a "rogue" or "disorderly person." The Slunzaks reciprocated with the pejorative "Wałach," that is, an "uncultured and uncivilized highlander" (Pallas, 1970: 75–76). Of course, this derisive term was derived from the East Silesian Slavicization of the ethnonym of the Vlachs, many of whom had merged with the Morawecs. Ironically, some of these Vlachs, especially in the southeast of East Silesia, also had assimilated with the Slunzaks as the so-called Silesian Highlanders (Szołtysek, 1998: 54).

The Slunzaks, especially those from the nonindustrialized areas, in encounters with Szlonzoks of the Upper Silesian industrial basin perceived their behavior as arrogant. On the other hand, the Slunzaks appeared to the Szlonzoks as backward "pampunie," that is, villagers or peasants. The infiltration of nationalisms into Austrian Silesia and Upper Silesia added a nationalist dimension to existing interethnic prejudices. Because Polish nationalism penetrated East Austrian Silesia more quickly than Prussian Upper Silesia, the Morawecs and, to a lesser degree, the Szlonzaks began to identify the Slunzaks not so much with the Poles as with the stereotypes of the Polish "uncivilizedness." These included "Galician poverty" or "polnische Wirtschaft."[8] Similarly, with the subsequent advances of Polish nationalism in Upper Silesia at the turn of the twentieth century, the Morawecs from the south of this region began to feel repugnance toward the Szlonzoks, who appeared to the former as "too Polish." The Morawecs shared this attitude with the Germans or German-speakers, who felt that the Szlonzoks increasingly succumbed to Polish tendencies, whether linguistic or national. At the same time, the Upper Silesian section of the Morawecs did not feel well disposed to Morawecs from Austria-Hungary, as many of the latter used the standard Czech language or espoused Czech nationalism. Thus, in the eyes of Upper Silesia's Morawecs, the consequence was that the Szlonzoks and the Austrian-Hungarian Morawecs shifted further away from them and drew closer to the "civilizationally inferior" Poles and Czechs. This coaxed the Upper Silesian Morawecs into gradually identifying themselves with the "civilizationally superior" Germans.

The aforementioned "contents" and borders of the three ethnic groups created mutually exclusive fields of communication. These fields undermined societal cohesion, creating a considerable degree of endogamy and, by the same token, a certain biological self-enclosure of these groups.[9]

The separation of these ethnic groups from the growing national groups was a result of ethnic borders. The Szlonzoks and the Slunzaks perceived Poles as alien and expressed their attitude in this regard with their specific use of the ethnonyms "Polok" (Pole) and "Galicjok" (Galician, an inhabitant of Galicia). In the Szlonzokian and Slunzakian usages, these ethnonyms functioned as strong pejoratives. No self-respecting Slunzak or Szlonzok would bear being called such names (Kaciř, 1997: 54).

On the other hand, Poles from Congress Poland, the Province of Posen, and Galicia did not consider the dialects of the Szlonzoks and the Slunzaks to be Polish (Pallas, 1970: 50). Poles from the Province of Posen also referred to the Szlonzoks with the pejorative "Odraks," that is, a "poor, uncultured folk," referring to their isolated location on the River Oder ("Odra" in Slavic), where many subsisted on tiny plots of land. The influence of the Polish language and culture on the Szlonzoks, which emanated from Galicia and Congress Poland, was limited by the international borders. In addition, Wielkopolska's Polish national movement's interest in the Szlonzoks emerged only at the close of the nineteenth century. Then, in an ethnic sense, the historic notion of the Prussian partition of Poland-Lithuania was extended to contain Upper Silesia, which had not belonged to the commonwealth when Russia, Prussia and Austria had erased it from the political map of Europe. The overwhelming majority of the Szlonzoks disagreed with this approach of Polish nationalism and continued to perceive their region as an integral part of Prussia/the German Empire. This perception of Upper Silesia as an entity separate from Poland has survived among the Szlonzoks, as evidenced by the expression "*jada do Polski*" (I'm going to Poland). It denotes a trip to the cities of Sosnowiec or Chrzanów across the small rivers of Brynica (Brinitza) or Przemsza (Przemsa), which until 1918 constituted the border between Prussia/Germany, and Russia (that is, Congress Poland) and Austria-Hungary (that is, Galicia).

It was relatively easy for the Polish language and nationalism to infiltrate East Austrian Silesia from its firm base in Galicia, even though the administrative border amounted to a barrier. However, the factor that limited incorporation of the Slunzaks into the Polish nation was the coupling of Polish nationalism with Catholicism. This repelled numerous Protestant and Catholic Slunzaks because they were raised with tradition of religious tolerance and mutually fruitful coexistence. The relatively higher level of development of Upper Silesia and East Silesia vis-à-vis the adjacent areas of Congress Poland and Galicia fortified the stereotype of "civilizational inferiority" of the Poles. Due to the stigma of Polishness, Galician migrant workers in the Ostrau-Karwin industrial basin were, for the most part, ennationalized into the German or Czech nations. Both these nations were perceived as "civilizationally superior" to the Polish one (Grobelný, 1992: 69).

The centers of the Czech national movement were relatively remote from the areas inhabited by the Morawecs, which delayed the spread of Czech nationalism among them. The center of Czech nationalism in Bohemia was associated with anti-Catholic Hussitism/Protestantism and as such was incompatible with the Morawecs' universalistic Catholicism. The Moravian language was another barrier, which the Morawecs perceived as different from standard Czech, which was based on the Slavic dialect of Prague. Additionally, the use of Gothic letters to write and print in Moravian made this language graphically similar to German. One cannot overestimate barriers in the form of administrative and international borders. Hence, the Czech national movement most easily penetrated the Moravian salient between West and East Silesia because the ethnic border between the Morawecs and the Slavic-speaking Moravians was rather blurry there. The Czech national message also spread in the Slavic-speaking areas around Troppau, which somehow "belonged" to Moravia due to the inclusion of all of Moravia, as well as the eastern half of West Austrian Silesia, in the Olmütz Archdiocese. It was more difficult for the Czech national movement to enter the west of East Silesia included in the Breslau Diocese. East Silesia in its entirety was contained in the Breslau Diocese. This contributed to making the border between the Morawecs and the Slunzaks less distinct, and brought about the counteraction on the part of the Polish national movement. Polish nationalists from Galicia considered not only the western part of East Silesia but the entire region to be "nationally theirs" as unambiguously "Polish" in character. Last but not least, the international Prussian/German–Austrian/Austro-Hungarian border, despite the ecclesiastical inclusion of the south of Upper Silesia in the Olmütz Archdiocese, did not allow Czech nationalism to penetrate this area until 1918. The mechanism used by the Morawecs to differentiate themselves from the Poles in East Silesia was the common stereotype that associated Polishness with a "low level of civilization." Sometimes the Morawecs also used this instrument to delineate their difference vis-à-vis the Slunzaks, whom they tended to identify with the Poles.

The Szlonzoks could separate themselves from the Germans by virtue of their Slavic speech. But until the *Kulturkampf* neither the linguistic nor the eligious difference tended to be politicized. So the Szlonzoks could easily identify themselves not only with their region but also with Prussia. The same was true in the case of the Morawecs from the south of Upper Silesia (Pallas, 1970: 39). The subsequent nationally homogenizing line of the *Kleindeutsch* nation-state directed against Catholicism and languages other than German caused the emergence of the stereotype that the German is a Protestant and the Szlonzok a Catholic. In addition, the Szlonzok used standard Polish in church and at school. This of course did not mean that he felt himself to be a Pole (Reiter, 1960: 7). However, the use of this standard language and the Szlonzoks' Catholic faith would later facilitate the task of Wielkopolska's Polish national movement, which, among others, drew on confessional divisions. These Polish national activists decided to promote the slogan "a Pole is a Catholic, while a German is a Protestant" in their effort to forge a clearly delineated Polish national group in Prussia/the German Empire.

Germans tended to use the terms "Wasserpolen" and "Wasserpolnisch" as pejorative labels for denoting the Szlonzoks and their language (Pallas, 1970: 39), which fortified the ethnic border between these two groups. These German terms also separated the Szlonzoks from the Poles, especially when Polish activists used the term "Wasserpole" in the meaning of a "renegade" to denigrate Szlonzoks who would not identify themselves as Poles (Kaciř, 1997: 54) or would dare to display the somewhat un-Polish constituents of their multiple identity.

The Protestantism that was made part and parcel of the ideological basis of the *Kleindeutsch* nation-state alienated the Morawecs (as it did the Szlonzoks) from the German nation, especially in that this newly founded nation-state limited the use of the Moravian language in the Morawecs' social life. On the other hand, their written language remained the paramount ethnic marker of the Morawecs in Austria-Hungary. At the turn of the twentieth century this language was reinforced in its function as an ethnic marker by the spread of *Kleindeutsch* nationalism. This ideology separated the Morawecs from their German-speaking neighbors ennationalized into the German nation. Another significant factor for the ethnic coalescence of the Morawecs was the Moravian *Ausgleich* (compromise) of 1905. It regulated the relations (that is, separateness as well as coexistence) between the Slavic- and German-speaking Moravians in the crownland of Moravia. As a result the infiltration of this region, either by Czech or German nationalism, was limited, allowing the Morawecs of the Moravian salient to preserve their ethnic identity or to modify it toward that of the Moravians.

What separated the Slunzaks from their German-speaking neighbors was the Slavic idiom of the former as well as the homogenous Catholicism of almost the entire German-speaking populace in Austrian Silesia. Geographical distance constituted another barrier. The extensive compact areas inhabited by German-speakers were only located well beyond the Moravian salient in West Silesia. The Germanophone island, centered on the East Silesian town of Bielitz and on the Galician town of Biała, was insulated by the vast Slavic-speaking areas around it.

The development of the national movements in Silesia prior to 1871 and the emergence of the ethnic groups shaped by the rise of nationalism have been discussed above. The relations among the ethnic and national groups were noted and the ethnic boundaries separating them analyzed. Now it is necessary to scrutinize the approximate numerical size and political influence of these national and ethnic groups.

As was said before, the persisting loci of identification *besides* the nation were the region, the monarch, the prenational state, the estate, the confession and the traditional way of life. The nation was of ever growing significance in the wake of the establishment of the *Kleindeutsch* nation-state and would overshadow all other non-national elements of one's identification. This happened after the international espousal of the national principle as the very instrument of political organization at the close of the Great War (1918). Bearing in mind this gradual transition from the non-national multiple identity (constructed from numerous malleable constituents) to the monistic one (composed from only one, national constituent that equals nationality), it comes as no surprise that national groups in Silesia grew with the unfolding of the corresponding national movements. On the other hand, the rise of these national groups incited the naissance and eventual coalescence of ethnic groups. They grew out of the opposition to ennationalizing endeavors that endangered the traditional ways of life on which these ethnic groups thrived. But in a way, it was modernization (cf. Waters, 1998: 13–19), broadly understood, that prepared the ground for the rise of national and ethnic groups. This modernization was due to increased spatial and social mobility and democratization. These phenomena brought about the gradual phasing out of the insulation of self-contained localities from the world around them, and the disappearance of estate divisions.

By 1871 this process had been largely completed in Lower Silesia, where the overwhelming majority of the populace felt themselves to be Germans, without, however, forgetting their keen attachment to their home region of Silesia and to Prussia. In addition, their traditional loyalty vested with the Prussian monarch extended to his new position as Kaiser of the German Empire.[10] But the Lower Silesians did not seem to interpret this development as requiring them to believe this empire to be identical with the notion of a German nation-state and its inhabitants with all the Germans. The Kaiser was not a ruler of Germany or the German nation but of an empire, even though its official name was modified with the adjective "German" (Görtemaker, 1996: 253). A similar process, as in the case of the Lower Silesians, unfolded in relation to the predominantly monolingual German-speaking Protestants of Upper Silesia. On the other hand, the Slavic/Polish-speaking Protestants of northeastern Lower Silesia gradually gravitated toward Germandom, and this process, facilitated by the grounding of Polish nationalism in Catholicism, was completed at the beginning of the twentieth century.

The Slavic/Polish-speaking and frequently bilingual (to a varying degree of linguistic competence in standard German and/or Upper Silesian German dialect) population of Upper Silesia was alienated from the *Kleindeutsch* nation-state by *Kleindeutsch* nationalism, founded on Protestantism and the German language. But it was true only in the period of the *Kulturkampf*. Afterward the Catholic Church reached a rapprochement with Berlin, and the language issue remained secondary to religion. The German Empire ceased to be an anti-Catholic juggernaut, so Polish nationalists could not use this argument in order to coax the aforementioned population to espouse Polish nationalism. All these ideological changes in the 1870s and 1880s rather increased their attachment to (Upper) Silesia and Prussia besides contributing to their coalescence into the Szlonzokian ethnic group. Prior to 1871, the mainstream Polish national movement's interest in Upper Silesia was minimal, and the region still was not considered part of the partition areas of erstwhile Poland-Lithuania to be redeemed as a fragment of a future Polish nation-state. Only with the forging of the ethnic definition of the Polish nation in the 1890s did Upper Silesia and the Szlonzoks enter the plans of the Polish nationalists in earnest. At the end of the period surveyed in part 1 of this study, only a very few educated locals (anywhere from a few dozen to perhaps a hundred) felt themselves to be Poles without severing their identificational links with their region and Prussia. Although some Szlonzoks could pass themselves off as Poles during their trips to the adjacent areas of Congress Poland and Galicia, they did not cherish Polishness as even a minor constituent of their multiple identity. That was due to the stereotypically pejorative perception of the Poles and the Galicians common in Prussia/Germany.

The Slavic/Polish-speaking population of Pleß County could have been a stronghold for the Polish national movement had they not been Protestants. Only across the border in East Austrian Silesia did Protestantism not bar one from becoming a Pole. It was the pragmatic approach of the local Polish nationalists. Having espoused the ideology of Polish nationalism from one of its centers, lo-cated in Cracow, they transplanted it to East Silesia, less its confessional element, in recognition of the religiously mixed character of the region. Some of these activists were Protestants, but they did not embark on the Polish national course so as to change their faith. This would actually lessen their ethnic distinctiveness vis-à-vis the overwhelmingly Catholic German-speakers in Austrian Silesia and Cisleithania.

The beginning of the Polish national group in East Silesia is connected to the Slavic/Polish-speaking (Slunzakian) activists who were students at the local Protestant secondary school (one of very few in the Habsburg Empire). Later they were joined by Catholics, who had to carry out the ennationalizing work further on when the ranks of Slavophone Protestants were depleted by the Silesian (Slunzakian) national movement at the end of the 1860s and beginning of the 1870s. East Silesia's German-speaking pastors headed this Slunzakian movement. Although the universalism of the Catholic Church (propagated in Austrian Silesia by the Breslau bishop[11]) toned down Polish nationalism in East Silesia, it did not prevent the crystallization of the educated elite of several dozen Polish national activists due to the active support flowing from the Polish national movement in Galicia. These Protestant and Catholic Polish national activists did constitute a percentage of the population in East Silesia that was considerably larger than that of their counterparts in Upper Silesia. Moreover, the East Silesian activists developed a more monistic identity, in which the confessional, dialectal and regional constituents were clearly subordinated to the Polish national constituent. In this manner, the other identificational constituents evolved into the basis of the specific kind of East Silesian Polishness, which never smacked of any foreignness in the eyes of Warsaw politicians despite its regional distinctiveness.

That was so because only a few thousand Germans lived in East Silesia, and upward social mobility in the Habsburg Empire/Austria-Hungary was not limited exclusively to the German language and culture as in Prussia/Germany. It became even less so with the introduction of Polish as the official language in neighboring Galicia in 1869. Hence, advancement through the Polish language and culture guaranteed by the Polish-language universities in Cracow and Lwów gradually became an even more enticing option, unlike in Upper Silesia. In this Prussian province the peer pressure of the German-speaking environment caused the vast majority of the few Slavic/Polish-speakers who gained secondary/university education to become Germans. It was the only way in which they could reaffirm their higher social status connected to their learned professions. That was not so much true of priests, who had to cater to all the linguistically variegated population of Upper Silesia. But the universalism of Catholicism largely discouraged them from espousing the particularism of any nationalism. Hence the message of Polish nationalism spread in Upper Silesia only in its tacit version, promoted by undereducated local lay teachers and journalists. They concentrated on winning acceptance for the limited public and educational use of standard Polish and can hardly be considered straightforward Polish nationalist activists.

Bohemia's Czech nationalism was forged in earnest only in the mid-nineteenth century, during which it became increasingly steeped in the Hussitic and Protestant tradition of the Bohemian noble *natio*. This confessional-ideological linkage hindered the spread of this ideology in homogeneously Catholic Moravia and West Austrian Silesia. However, several dozen Czech nationalist activists emerged at the end of the 1860s and the beginning of the 1870s, especially in the vicinity of Troppau. Then they made some incursions into the Moravian wedge between West and East Austrian Silesia and into the west of East Silesia. What encouraged them was the gradual waning of their earlier cooperation with Polish nationalist activists in East Silesia, which had formerly thrived due to the policy of Slavic reciprocity in the face of the ideological danger posed by the spread of German nationalism.

The then codified standard Czech language and culture gained fuller recognition only in Bohemia during the 1870s–1880s. The Moravian (Moravian-Slavic or Slavic) language, written and printed in the Gothic type, was employed by the Slavic-speakers in Moravia and especially in West Austrian Silesia. Consequently, social advancement was possible there through the German language and culture rather than the Czech counterparts, unless one was prepared to move to Bohemia.

The international Austrian-Prussian/German border and the universalistic policies of the Catholic Church also kept Czech nationalism at bay, so that it did not
penetrate the south of Prussian Upper Silesia until 1918.

Most German-speakers of Austrian Silesia, though aware of the goals of German nationalism, which resulted in the establishment of the successful *Kleindeutsch*
nation-state, were somehow repelled from this state and the ideology of *Kleindeutsch*
nationalism. First, the state was founded on the basis of politicized Protestantism,
and, second, this nationalism had brought about the defeat of the Habsburg Empire
at the hands of Prussia in 1866. It also endangered the existence of the Habsburg
Empire/Austria-Hungary and, by extension, of Austrian Silesia with the proposal
of splitting the empire and this crownland along the ethnic line that would separate "Germans" from "non-Germans." This program would destroy the established
imperial institutions and traditions alongside the lattice of traditional crownlands
with which the Austrian and Austrian Silesian German-speakers felt at home. It
was all they had, and so only with the advance of the Czech national movement in
Bohemia during the 1870s and 1880s, some of the German-speaking intellectuals
and journalists began to espouse the vague ideals of *Großdeutsch* nationalism.

This ideology was given a boost thanks to the rapprochement and subsequent
cooperation between Vienna and Berlin. The alliance took off in the 1880s and
1890s and was sealed by the spread of German nationalism in Cisleithania. *Großdeutsch* and *Kleindeutsch* nationalists found the common ground in anti-Semitism,
imperialism, Pan-Germanism and the struggle against the rapid proliferation of
various non-German nationalisms in Austria-Hungary. However, prior to 1871,
the majority of Austrian Silesia's German-speakers identified themselves as Aus-
trian/West/East Silesians, Silesian Austrians or, simply, Austrians. Straightforward
ethnic nationalism still had not won the day.

In East Austrian Silesia the situation was a bit different in the case of the
German-speaking area around Bielitz and of much smaller Germanophone islets
concentrated around the other towns. Most of those German-speakers were Protestants, and so some of them were quite quick to espouse *Kleindeutsch* nationalism,
especially if they lived in the localities close to the border with Prussia/the German
Empire, such as Oderberg. On the other hand, with the development of the Upper
Silesian and Ostrau-Karwin industrial basins, where the management and highly
qualified workers were almost exclusively German-speaking in the former case and
German- and Czech-speaking in the latter, the social and economic environment
fostered bilingualism. This linguistic adaptation technique spread most among the
Slavic-speakers, who often were unqualified or less qualified workers. Bilingualism
and multilingualism were also common in the milieu of traders and foremen, irrespective of their mother tongue. That was because the former wanted to sell their
wares to every client, regardless of his linguistic preferences, whilst the latter had

to issue unambiguous and comprehensible orders to be properly understood by everybody in their working units (Reiter, 1989: 123–124). In a longer view, the dynamics of these sociolinguistic relations gave birth to a Slavic-Germanic creole in the Upper Silesian basin and to related pidgins in the Ostrau-Karwin basin. They constituted mixed-language forms devised for successful communication across the language barrier. Those who hoped for social advancement through work or education, however, had to acquire standard German in the former industrial basin, and in the Ostrau-Karwin basin, either standard German or standard Czech. Later this necessity encouraged such enterprising individuals to become ennationalized into the German nation in Prussian Upper Silesia and into the German or Czech nation in Austrian Silesia.

To reiterate, most of the Slavic-speakers of Upper and Austrian Silesias belonged to one of the following three ethnic groups: the Szlonzoks, the Slunzaks, and the Morawecs. The German, Polish and Czech national movements undertook endeavors aimed at the ennationalization of the members of these ethnic groups into the respective nations. These movements' frequently clashing efforts canceled one another out, while the Silesian national movements in Upper Silesia and East Austrian Silesia improved the lots of the Szlonzoks and the Slunzaks, respectively. The policy of the state and of the Catholic Church that propagated the Moravian regional identity in Moravia and the Morawec ethnic identity in southern Upper Silesia, West Austrian Silesia and northern Moravia served the same end in the case of the Morawecs. The Catholic Church fostered all the aforementioned ethnic and regional identities, hoping to oppose the spread of the particularism of nationalisms, especially when the *Kulturkampf* endangered its autonomous existence. Following the rapprochement with the Prussian state, which ended the *Kulturkampf* in the mid-1880s, the Catholic Church duly recognized the economic, social and political achievements of the *Kleindeutsch* nation-state. From then on the church concentrated on protecting this nation-state as well as the traditional way of life of the Catholic faithful with non-national ethnic multiple identities. This shielded the population and the state from the potentially destructive incursions of Polish and Czech nationalisms. In this task the Protestant Church joined the Catholic hierarchy.

In Austrian Silesia the Catholic Church and the Protestant Church, without having had to suffer the interlude of the highly divisive *Kulturkampf*, jointly worked to preserve the existing social, economic, administrative and ethnic relations, and against the disruptive influence of nationalisms. But with the spread of non-German nationalisms, the German (both *Klein-* and *Großdeutsch*) nationalisms began to function as the bulwarks that protected the German Empire and Austria-Hungary. Then both the churches' aforementioned efforts, aimed at the preservation of the three ethnic groups in Upper and Austrian Silesias, inevitably contributed to the strengthening of these German nationalisms. This also made the ethnic groups more sympathetic toward Germandom than to Czechdom or Polishdom. In any event, Berlin and Vienna had provided these ethnic groups with significant economic and social prosperity vis-à-vis the bleak situation in the adjacent areas of Galicia and Congress Poland. This was achieved almost without any pressure on the members of the three ethnic groups to renounce their non-national identities and traditional ways of life. On the other hand, no one could be sure if the Polish and Czech national movements could offer anything better to the ethnic groups. That seemed rather unreasonable in light of the fact that no Czech or Polish nation-state existed at that time. Unlike German nationalism, in most cases Polish and Czech nationalists coaxed members of these ethnic groups to become Poles or Czechs without any regard for the ethnic identities, needs and beliefs of the Szlonzoks, the Slunzaks and the Morawecs. This approach could not be effective, even if applied to those members of these three ethnic groups who displayed some sympathy toward the national causes of the Poles and the Czechs.

Finally, before 1871, even the Germans of Lower and Upper Silesia did not clearly develop a monistic national identity. They continued to invest their regions and Prussia (submerged in the German Empire) with an important role in their self-identification. Across the border, their region remained the locus of identification for Austrian Silesia's German-speakers, besides Cisleithania and the emperor. It was even truer in the case of the members of the ethnic groups and of the few individuals who became the local founders and activists of the local Polish and Czech national movements. The region and the monarch still functioned as the instruments of ensuring social cohesion in Prussian and Austrian Silesias until 1871. The national and ethnic differences had to be further emphasized and supported from without before they gained momentum enough to unravel the old social bonds. This cataclysmic event took place at the turn of the twentieth century. The emergence of national divisions within the previously cohesive societies of Austrian Silesia and Prussian Silesia later contributed to the complete overhaul of the political map of central Europe after the Great War. It was redrawn in agreement with the national principle, that is, in service of an ideology, *not* of people.

PART II

1871–1918

CHAPTER 6

Nationalism in Central Europe and Silesia in the Period 1871–1918

The German national movement was the first to enter the fray in Silesia. It arose in first half of the nineteenth century and became the dominant ideology in Prussia/ Germany beginning in the 1860s. German nationalists successfully implemented their policies of national homogenization when the *Kleindeutsch* nation-state emerged under Prussian leadership. The groundwork for this achievement had been laid earlier when the majority of the rulers of the Germanophone polities had accepted this solution in 1866 and 1867. At that time they had made their polities into members of the North German Confederation (Norddeutscher Bund). In 1871 the breakthrough came when the German Empire was founded. Prussia had triumphed. Its archenemy, France, was defeated and isolated. The more inclusive and, thanks to its combination with the tradition of universalistic Catholicism, less nationalist concept of the *Großdeutsch* nation-state was decisively discarded. Having been defeated in the Seven Weeks' War of 1866 the Habsburgs also lost their bid for supremacy in the German-speaking world and in the whole of central Europe. With time they had to content themselves with a position secondary to that of hegemonic Prussia/Germany. As a consequence, support for universalistic Catholicism and for a corresponding empire that would transcend ethnic and confessional differences was gone.

The ideology of nationalism became firmly entrenched in central and east-central Europe. It grew stronger despite the procrastinating policies of Austria-Hungary, which wanted to maintain a prenational status quo among its numerous ethnic groups. With hindsight, one can say that it was a hopeless task. But Vienna's imperial administration could not know that when the empire still seemed a solid and vibrant polity, bound to last at least as long as its predecessor, the Holy Roman Empire. But suddenly all the social structures were in flux due to the progress of modernization. Invariably, this meant ennationalization too. National activists, impressed by the success of the Prusso-German example, sought to transform numerous ethnic groups into nations. The ethnicization of the political life and career opportunities largely reserved for the German-speaking Austrians and the Hungarians (that is, Magyars) caused the non-German- and non-Magyar-speakers to feel less and less at home under the monarchy. They felt their homelands had grown somehow foreign to them, and the ennationalization made the inhabitants of these areas into second-class citizens unless they had acquired the German or Hungarian language. The previously apolitical ethnic divides came to the fore in the development of Austro-Hungarian and central European politics. To be modern also meant to be of a nation. Should one be left out with no nation of one's own, one could not hope that one's voice would be heard. The way from an object to subject of politics led either through assimilation into the fold of established and dominant nations, or through involvement in the processes of nation-building that could result in the emergence of new nations with which one wished to be associated.

The aforementioned developments did not leave Silesia unscathed. The homogenizing policies of nation-state-building, applied in Germany and fortified by rapid industrialization, ejected the populace of the multiethnic parts of Silesia from the cozy niche of their immediate social and geographical environs. Suddenly they were confronted with the ethnic Other they had not even clearly realized had existed in Prussia. Many left the countryside for cities and the western regions of the German Empire to find a better life for their families. The labor-hungry Upper Silesian and Austrian Silesian industrial centers attracted engineers, managers and investors from the intellectual and financial centers of Germany and Austria-Hungary. Similarly, many workers came to Prussian Silesia across the border from Russia (mainly Congress Poland) and Austria-Hungary (mainly Galicia). They also arrived in Austrian Silesia, predominantly from Galicia, Bohemia and Moravia. The managerial stratum was usually comprised of German-speakers, and in the case of Austrian Silesia, also of Czech-speakers and a few Polish-speakers as well. Workers recruited by Upper Silesian industry were overwhelmingly Polish/Slavic- and German-speaking, though after 1905 a sizeable group of Ruthenian-speakers from eastern Galicia came too. The manpower of the Austrian Silesian industry tended to speak German, Czech/Slavic, and Polish/Slavic. This picture would not be complete without mentioning that the managerial and laboring strata in the industry of Austrian Silesia were mostly Catholic, while the managers of the Upper Silesian industry, more often than not, were Protestant Germans. Some assimilated Jews also participated in the economies of both Silesias. But with the exception of their origin and sometimes their faith or proficiency in Yiddish, they were hardly recognizable as different from Germans and German-speaking Austrians. However, some traditional Jewish traders and artisans of Hasidic custom came to East Austrian Silesia from Galicia, and the same process could be observed in the eastern section of Prussian Upper Silesia. In the latter case the creation of the Jewish pale of settlement in Russia (1882) restricted the geographical sphere of their economic activity and pushed them abroad in search of a better life. Some of them went to Prussian Upper Silesia (Pogonowski, 1993: 25).

As King (2002: 83, 113, 128) has shown for the southern Bohemian town of Budweis (České Budějovice) conscious self-realization of ethnic difference vis-à-vis coworkers, employers, shop assistants and neighbors became part and parcel of one's everyday experience among the swelling urban population. The constant proximity and high intensity of interpersonal contacts in cities necessitated one's continual interaction with people of different tongues, religions, customs and origins. Censuses and bureaucratic practices institutionalized this intensified feeling of ethnic difference. One constantly had to answer the question, "Who are you?" posed by friends, coworkers, foremen and civil servants. And the census-taker demanded the individual choose one's unambiguous nationality as specified by state statisticians. One could not be an unrecognized "Szlonzok" or "Morawec." The options available were "German," "Pole" or "Czech." This situation pressed the individual to renounce one's non-national multiple identity and to declare one's allegiance to some nation-in-making. Such a choice often coincided with one's desire for social and economic advancement.

However, the successful realization of such a wish was possible only through the language and culture of the Germans, who constituted the demographic basis of the German Empire. They also clearly dominated until the turn of the twentieth century in the Austrian half of Austria-Hungary. The state-controlled popular education, conscript army and administration contributed to this phenomenon, pushing the linguistically, culturally, and sometimes confessionally incompatible groups to the social and economic margins. This either accelerated their assimilation or bred discontent. Generally speaking, there were two main sources of this discontent. First, one's painful experience of rejection by the mainstream of German-speaking society barred one from the benefits of assimilation. Second, on ideological grounds one could oppose any prospect of assimilation. The latter attitude would arise during the time when the state became increasingly involved in devising and implementing the homogenizing policies aimed at "cleansing" the nation and its nation-state of "foreign elements."

In the 1870s Russia and the German Empire pursued such homogenizing policies with respect to the Polish-speaking population in Congress Poland and the Province of Posen, respectively (Pogonowski, 1988: 25). This contributed to the overhaul of the traditional Polish national movement, which, it was hoped, would recreate Poland-Lithuania as a Polish nation-state on the basis of civic values. The noble activists of this movement were not sure if the peasants should be included in such a Polish nation, but modernization decisively broadened the access the population had to politics, regardless of ethnic or social origin. There would be no return to the past. The Polish *natio* could not transform itself into a Polish nation. This realization caused the formation of the Polish ethnic national movement, which drew on the exemplars of German and western European nationalisms (Porter, 2000). This novel ethnic version of Polish nationalism emerged at the turn of the 1890s. Such a speedy reply to German nationalism and Russifying policies was largely possible thanks to the Polish political and cultural autonomy in Galicia granted between 1867 and 1873. As a result, the Austro-Hungarian crownland of Galicia became the unhampered and unquestioned center of Polish culture and learning. To some extent it also functioned as a semi-safe haven for Polish national-ist activists from the Russian and Prussian partitions of Poland-Lithuania, which earned Galicia the nickname of "Polish Piedmont."

The more accommodating attitude of the Habsburgs toward nondominant ethnic groups, taken after defeat in the 1866 war and the *Ausgleich* of 1867, contrib-uted to the development of the Czech national movement and others throughout the monarchy. During the 1880s and 1890s this situation caused the German national and Pan-German movements to appear in Austria-Hungary. The German-speakers noticed that their privileged status in the monarchy would be threatened should other national movements receive more equal treatment and representation in the state institutions of the Danubian monarchy. Subsequently, German nationalists from Austria-Hungary established closer links with their counterparts in Germany. When Vienna and Berlin entered a political alliance, this development sealed the ideological ties recently established by German nationalists from both these states. In addition, they found that various differences between these two groups could be easily overcome on the common platform of Pan-Germanism, underpinned by a virulent strain of modern anti-Semitism (cf. Görtemaker, 1996: 270–273). This unprecedented rise of Pan-Germanism to the rank of a significant ideological force in Austria-Hungary and the German Empire at the beginning of the twentieth century incited a brief revival of increasingly pro-Russian Pan-Slavism.

During the Great War a majority of European politicians, pressed or sup-ported in this respect by the U.S. scholar-turned-president Woodrow Wilson, accepted the national principle as the basis of European politics after 1918. The political, economic, social and cultural life of central Europe was recast in the national mold. The underlying belief of scholars and some politicians in the wake of the political trail blazed by Wilson was that nations are "natural phenomena." They trusted that if such nations were disentangled from one another and put into exclusively their own nation-states, then the ideal of lasting peace would be realized in Europe. The proponents of the national solution did not listen to the protests of advocates of federalism and multiculturalism who had failed at their task of saving Austria-Hungary. Their last-minute attempt at reworking the Dual

Monarchy into a federal state in 1918 did not work (Ehrich, 1992: 533). Thus the processes of nation- and nation-state-building won the day. Although the emergence of various national movements did not take place in Silesia, this phenomenon strongly influenced all aspects of social life in the rapidly industrialized borderlands of eastern Upper Silesia and East Austrian Silesia. The Upper Silesian and Ostrau-Karwin industrial basins became a veritable epitome of prenational central Europe, squeezed in the confluence of the imperial frontiers that divided the three empires of Germany, Austria-Hungary and Russia. The crumbling of these borders in the name of "modern" nation-states spelled the end of the prenational social reality in historical Silesia.

In Prussian Silesia the homogenizing policies of the state and the offer of full social and economic privilege to those who were German-speaking and confessed Protestantism caused the majority of the Polish/Slavic-speaking Protestants from northeastern Lower Silesia to assimilate with Germandom already at the turn of the twentieth century. This centering of the German national unity on language and religion triggered some discontent among the Upper Silesian population, which was multilingual and predominantly Catholic. As such it better fitted Austria's somewhat universalistic concept of *Großdeutschland* than the *Kleindeutsch* nation-state spurred into being by Prussia. Most Upper Silesians perceived the homogenizing efforts undertaken by the German Empire in the name of national unity as an attack on their religion and the customs of their ancestors. Ironically, this obsession of German and other central European nationalisms with language caused the Upper Silesians to see language as the ideological preserve of their established way of life. This made them into the obedient faithful of the Catholic Church, which promoted local vernaculars as the preferred medium of communication with its congregations. These vernaculars survived in the limited space of religious instruction as media of instruction after Berlin removed them from elementary education following the establishment of the German Empire.

The Slavic-speakers of Upper Silesia (that is, the Szlonzoks and the Morawecs) objected to these ennationalizing developments. Their discontent was quickly channeled into the political arena where, drawing on the 1871 introduction of popular male suffrage in the German Empire, a party system came into being. The Catholic Zentrum (Center) party first sought to protect the church from the excesses of the *Kulturkampf,* and second to create a political space for Catholics in the empire. It sought to de-ideologize religion so that Catholicism would not make one into a second-class citizen and Protestantism would not help to guarantee one a privileged position in society. In accordance with these broader goals the Upper Silesian Catholic clergy represented (often in the Reichstag and the Prussian Landtag) and protected the interests of their Slavophone faithful. Thanks to this principled stance, the Upper Silesian Catholics staunchly supported Zentrum politicians and the local Catholic clergy, as they readily identified with the non-national universalistic message of the Catholic Church.

This development caught nationalists unawares, much to the dismay of German nation-state builders and of Polish nationalist activists. It was a blow especially to the hopes of the Polish national activists from the Province of Posen. They wanted to win the Slavic/Polish-speaking Upper Silesians over to the causes of Polishdom and of reestablishing the Polish-Lithuanian state as a Polish nation-state. The ensuing ideological struggle for the national allegiance of the non-German-speaking or bilingual population of Upper Silesia was fought out among the Catholic Church and Polish and German nationalisms. At the beginning of the twentieth century this led to the politicization and preliminary proto-national polarization of the populace, especially in the ranks of the activists and their immediate followers.

However, the majority of the population remained in their non-national Catholic world of multiple identities, entrenched in closely-knit communities. But after 1918, in line with the national principle, they were forced against their will and better judgment to opt for German or Polish or Czech nationality. The new situation bred another wave of discontent, which was channeled into Upper Silesia's Szlonzokian national movement. However, it could not effectively contend with Polish and German nationalisms, which were internationally recognized and supported by the corresponding nation-states. Not surprisingly, these two forces effectively phased out Szlonzokian nationalism following the plebiscite (1921) and the division of Upper Silesia between Germany and Poland (1922[1]).

The situation that developed in Austrian Silesia after 1871 was even more confused. The nation-building policies gradually became popular among the German-speakers. They formed a minority in comparison to the predominantly Slavic character of this crownland's population. The German-speaking Austrian Silesians and their Slavophone neighbors had lived peacefully side-by-side in line with the prenational values, which did not divide people along ethnolinguistic lines. The change, spurred on by modernization, gradually pushed this traditional world of Austrian Silesia toward nationalism. The main beacons that stood out as guideposts for the change were the obvious successes of Prussia and Germany in the field of nation- and nation-state-building, which went hand-in-hand with economic progress, a higher standard of living and better employment opportunities. The German-speakers of Austrian Silesia observed this change just across the border. Another factor that coaxed a slow rise of German nationalism in Austrian Silesia was the steady spread of Czech nationalism and its Polish counterpart, which seeped in from Bohemia and Galicia, respectively.

The state was hardly interested in, let alone supportive of, the development of German nationalism in this region. Vienna preferred to maintain equilibrium among various ethnic groups and emergent nations in Austria-Hungary rather than risk dissolution of the monarchy through embarking on the task of reconstructing the polity as a nation-state. That would require privileging the largest but demographically nondominant ethnic group of Germans and German-speakers at the expense of the others. Even if such a project succeeded, it would not be possible without the agreement of the Magyars. But eventually this would necessitate the splitting of the monarchy into at least two nation-states, one of the Germans and the other of the Hungarians. But as Slavic nationalists became more culturally and economically visible during the 1880s, German nationalist and Pan-German groups began to form as a grassroots effort in Austrian Silesia. They actively sought contact with similar organizations throughout Austria-Hungary and Germany.

Czech nationalists confronted the German national movement in West Silesia and in the industrial basin of Ostrau-Karwin, where both groups of nationalists were locked in a struggle with their Polish counterparts. The object of their contentious ennationalizing was Polish-speaking Galician immigrant workers. More often than not they assimilated either to Germandom or to Czechdom so as to improve their social and economic status. Polishdom was no option to these workers at that time, since "being a Pole" was stereotypically connected to an unsatisfactory standard of living and low prestige in the context of Galicia's proverbial poverty (Nowak, 1995: 32). The Polish nationalists in East Silesia, even with aid from Cracow, could not undo this perception.

On top of that, East Silesia's Polish national movement weakened considerably in the closing decades of the nineteenth century. This was because Polish nationalism had become increasingly intertwined with the Polish Catholic Church. This created simplistic national stereotypes of "Pole-Catholic" and "German-Protestant." The development alienated the sizeable section of Polish/Slavic-speaking East Silesians who were Protestants. The Polish national movement split along the confessional line into Protestant and Catholic branches. The latter established firm links with Galician coreligionists and began denouncing the Polish/Slavic-speaking Protestants as pro-German due to the fact that they were coreligionists of many German-speakers of East Silesia and of the German Empire. The Protestant Polish/Slavic-speakers countered these accusations by promoting the novel stereotype of "Pole-Protestant." However, this thinking on Polishness that connected Polish national feeling with Protestantism remained current only in East Silesia (Nowak, 1995: 25).

The ideological-religious conflict within the Polish national movement in East Silesia allowed Czech national activists to campaign for their goals in "traditionally" Polish/Slavic-speaking areas of this region. But at the beginning of the twentieth century Polish nationalists successfully retaliated. The curious situation which developed in the forty years before the outbreak of the Great War seemed quite "unnatural" to many inhabitants with non-national multiple identities. Unlike their more nationally minded neighbors, they united in their attachment to their crownland and loyalty to the monarch. They chose to refer to themselves as Austrian Silesians or simply as Austrians. In the situation of escalating national conflict at the beginning of the twentieth century, they felt beleaguered by baffling nationalisms that did not relate to their tradition and seemed to offer nothing more than strife and division. The non-nationally oriented Austrian Silesians opposed the coming change. Their stance reinforced the Silesian-Slunzakian national movement. Thanks to this movement Austrian Silesians, especially Slunzaks, hoped to be able to preserve their presumably non-national way of life and to be in a position to access Germandom in search of economic and social advancement.

This movement attracted many Polish/Slavic-speakers along with German-speakers and those who were bilingual. Polish nationalists perceived this trend as pro-German and, as such, a danger that could deepen the already existing lines of division within the Polish national movement. Hence, local Polish nationalists decried the adherents of the Silesian-Slunzakian national movement as "worse than Czechs or Germans" (Nowak, 1995: 32), because its emergence complicated the already intricate pattern of Czech-German-Polish national confrontation in Austrian Silesia.

Similar social and political conditions contributed to the emergence of the Morawec national movement among the Moravian/Slavic-speaking population in the northeast of West Austrian Silesia and across the border in the south of the Ratibor county. In 1920 the Allies divided East Silesia between Poland and Czechoslovakia, and a year earlier they had transferred the region of Hultschin from Germany to Czechoslovakia. These decisions, made in a search for the "natural borders" between the three nations, did not solve the Polish-German-Czech national conflict, but they did contribute to the liquidation of the two aspirant national movements connected to the ethnic groups of the Slunzaks and the Morawecs. The majority of the members and sympathizers of the Silesian-Slunzakian national movement found themselves in Poland, where they became Polonized or Germanized. The Morawecs of the Prussian/German town of Hultschin and its vicinity, hailed by the ideologists of Czech nationalism as staunchly Czech, surprised everybody by turning swiftly to Germandom. Later they passed into history as the "Hultschiners." Most of the other Morawecs living in Austrian Silesia or Moravia either became Czechs or merged with the Moravians.

◆   ◆   ◆

The above is a synopsis of the subject matter presented and analyzed in depth in part 2 of the study. While focusing on the period 1871–1918, this part traces the pattern of the spread of the ideology of nationalism in Silesia as well as the effects of ensuing ennationalization with regard to this region and its inhabitants.

Part 1 of this work focused on the rise of the ideology of nationalism in central Europe. It was mainly connected to the German national movement in Prussia, which defined ethnicity as the foundation for this ideology, or more precisely, ethnicity expressed through language. Simultaneously, this kind of central European nationalism grew out of a multiplicity of ideologies and traditional approaches to politics into what was arguably the main instrument of statehood legitimization. The watershed was the establishment of the German Empire on such a national principle. This example in the context of Prussia/Germany's undisputable successes in the fields of the military, economy, politics and social services formed the model of development for other areas in central Europe. The Czech and Polish national movements, among others, largely emulated the main pattern of German ethnic nationalism.

Nations and ethnic groups are neither natural nor everlasting. However, this false premise, endorsed by western European and U.S. academics and politicians, gave rise to the idea that the demographic and territorial extent of nations should be measured with censuses, and that on the basis of the numerical data it would be possible to cram such delineated nations into the shells of their own nation-states. This intellectual fad, in combination with the ever growing number of central European ethnic national movements, brought about the disintegration of this part of the continent into a multitude of small nation-states after 1918. The Allies not only approved of this development but, to a certain extent, encouraged it.

In this manner, they achieved their strategic goals of weakening Germany and building a buffer zone between Russia and Germany. A modicum of the nineteenth-century European balance of power was re-established with the help of the ascending United States. However, contrary to the hopes of politicians and academics, this redrawing of the political map in accordance with the ethnonational principle did not produce lasting peace. In fact, it increased the state of chaos in relations between the newly established nation-states and in the states' domestic politics. Low-intensity warfare and prolonged enmity, maintained in order to achieve the "true overlapping" of state borders with imagined ethnic boundaries or in the name of national minorities enclosed in now foreign nation-states, became endemic.

As the period between the Great War and World War II amply showed, the model of the ethnically defined nation-state did not work. On average, the standard of living plummeted in the successor states of Austria-Hungary. The new state frontiers not only separated families and friends but also hindered commerce and industry. The "brave new national order" allowed these nations that the West handpicked for statehood to thrive in their familiar ethnic environments reinvented as "national cultures." The worst hand was dealt to the non-national ethnic groups and some aspiring nations which the West chose not to recognize, as was the case for the Szlonzoks, the Slunzaks, and the Morawecs. They had either to assimilate within the accepted nations (that is, the Czechs, the Germans or the Poles) or to accept their lot as second-class citizens.

In the new national reality of central Europe no place was left for regional identification either. The Allies gave little thought to the fact that through redrawing the borders they destroyed centuries-old regions such as Austrian Silesia and Upper Silesia. With one stroke of a fountain pen on the map, the homelands of the non-nationally and non-ethnically minded Upper Silesians and Austrian Silesians were gone. The members of these regional groups, along with those of the unrecognized ethnonational groups, fell through the cracks gaping between the new nation-states. The nation-planners wrote them out of the standard national picture of central Europe as the "nationally labile." They were expected to get their act together and to enter an internationally accepted nation or national minority.

There was no place left for those who stuck to the prior, non-national traditions. In this modern age of nationalisms they were not only "old-fashioned" in their persisting loyalty to nonexistent regions and monarchies, but this attitude made them "uncivilized" in the eyes of their nationally conscious neighbors and, even worse, the nation-states, which could not trust them and condemned these persons to the role of "national renegades" or "potentially subversive elements."

CHAPTER 7

German Nationalism after 1871

The founding of the German Empire in 1871 marked the success of the *Klein-deutsch* strain in German nationalism. This empire, modeled on the North German Confederation, took a similar form of confederation (*Bundesstaat*). It was composed of twenty-five federal states, four kingdoms and six grand duchies. However, the Kingdom of Prussia dominated this structure by virtue of its share of the empire's area and population, which amounted to 65 percent and 62 percent, respectively. The person of William I sealed this Prussian hegemony. He simultaneously acted as the German emperor, king of Prussia and supreme commander. This fact was symbolically reflected in the German imperial black, white and red tricolor. It simply took the colors of the Prussian flag (black and white or silver) and the Prussian royal standard (black, silver and red). The only difference showed in the imperial standard, for which the additional golden color was used (Anon., 1889h: 334–335).

The German Empire, though similar in structure, differed from the Northern German Confederation in that William I exercised tight control over the new state. He was solely responsible for convoking the Bundesrat (Federal Council, that is, the upper chamber of the parliament) and the Reichstag (lower chamber). He had the constitutionally enshrined power to dissolve the latter. Besides this, the Prussian monarch and German emperor in one person also enjoyed the exclusive right to nominate the chancellor. One can aptly describe the imperial chancellor as the emperor's right hand, because this politician simultaneously acted as the Prussian prime minister, the chairman of the Bundesrat, and the superior of the secretaries of state and of the imperial bureaucracy. With such wide-ranging imperial prerogatives and the unwavering support of Chancellor Otto von Bismarck (1815–1898), who was bent on transforming the collection of Germanophone states and statelets into a German nation-state, the emperor could wholeheartedly embrace this *Kleindeutsch* national program. Judging from the euphoria that a majority of his subjects displayed at the establishment of the German Empire, they perceived the goals of German nationalism as their own (Kinder, 1978: II 76–77).

The construction of the German nation-state entailed thorough homogenization in all aspects of state and national life in the empire. Standardization of variegated legal and economic systems posed the most daunting challenge. Various legal and economic practices prevailed in the empire's constituent entities, and stark differences in privilege existed even within the territories of these entities. Without successful homogenization in these spheres Germany could not even dream of competing with the leading powers of the times. This task was largely completed between 1871 and 1900 (Kinder, 1978: II 77). The ready-made framework of the nation-state was filled in with vibrant economic investment and trade, which accelerated industrialization. Paradoxically, the worldwide economic crisis of 1873 did not hinder but fostered the rapid growth of the German economy.

Urbanization and improvement in healthcare and sanitary standards accompanying technological development resulted in a significant population surplus. When former peasants brought their traditional procreation patterns to cities, their high rate of fertility was not curbed by high child mortality, as it was in the countryside. In the 1870s, 600,000 German citizens emigrated overseas, followed by 1.2 million in the 1880s. A quantum leap occurred in the 1890s, when German industry became fully capable of absorbing the excess population, which left for the Ruhr instead of the Americas. Even then, there was still much room left for immigrant workers in the expanding and labor-hungry economy (Turner, 1992: 113–114).

In terms of production Germany ranked third behind the United States and the United Kingdom in 1871. But by 1913 it trailed only the United States both in production and in terms of GDP. In 1913 Germany's share of world manufacturing was 14.8 percent. Britain lagged behind with 13.6 percent, whereas France's level of production was less than half that, at 6.1 percent. However, Britain's per capita income of $244 surpassed Germany's $153, though the GDPs of both the states were comparable: $12 billion in Germany and $11 billion in the United Kingdom. Germany's population soared from 41 million in 1871 to 67 million in 1914. In Europe this figure was second only to that of Russia. St. Petersburg, however, could not hope to compete. Although Russia had the larger population, this difference was easily offset in favor of Germany by its far higher levels of education, social provisions and per capita income.

Statistics on literacy aptly illustrate Germany's social and cultural achievements in comparison to western and central Europe. In 1913, 330 out of 1,000 recruits entering Italy's army were illiterate; the corresponding ratios were 220/1,000 in Austria-Hungary, 68/1,000 in France, and an astonishing 1/1,000 in Germany. The beneficiaries were not only the Prussian army but also the economy, which increasingly required skilled workers. The German educational system produced them in abundance. The growing level of education among the populace at large allowed for the application of the fruits of scientific research to agriculture and industry. The use of chemical fertilizers and large-scale modernization led to a significant increase in crop yields, which were much higher than in any other European or world power. Germany's coal output grew from 89 million tons in 1890 to 277 million tons in 1914. The German Empire was a close second behind Britain with its 292 million tons. Austria-Hungary with a coal output of 47 million tons was far behind, as was France with its 40 million tons and Russia with its 36 million tons. In steel production, the increase was even more spectacular. The 1914 German output of 17.6 million tons was larger than that of Britain, France and Russia combined. Germany also excelled in the newer twentieth-century industries: electrical appliances, optics and the production of chemicals. The tripling of Germany's foreign trade between 1890 and 1913 brought this state close to Britain as a leading world exporter (Czapliński, 1990: 541; Kennedy, 1989: 210–211, 243; Turner, 1992: 111–112).

Unlike Austria-Hungary or Russia, imperial Germany did not contain numerous ethnic or national minorities.[1] In 1900 they amounted to 3.7 million citizens, or 7 percent of the total population in 1900. The vast majority, three million, were Poles or Polish/Slavic-speakers (Czapliński, 1990: 570). A more significant cleavage was caused by religion. In 1914 Germany's population was composed of Protestants (63 percent), Catholics (36 percent) and Jews (1 percent) (Turner, 1992: 111–112). Bismarck sought to diminish the political significance of this confessional divide because it hampered the construction of a unified German nation. Moreover, the universalism of Catholicism still played into the hands of the Habsburgs and helped Vienna sustain its waning influence in southern Germany and Upper Silesia, areas mainly inhabited by Catholics. On the other hand, some intellectuals and politicians were still ready to cooperate with the Catholic Church, hoping for the future extension of *Kleindeutschland* into *Großdeutschland*.

The Protestant Church, on the other hand, had traditionally perceived Prussia and the Hohenzollerns as its protectors in the Germanophone states. Therefore, without hesitation this church accepted its role of the state church within the framework of *Kleindeutsch* nationalism. Protestantism fit nicely into, and simultaneously reinforced, the ideological pattern of *Kleindeutsch* homogenization, unlike Catholicism. The latter presented a danger to unified Germany and to the German nation-in-construction because both the Protestant Church and the Catholic Church organized popular education at the elementary and secondary levels and controlled the respective school curricula. Ideological tenets furthered by Protestant schools usually went in line with the general goals of German nationalism, but the universalism promoted in Catholic schools was perceived by authorities as possibly subversive to the ideal of the German nation-state.

The ecclesiastical administrative divisions of the Catholic Church did not always coincide with the existing state borders and were centered on the Holy See. This placed the church in a position where it had to compete with the nation-state in the field of administration. For instance, Catholic priests were responsible for controlling the institution of marriage as well as for registering births and deaths in Catholic areas. The educational system and administration (besides the conscript army and mass media) were the crucial institutions through which national ideals were instilled in society, and by virtue of which homogenization was carried out. Not surprisingly the state sought to minimize or phase out the increasingly limited leverage the Catholic Church might have enjoyed in these areas of social life. Bismarck and his colleagues believed that without separating the church from politics and nation-building, it would be impossible to consolidate the newly established German nation-state (Kinder, 1978: II 77; Michalkiewicz, 1976: 305).

Having recognized the Catholic Church as the most serious obstacle to nation- and nation-state-building, in 1871 Bismarck embarked on the policy of the *Kulturkampf* in Prussia. The origin of the term *Kulturkampf* ("war of cultures") is probably linked to the 1873 ordinance that obligated all the Catholic seminary graduates to pass the *Kulturexamen*—examinations in the German language, culture and history. That was the precondition for allowing the graduates to serve as priests in the territory of Germany (Czapliński, 1990: 549). The spark that triggered the *Kulturkampf* was the dogma of papal infallibility, which was declared at the Vatican Council in 1870 (Kinder, 1978: II 77). The Catholic Church, pursuing its universalistic goals, dared to compete with the nation-state in politics. Berlin could not permit such an intrusion, so the policy of *Kulturkampf* was pursued not only in Prussia but all across Germany. Anti-Catholic policies were legislated in other European states too, but they never reached the extremes of Prussia's *Kulturkampf*.

The protracted struggle to limit the social and political influence of the Catholic Church continued in Germany well into the mid-1880s. Then it was terminated thanks to an uneasy consensus facilitated by the conciliatory attitude of Pope Leo XIII (1878–1903). In the course of this strife the state wrenched control over the educational system away from the Catholic Church, imposed the German language as the sole medium of instruction in schools, introduced the institution of civil marriage, took over the registration of births, marriages and deaths, and strove to subordinate the Catholic clergy and hierarchy to the state administration.

Instead of full success, the restrictive measures brought about the creation of the Catholic Zentrum Party (1871), which transposed the confessional cleavage from society at large into the political sphere. The party reigned supreme in the Catholic areas of Germany and engaged itself in the protection of the use of minority languages in church and religious instruction. This did not happen in defiance of the German national program but in line with Catholic universalism (Bokenkotter, 1977: 308; Fischer-Wollpert, 1990: 299–300; Michalkiewicz, 1976: 329; Pater, 1993: 8–9).

Not being able to make the Catholic Church docile, Bismarck had to accept that it would be impossible to secure swift liquidation of the confessional cleavage in Germany. Hence, he struck a compromise in order to transcend the stalemate, which might hinder the further development of the German nation-state. The growing division between the state and the Catholic Church in Austria-Hungary facilitated this coming together of the state and the church in the German Empire. Vienna's termination of the concordat in 1868 indicated the growing divergence between the state and the church before it culminated in the "Away-from-Rome" (*los aus Rom*) movement. At the international level, supporters of the anticlerical movement appealed for closer links with Germany (Kinder, 1978: II 79). Consequently, during the 1880s the political dimension of Catholic universalism was just a shadow of its former self. In addition, the old rival of Prussia, the Habsburg Empire, overcame the short-lived anti-Prussian sentiment connected to the 1866 defeat, and Vienna had grown ever closer and more subordinate to Germany. The process started in earnest when the League of the Three Emperors was established in 1872, bringing together Germany, Austria-Hungary and Russia. Then the Pan-Germans of Austria-Hungary appealed for closer links with the German Empire and for further subordination of the Catholic Church to Vienna (Kinder, 1978: II 83).

Thus, politically, it was safe for Bismarck to cooperate with the Catholic Church, especially so in the face of the danger that the socialist movement posed to the conservative order. The rise of socialists during the 1860s and 1870s was connected to rapid industrialization. The equally unfavorable attitudes of the Catholic Church and of Bismarck toward the socialists facilitated passing of the antisocialist act. It barred socialist deputies from taking their seats in the Reichstag and the land diets between 1878 and 1890 (Czapliński, 1990: 568). The Breslau Bishop Georg Kopp (1837–1914) was, for Bismarck, a suitable partner on the part of the Catholic Church to work out a *modus vivendi* between this church and the state. In 1881 Kopp was the first bishop appointed in Germany since 1872. He took over the Fulda Diocese. In this manner his nomination, approved by Berlin, symbolically commenced the gradual termination of the *Kulturkampf*. Kopp greatly facilitated this process thanks to the fact that he also controlled the heart of German institutional Catholicism—the Fulda Diocese. In the town of Fulda the so-called Fulda Conference of the German bishops had assembled since 1848. Following the creation of the German Empire in 1871, it was established as a permanent organ the following year. The chairman of the conference (usually the doyen among the German bishops) still presides over the German Catholic Church, not unlike the primate in the case of the Polish Catholic Church (Anon., 1889j: 779–780; Pater, 1996: 189).

Emperor William II (reigned 1888–1918) perceived Kopp as one of the few German bishops who comprehended the empire's German *raison d'état*. Bismarck immediately noticed that with this Catholic hierarch he could achieve a compromise with the Vatican without having to enter into any compromising agreement with the Zentrum. So in 1884 Kopp became a member of the Preußischer Staatsrat (Prussian Council of State) and, two years later, of the Preußisches Herrenhaus (higher chamber of the Prussian Landtag). In 1887 he was appointed bishop of the Breslau Diocese. As the largest in Europe and second-largest in the world the significance of the diocese was heightened by the fact that the imperial and Prussian capital of Berlin was located on its metropolitan territory. Kopp headed the two most important German dioceses, and since 1887 had chaired the Fulda Conference. As an active pro-state Catholic politician, Kopp easily moved in the interface between the state and the Catholic Church. In this capacity, he strongly contributed to the passing of the 1886–1887 acts that abolished the *Kulturkampf*. Kopp's conciliatory stance helped lessen the political clout of the Zentrum, so that the party's leader, Ludwig Windthorst (1812–1891), reviled him as a *Staatsbischof* ("state bishop"). It also earned Kopp a warning from the Holy See that he should not weaken this Catholic party with his political decisions anymore. But in recognition of his merits, the pope also made Kopp a cardinal in 1893 (Czapliński, 2002: 325; Galos, 1992: 55; Neubach, 1995: 185; Pater, 1996: 188–189, Scheuermann, 1994: 832–833).

The policy of the *Kulturkampf* and the antisocialist legislation alienated Germany's Catholics and industrial workers. Catholics were also members of the working class, as in the case of the industrialized region of eastern Upper Silesia. But socialist beliefs did not take any strong root in the populace prior to 1900 thanks to the joint counteraction on the part of the state, the Catholic Church and the Zentrum (Schofer, 1974: 156; Wanatowicz, 1992: 65). Bismarck won the loyalty of Catholics and socialists after phasing out the *Kulturkampf* (in the 1880s) and passing the most progressive social security legislation in the world. The forerunner of this novel social security system had been Upper Silesia's *Knappschaftskassen* (security funds for the miners). They had sprung up at the close of the eighteenth century and covered all the miners regardless of their position in the mine, as well as their families. These funds made it possible to stabilize the volatile pool of scarce labor and made work in mining more attractive.

The Bismarckian social security system also gradually covered agricultural laborers and artisans. Among the most significant breakthroughs in social legislation were the acts instituting sickness insurance (1883), accident insurance (1884), a health and pension scheme for all state employees (1888), and old age and disablement insurance (1889) (Czapliński, 1990: 569; Davies, 1996: 630; Kinder, 1978: II 77). Prior to 1914 the social conditions of German workers vis-à-vis their European counterparts were succinctly summarized by the French statesman Georges Clemenceau (1841–1929): "Ce sont des bourgeois" ("They are bourgeois") (in

Conrads, 1995: 8). In this manner Bismarck and his successors managed to attract many proletarian supporters away from socialism through having provided them with legislative and economic solutions to the social ills brought about by industrialization. The socialist movement had promised the same, but after Bismarck's social reforms it did not matter any longer. Hence, the potential electorate of the socialist parties decreased, so that the antisocialist legislation could be revoked in 1890.

The following year Pope Leo XIII issued the bull *Rerum novarum,* in which he stated that clergy should mediate between workers and employers (Fischer-Wollpert, 1990: 85). This newly formulated opinion allowed the church to establish Catholic worker organizations and facilitated Kopp's activities in this field. Since the latter half of the 1880s he had engaged in founding Catholic worker societies (Pater, 1996: 190). In this way, the church strove to curb the influence of socialist ideas among the proletariat. The Catholic hierarchy perceived socialist thought as godless and as such dangerous to Catholicism, whatever good intentions socialists might have. In this manner, in the 1890s a large space of common interests arose within the framework of which the state, the Catholic Church and the Zentrum collaborated with increasing frequency. The direct by-product of this negotiated cooperation was the further consolidation of the German Empire as a nation-state.

The social reforms and the steady increase in absolute income per capita made the majority of the German population well disposed to Berlin's government and accelerated the process of nation-building. But the language policy, aimed at fortifying the official status of German as *the* pivotal element of Germandom at the cost of limiting the use of other languages, dramatically misfired. This was especially so in the Province of Posen, where Polish nationalism enjoyed a growing grassroots organizational network. The ideological framework of the Polish movement there was perfected and fine-tuned in conjunction with similar Polish movements in Galicia and Congress Poland. Polish nationalism reformulated along ethnic lines started looking at Upper Silesia as a possible part of a future Polish state (Mroczko, 1994: 82).

In turn, Upper Silesia's Catholic Polish/Slavic-speakers, who during the *Kulturkampf* painfully experienced their otherness vis-à-vis the German nation-state, began to perceive the empire with some distrust. Not surprisingly, the Szlonzoks became even more tightly linked to the Catholic Church as the guarantor of their non-national identity and traditional way of life. Their assessment of the situation was summed up in the new stereotype: the "German is rich and Protestant," and the "Pole is poor and Catholic" (Neubach, 1995: 200). It was a ready-made pattern waiting to be filled in with nationalist sentiment. In popular thinking the average German saw the Polish/Slavic-speaking Upper

Silesians simply as Poles—maybe a bit different from the Wielkopolska Poles, but decisively distinct from himself. This feeling of otherness also spread among the Szlonzoks themselves; however, it still did not translate into their identification with Polishdom.

The improved standard of living made most Szlonzoks into loyal German citizens, and being usually simple people it was unthinkable for them to engage in the cause of a nonexistent Polish nation-state. Despite that, Polish activists tried to channel the discontent felt by many Szlonzoks into gradual acceptance of the ideology of Polish nationalism. Accordingly these activists transferred some basic forms of Polish organizational life from the Province of Posen to Upper Silesia. During the 1880s and 1890s this phenomenon was coupled with the strengthening of the political position of non-German ethnic groups/nations within the political, economic and social framework of Cisleithania (Ehrich, 1992: 529). Another factor that played into the hands of Polish nationalists was statistically created data on demography. The demographic trends of the *Landflucht* and *Ostflucht* brought about by industrialization scared Berlin.

The former term denotes the "flight from the countryside," which is a usual phenomenon repeated time and again in the course of overall development. Better employment opportunities created by industrialization lured excess rural population to cities, where they found higher standards of living. Next, a reinforcing feedback set in. Increasingly fewer people could earn a living in the countryside because another effect of modernization, the agricultural revolution, made farming less labor-intensive. Improved efficiency and higher output in farm production caused the prices of agricultural products to drop or stagnate. In order to profit under such conditions, the farmer had to have large capital at his disposal so as to pay for fertilizers and harvesters as well as a considerable amount of land in order to provide him with suitable revenue. Consequently, eastern Germany (that is, the larger part of Prussia), which remained the empire's most agricultural area, was relatively denuded of its rustic population. The former villagers migrated en masse, usually to industrialized western Germany.

German politicians and statisticians christened this westward demographic shift the *Ostflucht*, or "flight from the East." It is estimated that the negative balance of "emigrants" over "immigrants" east of the Oder-Neisse line amounted to anything between 1.82 and 4 million between 1840 and 1910 (Brożek, 1966: 28) and to 610,121 between 1885 and 1890 (Jonca, 1958: 139). Actually between 1871 and 1918 the industrial counties of Upper Silesia were the only areas east of Berlin with surplus of "immigrants" over "emigrants" (Schofer, 1974: 20).

There is little doubt that the concepts of *Landflucht* and *Ostflucht* reflected certain demographic patterns. But besides that, they provided the German government and German nationalists with a "scientific instrument" to illustrate that Germandom was imperiled. The obvious nationalist interpretation of these demographic trends claimed that the wave of "barbarian Slavs" could soon engulf east Germany. This Pan-German thinking about eastern Europe and Russia as the place from where "uncivilized Asiatic barbarians" would come to destroy Germany and the West resurfaced at the beginning of the twentieth century in the discourse about the "yellow and Bolshevik perils." The ideological emphasis on the "Slav danger" eventually overshadowed the real-life demographic effects of the *Land-flucht* and *Ostflucht,* and this discourse began to shape political and social reality much more decisively than statistical data. Statistics had already been turned into an instrument of national politics.

The emergence and strengthening of non-German national movements in Germany and Austria-Hungary clashed with the basic goals of *Kleindeutsch* and *Groß-deutsch* nationalism. The *Landflucht* added to this ideological frustration because it dealt a blow to the cherished national mythology that linked the German nation and nation-state with their countryside "roots." These roots were imagined as solidly grounded in the customs and traditions of the "simple and hard-working rural *Volk*." The premise of this ethnonational idea assumed the existence of a "natural" link that connected a nation with its soil. This concept became firmly anchored in central European nationalist mythologies in emulation of the German example, offered by the potent image of *Blut und Boden* ("blood and soil"). This highly emotional notion symbolized the inalienable unity of the German nation (and, later, "race") with the German state. After 1933 it would even form the ideological legitimization for Germany's racist legislation (Kopaliński, 1991: 539).

Not surprisingly the *Ostflucht* served well to illustrate the "Polish or Slavic danger," whatever actual statistical data showed. In some east German rural areas percentages of Poles or Polish/Slavic-speakers went up slightly in relation to the corresponding percentages of Germans. But all in all the percentages of Germans in cities and towns grew steadily at the cost of Poles and Polish-/Slavic-speakers. The growth rate of the east German urban population lagged behind in comparison to that in western and central Germany but was accompanied by a similar tendency among the Polish and Polish-/Slavic-speaking population. Not unlike Germans, the latter also participated in the *Ostflucht,* looking for better employment and living opportunities (Michalkiewicz, 1985: 39, 52). Nonetheless, the concepts of the *Landflucht* and *Ostflucht* were enough for German and Pan-German nationalist organizations authoritatively to opine that the process of German nation-state-building as well as the position of Germandom in central Europe was imperiled.

Pan-Germanism (*Pangermanismus, Alldeutschtum*) grew out of the perpetually frustrated desire for German unification. Its early proponents, such as Friedrich Ludwig Jahn and Ernst Moritz Arndt, championed the *Großdeutsch* solution. Others also wished to include the Scandinavians in some would-be *Großdeutsch* nation-state. Lastly, such writers as Friedrich List (1789–1846), Paul Anton de Lagarde (1829–1891), and Konstantin Franz argued for German's hegemony over central and eastern Europe. They believed that only then would enduring peace in Europe be possible. At the ideological level these thinkers readily espoused the notion of the superiority of the "Aryan race" as proposed by Joseph-Arthur de Gobineau (1816–1882) in his *Essai sur l'inégalité des races humaines* (Essay on the Inequality of Human Races, 1853–1855). The forerunners of his thought on "races and inherent inequalities among them" were the Göttingen professor Johann Friedrich Blumenbach (1752–1840), the French baron G. L. Cuvier (1769–1852) and the French scholar Victor Courtet (1813–1867). The last one developed the notion of the "Caucasian race" (Davies, 1996: 734).

The Englishman Houston Stewart Chamberlain (1855–1927) fell under the spell of the concept of the "Aryan race" in 1878, when at Oxford he listened to the lectures of the German professor Friedrich Max Müller (1823–1900). Chamberlain espoused the tenets of "scientific racism" and propagated the idea of "racial struggle" in his writings. His thought and example resonated even more strongly among Pan-Germans, because Chamberlain married Richard Wagner's (1813–1883) daughter and wrote in German. The operas of his father-in-law loomed large as "pure musical manifestation of Germanness in its essence." Rabidly anti-English, Chamberlain became a naturalized German citizen in 1916.

Drawing on the ideological basis offered by Gobineau and Chamberlain among others, in 1891 the loosely organized Allgemeiner Deutscher Verband (General German League) came into being. In 1894 Ernst Haase, a Leipzig professor and, significantly, a member of the Reichstag, turned it into the influential Alldeutscher Verband (Pan-German League). The league's purpose was to heighten German national consciousness, especially among Germans/German-speakers outside Germany. In his three-volume work *Deutsche Politik* (German Politics, 1905–1907) Haase called for German expansion in Europe. His ideas prepared the ground for the rise of the organicist concept of *Lebensraum* (living space). It can be roughly defined as "space required by a nation for life and growth." *Lebensraum* became the leitmotif of Hans Grimm's seminal *Volk ohne Raum* (The Nation without Living Space, 1926). Ewald Banse repeated his theses six years later in *Raum und Volk im Weltkriege* (Space and Nation in the World War), before *Lebensraum* became the core of Hitler's national socialist ideology (Anon., 1992d: 103; Kinder, 1978: II 65; Thorne, 1975: 251).

In Austria-Hungary Georg von Schönerer (1842–1921) and Karl Hermann Wolf unleashed the "Away-from-Rome movement" in 1897. They attacked Jews and Slavs and appealed for closer links of the Austrian Germans/German-speakers with Germany. Schönerer and Wolf's ideological antecedent was the Protestant Evangelischer Bund (Evangelical Union), which had come into being in Silesia in 1886. The rise of this union was a response to the end of the *Kulturkampf*. This organization saw the state's rapprochement with the Catholic Church as a dangerous increase in the Holy See's influence in Silesia and Germany (Anon., 1992d:

103; Greenfeld, 1992: 378–386; Kinder, 1978: II 79; Neubach, 1995: 185; Prinz, 1995: 354, 358).

The spread of Pan-Germanism in Austria-Hungary contributed to the gradual forging of the concept of the Sudetenland ("Sudety" in Czech). It denoted the outlying and usually mountainous regions of Bohemia, Moravia and Austrian Silesia that were predominantly inhabited by German-speakers. This term was derived from Franz Jesser's (1869–1954) coinage of "Sudetendeutsch," which he used for the first time in 1902. It meant a German region of the Sudeten Mountains but within the borders of Austria-Hungary (Hemmerle, 1992: 218; Weger, 1998: 24). Initially, the concept of the Sudetenland gained political currency in the wake of the break-up of Austria-Hungary (1918). The German-speakers, left outside the tiny postwar Austria, strove to establish their own state, which would escape incorporation into the coalescing Czechoslovakia (Prinz, 1995: 381). Thus the four provinces of the Sudetenland (Austrian West Silesia), Deutsch-Böhmen (north and west Bohemia), the Böhmerwaldgau (south Bohemia) and Deutsch-Südmahren (south Moravia) came into being, and subsequently were suppressed by Czechoslovak troops in late 1918 and 1919 (Honzák, 1995: 477). The Sudetenland was reestablished as an administrative entity during World War II. The first two of the aforementioned provinces were organized as the Sudetenland-Gau. The third one was divided between the Bayerische Ostmark and the Oberdonau (previously Upper Austria), while the fourth was incorporated into the Niederdonau (previously Lower Austria) (Hemmerle, 1992: 433; Jähnig, 1991: 151; Wagner, 1991: 257).

The establishment of various German nationalist organizations in the German Empire followed the rise of Pan-German organizations. They aimed at supporting "endangered Germandom," especially in the Polish/Slavic-speaking areas of the Province of Posen and West Prussia. In this manner these organizations helped the state, which could not easily engage in assimilation endeavors without breaching the rule of law.[2] The process of passing the responsibility for further homogenization of the *Kleindeutsch* nation-state into the hands of grassroots associations started in earnest with the founding of the Gesellschaft für Verbreitung von Volksbildung und Volksspielgruppen (Society for Spreading Folk Education and Supporting Folk Amateur Theater Groups) in 1871. It mainly facilitated the development of small popular libraries. Ten years later the Allgemeiner Deutscher Schulverein (General German School Association) came into being. This association aimed at bolstering the network of German schools.

Thanks to the efforts of the former organization, the Verband oberschlesischer Volksbüchereien (Union of Upper Silesian Libraries) was established in 1903. It comprised seventy German-language libraries and successfully counteracted the influence of the Wielkopolska Towarzystwo Czytelni Ludowych (Society of Popular Reading Rooms), which had been active in Upper Silesia since the 1880s (Mroczko, 1994: 27). In 1908 the Allgemeiner Deutscher Schulverein was transformed into the Verein für das Deutschtum in Ausland (Association for Germandom Abroad) so as to fortify the position of Germans/German-speakers outside Germany, especially in Austria-Hungary and elsewhere in central and eastern Europe. In this manner, the association evolved from a German into Pan-German organization, one that survives to this day (Czubiński, 1991: 106; Lüer, 1995: 82).

Apart from the societies of gymnasts, singers, riflemen, voluntary firefighters and students (mentioned extensively in part 1), the societies of war veterans also strongly spurred mass mobilization for the goals of German nationalism. The first German organization of this kind sprang up in the Lower Silesian Regency of Liegnitz in 1839.[3] Interest in establishing war veterans' organizations returned after the Prussian wars of 1864 and 1866 and the Franco-Prussian War of 1870–1871. The Deutscher Kriegerbund (German Union of War Veterans) came into being in 1872. On the eve of its transformation into the more comprehensive and tightly organized Deutscher Reichs-Kriegerverband (Imperial German Union of War Veterans) in 1884, the Deutscher Kriegerbund boasted 157,721 members. At that time Prussia's other veteran organizations had a combined membership of 75,431. It is estimated that including other war veteran organizations (especially from Bavaria, Saxony and Württemberg), the count of German veterans active in their various organizations was close to half a million (Anon., 1888c: 209–210). The war veteran organizations became the natural recruitment pool for German nationalist associations.

In 1897 the Deutscher Reichs-Kriegerverband adopted a clearly nationalist slogan: "Ein Reich, ein Volk, ein Gott" (One empire, one people, one God). Soon Emperor William II (reigned 1888–1918) extended his patronage to the union, lending to it his imperial prestige. Membership in any other German organization could not rival that of the Deutscher Reichs-Kriegerverband. In 1903, the union comprised 55,784 veterans in 466 branches in the Oppeln Regency alone. This number surpassed the membership of all the Polish and Polish-language societies in Upper Silesia. In 1889, 64 Polish organizations of Upper Silesia claimed 13,622 members. Before the outbreak of the Great War in 1914 the number of these societies rose to 464, and their membership to 46,000 (Coetzee, 1990: 3–13; Figowa, 1966: 15; Migdał, 1965: 67).

Although the German state could not do much against its Polish/Slavic-speaking citizens without violating its own legislation too blatantly, Berlin was in a position to discriminate against foreigners who had not acquired German citizenship and did not possess valid residence permits (Schofer, 1974: 23). As a result, the 1885–1886 expulsion[4] of alien Poles/Polish-speakers and Jews who had arrived in Germany from Congress Poland and Galicia contributed to the closure of the German/Austrian-Hungarian border. Next, Germany's immigration regulations and customs procedure achieved the form that became the norm in today's Europe and elsewhere. The above-mentioned action brought about the removal of some 26,000 illegal immigrants. During the years 1885–1887, 5,239 Poles, Polish-speakers and Jews were expelled from Upper Silesia (Lis, 1993: 93). The clearly ethnonationalist basis for these expulsions was indicated by the fact that this measure was not applied to alien Germans or German-speakers from Austria-Hungary and Russia. Also alien non-Slavs and non-Jews were largely exempted from this measure. For these ethnic categories of aliens, legalizing their permanent residence in Germany was made easy.

These deportations (or *rugi*—expulsions as they are known in Polish historiography) expressed the will on the part of the German authorities to bolster the position of Germandom east of Berlin. The government clearly accepted the nationalist view that the phenomena of the *Landflucht* and the *Ostflucht* might imperil the German nation (Mroczko, 1994: 30; Rogall, 1993: 70). The Catholic Church did not condemn this action, which clashed with the principle of universalism. The hierarchy simply did not wish to endanger their shaky *modus vivendi* with the state. At that time only the most restrictive of the *Kulturkampf* policies had been terminated. However, what happened infuriated Polish nationalists. They made the expulsions into one of the very symbols of their "national struggle against the Germans." No further deportations followed this singular event. Moreover, Polish nationalists overlooked the fact that the 1885–1887 deportations were not only applied to ethnic Poles and Polish-speakers but to Jews as well. Subtlety is not the strong point of nationalist thinking; what counts is political efficacy.

In a way, this simplistic attitude of the Polish national movement to these deportations may be justified by what followed afterwards. In 1887 a total ban on teaching Polish was imposed (Wiskemann, 1956: 11), and a year earlier the König-lich Preußische Ansiedlungskommission (Royal Prussian Settlement Commission) had been established with its seat in Posen. This commission wielded influence and commanded resources thanks to the legislation that promoted German settlement in the provinces of West Prussia and Posen. In the period 1886–1914 it spent 480 million marks (or roughly three billion present-day euros) (Rogall, 1993: 74) on purchasing 461,000 hectares of land. Although the commission was to buy Polish farms in order to bolster the German element, ironically it obtained 334,000 hectares from German farmers and only 127,000 hectares from Polish farmers. This land was used for establishing 300 villages (that is, one-tenth of the original goal) and settling 154,000 persons. This effort did not manage to alter the declining percentage of Germans in the Wielkopolska population. First of all, 115,000 of the settlers came from this province, and 23,000 (15 percent) of them were ethnically Polish.[5] What is more, due to the gradual drop in the profits generated by agricultural production, many a German settler sold his land and left for western Germany (Rogall, 1993: 75–76; Zakrzewski, 1988: 45).

The conflict between Poles and Germandom, politicized by the *Kulturkampf*, restrictive language laws and the *rugi* mainly unfolded in Wilekopolska and West Prussia. By the 1880s the national struggle was transferred into the broader sphere of the economy. Numerous savings banks, cooperatives, shops and the like were divided along national lines. They tended to draw capital and customers from their "own" national groups. Artisans, agricultural and merchants associations deepened this cleavage, because they also catered to nationally differentiated memberships (Rogall, 1993: 74). This national struggle, waged with economic means, was dubbed the *Wirtschaftskampf* (economic war).

This strife must have fanned insecurity among the Germans, especially those living in the Province of Posen. Therefore, it is not surprising that in 1894 the Verein für Förderung des Deutschtums in den Ostmarken (Society for the Advancement of Germandom in the Eastern Marches) came into being in Posen, not Berlin (Tims, 1966: 29). This society was a grassroots response to the falling percentage of German inhabitants in the Province of Posen. The province's population was comprised of 40 percent Germans in 1871 but just 38 percent in 1910. Their share in its urban population remained at the level of 50 percent, though the number began to diminish, especially in smaller towns, at the beginning of the twentieth century (Rogall, 1993: 71). The *Verein* also aimed at countering the legacy of Chancellor Leo von Caprivi's (1890–1894) relaxed policies toward Poles and to the issue of teaching in Polish (Rogall, 1993: 71; Wiskemann, 1956: 11).

The society's name was shortened to the handy Deutscher Ostmarkenverein (Society of the German Marches) in 1899. Poles knew it as "HaKaTa" because of its distinctive logo, which combined the letters H, K, and T. They were derived from the initials of the *Verein's* founders, Ferdinand Hansemann, Hermann Kennemann, and Heinrich Tiedemann (Rogall, 1993: 72–73) and appeared on the title page of the society's press organ, *Die Ostmark*. The Ostmarkenverein hoped to provide economic aid to Germans living in eastern Germany and to fortify German national consciousness (Snoch, 1991: 45). In 1912, in the Province of Posen its 12,000 members included civil servants, teachers, doctors, jurists and middle-class artisans. All these professions, collectively known as the *Bildungsbürgertum,* or intelligentsia, were responsible for spreading nationalist ideology in Germany and elsewhere in central Europe during the second half of the nineteenth century (Rogall, 1993: 72).

The first branches of the Deutscher Ostmarkenverein sprang up in Silesia on the initiative of local industrialists in 1895 and 1896. The Schlesischer Landesauschuss des Deutschen Ostmarkenvereins (Silesian Regional Committee of the Society of the German Marches) was established in 1903 with its seat in Breslau. Its membership rose steadily from 7,500 in 1905 to 11,850 in 1913. But this regional committee devoted only a small part of its activities to Upper Silesia, despite the fact that the Oppeln Regency contained a third of all the Polish/Slavic-speaking population in Prussia, or, in other words, more than a million out of the three and a half million. This made Upper Silesia into the region of Germany with the highest concentration of Polish/Slavic-speakers per square mile. The difference between Poles and Polish/Slavic-speakers of non-national multiple identities was obfuscated or crudely simplified by the German nationalist propaganda for the sake of enhancing the message of "imminent Polish or Slavic danger." This official approach of Berlin to the Szlonzoks suited the Polish national movement well. Thanks to Berlin's position Polish nationalists could credibly claim Upper Silesia's Szlonzokian population as part of the Polish nation.

The authorities of the Province of Silesia remained aloof to the Deutscher Ostmarkenverein, since Breslau's overt support for this organization would amount to acknowledging the existence of a "Polish problem" in Silesia, a situation they wished to avoid. As the 1880 Austrian-Hungarian census made clear, any official recognition of ethnic or national difference did not serve to contain it but led to the creation of ethnic and national movements. The rise of these movements endangered the privileged position of the established dominant national group(s) and could delegitimize the further existence of the state. The logic of ethnic nationalism is such that if a state is organized as an ethnic nation-state and comprises a sizeable ethnic minority, this fact begs for separating a region as the minority's nation-state (Snoch, 1991: 45; Tims, 1966: 287–288).

The Ostmarkenverein inspired the expropriation act of 1908. It was applied in only four cases that involved 1,655 hectares of land belonging to Polish owners. The ensuing popular outcry against it brought about official condemnation and suspension of this practice in 1913. The Zentrum organized its branch in Posen in 1908, but this party did not manage to curb the swelling national conflict there on the basis of Catholicism and universalism, as had happened in Upper Silesia. Perceived by Poles as an instrument of Germanization and by German nationalists as a clandestine supporter of Polishdom, the Zentrum could not even garner enough support to launch its provincial press organ in Wielkopolska. However, due to the outbreak of the Great War the national conflict abated. The German government wanted to secure the loyalty of Poles for Germany's struggle against Russia. On the other hand, Wielkopolska's Polish national movement hoped that Berlin would allow for the creation of a Polish state in Congress Poland after the tsar was defeated (Rogall, 1993: 71; Snoch, 1991: 45; Wiskemann, 1956: 14).

The head-on collision between German and Polish nationalisms that unfolded in eastern Germany allowed both movements to forge clearly delineated and inevitably opposed versions of their ideologies. These ideologies thrived on the ethnic cleavage that had opened quite violently between the Germans and Poles during the 1880s. Besides, the young German nation-state and its equally new nation craved symbols that would make their "ancient glory" (cf. Hobsbawm, 1992) known to foreigners and especially to Germans themselves (cf. Hobsbawm, 1992; Mosse, 1975: 47–72).

In 1875 the Arminius monument (*Hermannsdenkmal*) was erected. It commemorated the success of the Teutons over the Romans in the battle of the Teutoburg Forest. The colonnaded pedestal supports a gigantic statue in beaten copper nearly 30 meters in height, which took nearly forty years to build. The statue represents the Germanic chieftain Hermann (Arminius), who annihilated the invading Roman legions in AD 9, though he was a Roman citizen himself (Davies, 1996: 827). The *Niederwald* monument, which opened in Rüdesheim in 1883, commemorates the "national war" of 1870–1871. It stands on the bank of the Rhine, where it was unveiled in the presence of all the German princes in 1883. The construction of the *Kyffhäuser* monument in Thuringia, which represents the equestrian figure of Emperor William I, was completed in 1897 (Davies, 1996: 827). War veteran associations bore a major part of the cost of the latter edifice, as they had done previously for the *Niederwald* monument, with its colossal statue of Germania. The construction of the monument, dedicated to the memory of the "Battle of the Nations" in Leipzig in 1813, which had sealed Napoleon's fate, proceeded between 1898 and 1913. The League of German Patriots, specially created for this purpose, and whose membership soared into the thousands, raised money for the erection of the monument (Alter, 1994: 46).

The centenary of the outbreak of the War of Liberation, when the ideology of German nationalism was clearly formulated for the first time, was most lavishly celebrated in Breslau. In the capital of Silesia Frederick William III had commenced the warfare with his famous appeal *Aufruf an Mein Volk* (To My People). On the occasion of these celebrations the imperial court was transferred from Berlin to Breslau. The massive modernist Jahrhunderthalle (Centennial Hall) was adorned with a dome that was the largest in the world at that time. It conveniently housed numerous exhibitions as well as thousands of visitors and revelers (Klemmer, 1993; Scheuermann, 1994: 666–667). The hall survived both the World Wars, and after 1945 in Poland its previously deeply felt German provenance was exorcised by renaming it the Hala Ludowa (People's Hall). This name directly alluded to the *People's* Polish Republic (1952–1989).

Not only were historical events used for boosting the national German past-under-construction, but also the figure of the hailed creator of the German Empire, Bismarck, lent itself to nationalist mythologization. Larger than life, the chancellor was the very icon of the success of Germany's nation- and nation-state-building. The Germans were reintegrated after the termination of the *Kulturkampf,* thanks to progressive social legislation and the soaring economic strength of their state, and Bismarck's seventieth birthday was celebrated as a great national event in 1885. Unfortunately, this event coincided with the 1885–1886 expulsion of alien Polish-speakers and Jews, which made the difference between Polish and German nationalisms even more pronounced in the two ideologies' completely different agendas for that year.

After the short reign of Frederick III (reigned 1888), who became known as the hope of liberals, his young son, William II (reigned 1888–1918), ascended to the imperial throne. The emperor resented Bismarck's independent and masterful ways, and the chancellor felt driven to resign in 1890 when William II decided to introduce a "personal regime." Despite a formal reconciliation in 1894, Bismarck remained a constant critic of the emperor and of successive chancellors. This could not prevent another national celebration of his birthday in 1895, though it was marred by the Reichstag, which refused to present an address of congratulation (Anon., 1908d: 188; Kinder, 1978: II 77). The death of Bismarck in 1898 sparked yet another wave of national feeling, which culminated in the construction of Bismarck towers throughout the empire, with active communal support on the grassroots initiative of various national, cultural and economic organizations.

An example of such a tower still survives in Scheersberg near Quern, Schleswig-Holstein. Lower Silesia also used to have its own Bismarck tower in the Eulengebirge (Góry Sowie) range of the Sudeten Mountains. Importantly, another one was constructed in Upper Silesia in 1907 (or perhaps 1903) in Slupna (Słupna, today a district of Mysłowice [Myslowitz]), close to the symbolic *Dreikaiserreichsecke*—"cornerstone" of the three empires of Russia, Germany, and Austria-Hungary, where their borders converged from 1846 to 1918. It is said that on Sundays German families frequented this over twenty-meter-high tower to show their children *"polnische Wirtschaft"* visible across the border river in Galicia and Congress Poland. In this manner, the youngsters were clearly to realize "how happy they were to have been born in united Germany." It was a deft method of instilling national consciousness and prejudice in new generations.

After the 1922 division of Upper Silesia between Germany and Poland, Slupna found itself within the Polish borders. Polish nationalists were not able to devise a clever method to overhaul the tower's German provenance so that it would start catering to the Polish national feeling. It was not enough to rename it after the Polish (national) hero as the Kościuszko tower. The structure gradually decayed due to neglect, and finally veterans of the three anti-German [Upper] Silesian uprisings (1919, 1920 and 1921) pulled it down at some point in the mid-1930s (Dziadul, 1996: 4; Pierzchała, 1997: 49; Reichling, 1977: 325).

To wrap up the discussion of the further development of German nationalism in the process of the post-1871 nation-state-building, the effects of this ideology on European and international relations must be outlined. In 1872, shortly after the establishment of the German Empire, Bismarck constructed the League of the Three Emperors—those of Germany, Austria-Hungary and Russia—to contain any attempt at revenge on the part of France. The Russo-Austrian rivalry in the Balkans strained this alliance. Germany stood fast by Austria-Hungary, which resulted in ever-closer relations between these two states. This newly established closeness found its full expression in the Dual Alliance of 1879. After conciliatory moves on the part of Berlin and Vienna, Russia joined in the renewed League of the Three Emperors in 1881. The following year Italy joined this alliance, and it was extended into the Triple Alliance, though tensions between the newcomer and Austria-Hungary remained.

In the 1880s the Austro-Russian struggle for influence in the Balkans flared up again and did not abate until 1887, when Germany concluded the Reinsurance Treaty with Russia. The alliance system that allowed Bismarck to keep France isolated was shattered after the emperor's dismissal of the "iron chancellor" in 1890. The pattern of the old balance of power was decisively overhauled in 1894, with Russia concluding the Dual Alliance with France after Germany did not renew the Reinsurance Treaty in 1890. This meant that Berlin joined Vienna in the latter's bid to broaden Austria-Hungary's sphere of influence in the Balkans at the tsar's expense (Kinder, 1978: II 83; Turner, 1992: 114–115). The ground for this change had been prepared by Germany's unwavering policy of bolstering the armed forces[6] and thanks to its sweeping successes in industrialization.

Despite Bismarck's insistence that Germany was a "satiated" power, grassroots pressure mounted to emulate the imperial expansion of other western European powers. In 1882 Germany's Colonial League came into being, and the "inventor of German imperialism," Carl Peters (1856–1918), established the Society for German Colonization in 1884. Bismarck reluctantly had to recognize this trend. The imperial capital housed the Berlin Conference (1884–1885), instigated by the Belgian king's colonial cravings. At a series of meetings the European colonial powers carved up Africa in a thinly disguised imperial scramble for domination over the continent. Germany joined in the race to build its own overseas empire. Berlin gained colonies in South-West Africa, Cameroon, Togo, East Africa and in the South Pacific. The effort, however, was hardly offset by revenues flowing from the new territories. The total area of the possessions was six times bigger than that of Germany, while the colonial population was six times smaller than that of their "mother country" (Kennedy, 1989: 211; Kinder, 1978: II 77, 108–109; Reader, 1997: 555–580; Sabin, 1990: 212).

Germany extended its colonial empire in the South Pacific and its sphere of influence in China throughout the 1890s. On the basis of the regulatory framework set up by the Berlin Conference, Berlin concluded a series of treaties with Britain (1890), the United States (1898) and Spain (1899) in an effort to legalize its overseas empire-in-construction (Muirhead, 1908: 467; Sabin, 1990: 212). The Alldeutscher Verband and other Pan-German and German nationalist organizations also urged the policy of overseas expansion, and members of colonial organizations were recruited from among their ranks. After 1895 the German ruling elite seemed convinced of the need for large-scale territorial expansion, which Admiral Alfred von Tirpitz (1849–1930) deemed "as irresistible as a natural law."

Tirpitz's idea of constructing a huge naval fleet found eager support on the part of the emperor and the Flottenverein (Naval League), and work began in 1898. On the eve of the Great War Germany's fleet was second only to that of Britain. Thus, with this potential behind him, in 1899 the soon-to-be Chancellor Bernhard von Bülow (ruled 1900–1909) called for a redivision of the globe that would take into consideration Germany's interests. Queen Victoria (reigned 1837–1901), being the mother-in-law of William I's son Frederick III and grandmother to William II, was not opposed to fulfilling the colonial dreams of the German branch of her family. Neither was the influential secretary of colonial affairs, Joseph Chamberlain (1895–1903), who held Pan-German views. Consequently British foreign policy went along with the needs and wishes of the Triple Alliance (1885–1892, 1895–1902) until the demise of Victoria.

At the beginning of the twentieth century London viewed the increase in Germany's colonial appetite with apprehension. Berlin set out to compete with Britain and other imperial powers in the Middle East. The balance of power changed quite decisively when Britain and France, having overcome their enmity, concluded the Entente Cordiale in 1904. In 1907 Russia joined this alliance, which was reformulated as the Triple Entente. Two years later the Entente concluded the secret Treaty of Racconigi with Italy, in which the signatories agreed to keep the status quo in the Balkans. Germany was left isolated. Berlin stood fast by its "Nibelungen alliance" with Austria-Hungary, through which it hoped to exert Germany's power in the Balkans and in Turkey. This was clearly against the wishes of Italy, Russia, France and England and caused bitter rivalry between these two groups of European imperial powers during the Balkan crisis of 1912–1913 (Anon., 1990g: 350–351; Davies, 1996: 1300–1301; Kennedy, 1989: 211–213; Kinder, 1978: II 83, 103, 109, 121).

These events prepared the scene for the imminent outbreak of the Great War, which closes the period covered in this work. The effects of World War I on the national situation in Silesia will be analyzed in chapter 10.

CHAPTER 8

Polish Nationalism
Enters Prussian Silesia

The processes of nation-, nation-state- and empire-building in Germany together with its European and worldwide repercussions created the context within which the development of Polish nationalism in the Province of Posen and Upper Silesia must be interpreted. After the repeated failures of Polish uprisings in 1830–1831, 1846 and 1863–1864, directed mainly against Russia as the partition power that had seized most of Poland-Lithuania's territory and population, Polish activists dreaming of the reestablishment of this polity as a Polish nation-state decided to channel their efforts into "organic work." The concept of "organic work" (*praca organiczna*) meant fortifying the Polish influence through gradual but steady accumulation of Polish capital as the basis for developing Polish factories and for modernizing the agriculture in Polish hands.

Most importantly, the adherents of this idea concentrated on spreading Polish-language and Polish national education as the basic tool of forging a Polish nation because Bismarck (conscious that unification of Germany had just commenced German nation- and nation-state-building) rightly remarked in 1873 that Polish leaders were just a "handful of truculent aristocrats and priests with no nation behind them" (Wiskemann, 1956: 10). Concentration of the Polish national endeavors in the field of education gained special significance in the face of Germanization and Russification. These policies aimed at incorporating the Polish-speaking population into either the German nation or the mainstream of Russian society. As a result of subscribing to organic work Congress Poland had been turned into the engine of the Russian economy before industrialization was transplanted eastward into the heartland of the empire in the 1890s (Smogorzewski, 1992: 951). Similarly, the Province of Posen became the stage upon which the nationalist *Wirtschaftskampf* (economic struggle) was played out and in which the local Poles were not altogether unsuccessful.

Galicia, with its cultural and linguistic autonomy, on the other hand, afforded a safe haven for developing the Polish national movement and instilling national feeling in the Polish-speaking populace. This situation was made possible by the Polish-language bureaucracy and educational system, though the spread of Polish nationalism was checked in the 1880s and 1890s by the emergence of its Ukrainian counterpart, especially in the eastern part of the crownland. The Polish count Kazimierz Badeni spearheaded the recognition of Ruthenian (Ukrainian) language rights. He served as the Galician governor (1886–1895) and even rose to the position of Austrian-Hungarian prime minister (1895–1897). His position in accommodating the linguistic needs of Ukrainians indicated that many Polish-speaking nobles of Galicia were still not nationalists, remaining entrenched in their loyalty to the monarchy and to their own estate.

The period of organic work came to a close with the coming of age of the new generation of Polish nationalist activists. They themselves had not experienced the defeat of the January Uprising and the subsequent consequences, ranging from expropriation to exile in Siberia. The approaching change gained momentum from numerous clandestine Polish-language circles that sprang up at secondary and tertiary schools, especially in Congress Poland during the 1880s. These circles formed the springboard for the socialist, nationalist and peasant trends in the overall Polish movement. The émigré and ex-insurrectionist Zygmunt Miłkowski (1824–1915), more widely known by his pseudonym Tomasz Teodor Jeż, furnished the nationalist trend, which is of prevalent concern to this work, with its first ideological framework. In his book *Rzecz o obronie czynnej i skarbie narodowym* (On Active Defense and the National Treasury, 1886) Miłkowski urged that funds be gathered for the struggle that would bring about the reestablishment of Poland-Lithuania as a Polish nation-state.

In the same year another Polish activist, Zygmunt Balicki (1858–1916), established the secret Związek Młodzieży Polskiej (Association of Polish Youth), known as the Zet. This association derived its name from the Polish letter "z" (*zet*) in the first word of the Zet's full name. The Zet constituted the organizational basis for the all-partition Liga Polska (Polish League), established in Switzerland in 1886–1887 on Miłkowski's initiative. This league's aim was to "reestablish" Poland within its prepartition boundaries. Such young nationalist activists as Balicki and Roman Dmowski (1864–1939) were not satisfied with the traditional legalistic approach, which became prevalent in the Polish national movement after the disastrous uprisings.

In 1893 they established the overtly nationalist Liga Narodowa (National League) with its seat in Congress Poland. Its narrow elite membership strove to gain control over the grassroots *wszechpolski* (All-Polish) movement, which spawned numerous cultural, social and economic societies in all three partition zones. Dmowski became the main ideologue of Polish nationalism. In his 1893 brochure *Nasz patriotyzm* (Our Patriotism) he argued that the interest of the Polish nation should take precedence over any other concerns of individual Poles. In 1903 in his *Myśli nowoczesnego Polaka* (The Thoughts of the Modern Pole)[1] Dmowski called for conscious nation-building that would obliterate the non-national differences that divided the Polish-speaking population.

Putting this theoretical framework to use, the Liga Narodowa advocated assuring the best possible conditions for the development of the Polish nation-in-construction. This meant founding the Polish nation-state within the combination of the political prepartition and ethnic borders. The latter type of boundary would include Upper Silesia in this state as well. In this case it is hard to speak of "reestablishing" Poland-Lithuania, as the territories of this erstwhile polity were not what Dmowski and his circle desired. They married the Polish-Lithuanian nobility's civic and aristocratic nationalism with the ethnic principle, hoping that this ideological concoction would spawn a Polish nation-state where the nobility-led uprisings had not been able to do so. But the Polish national discourse was obviously legitimized through referring to a would-be Polish nation state as "reestablished." German and Italian nationalists employed a similarly inaccurate term when they referred to the founding of their respective nation-states as "reunification" of the German Empire or of the Kingdom of Italy. These polities had *not* previously existed, but the political discourse at that time was such that western European politicians readily accepted these national movements that could credibly claim some not too distant tradition of statehood somehow connected to the history of their postulated nations.

During the 1890s the novel approach of Polish nationalists in combining political and ethnic borders led to a new understanding of the term "Prussian partition zone" among Polish national activists and intellectuals. It was no longer limited to former Poland-Lithuania's provinces of West Prussia and Posen, which Prussia had annexed from Poland-Lithuania. They maintained that this partition zone also included Upper Silesia, as it was inhabited by a sizeable Polish/Slavic-speaking population. Obviously this territory, like the rest of Silesia, had lost its last politically significant ties with the Kingdom of Poland in the thirteenth and fourteenth centuries (Anon., 1983c: 212; Anon., 1983d: 615; Anon., 1987: 879; Ślusarek, 1996: 1–5; Smogorzewski, 1992: 951; Snyder, 2003: 124–125).

The Liga Narodowa became the nucleus of the Stronnictwo Narodowo-Demokratyczne (SN-D, National Democratic Movement), which was established in Congress Poland in 1897 and became a legal party between 1903 and 1905. Many of the party's members were elected to the first Russian Duma (parliament) in 1905, where under Dmowski's leadership they formed the Polish Circle (1905–1917). This circle demanded Polish autonomy, hoping for a gradual reestablishment of the Polish state that Russia would support. The Stronnictwo Demokratyczno-

Narodowe (Democratic National Movement), established in 1905, represented the SN-D's line in Galicia. The Polskie Towarzystwo Narodowo-Demokratyczne (Polish National Democratic Society), founded in 1909, played a similar role in the Prussian partition zone.

The Polska Partia Socjalistyczna (PPS, Polish Socialist Party), established in 1892/1893, took a more radical stance against Russia. It was the strongest socialist party in the Russian Empire. Under the leadership of Józef Piłsudski (1867–1935) the PPS took part in the abortive 1905 revolution. This party struggled for the Polish cause, as it was against the "internationalist cooperation" between Polish and Russian socialists, unlike Rosa Luxemburg (1871–1919) and Julian Marchlewski (1866–1925). The latter two socialist leaders' rather insignificant Social-Demokracja Królestwa Polskiego i Litwy (Social Democracy of the Kingdom of Poland and Lithuania, founded in 1898) advocated the unification of all the workers' movements within Russia despite ethnic, national or confessional differences. The Galician counterpart of Piłsudski's PPS—the Polska Partia Socjal-demokratyczna Galicji i Śląska (Polish Social-Democratic Party of Galicia and Silesia,[2] established in 1892)—had to share its influence with the conciliatory Polskie Stronnictwo Ludowe (PSL, Polish Peasant Movement, founded in 1895). The PSL saw more advantage in maintaining the political status quo that emerged after the introduction of universal male suffrage in Austria-Hungary in 1907 than in contesting it for the sake of the Polish national cause. Peasants were pleased with full civil rights and Polish-language education provided in Galicia. They did not want to risk them for the chimera of a possible Polish nation-state (Anon., 1987a: 314; Davies, 1991: II xx–xxi; Jakóbczyk, 1989: 72; Ślusarek, 1996: 3; Smogorzewski, 1992: 951).

The SN-D gained more ground in Congress Poland after the PPS was compromised because its members took part in the failed revolution of 1905. Dmowski, even more pronouncedly, hoped for Polish autonomy within the Russian Empire, emphasizing that Germany was Polish nationalism's main opponent (Smogorzewski, 1992: 951). This judgment was based on the Germanizing endeavors, which were carried out more decisively and methodically in the Prussian partition zone than in Russia. The tsar actually had to make some democratic concessions after the 1905 revolution as his government strove for the implementation of systemic reforms that would modernize the backward empire. These changes, which were essentially half measures to keep a semblance of the ancien régime afloat, weakened the state and its economy. Subsequently, Russia became more absorbed with sustaining its shaky system of governance and production and less interested in containing Polish nationalism than the economically and systemically robust German nation-state was.

However, Polish national activists living in the German Empire perceived their situation in a different light. Sharing in the German economic and political success, they were far better suited to conciliation than revolution. The growing network of various Polish societies served by the burgeoning Polish-language press and publishing industry came into being especially during the 1840s, 1850s and 1860s. They did not disappear upon the founding of the German nation-state and the introduction of Germanizing measures. First of all, when German officialdom chose to harass Polish-speakers, Germanization was widely thought to be the natural destiny of all the Hohenzollerns' non-German-speaking subjects. After all, enlightened Englishmen and Americans of the same era largely assumed that all non-English-speaking inhabitants of their countries would eventually be Anglicized. Homogeneity was accepted as a legitimate necessity without which the modern (of course, nation-) state could not effectively compete in the international arena. This tacit acceptance of the principle lasted until ethnic and national minority leaders grasped its obvious link with nation- and nation-state-building. They then decided to use it to their own, often irredentist ends. Berlin's strong statement on the need for assimilating Polish-speaking Prussians played into the hands of Polish nationalists (Zakrzewski, 1988: 46–47), but only thanks to the *Kulturkampf* were they able to forge an effective national ideology by intertwining it with Catholicism.

During the difficult years of the *Kulturkampf* the Polish Primate Archbishop Mieczysław Ledóchowski (1822–1902) spent two years in a Prussian jail and was subsequently exiled to Rome. Ninety Polish priests shared his fate, and many more were harassed. This disrupted pastoral life of numerous parishes and simultaneously convinced lay Polish-speakers that they and the Catholic Church were "on the same side of the barricade" in the Protestant-oriented *Kleindeutsch* nation-state (Davies, 1991: II 122, 127, 130–131).

Berlin's Germanizing measures concentrated on language and the economy, which pointed to the clear influence of the thought of Herder and Friedrich List on the German government's policies. The Polish answer to the stereotype of *polnische Wirtschaft* and the activities of the Ansiedlungskommission was to outdo the Germans in the use of these novel economic weapons of industrial work, order and thrift. Many Polish entrepreneurs and companies won in the ensuing *Wirtschaftskampf*, which was especially visible in the poor performance of the Ansiedlungskommission despite lavish support from the state and the Deutscher Ostmarkenverein (Davies, 1991: II 122). Between 1871 and 1878 the Polish language was removed from secondary education, courts of law and administration. In 1885–1886 Polish public opinion was outraged at the expulsion of alien Polish-speakers and Jews, and after 1887 the only subject taught in Polish in elementary schools was religion. By 1900 religious instruction in Polish was limited to just the two lowest grades. Paradoxically, the altogether liberal 1908 act on associations included a clause providing that German should be used at all public gatherings in the counties (*Kreise*) where Polish-speakers did not constitute more than 60 percent of the population (Trzeciakowski, 1976: 553).

This anti-Polish language policy made it clear to Polish national activists that as the German language constituted the core of Germandom, they should develop Polish nationalism around the Polish language in order to be taken seriously by the German authorities. Polish nationalists concentrated on Polish-language newspapers. Aided by the largely Polish-speaking Catholic clergy and Church administration, they created dense networks of singing, peasant, economic and Catholic worker societies, as well as numerous branches of the influential Towarzystwo Oświaty Ludowej (Society for Popular Education), the Towarzystwo Czytelni Ludowych (Society for Popular Reading Rooms) and the Sokół (Falcon) gymnastic society.

The Sokół gymnastic society is a spectacular example of how closely central European Slavic nationalisms emulated their German counterpart. Between 1811 and 1871 the German gymnastic societies mobilized male youth, preparing them to become fighters or regular soldiers ready to die for their nation-in-the-making. The Czech nationalists had established similar societies under the name of Sokol (Falcon) already in 1862 (Polišenský, 1991: 98), and Polish activists followed closely. The first Sokół was established in Lemberg in 1867, which gave rise to the Galician network. In 1885 this organization made an appearance in the Prussian partition zone and in 1905 made an illegal entrée in Congress Poland. By 1914 the SN-D had dominated the Sokół network ideologically and by 1919 the Sokół had been turned into a paramilitary organization. Its members participated in Poland's numerous border wars after 1918, as their German forerunners had in the German wars of 1813–1815, 1864, 1866 and 1870–1871 (Anon., 1987b: 233).

The Sokól and other Polish grassroots national organizations did not limit their activities to the territory of the Prussian partition zone. Beginning in the 1880s they spread to Silesia and the Polish-speaking diaspora in Berlin, Westphalia and the Rhineland (Davies, 1991: II 124; Trzeciakowski, 1976: 555).

This was possible despite the unfavorable attitude of the German administration because Prussia (and later Germany) was a *Rechtstaat*, a political community which operated within the framework of law. Such possibilities for grassroots initiatives did not open up in the Habsburg Empire prior to the liberalizing reforms of the 1860s, and were unthinkable in the Russian Empire. Although numerous political institutions retained a visible degree of authoritarianism in Prussia/the German Empire, the political system operated through established procedures and by legal means. Under these conditions Polish nationalists could also develop their own activities within the confines of law without fear of being unjustly incarcerated or deported to such inhospitable places as Siberia, unlike their compatriots in Congress Poland. Actually, through their deputies to the Reichstag and the Prussian Landtag, who formed the Polish circle in Berlin, Polish nationalists were able to influence German and Prussian politics.

The anti-Polish rhetoric spearheaded by the Deutscher Ostmarkenverein was clearly expressed in 1895 by the famous sociologist Max Weber (1864–1920), who joined the Alldeutscher Verbund. He opined that "[o]nly we Germans could have made human beings out of these Poles." Soon petty anti-Polish measures intensified. Street names and official signs (including cemeteries or public lavatories) were Germanized. Even before 1878 the same had happened to hundreds of place-names that sounded "too Polish or Slavic." Poles replied in kind, but carefully so as not to breach law.

In 1906 and 1907 almost half of the schools in the Province of Posen were engulfed by strikes against the imposition of German as the medium of instruction for religious teaching. During the climax of these strikes 70,000 children protested in 950 schools in the Province of Posen and 19,300 children in 536 schools in the Province of West Prussia. Against the expectations of Polish nationalists the strike did not really spread into Upper Silesia, where it affected only 431 children.

Another weapon for opposing Germanization and an instrument of Polish nation-building was the celebration of various Polish anniversaries. In 1909 it was the centenary of the birth of the famous romantic poet Juliusz Słowacki (1809–1849). The following year was the 500th anniversary of the battle of Grunwald (1410) during which the Teutonic Knights (symbolic forefathers of Prussia and paragons of German nationalism in Polish nationalist propaganda) were defeated by the joint Polish-Lithuanian forces. The centenary of the birth of the most renowned Polish composer Frédéric Chopin (1810–1849) was also celebrated. Two years later the centenaries of the birth of another well-known Polish romantic poet, Zygmunt Krasiński (1812–1859), and of the birth of the prolific historical writer Józef Ignacy Kraszewski (1812–1887) were celebrated two years later. Interestingly, in 1867 he had settled in Saxony (Hargreaves-Mawdsley, 1968: 305) and continued to be involved in the Polish nationalist movement. He had strongly supported it with his historical novels, thus creating a glorious past for the emerging Polish nationalism. In 1913 another centenary took place, this time of the death of Prince Józef Poniatowski (1763–1813). He had been the commander-in-chief of the armed forces of the Grand Duchy of Warsaw and a marshal of France. This event coincided with the fiftieth anniversary of the outbreak of the January Uprising (Davies, 1991: II 116, 134; Jakóbczyk, 1989: 25, 67–68).

For the anniversary of the battle of Grunwald, a public subscription was launched in order to erect a monument in commemoration of the "Polish" victory over the "Germans." The acrimonious character of these celebrations, which aimed at deepening the cleavage between Polish and German nationalisms, caused the East Prussian provincial administration to react with such official hostility that the organizers of the scheme were obliged to erect their monument in Cracow, Galicia. The world-renowned pianist and composer and Polish nationalist activist Ignacy Paderewski (1860–1941) unveiled this monument to the strains the very anti-German "Rota" (Military Oath),[3] composed by the poet Maria Konopnicka (1842–1910):

We shall not yield our forbearers' land,
Nor see our language muted.
Our nation is Polish, and Polish our folk,
By Piasts constituted.
By cruel oppression we'll not be swayed!
May God so lend us aid.
We'll not be spat on by Teutons
Nor abandon our youth to the German!
We'll follow the call of the Golden Horn,
Under the Holy Spirit, our *Hetman.*
Our armed battalions shall lead the crusade.
May God so lend us aid.
By the very last drop of blood in our veins
Our souls will be secured,
Until in dust and ashes falls
The stormwind sown by the Prussian lord.
Our every home will form a stockade.
May God so lend us aid.

Despite such ideological displays of animosity, the Poles living in the German Empire continued to be modest in their political aspirations to the very end of the Great War. The recognition of the solid material benefits brought by the German nation-state was widespread. Combined with their hatred of Russia, it generated renewed loyalty to Prussia, which remained as strong as before. The Polish deputies to the Reichstag often voted in line with the government's wishes especially during the chancellorship of Caprivi (1890–1894). He granted the Polish-speaking population with some nominal concessions such as the possibility of giving private lessons in Polish.

Polish/Slavic-speaking Upper Silesians together with Poles and Polish-speakers from the Pomeranian, West Prussian, and Wielkopolska regiments marched through the Great War to the strains of "Preußens Gloria" with never a thought but to keep in step. They served on all fronts with distinction and there was never a hint of mutiny until the very end of the war. Only because of the vacuum left by the revolution in Berlin and the abdication of the Kaiser, the Poles of the Province of Posen were stirred into rebellion at the turn of 1918 and 1919. This took place at the instigation of Paderewski. On his way from Stettin (Szczecin) to Warsaw on December 26, 1918, he delivered a pro-independence speech in Posen (Davies, 1991: II 136–137; Ślusarek, 1996: 4).

The situation in Upper Silesia was markedly different. The influence of German and Polish nationalisms was not strong prior to 1871. Even after this date the concept of nation remained largely alien to the German- and Slavic-speaking local population who continued to ground their identity in the Catholic Church and their region, rather than in a nation. The Slavic-speaking Protestant minority in Upper Silesia[4] and the 120,000-strong group of their ethnically similar co-religionists in northeastern Lower Silesia followed this pattern. They then gradually aligned themselves with the German nation, repelled from emergent Polishdom by its strict association with Catholicism. The accession of these Protestant Slavic-speakers into the German nation was facilitated by the fusion of *Kleindeutsch* nationalism with Protestantism. By the same token the double barrier of faith and language barred the Catholic Slavic-speakers from embracing this nationalism. On top of that, attachment to one's locality and to the Prussian identity, symbolized by the Hohenzollern dynast, remained strong. This slowed down the inclusion of these Catholic Slavic-speakers into Germandom and left them immune to the few pro-Polish influences, which entered Upper Silesia mainly from Wielkopolska and, to a lesser degree, from Galicia and East Austrian Silesia.

The Upper Silesian Catholics' attachment to the ideals of religious universalism made their attitudes more congruent with Austria-Hungary's *Großdeutsch* concept of the German nation-state than with that of Prussia's/Germany's. The establishment of the German nation-state in 1871 proved to be an ideological shock to them. Bismarck set out on the daunting task of homogenizing Germany in accordance with the tenets of *Kleindeutsch* nationalism, steeped in German language and Protestantism. The center of the newly founded nation-state was conveniently Protestant. But West Prussia, western East Prussia, the Province of Posen, and Silesia, as well as southwestern and western Germany, remained strongly Catholic. In 1871 the German Empire's population consisted of 62.3 percent Protestants, 36.2 percent Catholics and 1.3 percent Jews (Anon., 1891: 816–817). In this initial phase of nation-state-building, the Catholic Church, with its pro-Austrian and universalistic leanings, presented itself as the primary enemy of *Kleindeutsch* nationalism. The process of vigorous nation-state-building quite understandably turned against this obstacle with the sweeping policies of the *Kulturkampf* aimed at the Catholic Church. In the end this policy proved to be futile. Cooperation between the German Catholic Church and the state had to be resumed, and there was almost no change in the confessional pattern. In 1880 it looked the same, with 62.6 percent Protestants, 35.9 percent Catholics and 1.2 percent Jews (Anon., 1891: 817).

The consolidating endeavors of the *Kulturkampf* were deeply felt in Silesia. In 1885, Catholics, numbering 2,156,578 (52.4 percent), prevailed, as opposed to Protestants, who accounted for 1,897,002 (46.1 percent)[5] (Michalkiewicz, 1976: 60). Silesian Catholics were concentrated mainly in Upper Silesia and the Glatz (Kłodzko) Margravate. Both these areas housed less than 10 percent Protestants. Due to the higher growth rate in the Oppeln Regency than in the rest of Silesia, the percentage of Silesia's Catholics grew to 56.7 percent (2,962,783) and Protestants fell to 42.1 percent (2,199,114) by 1910. In the Oppeln Regency there were 2,000,066 (90.6 percent) Catholics and 187,751 (8.5 percent) Protestants.

The figures for the Breslau Regency were 751,562 (40.8 percent) and 1,055,570 (57.3 percent), respectively, while for the Liegnitz Regency, 211,155 (18 percent) and 955,793 (81.2 percent) (Michalkiewicz, 1985: 58–59). Out of the 44,985 Jews constituting 0.8 percent of the Silesian population, 18,268 inhabited the Oppeln Regency, 23,161 the Breslau Regency and 3,556 the Liegnitz Regency. They amounted to 0.8 percent, 1.3 percent and 0.3 percent of the three regencies' populaces, respectively. Those included in the "others" rubric accounted for 19,080 persons in the entire province. This category was the least numerous in the Oppeln Regency (Michalkiewicz, 1985: 58).

Understandably, the brunt of the *Kulturkampf* measures was felt in the Oppeln Regency. Besides being staunchly Catholic this province also housed the majority of Silesia's Slavic-speakers. In 1861 the regency's German-speakers amounted to 36.4 percent of its population, whereas Polish/Slavic- and Czech/Slavic-speakers made up 59.1 percent and 4.5 percent, respectively (Michalkiewicz, 1976: 48). In 1890 the figures were 36.3 percent (572,281) German-speakers, 59.2 percent (934,601) Polish/Slavic-speakers and 3.8 percent (59,243) Czech/Slavic-speakers; in 1910 the figures were 39.2 percent (865,780), 53 percent (1,169,340) and 2.6 percent (57,347). The 1910 census also registered 88,802 (4 percent) bilingual Polish/German-speakers and 571 bilingual Czech/German-speakers.

On the other hand, in the Breslau and Liegnitz Regencies, German-speakers were clearly the dominant group. In 1890 they amounted to 94.6 percent (1,512,397) in the former regency and 96.2 percent (1,007,184) in the latter one. In 1910 these figures were 94.5 percent (1,739,299) and 95.6 percent (1,124,284), respectively. In 1890 the Slavic populace of the Breslau Regency included 54,038 (3.4 percent) Polish/Slavic-speakers and 9,704 (0.6 percent) Czech/Slavic-speakers. The 1910 census-takers reported 51,931 (2.8 percent) Polish/Slavic-speakers and 11,564 (0.6 percent) bilingual Polish/German-speakers. In 1890 the Liegnitz Regency housed 27,255 (2.6 percent) Sorbian-speakers, and in 1910 it housed 26,576 (2.3 percent) Sorbian-speakers, as well as 1,178 bilingual Sorbian/German-speakers and 1,739 (0.1 percent) bilingual Polish/German-speakers.

In 1890, in the context of the entire Province of Silesia, the Polish/Slavic-speakers added up to 994,961 (23.6 percent of the whole population), Czech/Slavic-speakers to 70,333 (1.7 percent), Sorbian-speakers to 27,320 (0.6 percent), and bilingual Polish/German-speakers to 83,333 (1.8 percent), while German-speakers numbered 3,091,862 (73.2 percent). In 1910 the number of Polish/Slavic-speakers grew to 1,236,328 (23.7 percent), Czech/Slavic-speakers relatively decreased to 71,436 (1.4 percent), Sorbian-speakers went down to 26,650 (0.5 percent), and the number of bilingual Polish/German-speakers increased to 102,194 (2 percent).

In 1905 the categories of bilingual Sorbian/German- and Czech/German-speakers were introduced. In the 1910 census they added up to 2,117 and 1,162, respectively. Lastly, Silesia's German-speaking population shrank most decisively, by 1.8 percent to 3,729,363 (71.4 percent). In considering the Jewish populace, it is important to remember that thanks to the concurrent processes of emancipation and the Haskalah (Jewish Enlightenment), they largely assimilated into mainstream German life. The only exception was religion, which still distinguished Jews from Germans. In 1890 they numbered 48,003 (1.1 percent) in all of Silesia, and in 1910 44,985 (0.9 percent). Silesian Jews were concentrated in and around Breslau and in Upper Silesia. In 1890 there were 22,232 (1.4 percent) of them in the Breslau Regency, 21,147 (1.3 percent) in the Oppeln Regency and only 4,624 (0.4 percent) in the Liegnitz Regency. In 1910 the numbers were: 23,161 (1.3 percent), 18,268 (0.9 percent) and 3,556 (0.3 percent), respectively (Kokot, 1973: 77; Michalkiewicz, 1985: 52).

The *Kulturkampf* commenced immediately after the founding of the German Empire, followed by the liquidation of the Catholic Department in the Prussian Ministry of Religious Affairs (Kultusministerium). Bismarck issued the famous ordinance that prescribed up to two years in prison for any clergyman who used his church function to comment on matters of the state. In 1872 the Silesian Protestant Adalbert Falk (1827–1900) was nominated to be the Prussian minister of religious affairs. In that same year the Jesuits and similar orders were banished from the German Empire. This move considerably weakened the Catholic Church's hold on the educational system in the empire. In 1873 the bubble of the speculative boom of the *Gründerzeit* (founders' years) burst. The crash stimulated a revival of anti-Semitism and deepened suspicion toward the Catholic Church that was considered to be supportive of Polish nationalism.

The ensuing frantic search for a scapegoat soon spawned the concept of the "enemy within," supposedly acting in line with external foes of the German Empire. This tension facilitated the passing of a comprehensive portfolio of May Laws in 1873, amounting to a declaration of war on the Catholic Church. Overnight the state gained the right to control all church nominations and Catholic seminaries. The educational system, deemed a significant instrument of nation-building, was also wrenched away from the Catholic Church. In 1875 the Reichstag passed an act on compulsory civil marriages. As a consequence, the task of registering marriages, births and deaths shifted to the hands of the state. Without fulfilling this function, the state would not have been able to build an effective homogenous bureaucratic apparatus for the control of the population (Bahlcke, 1996: 103; Fischer-Wollpert, 1990: 299–300; Fulbrook, 1990: 131–133; Michalkiewicz, 1976: 302; Scheuermann, 1994: 292).

The *Kulturkampf* led to serious disorganization of the Catholic Church in the German Empire. In 1878 one-third of the dioceses had to function without bishops (Fischer-Wollpert, 1990: 300). In 1875, the harassed Breslau Bishop Heinrich Förster (1799–1881) had to flee to the Austrian Silesian part of his diocese, where he stayed until his demise. In 1876 the authorities closed the Breslau seminary[6] and its students had to continue their theological education in Austria-Hungary (Pater, 1996a: 103–104; Hepa, 1994: 6–7). As a result, more than one-quarter of the Silesian parishes were deprived of their priests and pastoral services (Neubach, 1995: 184).

With this situation the Silesian Catholics were not well-disposed to the new state, especially in Upper Silesia, where language-homogenizing policies accompanied the *Kulturkampf*. The 1872 ordinances of the administrations of the Oppeln and Breslau regencies removed from elementary schools all other languages than German, that is, standard Polish and Czech/Moravian in the south of the Ratibor county. These languages functioned as auxiliary ones in the lowest grades and continued to be used during religious instruction up to 1875, when new ordinances imposed German as the sole medium of instruction in all the schools (Michalkiewicz, 1976: 304; Plaček, 1996a: 8).

Förster and the Catholic hierarchy vehemently opposed the implementation of these decisions in the Oppeln Regency. The majority of Polish/Slavic- and Czech/Slavic-speakers of the Breslau Regency were Protestants, so the Catholic Church was not very interested in them. To counter the effects of the *Kulturkampf* in education, the Catholic hierarchy supported the development of the extramural system of teaching religion in Slavic languages, but it would become fully operational only in the 1880s (Pater, 1993: 21). The Catholic Church also appealed to parents to teach their children how to read and write in their respective languages. The Catholic Church believed that the spread of the German language would facilitate expansion of Protestantism in traditionally Catholic Upper Silesia. In this manner the clash between Catholic universalism and German nationalism unwittingly hinged on the language cleavage, which spawned the self-reinforcing stereotype of the "Catholic Pole" and "Protestant German" (Michalkiewicz, 1976: 305, 478; Pater, 1993: 21; Pater, 1996a: 104).

The *Kulturkampf* policies did not inspire any active political opposition on the part of the Slavic/Polish-speaking Upper Silesian Catholics, often disparagingly denounced as the "tool of the clergy" and "agents of Rome" (Schofer, 1974: 154; Wanatowicz, 1992: 42). But soon they formed the loyal electorate of the Zentrum Party, which strove to protect the Catholic Church and its universalistic principles against the onslaught of German nationalism. The Silesian branch of this party was organized by one of the biggest Upper Silesian land owners as well as a captain of industry and aristocrat, namely Count Franz von Ballestrem (1834–1910). Thanks to his efforts and to the support of the Upper Silesian Catholics, in 1881 all twelve Upper Silesian constituencies were represented in the Reichstag by Zentrum deputies. In this year the party also gained four mandates out of the twelve in the Breslau Regency. As a result the Zentrum held the relative majority in Silesia with a total of fifteen deputies, surpassing the influence of the Fortschrittspartei (Progressive Party) with thirteen mandates, the conservative parties with three mandates, and the Reichspartei (Imperial Party) with three mandates.

The Zentrum had maintained relative dominance in Silesia since 1878. The situation looked different in the case of the Prussian Landtag, where conservative deputies dominated with thirty mandates over the Zentrum's twenty mandates in 1888. But the latter party clearly held sway in the Oppeln Regency with twenty mandates out of twenty-one. In sum the Zentrum was a party to be reckoned with, as it had enjoyed a relative majority in the 397-seat Reichstag since 1878. In 1888 it had 101 deputies—well ahead of the conservatives with 77 seats—but rivaled by the national liberals, whose number of deputies fluctuated from 150 in 1874, to 45 in 1881, and to 100 in 1888. The Zentrum remained alternately the first- or second-largest party in the Reichstag until the last elections of 1912 (Anon., 1889m: 688; Bahlcke, 1996: 103; Czapliński, 1990: 536; Fuchs, 1994: 598; Gross, 1995: 58; Michalkiewicz, 1976: 316–317).

The social and cultural interests of the Upper Silesian population were well served by the Zentrum. Beginning in 1879 the party was instrumental in bringing about the dismantling of the *Kulturkampf* policies (Wanatowicz, 1992: 43). But in the context of the Junkers' (landed gentry) domination over German political life (Fulbrook, 1990: 144), later polarization of politics was inescapable in the Oppeln Regency. Upper Silesia was the part of Germany where feudal and industrial relations tightly intertwined, which opened an extremely deep social cleavage. For instance, 51 percent (5,255 sq km) of the arable land in the Oppeln Regency belonged to a handful of agricultural-industrial magnates (Neubach, 1995: 185). Seven of them alone shared as much as 26.4 percent (2,720 sq km) of this land (Weber, 1913: 21).

In the meantime, the Catholic Slavic/Polish-speakers of Upper Silesia stuck fast to the Zentrum and the Catholic Church as the sole guarantors of their traditional way of life. This is easy to understand in light of the change in the state's policies, which were incomprehensible to these Catholic Slavic/Polish-speakers. They could not understand why Prussia's success at building the German Empire should deprive them of religious service and do away with bilingualism in education and social life. The elimination of standard Polish and the Moravian language from elementary schools was accompanied by a string of similar decisions in other fields. In 1871 the Higher Mining Office forbade hiring supervisors who spoke only Polish (Schofer, 1974: 153). Five years later German became the only language of government and administrative offices. In 1886 it was forbidden to employ clerks who spoke Polish or Czech/Moravian only, whereas those who had joined the civil service earlier and had not acquired a good command of German were dismissed (Klein, 1972: 11–12).

In order to offset the adverse effects of the *Kulturkampf* in Upper Silesia, the

Catholic Church, together with the Zentrum, entered a symbiosis with the Polish-language Catholic press. The most important title was Miarka's *Katolik*. This "triple alliance" actively supported the development of Catholic organizations. The organizations and the press were responsible for spreading literacy in standard Polish and Moravian. They also assisted in the educational endeavors of the church and helped parents of non-German-speaking children. These adults formed an important self-help basis, because prior to 1872 many had acquired literacy in standard Polish and Moravian at Prussia's bilingual elementary schools (Michalkiewicz, 1976: 306–308). Already in 1872 there were 26 various Catholic organizations in Upper Silesia, and two years later 94 with 11,065 regular and 942 honorary members, according to hasty estimates of the Oppeln Regency's authorities, who seem not to have included all of them. It is impossible to assess how many of the members were Polish/Slavic-speakers and how many German-speakers or bilinguals. At that time thinking along national/ethnic lines was still unusual in this region.

It was a conflict between Catholic universalism and *Kleindeutsch* nationalism that produced this broad Catholic social movement, *not* any national conflict (Pater, 1993: 77–79). Obviously, with standard Polish and Moravian having been eliminated from education and administration, the sphere of their use was transferred to many of the organizations that the Catholic Church and the Zentrum co-established for this purpose. Thus the party, wishing to remain in close rapport with its Polish/Slavic-speaking electorate, in 1879 supported, from among its ten Reichstag and seventeen Landtag deputies from the Oppeln Regency, at least eight who had a reasonable command of Polish (Hytrek, 1996 [1879]: 64; Michalkiewicz, 1976: 316–317). One of them was the prelate and Polish prince Edmund Wiktor Radziwiłł from Posen. Although he followed the Zentrum's line of not joining the Reichstag's Polish Circle, which grouped Polish deputies from the Province of Posen, he did stress the common origins of the Polish/Slavic-speaking Upper Silesians and the Poles of Wielkopolska (Wanatowicz, 1992: 40).

The model of mobilizing the population through political rallies, popular in Bohemia, Moravia and Austrian Silesia, was transplanted to Upper Silesia. These rallies involved several thousand peasants and attracted participants from Galicia and Wielkopolska (Hytrek, 1996 [1879]: 38–39). Despite the tightening of border controls Upper Silesians, though in smaller numbers, continued to go on pilgrimages to Częstochowa in Congress Poland and especially Cracow in Galicia. For example, in 1879, 200 of them visited the tomb of St. Stanisław in Cracow (Pater, 1993: 107). The reinvigoration of Polish-language social life brought about by the *Kulturkampf* was bolstered by Polish periodicals from Wielkopolska, as well as Polish and Czech publications from Austrian Silesia (Hytrek, 1996 [1879]: 36).

Soon *Katolik* took over their role. Its runs grew steadily from 4,000 in 1874 to 24,000 in 1911 (Gröschel, 1993: 144), rivaling the largest Silesian newspaper in German, *Schlesische Zeitung* (Silesian Newspaper), which had runs of 12,742 in

1872 and of 18,089 in 1906 (Fuchs, 1994: 594). *Katolik* also got involved in the activity of spreading education in Polish by publishing, between 1876 and 1880, the educational weekly *Monika* (Monica), to which nearly 2,000 readers subscribed (Gröschel, 1993: 226–227).

The *Kulturkampf* caused the emergence of a symbiosis between political Catholicism and the largely educational-devotional Polish-language movement in Upper Silesia. This alliance of convenience endangered the process of German nation-state-building with the prospect of giving rise to a full-fledged Polish national movement, as had already happened in the Province of Posen. To forestall this possibility, the authorities tried to discourage Miarka and harassed him with no less than sixteen trials between 1869 and 1882 (Michalkiewicz, 1976: 309). He was forced to resign from the editorial board of *Katolik* and moved to Teschen, where he died in 1882 (Brożek, 1995: 61). Similar trials were staged against Miarka's collaborators and priests who engaged too much in this Polish-language movement and, through their activities, violated the *Kulturkampf* laws (Pater, 1996b: 333).

The authorities also supported the publication of the bilingual weeklies *Prawda/Wahrheit* (Truth, 1871–1877) and *Szlązak/Schlesier* (The Silesian, 1872–1880). The former was an organ of the Polish/Slavic-speaking Old Catholics in Upper Silesia, while the latter propagated the idea of ethnic and regional difference between the Szlonzoks and Wielkopolska's Poles. Both these periodicals advocated the government's official line. Hence, the Upper Silesian populace distrusted them, and these weeklies went defunct (Glensk, 1992: 18; Gröschel, 1993: 115, 225–226; Michalkiewicz, 1976: 309–310).

Interestingly, some clergymen, having noticed that Polish agitators from Wielkopolska had to switch to German in order to communicate with Upper Silesians speaking in their Slavic-based creole (Osborne, 1921: 47), embarked on the task of codifying an Upper Silesian language on this basis. Such a language could have allowed the Catholic Church to check the swelling flow of publications in standard Polish from Wielkopolska. They realized only too well that Moravian publications printed in Gothic type effectively stemmed the influx of any books and periodicals in standard Czech to southern Upper Silesia. The Silesian language printed in the same Gothic type would have probably had a similar effect of insulating the Szlonzoks from publications in standard Polish. However, the project of codifying the Silesian language never took off in earnest (Wanatowicz, 1992: 51).

The fate of the aforementioned bilingual periodicals would also befall the biweekly *Gazeta Górnoszląska* (Upper Silesian Newspaper, 1874–1886). Father Franciszek Przyniczyński (1844–1896) from Wielkopolska established it with the financial support from the Cracow Bishop Albin Dunajewski. They wished to weaken the position of *Katolik* in order to transplant the ideas of the Posen Polish movement to Upper Silesia. They even started the abortive monthly *Nowy Katolik*

(New Catholic, 1883). In both their newspapers they agitated for the Polish national movement and maintained that the Polish/Slavic-speakers of Upper Silesia were part of the Polish nation. The goal of Przyniczyński and Dunajewski was to merge the Upper Silesian Polish-language movement with the straightforward Wielkopolska Polish national movement.

The Polish nationalist rhetoric, with its anti-Zentrum overtones, was alien to Upper Silesian readers. Despite Przyniczyński's attempts, his weekly did not receive the Catholic Church's approval from Bishop Förster, as *Katolik* had. Furthermore, Przyniczyński's 1881 campaign for Polish-language candidates to the Reichstag who would not be Zentrum members failed utterly (Glensk, 1992: 19; Gröschel, 1993: 38–39; Pater, 1996b: 333). Przyniczyński and his brother, who helped him with managing the two periodicals, failed to take into account several facts. They directed their nationalist message to the Upper Silesian Polish-language middle class, but at that time there was none. Upgrading one's social status was possible only through the German language and assimilation with the German nation-in-making (Reiner, 1966: 117).

Most Upper Silesian priests, who held the greatest influence over the Polish/Slavic-speaking Upper Silesians, did not involve themselves in either the Polish or German national movements. Simultaneously, they discouraged any national feeling among their parishioners. The priests espoused Catholic universalism and spoke strongly against nationalism. They feared that this ideology could split their flocks along ethnic/national lines and draw them away from the fold of the Catholic Church (Pater, 1993: 121).

On the other hand, with the advance of the press and education, Upper Silesia's Polish/Slavic-speakers and the Wilekopolska Poles became consciously aware of one another. They chose, however, not to identify themselves as belonging to the same ethnic or national group. This is clearly evident in the fact that the use of the ethnonym "Pole" was considered pejorative by the Upper Silesian if applied to him (Wanatowicz, 1992: 76). The Polish-speakers of Wielkopolska retorted by speaking contemptuously of Polish/Slavic-speaking Upper Silesians as "Odraks" (literally, inhabitants of the lands along the banks of the Oder River) (Osborne, 1921: 50–51).

The tenuous links between Upper Silesia and Galicia, the Province of Posen, and even Congress Poland arose thanks to pilgrimages, a few personal contacts between Polish national activists, and the dealings of the intra-Catholic Church administration. The active involvement of Wielkopolska's Polish nationalists gradually altered the situation and embedded Silesia in the Polish national network. The Przyniczyński brothers sent out the first feelers through their newspapers. During the great 1879 famine Miarka organized the Komitet Głodowy (Hunger Committee), which appealed for aid from the Province of Posen, Galicia, Congress Poland,

and Polish organizations in the United States. Miarka illegally used the remaining resources for financing the distribution of Polish-language periodicals (Brożek, 1995: 61–62; Snoch, 1991: 89).

After the 1881 failure to field local non-Zentrum Polish candidates in the Reichstag elections, some Polish national groups, who agreed with the Przyniczyńskis' thesis that the Polish/Slavic-speaking Upper Silesians were part of the postulated Polish nation, could not help noticing that there was no clear-cut Polish national movement in Upper Silesia. These groups decided that the situation would change only with the immigration of Polish national activists, intelligentsia and middle class from Wielkopolska (Wanatowicz, 1992: 48). Many of them arrived in Silesia during the 1880s and 1890s (Glensk, 1995: 90), but most came because of economic, not ideological, reasons. In 1907 they constituted the largest group of "immigrants" in Silesia, amounting to 58,795 persons. Obviously they were internal migrants within the German borders. But the term "immigrant" prevented commonality with the German nation, which was in line with the thinking of Polish and German nationalists.

In the period of the intensified *Ostflucht*, Germans were not attracted to Upper Silesia. In their eyes this region remained somewhat alien, if not foreign, because of bilingualism. Moreover, the standard of living and wage levels were lower in Upper Silesia than in central and western Germany. However, what was linguistically and culturally alien to Germans was familiar to the Polish-speaking inhabitants of the Province of Posen. It was easier for them to adapt to the living conditions in Upper Silesia than for those in the homogenously German-speaking areas. Out of the Wielkopolska "immigrants," 7,048 worked in the civil service or practiced their professions (Michalkiewicz, 1985: 43). But as few as 200 of those who moved to Upper Silesia between 1885 and 1914 could be classified as intelligentsia, that is, doctors, lawyers, journalists, or university graduates (Wanatowicz, 1992: 74). The 200 members of Wielkopolska's Polish middle class and intelligentsia who settled in Upper Silesia facilitated the spread of the so-called *Großpolnisch* agitation.

The German adjective *großpolnisch* is ambiguous. Its basic meaning is "of the region of Wielkopolska," which translates as *Großpolen* in German or "Great(er) Poland" in English. The other meaning of the adjective *großpolnisch* is "All-Polish." It alludes to the *Wszechpolski* (All-Polish) movement, which emerged in the 1890s and was just one of the numerous forms of early Polish ethnic nationalism. This movement gained its peculiar name due to its association with the Galician periodical *Przegląd Wszechpolski* (All-Polish Review, 1895–1905). Dmowski founded the publication in order to popularize Polish nationalism among the young members and sympathizers of the largely elitist Liga Narodowa. In popular usage, the adjective *großpolnisch* denoted the Polish national movement from Wielkopolska (Osborne, 1921: 49; Tobiasz, 1947: 25; Wanatowicz, 1992: 137).

The most visible Polish influence arrived in Upper Silesia from the Province of Posen in the form of small libraries. They were established by the Towarzystwo Czytelni Ludowych (TCL, Society for Popular Reading-Rooms), which had come into being in 1880 (Davies, 1991: II xxii). In 1887 there were thirty such libraries in Upper Silesia and two in Lower Silesia (Jakóbczyk, 1989: 30). Altogether, in combination with local initiatives, 175 Polish-language libraries were founded in 166 Upper Silesian localities between 1879 and 1893. On average, each library housed 300–400 volumes. In the same period, 214 Polish national and Polish-language Catholic organizations, active in the economic, social, and cultural fields, came into being in about 100 localities. They formed a tentative Polish-language environment, which generated audiences for 932 Polish-language amateur theatrical productions between 1870 and 1900 and customers for Polish cooperative shops, of which there were 97 between 1885 and 1902 (Michalkiewicz, 1976: 345, 347–348; Mykita-Glensk, 1988: 18).

Now the question arises as to how large this potential Polish national movement was in numerical terms. According to Polish estimates 13,622 members belonged to 64 clearly pro-Polish organizations in 1898 (Figowa, 1966: 15). However, one should bear it in mind that during the 1880s and even during the 1890s it was still rather difficult to decide which organization was pro-Polish and which pro-German. Political Catholicism discouraged splitting the faithful along ethnic or national lines. This non-national orientation, encouraged by the Catholic Church, began to wane only after the German branch of the church under Bishop Kopp's leadership had managed to patch up its relations with the state between 1885 and 1887. Berlin could no longer disregard the Zentrum's political clout. Priest teachers had started returning to schools as early as 1876, and the process continued until 1890 (Michalkiewicz, 1976: 89, 480–481).

With the *Kulturkampf* a thing of the past, the Catholic Church and the Zentrum ceased to support the cause of Polish-language education so vociferously. Obviously, they did not refrain from using Polish during religious instruction and continued to point out the advantages of bilingualism. The church and the Zentrum's members also emphasized the fact that in Upper Silesia, as elsewhere in the German Empire, one could succeed in life only through acquiring a good working command of the German language (Wanatowicz, 1992: 44). Father Norbert Bonczyk (Boncek, Bontzek, 1837–1893), who strove to write Upper Silesia into the imagined past of the Polish nation with his epic poem *Góra Chełmska*[7] (Chełm Mountain, 1886), stated at an 1881 Catholic rally in Beuthen that "on two tongues man stands more firmly" (Pater, 1993: 121, 166). It seems that today's Polish interpretation of his works exclusively from the national point of view is not fully justified. His oeuvre also includes two collections of poems and a nonfiction book in German. Thus Bonczyk was a bilingual Catholic writer of universalistic persuasion, as were the majority of his Upper Silesian colleagues (Mandziuk, 1996: 44).

The inroads made by the Polish national movement in Upper Silesia were accompanied by the tentative idea of including Upper Silesia in a would-be Polish nation-state on the grounds of a proposed ethnic unity of the Polish/Slavic-speaking Upper Silesians with the rest of the Polish-speakers. This idea first appeared in Wielkopolska and was spread to Upper Silesia by Father Przyniczyński. In 1886 the same idea appeared in the Galician press (Kulak, 1990: 123) and a year later in Congress Poland (Suleja, 1992: 44; Wanatowicz, 1992: 59). By the end of the nineteenth century, Polish nationalists had started anachronistically thinking about Upper Silesia as an integral part of the Prussian partition zone. In this way they hoped to fortify the economic potential of a would-be Polish nation-state and to provide a strategic bridge that would conveniently connect Wielkopolska with Galicia (Wanatowicz, 1992: 62, 64). Polish nationalists were given an additional tool for including Upper Silesia in the mental picture of Poland in the form of the first Polish history of Silesia, *Dzieje Ślązka* (A History of Silesia, 1897), written by the scholar Feliks Koneczny (1862–1949), a professor from the Jagiellonian University, Cracow (Dyba, 1993: 33–34; Lubos, 1974: 524).

The changing role of Upper Silesia and its inhabitants in the plans of Polish nationalists, coupled with the spread of Polish-language organizations and the press in this region and with the statistically visualized and created *Ostflucht,* amounted to a national danger in the eyes of German politicians. The authorities decided to counteract this trend so as to ensure safety for the further construction of the German nation-state. School absenteeism among Slavic-speaking schoolchildren in Upper Silesia, which had increased after the commencement of the *Kulturkampf* (Michalkiewicz, 1976: 475), was to be curbed in line with the 1886 ordinance (Lis, 1993: 94). Another decision issued in the same year liquidated all the Polish/Slavic-language student organizations in Breslau, namely the Towarzystwo Literacko-Słowiańskie (1836–1886) and the Towarzystwo Górnoślązaków (1880–1886) (Michalkiewicz, 1976: 349–353; Świerc, 1964: 123). In the mid-1880s Kopp appealed for more extensive use of the German language in church and limited the use of standard Polish and Moravian in religious instruction (Michalkiewicz, 1976: 329, 480–481). Since 1894 this Breslau bishop had campaigned against Polish nationalism but advocated teaching Polish among Upper Silesians and German-speaking clergymen, doctors, and lawyers who, in the course of their daily business, interacted with Polish/Slavic-speakers (Galos, 1992: 57).

In 1891, in accordance with the decision of the Breslau Consistory, the weekly *Nowiny Szląskie* (Silesian News, 1884–1891)—the only periodical for the Polish/Slavic-speaking Protestants—was closed down. This weekly, like the majority of other Protestant publications for Polish/Slavic-speaking Silesians, was published in Gothic type, which was unambiguously associated with Germandom. After World

War II Polish settlers and expellees who found such publications in their new homes disposed of them, deeming them German. The closing of *Nowiny Szląskie* ensured the speedy assimilation of the Polish/Slavic-speaking Protestants into Germandom, to which they felt more affinity because of their confession than to Polishdom, which was steeped in Catholicism (Gröschel, 1993: 322; Michalkiewicz, 1985: 321; Szczepankiewicz-Battek, 1996: 10). In 1898 a circular letter was issued that obliged civil servants to support Germandom (Klein, 1972: 12).

To the official measures aimed at counteracting Polish nationalism, some historians also add Germanization of Slavic names and surnames in Upper Silesia. This process started in the 1860s and intensified after 1871. It is, however, an anachronistic interpretation of the past, as the process was not an orchestrated action. It came about due to the influx of German-speaking civil servants, who started arriving in Upper Silesia in large numbers in order to build the bureaucratic apparatus of the nation-state and to serve the growing industrial basin. They usually did not know Polish or Czech, so while beginning to institute the bureaucratic procedures that affected everybody, these civil servants had to write down names of Upper Silesians. They did so using German spelling, and they resorted to translating unpronounceable (to a German-speaker) Slavic names into German. The alterations can be classified as:

a. phonetic, brought about by the use of German spelling (*Kołoczek* > *Kolotzek*);
b. caused by translation (*Kowol* > *Schmidt* [Smith]); and
c. demanded by German usage.

German and English employ one form of surname for man and woman, unlike Slavic languages, which require different masculine and feminine forms of the same surname (for instance, m. *Markowski*, f. *Markowska*). In accordance with the German orthographic tradition, usually the masculine form (*Markowski*) was accepted both for man and woman in Upper Silesia (Jarczak, 1996: 12).

The Upper Silesians affected by this practice, hardly ever being fully literate in standard Polish and usually knowing better how to read and write in German, more often than not readily used the formalized written forms of their names as proposed or imposed by the civil servants (Jarczak, 1996: 12). One may even surmise that many an Upper Silesian, speaking the Upper Silesian Slavic-Germanic creole as his mother tongue but writing in German rather than in Polish, would have found the Polish spelling of his surname awkward.

The provision of more financial resources for Protestant schools than Catholic ones in Upper Silesia seems to have constituted another instrument of harassment that emanated from the atmosphere of the *Kulturkampf* rather than from a conscious effort to contain the Polish-language movement (Schofer, 1974: 153). However, the German action most decried by Polish nationalists were the

1885–1887 expulsions of alien Polish-speakers and Jews originally from Congress Poland and Galicia. Polish nationalist historians made these expulsions the very symbol of the struggle between Germandom and Polishdom. Leaving aside the rhetoric, it seems that what moved the authorities to take such an action was a fear of socialist or revolutionary influences coming from Russia as well as the need to deal with the cases of foreign residents whose residential status was incongruent with German law. The German Empire's approach to immigrants simultaneously was homogenized and produced a unified legal framework for the nation-state that clearly drew the line between citizens and unwanted aliens. At present the very same concept, together with the right to expel unwanted aliens, is employed by a majority of states worldwide. In sum, 25,914 aliens were expelled from the eastern provinces of Germany, but 10,162 were allowed to stay. Another 6,624 were expelled from Silesia and 5,758 from the Oppeln Regency, whereas 2,389 were permitted to remain in the province, including 1,975 in Upper Silesia (Brożek, 1863: 28, 37; Lis, 1993: 93; Rogall, 1993: 70).

The antisocialist laws instituted by Bismarck in 1878 were to eliminate from politics the *Reichsfeinde* (enemies of the empire), that is, the Sozialdemokratische Partei Deutschlands (SPD, German Social Democratic Party). The party's attraction had dramatically increased since its inception three years earlier, which could unbalance the established shape of the political forces in the empire. The authorities wished to prevent this, as they saw any political instability as a threat to the process of German nation-state-building that had just begun. The antisocialist measures were annulled only after Bismarck's resignation in 1890. Prior to that time these laws had constituted an additional platform of rapprochement between the state and the Catholic Church, because the church did not sympathize with any organized worker movements until the publication of the groundbreaking encyclical *Rerum novarum* in 1891 (Fulbrook, 1990: 133–134).

Neither antisocialist measures nor more stringent immigration regulations could curb the development of the Polish national movement, which was largely transplanted to Upper Silesia from outside. Nobody wanted to introduce more radical steps to this end, because they would have had to breach the constitution. As such they would undoubtedly have shattered the underlying framework of the *Rechtstaat,* which functioned as the powerful legitimizing basis for the German nation-state. Hence the limits imposed on Polish-language social life, together with Bismarck's addresses emphasizing the need for homogeneity of the citizenry within the empire's borders, solidified the opposition of the few Polish nationalist activists. They steeled themselves for the task of instilling Polish national identification among Upper Silesians (Machray, 1945: 26).

In 1889 Adam Napieralski (1861–1928), from the Province of Posen, arrived in Beuthen to take up the position of the editor of *Katolik.* He continued the weekly's universalistic line, rightly convinced that the Polish/Slavic-speaking Upper Silesians did not consider themselves Poles as some Polish activists hoped (for instance, Przyniczyński). But Napieralski gradually broadened the organizational framework of the Polish-language movement, which later would be utilized by more radical Polish nationalists. He established the first two Polish credit banks in Upper Silesia in 1895 and 1900 (Snoch, 1991: 95). In this manner Napieralski introduced the basic tenets of *Wirtschaftskampf*, developed by Polish activists in the Province of Posen.

The clearly Polish nationalist streak of activism that came into being in Upper Silesia is connected to two Wielkopolska journalists, Jan Karol Maćkowski (1865–1915) and Bronisław Koraszewski (1864–1924). In 1890 the latter founded *Gazeta Opolska* (Opole [Oppeln] Newspaper, 1890–1923) with financial resources he had received from the Liga Polska. A year later Maćkowski probably received a subsidy from the Upper Silesian medical doctor and Polish national activist Józef Rostek (1859–1929) to purchase *Nowiny Raciborskie* (Racibórz News, 1889–1921) and turn it into a Polish national newspaper similar to Koraszewski's *Gazeta Opolska*. Interestingly, Rostek was one of the very few Polish-speaking Upper Silesians who attended a university and graduated from a department other than that of theology. Even more surprisingly, in the course of his university education and professional life he did not take on a German national identity. On the contrary, he became a Polish national activist, and in 1880 he established the Towarzystwo Polskich Górnoślązaków in Breslau (Gröschel, 1993: 197–198, 238; Snoch, 1991: 67, 87, 122; Tobiasz, 1947: 22).

The relaxed attitude toward the Polish movement in Germany during Leo von Caprivi's chancellorship (1890–1894) allowed for the establishment of new organizations. The Towarzystwo Naukowe Akademików Górnoślązaków (Scientific Society of Upper Silesian Students, 1892–1899) and the Kółko Polskie (Polish Circle, 1895–1906) of theological students sprang up in Breslau (Michalkiewicz, 1985: 358–359). More radical views were brought to the academic center in 1894 with the founding of the local Sokół organization, which drew on the experience and resources of similar gymnastic-nationalist organizations already existing in the Province of Posen. A year later one Posen activist established another Sokół branch in Beuthen. New branches proliferated, and in 1901 they were united as the Sixth (Silesian) Group of the Związek Sokołów Polskich w Państwie Niemieckim (Union of Polish Sokół Organizations in the State of Germany). Between 1894 and 1914 there were about 30 Silesian Sokół branches in existence (Michalkiewicz, 1985: 346–348; Ponczek, 1987: 3–5). This organization paved the way for various radical nationalist groups inspired by the Liga Narodowa and the Zet. The Zet's Breslau branch was launched in 1895. Other Polish national organizations proliferated in Silesia at the turn of the twentieth century, but they usually stuck to Breslau

(Michalkiewicz, 1985: 358; Świerc, 1964: 123; Tobiasz, 1947: 23). Their members, more often than not students, were responsible for spreading the message of Polish nationalism in Upper Silesia (Lis, 1993: 96).

The picture would not be complete without mentioning that Polish associations of singers had existed in Upper Silesia since 1883. In time they were radicalized and became a pool of recruits for more openly Polish nationalist organizations. This trend solidified after the 1910 unification of these associations under the umbrella organization of the Związek Śląskich Kół Śpiewaczych (Union of the Silesian Circles of Singers) (Hanke, 1997: 66; Michalkiewicz, 1985: 342–343). Polish women's organizations joined the national race beginning in 1900. Already in 1907 no fewer than 2,000 Upper Silesian women participated in the congress of the women's periodical *Przodownica* (Female Leader) in Cracow (Michalkiewicz, 1985: 348–350).

In the 1890s hundreds and even thousands of Upper Silesians went on pilgrimages to Cracow, and thanks to this Upper Silesian-Galician link, 74 Upper Silesian priests received their education in this city between 1892 and 1913 (Kwiatek, 1992: 80–82, 90). More nationally minded Upper Silesian activists also participated in Polish national anniversaries celebrated in Cracow—for instance, in the transfer of the remains of the greatest national Polish poet, Adam Mickiewicz (1798–1855), to the Wawel Royal Castle (1890); in the centenary of the Kościuszko Insurrection (1894); and in the five hundredth anniversary of the founding of the Jagiellonian University (1900) (Wanatowicz, 1992: 56).

These ties between Galicia and Upper Silesia developed in both directions. For instance, some participants of the January Uprising (1863–1864) fled from Russia to Romania, where they established their cultural center in Iași in 1866. It gathered significant capital and a library of 4,000 Polish-language volumes. Many of these insurrectionists left Romania for western Europe. In 1892, due to the rapid shrinking of the Polish community in Iași, this book collection and the financial resources were transferred to Beuthen. This made the city into the center of the Polish movement in Upper Silesia and gave rise to the Górnośląskie Towarzystwo Literackie (Upper Silesian Society of Literature). Not surprisingly, in such a friendly environment, this Polish library from Iași grew. In 1922, after the division of Upper Silesia, it became the core of the library of the Silesian autonomous Sejm in Katowice in the Polish section of Upper Silesia. In 1936 the library was transformed into the Silesian Public Library, and in 1952 into the Silesian Library. With its new imposing seat, opened in 1996, this library remains one of the most potent symbols of Polishdom in Upper Silesia (Anon., 1997: 4; Snoch, 1991: 11).

The unfolding of various links between Polish organizations from Galicia and Wielkopolska with Upper Silesia encouraged the establishment of more formal ties between Polish nationalist organizations and their fledgling counterparts in

Upper Silesia. For instance, after the annulment of the antisocialist laws in 1890, the SPD and its affiliated Towarzystwo Socjalistów Polskich (TSP, Society of Polish Socialists) became interested in Upper Silesia, where a significant strike had been staged a year earlier. Soon the TSP separated from the SPD. The TSP accepted the program of the Polska Partia Socjalistyczna (PPS, Polish Socialist Party, established in Paris in 1892) and cofounded the PPS Zaboru Pruskiego (PPSzp, PPS of the Prussian Partition Zone) in 1893. The PPSzp was active in the Province of Posen and Upper Silesia in line with the ethnic concept of Poland that included Upper Silesia. Moreover, the strength of the labor movement was so conspicuous in the Upper Silesian industrial basin that in 1901 the PPSzp's main press organ, *Gazeta Robotnicza* (Worker's Newspaper, 1891–1939), was moved from Berlin to Kattowitz (Davies, 1991: xx; Gröschel, 1993: 334; Lis, 1993: 94–95; Wanatowicz, 1992: 56, 65).

Other Polish political groupings did not share the PPSzp's rather unrestrained position that Upper Silesia was part of a future Polish nation-state. The Polish national conservatives stood on the ground of legalistic loyalty to the partition powers and opposed the inclusion of Upper Silesia in the schemes of Polish nationalism. These conservatives demanded the reestablishment of Poland-Lithuania in its pre-partition shape as the nation-state for the Polish nation. In 1872 the Wielkopolska conservatives stated that Silesia should exist for itself and not for the Polish nationalist cause (Wanatowicz, 1992: 71–72). They were afraid that Polish national agitation would contribute to establishing a strong socialist movement in Upper Silesia that would divert resources and attention from the national goal to worker internationalism propagated by socialists. The development they feared did occur at the turn of the century. So in 1901 the Polish Circle at the Reichstag strongly condemned Polish nationalist agitation in Upper Silesia, following the example set by the rector of the Jagiellonian University, Count Stanisław Tarnowski. At the 500th anniversary of the founding of this university (1900) he had refused to accept the coal bust of the Polish-Lithuanian King Władysław Jagiełło (reigned 1386–1434, the university's founder) from the hands of the Upper Silesian delegation (Wanatowicz, 1992: 69–70).

The lukewarm reception of the idea of Upper Silesia as part of a would-be Polish nation-state was caused by the fact that, from the historical point of view, this region had never been included in Poland-Lithuania. It was this state that Prussia, Russia, and the Habsburg Empire had partitioned in the second half of the eighteenth century and which the Polish national movement sought to restore. On the other hand, Polish nationalists were not sure if the Polish/Slavic-speaking Upper Silesians should be included in the postulated Polish nation on ethnic grounds. The Upper Silesian clergy quite accurately opined that their parishioners constituted a Polish/Slavic-speaking population of no national attachment. The

Zentrum modified this statement a little, claiming that they were Polish/Slavic-speaking Prussians, which largely reflected the thinking of the Polish/Slavic-speaking Upper Silesians about themselves (Wanatowicz, 1992: 110–111).

These opinions sounded like the words of Bismarck. In 1886 he said that the *Wasserpolnisches Volk*[8] were nationally indifferent. Later he commented that because of the local Polish language movement and the influence exerted by the Polish national movements, the *Wasserpolacken* were Polonized (Nicolai, 1930: 58–59). The effect of this process of Polonization of the Polish/Slavic-speaking Upper Silesians was quite optimistically assessed by Polish national sources. At the turn of the twentieth century they claimed that 20 percent of the Polish/Slavic-speaking Upper Silesians considered themselves to be Poles. More to the point was a conservative Polish statement in 1908 which held that only a handful of Polish/Slavic-speaking Upper Silesians identified themselves as Poles (Wanatowicz, 1992: 90, 123).

The Zentrum and the Catholic Church, which were still espousing universalistic views, could not remain neutral to the efforts aimed at establishing a Polish nationalist center in Upper Silesia on the basis of the Polish-language movement, which the party and the church had helped bring about themselves. Moreover, Kopp, having entered the Prussian governmental structures in the mid-1880s (Scheuermann, 1994: 832), paved the way for Zentrum politicians to obtain significant positions in the state. Von Ballestrem, the leader of the Silesian Zentrum, became the first Catholic vice-president of the Reichstag in 1890 (Gross, 1995: 58). Four years later the first Catholic, Prince Hermann von Hatzfeldt[9] (1848–1933), was nominated for the position of the *Oberpräsident* of the Province of Silesia (Kaczmarek, 1993: 19; Scheuermann, 1994: 521). In this situation the Silesian Catholic Church and the Zentrum could not compromise their position by supporting the Polish-language movement too vociferously, much less the local budding Polish national movement. Lending such support would have gone against the tenets of Catholic universalism and could have harmed the process of German nation-state-building.

In 1893 Kopp appealed to the kaiser for some concessions on Polish-language education, but to no avail. German nationalists strongly criticized him for this proposal. In 1902 the bishop opposed any transgressions on the part of the Deutscher Ostmarkenverein against the Catholic Church and the spiritual life of the faithful. Six years later, Kopp castigated the overtly anti-Polish laws that were issued after 1900. On the other hand, in 1890 the bishop recommended that the Silesian clergy use German in church life more often. As a member of the Austrian Silesian Landtag[10] he opposed giving official status to Czech and Polish in this crownland. In 1894 Kopp said that he aimed to sever any organizational ties between Upper Silesia and the historical partition lands of erstwhile Poland-Lithuania, but he had nothing against the Polish language in church life. In 1897 the bishop dissolved the pro-Polish Catholic Towarzystwo św. Alojzego (St. Aloysius Society)[11] and advised priests to resign from leadership positions in pro-Polish associations (Galos, 1992: 57; Galos, 1996: 190–191; Michalkiewicz, 1976: 481; Reiner, 1966: 113). Subsequently, the clergy remained staunchly universalistic and chose to display no national preferences. At the end of the nineteenth century only about 25 out of the 500 Upper Silesian priests were actively pro-Polish or entered the ranks of the Polish national movement in Upper Silesia (Tobiasz, 1947: 38).

This universalistic and pro-state attitude of the Catholic Church and the Zentrum displeased the radicalized Polish activists, and as a result the 1891 bilingual Zentrum/Catholic rally in Beuthen was the last in which a common position was adopted. In the 1893 elections to the Reichstag and the Prussian Landtag the rift appeared clearly when the Polish/Slavic-speaking Zentrum members put forward their own candidates against the wishes of the party's leadership. It was not a manifestation of support for Polish nationalism but of discontent with aristocratic candidates who did not fully represent the interests of the Polish/Slavic-speaking Upper Silesian peasants and workers. One candidate of the Polish/Slavic-speaking Zentrum faction was elected to the Landtag, and two more were successful in the 1894 and 1895 by-elections to the Reichstag. *Nowiny Raciborskie, Gazeta Opolska,* and even *Katolik* contributed to their success by campaigning for these candidates. This falling out between the Zentrum and the Polish faction made the party understand that it would lose its position in Upper Silesia without the full support of the Polish/Slavic-speaking Catholics grouped around *Katolik.* Consequently a compromise was worked out prior to 1897. Nevertheless, this could not prevent further bickering between these two groups at the close of the nineteenth century. However, Napieralski, the *Katolik* faction's[12] leader, noticed that in many constituencies Polish/Slavic-speaking Upper Silesians chose to vote for traditional German-speaking aristocratic candidates. This phenomenon cemented the increasingly uneasy alliance, which in the age of the intensifying nationalist Polish-German conflict survived well into the next century (Brożek, 1995: 62; Lis, 1993: 95–96; Michalkiewicz, 1985: 365–375; Wanatowicz, 1992: 70).

The rapprochement between the Zentrum and the *Katolik* faction did not please young radicals, who appeared among Upper Silesian Polish/Slavic-speaking students. They were influenced by Polish nationalist propaganda radiating from Wielkopolska and Galicia. Upper Silesians participated in Polish student meetings in Teschen (1899, 1909, 1910, 1912, 1913) and Cracow (1908), and they staged a similar meeting in Beuthen in 1911. The Liga Narodowa secured a significant influence among Polish/Polish-speaking students in Breslau after 1900 and established numerous organizations, usually affiliated with the Zet. In 1901 the Zet established the Polska Grupa Narodowa (Polish National Group), which in 1908 had 156 members: 87 from the Province of Posen, 37 from Silesia, 30 from Galicia and Congress Poland, and 2 from other states. The Polish nationalists organized summer camps for their supporters in Wielkopolska and, after 1910, in Lwów and infiltrated secondary schools in Silesia (Kwiatek, 1991a: 11; Michalkiewicz, 1985: 357–364).

The students spread Polish nationalist ideas to Upper Silesia. Consequently, the more radical faction of the local Polish-language movement, encouraged by the election successes of the Polish/Slavic-speaking candidates not approved by the Zentrum, distanced itself from the moderate stance of *Katolik*. They strove to establish links with the mainstream of the Polish national movement. In 1894 they took part in the Polish nationalist rally in Lwów (Neubach, 1995: 200–201), and in 1901 the leadership of pro-Polish and Polish-language organizations from Upper Silesia met in Beuthen (Kwiatek, 1991: 12). Having observed this increase of interest in matters Polish, Napieralski launched the first Polish-language daily, *Dziennik Śląski* (Silesian Daily, 1898–1931). The circulation rapidly rose to 6,000 in 1910 and to 10,000 in 1913. Five years later it was joined by another daily, the overtly pro-Polish *Głos Śląski* (Silesian Voice, 1903–1921)—whose initial high runs of 4,000 copies had risen only to 4,700 by 1914. The short-lived *Gazeta Polska* (Polish Newspaper, 1902) and *Iskra* (Spark, 1903) were connected with the Eleusis. This organization originated in Cracow and propagated the messianic strain of Polish nationalism, derived from the writings of Polish romantic poets. The Eleusis was promptly suppressed in 1904–1905, and its members continued their activities underground in conjunction with the Zet (Glensk, 1992: 20–21; Gröschel, 1993: 41, 83–84, 108–109; Kwiatek, 1991; Michalkiewicz, 1985: 354–355; Snoch, 1991: 30–31).

Since the turn of the twentieth century Polish periodicals, publications, bookshops, cooperatives, credit and saving banks/societies, trade unions, and cultural and other organizations proliferated. As usual the question arises as to what the extent of their influence was. In 1914 the various 494 Polish organizations boasted 45,760 members, and 85,129 readers belonged to Polish-language libraries in 1911–1912 (Michalkiewicz, 331–340). However, it would be an overstatement to claim that they were Poles. The majority of the Upper Silesians displayed unwavering loyalty to Prussiandom and their non-national Szlonzokian identity. The social dynamics of this ethnic identity was often incomprehensible to the outside observer in such situations when an Upper Silesian claimed to be a Pole and German simultaneously if pressed to reveal his national identity (Pater, 1993: 214). It was an unambiguous example of the non-national multiple identity whose constituents also included national identities promoted by the state and national movements. Thus, it is sobering to remark that, according to the contemporary police sources, there were only 120 Polish national activists in 1910 in Upper Silesia. Many of them came from the Province of Posen and Galicia, so that the indigenous contingent was even smaller. However, as was to be shown in later years, this relatively small number of local national activists was able to bring about quite radical changes. The same police sources indicated that in Wielkopolska Polish activists numbered 380 in 1905–1906, which is not a great deal more (Molik, 1993: 77).

The Polish national movement, commenced in earnest by *Gazeta Opolska* and *Nowiny Raciborskie* in the 1890s, could not effectively compete with the traditional and popular Catholic universalistic leanings that prevailed among the Upper Silesians until the appearance of the legendary figure of Wojciech (Albert) Korfanty (1873–1939). Many a German Silesian and historian considered or still considers him a "Deutschenhasser" (the embodiment of venomous hatred against the Germans) (Scheuermann, 1994: 834). Accordingly they dubbed Polish nationalism in Upper Silesia as the "böser Geist Korfantys" (evil spirit of Korfanty) (Bahlcke, 1996: 110). On the other hand, he is a paragon of Polishness to Polish nationalists (Wawryszyn, 1992) but an ambiguous figure to the Upper Silesians of no national preferences (Szlonzoks). To the Szlonzoks, Korfanty generally seemed to be a tragic politician who tried to secure some social and political space for the Upper Silesians of no national convictions, a space in the confines of which Szlonzoks could continue to live in accordance with their own non-national multiple identity in the rapidly modernizing world of clashing nation-states.

In sum, trying to satisfy the hopes of the Polish/Slavic-speaking Upper Silesians, the needs of the Polish state that emerged after 1918, and the expectations of the German minority that appeared in Poland's Silesian Voivodeship after the division of Upper Silesia in 1922, as well as his own political ambitions, Korfanty was doomed to take controversial decisions. More often than not, these decisions were perceived as anti-German by the Germans, pro-German or even anti-Polish by the Poles, and simultaneously pro-German and pro-Polish and, as a result, anti-Upper Silesian by the Szlonzoks (cf. Gross, 1995: 85–84; Snoch, 1991: 67).

Korfanty was born to a miner's family in the small worker settlement of Sadzawka (Sadzawki), located (quite symbolically) very close to the border of Congress Poland, from where his grandfather had arrived in search of employment. Presumably Korfanty was a brilliant and diligent student. He continued his education at the Kattowitz gymnasium,[13] which was extremely rare in the case of Upper Silesian Polish/Slavic-speaking (Szlonzokian) children, unless they wished to become priests. Initially, Korfanty had a better command of German than Polish, but his mother, with the use of religious books, taught him to read Polish. Later, he developed a "rebellious" taste for matters and publications in Polish, which led to his expulsion from the gymnasium with no right to continue his education at any secondary school in Germany. Thanks to aid from Wielkopolska Polish activists and especially from the Prussian Landtag deputy Józef Kościelski (1845–1911), Korfanty was able to pass his matriculation examination in 1895 without having attended a gymnasium. He continued his education in Berlin (1895–1898). Before leaving the imperial capital for Breslau he associated with Polish students,

Polish socialists, and Polish national activists. Probably already in Berlin Korfanty joined the Zet and continued his contacts with this organization when studying in Breslau (Scheuermann, 1994: 835–836; Kaczmarek, 1993: 20–21; Tobiasz, 1947: 18–23; Zieliński, 1983: 3).

At the turn of the twentieth century the Polish national newspapers—Galician *Przegląd Wszechpolski* (All-Polish Review) from Lwów, as well as *Gazeta Grudziądzka* (Grudziądz Newspaper) and *Praca*[14] (Labor) from the Province of Posen—began reaching Upper Silesia. Especially *Praca,* with its 2,000 subscribers in Upper Silesia, and the *Dziennik Berliński* (Berlin Daily) were responsible for propagating Polish nationalism in the Oppeln Regency. Collaborating with these two periodicals, in 1901 Korfanty declared in *Praca,* "we hate you Germans," and in the same year, on Korfanty's initiative, *Dziennik Berliński* published two brochures: *Baczność! Chleb drożeje!* (Attention! Bread Prices Rise!) and *Precz z Centrum!* (Away with the Zentrum!). These brochures were distributed in Upper Silesian industrial cities and towns. It was a deft stratagem calculated to draw the Polish/Slavic-speaking and Catholic Upper Silesian workers away from the Zentrum and win them for Polish ethnic nationalism with the help of the special attention paid to social concerns.

In this manner, seizing the opportunity of the deepening economic slump that followed the brief recovery of 1897 (Fulbrook, 1990: 143), Polish nationalists and Korfanty co-opted the socialist program. This commenced an open conflict between them and the socialists, who saw Korfanty's slogans and actions as contrary to the socialist movement's non-nationalist idea of internationalism. *Dziennik Berliński* and *Praca* fortified the influence of Polish nationalism among the Upper Silesians with further brochures. These publications popularized the idea of the Polish nation and defined it as consisting of all the speakers of the Polish language. Arndt's 1813 definition of the German nation was translated for the needs of Polish ethnic nationalism (Fishman, 1996: 166). In 1901 the elitist Liga Narodowa accepted Korfanty as a member, and he forcefully entered the fray the same year with an article in which he stated that "the Upper Silesians are Poles." This article appeared in the clearly Polish nationalist daily *Górnoślązak*[15] (Upper Silesian, 1901–1933). This daily's runs soared to 6,000 in 1902 and 9,400 in 1914, rivaling Napieralski's *Dziennik Śląski.* Between 1902 and 1905 Korfanty acted as the editor of the *Górnoślązak* (Glensk, 1992: 21; Gröschel, 1993: 119–120; Michalkiewicz, 1985: 366–368; Snoch, 1991: 42; Wanatowicz, 1992: 96; Zieliński, 1983: 4).

In 1902 the top ideologues of Polish nationalism, Dmowski, Balicki, Popławski and other Liga Narodowa members (including Korfanty), met in Cracow and decided to create a full-fledged Polish national movement in Upper Silesia. To this end, they established the Polskie Towarzystwo Wyborcze (PTW, Polish Election Society) in November 1902, with its seat in Gleiwitz, and published the PTW's program. This document emphasized that the PTW's Upper Silesian candidates were Poles and, if elected, would join the Polish Circle of the

Wielkopolska deputies to the Reichstag and Landtag. This program also included the slogan advocating that Polish-speaking Upper Silesians should vote for pro-Polish Polish-speaking deputies. In the 1903 Reichstag elections the PTW fielded seven candidates. Korfanty obtained a mandate as the *only one* in a runoff round of voting by the very narrow margin of 1.4 percent. To his advantage were intensive campaigning and the recession, which hit the German Empire that year causing bitter discontent in this highly industrialized constituency of Kattowitz-Zabrze.

As a thirty-year-old, Korfanty was the youngest Reichstag deputy, along with Matthias Erzberger. Korfanty, unlike the *Katolik* faction and Zentrum Polish-speaking deputies, joined the Polish Circle, tangibly showing the German public that he was serious about the idea of making Upper Silesians into Poles and incorporating their region into a future Poland. Korfanty's stance was made even clearer in 1904 when he was elected to the Prussian Landtag from a Wielkopolska, *not* Upper Silesian, constituency. These initial successes prompted Popławski to state that Upper Silesia shifted from the category of uncertain semi-Polish borderlands (*Kresy*) into the center of the Polish national/ethnic and political life. Apart from Upper Silesia these *Kresy* included most of the former Grand Duchy of Lithuania, Ruthenia (Ruś), Szepes (Spiš, Spisz), Arva (Orava, Orawa), and, perhaps, Teschen (East Austrian) Silesia (Fulbrook, 1990: 143; Kaczmarek, 1993: 20–21; Michalkiewicz, 1985: 382–383; Wanatowicz, 1992: 104, 108; Zieliński, 1983: 5).

In the year of the 1905 revolution in Russia, which directly influenced Upper Silesia across the border from Congress Poland, Korfanty's mandate was annulled. Using the unrest and the lingering economic recession that had set in in 1903, the PPSzp, with the SPD's support, put forward its own candidate in the ensuing by-election. The PPSzp hoped to add one of its own to the four SPD deputies who had gained their mandates in the Breslau Regency two years earlier. Korfanty won with a wide margin, having adopted the Zentrum's anti-socialist rhetoric, to which the Catholic Church also subscribed. Deeply religious Upper Silesian Catholics easily took on this conservative stance, as opposed to the prospect of a revolutionary order proposed by social democrats, which seemed to them ungodly and dangerous. Subsequently, having failed to gain expected support in Upper Silesia, the PPSzp folded into and again started functioning within the SPD's organizational framework.

Napieralski, having observed that the strain of unmitigated Polish nationalism attracted followers, took part in the 1906 by-election and was elected to the Reichstag (Lis, 1993: 110–111; Michalkiewicz, 1985: 270, 404). In 1905 Korfanty established the newspaper *Polak* (The Pole, 1905–1926) and adopted a less nationalist tone, not wishing to alienate the powerful *Katolik* faction. His attitude limited socialist influence and contributed to the consolidation of Upper Silesia's Polish camp around the Christian democratic values espoused by the middle class. In 1907, before the new elections to the Reichstag, Korfanty established the daily

Kuryer Śląski (Silesian Courier, 1907–1922). Korfanty, Napieralski and three other Polish candidates of the *Katolik* faction won mandates (out of the total of twelve) in the Oppeln Regency (Bahlcke, 1996: 110; Glensk, 1992: 21–22; Gröschel, 1993: 123–124). Polish nationalists rejoiced, and in his 1908 book, *Niemcy, Rosja i kwestia Polska* (Germany, Russia and the Polish Question), Dmowski demanded for a future Polish nation-state, among others, Upper Silesia, the Lower Silesian counties of Groß Wartenberg and Namslau (Namysłów), and all of Austrian Silesia (Mroczko, 1994: 97–98).

This successful offensive of Polish nationalism and the election results put the Zentrum on the defensive. The party won just five mandates and, in addition to that, one mandate went to a conservative candidate. Although the Polish movement and the Zentrum obtained five mandates each, the former received 39.5 percent of the votes and the latter only 31.7 percent, which made the Zentrum's loss even more acute (Lis, 1993: 112). However, the Polish movement, restricted by anti-Polish legislation, also felt uneasy. Thus, in 1908, the *Katolik* faction and the Zentrum, with nine mandates among them (Korfanty did not join this alliance), decided to form a coalition so as to ward off socialists and to campaign for scrapping these anti-Polish measures (Lis, 1993: 114; Michalkiewicz, 1985: 270; Wanatowicz, 1992: 120).

Korfanty also moved in the same direction, having renounced his ties with the Liga Narodowa and his staunchly anti-German program in the same year. Napieralski's pragmatic line bore more fruit, and Korfanty was rapidly losing support among the electorate. To preclude his obliteration from the political scene Korfanty reached an agreement with Napieralski in 1910. In the following year they established the Stronnictwo Polskie na Śląsku (Polish Party in Silesia) and broke the traditional ties between *Katolik* and the Zentrum. The *Katolik* press group continued monopolizing the Polish-language press in Upper Silesia through buying out independent Polish-language periodicals, including Korfanty's *Polak* (Figowa, 1966: 16).

The Zentrum distanced itself from *Katolik* in 1909, hoping that the split among the PPS and the nationalist and Catholic (universalistic) strains in the Polish movement would reduce the *Katolik* faction's appeal to the public at large. Moreover, the Silesian Zentrum leader von Ballestrem and his colleagues actively campaigned for structural and economic improvements in Upper Silesia, which disposed the electorate more favorably to the party. Subsequently, in the last Reichstag elections (1912) the Polish movement obtained only three mandates. In light of the Zentrum's success it is worthwhile mentioning that the plebeian strain, which had commenced in the party due to the rise of the Polish movement, prevented fielding even a single nobleman as a candidate in the 1912 elections in Upper Silesia (Bahlcke, 1996: 110). The political strength of Polish nationalism in Upper Silesia proved short-lived. The rapid growth in the number of votes cast in support of Polish candidates in the Oppeln Regency, from 17.7 percent in 1903 to a staggering 39.5 percent in 1907, was followed by a drop to 30.8 percent in 1912 (Długoborski, 1995: 15). Korfanty did not dare to participate in the 1912 elections, castigated by the PPSzp and the Liga Narodowa as a traitor to the Polish national cause. The following year in the Prussian Landtag elections not a single Polish candidate obtained a mandate (Bahlcke, 1996: 105; Kwiatek, 1982: 241; Kaczmarek, 1993: 22; Michalkiewicz, 1985: 411, 415; Wanatowicz, 1992: 121–122).

In 1912 the Zentrum's organ, *Der oberschlesische Kurier* (Upper Silesian Courier, 1906–1945), commented that Polish nationalism in Upper Silesia had been dealt a death blow and predicted its speedy demise due to the educational and economic improvements gradually introduced by the German government in the wake of the economic recovery (Bahlcke, 1996: 110; Gröschel, 1993: 150). This opinion drew on the same tenet as Polish national voices, which had maintained in 1907 that the presence of Polish nationalism in Upper Silesia had not been brought about by any local Polish revival but by cultural and educational influence from the outside. It had been also understood that this movement would vanish without continuous development of Polish cultural and social organizations (Wanatowicz, 1992: 118). Both these assessments proved to be right. The anti-Polish measures, coupled with the end of the recession and improved social conditions, did weaken the Polish movement, which was decisively muted by the outbreak of the Great War. New laws limiting activities of Polish organizations and weakening their membership through the military draft rendered the Polish movement extremely inactive. The war turned out to be a new variable in the Polish-German national conflict, which was to flare up only after the end of World War I (Lis, 1993: 116; Michalkiewicz, 1985: 421).

German nationalists felt endangered by the emergence of the Polish-language movement in the 1890s, and so did the German administration with the appearance of the Polish national movement after 1903. In their eyes the Polish successes imperiled the processes of German nation- and nation-state-building that the German public and politicians perceived as the greatest good. Accordingly, since the 1890s, German civil servants and professionals had been appealed to and economically incited to settle in the non-German-speaking areas (including Upper Silesia) of the German Empire. This was to strengthen Germandom and offset the influence of non-German national movements (Migdał, 1965: 73). As a consequence, the number of civil servants grew in these areas by 50 percent between 1895 and 1906, thanks to various financial incentives offered to them. In 1894 Emperor William II delivered an overtly anti-Polish speech in Thorn (Toruń), and in the same year the conciliatory Chancellor von Caprivi was removed from office.

Between 1895 and 1897 a new wave of expulsions of Polish-speaking and Jewish aliens (illegal immigrants) was conducted, though it involved considerably fewer persons than the 1885–1887 expulsions. The budget of the Royal Prussian

Settlement Committee (Königlich Preußische Ansiedlungskommission) was enlarged in 1898, and in the same year the ministerial circular letter recommended that civil servants living in the Polish-speaking regions enroll in various German organizations and actively participate in German cultural life. In 1900 Bülow became chancellor and started Berlin's more comprehensively anti-Polish line. He was clearly conscious that Polish nationalists wanted to attract the Upper Silesians into the fold of Polishdom in order to turn Upper Silesia into a territorial bridge between Wielkopolska and Galicia. The *Wirtschaftskampf* started in Upper Silesia in earnest in 1898 when the Prussian minister of state argued that the emerging Polish economic movement should be curbed. In 1901 the president of the Oppeln Regency, Ernst Holtz, appealed for the development of German cooperatives and savings banks, which he offered to support with special subsidies. The following year he issued a circular letter in which he forbade civil servants and their families to maintain any contacts with Polish banks and cooperative shops, and in 1902 and 1903 lists of such proscribed enterprises were compiled. Moreover, Polish credit and saving banks from Upper Silesia were forbidden to join the cartel union of similar banks in the Province of Posen (Molik, 1993: 63).

Special commissions to further German colonization commenced their activities in Upper Silesia in 1903. Two years later the Prussian government issued an order which stated that the emperor supported the idea of enlarging *Fideikommisse* to strengthen Germandom. *Fideikommiß* in German, or *fideikomis* in Polish, is derived from the Latin term *fidei commissum*. It denoted a hereditary land that could be sold only as a whole. *Fideikommisse* were the stronghold of Junkers and accounted for almost half the arable land in Upper Silesia (Snoch, 1991: 32; Tokarski, 1971: 216; Ullmann, 1985: 86). The 1904 amendment to the 1886 Colonization Act allowed the authorities to prohibit construction of houses in Polish-speaking areas, and in 1908 the Expropriation Act was passed, permitting removal of non-German property owners from border areas. The 1904 and 1908 laws, giving preferential treatment to German settlers who wished to purchase land, were more often enforced in the Province of Posen than in Upper Silesia, where there was little arable land and the majority of the workforce was employed in industry (Łukasiewicz, 1988: 82).

Actually the Expropriation Act was used only once in 1912 and applied to just four farms in the Province of Posen. Much more restrictive for Polish-language and Polish national life in Upper Silesia was another act of 1908. It forbade political organizations to recruit members younger than eighteen, and it established German as the language of meetings of all organizations in the counties where non-German-speakers did not constitute more than 60 percent of the populace. Languages other than German were allowed to be employed at such meetings only until 1928. All the restrictions were enforced by the obligatory presence of a policeman during meetings (Klein, 1972: 12–14; Michalkiewicz, 1985: 280–284). This situation led to numerous trials of Polish journalists, activists and organizations that transgressed these laws (Michalkiewicz, 1985: 285–287, 295), but local opposition was not very strong. For instance, the 1906 school strike against religious instruction in German was joined by at least 70,000 schoolchildren in 50 percent of the schools in the Province of Posen. At the same time in Upper Silesia only 431 children of several schools participated in this strike, due to the unfavorable opinion that the Zentrum as well as Napieralski and Korfanty voiced about this action (Jakóbczyk, 1989: 67; Reiter, 1966: 44–45).

In 1912 the "struggle for land" as conducted by the Königlich Preußische Ansiedlungskommission and Polish landowners in the Province of Posen also extended to Silesia through the Besitzfestigungsgesetz (Act on Strengthening the [German] Ownership of Land). This act, like the Colonization Acts, gave ethnic German farmers priority when it came to buying land on the market. Slavic-speakers' requests regarding the purchase of land could be considered only when no German farmer showed an interest. German farmers also obtained access to preferential loans (Brożek, 1966a: 17). The Besitzfestigungsgesetz covered those Prussian territories in which the Königlich Preußische Ansiedlungskommission did not have the statutory right to operate. The 1913 Prussian royal ordinance determined the areas of Silesia where this new act was to be applied. They included the entire Oppeln Regency with the exception of the overwhelmingly German-speaking counties of Leobschütz, Neisse and Grottkau. In the case of the Breslau and Liegnitz regencies all the counties next to the border of the Province of Posen were included (Brożek, 1966: 15–17).

Through adopting these measures, the authorities eventually accepted the stance of the German nationalists, who argued that Polish nationalism also endangered Silesia. But the land struggle never began in Silesia in earnest, because the Reichstag condemned Prussia's expropriation policy in 1913. And after the outbreak of the Great War neither the Prussian government nor German nationalists were interested in continuing the nationalist conflict, once faced with external enemies and the fortified socialist movement (Wiskemann, 1956: 14).

These official measures, aimed at limiting the development and influence of the Polish national movement, were accompanied by grassroots German activities. Already when *Nowiny Raciborskie* started promoting Polish nationalism, the Zentrum launched the short-lived biweekly *Gazeta Górnośląska Ludowa* (Popular Upper Silesian Newspaper, 1892–1893). By virtue of the initiative of the Industriellenbund (Union of Industrialists) the thrice-weekly *Der Oberschlesische Arbeiterfreund* (Upper Silesian Worker's Friend, 1900–1919) was established to offset the Polish influence among industrial workers. Its run soon reached over 20,000 copies (many of which were distributed free of charge), and the periodical was supplemented by the annual calendar *Arbeiterfreund-Kalender*. Generally, these German-language periodicals, which wanted to achieve financial success in

Upper Silesia, strove to remain ideologically neutral so as not to repel Polish/Slavic-speaking Upper Silesians.

Thanks to these tactics, the bilingual weekly *Der Oberschlesische Berg- und Hüttenmann* (Upper Silesian Miner and Metallurgical Worker, 1880–1899) reached sales of 3,000 copies per week, and the daily *Der Oberschlesische Wanderer* (Upper Silesian Wanderer, 1828–1945) grew to rank as the second-largest newspaper in Silesia at the beginning of the twentieth century, with a run of 20,000 copies in 1906 and 40,000 in 1914 (Glensk, 1992: 20, 24–25; Gröschel, 1993: 79–80, 119, 239; Schofer, 1974: 95). The influence of these periodicals was significant in drawing the Upper Silesians away from socialism and Polish nationalism. Since 1896 their efforts, as well as the official measures, had found an eager supporter in the person of Rudolf Küster. He was the director of the Department of Religious and Educational Affairs in the government of the Oppeln Regency.

The first popular German library was established in Tarnowitz (Tarnowskie Góry) in 1897, and in 1910 there were 146 stationary popular libraries and 939 traveling libraries with 120,825 members. In 1903 they were united in the framework of the Verband oberschlesischer Volksbüchereien (Union of Popular Libraries of Upper Silesia). Three years later this union started publishing its own bimonthly, *Die Volksbücherei in Oberschlesien* (The Popular Library in Upper Silesia, 1906–1922). The 1568 Upper Silesian elementary schools boasted 1,538 libraries of their own, which were supplied with 64,000 copies of *Kindergärtchen* (Kindergarten Children, 1893–1919) and *Der junge Oberschlesier* (Young Upper Silesian, 1894–1920) in 1910–1911 (Gröschel, 1993: 241, 326).

Schools also organized numerous extramural activities. For instance, in 1912 they staged skating and skiing events in 361 localities, which were attended by 19,778 children. In 1912 there were 614 continuing education schools that aimed at improving German literacy among the 35,061 youth working in shops, on farms and in crafts. In the same year there were also 20 factory schools, with 2,202 students. The Jung-Deutschland-Bund (Union of Young Germany) and the Mädchenheime (Girls' Club Rooms) spread the ideals of German nationalism among the school youth. The Deutsche Turnerschaft (Union of German Gymnastics) and the Oberschlesischer Spiel- und Eislaufverband (Upper Silesian Union of Sports Games and Skating) supported 516 organizations, with 37,312 members in 1912 in Upper Silesia. These two sports organizations enjoyed their own monthly *Oberschlesische Turn-Zeitung* (Upper Silesian Gymnastics Newspaper, 1907–1921) (Gröschel, 1993: 241). The Oberschlesischer Sängerbund (Upper Silesian Union of Singers), Schlesischer Sängerbund (Silesian Union of Singers), Männersingervereine (Societies of Male Singers) and the Oberschlesischer Arbeitersängerbund (Upper Silesian Workers' Union of Singers) boasted almost 12,000 members in 1912.

The Polish-language amateur theater was countered with state-subsidized productions in the theaters in Oppeln, Beuthen, Gleiwitz, Kattowitz and Ratibor, as well as with the activities of the Oberschlesisches Volkstheater (Popular Upper Silesian Theater), with its seat in Königshütte. What is more, the *Kriegsvereine* (veteran associations) and the Flottverein (Fleet Association) had 82,388 and 7,559 members, respectively, in 1912. The German nationalist society par excellence, the Deutscher Ostmarkenverein, was of little importance in Silesia, in contrast to its position in the Province of Posen, since the Silesian authorities held that there was no problem of Polish nationalism in their province. Hence any extensive official support for this association would amount to acknowledging the existence of Polish nationalism as a significant political force. But thanks to the patronage of Upper Silesian entrepreneurs, Silesia's first branches of the Deutscher Ostmarkenverein came into being in 1895–1896.

The situation changed after Korfanty's success in 1903, at which time the Schle-sischer Landesauschuss (Silesian Committee) of the Deutschen Ostmarkenverein came into being in Breslau. The association's membership rose from 7,500 in 1905 to 10,422 in 1909 and to 11,850 in 1913. In 1909, 6,150 persons belonged in Upper Silesia alone. This association actively supported all the anti-Polish measures introduced by the government and railed against any participation of German-speakers in Polish-language life, including publication of German enterprises' advertisements in the Polish-language press. The Schlesischer Landesauschuss's largest success was the organization of the all-German rally, which took place in Upper Silesia in 1909. The activities of the Deutscher Ostmarkenverein and of other German nationalist organizations almost ceased, as had those of their Polish counterparts, upon the outbreak of the Great War (Michalkiewicz, 1985: 296–309).

The pro-German initiatives in the field of politics and culture strongly attracted the Upper Silesian population to Germandom, despite the stunning successes of the Polish movement during the first decade of the twentieth century. This also showed in the Catholic Church statistics. Between 1867 and 1918 the ratio of monolingual German-speaking priests grew from 9.2 percent to 19.8 percent in Upper Silesia (Surman, 1992: 70). Despite Kopp's disapproval of the anti-Polish laws and the activities of the Deutscher Ostmarkenverein (Galos, 1992: 57), the Silesian Catholic Church continued to go along with the official line, which aimed at "civilizing" Upper Silesians through the medium of the German language and culture (Lüer, 1995: 82–83). Not surprisingly, German-language sermons were delivered in 120 Upper Silesian parishes in 1900, and in 231 parishes ten years later. Similarly, pre-First Communion instruction was provided exclusively in German in only 26 parishes in 1900, but in 46 parishes by 1910 (Michalkiewicz, 1985: 303).

The national conflict that unfolded at the turn of the century in Upper Silesia, as well as the *Ostflucht*, had a peculiar influence on the labor relations in the Upper Silesian industrial basin. The rapid development of Upper Silesian industry in the first half of the nineteenth century brought about staggering urbanization. Beuthen's population grew from 1,558 in 1795, to 15,711 in 1871, and to 63,110 in 1908 (Krause, 1995: 8; Weczerka, 1977: 23). Another city illustrating this process is Kattowitz. It achieved the status of town in 1865, and the number of its inhabitants soared from 675 in 1825, to 4,815 in 1865, and to 35,722 in 1905. In 1875 in this town's vicinity there were six iron and eleven zinc metallurgical works, as well as fourteen coal mines (Reichling, 1977a: 223). The ongoing industrialization brought about the 1873 division of the old county of Beuthen into the new counties of Beuthen, Kattowitz, Tarnowitz and Zabrze. In 1890 the county of Beuthen was split into the urban and land counties of Beuthen. The same process was applied to the county of Kattowitz in 1899, but one year earlier the county of Königshütte had been carved out from it (Stüttgen, 1976: 190, 197, 214, 217). All the counties, together with the counties of Tost-Gleiwitz (Toszek-Gliwice), Rybnik and Pleß, formed the Upper Silesian industrial basin (Schofer, 1974: 6).

Despite all these developments in industrialization and urbanization, the Ruhr became more productive and modern than Upper Silesia during the 1860s and 1870s. The Upper Silesian mining and metallurgical industries employed 18,717 workers in 1852, 36,306 in 1865, 77,464 in 1885, 122,540 in 1900 and 193,560 in 1913. On the other hand, the Ruhr mines alone gave work to 14,299 persons in 1851, 51,391 in 1870, 101,929 in 1885, 226,902 in 1900 and 382,951 in 1913 (Schofer, 1974: 14–15). In the German Empire, Upper Silesia became more peripheral than it had been in Prussia. The cost of transporting the industrial products was reflected in wages that were lower even than those earned by workers in the Lower Silesian mines of Waldenburg (Wałbrzych), and obviously the latter were surpassed by what the Dortmund employers offered (Fuchs, 1994: 561). The Silesian workers and miners had also to work longer shift hours than their Ruhr counterparts. Hence many Upper and Lower Silesians migrated westward in search of improved living and working conditions. This phenomenon intensified especially during times of economic crisis (1873, 1882, 1893, 1903), when laid-off workers rarely decided to return to the farms of their parents. Between 1871 and 1910 about 600,000 people left Silesia (Schofer, 1974: 20, 44, 115), or, more precisely, 250,000 from Upper Silesia, 220,000 from the Breslau Regency, and 166,000 from the Liegnitz Regency. The only counties with more migrants coming than leaving in the period 1871–1905 were those of Beuthen, Kattowitz and Zabrze (Wrzesiński, 1995: 182).

In 1907 there were 730,388 Silesians residing in the German Empire outside their province—297,350 in Berlin and Brandenburg, 162,312 in Saxony, 93,641 in Westphalia and the Rhineland, and 43,605 in the Province of Posen (Michalkiewicz, 1985: 41). Considering intra-provincial migrations, in 1900 there were 104,266 Upper Silesians in Lower Silesia, while there were only 58,000 Lower Silesians in Upper Silesia. On the other hand, in 1907, 200,000 non-Silesians resided in the province, though there were only 75,000 in the industrial region of Upper Silesia.

Regarding the 60,000 non-Silesians residing in the Oppeln Regency in 1900, none of the German provinces contributed more than 2,400 with the exception the Province of Posen (8,400). Thus in every census from 1871 to 1900, 95 percent of the population in the Upper Silesian industrial basin were listed as born in Silesia. No major alterations had taken place in this respect prior to 1914, when the war cut off any further major population shifts (Schofer, 1974: 22, 34–35).

The *Ostflucht,* which was perceived as one of the greatest dangers to Germandom, deepened with the influx of foreign workers. They came to work in Upper Silesian industry mainly from the outlying counties of Galicia and Congress Poland. In 1885 there were 3,178 such workers in the Oppeln Regency. Together with their family members they added up to 7,761, 60.7 percent of which were Russian citizens, and 39.3 percent Austro-Hungarian (Brożek, 1958: 5). Because only 2,851 of these foreign workers were employed in the Upper Silesian industrial area, at most they constituted a mere 3.7 percent of the workforce employed in the Upper Silesian mines and metallurgical works, a rather insignificant percentage (Brożek, 1958: 5; Schofer, 1974: 14). The 1885–1887 expulsions of foreign workers did not significantly lower the overall number of alien Polish-speakers in Upper Silesia and did not affect daily cross-border commuters. This cross-border traffic accounted for 8,000 people each day before 1885, and it continued to involve thousands of short-term migrants right up to 1914 (Schofer, 1974: 23).

The relative unattractiveness of Upper Silesia and the increasing production in the industrial basin resulted in a severe labor shortage. The Königlich Preußische Ansiedlungskommission did not manage to bring in the predicted number of settlers (Davies, 1991: II 129), which exacerbated the labor shortfall in the second half of the 1880s. Thus, despite the various proposals to employ Swedes, Lithuanians, Estonians, Finns, Byelorussians, Ukrainians, Germans from Hungary, Italians, and even Chinese, the fact had to be recognized that Galicia and Congress Poland were the natural economic hinterland of Upper Silesia. So when the border was opened to foreign workers in 1890 under pressure from employers, almost all the incoming foreign contract workers were Polish-speakers from these regions. That said, no Jews were allowed in, and in order to prevent naturalization, *Karenzzeit* (waiting period) was applied to them, as a result of which they had to leave the German Empire for several winter months each year (Brożek, 1958: 17; Schofer, 1974: 24–25). In 1894 the institution of *Karenzzeit* was applied also to Czechs and in 1902 to Lithuanians (Jonca, 1958: 150–151). In 1910, out of 30,000 Czechs/Czech-speakers working in Germany (predominantly in the Ruhr, where the waiting period did not apply), only 7,000 were employed in Silesia. Almost none of them came from the Ratibor county, where the ethnically related Morawecs resided (Schofer, 1974: 71).

After the initial upsurge of 5,267 foreign contract workers, the annual figure hovered between 200 and 1,000 in the period 1892–1895, and between 1,000 and

3,000 in the period 1896–1900 (Brożek, 1966a: 56). From 1900 to 1906, the total labor force grew swiftly, and the number of foreign workers increased to an annual average of 3,000 (Schofer, 1974: 25–26). Because the constant annual outflow of 5,000–6,000 Upper Silesian migrants to the Ruhr between 1898 and 1905 had drained the local workforce pool, a more decisive measure had to be introduced to alleviate the worsening shortage of labor (Schofer, 1974: 75). Opportunely, in 1905 a Greek Catholic priest, Hanyckyi, from the vicinity of Lwów organized recruitment of Ruthenian (Ukrainian) workers to Upper Silesia. The annual waiting period did not apply to them, so they proved to be popular among employers (Jonca, 1958: 152; Schofer, 1974: 72). Because of this influx, the number of foreign workers reached the significant figure of 9,466 (including 3,122 Ruthenians), that is, 10 percent of the total workforce in 1907. In due time Hanyckyi moved to join the Ruthenian faithful in Upper Silesia, and the number of foreign contract workers reached the unprecedented number of 19,366 in 1913.

Since 1908 there had been more or less equal numbers of alien Polish-speakers and Ruthenians employed in Upper Silesian industry because in this year the authorities had introduced a number of anti-Polish measures, and the Upper Silesian industrialists had been also cautioned against employing Polish workers from the Province of Posen. In 1913 the situation decisively changed in favor of Ruthenian workers, who numbered 10,627, whereas Polish foreign workers were only 7,648. Almost no Polish workers from Congress Poland were employed before 1908. After 1908 the number of Polish workers from Congress Poland and Galicia was more balanced, and in 1913 there were 3,735 of them from the former region and 3,913 from the latter one (Brożek, 1966: 57).

With the influx of foreign workers, the number of Polish-speaking cross-border commuters did not drop significantly but was maintained at the level of 6,419 (3,358 from Congress Poland and 3,061 from Galicia) in 1910 (Brożek, 1966a: 57, 65; Schofer, 1974: 26, 38, 72). In all likelihood there was not much social interaction between local and foreign workers due to the different (popularly perceived as "lower") cultural standards of the immigrants (Wanatowicz, 1992: 74–75). Thus the main cleavage was among the predominantly Polish/Slavic-speaking local workers and the overwhelmingly German-speaking ones. However, this divide was closed after 1910 due to the split in Upper Silesia's Polish movement and to the negative stance of Polish activists and the Zentrum toward socialism. Workers saw it as a lack of interest in their social problems on the part of the main political forces in Silesia and the German Empire. Hence, socialists eventually gained the upper hand in 1913. The Polish and German trade unions circumvented the simmering ethnic conflict, constantly stirred up by Polish and German nationalists, by creating all-German and all-Polish groups. Thus they were able to stage the first coordinated strike in Upper Silesia, involving some 55 percent of all the crews at one point in May 1913, although only about 15–20 percent of all Upper Silesian miners were unionized. Thus socialism was the winner of the ideological struggle in Upper Silesia prior to the outbreak of the Great War (Schofer, 1974: 156).

Before moving on to the problem of Austrian Silesia, it is worthwhile observing the Silesian contribution to the development of Jewish nationalism or Zionism. The term denotes the movement to unite the Jewish people of the diaspora and to settle them in Palestine. The Austrian Jewish philosopher Nathan Birnbaum (1864–1937) was the first to apply the neologism "Zionism" to this movement. "Zionism" is derived from the Hebrew word "Zion," which is the name of one of the hills of Jerusalem on which the city of David was built. The Zion hill became the center of Jewish life and worship. Later it acquired the symbolic meaning of the house of God, Israel and Judaism (Cohen, 1990: 161; Onions, 1983: 2595).

European Jewry began to be granted political equality in revolutionary France (1791). By 1871 this process had spread all over Europe with the notable exception of Russia. Emancipation, coupled with the Haskalah, brought about assimilation in Germany and Austria-Hungary during the second half of the nineteenth century (Cohen, 1990: 161–162; Kinder, 1978: II 62). However, this trend was hindered by the enduring existence of the pale of Jewish settlement in Russia. It was instituted in 1835 and reinforced by the repeated waves of pogroms of Russian Jewry (1881–1884, 1903–1906, 1917–1921) (Carr, 1996: 42; Davies, 1996: 844, 1311).

In the 1880s and 1890s the Austrian-Hungarian Pan-German movement under the leadership of Georg von Schönerer took up the anti-Semitism that was emanating from Russia. Afterward anti-Semitism grew increasingly strong in the Dual Monarchy and the German Empire (Anon., 1992d: 103). Consequently, Jewish activists put forward proposals that the Jews should establish their own homeland, preferably in Eretz Israel (the Land of Israel) (Cohen, 1990: 161). Although there were only 46,617[16] Jews in Silesia in 1871, and 45,692[17] between 1905 and 1910 (Kokot, 1973: 76–77), Upper Silesia proved to be a convenient venue for the famous Kattowitz Conference. It took place in this industrial city in 1884. Twenty-two delegates from nearby Russia attended, six from Germany, two from England, one from France and one from Romania. The conference's date was set on the one hundredth birthday of Sir Moses Haim Montefiore (1784–1885), an Anglo-Jewish philanthropist who, through his personal advancement in English society and his continuous endeavors, brought about emancipation of the British Jews in 1858. Between 1827 and 1875 he made seven journeys in the interest of Jewry in Congress Poland, Russia, Romania and Damascus (Kinder, 1978: II 62; Thorne, 1975: 904).

The Kattowitz Conference delegates represented the Hibbat Zion societies, which had come into being in the early 1880s in support of Jewish settlement in Eretz Israel. The movement aimed at settling Jews in Palestine. It had originated in the 1860s, when the first attempts to this end had been undertaken (Davies, 1996: 846). The Kattowitz Conference established an institution called Agudat Montefiore so as to promote farming among the Jews and support Jewish settlement in Eretz Israel. In sum, this conference laid out the foundations for organizing further Hibbat Zion societies, especially in Russia (Anon., 1972: 819–821).

The movement obtained its ideological basis in 1896 when the Budapest-born Viennese Jewish journalist Theodor Herzl (1860–1904) published his work *Der Judenstaat* (The Jewish State). In it he observed the limits of assimilation set by the trial of Dreyfus in France (1895). The following year Herzl organized the first Zionist Congress in Basel, Switzerland. In turn the congress founded the permanent World Zionist Organization. In the meantime the number of Jews in Palestine increased from 12,000 in 1845 to 85,000 in 1914. During World War I, the British wooed the Zionists in order to secure strategic control over Palestine and to gain the support of world Jewry for the Allied cause. The British government therefore issued the Balfour Declaration in 1917, officially supporting the idea of establishing a Jewish state in Palestine. Following the carving up of the Ottoman Empire and the establishment of British control over Palestine, in 1922 the League of Nations approved the terms of the declaration in the mandate for this land. During the British mandate in Palestine the *Yishuv* (Jewish community) grew to 600,000 people, and in 1948 the founding of Israel as a Jewish nation-state was achieved (Davies, 1996: 846; Carr, 1996: 42; Cohen, 1990: 162–163; Peretz, 1990: 306–307).

CHAPTER 9

Nationalisms in Austrian Silesia Prior to the Great War

Before focusing on Austrian Silesia, it is necessary to look at both the domestic situation in Austria-Hungary and Vienna's international relations during the years 1871–1914, since they comprise the indispensable background of the various developments that unfolded during that time in this crownland.

The 1867 *Ausgleich* (Compromise), which turned the Habsburg Empire into the Dual Monarchy, also paved the way for Hungarian politicians to engage in imperial politics. Count Gyula Andrássy (1829–1890), who was nominated the minister of foreign affairs in 1871, discarded the anti-Bismarck bias of his predecessor and sought friendship with the German Empire. The memories of the Seven Weeks' War of 1866 were gradually forgotten. Andrássy promised that the Danubian monarchy would not interfere in the German Empire's internal affairs. In return, Berlin backed Vienna's attempts to limit Russia's influence in southeastern Europe. In 1872, Francis Joseph I reciprocated by joining the League of the Three Emperors, in order to contain France.

The gradual decline of the Ottoman Empire led to the outbreak of numerous revolts and upheavals in the Balkans. Andrássy failed to induce the Ottoman government to adopt a reform program. By the next year, a Russian intervention seemed imminent. In order to placate Austria-Hungary, St. Petersburg offered Vienna part of the region after an eventual partition. Andrássy declined this proposal, based on the assessment that the Dual Monarchy would not be able to absorb new territory without upsetting the delicate internal balance between its various national and ethnic groups. Russia gave up its plans and in 1877 secured Austria-Hungary's neutrality during St. Petersburg's war against the Ottoman Empire. After victory in 1878, the Russians sought to acquire more than other European powers would allow. As a result, the situation in the Balkans was reorganized in a more balanced manner at the Congress of Berlin in the same year.

Austria-Hungary was allowed to occupy Bosnia-Herzegovina, which required significant military efforts and proved that Vienna was not in a position to absorb any more land and population effectively. Most importantly, Andrássy's endeavors were rewarded with the signing of the Dual Alliance between Germany and Austria-Hungary in 1879. Both emperors promised each other mutual support in case of Russian aggression. Although Austria-Hungary's hold on the Balkans solidified after Serbia became its client in 1881, Bismarck made the Dual Monarchy overhaul its foreign policy six year later so that it would comply with the German and Italian demand for the isolation of France.

Rome joined the Dual Alliance in 1882 and entered the Balkans as another player to which Vienna was expected to grant some concessions. On the basis of the First and Second Mediterranean Agreements of 1887, Great Britain joined Austria-Hungary and Italy in their efforts to block Russia from seizing control of the straits between the Black Sea and the Mediterranean. The Three Emperors' Alliance was allowed to expire after Bismarck's dismissal. Consequently, in 1897 Francis Joseph I and his foreign minister, Gołuchowski, traveled to St. Petersburg and signed agreements with the tsar to exclude Italy from Balkan affairs. They also sought to ensure the preservation of order in the region through bilateral cooperation between these two eastern monarchies rather than a multilateral alliance system.

In 1903, a major revolt occurred in Macedonia, and the Obrenović dynasty in Serbia was replaced by the Karađorđević dynasty in the wake of the assassination of King Alexander I (reigned 1889–1903). Serbia's relations with Austria-Hungary deteriorated. The economic pressure applied by Vienna did not crush this country, but instead pushed it into the Russian camp. After 1906, Vienna's new foreign minister, Count Aloys Lexa von Aehrenthal (1854–1912), sought to free Austria-Hungary from its submission to German interests. He also strove to pursue a more dynamic and independent Balkan policy. The combined Russian and Serbian opposition frustrated his endeavors.

In 1908, following a revolution in the Ottoman Empire, the Young Turk movement announced the reform of the Ottoman constitution. Because Bosnia-Herzegovina nominally remained under Ottoman suzerainty, Austria-Hungary was afraid that this constitutional change could undermine Vienna's control of the provinces. Thus, Austria-Hungary annexed Bosnia-Herzegovina in the same year, shattering Serbia's nationalist aspirations. Belgrade could not dream any more about enlarging its territory with Bosnia-Herzegovina as envisioned by Serbian nationalists. In addition, Berlin's 1909 ultimatum forced the Russians to withdraw their support from Serbia.

Serbia remained in a state of simmering conflict with Austria-Hungary. Consequently, Vienna became dependent on the German Empire's support again. In 1912, when the Italian-Ottoman conflict over Tripoli provoked anti-Ottoman sentiment in the Balkans, the international situation grew extremely tense. The ensuing Balkan Wars (1912–1913) forced the Ottoman Empire to abandon the majority of its remaining European possessions. The resulting rapid territorial growth of Serbia was especially unwelcome to Austria-Hungary. Vienna had twice threatened this country with an ultimatum to withdraw from its newly gained possessions. However, no military action ensued, since neither Germany nor Italy was willing to guarantee support.

By providing Bulgaria with aid against Serbia, Austria-Hungary alienated Romania. Bucharest had already shown resentment against the Habsburg Monarchy because of Budapest's treatment of the Romanian-speaking minority exposed to blatant Magyarization in Transleithania. Romania thus joined Italy and Serbia to facilitate organizing their respective ethnonational irredentist movements in the Dual Monarchy. By 1914, the leading Austro-Hungarian government circles were convinced that offensive action against the foreign protagonists of irredentist claims was essential for preserving the territorial integrity of the empire.

Disregarding warnings, Archduke Francis Ferdinand (1863–1914), the heir of Francis Joseph I, participated in the army maneuvers in Bosnia-Herzegovina. When on June 28, 1914, a Serbian nationalist assassinated the archduke and his wife in Sarajevo, Belgrade's attempts at conciliation were of no avail. The Austro-Hungarian Foreign Office decided to use this opportunity for a final reckoning with the Serbian threat that could disrupt the empire from without and from within. Austria-Hungary declared war on Serbia on July 28. Austria-Hungary hoped for a quick victory over Serbia in a contained local conflict, but this was impossible to achieve because of Russia's support for Belgrade.

Soon this regional conflict escalated into a continental war. In answer to Russian mobilization, Berlin declared war on the Russian Empire on August 1, 1914. When Paris declared that it would act "in accordance with its own interests," Germany preemptively declared war on France two days later. On August 2–3, German troops invaded Belgium, challenging the Allies' guarantee for the country's neutrality. Therefore, Britain presented Germany with an ultimatum on August 4 that amounted to a declaration of war. Other declarations of war followed in a quick succession: Serbia on Germany (August 6), Austria-Hungary on Russia (August 6), France on Austria-Hungary (August 11), and Britain on Austria-Hungary (August 12). Thus the stage was set for the transition of Europe and the world into the violent twentieth century (Ehrich, 1992: 527–528, 530–531; Kinder, 1978: II 83, 121–122).

Vienna's external politics were a reflection of its internal ethnic and national composition. The domestic tensions produced by the onset of the ideology of nationalism made the displeased groups, which could not realize their nationalist dreams within Austria-Hungary, look for outside allies along ethnic lines.

The Austro-Hungarian Germans developed a special affinity for Germany, the Czechs for Russia, the Southern Slavs for Serbia, and the Romanians for Romania (Walker, 1908: 605). Even the Poles and Hungarians, the most satisfied and loyal subjects of Francis Joseph I, were also ready to carve out their own independent states should an occasion arise, as evidenced by their actions at the close of the Great War. The happy days for Austria, when the slogan "Bella gerant alii; tu felix Austria, nube" (Let others fight, and thou, happy Austria, marry) held true, were long over.

In the second half of the nineteenth century, nationalism ruled supreme. Hence, the general development of German and Czech nationalist movements must be scrutinized as the context of the development of nationalist conflict in Austrian Silesia. Not much attention is devoted to Polish nationalism because (apart from its Magyar counterpart) it emerged under the best conditions possible for growth, complete with the Galician autonomy. Nowhere in Russia or Germany was the situation as convenient for Polish nationalists as in Austria-Hungary. It is not surprising that the Galician Poles did not seek any drastic alteration of their status quo, unlike the Czech and the Austrian Germans.

After Prussia's victory over France and the establishment of the German Empire, the finality of the Sadowa defeat of 1866 had to be accepted. The internal weakness of the Habsburg Monarchy, revealed in the course of the Austro-Prussian conflict, compelled Francis Joseph I to grant the Hungarians the *Ausgleich* in 1867. This document remodeled the Austrian Empire into bipartite Austria-Hungary and triggered resentment from the Poles and the Czechs, who demanded similar compromises the next year (Carter, 1992: 923). How to reorganize and make governable Cisleithania became an urgent issue because its German and Czech inhabitants accounted for 60 percent of the population (Waldenberg, 1992: 37). In 1867–1873, the Poles received full cultural autonomy within Galicia, and in 1871 a ministry for Galician affairs was set up. These developments turned the Galician Poles into the staunchest supporters of the monarchy and the government well into the Great War.

Francis Joseph I also wished to solve the Czech problem along the same lines. Meanwhile, the Franco-German War of 1870–1871 temporarily diverted public attention from Czech demands, but it also indicated potential divisiveness of ethnic cleavages when nationalist sentiment became involved. Austro-Germans celebrated the Prussian victories, whereas the Czechs and other Slavs were decisively pro-French. In 1870, František Rieger (1818–1903), Palacký's son-in-law and the leader of the Národní Strana (National Party) of the Old Czechs, protested in the name of the Czechs against the German annexation of Alsace-Lorraine (Elsaß-Lothringen). In 1871, the secret talks with Palacký and Rieger led to the issuance of an imperial rescript. Francis Joseph I promised the Czechs recognition of their traditional rights of the Czech Crown and showed his willingness to take the coronation oath in Prague.

The Czech leaders answered with a constitutional program set out in the Fundamental Articles. Accordingly, Bohemian affairs were to be regulated in the manner of the Magyars enjoying their Hungarian *Ausgleich*. This would have elevated Bohemia to a status equal to Hungary. The Austro-Germans and Hungarians rejected this program. The former were afraid to lose their privileged position in Bohemia, while the latter feared that this program would deprive them of their unique position in the Dual Monarchy and possibly incite minority groups in Transleithania. From that moment on, Cisleithania was governable only because of Polish support. The Czechs resorted to obstructionism. They withdrew from the Bohemian Landtag and again abstained from attendance at the Reichsrat (Ehrich, 1992: 527; Polišenský, 1991: 91).

The more radical Young Czech group gradually emerged in the Národní strana after 1863. But the watershed event was Vienna's rejection of the Fundamental Articles in 1867. This led to the open split upon the failure of the Old Czech conciliatory line. The Young Czechs established their Národní strana svobodomyslná (Liberal National Party) in 1874. During the subsequent period of political passivity and indecision, Rieger devoted his time to editing the first Czech-language encyclopedia (1859–1874), whereas the Young Czechs came to dominate the most influential press organ of Czech nationalism, *Narodní listy* (Carter, 1992: 923; Pokorný, 1993: 113).

The precarious position of the Austro-Germans improved after the conclusion of the Dual Alliance with the German Empire in 1879, which also temporarily placated the Austro-German liberals. They had opposed the 1878 annexation of Bosnia-Herzegovina and the subsequent redirecting of the Austro-Hungarian foreign policy toward the Balkans because these decisions brought about an increase in the number of Slavs living in the Dual Monarchy. But already in 1879, Austro-German politicians were put on the defensive when a "cabinet above parties" was formed by a coalition of clericals, German aristocrats and Slavs. The new prime minister, Eduard Taaffe (1833–1895), persuaded the Czechs to give up their boycott of the Bohemian Landtag and the Reichsrat.

In return, the Stremayr Language Act was passed. It made Czech and German equal languages in the "outer services" rendered by the civil service of Bohemia and Moravia. Significantly, this law did not apply to Austrian Silesia. After the passage of the act, a citizen could deal with any state office in these two crownlands either in German or Czech. But the German language still remained the sole medium of communication within civil service offices.

In 1882, Prague University was divided in order to furnish the Czechs with a national university. In the same year, Taaffe introduced electoral reform that enfranchised the more prosperous Czech peasants and weakened the hold of the German middle class on the government of Bohemia. Consequently, after 1882 Germans lost dominance in the Bohemian Landtag and in the Prague City Council, where no German aldermen sat between 1882 and 1918. In 1886 the Czech language was introduced to the supreme courts of Bohemia and Moravia in Prague and in Brünn. Nationalistically minded Austro-German politicians accused Taaffe of "Slavicizing Austria" (Ehrich, 1992: 528; Kořalka, 1995: 18–19; Prinz, 1995: 348–350; Schenk, 1993: 72).

The cabinet arrangements satisfied neither the Czechs nor the Germans. The Young Czechs started to gain increased support from the Czech-speaking electorate. At the same time, the Austro-German nationalists confronted the Austro-German conservatives and tabled the Linz program in 1882, in which the nationalists proposed restoration of German dominance in Cisleithania. This goal was to be achieved through detaching Galicia, Bukovina and Dalmatia from the monarchy, reducing relations with Hungary to a purely personal union, and establishing a customs union and other close links with the German Empire (Kinder, 1978: II 79). Because German-speakers tended to look for deliverance from Berlin rather than Vienna (Pokorný, 1993: 132), an encouraging environment for the emergence of Pan-Germanism developed. The movement's leader was Georg von Schönerer (1842–1921), a deputy to the Reichsrat, who also introduced a note of anti-Semitism into German nationalism. The first official Pan-German organizations were established in the early 1890s (Anon., 1992d: 103).

In the second half of the nineteenth century, the Czech national movement spawned numerous school, parish and county Czech-language libraries. A dense network of various organizations constituted the movement's framework. The most significant Czech national organizations of that time included the Matice česka (Czech Language Society), the Matice školska (School Society), the Živnostenská banka (Commercial Bank) and the Sokol (Falcon Gymnastic Association). In 1880 the Ustřední matice školská (Society for Secondary Schools) was established, and the Czech National Theater came into being the following year.

The Austro-Germans responded with their own national organizations, in order to safeguard their national interests in Austria-Hungary. They enjoyed their own Hypothekenbank (Mortgage Bank), founded in Prague in 1864. Their gymnastic associations were organized as the fifteenth branch of the Deutsche Turnerschaft. In 1880, the Deutscher Schulverein (German School Society) was established. Later the nationalist *Schutzvereine* (protection societies) followed, which included the Deutscher Böhmerwaldbund (German Böhmerwald Union, 1884) in Budweis, the Bund der Deutschen Nordmährens (Union of German Northern Moravia, 1886) in Olmütz, the Bund der Deutschen in Böhmen (Union of Germans in Bohemia, 1894) in Prague, the Bund der Deutschen Ostböhmens

(Union of Germans in East Bohemia, 1894) in Troppau, the Bund der Deutschen in Südmähren (Union of Germans in Southern Moravia, 1899) in Brünn, and the Bund der Deutschen der Iglauer Sprachinsel (Union of the Germans in the German-speaking Area of Iglau [Jihlava]) (Pokorný, 1993: 129, 134–135; Prinz, 1995: 355; Schenk, 1993: 77).

In the 1880s, the emergent socialist movement curbed some of the influence of the Czech and German nationalisms, but the resonance of ethnic cleavage prevailed. In 1890, Prime Minister Taaffe strove to negotiate an agreement between the Old Czechs and the German liberals, proposing to divide Bohemia along national lines for administrative and judicial purposes. This proposal threatened to weaken the position of the Austro-Germans in Bohemia, while it was insufficient to satisfy the Young Czechs. The latter hoped for officially accepted dominance of the Czech language and culture within the lands of the Czech Crown, which would be administratively united. In 1893 Taaffe's conciliatory endeavors incited riots in Prague. He had to resign, and the compromise project was shelved.

Interestingly, the Young Czechs, who had been gradually surpassing the Old Czechs since the 1880s, did not manage to retain their position after the Old Czechs had suffered a total defeat in the Reichsrat elections of 1891. Dissatisfied Czech peasants and workers turned away from the bourgeoisie-centered Young Czechs toward their own class movements. A similar phenomenon also took place among German-speaking peasants and workers of Bohemia and Moravia. This precarious calmness of counterbalanced nationalisms continued even when a Polish aristocrat, Kazimierz Badeni (1849–1909), became the prime minister in 1895.

Though unnoticed at that time, the appointment of Badeni symbolized the breakdown of German control over the Habsburg Monarchy. For the first time in Habsburg history, German-speakers controlled none of the key positions in the government. Not only was the prime minister a non-German but the finance minister (Biliński) and the foreign minister (Gołuchowski) were as well. Relying on support received from the Slav and conservative parties represented in the Reichsrat, Badeni dared to take up the Bohemian language question again. In 1897, seeking to achieve a consensus with the Young Czechs, he issued an ordinance that introduced Czech as a language equal to German even in the "inner service" of all the state offices in Bohemia and Moravia. It meant that every civil servant would have to master both languages by 1900. This decision put Germans, who refused to learn Czech, at a disadvantage, and it provoked widespread protests that climaxed in November 1897. Demonstrators took to the streets, not only in Vienna, but also in Graz and some German cities of Bohemia. Francis Joseph I had to dismiss Badeni, and his language ordinance was revoked in 1899 (Carter, 1992: 923; Ehrich, 1992: 528–529; Schenk, 1993: 75; Waldenberg, 1992: 45).

This stopgap solution did not satisfy German nationalists and turned Bohemia, the largest and richest crownland, into a trouble spot second only to the southern Slavic provinces after 1908 (Carter, 1992: 923; Prinz, 1995: 358). In 1910, the Czech lands—Bohemia, Moravia and Austrian Silesia—were responsible for 40 percent of the industrial production and 45 percent of revenue income of all Austria-Hungary. In addition, almost half of the Cisleithanian railway lines were located there. The number of Czech-language periodicals (indicative of the development of the mass Czech national movement) soared from thirty titles in 1861 to over 750 in 1905. Due to rapid industrialization, the percentage of Czechs began to increase in the predominantly German-speaking areas of the Czech lands, since the majority of factories and mines happened to be constructed in these Germanophone areas.

Furthermore, in 1900 there were 4.26 percent illiterate Czechs and 6.83 percent illiterate Germans in Cisleithania. More Czechs were employed in industry (26.2 percent) than Germans (25 percent). In 1913, the thirteen Czech banks had at their disposal 25 percent more capital than their German counterparts in the Czech lands. Practically, the social, cultural, political and economic situations of the Czechs and of the Germans in the Czech lands were equal prior to 1914. Since the beginning of the twentieth century, some held the opinion that Germans were even discriminated against. For instance, in 1903 out of 24,700 imperial civil servants in the Czech lands, only 5,400 were Germans, and Czech-language schools opened even in areas where Czechs were in the minority. On the other hand, Germans constituted 37 percent of the Bohemian population, but they paid 53 percent of the taxes. This indicates that Germans had effective control over a larger chunk of industry and commerce (Waldenberg, 1992: 41–47).

The inability of the authorities to alleviate nationalist conflicts became so pervasive and frustrating at the turn of the twentieth century that the Social Democratic Party developed and endorsed the Brünn Program during its congress in that city in 1899. This program presented a national reform based on democratic federalism. It proposed granting the right of national decision to territorial units formed on the basis of the national principle. Karl Renner (1870–1950) and Otto Bauer (1881–1936), who later became Austrian and German socialist leaders, drafted various programs for the solution of the nationality problem in their books and articles published between 1900 and 1910. Another model of dealing with these issues was actually implemented in the form of the Moravian *Ausgleich* (Compromise) of 1905.

The German-speakers had an absolute majority in the Moravian Landtag, though they constituted only 27 percent of Moravia's population. In 1896, they decided to work out a practical consensus with the local Czechs/Slavs in order to avoid nationalist conflicts, which had ravaged neighboring Bohemia's political and economic life. The following year, the Moravian Landeskulturrat (Council of Culture), which was responsible mainly for education, was divided into German and Czech sections. After nine years of work on it, the *Ausgleich* was ready in 1905, and was promptly endorsed by the Landtag and the monarch.

Moravia's Czechs/Slavs gained equal access to politics, a clear majority in the Landtag, and Czech (Moravian) and German were declared to be of equal importance in education and the civil service. The Brünn University was divided into German and Czech sections, furnishing the Czechs with their second national university. Proposals to introduce similar compromises in Bohemia and Austrian Silesia were not adopted (Ehrich, 1992: 531; Kořalka, 1995: 20; Kotzian, 1991: 9–10). Instead, under the influence of the 1905 revolution in Russia, Francis Joseph I sanctioned popular equal male suffrage two years later. It made the German deputies into a minority in the 516-seat Reichsrat, but in all events they still remained the strongest national group with 233 mandates.

Universal male suffrage brought about the expected decline in the influence of the nationalist parties, as the Christian Socialists and Social Democrats returned as the two strongest parties out of thirty-odd ones represented in the Reichsrat. These electoral results helped in transforming Austria-Hungary into a federal state. However, after 1908 the Balkan crises took precedence over internal reforms. The annexation of Bosnia-Herzegovina in 1908 contributed to the convening of another Pan-Slav congress in Prague, among other places, in support of Serbia. During the diplomatic crisis which ensued, as the Czechs took the side of the Serbs, martial law had to be declared in Prague on Francis Joseph I's sixtieth anniversary of accession to the throne. A small Czech party of intellectuals even demanded independence. They were in the minority, and a majority of Czech politicians opted for wide autonomy within the monarchy. If they did gain independence, there was a danger that the German Empire or Russia would quickly dominate such a Czech nation-state.

The situation became more difficult after the Reichsrat elections of 1911, when the Social Democrats lost half of their mandates. As a result, the influence of nationalist parties increased. Bohemia's Germans noticed that it would become increasingly difficult to retain their dominance over the crownland. The Germans were ready to accept the idea of administrative division of the Czech lands, but the Czech nationalists stood fast by their program of unifying all the Czech lands. The political and social tension that emerged as a result of this German-Czech nationalist conflict was not resolved by the failed attempt at reaching a Bohemian *Ausgleich* in 1912. The imminent conflict had to be ameliorated through the suspension of the Bohemian constitution and crownland autonomy the following year. This unresolved situation intensified, particularly at the close of World War I, contributing to the break-up of Austria-Hungary (Ehrich, 1992: 529–530; Herod, 1976; Kolejka, 1956; Kořalka, 1995: 19; Prinz, 1995: 361; Waldenberg, 1992: 37, 42, 47–49).

Constituting the smallest crownland, Austrian Silesia was administratively detached from Bohemia, Moravia and Galicia. But the Czech, Polish and German national movements started infiltrating this region as early as the 1860s. The establishment of the German Empire and triumph of *Kleindeutsch* nationalism just across the border did not leave the attitudes of the German-speaking Austrian Silesians unchanged. Taking into consideration the general indicators of overall development in Austrian Silesia and the emerging pattern of nationalist strife in Bohemia, there seemed ample potential for the emergence of nationalist, social and confessional conflicts in this crownland. Its population rose from 511,581 in 1869 to 756,948 in 1910. In 1869, 54.5 percent (279,024) inhabitants lived in West Silesia and 45.5 percent (232,557) in East Silesia. Due to rapid industrialization, which attracted many workers to the Ostrau-Karwin industrial basin, these ratios were completely reversed. In 1910, West Silesia housed only 42.6 percent (322,128) of the Austrian Silesians, while East Silesia had 57.4 percent (434,821).

According to the 1857 estimate, 51.1 percent of the Austrian Silesians were German-speakers and 48.9 percent Slavic-speakers (Jews usually spoke German), while other researchers estimate about 51 percent were Slavic-speakers, 48 percent German-speakers and 1 percent Jews. Thus it may be safely assumed that the numbers of German- and Slavic-speakers were almost equal at that time. According to the 1910 census there were 326,000 (43.9 percent) German-speakers, 235,000 (31.7 percent) Polish-speakers and 180,000 (24.3 percent) Czech-speakers in Austrian Silesia. Considering both parts of this crownland separately, West Silesia contained 18.9 percent Czech-speakers in 1880 and 20.1 percent in 1910, with the rest of its population composed of German-speakers. The situation was more complicated in East Silesia, where in 1880 there were 58.6 percent Polish-speakers, 27.4 percent Czech-speakers and 14.1 percent German-speakers. In 1910, the figures were 54.6 percent, 27.1 percent and 18 percent, respectively (Anon., 1992c; 61; Gerber, 1994: 30–31).

Sudden demographic changes in the mere span of three decades (especially in East Silesia) can be explained by the influx of migrants and immigrants to the Ostrau-Karwin industrial basin. In addition, the outflow of population to Vienna and other urban centers of the Dual Monarchy contributed to this process, as well as the relative novelty of the concept of nationality, which was first introduced in the official Austro-Hungarian census in 1880. The measuring of nationality varied, based either on a standard language as used within one's own family or on the one used to communicate with the census-taker. However, quite a sizeable chunk of the East Silesian population spoke mixed language forms belonging to the continua of transitional dialects and creoles. These continua extended among the homogenizing cores of the German, Polish and Czech national cultures. The speech of the East Silesians, who often were not fluent in any of these standard languages, was nevertheless classified as "belonging" to one of these three languages. Because dialects or creoles were not taken into consideration (Nowak, 1995: 33), there was considerable arbitrariness ingrained in census-takers' interpretations of which language was spoken by the families they investigated.

Because most census-takers were German-speakers, they could not distinguish among Slavic languages (let alone dialects), which added to this arbitrariness. On top of that their superiors and the census-takers themselves sometimes happened to support various national movements, which influenced their interpretation of the language situation in a locality or region where they carried out their duties. They also faced the technical problem of the widespread cases of bilingualism and multilingualism, as on census returns each person was to be identified as speaker of one language only.

Some available quantitative measures of shifting demographics can demonstrate the processes of migration within Austrian Silesia after 1871. In 1910, 76,000 Austrian Silesians lived in Vienna, and 58,545 Galicia-born Polish-speakers permanently resided within the industrial basin (Gerber, 1994: 30). The emerging national cleavages were made even more complicated because of the old divisions that continued along confessional lines. In 1910 the population of Austrian Silesia was 84.4 percent Catholic, 13.6 percent Protestant and 1.8 percent Jewish. Once again, differences between both the parts of this crownland were considerable. West Silesia's population was quite homogenous, with 96.3 percent Catholics, unlike East Silesia, with its 76 percent Catholics, 21.5 percent Protestants and 2.5 percent Jews. East Silesia's Protestants were predominantly German- and Polish-speaking, whereas its Jewish population included a sizeable community of Yiddish-speaking Hassidim from Galicia. They differed greatly from the more "enlightened" German-speaking Jews of West Silesia (Anon., 1992c: 61). From the contemporary point of view, the Czech-German national cleavage in West Silesia was alleviated by the unity of faith. Catholicism also united the majority of Czech-speakers in both parts of this crownland. Similarly, Protestantism held together the German-speakers of East Silesia, who concentrated in and around Bielitz (Wurbs, 1982: 84), but it split the Polish-speakers.

From a national point of view, the statistics illustrate the demographic decline of Austrian Silesia's German-speakers. Their percentage diminished from 51.1 percent in 1857 to 48.91 percent in 1880, and to 43.9 percent three decades later (Gerber, 1994: 30–31; Kořalka, 1995: 18; Anon., 1992c: 61). But these changes were not too clearly realized and officially noticed until the concept of nationality gained currency from 1880 onward. On the other hand, the crownland seemed a sure foothold for Germandom, since its percentage of German-speakers was the largest of all the lands of the Czech Crown. The number of German-speakers in Bohemia sank from 36.76 percent in 1880 to 31.17 percent in 1910. The corresponding figures for Moravia were even lower: 29.38 percent and 27.62 percent, respectively. Moreover, the demographic dominance of Czech-speakers in Bohemia and Moravia was not moderated by the strong presence of Polish-speakers, as in Austrian Silesia (Kořalka, 1995: 18).

The relative German dominance in Austrian Silesia ensured stability of the crownland's politics and consequently delayed emergence of national movements that largely had to be ignited from outside. Therefore it is surprising that in 1873 the crownland issued the ordinance instituting bilingual education with German as the leading medium of instruction in place of Polish- and Czech-language elementary schools (Anon., 1939: 1338; Michalkiewicz, 1985: 661). Perhaps it was a reaction to the intensifying national conflict with the Czechs after the failure of the proposed Bohemian *Ausgleich*. Another explanation claims that what encouraged this step in the interest of Germandom was the successful creation of the *Kleindeutsch* nation-state just across the border. Berlin's policies became the national standard to which the Austro-Germans tended to aspire. The most important policy in this regard seems to have been the barring of all languages other than German from elementary education in Prussian Silesia and elsewhere in the German Empire (1872). But this ordinance replacing monolingual Polish- and Czech-speaking elementary schools in Austrian Silesia with bilingual ones was not efficiently enforced (Michalkiewicz, 1985: 661).

Austrian Silesia was perceived as safely shielded against the Czech-German national conflict that made it difficult to govern Bohemia and, less so, Moravia. Hence, the Stremayr Language Act of 1880, which put Czech on equal footing with German in Bohemia and Moravia, was never extended to this crownland (Pokorný, 1993: 116). However, similar provisions were granted to the Austrian Silesians in 1882 when Moravia's supreme court in Brünn issued a decision that obliged all the Austrian Silesian courts to accept Czech and Polish as official languages in contacts with customers. The letter of this decision was frequently avoided because documents in Czech and Polish were indeed accepted but answers were invariably issued in German (Knop, 1992: 113). The language situation continued unchanged until the end of the century, since Badeni's dramatic equalization of German and Czech in inner service of the state administration did not apply to Austrian Silesia (Prinz, 1995: 356). However, in 1899, these languages were accepted in the crownland's financial and internal revenue offices in recognition of the need for wider use of Czech and Polish (Knop, 1992: 113).

Given the context of the development of Polish and Czech national movements in Austrian Silesia and the influx of Polish-speaking migrants from Galicia in the 1880s and 1890s (Nowak, 1995: 29), these language decisions were less vehemently criticized than the 1880 and 1897 language acts that introduced Czech into the administration in Bohemia and Moravia. One of the main critics of including Czech and Polish in the institutions of Austrian Silesia was the Breslau Bishop Georg Kopp. His diocese contained all of East Silesia and one-third of West Silesia. In 1888, he urged the pope to oppose the idea of language rights for Slavic-speakers in Austrian Silesia. As a member of the Austrian Silesian Landtag, he voted against the 1899 decision allowing the official use of Polish and Czech in this crownland. He recommended that priests use German in religious instruction and ordered them to leave the boards of all Slavic societies, including the editorial board of *Gwiazdka Cieszyńska*. Kopp also opposed the spread of Polonization through the influx of Galician migrants, which entailed an increase in the Cracow bishop's influence in East Silesia. Kopp strongly contributed to the opening of the Catholic seminary in Troppau in 1899, whose graduates curbed the inflow of Czech-speaking priests from Moravia (Galos, 1996: 191; Golec, 1993: 178).

In addition, German-language and nationalist organizations began to emerge during the two last decades of the nineteenth century, in emulation of Polish and Czech national examples and due to Pan-German and *Kleindeutsch* influences stemming from Vienna and Berlin respectively. It is worth remembering, however, that since the first half of the nineteenth century, *Großdeutsch* associations of singers[1] and riflemen continued to exist, including similar extant associations of gymnasts and voluntary firemen that dated back to the mid-nineteenth century. They constituted the natural foundation for new organizations, which were to oppose the rise of Slavic nationalisms.

In 1880, the Deutscher Schulverein (German School Organization) was established in Austrian Silesia and its branches sprang up in other towns (Wurbs, 1982: 32; Zahradnik, 1992: 32). German political activists, who had traditionally supported Germany since the 1870–1871 war with France, gathered around the liberal periodical *Silesia*. In the 1880s, their left wing established the nationalist daily *Freie Schlesische Presse* (Free Silesian Press). At the beginning of the 1890s, the Pan-German, nationalist and anti-Semitic ideas propagated by Georg von Schönerer were taken up by some Austrian Silesian liberals who founded their nationalist weekly *Deutsche Wehr* (German Defense) in 1892. This telltale title spelled out the insecurity of the crownland's German-speakers vis-à-vis Slavic national movements and the increasing percentage of Austrian Silesia's Slavic inhabitants associated with these movements (Gawrecki, 1992: 62).

This deeply felt national insecurity caused German nationalists (for instance, W. Kudlich, E. Rochowanski) to establish the Bund der Deutschen Ostböhmens, with its seat in Troppau in 1894. Although it followed suit with similar organizations, which had emerged in Bohemia during the 1880s (Prinz, 1995: 355), the particular year of its birth was quite ominous. It coincided with the establishment of the Deutscher Ostmarkenverein in Posen (Snoch, 1991: 45) and of the Alldeutscher Verband (Anon., 1992d: 103). The Austrian Silesian organization became known as a *Schutzverein* (protective association), and subsequently its name was simplified to the Nordmark (Northern March). This German national organization operated in Austrian Silesia and in the Moravian salient between this crownland's two parts (Gawrecka, 1993: 69). In 1914, it boasted 25,000 members (Bein, 1995: 144), whereas the Deutscher Ostmarkenverein had just 11,850 members (1913) in all of Prussian Silesia (Snoch, 1991: 45). In 1897 the

Nordmark openly adopted *Großdeutsch* nationalism as its ideological stance with the appeal, "Let us become Germans *in toto,* but let us also remain true German Silesians" (Gawrecki, 1993: 57). German nationally minded socialists of Austrian Silesia joined the struggle of nationalist strife in 1907 when they launched their own newspaper, *Neue Zeit* (New Time) (Gawrecki, 1992: 62).

In 1905 the perceived threat posed by Slavic nationalisms caused the German-speaking Landtag deputies to turn down their Czech-speaking colleagues' proposal to work out an *Ausgleich* for Austrian Silesia modeled on the successful example of the Moravian *Ausgleich* (Kořalka, 1995: 20). This decision was quite understandable, because in the same year, the Galician Landtag appealed to the emperor to merge predominantly Slavic-speaking East Silesia with Galicia. The Austrian Silesian Landtag replied with a proposal to attach the predominantly German-speaking border areas of Galicia[2] to Austrian Silesia. Even so, the status quo remained because Francis Joseph I disregarded both the proposals and took no decision in this matter.

However, due to the overall language and national situation in Bohemia and Moravia, the Austrian Silesian Landtag could not avoid granting Slavic-speaking Austrian Silesians more language rights. In 1907, this diet decided that the self-governmental administrations of the communes (*Gemeinden*) would choose suitable languages of inner and outer administration, either German, Czech or Polish. Polish and Czech had already been allowed for use in minor communal affairs in 1901 (Knop, 1992: 113; Michalkiewicz, 1985: 714; Wurbs, 1982: 48–49). In 1910, the Landeskulturrat (Crownland Council of Culture) was divided into the three sections: German, Polish and Czech (Kořalka, 1995: 20). These sections received the official permission to reintroduce Czech- and Polish-language textbooks to Austrian Silesian schools (Fazan, 1991: 206).

In sum, the national movement manifested itself in various language-specific institutions. In 1910, there were six dailies in Austrian Silesia, including a Czech one and a Polish one (Gawrecki, 1992: 64). In 1880, West Silesia boasted eight exclusively German-language secondary schools, and by 1914 four new ones were added, two with Czech as the language of instruction and two with the German language in this function. In 1880, there were seven secondary schools in East Silesia, all of them with German as the medium of instruction. By 1914, fourteen new schools had been established: six with German, five with Czech and three with Polish as the medium of instruction (Gerber, 1994: 33). In 1917, the 306 elementary schools of East Silesia included 156 Polish-language, 76 Czech-language, 49 German-language, 21 Polish-German bilingual and 4 Czech-German bilingual schools. However, in order to finish elementary school, a student was required to attend the sixth and seventh grades either in a German-language or bilingual school. These forms were simply not available in Czech- or Polish-language schools (Michalkiewicz, 1985: 662).

Thus, the German language dominated in Austrian Silesia until 1918 (Kořalka, 1995: 20), unlike in Bohemia, Moravia or Galicia. On the other hand, Czech and Polish were allowed some official status, which was unthinkable just across the border in Prussian Silesia. Given the context of these gradually equitable language and national relations in Austrian Silesia, Polish and Czech nationalists from outside were increasingly less successful at promoting their nationalisms in this crownland. His hopes not daunted by this development, in 1908 Dmowski demanded, among other things, all of Austrian Silesia for a future Poland (Mroczko, 1994: 97–98). Prior to the outbreak of the Great War, in May 1914, a Young Czech activist and Masaryk's friend, Karel Kramář (1860–1937), propounded the idea of a Slavic federal state (ruled by the tsar), which would consist of Russia, Poland, Bulgaria, Montenegro, the South Slavic lands of Austria-Hungary, and the lands of the Czech Crown. In this respect, he demanded the Glatz (Kłodzko) Margravate from Prussian Silesia for Bohemia, and he decided that the eastern half of East Silesia would belong to Poland. Finally, on June 28, 1914, the day when Archduke Francis Ferdinand was assassinated in Sarajevo, a nationalist showdown was staged on the Austrian Silesian-Galician border. The Biala (Biała) River separated the Austrian Silesian city of Bielitz from the Galician town of Biała, though both of them formed a single urban complex.[3] In support of the Polish demands to merge East Silesia with Galicia, Polish activists of the Sokół and voluntary fire brigades marched onto the bridge spanning the two towns. But German gymnasts and athletes prevented them from crossing it. It was a bad omen for the coming years (Wurbs, 1982: 49–50).

Austrian Silesia's Polish national movement was concentrated in the center and east of East Silesia. Having come to the fore in 1848, it managed to maintain its continuity throughout the reactionary 1850s and became quite active at the end of the 1860s. In 1867, the first Polish-speaking deputy was elected to the Austrian Silesian Landtag and four further ones were elected in 1871. In the years between 1873 and 1879, the Mistrzowitz (Mistřovice) rich peasant and Polish activist Jerzy Cieńciała (1834–1913) was Austrian Silesia's first Polish-speaking member in the Reichsrat, where he joined the Polish Circle of the Polish deputies from Galicia (Golec, 1993: 71; Michalkiewicz, 1976: 359). For similar developments, Austrian Silesia's Czech-speakers had to wait until the 1890s and the turn of the twentieth century (Anon., 1939: 1338). The development of the Polish movement in Austrian Silesia was facilitated by the proximity of *the* Polish cultural center of Cracow, and by the wide-ranging cultural and political autonomy obtained by Galicia in 1867–1873. Neither Bohemia nor Moravia was granted such generous autonomy. It is not surprising that beginning with the 1870s, Polish activists from Galicia were bringing Polish national ideas to East Silesia (Wanatowicz, 1992: 75).

Polish activists also participated in Polish national meetings organized in

Cracow and Lwów in 1870 and 1871 (Grobelný, 1992: 72). Reverend Leopold Otto (1819–1882) gave a boost to the development of Polish nationalism among Polish-speaking Protestants. Although he was from German-speaking stock, Otto introduced Polish-language Protestant celebrations in Warsaw in 1849. After the fall of the January Uprising in 1864, he moved to Teschen, where he contributed to the establishing of numerous Polish organizations. He also published Austrian Silesia's only Polish-language Protestant periodical, *Zwiastun Ewangeliczny* (Evangelical Announcer, 1865–1875). Otto returned to Warsaw in 1875, but left behind the first inklings of Polish nationalism among East Silesia's Protestants. With time, this trend led to the atypical association of Polishdom with Protestantism, which did not resonate anywhere else among Polish-speakers (Golec, 1993: 213–214; Zahradnik, 1989: 224). Actually, the fact that the Polish/Slavic-speakers of northeastern Lower Silesia were Protestants caused them to become Germans. But that was not the case in East Silesia.

Considering the development of Polish organizations, the already existing reading rooms and small libraries as well as the Towarzystwo Rolnicze (Agricultural Society, 1868) were supplemented with numerous new ones. In 1872, Paweł Stalmach, still the publisher of *Gwiazdka Cieszyńska* and one of the leading Polish activists of East Silesia, founded the Towarzystwo Naukowej Pomocy (Aid Society for Students) to support poor Polish/Slavic-speaking students from East Silesia (Myška, 1993: 101; Snoch, 1991: 133). The following year, he contributed to the establishment of the Towarzystwo Oszczędności i Zaliczek (Society for Savings and Loans) (Zahradnik, 1992: 40). In 1861, Father Ignacy Świeży (1839–1902), together with his East Silesian friends, founded the Towarzystwo Narodowe (National Society) at the Catholic Seminary in Olmütz. In addition, he inspired them to establish the Polish-language Catholic publishing house Dziedzictwo bł. Jana Sarkandra (Blessed Jan Sarkander[4] Heritage). They drew on the example of a similar Czech-language publisher active in Bohemia and Moravia since 1835, named after the Czech patron saint Jan Nepomucen. By 1897, Father Ignacy Świeży's East Silesian publishing house had brought out thirty-three exclusively religious books with a run of 1,000 copies each, and twenty calendars with a run of 5,000 copies each (Pater, 1996b: 436–437).

Due to the Catholic-Protestant rivalry, the Polish movement split along confessional lines in the second half of the 1870s (Kaciř, 1996: 4; Lis, 1993: 99–100), and no Polish-speaking candidate managed to be elected to the Reichsrat in the 1879 elections (Golec, 1993: 71). In order to get better control of education, the Polish-speaking Protestants established their own Towarzystwo Oświaty Ludowej (Society for Popular Education) in 1881. The confessional split deepened in 1883 when the Związek Śląskich Katolików (ZŚK, Union of Silesian Catholics) came into being. It already boasted a membership of 2,000 within the next year and dynamically entered the social and political life of East Silesia. The ZŚK organized rallies and meetings and published brochures. The alienated Polish-speaking Protestants responded in 1884 with the founding of their Polityczne Towarzystwo Ludowe (PTL, Popular Political Society). This looming conflict was gradually terminated due to a reconciliation reached in the face of the 1884 Landtag elections and the 1885 Reichsrat elections. As a result, Father Świeży and P. Kania became members of the Landtag and the former also became a member of the Reichsrat (Pater, 1996b: 434). This electoral success, the example of the Matice opavská (1877), which founded the Czech gymnasium in Troppau (1883) (Gawrecki, 1992: 63), and the establishment of the Deutscher Schulverein (1881) caused Polish activists led by Paweł Stalmach and Father Świeży to found the similar Macierz Szkolna (School Organization) in 1885. In 1895, it eventually brought about the opening of the Polish gymnasium in Teschen (Lis, 1993: 100; Michalkiewicz, 1976: 357; Myška, 1993: 101).

On August 2, 1888, a terrible storm ravaged East Silesia. Because state aid did not amount to much, Father Świeży appealed for help from Polish organizations in Galicia and Congress Poland the next year. Miarka had used the same recourse in 1879 when Upper Silesia's Slavic/Polish-speaking peasantry's livelihood was wrecked by a draught. Świeży's initiative led to more contacts with Polish activists from these areas. As a result of the alleviation of the dramatic situation and Father Świeży's activities aimed at bridging the Protestant-Catholic rift, full reconciliation was reached in 1890. The ŚKL and the PTL agreed that they would field Father Świeży as their common candidate for the 1891 Reichsrat elections. Due to this new political and confessional consolidation, he received more votes than the German candidate and obtained the mandate. As a consequence, this event temporarily prevented the rise of full-fledged Polish nationalism by directing the Polish-language movement toward universalism. The weekly *Katolik* played a similar role in Upper Silesia by preventing the transformation of the Polish-language movement into a national one (Michalkiewicz, 1976: 360).

In 1890 the ŚKL and the PTL had also reached a compromise with Czech-speakers, which resulted in Czech-speaking candidates' becoming members of the Landtag for the first time. Thus, the three Polish-speaking deputies and the three Czech-speaking ones had formed an alliance, which had to be reckoned with by the German-speaking majority (Anon., 1939: 1338; Pater, 1996b: 435). Then cooperation with Czech-speakers continued, particularly in the context of emerging German nationalism. Polish activists gave access to the premises of the Dom Polski (Polish House) in Teschen to the Czech cultural and educational organization Snaha (Endeavor, established in 1882) during the 1880s (Zahradnik, 1992: 44). On August 1, 1897, 15,000 Polish- and Czech-speakers attended the Polish rally near Teschen. This demonstration incited German-speakers to organize a counter-rally in this town on September 12, 1897. But in comparison, the attendance of 800 was pitifully small. Polish and Czech activists responded with a joint Czech-Polish rally in which all the

Polish and Czech Landtag and Reichsrat deputies participated (Pater, 1996b: 436). In 1900, the Czech-speaker P. Cingr was elected to the Reichsrat with the support of Czech- and Polish-speaking social democrats (Kacíř, 1996: 5).

Later, Polish-Czech cooperation began to unravel when the nascent Czech national movement in Austrian Silesia became better organized. Polish activists perceived the rise of this national movement as Czechization when it started infiltrating East Silesia. Since the 1880s, Czech nationalists had been active in Teschen. In the early 1890s, the Czech organization Snaha expanded its activities in this town, and in 1895, the Czech-language weekly *Noviny těšínske* (Těšín News) began publishing (Grobelný, 1992: 73). Also in 1894, Bohemia's leading nationalist newspaper, *Narodní listy,* advocated making all of East Silesia into a truly Czech-speaking land (Zahradnik, 1992: 44), much to the horror of Polish nationalists. In the 1890s, they replied with their own program, proposing to make East Silesia into a homogenously Polish-speaking land up to the Ostrawica (Ostravice) River, that is, to East Silesia's western frontier. Czech nationalists continued establishing schools and organizations in the east and center of East Silesia. This sparked discontent on the part of Polish activists, who saw the central part of this region as "rightfully belonging" to the Polish nation. Czech activists disagreed with this view and pointed out that Czech national life had quickly developed in and around the rapidly industrializing city of Ostrau. Obviously, its location on the East Silesian-Moravian border facilitated the city's transformation into the center of Czech cultural and national life in western East Silesia and the Moravian salient that divided Austrian Silesia. The proliferation of Czech national influence emanating from Ostrau increased, especially after the Moravian *Ausgleich* of 1905. Then Czech/Slavic-speakers obtained more civil and language rights in next-door Moravia than Czech- or Polish-speakers enjoyed in Austrian Silesia (Grobelný, 1992: 73; Kacíř, 1996: 4). In 1902, numerous repeated instances of escalating Polish-Czech national tension caused Czech and Polish scholars and journalists to publish appeals for Czech-Polish cooperation in the Czech-language *Slovansky přehled* (Slavonic Review) and the Polish-language *Świat Słowiański* (Slavonic World). With an increase in the activities of German national activists prior to the outbreak of the Great War, Czech and Polish nationalists organized many joint protest rallies in East Silesia. The largest one took place in Michalkowitz (Michálkovice) (Grobelný, 1992: 75–76).

In 1898 Czech activists managed to establish the Slezská matice osvěty lidové (SMOL, Silesian Organization for Popular Education) in Teschen. But due to the growing strength of Polish nationalism, it had to be moved to Ostrau in 1908. The same fate met *Noviny těšínske,* which had been transferred to Friedek (Frýdek) (on the border with Moravia) a year earlier. In 1901 Ferdinand Pelc (1876–1932), a leading activist of the SMOL, stated that the "Polish danger was equal to the German one." His opinion found support in the emotive poetry of Petr Bezruč.[5]

In one of his poems, Bezruč commented that "one hundred thousand of us [that is, Czech-speakers of Austrian Silesians] were Germanized, and one hundred thousand Polonized." This line of reasoning was derived from Ignác Hořica's 1895 thesis that East Silesia's Polish-speakers were Polonized Moravians[6] who should be regained for Czechdom (Zahradnik, 1992: 44). These opinions were disheartening for Polish nationalists because they partially reflected the feelings of the Slavic-speaking East Silesians or Slunzaks. The latter, similar to the Slavic-speaking Upper Silesians or Szlonzoks, considered the labels "Pole" and "Galician" as offensive. This was due to the clearly lower standard of living and education of the Polish-speakers in Galicia. No East Silesian wanted to be associated with the proverbial *bieda galicyjska* (Galician poverty) or *polnische Wirtschaft*. Furthermore, because of this low status associated with these stereotypes, Galician migrants to the Ostrau-Karwin industrial basin did not wish to be identified as Poles either. They promptly got Germanized or Czechized, to the dismay of Polish national organizations (Kacíř, 1996: 3, 5).

Polish nationalists counteracted this trend with help from Galician activists. The Sokół opened its first East Silesian branch in Teschen in 1891. The Towarzystwo Szkół Ludowych (Society for Popular Schools), which commenced its activities in Cracow in the same year, founded its Teschen affiliate a year later. This branch facilitated the Macierz Szkolna's opening of the first Polish-language secondary school in Austrian Silesia in Teschen in 1895 (Fazan, 1991: 105, 122; Lis, 1993: 100). In reaction to the increasingly universalistic character of the Polish movement, resulting from cooperation of Catholic and Protestant Polish activists, Polish nationalists established the nonconfessional nationalist society Jedność (Unity) in 1897. The society's membership soared from 300 to 3,000 in 1907 (Fazan, 1991: 107–108).

After Vienna did away with legal restrictions, the social democratic movement developed dynamically in Austrian Silesia (not unlike in Upper Silesia), because this crownland was the most industrialized region of Austria-Hungary. It was responsible for 46.2 percent of the Dual Monarchy's total coal output and 97 percent of its coke production (Lis, 1993: 120–121). In addition, 39.4 percent of Austrian Silesia's workforce was employed in industry in 1910. In the second-most industrialized crownland, Bohemia, this number was lower, 36.6 percent (Bahlcke, 1996: 114). Seizing this opportunity, Polish social democrats from Galicia established the newspaper *Równość* (Equality, 1897–1901) in Teschen (Lis, 1993: 100; Zahradnik, 1989: 180), whereas Polish nationalists began publishing the weekly *Głos Ludu Śląskiego* (The Voice of the Silesian People, 1897–1920) in Freistadt (Fryštát) so as to prevent the Czechization or Germanization of Galician migrants. The Polish national center that developed in this town survived until 1912. In that year, the newspaper moved to Teschen in recognition of the successful inroads German and Czech nationalisms made there (Grobelný, 1992: 74; Zahradnik, 1989: 74–76).

The radical Polish nationalist group active in Freistadt, in cooperation with Polish activists from Galicia (including Dmowski), popularized Polish nationalism in the Ostrau-Karwin industrial basin. This intensified Polish-Czech national conflict in this area at the turn of the twentieth century. Less radical Polish activists, together with their Czech counterparts, strove to abate this tension. They insisted on the necessity of Slavic cooperation (reciprocity) in order to contain German nationalism in Austrian Silesia. To accomplish this goal, they agreed to concentrate Polish national and cultural life in Teschen in order to avoid conflict with Czech national centers in the west of East Silesia (Grobelný, 1992: 74–76; Michalkiewicz, 1985: 714).

The subsequent period of uneasy status quo between Czech and Polish nationalists was shaken by the 1905 revolution in Russia. Numerous Polish-speaking refugees from Congress Poland sought safe haven in Galicia and East Silesia, where they fortified the social democratic movement. Strikes engulfed East Silesia, and in the wake of this general social commotion and the introduction of popular male suffrage (1907), Polish activists from Galicia and East Silesia decided to establish overtly pro-Polish organizations in the latter region. In 1906, the PSL of East Silesia and the Polskie Stronnictwo Narodowe (PSN, Polish National Party) were established as respective offshoots of Galicia's PSL and SD-N. In this year, the social democratic movement of Austrian Silesia was divided along ethnic lines, which led to the emergence of the Polska Partia Social-Demokratyczna (PPSD, Polish Social Democratic Party) of East Silesia. It formed a single party with its mother Galician organization of the same name (Lis, 1993: 117–118; Myśliński, 1986: 9). Also in 1906, the PSN launched the first Polish-language daily in Austrian Silesia, *Dziennik Cieszyński* (Cieszyn Daily, 1906–1920) (Zahradnik, 1989: 53). The next year, Galicia-born Polish activist Franciszek Popiołek (1868–1960) founded the influential literary quarterly *Zaranie Śląskie* (Silesian Dawn, 1907–1938 and 1957–1992) and in 1913 wrote the first Polish history of Austrian Silesia, *Dzieje Śląska Austryackiego* (Lubos, 1974: 523; Zahradnik, 1989: 218). The influence of Galicia's Polish nationalism on East Silesia was so strong and perceived as "normal" after 1905 that the authorities did not object to the coupling of Galicia and East Silesia on a map reproduced in Polish-language textbooks. This amounted to a tacit endorsement of the Polish claim to this part of Austrian Silesia (cf. Haardt, 1907: 57).

In 1907, after the introduction of universal male suffrage, the Social Democrats won the first elections to the Reichsrat and gained 51 percent of votes in the Dual Monarchy. It was a blow to Polish radicals and universalistic Polish activists in Austrian Silesia (Gawrecki, 1992: 62–63; Lis, 1993: 118). In order to offset the social democratic influence,[7] the latter decided to mobilize Protestant-Catholic cooperation between the ZŚK and the PZN (Zahradnik, 1992: 47). They also started collaborating with Polish nationalists, which resulted in the 1907 merger of the Macierz Szkolna with the Jedność (Michalkiewicz, 1985: 714). In 1911, the PSL merged with the PSN to form the Polskie Zjednoczenie Narodowe (Organization of Polish National Unity). It cooperated closely with the ZŚK and the PZN. Together, these three organizations managed to weaken the social democrats and strove unsuccessfully to limit the influence of Josef Kożdoń's ethnic Slunzakian Śląska Partia Ludowa/Schlesische Volkspartei (Popular Silesian Party, established in 1909) in the 1911 elections. However, this unprecedented consolidation of the Polish movement in East Silesia (which excluded only the Polish social democrats) intensified the tension with Czech nationalists prior to the outbreak of the Great War. In 1909, it was tangibly exemplified by the opening of the two secondary schools, one Polish-language and the other Czech-language, in the same locality of Orlau (Orlová) (Gawrecki, 1992: 63–64; Lis, 1993: 119; Nowak, 1995: 31; Zahradnik, 1992: 47).

In examining the development of the Polish national movement in Austrian Silesia, it is necessary to investigate how influential it was prior to the Great War. The Sokół, which usually attracted nationalist-minded youth and students and provided closely knit cadres of pro-Polish fighters and organizers in Upper and Austrian Silesia after 1918, had 649 members in 1909. The size of the less nationalist and more universalistic Polish-language movement can be assessed by the membership of the Macierz Szkolna, which amounted to 5,144 in 1914 (Fazan, 1991: 122, 127). In 1910, the Polish-speakers of East Silesia were served by twenty-eight periodicals, including one daily, one semi-weekly, eight weeklies, six fortnightlies, six monthlies, one quarterly, and five irregular periodical publications (Zahradnik, 1989: 248). Therefore, it is possible to argue that the Polish national movement was considerably weaker than Austrian Silesia's German movement, represented by the Nordmark's 25,000 members. But the Polish/Slavic-speakers were concentrated in the central and eastern parts of East Silesia, where they constituted the majority of its inhabitants. In 1910 there were 233,850 (54.8 percent) Polish/Slavic-speakers in East Silesia as compared to 115,604 (27.1 percent) Czech/Slavic-speakers and 76,916 (18.1 percent) German-speakers. Clearly, the Polish/Slavic-speaking population had a numerical advantage in this area of Austrian Silesia (Zahradnik, 1992: 45).

To fully understand the national conflicts that were to tear East Silesia apart after 1918, it is worthwhile remembering that the west of East Silesia was dominated by Czech/Slavic-speakers, while German-speakers formed a majority in Bielitz and the vicinity. German- and Czech-speakers also prevailed in the Ostrau-Karwin industrial basin, though Polish/Slavic-speakers contested their dominance in Freistadt, Orlau and Karwin. In addition, instances of Polish-Czech national conflict were often more intense than their German-Polish or Czech-German counterparts (Gawrecka, 1993: 71). The explanation for this phenomenon may lie in the fact that all the Slavic-speakers of East Silesia were ethnically and linguistically quite homogenous. Hence Polish and Czech nationalists must have invested much effort in constructing the ethnic border between populations perceived as Czech- and Polish-speaking. In this task, they were unexpectedly assisted by the first Austro-Hungarian censuses that introduced the question on one's language as the indication of one's nationality in 1880. Statistics made visible this imagined but gradually actualized border. The maintenance of it, as well as any changes in this line, constituted the basis for nationalist acrimonies between Czech and Polish nationalists.

The Czech national movement of Austrian Silesia was more effectively suppressed during the reactionary 1850s than its Polish counterpart, which had retained its continuity since its emergence in 1848. Polish activists managed to found a Polish-language weekly in 1848 and later to preserve its publication in a less radical form up to 1920. In this respect, the Czech national movement can be considered discontinuous. Although it spawned some local activists and institutions, such as reading circles in and shortly after 1848, Czech nationalists did not produce effective mechanisms for the further forging and uniting of this fragmented movement within Austrian Silesia. Necessarily, this crownland's Czech nationalism fed on Czech-language publications from nearby Moravia and Bohemia. The popularity of Pan-Slavism among the Old Czechs caused many Czech activists in Austrian Silesia to cooperate with Polish-language groups and *Gwiazdka Cieszyńska*. This peaceful Slavic cooperation was fortified by the universalistic attitude of the Catholic Church, as a majority of Austrian Silesian Czech-speakers were Catholics. The situation continued unchanged until the beginning of the 1860s.

The subsequent political relaxation brought about by an attempt at constitutional reforms in the Habsburg Empire allowed the Troppau secondary school teacher Antonín Vašek (1829–1880) to establish in 1861 Austrian Silesia's first Czech-language periodical, the weekly *Opavský besedník*. It went defunct in 1865, breaching the continuity of the Czech national movement. The emergence of the Young Czechs in the latter half of the 1860s and the efforts to negotiate a Bohemian *Ausgleich* created an appropriate ambience for embarking on new initiatives. Vincenc Prasek (1843–1912), a graduate of the Troppau secondary school, where he was influenced by Vašek, worked in a Slavic[8] secondary school in Olmütz. He met there a Moravian-born Czech activist, Jan Zacpal (1844–1888), whom he inspired to found the Czech-language weekly *Opavský týdeník* (1870–1913) in Troppau. The Catholic Church also strove to adapt to the political changes. Hence the Katharein (Kateřinky) parish reading and singing circle was transformed into the Katolicko-politicka beseda (Catholic-Political Club) in 1870. But the *Opavský týdeník* became the first permanent institution of the Czech national movement in Austrian Silesia. This gave a new impetus to Troppau's Czech-speaking intelligentsia. In 1875, they brought about the introduction of Czech-language sermons in St. George Church in the Austrian Silesian capital and founded the Matice opavská (Opava Cultural Organization) two years later. The Matice opavská was destined to become the most influential organization of Austrian Silesia's Czech national movement, and it survives to this day under the changed name of the Matice Slezská (Silesian Cultural Organization) (Gawrecki, 1992: 63; Jakubíkova, 1994: 144–145; Myška, 1994: 94).

Until 1918, the Matice opavská remained the main organizer of Czech national life in Austrian Silesia. It founded, operated and aided Czech-language schools, libraries, kindergartens, museum rooms, and reading and singing societies. In 1878, the Matice opavská opened its own Czech-language library and started publishing Austrian Silesia's first Czech-language scholarly journal, *Vestník Matice opavské* (Bulletin of the Matice opavská). It was established as a regular periodical only in 1892 and continues publication to this day, though the name changed to *Slezský sborník* (Silesian Contributions) after 1945. With modest financial support from Prague, but mostly based on its own resources, the Matice opavská founded Austrian Silesia's first Czech-language secondary school in 1883. Vincenc Prasek was its first principal. The following year the Muzeum Matice opavské (Museum of the Matice opavská) opened its doors. Subsequently, this museum commenced the action of collecting various artifacts that would assist in "proving" that the crownland had "always been" a Czech land from an ethnic and historical point of view. Initially, the influence of the Matice opavská was limited to Troppau and the Czech-speaking areas in West Austrian Silesia, but over time, it contributed to the creation of the Czech national movement in northeastern Moravia and in the Moravian wedge between West and East Silesia (Anon., 1939: 1342; Bein, 1995: 144; Gawrecki, 1992: 63; Jakubíkova, 1994: 143, 149, 151).

In the 1880s, numerous Czech organizations were created, including the overtly nationalist Sokol. Czech activists established themselves in the western East Silesian border towns of Friedek and Ostrau, a city whose name constitutes a fine example of nationalist manipulation. There were actually two towns bearing the same name. The bigger one, Mährisch Ostrau (Moravská [Moravian] Ostrava), was located in the Moravian salient, and the smaller one, Polnisch Ostrau (Polská [Polish] Ostrava), across the border river of Ostrawitza (Ostravice) in East Silesia. Due to rapid industrialization, both cities had started functioning as single urban organism since the second half of the nineteenth century, but they were officially merged into one city only in 1945. In 1920 the Czech authorities altered the name Polská Ostrava, that is, *Polish* Ostrava, to the more neutral Slezská Ostrava or *Silesian* Ostrava, in order not to give the Polish authorities an additional argument for claiming this part of East Silesia as Polish. All the modifying labels disappeared in 1945 (Batowski, 1964: 44).

From the western borderland of East Silesia, Czech national movements began to infiltrate the center of this region. Already in 1883, Snaha was established in Teschen. When German aldermen began to dominate the Friedek town hall in 1884, Czech activists started operating more decisively in Teschen. The predominantly German-speaking authorities did nothing, as the Czech-Polish national conflict played into the hands of German nationalism (Gawrecki, 1992: 63; Zahradnik, 1992: 44). Thanks to the Polish-Czech pre-electoral campaign, three Czech-speaking and three Polish-speaking deputies entered the Landtag (Anon., 1939: 1338). This exemplary (Pan-)Slavic or universalistic cooperation faltered in the course of the 1890s due to the increased influence of Czech nationalists from Prague and their Polish counterparts from Cracow. These nationalists put forward mutually exclusive demands for East Silesia as an "inalienable part" of the prospective Czech and Polish nation-states, respectively.

The Czech-language universalistic Catholic political organization Jednota (Unity), which became active during the 1880s, could not effectively lower this tension through cooperation with its Polish counterpart the ZŚK. In 1894 *Noviny těšínske* was launched in Teschen, much to the criticism of *Gwiazdka Cieszyńska*, because Polish activists considered this town the center of the Polish nationalist movement. Thus, the Slezská matice osvěty lidové, which came into existence in this town in 1898, was also met with enmity by Polish activists. Due to this situation and the development of Polish nationalism, *Noviny těšínske* had to move to Friedek in 1907, and the Czech school organization moved to Ostrau a year later (Grobelný, 1992: 73; Zahradnik, 1992: 44).

Vincenc Prasek, in cooperation with the Matice opavská, strove to describe various aspects of the whole of Austrian Silesia in order to claim it for Czechdom through scholarship conducted in the Czech language. He planned ten volumes of the *Slezské vlastivědy* (Silesian Regional Studies), but only four were published. Their topics included the folklore of the Austrian Silesian Czech-speakers (1888), the historical topography of West Silesia (1889), the history of West Silesia up to 1813 (1891), and the history of East Silesia up to 1433 (1894) (Myška, 1994: 95). On the other hand, František Slama (1850–1917) and Adolf Emil Vašek (1881–1948) wrote fiction inspired by Austrian Silesian themes, while Jan Loriš (1860–1920) and Čeněk Ostravický (1869–1912) wrote poetry drawing on the local lore. They strove to construct Austrian Silesia into Czechdom through the means of literature. Petr Bezruč finally achieved this goal (Lubos, 1974: 610–621). His poems merged Silesian topics with industrial imagery, which proved quite effective in the period of rapid industrialization that spawned the social democratic movement.

In 1893, the Bohemia-born Petr Cingr (1850–1920) organized the worker movement in the Ostrau-Karwin industrial basin. In the same year, he also started publishing the periodical *Odborné listy* (Trade Union Newspaper). The miners' strikes of 1894 and 1896, as well as the general strike of 1900, indicated that the social democratic movement was temporarily stronger than the national movements. The cooperation of social democratic activists of Czech, German and Polish tongues ceased after the successful 1907 Reichsrat elections when they seized four of Austrian Silesia's seven mandates. The social democratic organizations split along ethnic lines and fully espoused the nationalist ideology after 1910 (Gawrecki, 1992: 63–64; Lis, 1993: 118; Myška, 1993: 24–25).

The nationalist tension was visible in the activities of Polish, German and Czech organizations, whose national interests clashed violently in this industrial basin. The Polish-Czech national conflict symbolically and practically culminated in the 1909 founding of one Polish- and one Czech-language secondary school in Orlau. Also in Orlau Czech activists had launched the previous year a weekly under the telltale title *Obrana Slezska* (Defense of Silesia) (Grobelný, 1992: 24). Austrian Silesian nationalist and universalistic activists of various tongues (among them Petr Bezruč) claimed that they wanted better social, cultural and educational standards for their fellow nationals. But the networks through which ideological, financial and cadre aid flowed from Prague, Cracow, Vienna and Berlin inextricably linked Austrian Silesia with the mainstreams of Polish, Czech and German nationalisms. These clashing ideologies set the scene for the partition of Austrian Silesia after 1918 (Pynsent, 1993: 44).

To understand the development of the Czech national movement in Austrian Silesia it is important to compare how strong it was vis-à-vis its Polish and German counterparts. This is clear from the following statistics: 20 percent of West Silesia's population were Czech/Slavic-speakers in 1910, and they made up 27 percent in East Silesia. From the point of view of the entire crownland, they were the smallest ethnic group, well behind the dominating German-speakers and Polish/Slavic-speakers. Because of the geographic distribution, German-speakers clearly dominated in the whole of West Silesia, with the exception of its eastern corner around Troppau. Polish/Slavic-speakers enjoyed a similar position in East Silesia, with the exception of its western section. But the Austrian Silesian Czech/Slavic-speakers inhabiting bordering parts of West and East Silesia were linked via the Moravian wedge, which was populated by Czech/Slavic-speakers as well. This salient gave them direct access to the Czech/Slavic-speakers of northeastern Moravia.

Thus, it is difficult to assess the development of Austrian Silesia's Czech national movement without taking into consideration the Moravian environment, where the conditions for Czech nationalism were quite congenial after the 1905 *Ausgleich*. But Troppau and Ostrau continued to function as the Czech cultural centers for northern Moravia well into the twentieth century, because the *Ausgleich* fortified the regional Moravian or ethnic Morawec identity instead of inspiring Czech nationalism. This actually blocked further development of Czech nationalism in this area. Hence, it is justifiable to say that the Czech nationalism of Austrian Silesia was weaker than its German and Polish counterparts (Gawrecki, 1992: 61; Zahradnik, 1992: 45; Wiskemann, 1938: map at end). Due to the lack of information on membership of the Czech national organizations of Austrian Silesia, it is important to note that in 1919 there were 25 German savings banks with deposits of 162 million crowns, and three Czech ones with deposits of 5 million crowns (Anon., 1919: 19). This shows that Austrian Silesia's Czech/Slavic-speakers lost the *Wirtschaftskampf* to the crownland's German-speakers, unlike the Czech-speakers of Bohemia and, less so, of Moravia (Waldenberg, 1992: 43).

Analyzing the development of the Czech national movement in Austrian Silesia, one has to pay some attention to the Czech/Slavic-speakers who lived in a compact area across the border in southern Upper Silesia. They spoke northern Moravian subdialects related to Czech but more similar to the spoken vernacular of their Szlonzokian neighbors. Like the majority of the dialectal Czech/Slavic-speakers of Austrian Silesia and Moravia, these Czech/Slavic-speakers of Upper Silesia considered themselves to be Morawecs. As a consequence, they called their speech the "Moravian language" (Kacíř, 1996: 3; Žáček, 1995: 152). The Prussian authorities (like their Habsburg counterparts in regard to Moravia) sought to fortify this regional identity by labeling the Morawecs in official documents and statistics as "Moravians" or "Moravian-speakers" (Gawrecki, 1992: 59).

However, it was their locally born priest Father Cyprian Lelek (1812–1883) who was most responsible for the development of the Czech national movement in this Upper Silesian area, and across the state border in Austrian Silesia and the Moravian salient. Lelek was the only Czech-speaking deputy of the German National Assembly in Frankfurt and the Prussian National Assembly in Berlin. In 1846, he published the first (and only) issue of *Holubice*, the first Czech/Moravian-language newspaper in Austrian and Prussian Silesias. In the same year, Lelek also wrote the first Czech/Moravian-language history of Silesia, before even the Czech- and Polish-language textbooks were introduced to Austrian Silesian elementary schools. At the beginning of the 1850s, he wrote a Czech/Moravian-language primer, which went through six editions during between 1846 and 1871. His interests were mainly folkloristic and his attitudes were universalistic, like Upper Silesia's Polish-speaking clergymen, so he shied away from the Czech national movement that emerged across the state border in Austrian Silesia during the 1860s and 1870s.

Lelek stuck to confessional loyalties, which still overrode ethnic lines in Silesia at that time. His universalistic stance was made easier by the fact that his Morawec faithful were Catholics (Myška, 1994: 74–75). But it was not satisfactory for the authorities of the newly formed German Empire during the *Kulturkampf*, since Berlin perceived Catholic universalism as a part of the Vienna-supported *Großdeutsch* nationalism. This universalism's association with the Slavic languages of Upper Silesia made it especially subversive in the eyes of the provincial administration. These languages clashed with the homogenously monolingual ideal of *Kleindeutsch* nationalism. No Czech- or Moravian-language periodical emerged in Prussian Silesia after 1848. As a consequence, Father Lelek ended up collaborating with several Austrian Silesian and Bohemian Czech-language newspapers. The Bohemian newspapers included *Hlasy* (Voices), *Národní listy*, and the Austrian Silesian ones: *Opavský besedník* and *Opavský týdeník* (Myška, 1994: 75). Father Lelek encouraged the faithful to subscribe to them and to purchase religious books in Moravian and Czech (Hytrek, 1996: 36; Myška, 1994: 74–75). Some of these publications contained the Czech national messages propagated by the Old Czechs. Hence, already in the 1860s the Prussian authorities (rather rightly) blamed Czech nationalists for striving to introduce ethnic cleavage. It would destroy Upper Silesia's peaceful centuries-long German-Morawec coexistence (Wanatowicz, 1992: 135).

The region's Morawecs, numbered 42,000 in 1840 (Kokot, 1973: 74) and formed a quarter of the population of the Ratibor county and 11 percent of the population in the Leobschütz county in 1875 (Reiner, 1971: 397). By 1905, their numbers had risen to 57,000 in the former county and to 5,000 in the latter (Gawrecki, 1992: 61). Their percentage in the populace of both these counties remained unchanged, though in the case of the Ratibor county, they amounted to 42.2 percent of the rural population and 4.4 percent of the urban population.[9] Morawecs were concentrated west of the line running from Oderberg to Bauerwitz (Baborów) in the southern section of the Ratibor county. A smaller region of Morawecs lay in the south of the Leobschütz county around the villages of Branitz (Branice), Nassiedel (Nasiedle) and Jakubowitz (Jakubowice) (Gregor, 1904). The policies of the *Kulturkampf,* which removed Polish from elementary education in Prussian Silesia after 1872 and from school religious instruction after 1875, were also applied to the Morawecs and the Moravian language. The only preserve of their language and customs remained the local Catholic churches (Plaček, 1996: 7–8).

Due to the anti-Catholic and anti-Slavic character of the *Kulturkampf,* the Morawecs, like the Polish/Slavic-speaking Upper Silesians or Szlonzoks, turned into loyal supporters of the Zentrum. However, the Morawecs' pro-German attitude remained quite strong, unlike that of some of the Szlonzoks and Slunzaks, because the Morawecs' religious books were published in their own written dialect, officially known as the Moravian language. It differed in spelling and usage from standard Czech because the latter had been modernized (changed) in the mid-nineteenth century. In addition, while Czech texts had ceased to be printed in Gothic characters in the 1820s and 1830s, Moravian-language publications made exclusive use of this Gothic type, which was unambiguously associated with Germandom (Triest, 1984: 657). This ethnocultural distinctiveness of the Morawecs vis-à-vis other nationally and ethnically differentiating inhabitants of Upper Silesia and Austrian Silesia was deepened by the fact that the Morawec-populated territories mainly belonged to the Olmütz Archdiocese. It comprised the south of Prussian Upper Silesia and the Moravian wedge between East and West Austrian Silesia, as well as the eastern section of West Silesia.

In order to insulate the Morawecs from the developing Slavic national movements in Upper and Austrian Silesias and to retain their unwavering loyalty to the Catholic Church and the Zentrum, the local clergy launched the weekly *Katolické Nowiny* (Catholic News, 1893–1920). It was published in the Moravian language and printed with the use of Gothic fonts. This weekly's runs soared from 420 copies in 1893 to 3,000 between 1911 and 1917. The editors of this newspaper, Father Arnošt Jureczka (1867–?), Josef Hlubek (1872–1951) and Josef Ottawa (1861–1921), were the main leaders of the nascent Morawec national movement. On the basis of the Treaty of Versailles, the larger part of the Upper Silesian territory inhabited by the Morawecs was transferred to Czechoslovakia in 1920. Because of the area's main town, Hultschin, it became known as the Hultschiner Ländchen (Hlučinsko). It measured 315.8 square kilometers and, according to the 1910 census, supported a population of 48,446, the majority of whom were Morawecs. The Czechs considered them "antiquated Czechs" who had to be modernized and integrated into the fold of the Czech nation. In 1920, the year when the *Katolické Nowiny* was closed down, standard Czech spelling and the Latin type were employed in this periodical so that the title read *Katolické noviny* (Gröschel, 1993: 240; Weczerka, 1977a: 199).

This sudden imposition of the Czech national identity on the Morawecs squelched the Morawec national movement and brought about an equally rapid reaction to Czechization. Gradually, the Morawecs started to identify themselves as Germans. According to the 1910 census, there were 19 percent Germans in the Hultschiner Ländchen, while the Czechoslovak sources estimated it at 20 percent[10] (Weczerka, 1977a: 200). Czechization, which continued unabated against the wishes of the *Hultschiners* (that is, the inhabitants of the Hlučinsko), caused 80 percent of them to vote for the Sudetendeutsche Partei (Sudeten German Party). Hence, prior to World War II, the majority of them identified themselves as Germans. In this process, the Morawec ethnic and national identity vanished. As an ironic observer rightly remarked: "Bismarck could not make the 'Hultschiner[s]' into Germans, but where he failed the Czechs have succeeded" (Wiskemann, 1938: 232–234).

Before moving to the problematic of the Slunzakian national movement, it is worth noting that in 1840, there were 8,500 Bohemian-speakers (or Czech-speakers stemming from Bohemia) living in the Breslau Regency. They were concentrated in the Glatz Margravate and in the counties of Strehlen (Strzelin) and Groß Wartenberg. About 1,000 of them also resided in the Liegnitz Regency, mainly in Hirschberg (Jelenia Góra), Jauer (Jawor) and Görlitz (Zgorzelec, Görlitz). By 1905 their number rose to 1,800 in the latter regency and to 10,000 in the former regency, where their presence became visible in the workforce of the Waldenburg-Neurode coal mining area (Kokot, 1973: 74). A majority of them were descendants of eighteenth-century Protestant refugees from Bohemia and Moravia. Because they lived in predominantly German-speaking areas, they were often bilingual. Furthermore, being Protestants and knowing German helped them very easily assimilate into *Kleindeutsch* Germandom, which was based on these two ethnocultural elements. It was more practical to be a German than a Czech (Bohemian) at that time in Prussian Silesia and the German Empire. Hence the Czech national movement did not influence these Czech/Slavic-speaking Bohemians. Like the Polish-speaking Protestants of northeastern Lower Silesia, almost all of these Lower Silesian Czech/Slavic-speakers became Germans by 1945. They only preserved some vague memories of their Czech ethnic or Bohemian regional origins. At the end of World War II, Soviet troops occupied the Glatz Margravate. Subsequently, the Polish administration took over this area and, together with the Soviets, carried out the expulsion of the margravate's German population in 1945–1946. Soon, there was no need for the use of the Czech language (cf. Großpietsch, 1994). Even those 2,000 to 3,000 local Bohemians, who declared themselves Czechs in the second half of the 1940s, decided to leave for Germany rather than Czechoslovakia after the communist takeover in the latter country in 1948 (Pałys, 1995: 39, 49).

A phenomenon similar to the Morawec national movement was the Slunzakian national movement. It slowly developed after 1848 in East Silesia as a reaction to the emergence of the Czech and Polish national movements, which aimed at homogenizing the population speaking their specific subdialects and practicing varied customs into the homogenous national worlds of the standard Polish and Czech languages and cultures. The beginning of this movement can be traced back to the decision of the local Catholic clergy to neutralize *Tygodnik Cieszyński* and the clearly Polish national activists who had launched it. To this end, the clergy established the Polish-language universalistic and pro-German weekly *Nowiny dla Ludu Wiejskiego* (1848–1849). This initiative was abandoned during the reactionary 1850s, but the development of the Czech and Polish national movements led to the establishment of the pro-German political weekly *Nowiny Śląskie* (Silesian News, 1868–1869). This periodical promoted the regional Austrian Silesian identity and loyalty to the Austrian half of the Dual Monarchy. Both of these newspapers appeared in Teschen and mainly sought readership in this town and its vicinity.

The Lemberg-born Reverend Theodor Haase (1834–1909) became the pastor of the bilingual Protestant Bielitz Parish in 1859. Later, he followed in the footsteps of Reverend Leopold Otto. After the latter left for Warsaw in 1875, Haase was nominated to the position of the Teschen pastor the following year. There was an ideological difference between these two pastors. Otto advocated the Polish national idea in East Silesia. Strangely enough, he managed to associate it with Protestantism, though elsewhere Polish nationalism and Protestantism were mutually exclusive because of the latter's unambiguous association with Germandom. Haase opposed this national line. He was elected to the Landtag in 1876, and three years later gained a Reichsrat mandate from the urban *curia*[11] constituency of Bielitz, Skotschau, Schwarzwasser (Strumień) and Jablunkau (Jabłonków). In 1882, he was also nominated to the position of the Moravian-Austrian Silesian superintendent of the Evangelical Church of the Augsburg Confession (Gawrecki, 1992: 62; Golec, 1993: 119; Weczerka, 1977b: lxxxv; Zahradnik, 1989: 122, 125). Haase was against all nationalisms because they introduced ethnic cleavage that cut across the Protestant faithful and, generally speaking, the Austrian Silesian population.

In his activities aimed against any ennationalization of his faithful, Haase was aided by the split in the Polish movement along confessional lines, which led to the emergence of the Catholic ŚKL and Protestant PTL during the first half of the 1880s. He commenced the publication of the pro-Austrian Silesian, Protestant and pro-German political weekly *Nowy Czas* (New Time, 1877–1920). Later it was combined with the more practically oriented biweekly *Przegląd Rolniczy* (Agricultural Review, 1887–1909). The run of the former periodical reached 1,500 in 1900. Haase also established the Protestant Reading Room in Teschen in order to limit the influence of similar Polish institutions in this region. In 1885, there were fourteen East Silesian pastors already cooperating with Haase, as opposed to the three who either stayed neutral or leaned toward the pro-Polish PTL. The long career of Haase was crowned in 1905, when was he made into a life peer to the Reichsrat's higher chamber, the Herrenhaus (House of Lords). It lent a considerable degree of respectability to the emerging Slunzakian movement and credibility that was not readily available either to the Polish or Czech camp (Nowak, 1995: 27–28; Zahradnik, 1989: 125–126, 153–154).

Industrialization contributed to the emergence and intensification of the national conflict in East Silesia during the 1880s–1910s. What made this process even more acute was the influence of Polish, German and Czech nationalisms that radiated from Cracow, Vienna and Prague, respectively. These developments could not be prevented or contained with Haase's traditional methods at the beginning of the twentieth century. In addition, the political situation grew more complicated and polarized with the unprecedented rise of the social democratic movement at the turn of the twentieth century.

The locally born Josef Kożdoń (1873–1949) offered a solution to this vexing debacle. Czech researchers spell his surname in accordance with the Czech spelling as "Koždoň," while Polish scholars employ the Polish-language version of his first name, "Józef." It is difficult to determine the correct form of this politician's name and surname, as there is no extant registration document of his birth. But after analysis of various German, Polish and Czech sources, it seems that the form "Josef Kożdoń" was used to sign official documents.

Kożdoń attended a Polish-language elementary school and later graduated from the Teschen teachers' seminary, where the medium of instruction was German, as in all the other Austrian Silesian teachers' seminaries at that time. In 1898, he started working at the elementary school in Skotschau. By birth, education and job, he was attached to this area of East Silesia toward which Haase had directed his efforts. Kożdoń subscribed to Haase's views and spoke against nationalisms. He especially opposed the Galician Polish-speakers, who, according to him, had nothing in common culturally with the East Silesian Polish-speakers. Kożdoń also spoke against the influx of the Czech intelligentsia attracted to East Silesia by industrialization. Thanks to German support, he was elected to the Landtag in 1907 (Golec, 1993: 161; Nowak, 1995: 29).

Soon, Kożdoń started building his electorate, especially in the region around Skotschau, Schwarzwasser and Bielitz (Nowak, 1995: 31). He consolidated this electorate around his political creed: "We, East Silesians, regardless of the language [we speak], call ourselves Austrians and repudiate any nationalistic chauvinism, be it Polish or German, and are bound with Vienna" (Kacíř, 1996: 3). This political program aspired to preserve the ethnic distinctiveness of the East Silesians (that is, mainly Slunzaks), firmly anchored in regionalism and loyalty to the Habsburg monarch. Such a political vision proved attractive as the Polish, Czech and German nationalists and the Catholic and Protestant churches contended for this population's identity against their wishes. In the process of industrialization, the Slunzaks entered into contact with arriving Czech-speaking intelligentsia and Galician Polish-speaking workers. Confronted with the Other, they expressly rejected the attempts to include them in Polishdom, considering the ethnonyms "Pole" and "Galician" as pejorative. The Czech nationalist influence was weakened in east and central East Silesia at the turn of the twentieth century, making goals of Czechdom no longer a viable option. On the other hand, centuries-long attraction to Austrian culture, based on the German language, did continue. Thus, Kożdoń and his Slunzakian followers, not wishing to transform their ethnic group into a full-fledged nation, decided that they felt more affinity to *Großdeutsch* Germandom from a cultural stance than to the then-coalescing Polishdom (Kacíř, 1996: 3; Nowak, 1995: 30). Consequently, the ethnic appeal of East Silesia's Slunzakian movement was confined to the rural areas, where the demographic patterns had not been transformed by industrialization. The Slunzakian ethnic identity was not an option to Galician migrants in the Ostrau-Karwin basin, who usually chose between assimilation into Germandom or Czechdom (Nowak, 1995: 32).

In 1909 Kożdoń, with the aid of the Protestant Church and local German activists, established the Śląska Partia Ludowa/Schlesische Volkspartei (ŚPL/SVP, Silesian People's Party) in Skotschau. In the same year, he was elected to the Landtag for another term (Gawrecki, 1992: 62; Kuhn, 1977: 508). Initially, this new party attracted 2,000 members, and in 1910 the electoral base of the ŚPL/SVP and the Slunzakian movement in general considerably broadened with the founding of the apolitical Związek Ślązaków/Bund der Schlesier (ZŚ/BdS, Union of the Silesians) (Nowak, 1995: 31). The Slunzakian movement also enjoyed its own weekly, *Ślązak* (Silesian, 1909–1923), which was simultaneously the ŚPL/SVP's press organ. Its run soon topped 3,400 copies (Zahradnik, 1989: 191). In 1911, the Slunzaks achieved a considerable success in the local elections when members of the ŚPL/SVP and ZŚ/BdS were elected to head thirty-six *Gemeinden* (communes). At that time, Austrian Silesia was divided into counties that were constituted from the *Gemeinden*. East Silesia housed the four counties of Bielitz, Teschen, Friedek and Freistadt, which shared among them 213 *Gemeinden* (Nowak, 1995: 26). In the Teschen county, where the Polish movement was the strongest, in 1907 administration was conducted in the Polish language at twenty-five *Gemeinden*, in Polish and German at eight *Gemeinden*, and exclusively in German at thirty-six *Gemeinden* (Grobelný, 1992: 75).

The pronounced lack of interest of the Slunzakian movement in ethnic nationalism was clearly displayed during the 1910 census. Kożdoń suggested that his supporters should indicate German or Polish as their *Umgangssprache,* or language employed in everyday situations (Nowak, 1995: 30). This anational but pro-German stance of the Slunzakian movement inescapably bred conflict with the Polish national movement. It considered East Silesia's northeastern corner, dominated by Kożdoń's adherents, as its own. Polish activists abused their Slunzakian counterparts with such labels as "renegades," "*kożdoniowcy*" (that is, "Kożdoń's men") or "*ślonzakowcy*." This latter, phonetically altered label is derived from the Polish word "*Ślązak*," meaning "Silesian," or rather "Slunzak" in this specific context. East Silesia's Polish activists reserved the word *Ślązak* as a term of reference to themselves and denied its use to the Slunzakian national movement[12] (Kacíř, 1996: 3). Polish nationalists also appealed for unrelenting struggle against the Slunzakian activists as "worse than Czech- or German-speakers" inhabiting East Silesia (Nowak, 1995: 32). As a consequence, not only straightforward Polish nationalists attacked the ŚPL/SVP but also the nationally oriented members of the PTL and ZŚK (Zahradnik, 1992: 47). Kożdoń answered by attacking the increasingly monolingual Polish-language libraries, which, because of this tendency, could not appropriately serve the multilingual population of East Silesia and popularized Polish nationalism (Fazan, 1991: 103, 174).

Due to the outbreak of the Great War in 1914, social and national conflicts in Austrian and Prussian Silesias were forgotten or largely swept under the carpet of the steadfast loyalty of all the populations to their respective emperors (Grobelný, 1992: 77; Lis, 1993: 116). The political and economic life of Austria-Hungary and the German Empire was fully subordinated to the war effort. Radical socialist and nationalist publications were suppressed with preventive censorship. Proponents of nationalist and socialist organizations were limited in their activities almost to a standstill by mobilization and wartime strictures. Soldiers of various tongues and ethnic backgrounds fought loyally at various fronts, remaining true to the tsar or the German and Austro-Hungarian kaisers.

For the time being, the general attachment of the populations to their respective dynasts successfully overrode ethnic cleavages up to 1917 and 1918. The Polish or Czech national question was more frequently toyed with by Moscow, Vienna and Berlin for the sake of winning the war than by those concerned. The latter only hoped to survive the nightmare and to be reunited with their families scattered in the course of the prolonged warfare. Sensibly, they had no wish to continue fielding more soldiers and fighting in order to facilitate emergence of nation-states, which national ideologues had devised. Mostly it was only these ideologues who impatiently awaited opportunities to force these yet unheard-of nation-states onto the political map of postwar Europe.

The situation changed with the gradual collapse of the prewar status quo in 1917 and 1918. In addition, the Allies accepted the national principle in the form of U.S. President Woodrow Wilson's dogma of self-determination of nations as the cornerstone of the political reorganization of the continent. This made many unwilling troops continue soldiering for numerous new "lords," be they various national or revolutionary movements, which followed in quick succession after the break-up of Austro-Hungary and the demise of the traditional power systems in the German Empire and Russia. The drawn-out end of this era spawned a dramatically new Europe of nation-states. It also resulted in a new partition of Silesia, simultaneously with the consolidation of nation-states whose emergence was demanded and justified by respective nationalist ideologies.

Regional identities and loyalties to multiethnic and multiconfessional political entities became passé. Ethnic, linguistic and, to a lesser degree, confessional homogeneity as the basis of nation- and nation-state-building won the day. Unavoidably, this meant the decline of the traditional way of life in Silesia, as in many other distinctively multicultural regions of central and eastern Europe. To understand this process, it is necessary to present a general overview of the activities of the Polish and Czech national movements. They were responsible for replacing the prenational and anational forms of identification with the "standard" national one. Simultaneously, these movements also seized the opportunity of the unexpected collapse of the prewar order in central Europe, which left the national movements the main actors on the political scene. This led to the creation of the new aspiring nation-states. They included Poland and Czechoslovakia, which were founded in 1918 at the cost, among others, of the German Empire and German nationalism. The subsequent struggle between the proponents of Czech(oslovak), German and Polish national dreams left an indelible scar on Silesia.

The following chapter offers a close scrutiny of this process in Silesia.

CHAPTER 10

World War I and the
National Question in Silesia

During the Great War, Silesia, because of its location, was linked to the vicissitudes of the dynamically changing Eastern Front. Possessing a larger standing army, which offset their slower mobilization procedures, the Russians assumed the offensive at the very beginning of the war. Already in August 1914, Russian armies advanced into East Prussia and Galicia. They were precariously held back from entering East Prussia, the Province of Posen, and Silesia, as well as from seizing Cracow. The chief aim of the three million Russian troops was to capture Upper Silesia, the second-largest industrial basin of the German Empire. Then the victory would have been complete with the projected fall of the Silesian capital of Breslau.

The possibility of losing Silesia to the Russians was so imminent that evacuation of the civil population started and destruction of industrial facilities was prepared. The desperation of the Germans was evidenced by the barbed wire fences put up east of Breslau in hopes of restraining the advancing Russian forces. General Remus von Woyrsch (1847–1920), in charge of the protection of his native province, deftly withstood the Russian onslaught. It was decisively stopped by General Paul von Hindenburg's (1847–1934) victory at Tannenberg (Stębark) in East Prussia (August 26–30, 1914) and his two further victories in the two battles of the Masurian Lakes (September 7–14, 1914; February 7–21, 1915). German nationalists regarded these victories as symbolic revenge for the 1410 battle of Grünfelde (Grunwald),[1] during which the Teutonic Order's forces had been defeated by the more numerous Polish-Lithuanian and Bohemian troops (Czapliński, 1990: 600). These successes were also commemorated in Upper Silesia. In 1915, Upper Silesia's largest industrial village of Zabrze was named after Hindenburg (it was elevated to the rank of a town only seven years later).

In April 1915, the German forces advanced into the Russian provinces of Lithuania and Courland, and the following month Galicia and Bukovina were regained. The Austro-German offensive launched on July 1 along the front line extending from the Baltic to the San River achieved a crossing of the Vistula at Ivanogrod (Dęblin) on July 29–30. This success led to the successive captures of Warsaw (August 8), Kovno (Kaunas) (August 18) and Brest-Litovsk (Brest) (August 25). The Russians managed to check this impetus in eastern Galicia. The four Russian offensives staged during the second half of 1916 only pushed back the Austro-German armies a bit.

Beginning in July 1917, the German and the Austrian armies recaptured almost all of Galicia and Bukovina. In September, the Germans took Riga and, the following month, occupied the greater part of Latvia. In further advances, they were helped by the increasing disorganization of the Russian state, brought about by the outbreak of the October Revolution in November 1917. On February 9, 1918, the Central Powers recognized the Ukrainian state and Ukrainian autonomy in eastern Galicia in exchange for the delivery of grain supplies. In the Treaty of Brest-Litovsk (March 3), Soviet Russia, embroiled in numerous internal and border conflicts, left the stage of the Great War entirely. St. Petersburg also surrendered other territories to the Central Powers—Livonia, Courland, Lithuania, Estonia and Congress Poland—and recognized Finland and Ukraine as independent states.

The Central Powers, eager to check the westward spread of bolshevism, maintained control of these vast eastern territories (with the exception of Finland) by the autumn of 1918. Then, many central and eastern European states declared their independence, and communist revolution was transplanted to the German Empire and Austria-Hungary. On October 16, 1918, Emperor Karl (reigned 1916–1918) issued a manifesto announcing the transformation of Austria-Hungary into a federal union. This long-overdue move could not forestall the breakup of the Habsburg realm. The Ottoman Empire also crumbled, and as the Allies made inroads into the lines of the Central Powers on the Western Front, Germany had to conclude an armistice with the Allies on November 11. The Great War was over.

On January 18, 1919, the peace conference convened in Paris to determine the new political terrain of Europe. Instead of substantively addressing the hostilities, this conference only obscured them with rhetoric. It dictated unduly harsh terms of peace to the German Empire, which was rather unjustly accused of having caused the war. The Allies also legitimized Germany's territorial losses to the new nation-states of Lithuania, Poland and Czechoslovakia. Cisleithania, formerly dominated by German-speakers, was limited to the tiny rump of old-Austria. These developments were a tragedy of *Kleindeutsch* nationalism and the dismantling of its *Großdeutsch* counterpart. As a result the Allies installed a "cold peace," which Berlin and Vienna saw as an "unjustified dictate [*Diktat*]." With the benefit of hindsight, one can remark that this conference simply delayed the resumption of military activity for two decades (Czapliński, 1993: 43; Ehrich, 1992: 533; Fuchs, 1994: 608–609; Kinder, 1978: II 125, 130–131; Neubach, 1992: 12; Scheuermann, 1994: 1980).

During the war the Polish question had been a trump card to be used in times of need by Russia and the Central Powers. On August 16, 1914, the Austrian government had allowed the formation of the Naczelny Komitet Narodowy (NKN, Supreme National Committee) in Cracow and of a Polish legion, to which soldiers were recruited from Józef Piłsudski's society of Polish riflemen and from among his other followers. Two days earlier St Petersburg had recognized the basic right of the Poles to autonomy. Then in November the Russian authorities allowed the founding of the Komitet Narodowy Polski (KNP, Polish National Committee) under Roman Dmowski's leadership. On Piłsudski's own initiative the clandestine Polska Organizacja Wojskowa (POW, Polish Military Organization) came into being in Warsaw in October. The NKN hoped to establish the Polish nation-state with the support of the Central Powers, while the KNP strove for the same, expecting Russian aid to this end.

The quick succession of the Central Powers' victories on the Eastern Front had made further concessions to the Poles unnecessary. Congress Poland was divided into two military occupation zones, with a German governor in Warsaw and an Austrian-Hungarian governor in Lublin. Dmowski's plans having been frustrated, he left for western Europe. Congress Poland's Polish activists established the Centralny Komitet Narodowy (CKN, Central National Committee) in December 1915. It accepted the NKN's program. However, the Central Powers were reluctant to contribute to the founding of an independent Poland in any substantial manner. They hoped to win the war soon and to reestablish the prewar status quo, possibly improved in their favor.

Thereafter the war of attrition set in, with no end in sight, and it overburdened the unprepared economies of the Central Powers to the point of collapse. On German initiative the Poles had to be won again for the war effort. The German and Austrian-Hungarian emperors proclaimed a new Kingdom of Poland on November 5, 1916. William II considered offering the Polish crown to the Prince of Pleß, Hans Heinrich XV von Hochberg (1861–1938), or to his eldest son. This prince was a renowned industrialist, large landowner, member of the upper chamber of the Reichstag, the deputy *Oberpräsident* of Silesia, the president of the elite Union-Klub in Berlin, a diplomat, and a trusted friend of the emperor. Hans Heinrich XV was one of the ten richest persons in the German Empire. He, like many other aristocratic families of Silesia, accepted the tradition of the Silesian Piasts as his own, visible in the symbolic use of the Polish/Slavic name Bolko in his family. Due to some distant genealogical connections with the Silesian Piasts, Hans Heinrich XV promoted the "Piast origin" of his princely dynasty. This justified his claim to the Polish throne, and many a contemporary Polish scholar espoused this point of view. After the 1922 division of Upper Silesia, the majority of Hans Heinrich XV's estates were included within the Polish borders. In order not to lose control over them, he accepted Polish citizenship and ranked as the fifth-richest person in Poland. But in the estimate of his Polish fortune, Hans Heinrich XV's Lower Silesian mansions in Germany were not taken into account (Polak, 1995: 200–201).

The Central Powers' proclamation of the Polish Kingdom did not fulfill the hopes of Polish nationalists. Berlin and Vienna envisioned it as consisting of Russia's Congress Poland only, without any possibility of attaching to it the rest of the Russian partition of erstwhile Poland-Lithuania, or Galicia, let alone the Province of Posen. This proclamation, however, did encourage Polish nationalists and caused the CKN (which controlled the then semi-legal POW) to undertake anti-Russian activities.

In the meantime, thanks to the personal contacts of the renowned Polish pianist Ignacy Paderewski (1860–1941) with U.S. President Woodrow Wilson (1856–1924), the latter stated on January 22, 1917, that the Allies and the Central Powers accepted the necessity to reestablish a "united, independent and autonomous Poland." On March 29 the Russian provisional government proclaimed that a Polish state in alliance with Russia would be created. Subsequently, Polish armies were formed in France and Russia. On August 15, 1917, Dmowski reestablished the KNP with its seat in Switzerland before the committee was moved to Paris. In Congress Poland Piłsudski's 20,000-strong Polish legion did not want to swear allegiance to the Central Powers, which led to his imprisonment on July 22. On October 15 Berlin and Vienna installed the Regency Council of the Kingdom of Poland. But this decision came too late and could not overcome the distrust that Polish nationalists now felt toward the Central Powers.

The national principle, encapsulated in the "right to self-determination of all nations," as stated by both Wilson and Lenin, was elevated to the rank of an internationally accepted guideline in accordance with which the political map of Europe was to be reorganized. On January 8, 1918, Wilson demanded an "independent Polish state" in his Fourteen Points speech. The military collapse of Austria-Hungary in October led to the formation of the Polska Komisja Likwidacyjna (Polish Liquidation Commission)[2] in Cracow on October 28. It was the first independent Polish administrative body. On November 7 the provisional government of the Polish Republic was established in Lublin.

Piłsudski was freed when the German Empire feared collapse in November 1918. Upon his return to Warsaw the aforementioned administrations put themselves under Piłsudski's control, and he became the unrivaled ruler of the forming Polish nation-state on November 11. This date is generally recognized as the day when the Second Polish Republic was founded. Interestingly, the name of this new nation-state construed it as the direct successor to the multiethnic and much more territorially extensive Commonwealth of the Kingdom of Poland and the Grand Duchy of Lithuania. In this manner, Polish nationalists claimed former Poland-Lithuania and denied its heritage to Lithuania, Belarus and Ukraine. In the interwar period, beginning in the 1930s, November 18 was celebrated as the Polish Day of Independence, as it is today following the collapse of communism in 1989 (Czubiński, 1976: 613–614; Schramm, 1989: 80–81; Smogorzewski, 1992: 951–952).

Prior to the Great War, the bitter Czech-German national conflict unfolded in Bohemia, which brought about the suspension of the crownland's constitution in 1913. These developments discouraged the Czech population from wholehearted participation in the war effort. Some Czech intellectuals of Pan-Slav leanings openly proclaimed that the war was not fought for the Czech national cause and that they should instead side with Russia. This disloyal stance brought about the incarceration of many pro-Russian Young Czechs, including Karel Kramář. Vienna was convinced of its position when some Czech units went over to the Russian side in 1915 during a time when St. Petersburg seemed close to achieving victory.

In December 1914, the Young Czech leader Tomáš Garrigue[3] Masaryk (1850–1937) was warned of his imminent arrest, abandoned his family and fled abroad, protected by a Serbian passport. Earlier, his career had been academically oriented. He had taught philosophy in Vienna, worked as a professor at the Czech Prague University since its inception in 1882, and served several terms as a deputy to the Reichsrat. Masaryk had opposed Pan-German policies that subjugated Austria-Hungary to the German Empire and disagreed with the aggressive Austro-Hungarian course in the Balkans. He had also contributed to the standardization of the Czech language and culture as an initial editor of the monumental *Ottův slovník naučny* (1888–1942). This thirty-volume encyclopedia remains unsurpassed in the Czech-language publishing world to this day. His escape from Austria-Hungary launched Masaryk on a political career that would make him "the father of Czechoslovakia," as well as into the first president of the Czechoslovak Republic (1918–1935).

Masaryk settled in London and began appealing to English intellectuals (including R. W. Seton-Watson[4] [1879–1951]) for the Czech national cause. In 1915 he was joined by his student Edvard Beneš (1884–1948), who had earlier established the secret organization Mafie (Mafia). Mafie opposed the official Austro-Hungarian anational line and served as a liaison between domestic and émigré Czech nationalist organizations. Masaryk at first was vague about what course of action to take. After the young Slovak astronomer and general in the French Army, Milan Rastislav Štefánik (1880–1919), offered his support, Masaryk settled on the idea of a Czechoslovak state. It was to include the historic Czech lands (Bohemia, Moravia and Austrian Silesia) as well as Upper Hungary (Slovakia).

The official commencement of the Czechoslovak independence movement is associated with the celebrations of the five hundredth anniversary of the death of Jan Hus (1369–1415) in Geneva on July 6, 1915. The grand monument in his honor, placed in the midst of the Old Town Square in Prague, still succinctly symbolizes this reformer's significance for the Czech national idea. The subsequent association of Czech nationalism with Hussitism, championed by Masaryk, made important representatives of the Czech Brethren into Czech national heroes, including Jan Žižka (1370–1424) and Jan Amos Komenský (Comenius) (1592–1670). The former is commemorated in a colossal equestrian statue. It represents him as a victorious one-eyed general of Bohemia's Hussites. Placed on the top of the high hill located in the district named after him, Žižkov, the statue overlooks all of Prague. Komenský added an intellectual dimension to this militaristic streak of Hussitism. Masaryk saw this intellectual, theological, original thinker and writer as the key figure in the history of Czech democracy and humanism. Hence Masaryk even entitled the first part of his memoirs *The Testament of Komenský* (Davies, 1996: 609).

This association of Czech nationalism with Hussitism allowed for differentiating the Czech nation vis-à-vis its neighbors, namely the Austro-Germans and the Poles who were Catholics, and the Lutheran and Catholic Germans. Yet the majority of the Czech- and Slovak-speakers were Catholics because of the successes of the seventeenth-century Counter-Reformation. This explains why this official kind of Czech nationalism made significant inroads in Moravia only during the time that the nation-state of Czechoslovakia existed. This region was much more traditionalistic and homogenously Catholic than Bohemia. On the other hand, the 1905 *Ausgleich* prevented the rise of politicized Czech-German national conflict in Moravia (Davies, 1996: 609).

In November 1915 the Československý výbor (ČV, Czechoslovak Committee) was founded and proclaimed as its goal the achievement of independence for a Czechoslovak nation-state within the framework of the Habsburg monarchy (Waldenberg, 1992: 48). However, already in 1916 Beneš had presented quite an uncompromising stance in his book *Détruisez l'Autriche-Hongarie* (Destroy Austria Hungary). Autonomy within the framework of reformed Austria-Hungary rapidly lost its appeal (Polišenský, 1991: 107). In February 1916 the ČV was transformed into the Československa národní rada (ČNR, Czechoslovak National Council), which began to cooperate with Polish and Romanian organizations abroad, as well as with the Yugoslav Committee.

The victories of the Central Powers at the Eastern Front convinced the Young Czechs that loyal support for the Dual Monarchy's war effort would better serve their cause. In 1916, together with other Bohemian political groups, they established the Český svaz (ČS, Czech Union), which organized the Czech deputies in the Reichsrat, and the Národní výbor (NV, National Committee). The NV was to act as the highest Czech national body in Bohemia.

The Czechs' relations with Vienna relaxed after the demise of Francis Joseph I in November 1916. The new emperor, Charles I, granted amnesty to political prisoners and attempted to reform the Dual Monarchy in accordance with the tenets of federalism. In reply to these initiatives, on January 24, 1917, the ČS declared that its goal was to "liberate the Czechs from the foreign state [of Austria-Hungary]." But as an afterthought the ČS added that it wanted to achieve this aim under Habsburg rule.

Next, the February Revolution swept Russia in March, and Washington declared war on Germany on April 6. These developments, coupled with the worsening economic situation, prevented Charles I from proceeding with his plans of domestic reforms. More Czech activists, not unlike other national politicians throughout Austria-Hungary, began concluding that it would be impossible to prevent the eventual breakup of the Dual Monarchy along ethnic lines.

In May 1917, when the last Reichsrat convened, Masaryk left London for Russia to speed up the organization of a Czechoslovak army made up of freed Czech and Slovak POWs in Russian captivity. A Czechoslovak brigade participated in the last Russian offensive against the Central Powers in the summer of 1917. After the outbreak of the Bolshevik Revolution in November, Masaryk left for the United States in order to campaign for the Czechoslovak cause. At the same time, the Czech troops struggled against the Bolsheviks and seized control of the Trans-Siberian Railroad.

On January 8, 1918, Wilson promulgated his Fourteen Points, the tenth of which called for the "freest opportunity of the autonomous development" for the peoples of Austria-Hungary. Two days earlier a demand for a sovereign state within the historic frontiers of the Czech lands and of Slovakia (Upper Hungary) had been made in Prague at the Epiphany Convention, which had been followed by anti-Austrian demonstrations.

Czech delegates participated in the Congress of Oppressed Nationalities assembled in Rome (April 1918), where the anti-Austrian final resolution was adopted. On April 30 the ČS demanded transformation of Austria-Hungary into a federal state, and in May the Slav national celebrations in Prague demonstrated the strength of the Czechoslovak and other Slav independence movements. In the same month the Allies began to support the possibility of allowing for the emergence of nation-states at the cost of the dissolution of Austria-Hungary.

On May 31, the Pittsburgh Convention was adopted. It favored a political union of the Czechs and the Slovaks. On July 13 the NV was reorganized in line with the results of the last (1911) Bohemian Landtag elections. In this manner the NV aspired to make Bohemia the third constituent part of the Dual Monarchy. At the same time France recognized the ČNR as the supreme body in charge of Czechoslovak national interests. Other Allies followed suit. On September 28, Beneš signed a treaty whereby France agreed to support the Czechoslovak national program at a postwar peace conference. The ČNR constituted itself as a provisional government on October 14, and, undeterred by Charles I's manifesto promising the transformation of Austria-Hungary into a federal state (October 16), on October 18 Masaryk and Beneš issued a declaration of Czechoslovak independence, simultaneously in Washington and Paris. The NV proclaimed the Czechoslovak Republic on October 28 in Prague. Two days later the Slovak Národní rada (National Council) acceded to the proclamation. On October 27 the last Austro-Hungarian foreign minister, Gyula Andrássy (1860–1929), accepted the existence of this independent Czechoslovak state.

After the signing of the armistice between the Allies and Austria-Hungary on November 3, Charles I relinquished his administrative powers on November 11. On the same day an armistice was concluded between the Allies and the German Empire. This date (which also officially saw the birth of independent Poland) marks the final—and today, largely forgotten—dismantling of Austria-Hungary (Carter, 1992: 923–924; Ehrich, 1992: 533–534; Pokorný, 1993: 141–142; Polišenský, 1991: 106–110).

The emergence of the new nation-states of Czechoslovakia and Poland meant that they would compete for the industrial and mineral wealth of Silesia, first with each other over East Silesia, and second with Germany over Upper Silesia. What encouraged Prague and Warsaw was the rapid and unpredicted breakup of Austria-Hungary, as well as the sharp decline in the military and political power of the German Empire and of Russia, which was embroiled in revolutions. However, before this process is analyzed in relation to its effects on Silesia, it is necessary to sketch the general situation in Prussian Silesia and Austrian Silesia during the Great War, with special attention paid to the activities of the Slavic national movements.

Prior to the outbreak of World War I, Polish activists strove to consolidate the Polish national movement in Germany and to merge it at the leadership level with the counterpart movements in Congress Poland and Galicia. In April 1913 the Rada Narodowa (RN, National Council) was established in Posen with four delegates from Upper Silesia, including Korfanty. Apart from the aforementioned goals, the RN also aimed at propping up Polishdom at the western and northern edges of the Province of Posen as well as in western East Prussia and in Upper Silesia. Polish activists perceived these territories as "Polish." They also saw the considerable percentage of German-speaking inhabitants living there, as well as the lack of Polish national identity among the Polish/Slavic-speaking inhabitants, as a "danger" to the Polish nation. Polish nationalists opposed this social and political reality, which they hoped to change in favor of the process of Polish nation- and nation-state-building (Jakóbczyk, 1989: 72; Michalkiewicz, 1985: 422; Wanatowicz, 1992: 129).

The leadership of the Liga Narodowa (LN) staged a meeting in Berlin in 1914 to convince LN activists in Germany that they should accept Dmowski's concept of creating Poland with the aid of Russia after St. Petersburg had defeated the Central Powers (Mroczko, 1994: 102). These moves, clearly disloyal to the German Empire for those LN members with German citizenship, were restrained by the tense political situation in 1913 and 1914. After the outbreak of the Great War such an alliance of the LN with Russia was not an option since the Central Powers gained the upper hand on the Eastern Front (Michalkiewicz, 1985: 421).

In August 1914 about sixty socialist and Polish activists were interned in Silesia. The kaiser introduced martial law so as to ensure the *Burgfriede* (civil peace). The subsequent clampdown on any political activities not controlled by the authorities, as well as military conscription, put an end to socialist and Polish nationalist initiatives. The press was censored and the majority of socialist organs were temporarily closed down, including the increasingly pro-Polish *Gazeta Robotnicza*. *Katolik* remained the only Polish-language newspaper that continued publishing in Upper Silesia at the beginning of the war (Fulbrook, 1990: 152; Glensk, 1992: 23; Kwiatek, 1991: 15–16).

Initially the inhabitants of Silesia, like those of all of eastern Germany, were united in the face of the Russian onslaught. The newspapers brought out by Napieralski's *Katolik* press group loyally supported the German war effort, and Korfanty also went along with this line (Figowa, 1966: 25, 29). After the Russians had been repelled in the spring of 1915, the imperial war headquarters were located in the Pleß palace in the immediate vicinity of the prewar German-Russian border. The headquarters remained there until the spring of 1917. It remained in close liaison with its Austro-Hungarian counterpart, which for this purpose had been moved to nearby Teschen, due to the military subordination of the Dual Monarchy to the German Empire (Ehrich, 1992: 532; Fuchs, 1994: 609).

The ensuing German and Austro-Hungarian occupation of Congress Poland brought almost all of the Polish-speaking population within the confines of the Central Powers and simultaneously insulated it from Russia. Berlin and Vienna could not ignore this human potential and put forward all kinds of incentives prior to the proclamation of the Polish Kingdom (1916). In this manner the German and the Austro-Hungarian governments hoped to win the Poles for the military struggle against Russia in this dangerously prolonged warfare (Wiskemann, 1956: 14).

Napieralski organized the pro-German Polish-language press in the occupied territories of Congress Poland. It propagated the view that, with German help, independent Poland could be founded within the boundaries of Congress Poland (Snoch, 1991: 95). Further links between the occupied territories and Upper Silesia were forged thanks to the merger of the occupied Dombrowa (Dąbrowa) industrial basin with Upper Silesian industry when the pre-1914 German-Russian border had disappeared (Fuchs, 1994: 610). The Upper Silesian coal field extended well outside the region's boundaries into the adjacent territories of Galicia and Congress Poland, which belonged to Austria-Hungary and Russia, respectively. Russia's part of this coal field was centered on the town of Dombrova (in the Russian language). Between 1915 and 1917, and then 1939 and 1945, the Germans named this town Dombrowa, and in the years 1918–1939 and after 1945 it has been known by its Polish name of Dąbrowa Górnicza. Consequently, this industrial basin, named for the town, is known as the Dąbrowa, Dombrowa and Dombrova industrial basin to the Poles, the Germans and the Russians, respectively (Batowski, 1964: 13).

Congress Poland and Galicia, through which the front lines swept on a scale unimaginable at the Western Front, suffered serious damage. Upper Silesian Polish activists who remembered the aid that had flowed from Congress Poland and Galicia to Upper Silesia during the 1879 famine decided to reciprocate. Napieralski's predominantly pro-German and universalistic *Katolik* camp, which worked for an independent Poland without Upper Silesia, worked hand in hand with the pro-LN nationalist faction. The latter, however, hoped for the inclusion of Upper Silesia in a would-be Poland. They gravitated around Bronisław Koraszewski's *Gazeta Opolska* and Zygmunt Seyda's (1876–1925) *Gazeta Ludowa*. The latter was an LN activist from the Province of Posen who organized and led the pro-LN Polish nationalist movement in Upper Silesia (Anon., 1987c: 161).

What motivated Napieralski in his cooperation with Polish nationalists was a Christian obligation to help coreligionists of the same language in occupied Congress Poland. Thanks to his Posen roots he also envisioned the creation of an autonomous or even independent Poland under the protection of the Central Powers. This accorded with Berlin's line and allowed Napieralski not to breach his loyalty to the German Empire, of which he was a citizen. These legalistic niceties were of no concern to the national radicals active in Upper Silesia. In the *Katolik* press group's control over the Polish-language press in Congress Poland, they saw the possibility of establishing, maintaining, and broadening contacts with national organizations from other Polish-speaking territories. Under more favorable conditions, Upper Silesia's Polish nationalists hoped to use these links as a springboard for establishing a Polish nation-state that would include Upper Silesia (Kwiatek, 1991: 19–20, 27; Mendel, 1987: 33–34, 37).

In 1914/1915 Korfanty distanced himself from the loyally pro-German stance represented by Napieralski (Figowa, 1966: 29), but he did not favor the Polish voluntary forces which Piłsudski formed in Galicia. Korfanty rightly observed that they would be utilized for the anti-Russian struggle and not for establishing a Polish nation-state. But he failed to predict that those involved would choose to disregard the Austro-Hungarian command at some point. The dominant attitude among the Polish nationalist radicals was that more would be gained if one calmly waited for the opportune moment. Wielkopolska and Upper Silesian

Polish nationalists were disillusioned by the NKN's position. In 1915/1916 this committee supported the idea of creating a Poland within the framework of the Dual Monarchy through a merger of Galicia with occupied Congress Poland. But the *Katolik* faction took this stance because it agreed with Napieralski's legalistic opinion. He stood for the territorial integrity of the German Empire and its German national character, which should not be compromised through incorporation of vast Polish-speaking territories (Kwiatek, 1991: 21–22, 25).

Because of the prolonged war of attrition, the economic situation in the Central Powers deteriorated, resulting in shortages of goods and high inflation, which made citizens hoard gold coins. The authorities responded with the introduction of token paper money and an increasing number of ersatz products (Mendel, 1987: 14, 16). This system functioned quite effectively until the winter of 1916–1917, when food shortages became acute all over the German Empire and Austria-Hungary (Fuchs, 1994: 612). Generally speaking, food rations and living conditions were much worse in Upper Silesia than in Lower Silesia (Gelles, 1978: 278). Due to conscription many factories (especially those producing consumer goods) had to limit or even cease production. The labor shortage was alleviated with POWs, who, for the most part, were employed in the mines of Upper Silesia. They numbered 1,195 in 1915, 28,004 in 1916, 34,330 in 1917 and 31,067 in 1918. Women began to enter the job market: 5,623 female workers were employed in the Upper Silesian mines in 1914 and 14,037 in 1918. They amounted to 4.6 percent and 9.4 percent of the mining workforce in these years, respectively. However, the plight of the populace did not improve, which triggered hunger marches in 1916 and 1917 and brought about broader acceptance of socialist ideals in other regions of Germany at this last stage of the war (Migdał, 1967: 12, 16, 18, 24–25).

These general difficulties allowed the LN Polish nationalist camp from Wielkopolska to form the clandestine Międzypartyjny Komitet Obywatelski (MKO, Multipartisan Civil Committee) in January 1916. A few Upper Silesians belonged to it. The MKO gradually transplanted Dmowski's idea to Wielkopolska that Poland should be established with the help of the Allies. In 1916 the Polish national movement definitely reemerged in the Province of Posen. But this phenomenon was not paralleled in Upper Silesia, where the LN camp was actually weakened when Seyda left this region. However, connections between Polish nationalists in Wielkopolska and Upper Silesia steadily grew stronger.

This process was highlighted in 1916 by the celebrations of the sixty-first anniversary of Mickiewicz's death, held in Posen and Beuthen with the mixed participation of Wielopolanians and Upper Silesians. Similar events facilitated establishing links between Polishdom and Upper Silesia's Polish nationalists. In 1916 it was the seventieth birthday of the immensely popular Polish nationalist writer and Nobel Prize winner Henryk Sienkiewicz (1846–1916). He wrote historical novels in which heroes, anachronistically defined as "Polish," successfully fought similarly anachronistically defined "German," "Swedish" or "Russian" enemies. Sienkiewicz sought to utilize the fictionalized past for building Polish nationalism (Hargreaves-Mawdsley, 1968: 494). The year 1917 was marked by the centenary celebrations of the death of the Polish and U.S. national hero Tadeusz Kościuszko (1746–1817).

In the course of these cultural and political events one of Wielkopolska's Polish nationalist leaders of universalistic leanings, Father Stanisław Adamski (1875–1967), commenced his numerous contacts with Polish activists in Upper Silesia. He was born in the Lower Silesian town of Grünberg, but because of his education and the course of his ecclesiastical career he was established in the Province of Posen. His support for the development of Polish nationalism in Upper Silesia resulted in his moving to the region after the war. As the bishop of Katowice he would facilitate the survival of the Polish clergy in Upper Silesia during World War II and oppose the subsequent atheization of this region, attempted by Polish communists after 1945 (Kwiatek, 1991: 28–30; Mendel, 1987: 35–36; Myszor, 1996: 6).

Upper Silesia's Polish national movement suddenly reemerged in 1917 following Korfanty's speech in the Prussian Landtag (January 19, 1917). He criticized the anti-Polish measures and presented the Prussian government with a catalog of Polish demands. Because Korfanty had entered the Landtag on a mandate from the Province of Posen, Napieralski maintained that Korfanty's opinion related to this province only. *Gazeta Ludowa* disagreed and opined that Korfanty's demands also extended to Upper Silesia. The general scandal caused by this speech propelled Korfanty onto the political stage once again (Kwiatek, 1991: 31).

Although probably unbeknownst to the general public, on January 11, 1917, Paderewski presented Wilson with a memorandum in which he portrayed Prussian Silesia and East Austrian Silesia as Polish (Mroczko, 1994: 110). At the end of March, Dmowski furnished the British foreign minister, Sir Arthur James Balfour (1848–1930), with a proposal that foresaw a future Poland that included Upper Silesia and East Silesia (Kulak, 1990: 211). Moreover, in June 1917 the ND activist Bolesław Jakimiak wrote *Zachodnia granica Polski* (Poland's Western Boundary), which was published in Moscow in 1918. He envisaged the Oder-Neisse line (without Stettin [Szczecin]) as the appropriate Polish-German border. It gave an early start to the idea that was actualized in 1945 (Kulak, 1990: 221–224). After the end of the Great War the aforementioned proposals made the Allies more prone to accept limited transfers of lands with Polish-speaking inhabitants, which had not constituted a part of erstwhile Poland-Lithuania, to the forming Polish nation-state.

In the meantime, on April 19, 1917, the Prussian government annulled the language clause in the Act on Associations of 1908. Once again Polish could be used as the medium of communication at meetings of Polish-language societies.

But this freedom was considerably curtailed in Upper Silesia, where the authorities noticed that Polish activists used standard Polish instead of the Upper Silesian Slavic dialect or the Slavic-Germanic creole known as *Wasserpolnisch*. Only *Wasserpolnisch* was considered indigenous and appropriate for use at the meetings of non-German-language associations in Upper Silesia (Klein, 1972: 22; Kwiatek, 1991: 33).

Napieralski and Father Jan Kapica (Kapitza) (1866–1930) strove to reestablish the alliance between Upper Silesia's Polish/Slavic-speakers and the Zentrum in May and June 1917, but the radicalized clergy and population did not see their hopes fulfilled and turned to socialists and Polish nationalists. The ordinance of April 23 allowed for conducting religious instruction in Polish in the Province of Posen. But the situation worsened in Upper Silesia because a parallel relaxation in language laws was not introduced for this region (Kwiatek, 1991: 33–35). It brought about demands for a modicum of recognition for Polish in Upper Silesia and led to the establishment of the ecclesiastical Towarzystwo Oświaty im. św. Jacka (TOśJ, St. Jacek [Hyacinth] Educational Society) in Oppeln in October and November 1917 (Mendel, 1987: 38).

In the latter half of 1917 the idea of self-determination grew in popularity among Polish nationalists in the German Empire. The overall political thaw in the face of economic problems and military failures suffered by the state allowed the Sokół and other Polish nationalists to operate in Upper Silesia quite freely (Kwiatek, 1991: 37–38).

In January 1918, the political basis of the European order was shaken by Wilson's Fourteen Points speech, in which he accepted the national principle implicit in the concept of self-determination. In this atmosphere, charged by the Bolshevik Revolution, during which Lenin paid lip service to the aforementioned principle, Korfanty demanded protection of minorities in the Prussian Landtag on January 11, 1918. In March, the TOśJ handed the Prussian Ministry of Education a memorandum including the demand for the reintroduction of Polish as a medium of instruction for religious instruction classes. In the context of the increasingly difficult economic and military situation, the Central Powers concluded peace treaties with Ukraine in February and with Soviet Russia in March. This dashed Polish nationalists' hopes for including some of the eastern territories of former Poland-Lithuania in a future Poland (Kwiatek, 1991: 39; Schramm, 1989: 81).

The German government, which still attempted to win the war and to preserve the territorial integrity of the German Empire, was not prepared to embark on experiments that might appease Polish activists in Upper Silesia. In addition, Berlin perceived this region as an integral part of the German Empire, and hence it considered any Polish nationalist demands with regards to Silesia as an indication of groundless Polish aggression (Lüer, 1995: 84). A change in this stalemate came in June 1918, thanks to the Reichstag by-election in the traditionally pro-Polish

Upper Silesian constituency of Gleiwitz-Lublinitz (Gliwice-Lubliniec). Polish nationalists, with the active involvement of activists from the Province of Posen, fielded Korfanty, who stood against the Zentrum candidate. Korfanty won with 62.5 percent of the votes (Kwiatek, 1991: 39–41; Zieliński, 1983: 5). The Upper Silesia-born socialist Józef Rymer (1882–1922) also participated in this election. He was a leader of the Zjednoczenie Zawodowe Polskie (ZZP, Polish Workers' Union), whose headquarters had been moved from Berlin to Kattowitz in 1911. The ZZP nationalist members formed the Narodowe Stronnictwo Robotników (NSR, Workers' National Party) in March 1918 in Posen. Rymer actively supported the connections between the ZZP and the NSR (Dubiel, 1993: 2; Kwiatek, 1991: 42).

It was the Sokół that organized Polish nationalist activities in Posen and Upper Silesia scheduled for the summer of 1918, which convinced the authorities not to authorize its rallies. On October 5 the Landtag's Polish Circle, including Korfanty and Seyda, demanded Prussia's ethnically Polish territories for a future Poland in accordance with Wilson's Thirteenth Point. Moreover, almost the entire Polish nationalist movement in Prussia, including its Upper Silesian branch, recognized the Wielkopolska Rada Narodowa (RN, National Council) as its administrative and national center (Kwiatek, 1991: 43–44).

On October 8 Dmowski handed Wilson a memorandum in which, among other things, Upper Silesia and three counties of the Breslau Regency were claimed for a would-be Polish nation-state. In the Reichstag on October 25 Korfanty demanded all the Prussian territories inhabited by Polish-speakers for this state (Kulak, 1990: 229–230). The following day, the Sokół-based Straż Obywatelska dla Górnego Śląska (SOdGŚ, Civil Guard of Upper Silesia) was created in anticipation of an insurrection that would allow seizing this region for Poland.

Revolutionary chaos began in Germany on November 3, 1918, when sailors rioted in Kiel (Kwiatek, 1991: 46–47). The international situation faced by Berlin became complicated after the break-up of Austria-Hungary and the emergence of Czechoslovakia on October 28. This new nation-state was seen as a greater danger to Silesia than Polish nationalism. In Lower Silesia, Prague demanded the border areas of Schreiberhau (Szklarska Poręba), Glatz Margravate, Landeshut (Kamienna Góra) and the Waldenburg-Neurode industrial basin, as well as the southeastern section of Upper Silesia (Wanatowicz, 1994: 23).

At that time many a Czech nationalist went so far as to appeal for the complete dismantling of the German Empire and Austria-Hungary "in the interest of world peace." In 1922 Hanus Kuffner (1861–1929) presented a comprehensive overview of such plans in his brochure Náš stát a světový mír (Our State and World Peace). He proposed to truncate the German Empire into the landlocked German Reserve, centered on Leipzig, Frankfurt and Munich. The remaining western and southern German territories he wished to apportion to Switzerland,

France, Belgium and The Netherlands. France would control the buffer statelet of Oberrhein. Northern Germany would be divided into the separate statelets of Pomerania, Oderelbe, Unterelbe and Weserland, whereas East and West Prussia would be partitioned between Poland and Soviet Russia. The Czech state would be satisfied with the lands of the former Czech Crown (Bohemia, Moravia and Austrian Silesia) together with all of Prussian Silesia, Lusatia, half of Slovakia, half of Hungary and the majority of the Austrian lands. The South Slavs, Romania and Soviet Russia would annex the rest of the Austrian lands and Hungary. Austria would be reduced to the minuscule Mittelmark, with Vienna and Salzburg as border cities, not unlike Hungary, whose capital of Budapest would be located on the border with the Czech and South Slav states. Ominously, many elements of this plan were actualized in 1918 and especially after 1945. But the Poles replaced the Czechs as the main beneficiaries, though in Kuffner's blueprint Poland was to remain a relatively small state (Hellriegel-Netzebandt, 1996: 169–181; Rösner-Kraus, 1989: 212–213).

Workers' and soldiers' councils came into being on November 5–8, 1918, in the north of the German Empire, on November 9 in the center and the south of this country, and the following day in the east, including Silesia (Kinder, 1978: II 130). Numerous *Bauernräte* (peasants' councils), *Volksräte* (people's councils), *Arbeiterräte* (workers' councils), and *Soldatenräte* (soldiers' councils) supplanted the official authorities in Silesia, as they did elsewhere in the German Empire. In Silesia the councils were subjected to the Volksrat zu Breslau–Zentralrat für die Provinz Schlesien (VzB, People's Council in Breslau: The Central Council for the Province of Silesia). It was established on November 10. The VzB functioned until December 31, 1919, and during this time it coordinated actions against Polish nationalists, hoping to retain all of Silesia for Germany (Lesiuk, 1982: 467–468).

In November the official authorities did not have at their disposal any troops to safeguard the Silesian borders against possible Polish or Czech incursions (Hauser, 1991: 18–19). This problem was solved through the inflow of *Freikorps*—counterrevolutionary voluntary corps (Biały, 1982: 129–131)—which were subordinated to the Grenzschutz-Division (Border Protection Division), with its seat in Gleiwitz (Hawranek, 1982: 158). The general feeling was that Silesia was being surrounded by Czechoslovakia in the south and Poland in the east. This did not allow for any greater concessions to the Polish-language movement in Upper Silesia other than the reintroduction of Polish for religious instruction in the first three grades of elementary school (December 20). And even this change took place only at the Breslau Bishop Adolf Bertram's[5] (1859–1945) insistence (Klein, 1972: 37).

Because the various aforementioned councils did not wish to promote the Polish national cause in Upper Silesia or elsewhere in the German territory, Polish activists started organizing *Polskie rady ludowe* (PRLs, Polish people's councils) in Upper Silesia beginning in November 1918. They existed until February 1920, and according to the Polish sources there were 500 different PRLs in Upper Silesia during this period (Wyglenda, 1982: 423–424). The PRLs constituted the grassroots basis for the Polish national movement, which rapidly coalesced in the German Empire thanks to the Wielkopolska Poles' unifying effort in the form of the Sejm Dzielnicowy (Regional Sejm [of the Prussian Partition Zone]), which convened in Posen on December 3–5. Out of the total number of 1,399 representatives, 431 came from Upper Silesia. This Sejm Dzielnicowy established its executive branch, the eighty-person-strong Naczelna Rada Ludowa (NRL, Supreme People's Council), which comprised twenty-nine Upper Silesian representatives. The NRL was headed by a six-person commissariat that included two Upper Silesians: Korfanty and Rymer (Wanatowicz, 1994: 23).

The clandestine, eight-person Naczelna Władza dla Górnego Śląska (Supreme Governing Authority in Upper Silesia) came into being in Beuthen on November 19, 1918. It was renamed the Naczelna Rada Ludowa (Supreme People's Council) in December. Later this body accepted the authority of the Wielkopolska NRL (Wyglenda, 1982a: 321) and was transformed into the Upper Silesian Subcommissariat of the NRL on January 3, 1919. Because of the hurdles put in its way by the German authorities, the subcommissariat opened its branch across the border in the already Polish-held city of Sosnowiec, located in former Congress Poland. After the subcommissariat was banned in Germany on May 14, 1919, it was moved to this city for good (Wyglenda, 1982b: 407–408).

The forging of the political structures that merged the various strains of the Polish national movement was the first step. Popular support for these structures in the Province of Posen and Upper Silesia allowed for taking the second step, finalized with the emergence of paramilitary structures. They were organized in anticipation of armed struggle that would detach Upper Silesia from the German Empire and incorporate it into Poland. The Polish *Związki Wojackie* (ZWs, Veteran Associations) came into being in December 1918, emulating the model set by the German *Kriegervereine*. The entire focus of Polish nationalists was on organizing the legal ZWs after the German authorities had discovered the illegal SOdGŚ, as a result of which SOdGŚ members had decided to dissolve it on December 12 (Wyglenda, 1982c: 670).

At that time the nascent Polish central government did not wish to venture into any conflict with the German Empire over the Province of Posen or any other Polish-speaking regions within the German boundaries. This government had its hands full with the task of securing other regions much more significant for forming a Polish nation-state. First, Warsaw had to liquidate the German and Austro-Hungarian occupation of Congress Poland and to take western Galicia over from the Austro-Hungarian administration. Second, the Polish government was engaged in military conflict over eastern Galicia with the West Ukrainian

Republic and was competing for East Austrian Silesia, Arva (Orawa, Orava) and Szepes (Zips, Spisz, Spiš) with Czechoslovakia (Davies, 1991; 395).

The Wielkopolska NRL was displeased by this stance of Warsaw (Kwiatek, 1991: 54), but, on the other hand, it did not want to take any decisive actions on its own. However, the nationalist tension that had mounted in Wielkopolska since the beginning of November 1918 became uncontrollable after Paderewski's visit to Posen (December 26–27, 1918). The Wielkopolska Uprising broke out on December 27. On January 8, 1919, the NRL superseded the German authorities. This uprising did not spread to any other German provinces but ended on February 16 when the prolongation of the armistice between the Allies and the Central Powers was signed in Trier. The NRL government became independent of Berlin, and the temporary border placed a majority of the territory of the Province of Posen under the NRL's authority (Brożek, 1982: 438).

On November 28, 1918, Piłsudski, in his capacity as the Naczelnik Państwa (State Leader), issued the Constituent Sejm's Electoral Act. In a symbolic rather than practical manner, this act's provisions extended to the Province of Posen, the Oppeln Regency, some areas of the Breslau Regency, and some areas of East Prussia. The German authorities protested Warsaw's clear infringement of the existing borders. All the above-mentioned territories still remained under German control until the time when the peace conference would decide otherwise. The elections to the Constituent Sejm were to take place on January 26, 1919. As a preemptive measure the German authorities issued regulations on the basis of which any attempt to stage these elections within the German borders would be treated as high treason. These regulations also preempted possible obstacles that Polish nationalists could have posed with their appeals for boycotting the elections to the German National Assembly (January 19) and to the Prussian Landtag (January 26) (Hauser, 1991: 42; Wyglenda, 1982d: 15).

Piłsudski, encouraged by the successes of the Wielkopolska Uprising, decided to fulfill the largely symbolic letter of the Electoral Act in the context of the German territories claimed by Warsaw. He invited pro-Polish Landtag and Reichstag deputies from these territories to become members of the Polish Constituent Sejm without actually being elected. Five of the deputies came from Upper Silesia (including Korfanty) and soon Rymer joined them too. The presence of the Upper Silesian deputies indicated that Poland was willing to treat the question of Germany's Polish/Slavic-speaking territories as its domestic affair (Kwiatek, 1991: 68). This encouragement was incentive enough to cause the members of the Sokół and the ZWs to establish a secret military organization based on the model of Piłsudski's POW (Davies, 1991: II 381).

In January 1919 the POW for Upper Silesia was organized, with its headquarters in Beuthen. The Sosnowiec-based Subcommissariat of the Wielkopolska NRL, headed by Korfanty, controlled this Upper Silesian POW. The POW's ranks swelled with young Polish/Slavic-speaking Szlonzoks, who had been radicalized through the postwar commotion, revolution, and the disruption of the traditional administrative and social structures. On top of that, many of these young men were embittered by unpleasant experiences they suffered in the German Imperial Army, where often they were derisively referred to as *"Wasserpolacken,"* meaning "uncivilized peasants" or "not real Germans." They yearned for a change. So the POW's membership quickly rose to 5,000 in March 1919 and to 14,000 in May (Kwiatek, 1991: 74).

The traditional links of the Upper Silesian Polish movement with its Wielkopolska counterpart facilitated the forging of military, political and personal contacts between the former and the Polish government. At that time Berlin was busy suppressing the revolution and stabilizing the difficult economic and social situation so as to offset the possibility of the breakup of the state, as had already happened in the case of its ally, Austria-Hungary. Hence, the German government had no means effectively to curb the development of Polish irredentism in Upper Silesia. The overall situation in Silesia worsened with the unprecedented wave of strikes in late 1918 and early 1919. From the military point of view Silesia also became seriously endangered when the Poles seized the Province of Posen. Suddenly Silesia was surrounded by Czechoslovakia to the south and by Poland to the east and north (Hauser, 1991: 47).

This necessitated the introduction of martial law on January 3, 1919, in the most troubled spots of the Upper Silesian industrial basin (Wanatowicz, 1994: 26) because even the Grenzschutz-Division, with its 2,000 troops at the end of January, was too small to deal effectively with the looming disaster. Moreover, the Breslau VzB unrealistically aspired to control the entire Province of Posen. As a result it was entrusted with the governance of the Wielkopolska counties of Lissa (Leszno), Frauenfeld (Wschowa), and Rawitsch (Rawicz), which were not engulfed by the Poles in the course of the Wielkopolska Uprising. But this meant that the Breslau provincial administration had even less means to spare for securing the German hold on Upper Silesia (Hauser, 1991: 51). The Polish-Soviet War (February 1919–October 12, 1920) prevented the danger of further Polish offensives against Germany, especially in Upper Silesia.

This war broke out when German troops had withdrawn from the intervening zone of occupation, the Land Ober-Ost (Davies, 1991: II 396). Using this opportunity to seize more territory of former Poland-Lithuania, Polish troops engaged in a struggle with Soviet Russia while they continued to fight with the Western Ukrainian Republic. Warsaw's heavy military involvement in the east gave Berlin some breathing room. Prague also saw in this an opportunity for Czechoslovakia. The Czechoslovak army, supported by France, attacked the Polish section of East Austrian Silesia on January 23, pushing the Polish-Czechoslovak partition line eastward at the expense of Poland (Wanatowicz, 1994: 16). This event played into

Berlin's hands, because under these circumstances it was unlikely that Warsaw would launch any offensive in order to secure the Prussian Silesian territories that it claimed. In this period of respite, the German authorities attracted as many volunteers as possible to protect Silesia. Their numbers already topped 40,000 at the beginning of February (Hauser, 1991: 52).

German control of the province was thus ensured against any foreign military incursions. But the final fate of Silesia was to be decided at the peace conference (January 18, 1919–January 21, 1920). Although the analysis of the subsequent events does not, strictly speaking, belong to this work's scope, it is necessary to remark that by that time the German Empire had already lost the control of all its industrial basins, with the exception of Upper Silesia. Understandably, in this situation Berlin would do whatever it could to protect the latter from passing into Polish or Czechoslovak possession. Giving up Upper Silesia would have meant the immediate economic collapse of the German Empire, which was suffering under the blockade imposed by the Allies at the end of 1918 and beginning of 1919. On the other hand, the growing strength of the Polish national movement in Upper Silesia could not be denied. Although numerous Szlonzoks started thinking of themselves as Poles, the vast majority of them stuck to their non-national multiple ethnic identity. The Szlonzoks hoped for reestablishment of their traditional way of life after the war and did not wish to be forced to choose between Germandom or Polishdom. This situation gave rise to the Szlonzokian national movement. Much earlier a similar encounter of the Slunzaks of East Austrian Silesia with the Czech-German-Polish national conflict had spawned the Slunzakian national movement. Kożdoń and his Slunzakian supporters strongly voiced the opinion that "[East or Austrian] Silesia should be for the [East or Austrian] Silesians only." The Szlonzoks followed the same line, and the slogan "Upper Silesia for the Upper Silesians" became common at the end of 1918 (Hauser, 1991: 40).

The origins of the Szlonzokian national movement must be sought in the rapid success of *Kleindeutsch* nationalism, which had led to the founding of the German Empire in 1871. This newly created German nation-state involved in nation- and nation-state-building based these endeavors on the German language and Protestantism. Necessarily, these officially espoused ideological goals of the German national policies gradually alienated the non-German-speaking Upper Silesians as well as many an Upper Silesian and Silesian Catholic, regardless of language. The ensuing anti-Catholic *Kulturkampf* fortified the hold of the universalistic Zentrum on Upper Silesia, and to a lesser degree on the Breslau Regency. This facilitated the rise of the language-based strain of relatively mild Polish nationalism in Upper Silesia, which received strong organizational and financial support from the Province of Posen.

At that time, the pro-German bilingual weeklies *Prawda/Wahrheit* (1871–

1877) and *Szlązak* (1872–1880) were launched. The former aimed at winning over the Polish/Slavic-speaking Upper Silesians (that is, Szlonzoks) to pro-state Old Catholicism, while the latter worked for the universalistic Zentrum, operating in conjunction with the mainstream Catholic hierarchy (Gröschel, 1993: 115, 225–226). But above all both these newspapers fortified the ethnic identity of the Szlonzoks. These periodicals also made the Szlonzoks well-disposed toward Germandom, simultaneously pitting them against Polish nationalism, which the press organs presented as an alien influence. The end of the *Kulturkampf* commenced the age of peaceful "cohabitation" of the state and the Catholic Church in the German Empire and in Upper Silesia. The Zentrum, which emerged as an opposition party, became one of the most significant ruling parties. As such the Zentrum increasingly engaged itself in the process of German nation-state-building. Hence, it ceased lending its wholehearted support to the particularistic interests of the Polish/Slavic-speaking Szlonzoks. But the Catholic Church and the Zentrum still continued to accommodate the specific needs of the Szlonzoks when various acts aimed at curbing the use of Polish and the Szlonzokian creole/dialect were issued in especially quick succession at the beginning of the twentieth century. Even the Zentrum and the Catholic Church strongly opposed the most oppressive of these measures, but the damage had already been done, opening the way for the infiltration of Polish nationalism into Upper Silesia and among the Szlonzoks.

Berlin's record of relative military success during the Great War stemmed the tide until 1917/1918, when economic difficulties mounted and, coupled with the breakup of Austria-Hungary, led to the unexpected founding of Czechoslovakia and Poland. The very existence of these new nation-states advanced the interests of Slavic nationalisms better than any prior nationalist rhetoric. Furthermore, the social, political and economic commotion that broke out at the end of the Great War worsened under the strain of the influenza pandemic and the disruption of the old order.

The revolutionary impetus emanating from Soviet Russia also brought about the collapse of traditional social structures in the German Empire, and it triggered the creation of various soldiers', workers', people's, and even peasants' councils. They seized effective control over the army and various areas in the empire. The defeat, which was sealed by the armistice of November 11, toppled the monarchy and empire on November 9, when a republic was proclaimed, due more to a blunder in a political speech than to any real intent (Turner, 1992: 116). These events deprived Silesia of any effective military shield against the anticipated Czechoslovak attack and, on the other hand, they radicalized the populace. In Upper Silesia waxing Polish and waning German nationalisms clashed. This endangered the traditional influence of the Catholic Church and the Zentrum, which had presented a largely anational political line. The possibility of the Polish annexation of Upper Silesia loomed large, and it became imminent at the end of 1918 and beginning of 1919, when the Wielkopolska Uprising erupted.

An additional dimension to this dire social and political situation was created by the Prussian government's November 15 decision to separate the civil and educational systems from either church. The Silesian Catholic Church and the Zentrum protested this move, as did the overwhelmingly Catholic Upper Silesian population which, in addition to the scrapping of this decision, demanded the introduction of religious instruction in the appropriate mother tongues to schools (Hauser, 1991: 25). Once again the Zentrum and the Polish/Slavic-speaking Szlonzoks united around the same political goal. They wished to weaken the influence of Polish and German nationalisms in Upper Silesia.

In order to strengthen the position of universalistic Catholicism in Silesia, Zentrum activists proposed excluding Silesia from Prussia and turning it into a separate German state (*Land*). The Breslau VzB also supported this position. To this end the VzB proposed making Silesia temporarily independent of Berlin so as to prevent the infiltration of the socialist revolutionary influences spread by the influential Spartakusbund (Spartacus Union). The idea of a temporary independence for Silesia found no support in the army, which decided that such an entity would not be militarily viable, especially if attacked by the Poles or the Czechs. Thus, in December 1918 the VzB abandoned this plan and simultaneously demanded a degree of autonomy in the spheres of language and religion for Upper Silesia.

The idea of *Oberschlesien als selbständiger Freistaat* (Upper Silesia as an independent free state) found its advocates among the Upper Silesian industrialists. They were afraid that Friedrich Ebert's (1871–1925) Social Democratic government was not strong enough to tame revolution and keep Upper Silesia within Germany. Moreover, these industrialists believed that as an independent state Upper Silesia would not have to share the burden of war reparations imposed on Germany. They started cooperating with the pro-independence activists already at the end of November 1918. The most well-known of these activists were Ewald Latacz, the chairman of the Loslau soldiers' council; Jan Reginek, the chairman of the Ratibor workers and soldiers' council; and Jan's brother Father Thomas (Tomasz) Reginek (1887–1974).

They wanted to model an Upper Silesian state on the Swiss political system. Initially, the proponents of independent Upper Silesia actively campaigned for support in Prague. They hoped that the Czechoslovak government would facilitate their contacts with the Allies, but this scheme did not work out. On December 20, 1918, the *Oberschlesischer Kurier* (Upper Silesian Courier, 1908–1945) published an emotional appeal to the Upper Silesians, that is, the Szlonzoks. It stated that they had been treated as second-class citizens in Germany but reminded them that also the Poles had laughed at their language. This appeal advised the Szlonzoks not to trust either the Poles or the Germans, who wanted to control Upper

Silesia solely for its mineral wealth and industry. The appeal's authors concluded that the Szlonzoks should stand fast for an independent Upper Silesian state. On December 28, the VzB decided to avert the possible separation of Upper Silesia and promised to proclaim a Silesian republic on December 30. Such a republic would be headed by an SPD government, which would ensure retaining a partisan connection with the Berlin SPD government (Hauser, 1991: 28–31).

The Breslau conference of December 30, 1918, which focused on the possibility of separating Upper Silesia from Germany, did not generate enough official support for such a plan, especially in the context of the December 28 decision that had cancelled the planned separation of church and state. The main bone of contention had already disappeared, whereas external dangers contributed to the opinion that Upper Silesia should be retained within the borders of the German Republic. However, to ensure the loyalty of the independence-minded Szlonzoks, the conference adopted the so-called *Breslauer Beschlüsse* (Breslau Resolutions), which gave cultural autonomy to Upper Silesia. These resolutions established, among other things, that Catholics with knowledge of standard Polish would be nominated to high administrative positions in the Oppeln Regency, religious instruction would be conducted in schools in children's mother tongues, a separate Catholic Church delegation (ersatz diocese) would be established for Upper Silesia, and the position of the Upper Silesian commissar would be created in the provincial government. The resolutions were displayed in the form of posters all over the Oppeln Regency. On January 4, 1919, the Prussian government accepted all of these resolutions, but ignored the demand requiring high regency officials to have a working command of Polish, as well as the decision to form a separate Catholic Church delegation in Upper Silesia (Hauser, 1991: 39–42).

In the meantime, the internal situation deteriorated. In addition to the Polish nationalist and separatist trends, the radical non-ethnically and non-nationally oriented Kommunistische Partei Oberschlesiens/Komunistyczna Partia Górnego Śląska (Communist Party of Upper Silesia, that is, a branch of the Spartakusbund) had come into being on December 20, 1918, in Beuthen. Its membership soared to 16,000 at the beginning of 1919 and to 25,000 by the middle of the same year (Hawranek, 1982a: 232). In order to prevent an outbreak of a socialist revolution martial law was introduced in some areas of the Upper Silesian industrial basin. Later it was gradually extended to other areas of Upper Silesia when the Spartacist revolt broke out in Berlin on January 6, 1919 (Turner, 1992: 117; Wanatowicz, 1994: 26).

The internal instability, external dangers and the coming to terms with some of the demands posed by the Szlonzokian national movement convinced the Upper Silesian Catholic clergy and the Katholische Volkspartei[6] (Catholic People's Party) to support rather than boycott the January 1919 elections to the German National Assembly and the Prussian Landtag. Hence, despite Polish nationalists' appeals not to vote, many Polish/Slavic-speaking Szlonzoks did take part in these elections; 59 percent of the eligible voters cast their ballots. In January 1919, the Polish danger was averted when the Polish troops became engaged in western Ukraine and in Wielkopolska. The Czechs were also unlikely to attack while they were struggling with the Poles over East Austrian Silesia and with Austro-Germans over the Sudetenland. The Spartacist revolt was suppressed after a week of disturbances, and a modicum of internal stability was reintroduced. The growing ranks of the various *Freikorps* and of the Grenzschutz-Division provided the Silesian populace with more security.

But this improved situation and the Oppeln Regency president Walther von Miquel's ban on propaganda advocating Upper Silesian autonomy (December 31, 1918) did not stop the rapid growth of the Szlonzokian national movement. It had become increasingly strong during the last quarter of 1918, and the regency authorities' decision to consider agitation for Upper Silesian autonomy as high treason could not deter the populace from joining the Szlonzokian national movement. One wing of the movement, headed by the Rybnik *Landrat* (county governor) Hans Lukaschek (1882–1960), demanded autonomy for Upper Silesia within Germany. This strain of Upper Silesian autonomists soon merged with the mainstream of postwar German politics. The faction worked for the founding of a *Freistaat Oberschlesien* (Free State of Upper Silesia) (Cimała, 1982: 23).

At the beginning of January 1919, the Bund der Oberschlesier/Związek Górnoślązaków (BdO/ZG, Union of the Upper Silesians) came into being. Soon its membership topped 150,000 and then grew to half a million, according to the BdO/ZG, or to 300,000, according to the Prussian government. The BdO/ZG, in accordance with its main slogan, "Upper Silesia for the Upper Silesians," demanded the nullification of all the anti-Polish-language acts and full equality of the Polish and German languages, and that civil servants should be bilingual, that civil service nominations would reflect the confessional structure of Upper Silesia, and that there would be a separate Catholic Church delegation for Upper Silesia, complete with its own bilingual bishop. Last but not least, the BdO/ZG also demanded an official guarantee that if Upper Silesia should gain autonomy or independence, it would not be divided (Hauser, 1991: 43; Schmidt-Rösler, 1999; Wanatowicz, 1994: 25).

Initially, the BdO/ZG popularized its goals in the Zentrum's premier press organ, *Schlesische Volkszeitung*. Then the BdO/ZG founded its own bilingual weekly, *Der Bund/Związek* (The Union, 1920–1922), whose run soared from 20,000 in 1920 to 40,000 prior to the plebiscite in 1921 (Gröschel, 1993: 50–51). The BdO/ZG's first secretary general, Father Thomas Reginek, had to flee Upper Silesia at the beginning of 1919 because he faced the danger of being arrested by the Grenzschutz-Division due to his firm stance on Polish language rights. As one of the leaders of the Szlonzokian independence/autonomist movement, he also faced the danger of being tried for high treason. In Berlin, Reginek probably met Korfanty, and in Paris he talked to Dmowski concerning social-economic autonomy for Upper Silesia. This must have been one of the significant factors in convincing Warsaw to grant the future Polish part of Upper Silesia wide-ranging autonomy. It was strangely atypical in the highly centralized Polish nation-state, which was shaped after the model of the French state. The Polish government, however, was eager to pay the price in order to placate Szlonzokian nationalism, so as to be able to secure as large a slice of the Upper Silesian industry for Poland as possible. Simultaneous struggles with Berlin and the Szlonzoks would have made it impossible for Warsaw to secure any fragment of this region for Poland (Cimała, 1982a: 474; Wycisło, 1996: 346).

After this presentation of the multifaceted struggle for the control of Prussian Silesia, and especially of Upper Silesia, it is time to turn to Austrian Silesia. The tragic vagaries of warfare and the subsequent dismemberment of Austria-Hungary sparked antagonisms similar to those that unfolded in Upper Silesia. And in this crownland national movements increased these tensions as well. Although the actors were different from those in the case of Prussian Silesia, the main bone of contention remained the same: the rich coal seams and heavy industry conveniently concentrated in the Ostrau-Karwin industrial basin.

Prior to the outbreak of the Great War, the Czech national movement in Austrian Silesia was consolidated under the umbrella organization of the Nar-odní rada (National Council, 1907), while its Polish counterpart, the Austrian Silesian section of the NKN, was formed at the end of August 1914. Ostrau, the main urban center of the industrial basin, became the stage on which the national conflict unfolded. This could have threatened industrial production, so vital for the Austro-Hungarian war effort. Hence the gradual cessation of the activities of nationalist organizations, caused by the military draft, was effected through the militarization of the steel and mining industry, beginning in the autumn of 1914. The volatility of the Eastern Front and the necessity of maintaining close cooperation with Germany so as to ward off Russian attacks made it essential to move the imperial-royal military headquarters to Teschen.

Fighting in close alliance with the German Empire was especially attractive for Austrian Silesia's German-speakers. They anticipated a speedy victory and fortification of their position vis-à-vis the strengthening Slavic national movements in the crownland. Some Austrian Silesian Polish/Slavic-speaking Slunzaks and straightforward Polish nationalists welcomed the idea of forming a Polish state from Galicia and Congress Poland, a state that obviously would be incorporated into Austria-Hungary. To support this goal, volunteers from East Austrian Silesia joined Piłsudski's Polish legion. Austrian Silesia's Moravian/Slavic-speaking Morawecs and Czech nationalists thought of the war as not their own and unfavorable to their cause. Moreover, in light of Czech nationalism's traditional affinity to Pan-Slavism, it is not surprising that many a young Russophile of this crownland volunteered for the Czech legions organized in Russia.

As was the case for the German Empire, the war of attrition led to the difficult economic situation in Austrian Silesia, as elsewhere in Austria-Hungary. As a result, numerous strikes flared up in 1916 and 1917, especially in the industrial centers. In the spring of 1917 the government could not prevent the reemergence of political life in its prewar manifestations if Vienna wished to continue maintaining, at the very least, the prewar status quo. Nationalist tensions soon reappeared as well. In January 1918 municipalities of the majority of the Austrian Silesian towns, in conjunction with the Landtag, issued a memorandum calling for fortification of the German character of the crownland. In the same document they also protested the idea of merging East Silesia with Galicia as part of a postulated Polish nation-state. Polish and Czech activists had striven to undertake a joint action against this growing German influence already in 1917. But in 1918 the viable prospect of establishing an independent Poland and a separate Czech(oslovak) state pitted these two nationalist groups against each other. They were locked in conflict over the future of East Austrian Silesia as both national camps claimed this region with Austria-Hungary's largest industrial basin (Gawrecki, 1992: 64–65; Grobelný, 1992: 77).

After the outbreak of the Bolshevik Revolution in Russia, the social situation became radicalized in the crownland during 1918. The socialist movement grew rapidly in industrial centers, where trade unions staged numerous strikes against continuing the war. But soon the socialist slogans of these demonstrations were imbued with Czech and Polish pro-independence elements. The prospective Czechoslovak authorities stabilized and gained international recognition more quickly than its Polish counterparts. Hence branches of the ČNR were formed in Austrian Silesia equally swiftly, which gave Czech nationalists the advantage of an early start in this region. They used it deftly. On September 22, 1918, Czech activists organized the national rally in Ostra Hůrka, near Troppau, where they proclaimed the right of self-determination for the "Czechoslovak nation."[7] Soon after, on October 28 Czechoslovakia came into being, whereas the Polish nation-state was to emerge only on November 11 (Gawrecki, 1992: 65; Grobelný, 1992: 78).

The crownland's German-speakers opposed this Czech proclamation. They were apprehensive of the possibility of being included in a Czech(oslovak) nation-state as a minority. They would lose their privileged status, shared with other Austro-Germans in Cisleithania, and would have to trade places with the Czechs, who, so far, had been a largely powerless minority in Austria-Hungary. Thus, the prospect of subjection of the crownland to Prague did not look auspicious to the Austrian Silesian German-speakers. On October 15, 1918, they organized a *Volkstag* (people's rally) in Troppau (Opava) in order to show their willingness to stand for Germandom (Gawrecki, 1992: 65). Later their moves were orchestrated with the events that unfolded in Vienna after the de facto breakup of the Dual Monarchy.

Cisleithania could not escape the fate of the disintegrating Dual Monarchy. Prior to Austria-Hungary's signing of the armistice with the Allies on November 3, 1918, the 210 German members of the Reichsrat formed themselves into the National Assembly for Deutschösterreich, or German-Austria. On October 30, they proclaimed it an independent state. In the wake of the revolutionary events in Vienna and in the German Empire the National Assembly resolved that "German-Austria is a democratic republic." This proclamation was issued on November 13, that is, one day after Emperor Charles I's abdication (Ehrich, 1992: 534).

In the meantime, on October 29, 1918, that is, one day after the founding of Czechoslovakia, the Reichsrat's German members from Bohemia proclaimed the independence of Deutschböhmen, or German-Bohemia, with its capital in Reichenberg (Liberec). It consisted of the predominantly German-speaking western and northern peripheries of this crownland. On the following day the province of the Sudetenland was proclaimed in Troppau. It contained West Austrian Silesia and the predominantly German-speaking areas of northern Moravia. The Sudetenland's area was 6,534 square kilometers, and its population included 643,804 German- and 25,028 Czech-speakers. Robert Freißler (1877–1950), a member of the Austrian Silesian Landtag, was nominated to the position of the provisional *Landeshauptmann* (governor). Together with his deputy, Hans Jokl (1878–1935), he started organizing the new province. It was difficult to turn the Sudetenland into a viable region due to transportation, food supply and economic problems; but above all, the Sudetenland lacked anything more than verbal support from Vienna. Despite all the odds, the province's Volkswehr (People's Guard) rapidly grew to 6,700 troops (Bahlcke, 1996: 146; Gawrecki, 1992: 65; Prinz, 1995: 381; Rothschild, 1992: 78–79). On November 22, the National Assembly claimed for German-Austria all the Habsburg lands in which the majority of the population was made up of Germans or German-speakers. This assembly demanded, among other things, German-Bohemia and the Sudetenland, as well as the Böhmerwaldgau (Bohemian Forest District) and Deutschsüdmähren (German Southern Moravia). These two latter provinces were founded at a later date with the intention of incorporating them into adjacent Lower and Upper Austria (Breugel, 1973: 22–23; Ehrich, 1992: 534).

These four short-lived German-speaking provinces were referred to as "the Sudetenland." It added to the terminological confusion because one of these provinces bore the same name of "the Sudetenland." And another significantly different Sudetenland province was created in 1938 from these Bohemian and Moravian-Silesian lands of Czechoslovakia, which the Munich Agreement transferred to Germany. The tradition of calling Bohemia, Moravia and Austrian Silesia the "Sudetenländer" (Sudeten Lands) developed at the beginning of the twentieth century, probably in defiance of and as a reply to the Czech national penchant for lumping these areas together as the lands of the Czech Crown (Breugel, 1973: 22–23; cf.: Haardt, 1907: 53).

Considering the actual post-Great War province of the Sudetenland, its authorities planned to take into consideration possible national and linguistic demands of the Czech-speakers, Polish-speakers, Slunzaks, Morawecs and Jews who lived in the territory. This shows that the authorities clearly realized that the Sudetenland was not ethnically homogenous and could not exist without the active participation and consent of the inhabitants from non-German-speaking stock (Breugel, 1973: 23). However, from the inception of this province, the Czech/Slavic-speaking areas of West Silesia and the entirety of overwhelmingly Slavic East Silesia (including the industrial basin) were consciously excluded from the Sudetenland. This was done in order to preclude the possible wrecking of this province through widespread ethno-national tensions (Prinz, 1995: 381; Wurbs, 1982: 52).

German-Bohemia and the Sudetenland adjoined Germany rather than German-Austria, from which they were separated by the broad Czech heartland. It did not matter, however, because the established assumption was that the Allies would eventually allow for an early incorporation of German-Austria into Germany, which as a result would be transformed into the first truly *Großdeutsch* nation-state. This hope remained unrealized, as the Allies actually prevented the creation of a Greater Germany. What is more, they did not answer the repeated requests for the endorsement of the German Sudeten provinces in agreement with the Wilsonian principle of self-determination. At that moment Berlin was not much interested in the fate of the Sudeten Germans, who had not belonged to the German Empire. The German government had its hands full dealing with the aftermath of the defeat, the revolutionary movements and the dangers posed to the territorial integrity of Germany.

Hence, neither the Allies nor Berlin offered the Sudeten Germans any serious support when Czech legionaries, recently returned home from France and Italy, proceeded to occupy the self-proclaimed German provinces. Thus Prague reasserted the territorial integrity of the historical lands of the Czech Crown—the very ideological basis of Czech nationalism. Reichenberg fell to the Czechs on December 16 and Troppau two days later. By the end of December the western section of West Austrian Silesia was taken, and the Sudetenland government assembled for the last time on February 18, 1919. The absence at this time of military resistance on the part of the local German-speakers to this Czech occupation entailed not only their weakness; the Sudeten Germans also trusted that at the peace conference the Allies would order plebiscites in their homelands. The German-speakers were sure that the results of such plebiscites would prove decisive and to their liking.

Three months later, when it was clear that such expectations were erroneous, the Sudeten Germans belatedly staged protest demonstrations with scattered marches on Czechoslovak gendarmerie barracks. A number of these protests took place on March 4, 1919. It was the day the new German-Austrian National Assembly convened in Vienna. The Sudeten Germans had not participated in the elections to this body because Prague had not allowed it. In the course of dispersing the demonstrations, fifty-two Germans were killed and eighty-four wounded. Of all non-German-speaking states, Czechoslovakia, with 3,232,000 Germans (3,051,000 in the Czech lands and 148,000 in Slovakia), contained the numerically largest ethnic German minority, which amounted to 22.3 percent of the state's total population in 1930 (Lemberg, 1995: 34). Due to its sheer size, this minority inevitably exerted a destabilizing effect on the newly founded ethnic nation-state. It could not be otherwise in the interwar period when the ethnonational principle ruled supreme in European and especially in central European politics (Bahlcke, 1996: 146; Rothschild, 1992: 79).

A still more complicated situation unfolded in East Silesia, especially in the context of the mutually exclusive Polish and Czech claims to the whole of this region. Already before the capitulation of Austria-Hungary, a majority of local Polish and Czech parties supported the demands of the respective national movements. This suddenly reintroduced nationalist tension, which the war had previously dulled. On October 10, 1918, Polish members of the Reichsrat convened in Cracow and decided to take some steps to secure East Austrian Silesia for the emerging Polish nation-state. On the basis of Charles I's proclamation of October 16, which promised to turn the Dual Monarchy into a federal state, the Rada Narodowa Księstwa Cieszyńskiego (RNKC, National Council of the Cieszyn [Teschen] Principality) came into being. This body represented the Poles of East Silesia. On October 30 it published its manifesto announcing that East Silesia would belong to Poland, though the eventual border would be negotiated with the Czechs. The board of the RNKC was constituted of Father Londzin, Jan Michejda and Tadeusz Reger. On the night of October 31 and morning of November 1, Polish officers from the Austro-Hungarian Army conducted a coup in Teschen. It allowed the RNKC to seize the majority of the territory and to start organizing its own military branch in the form of civil militia. Soon the militiamen numbered between 2,000 and 2,500 (Wurbs, 1982: 52). The Polish national authorities in Warsaw and Cracow accepted the RNKC as the legitimate representative of the Polish government (Gawrecki, 1992a: 80; Wanatowicz, 1994: 14–15).

Understandably, the RNKC was not supported either by the local Czech/ Slavic-speakers subscribing to the Czech national program, or by the members of Kożdoń's ŚPL/SVP, who stood for the indivisibility of East Silesia. On October 28, that is, the day Czechoslovakia officially came into being, the Zemský národní výbor pro Slezsko (ZNV, Regional National Committee for Silesia) was established in Troppau. It immediately started fortifying its power and infrastructure basis, hoping to secure for Czechoslovakia both West and East Austrian Silesia, which at that time were controlled by the Sudetenland and the RNKC, respectively. To this end, on November 1 in Ostrau the ZNV proclaimed that it was entitled to exercise its authority in the whole crownland of Austrian Silesia. In reality, before the Sudetenland was seized by Czech troops in December, the ZNV's influence had been limited to the counties of Friedek and Freistadt, located in the west of East Silesia. And, on top of that, the Poles strongly contested national ownership of the latter county.

The ensuing escalation in the nationalist tension was abated by the agreement on the provisional division of East Silesia, which the ZNV and the NRKC signed on November 5, 1918. Czechoslovakia received 519 square kilometers and Poland 1,762 square kilometers of East Silesia (Wurbs, 1982: 53). The majority of the industrial basin was included in the Czech part. But the strategic Kassa (Kaschau, Košice)-Oderberg railway, which constituted the sole reliable transportation route between the Czech lands and Slovakia, remained in Polish hands because it crossed the preliminary division line in East Silesia.

This division line was neither economically nor strategically viable for Czechoslovakia. In Prague one could hear strong appeals for a redivision more attuned to Czechoslovak interests (Gawrecki, 1992: 66; Wanatowicz, 1994: 14–15). In this case, as in the Polish-Czechoslovak disputes over Zips and Arva, each of the nation-states involved wished to see the other confined to ethnic frontiers, lest its neighbor became a source of irredentist instability in postwar Europe. On the other hand, every one of the concerned nation-states reserved for itself the special right to claim "historical," "strategically sensible" or "economically rational" frontiers (Rothschild, 1992: 85). This application of different standards to one's own nation-state and to the neighboring nation-state led to the typical coolness in the bilateral relations between Poland and Czechoslovakia between the two world wars. This coolness persisted despite the relatively small size of the territories involved.

The letter of the provisional agreement of November 5 was violated by Warsaw's November 28 decision to conduct the January 26, 1919, elections to the Polish Constituent Sejm in the whole of East Silesia, as well as in Csaca (Čadca, Czadca), Zips and Arva. The Czechoslovak government rightly interpreted this move as Poland's usurpation of the territories, whose fate, it was believed, would be decided at the peace conference. Both sides began to fortify their military forces in East Silesia in anticipation of a military solution.

In December 1918 the ZNV's position improved when its power extended over all of West Austrian Silesia in the wake of the Czechoslovak annexation of the Sudetenland. Then the ZNV could afford to question the legitimacy of the RNKC. At that time Poland's conflict with Western Ukraine drew Warsaw's attention away from East Silesia, which was just one of Poland's numerous unresolved border questions, and a rather insignificant one in comparison to Polish ambitions in the east. Simultaneously, Prague's perception of the East Silesian issue was completely different. The economic survival and well-being of Czechoslovakia hinged on East Silesia, with its industrial basin and the railway link between Slovakia and the Czech lands.

The French supported Poland in its conflict with Germany over Upper Silesia in order to weaken the latter. But in the case of East Austrian Silesia, Paris assisted Czechoslovakia against Poland with the same goal in mind. Without East Silesian industry Czechoslovakia would not have been able effectively to deter Germany. On January 23, 1919, the Czechoslovak army, with the support of French and Italian troops, launched an attack. It was not as swift as Prague envisioned, and it did not lead to the complete removal of the Polish troops from East Silesia. This was due to the staunch opposition staged by Polish soldiers, local civil militias, and the Polish/Slavic-speaking miners of the Ostrau-Karwin industrial basin. After the battle of Skotschau (January 28), the front stabilized along the Vistula River. Prague and Warsaw signed an armistice on January 30. This brief Czechoslovak-Polish War resulted in 150 casualties and 1,000 wounded (Wanatowicz, 1994: 17).

After this conflict, the question of East Silesia became part of the agenda of the peace conference, which had convened in Paris on January 18, 1919. On February 3 the new division line, more favorable for Czechoslovakia, was established. The Czechs moved up to this new provisional border on February 25, but they remarked that ethnic borders did not always make sense, as some of those who spoke local Slavic subdialects or the Slavic-Germanic creole did not feel Polish or Czech. They chose instead to identify themselves as East Silesians or Slunzaks. This opinion added a new argument to the ongoing discussion of who had a "greater right" to East Silesia, Poland or Czechoslovakia (Gawrecki, 1992a: 81–82; Roucek, 1945: 148; Wanatowicz, 1994: 15–16).

It is also necessary to observe what reactions the Polish-Czechoslovak conflict elicited among the local Austro-Germans and the Slunzaks of East Silesia. In October 1918 the idea appeared that the German-speaking territories of Bohemia, Moravia and Austrian Silesia should be separated from a future Czech nation-state. On October 19 at the meeting in Teschen, Kożdoń's ŚPL/SVP supported the German program of including East Silesia in German-Austria. Adam Sikora's ŚPL/SVP splinter group favored a different solution: the transfer of East Silesia to Poland. In this manner Sikora hoped to secure a wide autonomy for his homeland, comparable to that which Warsaw later offered to the Szlonzoks of Upper Silesia. When Czechoslovakia commenced the offensive against the Sudetenland and other breakaway German provinces, it became obvious that East Silesia, which had not even been incorporated into the short-lived Sudetenland, did not stand a chance of becoming part of German-Austria. The local Germans and the mainstream ŚPL/SVP proposed establishing a neutral republic that would consist of Austrian Silesia and the Moravian wedge, which separated West Silesia from East Silesia. Some also spoke in favor of a joint Austrian-Polish-Czechoslovak condominium over this territory.

On November 30, 1918, Kożdoń was arrested by the Poles on the charge of pitting the populace against the RNKC. His movement fell into disarray. Meanwhile, the German-speakers of northeastern East Silesia, who could not secure the attachment of East Silesia to the Sudetenland or turn it into a separate political entity, decided to swear an oath of allegiance to the Polish authorities. This event took place at the beginning of December 1918 and prevented dragging the popular guards of these German-speakers into the Polish-Czechoslovak conflict. Following this line, the still-preliminary division of East Silesia was enough to convince the East Silesian German-speakers living in Ostrau and the vicinity to follow suit and pledge loyalty to the Czechoslovak authorities.

On the intercession of Londzin and Michejda, Kożdoń was released and moved to Ostrau. In Ostrau Kożdoń resumed the publication of his weekly, *Ślązak*. Now he campaigned for creating a neutral East Silesian republic or for transferring the whole of East Silesia to Czechoslovakia rather than to the "civilizationally inferior" Poland. His top priority was to prevent division of "his Silesia." The Polish-Czechoslovak conflict played into the hands of Kożdoń and the local German-speakers. The problem of East Silesia was internationalized. The Interallied Commission arrived there to make detailed inquiries. For the first time after the end of the Great War, Kożdoń and the German-speakers could present their own point of view at an international forum. They proposed turning East Silesia into a joint U.S.-British mandate, and on February 7, 1919, Kożdoń handed the commission a memorandum. In it he stated that East Silesia should become a neutral state, and if that were impossible, the land ought to be incorporated into Czechoslovakia (Nowak, 1995: 33; Wotawa, 1919; Wurbs, 1982: 53–54).

At the onset of the peace conference, a complicated pattern of claims and counterclaims to Upper and East Silesia developed. Poland and Germany competed for Upper Silesia. Prague abandoned its initial involvement in this so that the Czechoslovak government could make a stronger bid for East Silesia. East Silesia constituted the bone of contention for the Czechs and the Poles. The local Austro-Germans took a back seat when Czechoslovakia seized their Sudetenland. Without the help of Vienna or Berlin they could not do anything to influence events. The Trojan horse in these conflicts for control of both the industrial basins appeared in the form of the Szlonzokian and Slunzakian national movements. The BdO/ZG and the ŚPL/SVP generally viewed Poland quite unfavorably.

The leaders and members of these movements perceived the new Polish nation-state through the pejorative stereotypes of "Galician poverty" and "*polnische Wirtschaft*." They still considered the ethnonym "Pole" a pejorative label and associated Poland with "lower culture," as opposed to the "higher cultures" of Germany or Czechoslovakia. Thanks to its longer organizational tradition, the Slunzakian movement of East Silesia proved more consistent than its Szlonzokian counterpart, which was founded at the end of 1918. Due to this fact, while Berlin and Warsaw tried to negotiate with Kożdoń's ŚPL/SVP, they often considered the Szlonzokian BdO/ZG an irritation, if not a menace, that should be altogether removed from the political arena.

Ethnic and national cleavages deepened in Upper and East Silesia, especially in the revolutionary atmosphere that followed the end of the Great War. The situation worsened under the influence of socialist and nationalist propagandas, and also because of various violent actions staged by different worker organizations and national paramilitary organizations. In the case of Upper Silesia these paramilitary organizations were directed and financed by Posen, Berlin and Breslau, and, in the case of East Silesia by Vienna, Prague and Cracow. Thus, the stage was set for internecine fighting. It almost erupted when Prague seized the Sudetenland and decisively broke out in the course of the Polish-Czechoslovak war over East Silesia.

The premonition of a similar fate awaiting Upper Silesia came with the Wielkopolska Uprising. It could have easily spilled over into Silesia. Decision-makers slowly began to realize that the idealistic quest for peace and justice through standing fast for the unwavering application of the principle of national self-determination would probably not produce a better world. The planned and thorough ethnic cleansing conducted in the Province of Poznań (Posen) after the Wielkopolska Uprising was not something they could happily reflect on. Dividing populations along politicized ethnic lines cost lives and caused innumerable human tragedies.

The first concentration camps in Wielkopolska were organized for interning the most significant German civil servants, intellectuals and political leaders. In the two largest camps, located in Szczypiorno and Strzałkowo (Stralkowo), about 16,000 Germans were detained until July 1919. On June 2, 1919, all the communal German civil servants were dismissed from the public administration, which, together with their families, amounted to 100,000 persons. The new Polish administration treated as foreigners all the Germans who had moved to the Province of Posen after January 1, 1908. Those who had established their place of residence in this region prior to this date could opt either for German or Polish citizenship. Between 150,000 and 175,000 persons took advantage of the situation and chose to become German citizens. In the eyes of Polish law this made them foreigners. All of these "foreigners" eventually had to leave Poland. They added to the number of those who had left for central Germany immediately after the outbreak of the Wielkopolska Uprising or because of the introduction of the stern Polonizing measures.

In 1919 Wielkopolska's Polish-language mass media and, at a later stage, Polish historians attempted to "justify" the harsh treatment of the province's Germans by producing evidence of crimes that German troops and volunteers committed on the Polish population during the Wielkopolska Uprising (Tomkowiak, 1994). However, in light of the quick Polish victory, there was not much time for such atrocities to take place. On the other hand, Wielkopolska's German civilian population also suffered tribulations, as usually happens in the course modern warfare, especially if an ethnic or national conflict underpins it.

The Polish appeals that Wielkopolska Germans should pledge allegiance to Poland and join the Poles in their endeavors for the common good did not sound convincing to the German ear. The above-described methods of discrimination and ethnic cleansing amounted to a "war on Germandom." A Polish organization active in Poznań made it crystal clear with its telltale name: the Centralna Organizacja dla Oczyszczenia Poznania od Żydów i Niemców (Central Organization for Cleansing Poznań of Jews and Germans) (Rogall, 1993: 125, 130–131).

The number of the Wielkopolska Germans, which had steadily grown from 218,393 (27.7 percent) in 1816 to 806,504 (38.4 percent) in 1910 (Kozłowski, 1994: 18), sharply declined after the war to 327,846 in 1921 (Hauser, 1994: 44) and 224,254 in 1926. Their percentage in the population of Poland's Poznań Voivodeship sank to 11 percent. The change was even more dramatic in the cities. The percentage of Germans living in Poznań dropped from 42 percent in 1910 to 2 percent in 1931, and from 77.5 percent in 1910 to 8.5 percent in 1931 in Bydgoszcz (Bromberg) (Rogall, 1993: 130).

The homogenizing nature of the ethnic nation-state prevented the reestablishment of even a modicum of prewar peace, prosperity and stability. The long *belle époque* of the nineteenth century was definitively over. The "poverty of small [nation-]states"[8] engulfed central Europe and gave the foretaste of what the twentieth century was to be about, namely genocide, ethnic cleansing and mass expulsions.

In this context it is worth remembering that the various nationalisms which infiltrated Upper Silesia and Austrian Silesia usually came from without. These national ideologies mobilized small groups of locals who often happened to be somehow estranged from the social and political mainstream. For them it was easy to shun the traditional way of life that ensured the persistence of non-national multiple identities, identities that grew from one's everyday attachment to one's village, town, region, religion or monarch (Wanatowicz, 1994: 12).

The situation gradually changed after the divisions of Austrian Silesia and Upper Silesia. The ennationalizing policies of Germany, Poland and Czechoslovakia eliminated the possibility of non-national identification. This process accelerated, prodded by the totalitarian methods of social engineering employed during World War II and after. Millions of people were expelled, while hundreds of thousands were incarcerated or sent to forced labor camps. National "reeducation" progressed with the use of language bans and rampant discrimination. The possibility of a meaningful career and family life was closed to those who failed or refused to acquire the "appropriate" national identity. But due to the peripheral location of Upper Silesia and Austrian Silesia, ethno-national homogenization of these regions has never been complete. To this day, 40,000 Slunzaks survive in Czech Silesia and 200,000 Szlonzoks in Poland's Upper Silesia.

CHAPTER 11

National and Ethnic Groups in Silesia, 1871–1918

The ethnic relations in Silesia, especially in Upper Silesia, underwent a dramatic change after the founding of the *Kleindeutsch* nation-state in 1871. This success of German nationalism made the majority of the Silesian German-speakers into Germans. Looking at this development through the spectacles of Miroslav Hroch's scheme, they entered the mainstream of the German national movement, which at that time reached phase C.

This rather straightforward consequence of the establishment of the German Empire had a mixed result on the province of Silesia as a whole. The social change in Lower Silesia followed the general pattern observed elsewhere in the country, though not in the ethnically diverse Oppeln Regency. In addition, the overwhelming majority of the regency's inhabitants confessed Catholicism. The conflict between this religion, connected to the universalistic ideals and hierarchically centered on the Holy See, and the new nation-state, which attached Protestantism to its national ideology, was inescapable.

The long years of the *Kulturkampf* did not ennationalize German Catholicism or even subject it to Berlin's will. But a *modus vivendi* between the Catholic Church and the German Empire was reached in the second half of the 1880s. In the non-German-speaking areas, the *Kulturkampf* policies, aimed at limiting the social and political influence of the Catholic Church, were coupled with the propagation of the German language as another equally significant foundation of German nationalism. This led to instituting further measures against Catholics who happened not to speak this language.

Inescapably, the *Kulturkampf* antagonized the Polish/Slavic-speakers in the Province of Posen and in Upper Silesia. The measures directed against Polish and all other languages that could not be classified as German were retained after the official termination of the *Kulturkampf* in 1885 and 1886. They became steadily harsher in the period between 1890 and 1914. Not surprisingly then, this ennationalizing pressure caused the Wielkopolska Polish national movement to move to the transitional zone between phases B and C. Its tendency to progress speedily to phase C was frustrated by the German authorities and the continuing division of all the Polish-speakers among the partition powers of Russia, Prussia (the German Empire) and Austria.

In this situation, one could not hope that these Polish-speakers, defined as a nation, would be granted their own nation-state anytime soon. This would necessitate a dramatic change of the political map of central Europe. Such a previously unthinkable opportunity arose in the course of the Great War. The Polish national movement deftly utilized the collapse of tsarist Russia, the breakup of Austria-Hungary, and the near-collapse of the German Empire to establish the Polish nation-state in 1918. Under the influence of this impressive achievement, the Wielkopolska Polish national movement decisively moved to phase C during the Wielkopolska Uprising (1918–1919). This event, which took Berlin unawares, allowed for the swift incorporation of Wielkopolska into the new Poland.

The Wielkopolska Polish activists strove to spread the Polish national idea to other Polish/Slavic-speaking areas in Prussia, including Upper Silesia. The influence of the Polish national movement from East Austrian Silesian on Upper Silesia diminished at the turn of the 1880s when it split along the confessional cleavage. The Polish activists established their separate Catholic and Protestant organizations and, through their grounding in religion, contributed to the sidelining of the usual nationalist message. For the time being, Catholic universalism and Protestant loyalty to the state took the upper hand.

Faced with these developments, the Galician Polish nationalists, concentrated in Cracow, could hardly spare time and resources on Upper Silesia, a region that still seemed so un-Polish. The tightening of control over the international border separating the German Empire from Austria-Hungary did not help either. Hence Cracow Polish activists decided to focus their efforts on the reconstruction of the Polish national movement in East Austrian Silesia. This region was easy to reach from Galicia. In addition, Polish nationalism had previously achieved such successes there that one could not even dream that they might be repeated in Upper Silesia anytime soon.

The radical national influence from Wielkopolska on the nascent Polish movement in Upper Silesia did not bear any immediate fruit, despite the fact that the region's Polish/Slavic-speakers were much displeased with the *Kulturkampf* and the laws banning standard Polish from all aspects of public life, with the exception of sermons said during mass.[1] Furthermore, the universalistically minded Catholic Church sought to retain the unity of all the Upper Silesian faithful, whatever languages they happened to speak or write. The clergy moderated the impact of state-supported *Kleindeutsch* nationalism and of Polish nationalism radiating from

274 ◆ CHAPTER 11

the Province of Posen. As a result, the Polish national movement of Upper Silesia remained in the transitional zone between phases A and B until the 1890s.

Later the radical trend of Polish nationalism gained a tentative foothold in the industrial basin of Upper Silesia. It was possible due to the growing concentration of the urbanized population, which had better access to the press and politics than had been the case among the traditionally rural Upper Silesians. The vagaries of city life on weekly wages easily radicalized the inhabitants of industrial cities during times of economic crisis, price hikes and shortages of goods. Hardships led to strikes and demonstrations, not the passivity characteristic of the countryside. Radicalized labor was a force to be reckoned with.

Polish nationalism achieved its initial breakthrough in Upper Silesia when Korfanty was elected to the Reichstag in 1903. However, it was not a straightforward shift of the Polish national movement from phase A to phase B, but instead represented a split. The majority of the Polish/Slavic-speakers or Szlonzoks retained the steadfast loyalty to Napieralski's Zentrum/*Katolik* faction. With regard to Polish nationalism, this small group remained between phases A and B well into the Great War. At the same time Korfanty's rather elitist pro-LN camp progressed into phase B, however with a substantial loss of its relatively few supporters. This situation continued until 1914.

The destabilizing effect of the Great War and the emergence of the Polish nation-state brought about a considerable increase in the ranks of Korfanty's supporters. The position of his group grew even stronger due to the ideological and material aid flowing from the Province of Posen. This quickly pushed Korfanty's section of Upper Silesia's Polish national movement to the transitional zone between phases B and C. Many Polish-oriented members of Napieralski's camp also switched their allegiance to Korfanty. Thus, the final fate of the Polish national movement in Upper Silesia was to be influenced by the decisions of the peace conference.

The Germans, anxious about the possibility of losing all of Silesia or Upper Silesia, put forward plans of autonomy or even separate statehood for the entire province or the Oppeln Regency. The Catholic universalistic activists, even if sympathetic to the Polish cause, supported the Germans in their efforts to grant Silesia or Upper Silesia a degree of separate statehood or autonomy. These activists—mainly Catholic clergymen—had a vital interest in retaining the social cohesion of their parishes and the Catholic faithful. This translated into the clergy's efforts to work out such a political solution that would secure the continuation of the traditional, non-national way of life for their parishioners. This non-national way of life had served them well for centuries, and the prospect of retaining it was preferable to the inescapably painful process of national assimilation into either Germandom or Polishdom.

This universalistic and, simultaneously, anational program proved attractive to the Szlonzoks. A powerful Szlonzokian national movement reemerged. It had earlier appeared during the 1870s but had gone into oblivion after *Szlązak* had gone defunct in 1879. German and Polish attempts to sway this young Szlonzokian national movement into the direction of Germandom or Polishdom stalled its meteoric rise. However, the undeniable importance of the Szlonzokian national movement continued until the plebiscite (1921) that preceded the division of Upper Silesia between Germany and Poland in 1922.

The disappearance of the BdO/ZG after this division meant the end of the organizational life of the Szlonzokian national movement, but it remained a distinct social and political force, ready to reappear from underneath the official surface of the German or Polish nation. Szlonzokian nationalism continued to exert variegated influence on the political life of divided Upper Silesia between 1922 and 1939. In a nutshell, the Szlonzokian national movement dashed from phase A to phase B in 1918/1919. It attempted to cross the threshold of phase C in 1919, but the lack of international recognition for this national cause, combined with the division of the Szlonzokian homeland, made this movement retreat into the gray zone between phases A and B after 1921.

In Austrian Silesia, the Polish and Czech national movements developed fully during the liberal 1860s. They were dealt a serious blow when Vienna introduced bilingual (German-Slavic) education in the 1870s. This decision met the practical needs and the demands of the Slavophone populace, who realized that their children could not count on any meaningful career in Austria-Hungary unless they acquired a passable command of German. This development also prevented the radicalization of this population, which would have been unavoidable if their children had received education solely via the medium of a Slavic language. Without any knowledge of German and with no possibility to use the Slavic languages in public life or even in their professions, they would have pressed the crownland authorities for the introduction of these Slavic tongues as official languages of Austrian Silesia, in addition to German. The predictable altercations would have opened the space of social instability that nationalisms would have been quick to enter.

On the other hand, the *Ausgleich* of 1867 for the first time seriously limited the influence of the German-speakers in the Danubian monarchy, which had been transformed into Austria-Hungary. This concession rather imperfectly reflected the multiethnic character of this polity. After the military failures of the mid-nineteenth century, Vienna became convinced that it would be impossible to govern the empire based solely on the loyalty and political support of the German-speakers. Although the Austro-Germans were the dominant group, they did not constitute the majority of the empire's inhabitants.

The authorities attempted to secure the loyalty of the Czechs inhabiting Bohemia and Moravia—the empire's richest crownlands. At the beginning of the 1870s, Vienna offered them an *Ausgleich* similar to the one granted to the Magyars in 1867. This would make Cisleithania governable and more democratic, even though it could require the transformation of the Dual Monarchy into a triple one. This attempt faltered due to the staunch opposition expressed by the political circles of the Hungarians and the German-speakers. They were afraid of losing their privileged position in Austria-Hungary, with Transleithania and Cisleithania functioning as their quasi-nation-states.

Eventually, Vienna had no choice but to hinge the stability of the political system of Austria-Hungary on the Poles. The emperor granted them a wide-ranging autonomy in Galicia. Thanks to this development, they stood fast by the empire. Unlike in the German Empire or Russia, the Polish national movement enjoyed best conditions in Austria-Hungary's Galicia. In addition, unlike the Czechs, the Polish nationalists of Galicia did not canvass for establishing a Polish nation-state within the empire. They placed their hopes on recreating Poland-Lithuania as a Polish nation-state. In Vienna's eyes, this was a long shot because the contemporary political situation offered no such opportunity to the Poles in the foreseeable future. This would have demanded full or partial dismembering of the German Empire and Russia, which did not look plausible at the time. So it was safe to accept and even foster the rise of Polish nationalism in Galicia as a counterforce to the perceived "disloyalty" of the Czech national politicians. Possible excesses of Polish nationalism were curbed by Vienna's encouragement for the rise of Ruthenian (Ukrainian) nationalism in eastern Galicia.

Bohemia's Czech activists obstructed the monarchy's political life. They were displeased at Vienna's tactical exclusion of the Czechs from political considerations in favor of the Poles and the Hungarians. In this situation, the Czech politicians continued to pursue even more relentlessly the idea that the unity of the Czech lands should be administratively and politically reaffirmed. This contributed to the fortification of the Czech national movements in Moravia and Austrian Silesia, and the establishment of numerous links between these movements and their ideological base in Bohemia.

As a consequence, the moderate Old Czechs lost power to the radical Young Czechs in the 1870s and 1890s. The Young Czechs pushed Bohemia's Czech national movement into phase C at the beginning of the 1890s. Beginning in the 1880s, they had gradually won an increasing number of linguistic and cultural concessions for the Czechs of Bohemia and Moravia. But all these concessions always fell short of the sought-after unity of the lands of the Czech Crown. Since the 1890s, Bohemia's Czech nationalists had been seriously weakened by the rise of social democrats and Pan-Germanism. Moreover, a retreat toward the non-national sphere of regional and ethnic identities took place in Moravia after the celebrated 1905 *Ausgleich*. Suddenly, a Slavic-speaking Moravian could use his language in public life without having to become a Czech.

Hence, Bohemia's Czech national movement retreated to the transitory zone between phases B and C. Moravia's Czech national movement remained in phase B and partly became "denationalized," thanks to successful collaboration with the local German-speakers. This increasing attraction of regionalism ideologically distinguished Moravia's Czech national movement from its Bohemian counterpart.

These discrepancies present in Czech nationalism exerted a strong influence on the development of Austrian Silesia's Czech national movement. This movement reached phase B during the 1870s especially due to the founding of the Matice opavská in 1877. Rapid industrialization provided Bohemia's Czech nationalists with the means of developing and spreading their activities, usually to adjacent northern Moravia. However, the relative isolation from Prague and lack of interest on the part of Moravia's Slavophone elites kept the Czech national movement of Austrian Silesia in phase B. Its further growth was also stunted by the general decline of the mainstream Czech national movement at the turn of the twentieth century. The rise of Austrian Silesia's German national movement also frustrated the spread of its Czech counterpart as well.

The German-speakers progressed with the organizing of their own national movements because they were apprehensive of the growing political and cultural strength of the Czech-speakers in Bohemia and Moravia. The position of the German activists was bolstered by the successes of *Kleindeutsch* nationalism, clearly visible across the border after the founding of the German Empire. The rise of the Slavic and Hungarian national movements in the Dual Monarchy, coupled with Vienna's eagerness to accommodate their needs and aspirations within the existing political framework, put the German-speakers at a relative disadvantage. They interpreted these developments as discrimination and answered by turning to a *Großdeutsch* nationalism of their own during the 1870s–1890s.

Afraid to lose their still-dominant position in Austria-Hungary, the Austro-Germans reached phase B in the 1890s all over Austria-Hungary, including Austrian Silesia. Prior to 1914, Austrian Silesia's German national movement moved to the transitory zone between phases B and C. The movement strove to emphasize and maintain the German character of this crownland. They had a chance to achieve this goal because German-speakers constituted a plurality of this crownland's population. However, the number of Austro-Germans in Austrian Silesia was numerically smaller than that of all the Slavic-speakers combined. But the maintenance of the privileged position of this crownland's Austro-Germans was facilitated by the intensification of the conflict between the Polish and Czech national movements over East Silesia. Struggling with each other, these two Slavic national movements mutually cancelled out most of their influence in this effort.

The overwhelming political, economic and numerical strength of Austrian

Silesia's German-speakers, especially felt in West Silesia, made some Czech activists look for cooperation with their Polish counterparts. This coalition often was sought in the name of Slavic reciprocity (cooperation) or even Pan-Slavism. The trend largely disappeared during the 1870s–1890s, when the Czech and Polish national movements started developing similar forms of organizations and institutions in the field of culture, politics and education. This opened a cleavage between both these national movements in East Silesia, whereas Polish activists did not operate in West Silesia.

Polish activists had the advantage of neighboring Galicia and Cracow, where the Polish national movement remained safe and satisfied with its position in the transitory zone between phases B and C. However, the potential strength of East Silesia's Polish movement weakened at the turn of the 1880s when it split into the opposing Catholic and Protestant factions. Eventually this event confined the movement to phase B. The failure of East Silesia's Polish activists at consolidating their local movement was amply illustrated by their inability to prevent assimilation of Polish/Slavic-speaking migrants from Galicia into Germandom or Czechdom at the turn of the twentieth century.

The negative stereotypes associated with the Galicians also kept many East Silesian Polish/Slavic-speakers or Slunzaks from identifying with the Poles and Polish nationalism in general. Between 1905 and 1910, the situation created the springboard for the successful launch of the Slunzakian national movement. This movement had earlier appeared ephemerally at the turn of the 1850s, as well as during the 1870s. The mass appeal of the Slunzakian national movement became obvious in the northeast of East Austrian Silesia in the years 1910–1914. The movement's success was even more visible when seen in the context of the relatively weakened Polish and Czech national movements. The Slunzakian national movement rapidly reached phase B and stopped short of demanding autonomy or a nation-state for the Slunzakian nation. Instead, the movement chose cultural and political alliance with Germandom within the borders of Austria-Hungary.

The Great War submerged various nationalisms in the superficial loyalty and unity conditioned by military rule. But in the long run, this conflict and its aftermath actually exacerbated national and ethnic cleavages, especially in the face of the German–Austro-Hungarian alliance. It gave German nationalists hope that a truly German nation-state of Greater Germany would soon be built through a merger of the *Großdeutsch* and *Kleindeutsch* strains of German nationalism. Such a prospect was not appealing to a majority of the non-German national movements. The discontent of these movements erupted in the last years of the prolonged warfare marked by social, economic and political commotion.

The acceptance of the national principle in the guise of the Wilsonian notion of national self-determination led to the fall of the Dual Monarchy. This event imperiled Germandom, since the Allies favored satisfying the non-German national movements. The success of these movements was solidified when the Allies ordained and recognized the coming into being of the emerging nation-states. Thus, the Polish and Czech(oslovak) national movements of Austrian Silesia reached phase B and engaged in the venture of seizing this crownland for their respective nations, despite the local Austro-Germans' opposition.

German nationalists responded with a tacit proposal to create a *Großdeutsch* nation-state through uniting Germany with the predominantly German-speaking areas of Austria-Hungary. Following this line of defense, Austrian Silesia's German national movement reached phase C and participated in the establishment of the Sudetenland.

Czech nationalists of the Sudetenland were displeased with this development because of their own phase C-aspirations, encouraged by their full organizational and ideological merger with the mainstream of Czech nationalism. As a consequence, Prague saw to the dismantling of the Sudetenland and engaged in a bitter conflict over East Silesia with the local Polish national movement, which was actively aided by Warsaw. Through a full fusion with the Galician and mainstream Polish national movement, the Polish activists of East Silesia also reached phase C, like their Czech counterparts.

Only the Slunzakian national movement proved rather reluctant to embark on the full-fledged process of nation- and nation-state-building. As a result, the movement hovered between phases B and C. The Slunzakian activists hoped to save the traditional political and ethnic structure of East Silesia by making it into a neutral state. Alternatively, they would agree to attach their homeland to a Greater Germany or Czechoslovakia as an indivisible autonomous region. At most, they wanted to avoid incorporation of East Silesia into Poland or any division of their land.

The pattern of national conflicts was set at the end of the Great War due to the Polish and Czech national movements, as well as the German national movement of Austria-Hungary, which had crossed the threshold of phase C. This phenomenon had a direct bearing on Upper and Austrian Silesias, where the local national movements were quickly subjugated to the mainstream national movements, with their respective centers in Berlin, Warsaw and Prague. This immediately transplanted the generalized conflicts played out among the Czecho(Slovak), German and Polish nation-states to Upper and Austrian Silesias, aggravating national tensions already brewing in both these regions.

The Szlonzokian and Slunzakian national movements staged short-lived local opposition to these ennationalizing developments, which spread instability and national strife. But both these movements were swiftly suppressed or subjugated by their Czech, German and Polish counterparts, because the Szlonzokian and Slunzakian leaders and parties lacked the resources and outside support to make their voices heard at the international level. In addition, the influence of the local Czech, German and Polish national movements subsided. Their opinions were merely of advisory significance. The governments of Czechoslovakia, Germany and Poland did the talking at the peace conference. The governmental delegations negotiated the interwar shape of Upper and Austrian Silesias. Consequently, the local Czech, German and Polish national movements largely disappeared after 1919 in Austrian Silesia, and after 1921 in Upper Silesia. They became integral branches of the respective mainstream national movements of Czechoslovakia, Germany and Poland.

Even the minority national movements started taking irredentist orders from Berlin and Warsaw. Prague was excluded from this arrangement because no significant Czech minorities remained outside of Czechoslovakia. In Silesia, a sizeable German minority existed in the Silesian Voivodeship, Poland's region consisting of the Polish sections of Upper Silesia and East Austrian Silesia. Across the new Polish-German border that crisscrossed Upper Silesia, a Polish minority persisted in Germany's truncated Oppeln Regency. Czech Silesia, consisting of Austrian Silesia (less Poland's section of East Silesia) and the Hlučínsko, detached from Upper Silesia, also housed other significant German and Polish national minorities.

Czech Silesia's German minority was exceptional on several counts. First, it demographically dominated the region and formed the absolute majority of the population in former West Austrian Silesia. Second, after 1918, this minority joined the Sudeten German national movement in the hopes of being included in the fold of the German-Austrian nation-state. Only when it became apparent that the Allies would not allow merging Vienna-led German-Austria with the German Republic, Sudeten German activists gradually redirected the affiliation of their movement from Austria toward the politically stronger and geographically adjacent Germany. Consequently, the irredentist urges of Czech Silesia's Germans were ideologically connected to Vienna before this minority began to look to Berlin for guidance and leadership.

The Szlonzokian and Slunzakian national movements took a back seat in the hostile atmosphere of ennationalizing endeavors fostered by the Czechoslovak, German and Polish nation-states. However, political remnants of these two national movements persisted after the 1920 division of East Austrian Silesia and the 1922 division of Upper Silesia. That was possible because of the varying degrees of cultural and political autonomy employed in Czech Silesia, the Upper Silesian section of Poland's Silesian Voivodeship, and Germany's new Province of Upper Silesia.

From time to time, the Szlonzokian and Slunzakian national movements also grew stronger at the grassroots level with additional support of some previous supporters of the Czech, German or Polish national movements. They were usually ethnic Szlonzoks and Slunzaks who had become disenchanted in the course of their involvement with Czech, German or Polish nationalism. They noticed that Warsaw, Prague and Berlin tended to enforce ennationalization without any concern for local particularisms, contrary to the capitals' initial pledges to institute autonomous arrangements. These threatened particularisms constituted the fabric of the traditional way of life and underpinned regional identities still prevalent among the inhabitants of Upper and Austrian Silesias. These composite (multiple), local identities persisted because few persons replaced them with novel attachment to one nation or another. And even in such cases, the national identification often functioned as just another component of the Szlonzokian or Slunzakian multiple identity.

Losing or forsaking one's traditional way of life and non-national multiple identity is always a painful process, even when a person makes a conscious and calculated decision for the sake of the most appealing "nationhood." Regrets caused by abandoning one's anational childhood, kin, friends, multiethnic homeland, and specific dialect or creole frequently plague a person after changing one's identity. To become a member of a nation one must leave the traditional safety net ensured by the closely knit social environment extant in a region for an abstract and distant, though highly attractive, idea of a nation and its nation-state. However, the logic of modernization accompanying ennationalization extends the promise of recreating the *Gemeinschaft* (traditional community) in the modern world, but always fails to deliver. What nationalism provides is modern *Gesellschaft* (society) clad in the national rhetoric of *Gemeinschaft*. The traditional inescapably disappears, and in the end one enters the straightforward world of nations. As a result, when crossing the line between the pre- or anational to the national one has to learn how to live and function in the dramatically different social environment.

This phenomenon of sudden realization that one's ethnic world is coming to an end was clearly visible in the case of the Morawec national movement, which used to thrive in the southern part of Upper Silesia. This movement emerged in the 1840s, largely due to Cyprian Lelek's efforts. The protection and insulation from the outside world, granted by the Catholic Church to the Morawecs secured a low-key but guaranteed existence for their national movement. The Moravian language functioned as the medium of instruction in elementary schools, sermons were delivered in this language in churches, and predominantly religious books continued to be printed in Moravian. The *Kulturkampf* severed this tentative continuity of the Morawec movement, and the Catholic Church became its last refuge.

This situation lasted until the founding of the first and only Moravian-language periodical, *Katolické Nowiny* (1893–1920). The publication of this weekly heralded the shift of the Morawec national movement from phase A to phase B. This movement remained at this level, untroubled by the outside world because the Morawecs' relatively distant region was located beyond the commuter networks that fed the centers of industrialization in Upper and Austrian Silesias. No railway links connected their homeland to these centers. Agriculture secured for them a standard of living which the Morawecs expected and accepted. This insulation entrenched the Morawecs in the rural way of life and in Catholicism.

The dramatic changes at the end of the Great War and Czech nationalists' claims to their homeland appeared unseemly and largely incomprehensible to the Morawecs. They had a hard time identifying with any nationalism, especially the ethnically close nationalism of the Czechs. The latter ideology was steeped in the Hussitic tradition of Protestantism, inimical to the Morawecs' strong attachment to Catholicism. These events at the end of the Great War alienated many a Morawec. Prague seized and subsequently closed their only newspaper, *Katolické Nowiny*. Simultaneously, the Allies ordered the transfer of most of the Morawecs' homeland—the Hultschiner Ländchen—to Czechoslovakia.

In self-defense, the Morawecs closed themselves within their ethnic parochialism and frustrated Prague's attempts to Czechize them. Most of the Morawecs actually opted for Germandom, exemplified in their eyes by the culturally and confessionally close Sudeten Germans. The Morawec national movement disappeared after 1918, but contrary to Czech expectations, the Morawecs predominantly chose to become Germans, not Czechs. Despite this national choice, the Morawecs retained their multiple identity, which allowed them to function as Czechs among Czechs, Germans among Germans, and Morawecs in their home environment.

The end of part 2 of this study requires a brief reiteration of the policies of ethnic cleansing that, prior to 1918, Germany and Austria-Hungary employed in Prussian and Austrian Silesia, respectively. It ought to be borne in mind, however, that the methods and techniques used to this end were quite subtle and rarely amounted to such typically twentieth-century measures as expulsion, genocide, or totalitarian liquidation of cultures and languages.

The nation-building policy of the *Kulturkampf* was to weaken Catholicism in favor of Protestantism, as only the latter was believed to be fully compatible with *Kleindeutsch* nationalism. Catholicism smacked of "cosmopolitanism," defined as inimical to the task of German nation-state-building. The policy of the *Kulturkampf* failed due to the staunch opposition of the faithful and their Catholic Church. This required reaching a consensus between Berlin and the church, which led to a mutually fruitful modus vivendi. In addition to the conflict with the Catholic Church, the *Kulturkampf* displayed some ethnic overtones in Upper Silesia and the Slavic-speaking areas of the Breslau Regency.

All languages other than German were gradually banned from state offices, education and school religious instruction in the 1870s. On a limited scale the Catholic Church functioned as a haven for these banned languages, dialects and creoles. The clergy published books and periodicals in these language forms and employed them in the course of pastoral services and sermons. This situation lasted only until the 1890s, when even the Catholic Church joined Berlin in the task of nation- and nation-state-building. The church promoted Germandom and the German language but fell short of suppressing religious services in Polish (meaning not only the standard language but also the Slavic dialect and the Slavic-Germanic creole) or Moravian in the case of Upper Silesia.

The process of rapid industrialization facilitated the implementation of the German Empire's language policy. The dramatic change that overhauled the social world of Upper Silesia necessitated in-migration of numerous German (and usually Protestant) civil servants, engineers and other professionals. They came from the German-speaking hinterland, together with their families. This entailed a gradual transformation of the region's ethnic make-up. The rise of an industrial economy provided Berlin with indispensable instruments for pursuing the further processes of nation- and nation-state-building. In its course the state rarely alienated the non-German-speakers, because despite the limits imposed on the official use of their languages, they still enjoyed much higher standards of living than Polish-speakers in neighboring Congress Poland and Galicia, or even Czech-speakers in the rural areas of Bohemia and Moravia.

The German-language school system, mass media, conscription army, and civil service gradually nudged the multiethnic and multilingual culture and society of Upper Silesia toward Germandom. The locals themselves saw the German language not as a simple imposition but as an opportunity. Having acquired a working command of German, they could look for a job anywhere in the German Empire and Austria-Hungary. In addition, they could continue their education and embark on a white-collar career. Clerks stationed in Upper Silesia often unwittingly altered Slavic personal names and place-names. What they heard they wrote down according to German spelling and usage. This made Upper Silesia more "German-sounding" that it had been before.

A backlash on the part of Upper Silesia's Slavophone population came during the 1890s. At that time Berlin attempted to limit the use of non-German languages in churches, but this was too deep an intrusion immediately after the wrapping up of the *Kulturkampf*. Simultaneously, this decade saw the rise of radical German nationalism, which engaged Polish nationalism in the *Wirtschaftskampf*. Although this national-economic conflict was played out mainly in the Province of Posen, its effects also radiated to Upper Silesia.

The *Wirtschaftskampf* resulted in the birth of the non-universalistic and secular Polish national movement in Upper Silesia. The movement's successes culminated in the 1903 election of Korfanty to the Reichstag. The growing irredentism of the Wielkopolska Polish nationalism and the emergence of the Polish national movement in Upper Silesia as a political force necessitated a reaction on the part of the German authorities. Berlin was quick to support German cultural organizations and German-language libraries. The German government also issued new laws directed at countering the "Polish danger." In the first decade of the twentieth century they limited the use of Polish during meetings of Polish-language organizations and narrowed the sphere of economic freedom enjoyed by non-German-speaking German citizens. This blatant employment of law for the purpose of ennationalizing reached its logical conclusion in the Expropriation Act. However, it was never applied in Upper Silesia, and it soon became a dead letter due to vehement criticism voiced by the Catholic Church and liberal politicians.

The outbreak of the Great War did not alter the official language policies in Upper Silesia, but censorship ensured that the Polish-language press remained loyal to the kaiser and the state. The authorities ordered preventive internment of the leaders of the socialists and the Polish nationalists so that they could not complicate the situation with their activities. In the past, compulsory military service had facilitated assimilation of young Upper Silesian males into Germandom or at least furnished them with a command of the German language. During wartime, compulsory military service and the draft deprived the national movements of their most dynamic members. This situation remained unchanged until the last years of the war. Economic difficulties and the exigencies of the war of attrition brought about radicalization of the soldiers and the population.

The authorities had to do something in order to offset the danger of growing anti-German feeling among the non-German-speaking/bilingual groups of the Szlonzoks and the Morawecs. In 1917, use of Polish and Moravian at the meetings of Polish- and Moravian-language organizations was permitted. Oppeln and Breslau also attempted to employ civil servants who, along with German, would be able to communicate in Polish or Moravian. At the end of 1918, Polish and Moravian were reintroduced as languages for religious instruction in the first three grades of elementary school. Finally, article 113 of the constitution of the Weimar Republic guaranteed language and minority rights for non-German ethnic/national groups living in Germany (Klein, 1972: 37–50). However, any consistent minority policies began to emerge in Upper Silesia only after the division of this region between Poland and Germany in 1922.

In Austrian Silesia, Czech and Polish (or rather the local dialects classified as such) briefly enjoyed the status of official crownland languages between 1849 and 1851. Thereafter German ruled supreme in this capacity. Polish and Czech continued to be used in the schools until the 1870s, when the bilingual (German-Slavic) system of education replaced Slavophone elementary schools. This change was not fully successful, since many teachers and schools boycotted it. Soon the Matice opavská (1877) and the Macierz Szkolna (1885) came to their aid. Vienna had no choice but to retract its decision and to allow the opening of exclusively Czech- and Polish-language secondary schools between 1883 and 1914, along with Czech- and Polish-language elementary schools, which had returned to Austrian Silesia even earlier.

Actually, after the 1870s the central government or the crownland authorities hardly ever pursued any policies that could be seen as an attempt at ennationalization. The non-German-speakers were gradually granted more cultural and language rights up to the breakup of the Dual Monarchy in 1918. However, Austrian Silesia's non-German-speakers (or at least their nationalist-minded elites) felt discriminated against when they compared their situation to that of the non-German-speakers in Bohemia, Moravia or Galicia. The authorities could not allow similar concessions in Austrian Silesia because they would have alienated the German-speakers, who constituted almost half of the crownland's population (Kořalka, 1995: 18). In addition, such concessions would have also precipitated nationalist and ethnic conflicts. On the other hand, the crownland's Czech and Polish nationalist activists did not have enough economic and political power to coax the Landtag or the Reichsrat to grant them more linguistic and political rights.

Some say that during the period 1867–1918 the Habsburgs saw to the peaceful dismantling of Austria-Hungary and that the Hungarian *Ausgleich* had begun this process. In this vein one might infer that all the various ethnic or national groups inhabiting the empire opted for independence when Vienna had nothing more to concede to them. This teleological assumption, derived from the hindsight enjoyed by authors writing after 1918, was not that apparent during the existence of Austria-Hungary. The author even doubts if this thesis is entirely true. The Dual Monarchy, at least in Cisleithania, secured so many political rights for its citizens that the government could not prevent them, if they chose to, from pursuing various ethnic nationalisms. Belatedly, Vienna attempted to maintain the unity of the empire through overhauling it into a federation in mid-October 1918. This endeavor could have even succeeded had not, after the Great War, the logic of national self-determination been against multiethnic polities in general. Thereafter it turned out that national and ethnic minorities in the new nation-states faced discrimination unthinkable in Austria-Hungary.

Conclusion

This study constitutes an attempt at a diachronic presentation and analysis of the emergence of national and ethnic groups in Silesia. It is contextualized against the development of German, Polish and Czech nationalisms, and the findings are organized with the use of the theoretical model worked out by the Czech scholar Miroslav Hroch (1985). This model proved a deft instrument for analyzing the rise of ethnic nations and ethnic groups, as suggested by Hroch himself. But it also became evident that the model can be fruitfully applied to explain the rise of national groups, that is, regional branches of larger national movements or ethnic nations-in-making.

The semi-success of German nationalism brought about the founding of the *Kleindeutsch* German nation-state in 1871 and was followed by a gradual increase in national tensions. Their root cause was the unceasing contest over Silesia played out by Czech, German and Polish national activists at the close of the nineteenth century and at the beginning of the twentieth century.

U.S. president Woodrow Wilson seemingly put an end to this conflict, having coaxed the Allies to accept the national principle as the basis for the post-Great War political reorganization of Europe and, later, of the whole world. However, the carving-up of Silesia among Germany and the two newly emergent nation-states of Czechoslovakia and Poland did not do away with national tensions. On the contrary, this decision contributed to fortifying them. After the League of Nations had lost its power and legitimacy to enforce the interwar order set at Versailles, these and other national tensions precipitated the outbreak of World War II. Berlin was free to set out on its project of creating a *Großdeutsch* nation-state and a Germanic empire that would insulate and protect the former from the outside world.

So far scholarly efforts devoted to the history of Silesia have shied away from producing a synthetic study about the past of this land and the ethnicity of its population. This is perhaps not surprising in that such a synthesis would have to be written from one of the three available national points of view. Otherwise, it would compromise the established and prevalent national beliefs through providing a picture of Silesia which was not Polish, German or Czech. Before the commencement of various ennationalization projects aimed at merging Silesia and its inhabitants into Germandom, Polishdom or Czechdom, they and their land were more Silesian than anything else.

Nowadays, the parallel processes of globalization and regionalization[1] reduce the role of the nation-state. As a consequence, it ceases to be the sole legitimate player in the field of international relations, as well as the main focus of research for social sciences. Regional and suprastate forms of political, social and economic organization of human activities gain increasingly more significance along with the nation-state. Subsequently, new actors enter the stage of international relations, for instance, NGOs, the European Union, NAFTA, transnational and multinational corporations and even the individual within the European regime of human rights protection. Simultaneously, the bond between social sciences and the nation-state has unraveled somewhat, though it used to be extremely strong due to the fact that these sciences came into being in the already ennationalized West of the nineteenth century.

Nowadays, when regional and suprastate forms of social and political organization become more apparent, the social scientist does not necessarily have to devote one's research to national society (that is, nation) as the most important form of social organization. No longer do scholars have to contribute through research to the construction of their respective nation or nation-state. The same applies to the artist. Especially in central and eastern Europe as well as in the decolonized areas, since the times of Romanticism, artists have been traditionally expected to sacrifice their art at the national altar.

Beginning in the nineteenth century the lenses of the nation and the nation-state have been the only ones through which scholars have tended, or even been allowed (by peer pressure), to perceive and interpret the past. This led to the obvious anachronism of interpreting the prenational past in the nationalist manner, despite the fact that before the French Revolution no self-consciously defined nation-state had likely existed in Europe. Obviously, England and the Netherlands had come into being as nation-states earlier than France, but England became insulated in the broader framework of Great Britain, whereas the Netherlands' borders were redrawn quite often. Thus France emerged as the first and *par excellence* model nation-state, which aspirant nationalists attempted to emulate elsewhere.

By the same token no nation-state had come into being in central Europe prior to the founding of the *Kleindeutsch* nation-state, unless one takes into account the Balkan nation-states of Greece, Montenegro, Serbia and Romania. Thus prior to the nineteenth century there were no Poles, Germans and Czechs in Silesia who would claim to be members of the Polish, German and Czech nations, respectively, because such nations did not exist. Obviously, *nationes* were present, but they comprised a relatively narrow demographic stratum of the estate members. Their identity, however, was not based on language or state but rather on loyalty to the monarch and religion. In Silesia before the nineteenth century, the members of the *natio* of the Holy Roman Empire represented this group. In the process of modernization they had already started to be transformed into the *Bildungsbürgertum*, that is, the educated bourgeoisie and nobility who spoke standard German. They constituted the social and political springboard for the construction of the German nation.

The remaining majority, without the *natio* or *Bildungsbürgertum*, was *populus*, or peasantry, with no political influence under the serfdom system. Their identity focused on their insulated community (*Gemeinschaft*), bound with the corresponding immediate locality of a village or a group of villages organized as a parish. They also were staunchly loyal to the monarch, who represented the state, and, in the case of Catholics, also to the bishop, who headed the local diocese. In Silesia the monarch equaled Prussia or the Austrian Empire, while the bishop equaled Silesia, roughly coterminous with the Breslau Diocese even after the 1740 division of the region between Berlin and Vienna.

In addition to industrialization and popular elementary education, modernization brought about a higher standard of living, popular literacy and numeracy. It, too, increased social and spatial mobility as well as the overall intensity of communication in and among all strata of the population. In turn, these phenomena caused the *populus* to identify more strongly with their states and regions of residence. Simultaneously, they were molded into a single society, having gradually become a pool of culturally standardized, interchangeable labor, endowed with generic skills. This trend was crowned when the *populus* was granted civic rights that made it into citizenry. The legal status of this enfranchised *populus* was increasingly equalized with the privileged strata of the aristocracy, nobility clergy, landed gentry (*Junkers*) and bourgeoisie (that is, *Bildungsbürgertum*). Equality before the law and the same kind of cultural standardization shared by the members of the erstwhile *natio* and *populus* in Prussian Silesia formed the basis for the commencement of nation- and nation-state building.

What was missing was a way to ignite this potential process of nation- and nation-state-building. This came at the beginning of the nineteenth century, when central Europe was faced with the ultimate Other in the form of the French invading armies and the French occupation administration. German nationalism coalesced in the confrontation of Vienna and Berlin with France. The first important victim of this struggle was the Holy Roman Empire—the erstwhile mainstay of its *natio* and the estate structures. The *populus* shared in this shock, having to deal with Frenchmen and the constantly changing figures of new sovereigns. This increasingly made the *populus* aware of its ethnic, social and political distinctiveness. The equally traumatic experiences of the *natio* and the *populus* were consolidated in the War of Liberation (1813–1815). This event also made German nationalism into a permanent social-political force.

In the wake of the Congress of Vienna, which tried to reestablish a semblance of the pre-Napoleonic *status quo* in central Europe, nationalism was suppressed. It went against the doctrine of the divine legitimization of rule customarily enjoyed by numerous princes, kings and the Austrian emperor in the polities located between France and Russia. Seeking legitimization of their power in the will of the populaces who happened to inhabit their realms seemed to be a vulgar idea to the rulers. Moreover, it amounted to a violation of the traditional order and, as such, could bring about another revolution like the French model.

Therefore, German nationalism, cherished by poets, artists and broad circles of intellectuals, did not belong to the mainstream of political life until the 1840s. Then in the process of building the French nation-state, Paris demanded the border on the Rhine. This caused a popular outcry among the *Bildungsbürgertum*. The Prussian king Frederick William IV chimed in and actively supported the creation of some symbols of the postulated German nation. However, he was reluctant to grant his subjects a constitution and to recognize the will of the people as the source of legitimization of his rule.

In 1848 the February Revolution not only reestablished a republic in France, but it also triggered similar revolutions in the German Confederation as well as in the eastern half of the Austrian Empire (that is, the Kingdom of Hungary), which was not included in this confederation. Besides democratization, nationalism featured prominently on the agendas of these revolutions. National goals were not so significant in the case in France, which had been forged into a nation-state at the turn of the nineteenth century.

Having observed the rise of non-German nationalisms in the Austrian Empire, Vienna strongly opposed the prospect of establishing a *Großdeutsch* nation-state. It would mean the end of this empire. Eventually, a *Kleindeutsch* solution seemed more probable to the German National Assembly convened in Frankfurt am Main. In addition, a *Kleindeutsch* nation-state could be conveniently based on the structure of the German Customs Union. Such an arrangement would improve the overall viability of the planned nation-state. But Frederick William IV rejected the offer of the imperial crown of the planned *Kleindeutsch* empire. Instead he advocated a union of princes, but this idea came to nothing, because Vienna managed to reestablish the old order, complete with the German Confederation in place of the defunct Holy

Roman Empire. The Catholic Church agreed with this course of action because it feared emergence of a *Kleindeutsch* nation-state that would be rooted in Protestantism, which was the prevalent confession in the northern German-speaking polities and Prussia.

Understandably, due to its predominantly German-speaking and Protestant character, Lower Silesia fit the *Kleindeutsch* solution, while multilingual and overwhelmingly Catholic Upper Silesia was opposed to it and sided with Vienna's position. But the dominance of the Austrian Empire waned during the 1860s. The empire could not compete with rapidly industrializing Prussia. It was not the military or great palaces, but the economy, that won the day. Berlin aimed at achieving German national unity through the creation of a German national economy as proposed by Friedrich List. The eventual confrontation between Vienna and Berlin in 1866 sealed the downfall of the Austrian Empire and the dissolution of the German Confederation, which Vienna dominated. This momentous event paved the way for the *Kleindeutsch* nation-state. First, the North German Confederation (1866) was established on the basis of the German Customs Union. Five years later, the German Empire came into being.

Finally, German nationalists achieved their goal of establishing a German nation-state so as to house the postulated German nation. But only partially. Cisleithania, or the western section of the Austrian Empire (as of 1867, Austria-Hungary) included in the erstwhile German Confederation, remained outside this new nation-state. National activists still hope that the *Kleindeutsch* nation-state was a step toward the holy grail of a *Großdeutsch* nation-state.

Ennationalizing pressure exerted by the *Kleindeutsch* nation-state's administration was generally agreeable to Lower Silesia. The ethnic and confessional character of this region fit *Kleindeutsch* nationalism well. On the other hand, the policy of ethnic homogenization clashed with the Catholic and multilingual make-up of Upper Silesia. Similar tensions were to be felt in Austrian Silesia, but only beginning in the 1890s. This was not a consequence of any state-ordained ennationalizing policies. Vienna strove to retain the prenational status quo until 1918, but that was not enough to prevent the rise of rival nationalisms that claimed Austrian Silesia or parts thereof for Germandom, Czechdom and Polishdom.

Polish and Czech nationalisms entered Silesia much later than their German counterpart. Until the failure of the anti-Russian January Uprising (1863–1864) the attraction of Polish nationalism was limited only to the *natio* of erstwhile Poland-Lithuania and the intelligentsia this *natio* had spawned in the course of the nineteenth century. Only then was it realized that the program of restoration of Poland-Lithuania in the form of a Polish nation-state would not be possible without including all Polish-speakers, irrespective of their social status, in the postulated Polish nation. Polish nationalists expressed little interest with regard to Silesia because this region had not formed part of Poland-Lithuania when the commonwealth had been partitioned at the end of the eighteenth century. Hence, claims to Silesia for a planned Polish nation-state would be incongruent with the scheme of basing the construction of this state on the territory of former Poland-Lithuania.

This predicament was overcome at the close of the nineteenth century. Roman Dmowski and some other young Polish nationalists proposed building a Polish nation-state from the territories inhabited by a Polish-speaking population. The subsequent cross-pollination between the historic (Jagiellonian) and ethnic (Piast) approach to the question of the Polish nation-state allowed for the extension of the concept of the Prussian partition zone to cover Upper Silesia, and of the Austrian partition zone to cover East Silesia.

Catholicism constituted the foundation of Polish nationalism, even more so than Protestantism in the case of *Kleindeutsch* nationalism. The Polish primate not only headed the Polish Catholic Church but traditionally was also entrusted with the role of the *interrex*, or guardian of royal rule during interregna. In line with the decisions of the Congress of Vienna, tsars were crowned as kings of the Congress Kingdom of Poland until its dissolution in 1864. No pretense of continuity with the royal prerogatives of the elected kings of Poland-Lithuania was maintained. This Congress Kingdom comprised only a small fragment of the lands of former Poland-Lithuania. On the other hand, the largely surviving territorial structure of the Polish-Lithuanian Catholic Church seemed to be the base on which a Polish nation-state would be built.

The Breslau Diocese was formally excluded from the largely formal jurisdiction of the Polish primate, with his seat in Gnesen, only in 1821. At the same time the eastern sliver of Upper Silesia was transferred from the Cracow Diocese to the Breslau Diocese. From 1849 to 1873 standard Polish was used in elementary schools in the Slavic-speaking areas of the Oppeln Regency that formed part of the territory of the Breslau Diocese. Reflecting on these ecclesiastical links between Silesia and the Polish Catholic Church, as well as on the use of Polish in Upper Silesian schools, some Polish nationalists took these as the "proof" of ethnic commonality between the Polish nation and the Slavophone Upper Silesians. These nationalists came mainly from Wielkopolska, and acting on the above-described premise, they spread Polish nationalism in Upper Silesia, especially beginning with the last three decades of the nineteenth century.

Similar developments occurred in East Austrian Silesia, which was separated from Galicia only by an administrative border, as was Prussian Silesia from Wielkopolska. But in contrast to Upper Silesia, East Silesia was of mixed Catholic-Protestant character. Thus, although East Silesia was also part of the Breslau Diocese, initially, local Catholic and Protestant activists worked together to spread Polish influence there. The use of Polish and Czech (or, more correctly, the local

Slavic dialects identified as these two languages) was allowed in Austrian Silesia only briefly during the years 1849–1851. And even then, German remained the dominant language of public life in this crownland. The Polish/dialect press commenced during the 1840s and survived the post-1848 repressions. What is more, with the liberalization of the 1860s more publications in Polish appeared. Later, thanks to the introduction of Polish autonomy in Galicia and to the proximity of Cracow, Polish nationalism started infiltrating East Austrian Silesia. This process was stalled somewhat by growing disunity between Catholics and Protestants at the close of the nineteenth century as well as by the emphasis on the maintenance of organizational unity of the emerging worker movement, despite any ethnic or linguistic differences. However, unlike in Prussia/the German Empire, Vienna did not pursue policies of ennationalization. This facilitated the development of various nationalisms—except the German, which, due to the lack of support on the part of the state, took off in earnest only during the 1890s.

The third player, Czech nationalism, reached its mature ideological form during the 1848 events in Bohemia. After the Battle of White Mountain (1620) the *natio* of the Czech Crown gradually waned. First, this was due to massive expulsions and emigration of Protestant and mainly Czech-speaking nobility that involved up to 150,000 persons. A second cause was the gradual dissolution of the administrative distinctiveness of the lands of the Czech Crown in the Alpine-Czech land complex of the Habsburgs. Joseph II continued the reforms of his mother, Maria Theresa, through which he hoped to modernize the Habsburg hereditary lands. Without achieving this paramount goal, his empire would not be able to compete with Prussia. One of the tenets of modernization was centralization of power and elimination of regional particularisms.

In recognition of these aims, Joseph II was the first emperor who refused to be crowned with the Czech Crown of St. Wenceslas. Although his successor submitted to the pressure of the Bohemian estates and accepted this crown, the absolutist policy of centralization pursued during the first half of the nineteenth century nullified this act. Not surprisingly then, when the longest-reigning Austrian emperor, Francis Joseph II, experienced the rise of various nationalisms that threatened his realm with breakup during the second half of the nineteenth century, he never agreed to be crowned with the Czech Crown. His position became even stauncher after the 1867 *Ausgleich* because such a coronation would have compromised the dual character of this monarchy, and only this ensured the loyalty of the Hungarians.

The Czech-speaking bourgeoisie and intelligentsia experienced the attempt at building a central European *Großdeutsch* nation-state as an encounter with the Other. Predictably, they countered it with the program of Austroslavism as well as that of the restoration of the administrative unity of the lands of the Czech Crown. Eventually, the Czechs' political movement acquired the Pan-Slav orientation with emphasis on the concept of Slavic cooperation (reciprocity), which slowed down the development of straightforward Czech nationalism. The Czech national movement was concentrated in Bohemia. It spread to Moravia and Austrian Silesia, but not very dynamically. This was so because in the last decades of the nineteenth century Czech nationalism became grounded in the historical and intellectual tradition of Hussitism. This essentially Protestant turn in Czech nationalism was not acceptable to Moravians and Austrian Silesians, who were overwhelmingly Catholic. For them the politicized Czechs of Bohemia, who shunned or sidelined Catholicism, were the Other as well.

In the southern sliver of Prussian Upper Silesia, belonging to the Olmütz Archdiocese, between 1849 and 1873 the Moravian language (that is, the partly standardized local Slavic dialect employed for writing and printing) was made into a medium of instruction in elementary education. A similar development occurred across the state border in Austrian Silesia during the brief period 1849–1851, when the local dialect entered elementary schools under the name of the Czech language. The situation was repeated beginning in the liberal 1860s; however, at that time the dialect gravitated more toward standard Czech.

When Czech nationalism grew stronger and stronger in the last three decades of the nineteenth century, Upper Silesia found itself isolated from the influence of this ideology by the state border and the ennationalizing policies of the *Kleindeutsch* nation-state. But this nationalism made some inroads into Moravia and into Austrian Silesia, especially during the 1870s. In the case of the former region, the Moravian *Ausgleich* of 1905 limited the impact of Czech nationalism. In East Austrian Silesia the spread of this nationalism was checked by the clash with its Polish counterpart, especially in the 1890s. Likewise Czech nationalism had problems gaining the upper hand in West Austrian Silesia due to the opposition staged by the German national movement, which fully developed there only at the close of the nineteenth century.

Interestingly, the cause for the rise of German nationalism in Austrian Silesia as well as elsewhere in Cisleithania was not only the emergence of different nationalisms in the Austrian Empire/Austria-Hungary. An equally important factor that contributed to the rise of this ideology was the military, economic, political and colonial successes of the *Kleindeutsch* nation-state, which German-speaking Austrian Silesians could observe just across the state border.

As can be seen from the situation described above, nationalisms penetrated Silesia from outside mainly due to the peripheral location of this region in the polities that controlled it. This thesis is rather tentative in the case of Lower Silesia, since at the beginning of the nineteenth century this region was one of the places where German nationalism was forged. But though it was a university and trade center, Breslau remained peripheral in relation to the further development of German nationalism later in this century prior to the founding of the *Kleindeutsch* nation-state in 1871.

The policy of the Catholic Church, promoting the use of standard Polish and the Moravian language in Upper Silesia as well as Slavic dialects in Austrian Silesia, was not dictated by any sympathy for non-German nationalisms. It stemmed rather from the church's desire to limit the spread of Protestantism, which could accompany the infiltration of Upper Silesia by German nationalism. What is more, from the pragmatic point of view the use of these two Slavic languages allowed for better communication with the faithful in the rapidly changing world of increased social and spatial mobility. Communication was also of paramount significance for the Catholic and Protestant churches in Austrian Silesia. Without that the churches could not hope to shield the faithful from the secular trends and ideologies deemed harmful to the churches' pastoral work. On the ideological plane, the overall goal of the Catholic Church was to maintain its universalistic dimension in spite of the particularistic character of the nationalisms that were gradually taking over political and social life in central Europe.

Modernization and the spread of nationalisms encroached on the traditional way of life of the Slavic-speaking population, who felt themselves to be Catholics, Silesians and Prussians in Upper Silesia, and Catholics/Protestants and Austrian Silesians in Austrian Silesia. Ennationalization into Germandom did not proceed successfully in Upper Silesia because the Catholic Church protected the local population from the influence of German nationalism. In addition, a canceling-out effect occurred in the course of the confrontation of German nationalism with its Polish counterpart at the end of the nineteenth century and the beginning of the twentieth. Another element that limited the influence of any nationalism was the workers' movement, which emphasized its unity over any ethnic cleavages. Similar developments were apparent in Austrian Silesia, where the canceling-out effect was even more prominent, since Vienna conducted no ennationalizing policy comparable to that of Berlin.

Thus prior to 1918, Upper Silesia and Austrian Silesia were populated mainly by inhabitants who cherished non-national multiple identities. Because of the ennationalizing pressure and/or intensifying national conflicts, many of them gradually coalesced into the ethnic groups of the Szlonzoks, the Morawecs and the Slunzaks during the second half of the nineteenth century.

The first group was composed of Slavic-speaking, bilingual, and later, creole-speaking[2] Catholics living within the Upper Silesian perimeter of the Breslau Diocese. The Morawecs were comprised of Slavic-speaking Catholics from the territory of the Olmütz Archdiocese, which coincided with the southern sliver of Upper Silesia, the eastern half of West Austrian Silesia, as well as the Moravian salient between West and East Austrian Silesia. They also lived in the westernmost sliver of East Silesia, though this area was included within the borders of the Breslau Diocese. On the other hand, the Slunzaks differed from the Szlonzoks and the Morawecs in that that they were of mixed Catholic-Protestant character. They lived in East Austrian Silesia and across the border in the southeastern corner of Upper Silesia, both within the Breslau Diocese.

Regarding the national groups, the first one to emerge was obviously the German national group. Germans predominated in Lower Silesia. In Upper Silesia they mainly coincided with German-speaking Protestants, who formed fewer than 10 percent of the Oppeln Regency's population. This national identification steadily spread to all the German-speakers in this region, especially after 1871. On the other hand, if a Slavic/Polish-speaker gained secondary or university education, one usually became a German, with the tentative exception of Catholic priests. The latter had to return to and live in the traditionally Szlonzokian and Morawec localities, which helped and motivated the priests to retain their non-national ethnic identity. The same was true of Catholic priests and Protestant pastors of Morawec and Slunzakian background in Austrian Silesia. What is more, faced with the inroads made by Polish nationalism in East Austrian Silesia, the local pastors supported the development of the Slunzakian national movement at the turn of the twentieth century.

The relative freedom of operation for nationalists in Austrian Silesia allowed for the development of a sizeable Polish national group in East Silesia. They were more nationally conscious than their less numerous counterparts in the industrialized counties of eastern Upper Silesia, as the former enjoyed direct contact with Galicia—the "Polish Piedmont." Because technical and managerial workers of the Ostrau-Karwin industrial basin were German- and Czech-speaking, upward social mobility of Slavic-speakers in the Moravian salient and the western half of East Austrian Silesia was usually connected to ennationalization either into Germandom or Czechdom. The same options were opened to Slavic-speakers in the eastern half of West Austrian Silesia, but Germandom proved more enticing. This was the case because the west and the center of West Silesia were homogeneously Germanophone. As a result, at the turn of the twentieth century this area formed the springboard for the rise of the German national group, not unlike what had earlier happened across the state border in Lower Silesia.

However, regarding these two German national groups of Austrian and Lower Silesias, it is worthwhile remembering that their identities were not purely monistic, as currently demanded by the national orthodoxy. It is typical that even nowadays a German, besides feeling attachment to Germandom, still cherishes his regional identity complete with a specific dialect (often written and then known as *Kultursprache* [language of culture]) as well as regional traditions and values. Thus, in the nineteenth century the national and regional identities were even more on a par. A German of Prussian Silesia also felt himself to be a Silesian and Prussian; and his counterpart from Austrian Silesia, an Austrian and/or (East, West, Austrian) Silesian. The same was true, but perhaps to a lesser degree, of Poles and Czechs in Prussian Silesia and Austrian Silesia. Initially, before the national and ethnic cleavages became too deep to be easily crossed, the regional-confessional identity had allowed for relatively high cohesion of the populaces of Prussian Silesia and Austrian Silesia, especially during the first half of the nineteenth century.

The sudden change came with the end of the Great War, which precipitated the breakup of the Dual Monarchy and the establishment of the new nation-states in central Europe in line with the national principle. This necessitated partition of Upper Silesia and Austrian Silesia among Germany, Poland and Czechoslovakia as the first step in carrying out the respective three projects of ennationalization. The projects aimed to make the territories of these nation-states and their correspond-ing populations ethnically homogenous in agreement with the guiding tenets of corresponding nationalisms. The policies of ennationalization made almost all the Slunzaks and Morawecs into Poles and Czechs, respectively. Those who successfully resisted ennationalization were some Slunzaks who remained in Czechoslovakia's part of East Austrian Silesia, and the Morawecs from the Hlučínsko. The latter, under the unwanted pressure of Czech(oslovak) ennationalization, became pro-German Hultschiners or, simply, Hultschiner Germans.

Although some Szlonzoks became Poles, most in Poland's Silesian Voivode-ship were repelled from Polishdom by the crude ennationalization pressure that state administration directed at them. They also disagreed with the mistreatment of Germans at the hands of Polish officialdom and were disenchanted with the poor economic performance of the Polish nation-state. It had been the promise of well-being, comparable to that from the period before 1914, which had enticed some Szlonzoks to participate in the anti-German Silesian Uprisings on the Polish side. It is an empirical error to state, as some Polish scholars do, that the Silesian Voivodeship was the best-developed of all the voivodeships in interwar Poland. Technically it is correct, but completely irrelevant to the question of Polishdom in Upper Silesia. Szlonzoks living in the voivodeship compared their situation to that of their kin in Germany's interwar Province of Upper Silesia. The economy on the German side of the border that split Upper Silesia improved more rapidly than in the voivodeship. Consequently, the more flexible ennationalizing policy of Berlin, coupled with rapid economic advancement after 1933, achieved more success at making Szlonzoks into Germans than the Polish administration into Poles. Warsaw wished to immediately ennationalize Szlonzoks into Poles without taking into consideration their ethnic specificity and aspirations.

In the Third Silesian Uprising of 1921 some 50,000 Szlonzoks and Poles fought on the Polish side, and around 40,000 Szlonzoks and Germans on the

German side. These numbers are quite large, but they pale in comparison with the membership of the BdO/ZG, which gathered between 300,000 and half a million Szlonzoks prior to the division of Upper Silesia in 1922. It was the expression of a coalescing Szlonzokian nationalism that called for the transformation of Upper Silesia into a separate polity, probably a Szlonzokian nation-state.

The reader may ask about estimates, if not exact numbers, with regard to the demographic size of the analyzed national and ethnic groups. It is a tricky question, and on several counts so. First, as it has been repeated throughout this study, the salient trait of the prenational identity is its multiple or composite characteristic. The member of a nation conditioned by school, mass media and politics to believe that one's identity should be composed from one and only one national constituent is flabbergasted that a Szlonzok may sometimes behave as a German or a Pole, while at another time as a Czech or a Szlonzok. On the other hand, for another Szlonzok or any member of an ethnic group, this is just the natural dynamics of his multiple identity.

Second, neither in Prussia/the German Empire nor Austria-Hungary did the censuses attempt to measure the demographic size of the ethnic groups of the Szlonozks, the Slunzaks or the Morawecs. At that time civil servants did not perceive these groups as "national," and only this would have made them eligible for inclusion in census questionnaires. Quite simply, the sociopolitical and national movements of the Szlonzoks, the Slunzaks and the Morawecs appeared much later than those of the Germans, the Poles and the Czechs. Nationalisms of the latter had started coalescing at least one century earlier than Szlonzokian, Slunzakian and Morawec nationalisms. At the beginning of the twentieth century the Czechs, the Germans and the Poles were fully recognized nations in the eyes of the West. After World War I the Allies decided that central Europe was to be split among them, along with the Hungarians and the Slovaks. The Western powers were not willing to recognize any further aspirant nations, as this would have necessitated another round of increasingly intricate international bargaining and border wars before the final political map of this region could be established. At that time the international recognition of a group as a nation was tantamount to allowing it to seize the territory inhabited by its members as the group's legitimate nation-state.

The above has been said as a caveat in order to caution the reader about the epistemologically complicated nature of the estimates that follow.

Taking into consideration the number of the Polish national activists in Upper Silesia prior to the outbreak of the Great War, as well as the membership of the Polish-language associations, it may be inferred that the size of the Polish national group in this region amounted to 40,000–50,000 persons. Hence, this group accounted for 2 percent of Upper Silesia's population. Before 1914 the Slavophone inhabitants of Upper Silesia, less the members of the Polish national group and

the Morawecs, numbered 1.1 million, or 50 percent of the populace. These estimates represent the numerical strength of the Szlonzoks. Regarding the German
national group, it is safe to assume that at that time its membership corresponded
to the number of Upper Silesia's German-speakers, that is, 1 million people, or 45
percent of the population. Between 50,000 and 60,000 Morawecs constituted the
remaining 2.5 percent of the Upper Silesian inhabitants.

In Austrian Silesia, prior to the outbreak of the Great War the numbers of
people connected to the respective national movements allow for estimating the
demographic sizes of the national groups at 25,000 Germans, 5,000 to 10,000
Poles, and 3,000 to 5,000 Czechs. These three groups constituted 3 percent, 1 to
2 percent, and 0.5 to 1 percent of this crownland's population, respectively. After
having compared these data with the contemporary language statistics, one may
surmise that Austrian Silesia also housed 225,000 Slunzaks, 170,000 Morawecs,
and 300,000 Germanophone Austrian Silesians whose identity was connected to
the region. These two ethnic groups and one ethnoregional group accounted for 30
percent, 23 percent and 40 percent of Austrian Silesia's population, respectively.

This study could not give an account of further developments that influenced
the ethnic and national groups in Silesia after World War I without making it
unduly bulky and depriving this book of its theoretical focus. However, to allow
the reader to link the emergence of the national and ethnic groups in Silesia with
the present-day ethnic situation in this region, it is briefly noted what happened
to the Silesian population after World War II.

Most significantly, almost all of Silesia remaining in Germany was transferred
to postwar Poland, while the Allies decided to move the latter state's borders 300
kilometers westward. Internationally condoned expulsions and forced emigration
(that can be described more aptly as "ethnic cleansing") followed. These instruments
of ethnodemographic policy were applied to postwar Poland and Czechoslovakia
and helped denude Lower Silesia and the western section of Czech Silesia (former
West Austrian Silesia and the western half of erstwhile East Austrian Silesia) of
population. In their stead, ethnically Polish and Czech settlers arrived. The prewar
segments of the population were preserved, in varying degrees, only in the eastern
half of Upper Silesia (which coincides with the territory of the interwar Silesian
Voivodeship and the eastern section of Germany's prewar Province of Upper Silesia), the Czechoslovak and Polish sections of former East Austrian Silesia, in the
Hlučínsko, and in the rural vicinity of Opava (Troppau).

❖   ❖   ❖

The author trusts that this diachronic analysis of the emergence and development
of national and ethnic groups in Silesia will not be of interest to historians only. It
is hoped that this study will also serve as a springboard for further research into the
problem of ethnicity and nationalism in Silesia and elsewhere. When the need arises,

this work could also become an instrument for predicting further developments vis-à-vis regional, ethnic and national identities in Silesia today. State administrations neglect peripheries at their peril. Had the data gathered in this book been available to decision-makers in Warsaw or Prague, there would not have been so much surprise at the fact that in the 1991 Czechoslovak census 44,000 persons declared that they were of Silesian (that is, Slunzakian) nationality, or that the 2002 Polish census recorded 173,000 persons who declared their nationality to be Silesian (that is, Szlonzokian). These censuses were conducted after the fall of communism in 1989, which meant that people could write in the census returns what they thought without the danger of administrative reprisals, while the administrations could not massage the results to their liking any more.

Moreover, the author hopes that the interdisciplinary and diachronic character of this study will contribute to the development of a new approach to the question of ethnicity and identity in Poland, an approach that would strive to describe social reality rather than attempt to overhaul it in the interest of this or that nationalism. Until 1989, in line with the myth of the national and ethnic homogeneity of Poland, ethnic groups had been considered unambiguous parts of Polishdom, while the existence of any substantial national minorities was generally denied. The end of communism brought about relaxation in the state-ordained rigors of national mythologizing so as to foster a political and economic transition that would not marginalize or exclude some groups on the basis of ethnicity.[3]

The author has used varied theoretical instruments to analyze the ethnic problematic in the entire historical region of Silesia from the emergence of the national movements to the establishment of the nation-states that were to contest ownership of this region after 1918. The author has contextualized this study against the development of German, Polish and Czech nationalisms with the inclusion of the influence of these three national movements on the ethnic situation in Silesia. As a background, the political, administrative and ecclesiastical divisions of this region were also presented. What is more, the author has not concentrated solely on one ethnic or national group but on all the ethnic and national groups that emerged in Silesia during the second half of the nineteenth century. He has also analyzed the relations among these groups and the ethnic boundary mechanisms that allowed them to maintain their distinctiveness vis-à-vis one another.

Last but not least, the author wrote this study in English. Hence he hopes, in this manner, not only that it will become available to the world-wide community of learning, but that it also will contribute some valuable empirical material for the sake of more fruitful theorizing in the field of the comparative study of nationalism and ethnicity.

Notes

Notes to Introduction

1. One tends to forget that the victims of the Holocaust were not only Jews and Roma, but also homosexuals and, to a lesser degree, the mentally ill. All of them were considered "inflammatory elements" that the state had to remove from the German nation's "healthy tissue."

2. This neologism allows one to distinguish between the two different meanings of the verb "to nationalize." The usual one current in economics denotes the state's takeover of previously private means of production and property. However, the meaning intended here is the overall process of ethnic, cultural and linguistic assimilation intended to make the individual or a group of them into an indistinguishable part of a nation.

3. Earlier, this land was contested in the more straightforward military manner associated with the construction of dynastic-feudal realms. Hence ideology in the form of religious discord also tore at Silesia during the times of the Protestant-Catholic strife.

4. *Großdeutsch* (Greater German) nationalism aimed at uniting all the German-speaking lands (including those of Austria) into a single nation-state.

5. The *deutsche Ostgebiete* are the German territories east of the Oder-Neisse line, which, in 1945, the Allies agreed to transfer to postwar Poland and the Soviet Union.

6. Place names are given in these linguistic forms, which were official in the period covered in this work. In order to make it possible for the reader to find these locations on present-day maps, the initial appearance of every place name includes the modern form in parentheses. However, the author also uses the customary anglicized forms of place names if they exist (for instance, Cracow *not* Kraków).

7. *Natio* is the Latin term sometimes misleadingly translated as "political nation." In pre-modern and early modern European states it denoted all the estates of a polity functioning as a political group. They formed several percent of the population in western Europe and up to 20 percent in some regions of central Europe (for instance, in Mazovia) (Zientara, 1996: 11–25).

8. *Populus* is a Latin term often misleadingly translated as "a people" or "people." It denoted all the population of a state without the estates. This is the vast majority of a

state's population who had no influence on politics and were confined to agricultural work as peasants. In central Europe, the peasantry was not freed from serfdom until the first half of the nineteenth century (Zientara, 1996: 11–25).

9. *Bildungsbürgertum* refers to the educated city-dwellers (of various social origins) that in German-speaking polities emerged as the elites and the nation-forming agent in the course of the nineteenth century (Greenfeld, 1992: 293–310).

10. The *Kleindeutsch* (Little German) option was Prussia's hope to create a German nation-state from the northern German-speaking states to the exclusion of the Germanophone areas of Austria-Hungary.

11. Szlonzoks /shlonzoks/ (the second element indicates the Polish pronunciation) refers to the ethnic group meaning the "Silesians." But translating this ethnonym into English would be impractical, as it would not allow for retaining the difference between the Szlonzoks and the Silesians, that is, the people who, irrespective of language and religion, identified themselves with the whole region. What is more, the ethnonym of the ethnic group of the Slunzaks also means "Silesians."

12. The Slunzaks /sloonzakhs/ is the ethnic group related to the Szlonzoks.

13. The ethnonym Morawecs /moravetss/ means "Moravians," but translation would be confusing because, as in the case of Silesia, there was a large group of the Moravians who, despite linguistic and confessional differences, identified themselves with the whole Austrian crownland of Moravia.

Notes to Chapter 1

1. The *Vormärz* is the "period before March" of 1848 when revolutions broke out in Berlin and Vienna. The use of this term in German historiography emphasizes the fact that the events which took place from 1830 to 1848 prepared for the outbreak that led the way to new nation-states and a more democratic Europe (Neubach, 1995: 155).

2. After 1815 Prussian provinces were headed by *Oberpräsidenten* (senior presidents), while regencies were headed by *Präsidenten* (presidents).

3. He was the longest-serving *Oberpräsident* (1816–1845) in the history of Silesia (Stüttgen, 1976: 28), and his career may be likened to that of Metternich.

4. The feudal character of land ownership in Silesia persisted up to 1848, when the situation changed in Lower Silesia. But it was less true of Upper Silesia, where aristocratic latifundia survived largely uncurbed until 1945, as in East Prussia (Michalkiewicz, 1970: 163).

5. The villages were, in reality, industrial towns. Langenbielau for a long time remained the largest village of Prussia, with its population of 7,840 in 1825 and 12,939 in 1861 (and probably 14,000 in the 1840s) (Weczerka, 1977: 267–268). At that time, these numbers surpassed the population of the largest Upper Silesian town, Oppeln, with a population of 5,978 in 1825, 6,969 in 1840, and 10,000 in 1861 (Steinert, 1995: 319).

6. The uprising is still remembered thanks to the Silesian Nobel prizewinner Gerhart Hauptmann's (1862–1946) play *Die Weber* (*The Weavers*) (Herzig, 1994: 505).

7. That is, Russia, Austria and Prussia, which had partitioned Poland-Lithuania in the second half of the eighteenth century.

8. Its symbolism was so strong that it even earned its own name—the *Dreikaiserreichsecke* (triangle of the three empires).

9. The development of railways in Austrian and Prussian Silesia was quite rapid if one compares it to the first railroad, which opened in 1830 between Manchester and Liverpool, and the first one on the continent, between Linz and Budweis (České Budějovice) in 1832 (Kinder, 1978: II 43).

10. The term "Germany" is put in quotation marks because this usage is only a convenient shorthand that did not correspond to any polity at that time.

11. Mierosławski had considered carrying out some military actions in Silesia in order to engage as many Prussian troops as possible, thereby obstructing a Prussian intervention against the planned uprising. He also intended to conscript soldiers from Silesia and to establish a Silesian corps. In the Polish National Government, which came into being after the abortive Cracow Uprising of 1848, there was a seat reserved for a representative from Silesia, but this position remained vacant (Lis, 1993: 78). This renowned Polish nationalist and professional revolutionary, ironically (but maybe *not* surprisingly) was only "half-Polish," as his mother was French (Namier, 1992: 15).

12. Hence the body is sometimes referred to as the Frankfurt Parliament or Assembly.

13. Hans Kudlich was born on October 25, 1823 in Lobenstein (Úvalno), West Austrian Silesia, the third of eight children of a peasant family. He studied in Vienna in the years 1842–1848. He ceaselessly appealed for full emancipation of peasants, which the imperial patent of November 7, 1848 eventually guaranteed. Due to this success he was hailed *"Bauernbefreier"* (liberator of peasants). But after the suppression of the Reichstag he escaped to Prussian Silesia. Later he studied in Zurich before moving to the United States. After the amnesty of 1867 he wanted to return to the political scene in Austria-Hungary but without any success, so he returned to the United States. He died on November 11, 1917 in Hoboken, New Jersey, near New York City (Plaček, 1996; Prinz, 1995: 325).

14. Vienna abolished this constitution already in 1851, commencing the era of neo-absolutism in the Habsburg Empire (Kinder, 1978: II 61).

15. In German the term "Pan-Germanism" appears as *Pangermanismus* or *Alldeutschtum;* analogically this event became known as the Pan-Slav (*panslawisch*) or All Slav (*allslawisch*) Congress.

16. Dobrovský wrote on matters Slavic but exclusively in German. Considering his identity Josef Jungmann called him "a German of Slavic sympathies" (Jungmann, in Szyjkowski, 1948: 13).

17. The picture readily reminds one of the earlier depiction of Europe as a Christian queen who was to promote the interests of the Habsburgs. In the latter image Spain was the head and Bohemia the heart within the main bulk of the body—the Habsburg Empire.

18. After the clear manifestation of Czech nationalism in 1848, Palacký started broadening and translating his work into Czech. The Czech-language version was published between 1848 and 1876 (Szyjkowski, 1948: 55).

Notes to Chapter 2

1. Notably, Herder was one of the first European thinkers who employed the term "nationalism." He used it in his writings already in 1774 (Alter, 1994: 3).

2. Not unlike its preference for *"Volk"* over *"Nation,"* German nationalist thought did not internalize the notion of "culture" in its meaning and form as used in western Europe. The specific connotations of *"Kultur"* emphasized efficiency as the tool of national advancement and unique "civilizedness" of the Germans, which they had the duty to pass on to the "primitive" Slavs, Hungarians and colonial peoples worldwide. This conviction about the uniqueness of German *Kultur* led, in the first half of the twentieth century, to the rise of the coining of terms such as *Kulturstaat* (a civilized country) and *Kulturträger* (an upholder, defender and "carrier" of civilization) (Anon., 1888a: 293; Gove, 1966: 1257; Simpson, 1991: 929).

3. Such Polish romantic poets as Adam Mickiewicz (1798–1855), Juliusz Słowacki (1809–1849) and Zygmunt Krasiński (1812–1859) popularized this model through their own writings, and Polish nationalists enacted it in the ill-fated risings of 1830–1831, 1846 and 1863–1864.

4. Riflemen's associations (*Schützengesellschaften* or *Schützengilden*) emerged from groups of richer burghers (usually of the same trade) banded together and obliged by the city council to defend a specific section of the city walls (Anon., 1889: 670–671).

5. Singers' associations (*Sängergesellschaften*) emerged from church choirs.

6. The first one, *Teutonia Burschenschaft,* was organized in the autumn of 1814 in Halle, and numerous others followed in 1815 (Czapliński, 1990: 453; Kinder, 1978: II 47).

7. The initial success of the anti-Napoleonic rising was ensured by regular shipments of weaponry that the nascent Upper Silesian industry produced. Weapons were transported via the Klodnitzkanal (Klodnitz [Kłodnica] canal), which in 1812 connected Gleiwitz (Gliwice) with the Oder (Enden, 1977: 231). What is more, the *Eisernes Kreuz* (iron cross)—one of the most significant Prusso-German orders, was, for the first time, produced at a Gleiwitz foundry in 1813 (Breit, 1998: 29; Ullmann, 1985: 105).

8. *Vallhöl*—in Germanic mythology, the heaven of the brave, that is, the hall of fame for those who fought bravely and fell in battle (Anon., 1890b: 359).

9. The supposedly *German* victory over Napoleonic France inspired the Bavarian King Ludwig I to order the construction of this monumental structure (Anon., 1890b: 360).

10. The association's periodical, the *Zeitschrift des Vereins für die Geschichte Schlesiens,* appeared from 1855 to 1943 (Herzig, 1994: 524).

11. List was an ardent believer in nationalism as attested by his own words: "between the individual and humanity stands the nation" (List, in Szporluk, 1988: xii).

12. Nationalists tended to dub the central European events of the revolutionary year of 1848 with this name, which the region's historiographies continue to employ to this day.

13. In 1868, it was turned into a more structured organization under the new name Deutsche Turnerschaft (Organization of German Gymnasts) (Anon., 1889b: 945).

14. In 1863, 43 percent of the Prussian budget (that is, 40.7 million thalers) was allocated to military expenses (Biały, 1990: 265).

15. Constitutions, besides national flags, coats-of-arms and anthems, have been potent national symbols since the first went into force in the United States (1789).

16. This is an anachronistic use of the term "national minority" that the author applies with the hindsight of the twentieth century. Obviously, minorities began to be perceived in national terms only after the creation of the central European nation-states in 1918.

17. The term "nationality"(*Nationalität*) in this quotation is a synonym for "ethnic nation." However, not a single full-fledged nation of this type existed in Austria-Hungary at that time, with the exception of the Magyars (Hungarians). Vienna did not use the term "nation" (*Nation*), as this would entail the right to sovereignty.

18. National academies of sciences, not unlike universities and other national centers of learning, were of special significance for national movements in central and eastern Europe. Scholars employed by the institutions busied themselves with inventing national traditions and histories.

19. With the term "Prusso-German national feeling" the author emphasizes the attitude of the inhabitants of Prussia, the largest constituent of the German Empire. Usually they conflated their attachment to Prussia with that to Germany without differentiating between the two states.

20. Interestingly, the first Russian census during which the question about language was asked took place in 1897.

21. The term "language planning" denotes the totality of the nation-state's linguistic policies aimed at homogenizing and standardizing language use within the state's borders. The usual instruments to this end include the educational system, mass media, army, publishing industry, and national academy of sciences. The last institution often is endowed with the responsibility for devising officially espoused linguistic standards and guarding the "purity" of the national language (Crystal, 1987: 364–367).

Notes to Chapter 3

1. The non-German-speaking population is denoted here with the phrase "Polish/Slavic-speaking." The author introduced this awkward usage because these people were traditionally considered Polish-speaking, though in reality they spoke subdialects from the West Slavic dialect continuum and did not know the standard Polish language (Kamusella, 1998).

   Although there was a continuity of settlement between these two Polish/Slavic-speaking populations, religion divided them. The larger, Upper Silesian one professed Catholicism, while the smaller one, in the northeast of Lower Silesia, confessed Protestantism. And significantly, the vernacular of the Slavic-speakers in the southern sections of the Ratibor (Racibórz) and Leobschütz (Głubczyce) counties was closest to the speech of the Slavic-speaking inhabitants of Austrian Silesia and northern Moravia who lived across the border in the Habsburg empire.

2. It was a Polish version of the German-language periodical *Schlesische Volkszeitung zum Nutzen und Vergnügen* (Silesian Folk Newspaper for Use and Fun) (Snoch, 1991: 35).

3. Johann Jacob Korn established his Korn publishing house in Breslau in 1732. After Prussian annexation of Silesia he obtained the exclusive privilege to publish newspapers in the province. In 1742 Korn took over the first full-fledged Silesian paper, *Schlesischer Nouvellen-Courier* (Silesian News Courier, 1708), and published it until 1945. In 1848 the daily's title changed to *Schlesische Zeitung* (Silesian Newspaper). Korn, once the most important publishing house of Silesia, today survives in Germany in Würzburg under the name of the Bergstadverlag Wilhelm Gottlieb Korn (Scheuermann, 1994: 838–839; Schulz, 1991).

4. Bandtke dedicated it to Frederick William III (Lubos, 1974: 499).

5. The partition territories of former Poland-Lithuania, carved up among Russia, Prussia and the Habsburg Empire, did not include any part of Silesia because this land had never belonged to the Polish-Lithuanian Commonwealth. Only at the close of the nineteenth century did some Polish ethnic nationalists resolve to subsume Upper Silesia into the concept "Prussian partition." In this manner, they claimed this region for a future Poland and simultaneously legitimized this claim in pseudo-historical terms. Analogously, they included East Austrian Silesia within the scope of the Austrian Partition.

6. Marzanna is a female Slavic name.

7. This event commenced limited male suffrage in Prussia and in other Germanophone states. Male suffrage became universal when the German Empire came into being (1871). Women, however, obtained the right to vote only in 1919 with advent of the Weimar Republic (Davies, 1996: 1295).

8. This demand might have been influenced by the predicament of another Upper Silesian deputy to the Prussian National Assembly, Kiołbassa (Kiolbassa). He could hardly follow the proceedings, not having a good command of German. Because of this, there was even an attempt to exclude him from the assembly (Brożek, 1969: 4–5).

9. He supported the Polish national movement because he had discovered that his family descended from Polish nobility (Snoch, 1991: 67–68). Similar pro-Polish persons, although by no account numerous, appeared among the Silesian nobility in the second half of the nineteenth century—for instance, Alfred von Olschewski (Olszewski) from Eichholz (Warmątowice) near Liegnitz (Legnica). Under the influence of the writings of the national Polish writer Henryk Sienkiewicz (1846–1916), who glorified the Polish and Polish-Lithuanian past, Olschewski made the writer his only heir unless his children learned the Polish language and culture before the age of thirty. Sensibly, the writer renounced his right to this legacy in 1909 (Lis, 1988: 18–19). The crowning of this Herderian strain among German-speakers came with Alexander (Aleksander) Brückner (1856–1939). Born to a German family in Tarnopol in eastern Galicia, he headed the Department of Slavic Languages and Literatures at the Berlin University. At the beginning of the twentieth century he started writing in Polish and produced an immense number of books and articles, including classical works on the history of the Polish language, culture and literature (Anon., 1983: 370). Eventually, Brückner became an "honorary Pole" and even demanded to be buried in Poland. Due to the tense international situation in 1939 prior to the outbreak of World War II, and because of his children's opposition to this idea, Brückner's mortal remains stayed in Berlin (Kosman, 1989: 5–18).

10. A character from an apocryphal story about the biblical King Solomon, in the Middle Ages he was presented as a merry and smart peasant, a paragon of folk wisdom and humor.

11. Here the term "Polish-speaker" makes an appearance, as it was the category used in the census. For those speaking Slavic dialects akin to the ones spoken in Bohemia or Moravia and Austrian Silesia, the categories of "Bohemian-speakers" and "Moravian-speakers" were reserved.

12. A citizen of Poland-Lithuania who simultaneously belonged to the regional Prussian and/or German *estate natione.*

13. Due to his pro-Polish activities, simplistically perceived as anti-state by the Prussian school authorities, Lompa was discharged from his teaching position without the right to receive his pension and died in poverty (Snoch, 1991: 83). Polish national historians have glorified his sad fate, making Lompa into a martyr and legendary figure of the Polish national movement in Silesia. In fact, such a movement hardly existed in Prussian Silesia prior to 1871.

14. Upper Silesian men mastered the German language during their compulsory military service. They were stationed far away from home, all over Prussia and even abroad. As a consequence, they spoke the language much better than Upper Silesian women.

15. In 1827, the first provincial diet of the grand duchy convened (Jakóbczyk, 1989: 2).

16. As a journalist and publisher he actively supported and organized the Polish national movement. From 1868 to 1871 he managed a Polish bookshop at Culmhof and edited numerous Polish-language periodicals, including *Gwiazdka Cieszyńska* in 1861–1862 (Anon., 1983a: 468).

17. He edited *Przyjaciel Ludu* (Friend of the Common Folk), the most popular Polish-language Posen periodical in Silesia.

18. In 1848–1852 he was a deputy to the Prussian National Assembly. Beginning in 1863 he started publishing cheap Polish books in Posen. They were also distributed in Silesia (Anon., 1983b: 243–244).

19. Czech national activists pioneered the use of the rally to imbue masses with national consciousness in a congenial outdoor environment. They called such rallies *tabors* (camps), associating them with the Hussite tradition in an endeavor to differentiate Czech na-

tionalism from the Austrian tradition of political Catholicism (Waldenberg, 1992: 41).

20. He was a smith, poet and playwright as well as the Upper Silesian correspondent for *Przyjaciel Ludu* (Pater, 1991: 203; Snoch, 1991: 80).

21. The party's informal ideological and political origins date back to 1852. The deputies of the Prussian Landtag who did not espouse liberalism or conservatism belonged to the pro-Catholic faction. After 1859 they started opposing the *Kleindeutsch* Protestant homogenizing policies aimed at culture and education (Kinder, 1978: II 61).

Notes to Chapter 4

1. Land (regional) identity is a literal translation of the German term *"Landesbewußtsein"* or *"Landespatriotismus"*—that is, regional identity based on the administratively recognized regions (*Länder*). In the case of the Habsburg Empire, such regions were known as "crownlands."

2. At that time the official languages of Lower Silesia were Latin and German.

3. The educated of the Middle Ages and also of later epochs through the Enlightenment signed their names in Latin. The current ennationalizing spelling games played by the linguistic traditions of various ethnic provenances too easily overlook this fact. Those who get involved in these games are bent on "proving" that this or that person belonged to this or that specific nation, though it is obvious that the nation did not even exist at the time when the person concerned lived.

4. He signed his surname using this spelling (Myška, 1993: 92).

5. In this work they are referred to as *Morawecs,* as explained in the Introduction and later in this chapter.

6. Today it is the oldest museum in the Czech Republic (Gawrecki, 1993: 53).

7. It was the official name of Austrian Silesia and remained unchanged until 1918. The Habsburgs (as other dynasts) in this manner expressed their standing claims to various territories to which they were entitled in one way or another. As a consequence, among numerous official titles, the Austrian emperor also maintained that of the Herzog von Ober- und Niederschlesien (cf. Kracik, 1996: illustration).

8. This section gathered Polish and Ruthenian (future Ukrainian) representatives because they came from Galicia, which was an ethnically Polish-Ruthenian crownland.

9. Czech/Slavic-speakers lived around Troppau in West Silesia and in the westernmost sliver of East Silesia. Overwhelmingly Catholic, they differed from the mixed Catholic-Protestant Polish/Slavic-speaking population who inhabited the rest of East Silesia. Together with the ethnically related population residing in the Moravian salient between West and East Silesia, these Czech/Slavic-speakers differed linguistically from the German-speaking population of West Silesia and northern Moravia. This Germanophone population separated Austrian Silesia's Czech/Slavic-speakers from the Slavic-speakers of Bohemia and Moravia. Hence, in their identity the former remained similar to the Morawecs of Prussian Upper Silesia.

10. The holdings of the Polish library were incorporated into the Sherschnik library, which was not a public institution (Fazan, 1991: 65).

11. The Germans of Galicia and Austrian Silesia appealed for such a move so as not to allow this university to become a Polish-language institution due to the Polonization of Galicia in the wake of the cultural autonomy introduced in this province between 1867 and 1873 (Buszko, 1989: 6).

12. It is often forgotten that to avoid galvanizing Polishdom in Galicia too much, Vienna granted Ruthenian (future Ukrainian) the status of a crownland language in Galicia.

Elementary education in this language developed quite dynamically in eastern Galicia (Buszko, 1989: 33).

Notes to Chapter 5

1. Czech had not been fully standardized then, so the local written dialect (known as Moravian) was used as the medium of instruction at elementary schools in the south of Upper Silesia, as was also the case in the Slavic-speaking areas in Austrian Silesia (Knop, 1967: 25–26).
2. In the thirteenth century the Silesian principalities were largely independent, as no unified Kingdom of Poland existed. At that time the legal construction of the Polish *natio* became secondary to the local *gentes* of Mazovia, Małopolska, Silesia and other regions.
3. Cisleithania was the Austrian part of Austria-Hungary, located "before" the Leitha River. Analogously, Transleithania was the Hungarian part of this empire beyond this river. Obviously, the point of reference is imperial Vienna.
4. The Sorbian-speakers of Lusatia partitioned among Saxony, Brandenburg and Silesia in Prussia also started developing their own national movement, becoming Sorbs rather than Germans. However, this problem is not encompassed within the scope of this study.
5. The origins and pronunciation of this ethnonym and those that follow were explained in the Introduction.
6. Cf. the well-documented cases of how the Xhosas and the Zulus came into being (Krige, 1975: 598; Hammond-Tooke, 1975: 550–1)
7. The name *Kobylorze* is derived from *"kobyła"* (mare). It indicates they specialized in horse-breeding. The *Golocy* farmed on the *"gola,"* that is the plain left after a felled forest.
8. Literally, the term means "Polish economy," but in the German language this phrase denotes "disorder, filth, dilapidation and backwardness" (Orłowski, 1998).
9. On the influence of language and socially or culturally determined behavior on the emergence and maintenance of biological (that is, genetic) separateness of various human groups, see Cavalli-Sforza (1981), Cavalli-Sforza (1991), Dunbar (1993) and Liebermann (1994: 126–127).
10. Over time there was much change in the relation of the Hohenzollern monarchs with their Prussian state. The royal title assumed by Frederick I at his coronation in 1701 was King *in* Prussia; but in his province of Brandenburg, located in the Holy Roman Empire, he remained a mere prince. Frederick II became King *of* Prussia in 1772 (the year of the first partition of Poland-Lithuania) (Morby, 1994: 137). Thus, the Hohenzollerns had been *Prussian* kings only since 1772.
11. Two-thirds of Austrian Silesia was included within the borders of the Breslau Diocese.

Note to Chapter 6

1. The division of Upper Silesia was conducted cartographically in 1921 and was carried out in practice in 1922 when the Allied forces passed the respective fragments of this region to Germany and Poland.

Notes to Chapter 7

1. The use of the term "national/ethnic minority" is somewhat anachronistic in the period prior to the peace conference in Paris (1919). Only then did it enter the lexicon of international politics for good. However, the first international treaties aimed at pro-

tecting religious minorities were concluded in the seventeenth century. This confessional dimension of minority protection was extended into other aspects of social and political life, tentatively at the Congress of Vienna (1815), and decisively after World War I. This new aspect of minority protection tended to coincide with the ethnic dimension (Girasoli, 1995: 5–7).

2. Such considerations never played a big role in the ennationalizing efforts of St. Petersburg in its partition zone of erstwhile Poland-Lithuania.

3. It was predated by a similar organization in the Habsburg Monarchy that came into being in Bohemia in 1821 (Anon., 1888c: 210).

4. Today such forced but legal removals or expulsions of aliens pass under the bureaucratic name of "deportation of illegal aliens."

5. The rest of these settlers arrived from Westphalia, Saxony and Pomerania. After 1904 ethnic Germans from Galicia, Congress Poland and Volhynia had also started arriving in Germany (Rogall, 1993: 76).

6. With the exception of Britain, Germany bore the cost of its armed forces more easily than any other European state. Berlin spent just 4.6 percent of its GDP on defense in 1914, whereas Russia's expenditure in this field consumed 6.3 percent of its GDP, which caused a serious strain on its economy and populace (Kennedy, 1989: 212).

Notes to Chapter 8

1. Not unlike German nationalist propaganda of that time, Dmowski's book was rabidly nationalist, racist and anti-Semitic. For instance, he referred to the Aborigines of Australia as "tree-living half-monkeys" (1996: 92) and accused Jews of hindering development of the Polish national movement (1996: 119).

2. This party wished to exert its influence not only in Galicia but also in East Austrian Silesia (*not* Germany's Upper Silesia).

3. This poetic creed of Polish nationalism, which defined Polishdom through enmity to all things German, was customarily sung at Polish schools during the communist period (1947–1989). The purpose was to divert the attention of the public from the equally "traditional Polish-Russian enmity." Unfortunately, some nationalistically minded Polish teachers of history and literature still utilize this song during their classes.

4. The local Protestant population of Upper Silesia amounted to 4 percent in 1800. With industrialization and the influx of German-speaking engineers, teachers and clerks it grew to 9 percent in 1871 and remained unchanged until 1914. According to the 1910 census there were 187,751 Protestants in Upper Silesia out of the total population of 2,207,981. Probably half of them were Slavic-speakers (Michalkiewicz, 1985: 58; Szczepankiewicz-Battek, 1996: 10).

5. The rest of the total population of 4,112,219 was composed of 51,481 Jews (1.3 percent), 7,048 other Christians (1.3%) and 110 persons included in the "others" rubric (Michalkiewicz, 1976: 60).

6. It was opened again only in 1886 (Pater, 1996a: 104).

7. Chełm is the old name of St. Annaberg (Góra św. Anny or, literally, St. Anne Mountain), which houses the most important Catholic shrine of Upper Silesia.

8. This term can be rendered in modern terminology as the "Upper Silesian Polish/Slavic-speaking ethnic group," that is, the Szlonzoks.

9. Von Hatzfeldt belonged to the Reichspartei (Scheuermann, 1994: 520).

10. Because the Breslau Diocese included all of Austrian East Silesia and one-third of Austrian West Silesia, the Breslau bishop had a guaranteed seat in the Austrian Silesian Landtag (Dąbrowski, 1922: 176; Galos, 1996: 191).

11. In 1871 Father Bonczyk (Boncek, Bontzek) founded this society named after St. Aloy-sius (1568–1591), an aristocratic Jesuit novitiate who died a victim of his labors among the plague-stricken in Rome (Attwater, 1983: 37–38). In Upper Silesia it was the first Polish-speaking youth organization. It conducted cultural and educational activities in standard Polish, in defiance of the *Kulturkampf* (Snoch, 1991: 150).

12. The Zentrum's Polish or Polish-language faction was described in this way due to the significance of *Katolik* as this faction's mouthpiece and ideological backbone.

13. After the 1922 division of Upper Silesia, Kattowitz was transferred to Poland. This gymnasium to serve nascent Polishdom in the Silesian Voivodeship was exorcised of its German origin, having been renamed after Adam Mickiewicz, Poland's greatest national poet.

14. The Upper Silesian Marcin (Martin) Biedermann founded it in 1896 (Michalkiewicz, 1985: 376).

15. Marcin Biedermann established this periodical in Posen. It was transferred to Kattowitz in 1902 (Snoch, 1991: 42).

16. Of this number 22,764 Jews lived in the Oppeln Regency, 19,189 in the Breslau Regency and 4,664 in the Liegnitz Regency (Kokot, 1973: 76).

17. Of this number 18,268 lived in the Oppeln Regency, 23,564 in the Breslau Regency and 3,860 in the Liegnitz Regency (Kokot, 1973: 77).

Notes to Chapter 9

1. Actually, the oldest Cisleithanian German association of singers was founded in Bielitz in 1834 (Wurbs, 1982: 34).

2. These German-speaking areas of Galicia, extending from Oświęcim (Auschwitz) to Żywiec (Saybusch), constituted the Oświęcim principality within the borders of Po-land-Lithuania. After the first partition of Poland-Lithuania (1772), this principality was allocated to Austria. Vienna turned it into a separate crownland, which in 1773 was incorporated into the lands of the Czech Crown. As such, this erstwhile principal-ity also became part of the German Confederation, but only in 1818, three years after the establishment of this confederation. Hence, this land was treated as part of the "German lands" and was indeed the smallest crownland of the Austrian Empire until 1850, when it was merged with Galicia in order to streamline the administration of the former Republic of Cracow, which Vienna had annexed in 1846. Therefore, since the mid-nineteenth century, it had not been clear if this erstwhile Auschwitz crownland was a German land or not (Jähnig, 1991: 121; Snoch, 1991: 73).

3. In 1951 both towns were officially merged into Bielsko-Biała (Anon., 1983e: 233).

4. Father Jan Sarkander, (1576–1620) born in Skotschau, East Silesia, strove to regain the faithful for Catholicism in several largely Protestant parishes in Moravia where he worked as a priest. In the course of religious strife, he was tortured to death in the North Moravian town of Holleschau (Holešov). In 1855 Sarkander was beatified, and in 1995 Pope John Paul II canonized him (Golec, 1993: 236).

5. Petr Bezruč ("without hands") is the pen name of Vladimír Vašek (1867–1958), a son of the Czech activist Antonín Vašek, who founded the first Austrian Silesian Czech-language periodical, *Opavský besednik,* in 1861. Bezruč established his position with a collection of artistically original and highly political poems, entitled *Slezské písně* (Silesian Songs, 1909). Half of these poems had been published in an earlier collection in 1903. He sympathized with the Austrian Silesian Czech-speaking poor, and he was vociferously anti-Bohemian, anti-German and anti-Polish. His highly dialectal poetry and political views contributed to the rise of the Silesian feeling sympathetic to, but

not uncritical of, Czech nationalism (Myška, 1994: 75; Pynsent, 1993: 44; Urbanec, 1965: 5–6).

6. The Czech/Slavic-speakers of Austrian Silesia and the Upper Silesian county of Ratibor tended to identify themselves as "Morawecs," similar to the Czech/Slavic-speakers of Moravia, who referred to themselves as "Moravians" (Kacíř, 1996: 3; Žáček, 1995: 152–153).

7. Notably, none of the main Polish proponents of social democracy stemmed from Austrian Silesia—neither Tadeusz Reger (1872–1938), nor Ryszard Kunicki (1873–1960), nor Ignacy Daszyński (1866–1936), who was destined to become one of the most influential politicians in interwar Poland (Golec, 1993: 172; Lis, 1993: 118).

8. The language forms used by the inhabitants of Moravia were officially known as "Slavic" or "Moravian Slavic," though they did not differ much from the standard Czech of Prague. This strengthened the regional and ethnic Moravian identity and, as a consequence, prevented the spread of the Czech national movement that spread from Bohemia (Žáček, 1995: 152–153).

9. Polish/Slavic-speaking Szlonzoks constituted 47.9 percent of the county's rural population, whereas German-speakers made up 9.4 percent. The corresponding numbers for the urban population were 30.7 percent and 64.9 percent, respectively (Gregor, 1905).

10. It seems that official Czechoslovak statistics on the nationality of the inhabitants of the Hlučinsko were frequently massaged. The photocopies of documents in possession of Andreas Götze (Freie Universität Berlin) unambiguously indicate that Czechoslovak census officers often altered the Hultschiners' increasingly more numerous declarations for Germandom by striking the latter's statements and entering, in official hand, answers that made these Hultschiners, against their will, into Czechs.

11. In the Habsburg Monarchy deputies were elected to the Landtage and the Reichsrat in accordance with the various types of limited enfranchisement. The constituencies corresponding to these different types of election rules were organized in *curiae*. Usually more votes were needed for electing a deputy from the countryside or urban *curia* than from the ecclesiastical *curia* or the *curia* of great landowners and aristocrats. Moreover, the two former *curiae* had fewer deputies to themselves than the two latter ones. As a consequence, the more privileged were represented by a larger number of deputies than those with fewer entitlements, even though the latter were more numerous.

12. Slunzaks aspiring to preserve their specific identity described themselves in their own Slavic dialect as "*Szlonzaki, Ślunzoky* or *Schlonsaken.*" These three words phonetically are almost the same and mean "the Silesians," that is, "the Slunzaks." They appear different in writing because, in the absence of a standardized Szlonzokian language, they are rendered in the spelling systems of standard Polish, standard Czech and standard German (Kacíř, 1996: 3).

Notes to Chapter 10

1. Stębark is located near Grunwald.

2. It was to liquidate the foreign administration and rule in the territories that this commission controlled.

3. Garrigue—the surname of his American wife, which Masaryk accepted at marriage in addition to his own.

4. He was the first major western European historian of the Slavic peoples of central and eastern Europe as well as a prolific commentator on their national movements. His son

Hugh Seton-Watson (1916–1984) built upon his father's studies and laid the foundations for the study of ethnicity and nationalism in this part of the old continent.

5. Bertram (1859–1945) was consecrated as the Hildsheim bishop by the Breslau Bishop Kopp. After Kopp's death in 1914, the church authorities nominated Bertram to the position of bishop of Breslau. He retained this bishopric until his death at the end of World War II (Pater, 1996b: 25).

6. The Zentrum adopted this new name in Upper Silesia on December 16, 1918, in preparation for possible autonomization of Upper Silesia or even for its separation from Germany (Hauser, 1991: 42).

7. The concept of the Czechoslovak nation that underlay the establishment of Czechoslovakia never came to fruition. The Czech and Slovak nations continued to develop separately instead of officially merging into the postulated "Czechoslovaks" who would speak in some common "Czechoslovak language" as prescribed in the 1921 constitution. The failure of Czechoslovak nationalism became clear in 1939 when the independent Slovak nation-state came into being, as much a result of Berlin's instigation as at the Slovaks' displeasure with the dominant position of the Czechs in erstwhile Czechoslovakia.

8. The seminal Hungarian thinker István Bibó (1911–1979) coined this phrase in his 1946 essay (Bibó, 1995).

Note to Chaper 11

1. The liturgy of the holy mass continued to be conducted in Latin until the implementation of the decisions of Vatican II (1962–1965). In the case of Poland (which incorporated all of Upper Silesia and Lower Silesia in 1945) this change took place at the beginning of the 1970s.

Notes to Conclusion

1. On the theories and analysis of globalization and regionalization, see Featherstone (1990) and Waters (1995).

2. The Upper Silesian Slavic-Germanic creole developed to its fullest in the industrial basin in the closing decades of the nineteenth century.

3. This qualitatively new situation permitted Polish scholars to produce initial monographs on such ethnic groups as the Mazurs (Sakson, 1990), the Warmiaks (Ermlanders) (Szyfer, 1996), the Lemkos (Michna, 1995; Sitek, 1996) and the Kashubs (Latoszek, 1990; Synak, 1998). Also quite a good number of studies have been devoted to the ethnic and regional problem in Upper Silesia (Frysztacki, 1998; Łęcki, 1992; Sitek, 1992, Szczepański 1993; Świątkiewicz 1995; Wódz, 1995). However, the author believes that these monographs are somewhat deficient. First, they are written mainly from the sociological point of view. This indicates that sociologists more than other social scientists are aware of the fact that social reality cannot be explained only through the lenses of the nation-state and the nation. But this sociological predilection breeds disregard for other sets of analytical spectacles offered by political science, international relations, historiography, anthropology, sociolinguistics, and the study of nationalism and ethnicity. Significantly, in the last three decades students of these disciplines enumerated above have produced many theoretical blueprints and case studies useful for description and analysis of the ethnic problem. Second, the analyses presented in the above-mentioned monographs are predominantly synchronic and devoted to the recent years or decades. Thus, they lead the reader to believe that the context of nationalism and the nation-state is a constant that can be projected even into the distant

past. Third, these monographs are also quite selective. They focus either on a regionalism, an ethnic group or an ethnic identification without any attempt to merge these and other elements into a more multidimensional picture. Fourth, the studies hardly ever probe into the questions of neighboring ethnic groups, nationalisms and regionalisms, though it is obvious that these external ethnic and national influences do alter the analyzed problem at the diachronic level. Fifth, the authors of these works usually employ the monistic model of identity. This often leads the reader to believe that ethnic groups must eventually merge with one nation or another and that they cannot transform into nations on their own, or that people cannot simultaneously be members of their specific ethnic groups and some nation.

Works Cited and Consulted

Adamczyk-Grabowska, Monika. 1994. *Polska Isaaca Bashevisa Singera* [The Poland of Isaac Bashevis Singer]. Lublin: Wydawnictwo Uniwersytetu Marii Curie-Skłodowskiej.

Adamson, Lilian, and Rossem, Cefas van. 1995. Creole Literature (pp. 75–84). In Arends, Jacques et al., eds., *Pidgins and Creoles: An Introduction*. Amsterdam: John Benjamins Publishing Company.

Alter, Peter. 1994. *Nationalism*. London: Edward Arnold.

Altermatt, Urs. 1996. *Das Fanal von Sarajevo: Ethnonationalismus in Europa* [The Warning of Sarajevo: Ethnonationalism in Europe]. Zürich: Neue Zürcher Zeitung.

Anderson, Benedict. 1991. *Imagined Communities: Reflections on the Origin and Spread of Nationalism*. London and New York: Verso.

Anon. 1888. Jahn, Friedrich Ludwig (9: 133/134). In *Meyers Konversations-Lexikon* [Meyer Encyclopedia]. Leipzig: Verlag des Bibliographischen Instituts.

Anon. 1888a. Kultur [Culture] (10: 293). In *Meyers Konversations-Lexikon* [Meyer Encyclopedia]. Leipzig: Verlag des Bibliographischen Instituts.

Anon. 1888b. Lützow, Ludwig Adolf Wilhelm, Freiherr von (10: 1030–1031). In *Meyers Konversations-Lexikon* [Meyer Encyclopedia]. Leipzig: Verlag des Bibliographischen Instituts.

Anon. 1888c. Kriegervereine [Associations of War Veterans] (10: 209–210). In *Meyers Konversations-Lexikon* [Meyer Encyclopedia]. Leipzig: Verlag des Bibliographischen Instituts.

Anon. 1889. Schützengesellschaften [Riflemen's Associations] (14: 670–671). In *Meyers Konversations-Lexikon* [Meyer Encyclopedia]. Leipzig: Verlag des Bibliographischen Instituts.

Anon. 1889a. Statistik [Statistics] (15: 241–243). In *Meyers Konversations-Lexikon* [Meyer Encyclopedia]. Leipzig: Verlag des Bibliographischen Instituts.

Anon. 1889b. Turnkunst [Gymnastics] (15: 943–944). In *Meyers Konversations-Lexikon* [Meyer Encyclopedia]. Leipzig: Verlag des Bibliographischen Instituts.

Anon. 1889c. Nationalgarde [National Guard] (12: 3). In *Meyers Konversations-Lexikon* [Meyer Encyclopedia]. Leipzig: Verlag des Bibliographischen Instituts.

Anon. 1889d. Nationalverein, deutscher [National Society, German] (12: 4). In *Meyers Konversations-Lexikon* [Meyer Encyclopedia]. Leipzig: Verlag des Bibliographischen Instituts.

Anon. 1889e. Nationalfarben [National Colors] (12: 3). In *Meyers Konversations-Lexikon* [Meyer Encyclopedia]. Leipzig: Verlag des Bibliographischen Instituts.

Anon. 1889f. Nationaltheater [National Theater] (12: 4). In *Meyers Konversations-Lexikon* [Meyer Encyclopedia]. Leipzig: Verlag des Bibliographischen Instituts.

Anon. 1889g. Eisenbahn [Railway] (5: 428–447). In *Meyers Konversations-Lexikon* [Meyer Encyclopedia]. Leipzig: Verlag des Bibliographischen Instituts.

Anon. 1889h. Flagge [Flag] (6: 334–336). In *Meyers Konversations-Lexikon* [Meyer Encyclopedia]. Leipzig: Verlag des Bibliographischen Instituts.

Anon. 1889i. Freiekonservative [Free Conservatives] (6: 650). In *Meyers Konversations-Lexikon* [Meyer Encyclopedia]. Leipzig: Verlag des Bibliographischen Instituts.

Anon. 1889j. Fulda (6: 779–780). In *Meyers Konversations-Lexikon* [Meyer Encyclopedia]. Leipzig: Verlag des Bibliographischen Instituts.

Anon. 1889k. Niederwald (12: 163–164), In *Meyers Konversations-Lexikon* [Meyer Encyclopedia]. Leipzig: Verlag des Bibliographischen Instituts.

Anon. 1889l. Deutschland [Germany] (4: 800–912). In *Meyers Konversations-Lexikon* [Meyer Encyclopedia]. Leipzig: Verlag des Bibliographischen Instituts.

Anon. 1889m. Reichstag [Imperial Diet] (13: 687–688). In *Meyers Konversations-Lexikon* [Meyer Encyclopedia]. Leipzig: Verlag des Bibliographischen Instituts.

Anon. 1890. Volkslied [Folk Song] (16: 265–268). In *Meyers Konversations-Lexikon* [Meyer Encyclopedia]. Leipzig: Verlag des Bibliographischen Instituts.

Anon. 1890a. Volkszählungen [Censuses] (16: 275–276). In *Meyers Konversations-Lexikon* [Meyer Encyclopedia]. Leipzig: Verlag des Bibliographischen Instituts.

Anon. 1890b. Walhalla [Valhalla] (16: 359–360). In *Meyers Konversations-Lexikon* [Meyer Encyclopedia]. Leipzig: Verlag des Bibliographischen Instituts.

Anon. 1905. Slezsko [Silesia] (23: 365–389). In *Ottův slovník naučny* [Otto Scholarly Encyclopaedia]. Prague: J. Otto.

Anon. 1908. Panslavism (7: 735). In *Chambers's Encyclopaedia: A Dictionary of Universal Knowledge*. London and Edinburgh: Chambers; and Philadelphia: Lippincott.

Anon. 1908a. Census (3: 61–62). In *Chambers's Encyclopaedia: A Dictionary of Universal Knowledge*. London and Edinburgh: Chambers; and Philadelphia: Lippincott.

Anon. 1908b. Statistics (9: 695–696). In *Chambers's Encyclopaedia: A Dictionary of Universal Knowledge*. London and Edinburgh: Chambers; and Philadelphia: Lippincott.

Anon. 1908c. National Hymns (7: 406–407). In *Chambers's Encyclopaedia: A Dictionary of Universal Knowledge*. London and Edinburgh: Chambers; and Philadelphia: Lippincott.

Anon. 1908d. Bismarck-Schönhausen, Otto Eduard Leopold, Prince von, Duke of Lauenburg (2: 187/188). In *Chambers's Encyclopaedia: A Dictionary of Universal Knowledge*. London and Edinburgh: Chambers; and Philadelphia: Lippincott.

Anon. 1919. *The Germans in Bohemia, Moravia and Silesia*. Berlin: Staatsdrückerei.

Anon. 1939. Slezsko [Silesia] (Dodatký [Addenda], vol. 5, part 2: 1337–1345). In *Ottův Slovník Naučny* [Otto Scholarly Encyclopaedia]. Prague: Novina.

Anon. 1972. Kattowitz Conference (10: 819–821). In *Encyclopaedia Judaica*. Jerusalem: Keter Publishing House; and New York: Macmillan.

Anon. 1983. Brückner, Aleksander (1: 370). In Łąkowski, Rafał, et al., eds., *Encyklopedia Powszechna PWN* [PWN's Universal Encyclopedia]. Warsaw: PWN.

Anon. 1983a. Chociszewski, Józef (1: 468). In Łąkowski, Rafał, et al., eds., *Encyklopedia Powszechna PWN* [PWN's Universal Encyclopedia]. Warsaw: PWN.

Anon. 1983b. Bażyński, Franciszek (1: 243–244). In Łąkowski, Rafał, et al., eds., *Encyklopedia Powszechna PWN* [PWN's Universal Encyclopedia]. Warsaw: PWN.

Anon. 1983c. Balicki, Zygmunt (1: 212). In Łąkowski, Rafał, et al., eds., *Encyklopedia Powszechna PWN* [PWN's Universal Encyclopedia]. Warsaw: PWN.

Anon. 1983d. Dmowski, Roman (1: 615). In Łąkowski, Rafał, et al., eds., *Encyklopedia Powszechna PWN* [PWN's Universal Encyclopedia]. Warsaw: PWN.

Anon. 1983e. Bielsko-Biała (1: 233–234). In Łąkowski, Rafał, et al., eds., *Encyklopedia Powszechna PWN* [PWN's Universal Encyclopedia]. Warsaw: PWN.

Anon. 1984. Lompa, Józef Piotr (2: 762–763). In Łąkowski, Rafał, et al., eds., *Encyklopedia Powszechna PWN* [PWN's Universal Encyclopedia]. Warsaw: PWN.

Anon. 1984a. Lubomirski, Jan Tadeusz (2: 777). In Łąkowski, Rafał, et al., eds., *Encyklopedia Powszechna PWN* [PWN's Universal Encyclopedia]. Warsaw: PWN.

Anon. 1985. Powstania Wielkopolskie [Wielkopolska Uprisings] (3: 717). In Łąkowski, Rafał, et al., eds., *Encyklopedia Powszechna PWN* [PWN's Universal Encyclopedia]. Warsaw: PWN.

Anon. 1985a. Rieger, František (3: 889). In Łąkowski, Rafał, et al., eds., *Encyklopedia Powszechna PWN* [PWN's Universal Encyclopedia]. Warsaw: PWN.

Anon. 1985b. Miłkowski, Zygmunt (3: 112). In Łąkowski, Rafał, et al., eds., *Encyklopedia Powszechna PWN* [PWN's Universal Encyclopedia]. Warsaw: PWN.

Anon. 1987. Związek Młodzieży Polskiej 'Zet' [The 'Zet' Union of Polish Youth] (4: 879/880). In Łąkowski, Rafał et al., eds., *Encyklopedia Powszechna PWN* [PWN's Universal Encyclopedia]. Warsaw: PWN.

Anon. 1987a. Stronnictwo Narodowo-Demokratyczne [The National Democratic

Movement] (4: 314). In Łąkowski, Rafał, et al., eds., *Encyklopedia Powszechna PWN* [PWN's Universal Encyclopedia]. Warsaw: PWN.

Anon. 1987b. Sokół (4: 233). In Łąkowski, Rafał, et al., eds., *Encyklopedia Powszechna PWN* [PWN's Universal Encyclopedia]. Warsaw: PWN.

Anon. 1987c. Seyda, Zygmunt (4: 161). In Łąkowski, Rafał, et al., eds., *Encyklopedia Powszechna PWN* [PWN's Universal Encyclopedia]. Warsaw: PWN.

Anon. 1990. Serbia (23: 309–311). In Bram, Leon L., and Dickey, Norma H., et al., eds., *Funk and Wagnalls New Encyclopedia*. Columbus, OH: Funk and Wagnalls L.P.

Anon. 1990a. Greece (12: 162–185). In Bram, Leon L., and Dickey, Norma H., et al., eds., *Funk and Wagnalls New Encyclopedia*. Columbus, OH: Funk and Wagnalls L.P.

Anon. 1990b. Holy Alliance (13: 162/163). In Bram, Leon L., and Dickey, Norma H., et al., eds., *Funk and Wagnalls New Encyclopedia*. Columbus, OH: Funk and Wagnalls L.P.

Anon. 1990c. France (10: 405–448). In Bram, Leon L., and Dickey, Norma H., et al., eds., *Funk and Wagnalls New Encyclopedia*. Columbus, OH: Funk and Wagnalls L.P.

Anon. 1990d. Belgium (3: 398–410). In Bram, Leon L., and Dickey, Norma H., et al., eds., *Funk and Wagnalls New Encyclopedia*. Columbus, OH: Funk and Wagnalls L.P.

Anon. 1990e. Italy (14: 327–358). In Bram, Leon L., and Dickey, Norma H., et al., eds., *Funk and Wagnalls New Encyclopedia*. Columbus, OH: Funk and Wagnalls L.P.

Anon. 1990f. Switzerland (25: 58–69). In Bram, Leon L., and Dickey, Norma H., et al., eds., *Funk and Wagnalls New Encyclopedia*. Columbus, OH: Funk and Wagnalls L.P.

Anon. 1990g. Germany (11: 332–355). In Bram, Leon L., and Dickey, Norma H., et al., eds., *Funk and Wagnalls New Encyclopedia*. Columbus, OH: Funk and Wagnalls L.P.

Anon. 1990h. Masaryk, Tomáš Garrigue (17: 62). In Bram, Leon L., and Dickey, Norma H., et al., eds., *Funk and Wagnalls New Encyclopedia*. Columbus, OH: Funk and Wagnalls L.P.

Anon. 1992. Prussia (11: 751–753). In McHenry, Robert, et al., eds., *The New Encyclopaedia Britannica*. Chicago: Encyclopaedia Britannica, Inc.

Anon. 1992a. Pan-Germanism (9: 103). In McHenry, Robert, et al., eds., *The New Encyclopaedia Britannica*. Chicago: Encyclopaedia Britannica, Inc.

Anon. 1992b. Conscription (3: 552–553). In McHenry, Robert, et al., eds., *The New Encyclopaedia Britannica*. Chicago: Encyclopaedia Britannica, Inc.

Anon. 1992c. *Slezsko* [Silesia]. Opava: Matice slezská.

Anon. 1992d. Pangermanism (9: 103). In McHenry, Robert, et al., eds., *The New Encyclopaedia Britannica*. Chicago: Encyclopaedia Britannica, Inc.

Anon. 1996. Minister Bohl würdigt Verdienst der Heimatvertribene. 25. Bundestreffen der Landmannschaften der Oberschlesier [Minister Bohl Pays Tribute to the Merits of the Expellees. The 25th Federal Meeting of the Homeland Organization of the Upper Silesians] (pp. 7–8). *Deutscher Ostdienst.* No. 23, Jun. 7.

Anon. 1997. GTL po czterech latach [The GTL after Four Years] (p. 4). *Śląsk.* No. 2, Feb.

Armstrong, John. 1982. *Nations before Nationalism.* Chapel Hill, NC: University of North Carolina Press.

Attwater, Donald. 1983. *The Penguin Dictionary of Saints* (Ser.: Penguin Reference). Harmondsworth: Penguin Books.

Babiński, Grzegorz. 1997. *Pogranicze polsko-ukraińskie. Etniczność, zróżnicowanie religijne, tożsamość* [The Polish-Ukrainian Borderland: Ethnicity, Religious Differentiation, Identity]. Cracow: Nomos.

Bahlcke, Joachim. 1996. *Schlesien und die Schlesier* [Silesia and the Silesians] (Ser.: Vertreibungsgebiete und vertriebene Deutsche [Expelled Germans and the Territories from Which They Were Expelled], vol. 7). Munich: Langen Müller.

Banks, Marcus. 1996. *Ethnicity: Anthropological Constructions.* London: Routledge.

Barran, Fritz R. 1993. *Städte-Atlas. Schlesien* [The Atlas of Cities and Towns: Silesia]. Leer: Rautenberg.

Barth, Frederik. 1969. Introduction (pp. 9–38). In Barth. Frederik, ed., *Ethnic Groups and Boundaries: The Social Organization of Culture Difference.* Oslo: Universitetsforlaget.

Bartz, Brunon. 1995. *Exodus: integracja wysiedleńców jako wyzwanie dla polityki społecznej RFN* [Exodus: Integration of the *Aussiedlers* as a Challenge to the Social Policy of the FRG]. Tarnobrzeg: Historica.

Batowski, Henryk. 1964. *Słownik nazw miejscowych Europy Środkowej i Wschodniej 19 i 20 wieku* [The Dictionary of Central and Eastern European Place Names in the 19th and 20th Centuries]. Warsaw: PWN.

Battek, Marek J., and Szczepankiewicz, Joanna. 1998. *Słownik nazewnictwa krajoznawczego. Polsko-niemiecki, niemiecko-polski* [The Polish-German and German-Polish Dictionary of Place Names]. Wrocław: Silesia.

Bein, Werner. 1995. Das Schicksal Österreichisch-Schlesiens (bis zum Ende des Zweiten Weltkrieges) [The Fate of Austrian Silesia (Up to the End of the Second World War)]. In Irgang, Winfried, Bein, Werner, and Neubach, Helmut. *Schlesien: Geschichte, Kultur und Wirtschaft* [Silesia: History, Culture and Economy]. Cologne: Verlag Wissenschaft und Politik.

Bělina, Pavel, and RAK, Jiří. 1993. Léta 1815–1867 [Years 1815–1867] (pp. 11–59). In Bělina, Pavel, et al., eds., *Dějiny zemí Koruny České* [History of the Lands of the Czech Crown] (vol. 2). Prague and Litomyšl: Paseka.

Bell, Daniel. 1976. *The Coming of Postindustrial Society.* New York: Basic.

Bell-Fialkoff, Andrew. 1996. *Ethnic Cleansing.* London: Macmillan.

Berdychowska, Bogumiła, et al., eds. 1995. *Mniejszości narodowe w Polsce.*

Informator 1994 [National Minorities in Poland: A 1994 Guidebook]. Warsaw: Wydawnictwo Sejmowe.

Berger Stefan, et al., eds. *Writing National Histories: Western Europe since 1800.* London: Routledge.

Berlin, Isaiah. 1981. Nationalism: Past Neglect and Present Power. In H. Hardy, ed., *Against the Current.* Oxford: Oxford University Press.

Berlińska, Danuta. 1993. [Unpublished ms.]. Stosunki etniczne i postawy polityczne mieszkańców Śląska Opolskiego [The Ethnic Relations and the Attitudes of the Inhabitants of Opole Silesia]. Opole: Instytut Śląski.

Berlińska, Danuta, and Madajczyk, Piotr. 1998. Mniejszość niemiecka w Polsce [The German Minority in Poland] (pp. 83–141). In Berdychowska, Bogumiła, ed., *Mniejszości narodowe w Polsce. Praktyka po 1989 roku* [The National Minorities in Poland: Practice after the Year 1989]. Warsaw: Wydawnictwo Sejmowe.

Biały, Franciszek. 1982. Freikorps (pp. 129–131). In Hawranek, Franciszek, et al., eds., *Encyklopedia Powstań Śląskich* [The Encyclopedia of the Silesian Uprisings]. Opole: Instytut Śląski.

Biały, Franciszek. 1990. Wojny lat 1864, 1866 i 1870/1871 a wzrost tendencji nacjonalistycznych na Śląsku [The Wars of 1864, 1866 and 1870/1871, and the Increase in the Nationalist Tendencies in Silesia]. *Zaranie*. Nos. 3–4.

Bibó, István. 1991. The Distress of the East European Small States (pp. 13–88). In Bibó, István. *Democracy, Revolution, Self-Determination: Selected Writings* (ed. Nagy, Károly) (Ser.: East European Monographs, no. 317). Boulder, CO: Social Science Monographs.

Bibó, István. 1995. Nędza małych państw [Poverty of the Small States]. *Gazeta Wyborcza* (Section: Gazeta Środkowoeuropejska [Central European Newspaper]). Aug 19–20.

Bidelux, Robert, and Jeffries, Ian. 1998. *A History of Eastern Europe: Crisis and Change.* London: Routledge.

Bienek, Horst. 1993. *Reise in die Kindheit—Wiedersehen mit Schlesien* [The Journey into Childhood—A Meeting with Silesia]. Munich: Carl Hanser Verlag.

Billig, Michael. 1995. *Banal Nationalism.* London: Sage.

Birke, Ernst. 1968. *Silesia: A German Region.* Munich: Delp.

Black, Henry Campbell, et al. 1990. *Black's Law Dictionary: Definitions of the Terms and Phrases of American and English Jurisprudence, Ancient and Modern.* St. Paul, MN: West Publishing.

Bloom, William. 1990. *Personal Identity, National Identity and International Relations.* Cambridge: Cambridge University Press.

Blumenwitz, Dieter. 1989. *What Is Germany? Exploring Germany's Status after World War II.* Bonn: Kulturstiftung der deutschen Vertriebenen.

Böckh, Richard. 1866. Die statistiche Bedeutung der Volksprache als Kennzeichen der Nationalität [The Statistical Significance of Language as an Indicator of Nationality] (pp. 259–402). *Zeitschrift für Völkerpsychologie und Sprachwissenschaft*. No. 4.

Bogar, Karel, ed. 1992. *Umělecký a lidský odkaz básníka Óndry Łysohorského* [Artistic and Humane Legacy of the Poet Óndra Łysohorsky]. Frýdek-Místek: Muzeum Beskyd.

Bokenkotter, Thomas. 1977. *A Concise History of the Catholic Church*. Garden City, NY: Doubleday.

Borek, Henryk, and Brożek, Andrzej. 1979. Korespondencja z Teksasu do *Gazety Polskiej* w Chicago (1875) [A Letter from Texas to the Periodical *Gazeta Polska* in Chicago (1875)] (pp. 53–66). *Kwartalnik Opolski*. No. 4.

Breit, Holger. 1998. *Die Deutschen in Oberschlesien* [The Germans of Upper Silesia]. Munich: Grafik + Druck.

Breugel, J. W. 1973. *Czechoslovakia before Munich: The German Minority Problem and British Appeasement Policy*. Cambridge: Cambridge University Press.

Breuilly, John. 1993. *Nationalism and the State*. Manchester: Manchester University Press.

Breytenbach, Willie. 1997. *Democratisation in Sub-Saharan Africa: Transitions, Elections and Prospects for Consolidation*. Pretoria: African Institute of South Africa.

Bromley, Yulian. 1974. The Term *ethnos* and Its Definition (pp. 48–73). In Bromley, Yulian, ed., *Soviet Ethnology and Anthropology Today*. The Hague: Mouton.

Brożek, Andrzej. 1958. *Napływ robotników spoza zaboru pruskiego na Górny Śląsk w latach 1870–1914* [Immigration of Workers from Outside the Prussian Partition to Upper Silesia in the Years 1870–1914] (Ser.: Biblioteczka wiedzy o Śląsku, seria historyczna [Library of Information on Silesia, Historical Section], no. 1). Katowice: Śląski Instytut Naukowy.

Brożek, Andrzej. 1963. *Wysiedlenia Polaków z Górnego Śląska przez Bismarcka (1885–1887)* [Bismarck's Expulsions of Poles from Upper Silesia (1885–1887)]. Katowice: Śląsk.

Brożek, Andrzej. 1966. *Ostflucht na Śląsku* [Ostflucht in Silesia]. Katowice: Śląsk.

Brożek, Andrzej. 1966a. *Robotnicy spoza zaboru pruskiego w przemyśle na Górnym Śląsku (1870–1914)* [Workers from Outside the Prussian Partition in the Industry of Upper Silesia (1870–1914)] (Ser.: Monografie Śląskie Ossolineum [Ossolineum's Monographs on Silesia], vol. 12). Wrocław, Warsaw and Cracow: Ossolineum.

Brożek, Andrzej. 1969. [Unpublished ms.]. Emigracja zamorska z Górnego Śląska w II połowie 19 wieku [Overseas Emigration from Upper Silesia in the Second Half of the 19th Century]. In Anon., ed. *100 lat Polonii brazylijskiej* [Centenary of Polish Settlement in Brazil]. Opole: Instytut Śląski.

Brożek, Andrzej. 1972. *Ślązacy w Teksasie* [Silesians in Texas]. Opole: Instytut Śląski; and Warsaw: PWN.

Brożek, Andrzej. 1982. Powstanie Wielkopolskie [Wielkopolska Uprising] (p.

438). In Hawranek, Franciszek, et al., eds., *Encyklopedia Powstań Śląskich* [The Encyclopedia of the Silesian Uprisings]. Opole: Instytut Śląski.

Brożek, Andrzej. 1988. *Polish Americans, 1854–1939*. Warsaw: Interpress.

Brożek, Andrzej. 1995. *Po pięćdziesięciu latach. Wokół Stanisława Wasylewskiego i jego* Na Śląsku Opolskim [Fifty Years Later: On Stanisław Wasylewski and His *In Opole Silesia*]. Opole: Instytut Śląski.

Bryce, James. 1919. *The Holy Roman Empire*. London: Macmillan.

Brubaker, Rogers. 1992. *Citizenship and Nationhood in France and Germany*. Cambridge, MA: Harvard University Press.

Bunsen, Christian Charles Josias. 1858. Preface (pp. vii–xxii). In Freytag, Gustav, *Debit and Credit*. New York: Harper and Brothers.

Burszta, Wojciech J. 1998. *Antropologia kultury* [Anthropology of Culture]. Poznań: Zysk i S-ka.

Buse, Dieter K., and Doerr, Juergen C. 1985. *German Nationalisms: A Bibliographical Approach*. New York: Garland Publishing.

Buszko, Józef. 1989. *Galicja 1859–1914. Polski Piemont?* [Galicia 1859–1914: A Polish Piedmont?] (Ser.: Dzieje narodu i państwa polskiego [History of the Polish Nation and State], vol. 3, part 56). Warsaw: KAW.

Carr, Raymond. 1996. Keep the Homeland Fires Burning (pp. 42–43). *The Spectator*. July 13.

Carter, Francis William, Zeman, Z.A.B., Odlozilik, Otokar, et al. 1992. Czechoslovakia (16: 905–930). In McHenry, Robert, et al., eds., *The New Encyclopaedia Britannica*. Chicago: Encyclopaedia Britannica, Inc.

Cavalli-Sforza, Luigi Luca, and Feldman, M. W. 1981. *Cultural Transmission and Evolution: A Quantitative Approach*. Princeton: Princeton University Press.

Cavalli-Sforza, Luigi Luca. 1991. Genes, Peoples and Languages (pp. 104–111). *Scientific American*. No. 11.

Černý, Václav. 1995. *Vývoj a zločiny panslavisnu* [The Development and Crimes of Panslavism]. Prague: Institut pro středoevropskou kulturu a politiku.

Chałasiński, Józef. 1935. *Antagonizm polsko-niemiecki w osadzie fabrycznej 'Kopalnia' na Górnym Śląsku* [The Polish-German Antagonism in the Industrial Township 'Kopalnia' in Upper Silesia]. Warsaw: Dom Książki Polskiej.

Chlebowczyk, Józef. 1966. *Wybory i świadomość społeczna na Śląsku Cieszyńskim w drugiej połowie 19 wieku* [Elections and Social Consciousness in Cieszyn Silesia in the Second Half of the 19th Century]. Cracow: PWN; and Katowice: Śląski Instytut Naukowy.

Chlebowczyk, Józef. 1980. *On Small and Young Nations in Europe*. Wrocław: Ossolineum.

Chlebowczyk, Józef. 1983. *O prawie do bytu małych i młodych narodów* [On the Small and Young Nations' Right to Existence]. Warsaw: PWN and ŚIN.

Chocholatý, František. 1991. "Slezsko" [Silesia] (part 4) (pp. 76–97). *Střední Evropa*. No. 20.

Cholewa, Krzysztof. 1998. Najważniejszy argument [The Most Significant Argument] (pp. 1 and 3). *Schlesisches Wochenblatt*. No. 4, Jan. 22–29.

Choroś, Monika, and Jarczak, Łucja. 1995. *Słownik nazw miejscowych Dolnego Śląska. Polsko niemiecki i niemiecko-polski* [The Polish-German and German-Polish Dictionary of the Names of the Localities in Lower Silesia]. Opole: Instytut Śląski.

Choroś, Monika, Jarczak, Łucja, and Sochacka, Stanisława. 1997. *Słownik nazw miejscowych Górnego Śląska. Polsko-niemiecki i niemiecko-polski* [The Polish-German and German-Polish Dictionary of the Names of the Localities in Upper Silesia]. Opole: Instytut Śląski; and Kluczbork: Księgarnia Minerva.

Cimała, Bogdan. 1982. "Autonomiści górnośląscy" [Advocates of an Upper Silesian Autonomy] (p. 23). In Hawranek, Franciszek, et al., eds., *Encyklopedia Powstań Śląskich* [The Encyclopedia of the Silesian Uprisings]. Opole: Instytut Śląski.

Cimała, Bogdan. 1982a. Reginek, Tomasz (p. 474). In Hawranek, Franciszek, et al., eds. *Encyklopedia Powstań Śląskich* [The Encyclopedia of the Silesian Uprisings]. Opole: Instytut Śląski.

Clark, Colin. 1997. "New Age" Travellers: Identity, Sedentarism and Social Security (pp. 125–141). In Acton, Thomas, ed., *Gypsy Politics and Traveller Identity*. Hatfield, Hertfordshire: University of Hertfordshire Press.

Coetzee, Marilyn Shevin. 1990. *The German League: Popular Nationalism in Wilhelmine Germany*. New York and Oxford: Oxford University Press.

Cohen, Michael Joseph. 1990. Zionism (28: 161–164). In Bram, Leon L., and Dickey, Norma H., et al., eds., *Funk and Wagnalls New Encyclopedia*. Columbus, OH: Funk and Wagnalls L.P.

Connor, Walker. 1994. *Ethnonationalism: The Quest for Understanding*. Princeton, NJ: Princeton University Press.

Conrads, Norbert, ed. 1994. *Schlesien* [Silesia]. Berlin: Siedler.

Conrads, Norbert. 1995. Die sozialpolitische Lage Schlesiens, Ende des 19. und Anfang des 20. Jahrhunderts (pp. 8–9). *Hoffnung*, nos. 26–27.

Crystal, David. 1987. *The Cambridge Encyclopedia of Language*. Cambridge: Cambridge University Press.

Czajkowski, Andrzej, and Kulkowski, Andrzej. 1996. *Słownik gwary śląskiej* [The Dictionary of the Silesian Dialect]. Katowice: Columb.

Czapliński, Marek. 1974. *Adam Napieralski 1861–1928. Biografia polityczna* [Adam Napieralski 1861–1928: A Political Biography]. Wrocław: Ossolineum.

Czapliński, Marek. 2002. Dzieje Śląska od 1806 do 1945 roku [History of Silesia, 1806–1945] (pp. 250–425). In Czapliński, Marek, ed., *Historia Śląska* [History of Silesia]. Wrocław: Wydawnictwo Uniwersytetu Wrocławskiego.

Czapliński, Władysław, Galos, Adam, and Korta, Wacław. 1990. *Historia Niemiec* [A History of Germany]. Wrocław, Warsaw and Cracow: Ossolineum.

Czapliński, Władysław, and Ładogórski, Tadeusz. 1993. *Atlas historyczny Polski* [A Historical Atlas of Poland]. Warsaw and Wrocław: PPWK.

Cząstka-Szymon, Bożena, and Synowiec, Helena. 1996. *Polszczyzna w szkole śląskiej* [The Polish Language in the Silesian School]. Katowice: Śląsk.

Cząstka-Szymon, Bożena, and Synowiec, Helena. 1996a. *Polszczyzna w szkole śląskiej, Ćwiczenia dla uczniów* [The Polish Language in the Silesian School. Student Workbook]. Katowice: Śląsk.

Czubiński, Antoni. 1976. Polska w okresie dwudziestolecia międzywojennego [Poland During the Two Interwar Decades] (pp. 612–788). In Topolski, Jerzy, ed., *Dzieje Polski* [Poland's Past]. Warsaw: PWN.

Czubiński, Antoni. 1991. *Miejsce Polski w niemieckich planach aneksji i podbojów 1914–1945* [The Place of Poland in the German Plans of Annexations and Conquests]. Opole: Instytut Śląski.

Dąbrowski, Włodzimierz. 1922. *Zbiór praw konstytucyjnych i administracyjnych Województwa Śląskiego* [A Collection of Administrative and Constitutional Laws of the Silesian Voivodship]. Katowice: Urząd Wojewódzki.

Darby, H. C., and Fullard, Harold. 1978. *Atlas. The New Cambridge Modern History* (vol. 16). Cambridge: Cambridge University Press.

Davies, Norman. 1991. *God's Playground: A History of Poland* (vol. 1: The Origins to 1795; vol. 2: 1795 to the Present). Oxford: Clarendon Press.

Davies, Norman. 1996. *Europe: A History*. Oxford and New York: Oxford University Press.

Deletant, Dennis, and Hanak, Harry, eds. 1988. *Historians as Nation-Builders: Central and South-East Europe*. London: Macmillan Press in association with the School of Slavonic and East European Studies, University of London.

Deist, Ferdinand. 1984. *A Concise Dictionary of Theological Terms with an English-Afrikaans List*. Pretoria: J.L. van Schaik.

Deutsch, Karl W. 1966. *Nationalism and Social Communication: An Inquiry into the Foundations of Nationality*. Cambridge, MA: MIT Press.

Deutsch, Karl W. 1969. *Nationalism and Its Alternatives*. New York: Knopf.

Długajczyk, Edward. 1993. *Tajny front na granicy cieszyńskiej. Wywiad i dywersja w latach 1919–1939* [The Secret Front at the Cieszyn Border: Intelligence and Subversion in the Years 1919–1939]. Katowice: Śląsk.

Długoborski, Wacław. 1995. Górny Śląsk na tle innych ziem polskich w początku 20 wieku: gospodarka, społeczeństwo, kultura [Upper Silesia Contextualized against Other Polish Lands at the Beginning of the 20th Century: Economy, Society, Culture]. In Wanatowicz, Maria Wanda, ed., *Rola i miejsce Górnego Śląska w Drugiej Rzeczypospolitej* [The Role and Place of Upper Silesia in the Second Polish Republic]. Bytom: Muzeum Górnośląskie; and Katowice: Muzeum Śląskie.

Dmowski, Roman. 1996. [1903]. *Myśli nowoczesnego Polaka* [The Thoughts of the Modern Pole]. Wrocław: NORTOM.

Dokupil, Lumír, and Barteček, Ivo, eds. 1993. *Biografický slovník Slezska a severná*

Moravy [The Biographical Dictionary of Silesia and Northern Moravia] (vol. 1). Opava: OPTYS; and Ostrava: Ostravská univerzita.

Drabble, Margaret, ed. *The Oxford Companion to English Literature*. Oxford: Oxford University Press.

Dralle, Lothar. 1991. *Die Deutschen in Ostmittel- und Osteuropa* [The Germans in East-Central and Eastern Europe]. Darmstadt: Wissenschaftliche Buchgesellschaft.

Drews, Robert. 1988. *The Coming of the Greeks: Indo-European Conquests in the Aegean and the Near East*. Princeton, NJ: Princeton University Press.

Dubiel, Jacek. 1993. *Józef Rymer (1882–1922), pierwszy wojewoda śląski* [Józef Rymer (1882–1922), the First Silesian Voivode] (Ser.: Centrum Dokumentowania Losów Mieszkańców Górnego Śląska [The Documentation Center of Life Vicissitudes of the Inhabitants of Upper Silesia], vol. 3). Katwice: Towarzystwo Zachęty Kultury; and Gliwice: Muzeum w Gliwicach.

Dunbar, R. I. M. 1993. Coevolution of Neocortical Size, Group Size and Languages in Humans (pp. 681–735). *Behavioral and Brain Sciences*. No. 16.

Düspohl, Martin. 1995. Arbeitsmigration nach Berlin im 19. Jahrhundert/Imigracja zarobkowa do Berlina w XIX w. [Work Migration to Berlin in the 19th c.] (pp. 190–203). In Bździach, Klaus et al., eds., *'Wach auf, mein Herz, und denke'. Zur Geschichte der Beziehungen zwischen Schlesien und Berlin-Brandenburg von 1740 bis heute/ 'Przebudź się, serce moje, i pomyśl'. Przyczynek do historii stosunków między Śląskiem a Berlinem-Brandenburgią od 1740 do dziś* ['Wake Up, My Heart, and Think': A Contribution to the History of the Relations between Silesia and Berlin-Brandenburg from 1740 until Today]. Berlin: Gesellschaft für interregionalen Kulturaustausch; and Opole: Instytut Śląski.

Dyba, Marian. 1993. *Kształtowanie się środowiska historycznego na Śląsku w latach 1918–1939* [The Emergence of the Milieu of Polish Historians in Silesia in the Years 1918–1939]. Katowice: Uniwersytet Śląski.

Dziadul, Jan. 1996. Śląsk: Puste cokoły [Silesia: Empty Plinths] (pp. 4–5). *Polityka*. No. 29, Jul. 20.

Dziadul, Jan. 1997. My, naród śląski [We, the Silesian Nation] (p. 21). *Polityka*. No. 24, Jun. 14.

Edwards, John. 1994. *Multilingualism*. London and New York: Routledge.

Ehrich, Frederick F. 1992. Austria (4: 501–538). In McHenry, Robert, et al., eds., *The New Encyclopaedia Britannica*. Chicago: Encyclopaedia Britannica, Inc.

Eichler, Ernst. 1987– . S*lawische Ortsnamen zwischen Saale und Neisse. Ein Kompendium* [Slavic Place Names Between the Saale and the Neisse: A Compendium] (2 vols. published so far, A–J, K–M). Bautzen: Domowina-Verlag.

Eisler, Jerzy. 1995. *Marzec '68* [The March of '68]. Warsaw: WSiP.

Eitzen, Wilhelm. 1923. Preface (pp. 5–10). In Eitzen, F. W., *Commercial Dictionary* (part 2: English-German). Leipzig: H. Haessel Verlag.

Enden, Hans. 1977. "Klodnitzkanal" [Klodnitz Canal] (pp. 231–232). In Weczerka, Hugo, ed., *Schlesien* [Silesia] (Ser.: Handbuch der historischen Stätten [Handbook of Historical Places]). Stuttgart: Körner.

Eriksen, Thomas Hyland. 1992. *Us and Them in Modern Societies: Ethnicity and Nationalism in Trinidad, Mauritius and Beyond.* Oslo: Scandinavian University Press.

Eriksen, Thomas Hylland. 1993. *Ethnicity and Nationalism: Anthropological Perspectives.* London: Pluto Press.

Falęcki, Tomasz. 1997. *Jak rządzić Śląskiem? Polskie spory i opinie okresu międzywojennego* [How to Govern Silesia? Polish Disagreements and Opinions from the Interwar Period]. Kielce: Szumacher.

Faruga, Arkadiusz. 2004. *Czy Ślązacy zą narodem? Przemilczana historia Górnego Śląska* [Are the Szlozoks a Nation? Forgotten History of Upper Silesia]. Radzionków: Rococo.

Fazan, Mirosław. c. 1991. *Polskie życie kulturalne na Śląsku Cieszyńskim w latach 1842/48–1920* [Polish Cultural Life in Cieszyn Silesia in the Years 1842/48–1920]. Wrocław and Warsaw: Volumen.

Featherstone, Mike, ed. 1990. *Global Culture: Nationalism, Globalization and Modernity.* London: Sage.

Fiedler, Robert. 1987. *Tam jeszcze kęs polactwa. Wybór pism pastora z Międzyborza* [There Is Some Polishness Remaining There. The Selected Writings of the Pastor from Międzybórz] (ed. Gajda, Stanisław). Opole: Instytut Śląski.

Figowa, Felicja. 1966. Z działalności prasowej Adama Napieralskiego poza Górnym Śląskiem [From Adam Napieralski's Journalistic Activities Outside Upper Silesia] (pp. 13–30). *Kwartalnik Opolski.* No. 2.

Fischer-Wollpert, Rudolf (with additions on the Polish Church by Mazur, Zygmunt). 1990. *Leksykon papieży* [*Lexikon der Päpste.* 1985. Regensburg: Verlag Friedrich Pustet] [A Lexicon of the Popes]. Cracow: Znak.

Fishman, Joshua. 1996. Language and Nationalism (pp. 155–170). In Woolf, Stuart, ed., *Nationalism in Europe, 1815 to the Present: A Reader.* London and New York: Routledge.

Fras, Zbigniew. 1992. Problematyka śląska na łamach prasy galicyjskiej w okresie Wiosny Ludów [Silesian Matters in the Galician Press during the *Völkerfrühling*] (pp. 11–26). In Smołka, Leonard, ed., *Śląsk a czynniki zewnętrzne w 19–20 wieku* [Silesia and Outside Influences in the 19th and 20th Centuries]. Wrocław: Oficyna Wydawnicza Sudety and Oddział Wrocławskiego PTTK.

Frysztacki, Krzysztof, ed. 1998. *Polacy, Ślązacy, Niemcy. Studia nad stosunkami społeczno-kulturowymi na Śląsku Opolskim* [Poles, Silesians, Germans: Studies on the Socio-Cultural Relations in Opole Silesia]. Cracow: Universitas.

Fuchs, Konrad. 1990. *Aus Wirtschaft und Gesellschaft. Beiträge zur Geschichte Schlesiens vom 18. bis 20. Jahrhundert* [On Economy and Society: Contributions on Silesian History during the 18th–20th Centuries] (Ser.: Veröffentlichungen der Forschungsstelle Ostmitteleuropa und der Universität Dortmund, Reihe

A—Band 50 [Research Unit of East Central Europe at the University of Dortmund, subseries A, vol. 50]). Dortmund: Universität Dortmund.

Fuchs, Konrad. 1994. Vom deutschen Krieg zur deutschen Katastrophe (1866–1945) [From the German War to the German Catastrophe (1866–1945)] (pp. 554–692). In Conrads, Norbert, ed., *Schlesien* [Silesia] (Ser.: Deutsche Geschichte im Osten Europas [German History in Eastern Europe]). Berlin: Siedler.

Fulbrook, Mary. 1990. *A Concise History of Germany* (Ser.: Cambridge Concise Histories]. Cambridge: Cambridge University Press.

Fulbrook, Mary. 1991. *The Fontana History of Germany 1918–1990: The Divided Nation.* London: Fontana.

Gajda, Stanisław. 1987. Wstęp. Pastor Robert Fiedler z Międzyborza i jego polonofilska działalność [Introduction: Rev. Robert Fiedler from Międzybórz and His Pro-Polish Activities] (pp. 7–53). In Fiedler, Robert, *Tam jeszcze kęs polactwa. Wybór pism pastora z Międzyborza* [Some Polish Traces Still Survive There: A Choice from the Writings of the Pastor from Międzybórz]. Opole: Instytut Śląski.

Galos, Adam. 1992. Kardynał Kopp—postać fascynująca i kontrowersyjna [Cardinal Kopp—A Fascinating and Controversial Figure] (pp. 53–60). In Matwijowski, Krystyn, ed., *Ludzie Kościoła katolickiego* [People of the Catholic Church]. Wrocław: Centrum Badań Śląskoznawczych i Bohemistycznych, Uniwersytet Wrocławski.

Galos, Adam. 1996. Kopp Georg (Jerzy) (pp. 188–192). In Pater, Mieczysław, ed., *Słownik biograficzny katolickiego duchowieństwa śląskiego 19 i 20 wieku* [The Biographical Dictionary of Silesia's Catholic Clergy of the 19th and 20th Centuries]. Katowice: Księgarnia Św. Jacka.

Gawrecka, Maria. 1993. Problematyka narodowościowa Śląska austriackiego w latach 1742–1914 [The National Questions of Austrian Silesia in the Years 1742–1914] (pp. 61–74). *Studia Śląskie.* Vol. 52.

Gawrecki, Dan. 1992. Dějiny Slezska: Slezsko po roce 1742 [History of Silesia: Silesia after the Year 1742] (pp. 74–87). In Anon., ed., *Slezsko* [Silesia]. Opava: Matice Slezská.

Gawrecki, Dan. 1992a. Śląsk Cieszyński w okresie międzywojennym (1918–1938) [Cieszyn Silesia in the Interwar Period (1918–1938)]. In Anon., ed., *Zarys dziejów Śląska Cieszyńskiego* [An Outline of History of Cieszyn Silesia]. Ostrava and Prague: Komitet Czeskiej Administracji Terenowej.

Gawrecki, Dan. 1993. Śląskość w państwie Habsburgów [Silesianity in the State of the Habsburgs] (pp. 47–60). *Studia Śląskie.* Vol. 52.

Gawrecki, Dan et al., eds. 2003. *Dějiny Českého Slezska 1740–2000* [History of Czech Silesia, 1740–2000]. Opava: Sleszká univerzita v Opavě.

Geertz, Clifford. 1973. The Integrative Revolution: Primordial Sentiments and Civil Politics in the New States (pp. 255–310). In Geertz, Clifford, *The Interpretation of Cultures.* New York: Basic Books.

Gelles, Romuald. 1978. Położenie ludności Wrocławia w latach I wojny światowej [The Situation of the Wrocław Inhabitants during World War I] (pp. 253–279). *Studia Śląskie*. Vol. 34.

Gellner, Ernest. 1983. *Nations and Nationalism*. Oxford: Blackwell.

Gellner, Ernest. 1997. *Nationalism*. London: Weidenfeld and Nicolson.

Gerber, Michael R. 1994. *Österreichisch-Schlesien von 1742 bis zum Ende des Ersten Weltkrieges. Ein historischer Abriß* [Austrian Silesia from 1742 until the End of World War I: A Historical Outline]. Würzburg: Stiftung Kulturwerk Schlesien.

Gerlich, Marian Grzegorz. 1994. "Śląska krzywda"—przejaw zbiorowego poczucia poniżenia wśród górnośląskiej ludności rodzimej (okres międzywojenny) [The "Silesian Injustice": The Indication of the Group Feeling of Humiliation among the Indigenous Upper Silesian Population (in the Interwar Period)] (pp. 5–23). *Etnografia Polska*. Nos. 1–2.

Giddens, Anthony. 1985. *The Nation-State and Violence*. Cambridge: Polity.

Gill, David. 1984. Pits and Pitfalls: The Fate of Ondra Lysohorsky (pp. 27–44). *Scottish Slavonic Review*. No. 3, Autumn.

Girasoli, Nicola. 1995. *National Minorities: Who Are They?* Budapest: Akadémiai Kiadó.

Glensk, Joachim. 1992. Rozwój prasy lokalnej na obszarze styku dwóch narodowości (na przykładzie subregionu górnośląskiego) [Development of the Local Press at the Interface Between Two Nations (Exemplified by the Upper Silesian Region)] (pp. 12–32). In Glensk, Joachim, ed., *200 lat prasy polskiej na Śląsku* [200 Years of the Polish Press in Silesia]. Opole: Instytut Śląski.

Glensk, Joachim. 1995. Die oberschlesische Presse und die nationalpolnische Bewegung/Prasa górnośląska i polski ruch narodowy [The Upper Silesian Press and the Polish National Movement] (pp. 88–95). In Bździach, Klaus et al., eds., *'Wach auf, mein Herz, und denke'. Zur Geschichte der Beziehungen zwischen Schlesien und Berlin-Brandenburg von 1740 bis heute/ 'Przebudź się, serce moje, i pomyśl'. Przyczynek do historii stosunków między Śląskiem a Berlinem-Brandenburgią od 1740 do dziś* ['Wake Up, My Heart, and Think': A Contribution to the History of the Relations Between Silesia and Berlin-Brandenburg from 1740 until Today]. Berlin: Gesellschaft für interregionalen Kulturaustausch; and Opole: Instytut Śląski.

Golachowski, Stefan. 1950. *Materiały do statystyki narodowościowej Śląska Opolskiego z lat 1910–1939* [Sources Relating to the Nationalities Statistics of Opole Silesia in the Years 1910–1939]. (Ser.: Materiały do Dziejów Nowożytnych Ziem Zachodnich [Sources on the Modern History of the Western Lands], vol. 1). Poznań: Instytut Zachodni.

Golec, Józef, and Bojda, Stefania. 1993. *Słownik biograficzny Ziemi Cieszyńskiej* [The Biographical Dictionary of the Cieszyn Land], vol. 1. Cieszyn: published by the authors.

Görtemaker, Manfred. 1996. *Deutschland im 19. Jahrhundert. Entwicklungslinien* [Germany in the 19th Century: The Lines of Development]. Bonn: Bundeszentrale für politische Bildung.

Gove, Philip B., et al., eds. 1966. *Webster's Third New International Dictionary of the English Language. Unabridged, with Seven Language Dictionary* (vols. 1–3, continuous pagination). Springfield, Mass.: Merriam-Webster; and Chicago: Encyclopaedia Britannica.

Greenfeld, Liah. 1992. *Nationalism: Five Roads to Modernity.* Cambridge, MA: Harvard University Press.

Greenfeld, Liah. 2001. *The Spirit of Capitalism: Nationalism and Economic Growth.* Cambridge, MA: Harvard University Press.

Gregor, J. 1905. *Mapa Górnego Śląska z uwzględnieniem stosunków językowych, granic powiatowych i kolei żelaznych* [The Map of Upper Silesia with the Presentation of the Language Relations, County Borders and Railways]. Nicolai: K. Miarka.

Grobelný, Andělin. 1992. Śląsk Cieszyński od Wiosny Ludów do samodzielnych państw (1848–1918) [Cieszyn Silesia from the Revolution of 1848 up to the Time of Independent States (1848–1918)]. In Anon., ed., *Zarys dziejów Śląska Cieszyńskiego* [An Outline of History of Cieszyn Silesia]. Ostrava and Prague: Komitet Czeskiej Administracji Terenowej.

Gröschel, Bernhard. 1993. *Die Presse Oberschlesiens von den Anfängen bis zum Jahre 1945. Dokumentation und Strukturbeschreibung* [The Upper Silesian Press from the Beginnings Up to the Year 1945: Documentation and Description of Its Structure] (Ser.: Schriften der Stiftung Haus Oberschlesien, Landeskundliche Reihe [Publications of the Haus Oberschlesien, Series of Regional Studies], vol. 4). Berlin: Mann.

Gross, Herbert. 1995. *Bedeutende Oberschlesier* [Renowned Upper Silesians]. Dülmen: Laumann.

Großpietsch, Peter. 1994. *Die Grafschaft Glatz/Schlesien 1945/1946. Vom Kriegsende bis zur Vertreibung* [The Glatz Margravate, Silesia in 1945/1946: From the End of the War to the Expulsion]. Lüdenscheid: Zentralstellle Graftschaft Glatz/Schlesien.

Guibernau, Montserrat. 1996. *Nationalisms: The Nation-State and Nationalism in the Twentieth Century.* Cambridge: Blackwell.

Haardt, W., and Gustawicz, B. 1907. *Kozenna Atlas Szkolny* [Kozenna School Atlas]. Vienna: Edward Hölzl Geographisches Institut.

Hahm, Chaibong. 1997. The Clash of Civilizations Revisited: A Confucian Perspective (pp. 109–129). In Rashid, Salim, ed., *"The Clash of Civilizations"? Asian Responses.* Karachi: Oxford University Press.

Hajduk, Ryszard. 1982. Problem Polaków byłych żołnierzy armii niemieckiej na posiedzeniach Komisji Wojskowej Rady Narodowej Rzeczypospolitej Polskiej w Londynie [The Problem of the Poles, Former Soldiers from the German Army as Discussed at the Meetings of the Military Commission of the National Council of the Republic of Poland in London] (pp. 328–384). *Studia Śląskie*. Vol. 40.

Halecki, Oskar. 1950. *The Limits and Divisions of European History*. London: Sheed and Ward.

Hall, John, ed. 1998. *The State of the Nation: Ernest Gellner and the Theory of Nationalism*. Cambridge: Cambridge University Press.

Hammond-Tooke, W. D. 1975. Xhosa (11: 549–568). In Potgieter, W. D. J., et al., eds., *Standard Encyclpaedia of Southern Africa*. Cape Town: Nasou.

Hanich, Andrzej, and Bujak, Adam. 1985. *Góra Świętej Anny. Sanktuarium Diecezji Opolskiej* [Góra Świętej Anny: The Shrine of the Opole Diocese]. Aschaffenburg: Paul Pattloch Verlag.

Hanich, Andrzej. 1997. *Skorowidz nazw miejscowości diecezji opolskiej. Polsko-niemiecki i niemiecko-polski* [The Polish-German and German-Polish List of the Names of the Localities in the Opole Diocese]. Opole: Solpress.

Hanke, Rajmund. 1997. Zmarzlaki nie śpiewają [Those Who Get Cold Easily Do Not Sing] (pp. 66–68). *Śląsk*. No. 1, January.

Hann, Chris. 1995. Intellectuals, Ethnic Groups and Nations: Two Late-twentieth-century Cases (pp. 106–128). In Sukumar, Periwal, ed., *Notions of Nationalism*. Budapest: Central European University Press.

Hannan, Kevin. 1996. *Borders of Language and Identity in Teschen Silesia* (Ser.: Berkeley Insights in Linguistics and Semiotics, vol. 28). New York: Peter Lang.

Hargreaves-Mawdsley, W. N. 1968. *Everyman's Dictionary of European Writers* (Ser.: Everyman's Reference Library). London: Dent; and New York: Dutton.

Hastings, Adrian. 1997. *The Construction of Nationhood: Ethnicity, Religion and Nationalism*. Cambridge: Cambridge University Press.

Haugen, Einar. 1966. Dialect, Language, Nation (pp. 922–935). *American Anthropologist*. No. 68.

Hauser, Przemysław. 1991. *Śląsk między Polską, Czechosłowacją a spearatyzmem. Walka Niemiec o utrzymanie prowincji śląskiej w latach 1918–1919* [Silesia among Poland, Czechoslovakia and Separatism: Germany's Struggle to Retain the Province of Silesia in the Years 1918–1919] (Ser.: Historia [History], no. 168). Poznań: Wydawnictwo Naukowe UAM.

Hauser, Przemysław. 1994. Mniejszość niemiecka w Wielkopolsce i na Pomorzu w okresie II Rzeczypospolitej [The German Minority in Wielkopolska and Pomerania in the Second Republic]. In Sakson, Andrzej, ed., *Polska-Niemcy-mniejszość niemiecka w Wielkopolsce. Przeszłość i teraźniejszość* [Poland-Germany-the German Minority in Wielkopolska: The Past and the Present] (Ser.: Studium Niemcoznawcze Instytutu Zachodniego [German Studies Center of the Instytut Zachodni], no. 67). Poznań: Instytut Zachodni.

Hawranek, Franciszek. 1973. *Polityka Centrum w kwestii górnośląskiej po I wojnie światowej* [The Upper Silesian Policy of the Centrum after World War I]. Opole: Instytut Śląski.

Hawranek, Franciszek. 1982. Grenzschutz (p. 158). In Hawranek, Franciszek, et al., eds., *Encyklopedia Powstań Śląskich* [The Encyclopedia of the Silesian Uprisings]. Opole: Instytut Śląski.

Hawranek, Franciszek. 1982a. Komunistyczna Partia Górnego Śląska (Związek Spartakusa) [The Communist Party of Upper Silesia (the Spartacus Union)] (p. 232). In Hawranek, Franciszek, et al., eds., *Encyklopedia Powstań Śląskich* [The Encyclopedia of the Silesian Uprisings]. Opole: Instytut Śląski.

Hellriegel-Netzebandt, Friedrich, ed. 1996. *Deutscher National-Atlas: Schwerpunkte deutscher Geschichte im Kartenbild. Von der Frühzeit bis zur Gegenwart* [The German National Atlas: The Most Important Moments of German History in Maps. From the Earliest Times to the Present Day]. Munich: DSZ Verlag.

Hemmerle, Rudolf. 1992. *Sudetenland-Lexikon für alle, die das Sudetenland lieben* [The Lexicon of Sudetenland: For Everybody Who Loves Sudetenland]. Würzburg: Kraft.

Henzler, Marek. 1994. "Zawód ekscelencja" [Bishop: The Profession] (pp. 14/15). *Polityka*. No. 12, Mar. 19.

Hepa, Mikołaj. 1994. Wstęp [Foreword]. In Chrząszcz, Johannes, *Historia miast Pyskowice i Toszek* [A History of the Towns of Pyskowice and Toszek]. Pyskowice: Urząd Miasta.

Herod, Charles C. 1976. *The Nation in the History of Marxian Thought: The Concept of Nations with History and Nations without History*. The Hague: Martinus Nijhoff.

Herzig, Arno. 1994. "Die unruhige Provinz Schlesien zwischen 1806 und 1871" [The Troubled Province of Silesia between 1806 and 1871] (pp. 466–552). In Conrads, Norbert, ed., *Schlesien* [Silesia] (Ser.: Deutsche Geschichte im Osten Europas [German History in Eastern Europe]). Berlin: Siedler.

Herzig, Arno. 1995. Die Friedrich-Wilhelm-Universität Breslau/Uniwersytet Fryderyka Wilhelma we Wrocławiu (pp. 124–136). In Bździach, Klaus, et al., eds., *'Wach auf, mein Herz, und denke'. Zur Geschichte der Beziehungen zwischen Schlesien und Berlin-Brandenburg von 1740 bis heute/ 'Przebudź się, serce moje, i pomyśl'. Przyczynek do historii stosunków między Śląskiem a Berlinem-Brandenburgią od 1740 do dziś* ['Wake Up, My Heart, and Think': A Contribution to the History of the Relations Between Silesia and Berlin-Brandenburg from 1740 until Today]. Berlin: Gesellschaft für interregionalen Kulturaustausch; and Opole: Instytut Śląski.

hk. 1998. Ein Viertel weniger Spätaussiedler [One Quarter Less of *Spätaussiedlers*] (p. 14). *Schlesisches Wochenblatt*. No. 3, Jan. 18–22.

Hobsbawm, Eric John. 1990. *Nations and Nationalism since 1780: Programme, Myth, Reality*. Cambridge: Cambridge University Press.

Hobsbawm, Eric, and Ranger, Terence, eds. 1992. *The Invention of Tradition*. Cambridge: Cambridge University Press.

Hobsbawm, Eric. 1996. *The Age of Extremes*. New York: Vintage.

Honzák, František, Pečenka, Marek, and Vičková, Jitka. 1995. *Evropa v proměnach staletí* [Changes in Europe during the Centuries]. Prague: Libri.

Horowitz, Donald. 1985. *Ethnic Groups in Conflict*. Berkeley, CA: University of California Press.

Hosák, Ladislav, and Šrámek, Rudolf. 1970–1980. *Místní jména na Moravě a ve Slezsku* [Place Names in Moravia and Silesia] (2 vols.). Prague: ČSAV.

Hrabovec, Emilia. 1996. *Vertreibung and Abschub. Deutsche in Mähren 1945–1947* [Expulsion and Escorted Evacuation: Germans in Moravia 1945–1947] (Ser.: Wiener Osteuropa Studien [Viennese Studies on Eastern Europe], vol. 2). Frankfurt am Main: Peter Lang.

Hroch, Miroslav. 1985. *Social Preconditions of National Revival in Europe: A Comparative Analysis of the Social Composition of Patriotic Groups among the Smaller European Nations*. Cambridge: Cambridge University Press.

Hroch, Miroslav. 1994. *The Social Interpretation of Linguistic Demands in European National Movements* (Ser.: EUI Working Paper EUF no. 94/1). Florence: European University Institute.

Hytrek, Adolf. 1996. [Reprint of the 1879 ed.]. *Górny Szlązk pod względem obyczajów, języka i usposobienia ludności* [Upper Silesia in the Mirror of the Customs, Language and Temperament of Its Population]. Opole: Koło Związku Górnośląskiego w Opolu.

Jähnig, Bernhart, and Biewer, Ludwig. 1991. *Kleiner Atlas zur deutschen Territorialgeschichte* [A Small Atlas of German Territorial History]. Bonn: Kulturstiftung der deutschen Vertriebenen.

Jakóbczyk, Witold. 1989. *Przetrwać nad Wartą* [To Survive at the Warta River] (Ser.: Dzieje narodu i państwa polskiego [History of the Polish Nation and State], vols. 3–55). Warsaw: KAW.

Jakubíková, Renata. 1994. Vznik a počátky Matice opavské 1877–1884 [The Establishment and the Beginnings of the Matica opavská 1877–1884] (pp. 143–154). *Časopis slezkého zemského muzea: védy historické*, series B. no. 2, vol. 43.

Janicka-Krzywda, Urszula. 1988. *Poczet harnasi karpackich* [The Companion to the Carpathian Robber Leaders]. Warsaw: PTTK 'Kraj'.

Jarczak, Łucja. 1996. O śląskich nazwach osobowych [On Silesian Personal Names] (pp. 9–12). *Śląsk Opolski*. No. 1.

Johnson, Lonnie R. 1996. *Central Europe: Enemies, Neighbors, Friends*. New York: Oxford University Press.

Jonca, Karol. 1958. "Imigracja robotników polskich na Śląsk w końcu 19 i w początku 20 wieku" [Immigration of Polish Workers to Silesia at the Close of the 19th and at the Beginning of the 20th Century] (pp. 139–158). *Studia Śląskie*. Vol. 1.

Jonca, Karol. 1970. *Polityka narodowościowa III Rzeszy na Śląsku Opolskim w latach 1933–1940* [The National Policy of the Third Reich in Opole Silesia in the Years 1933–1940]. Katowice: Śląsk.

Kacíř, Petr. 1996. Národnostní problematika Těšínského Slezska druhé poloviny

19. a počátku 20. stol. v české historiografii [The National Problematic of Těšín Silesia in the Second Half of the 19th and at the Beginning of the 20th Centuries in Czech Historiography]. Paper presented at The Phenomenon of Modern Nationalism in Central Europe, conference organized by the Friedrich-Ebert Stiftung and the Freie Universität Berlin, Gliwice, Poland, October 9–11.

Kacíř, Petr. 1997. Problematyka narodowościowa na Śląsku Cieszyńskim w drugiej połowie 19 w. i na początku 20 w. w ocenie czeskiej historiografii [The National Problematic in Cieszyn Silesia in the Second Half of the 19th Century and at the Beginning of the 20th Century as Assessed by Czech Historiography] (pp. 52–60). In Linek, Bernard, et al., eds., *Fenomen nowoczesnego nacjonalizmu w Europie Środkowej* [The Phenomenon of Modern Nationalism in Central Europe]. Opole: Instytut Śląski.

Kaczmarek, Ryszard. 1993. Wojciech Korfanty w systemie politycznym Rzeszy Niemieckiej [Wojciech Korfanty in the Political System of the German Reich] (pp. 17–23). In Rott, Dariusz, and Skorwider, Eugeniusz, eds., *Wojciech Korfanty. Rozprawy i szkice historyczno-literackie* [Wojciech Korfanty: Historical and Literary Contributions and Sketches] (Ser.: Zeszyty Humanistyczne [Publications in Humanities], no. 1). Katowice: Pałac Młodzieży w Katowicach and Śląskie Towarzystwo Naukowo-Literackie.

Kaemmerer, M. 1988. *Ortsnamenverzeichnis der Ortschaften jenseits von der Oder und Neisse* [The List of Names of the Localities Beyond the Oder and the Neisse]. Leer: Rautenberg.

Kamenka, Eugene, ed. 1976. *Nationalism: The Nature and Evolution of an Idea.* London: Edward Arnold.

Kamusella, Tomasz. 1996. Geneza i anatomia wysiedleń przeprowadzonych na Górnym Śląsku w końcowym stadium i po zakończeniu 2 wojny światowej [The Origins and Anatomy of the Ethnic Cleansing Conducted in Upper Silesia at the Close of and after World War II] (pp. 112–129). In Nycz, Edward, ed. *Historyczne i współczesne problemy miasta i jego mieszkańców* [The Historical and Current Problems of the Town and Its Inhabitants]. Opole: Instytut Śląski.

Kamusella, Tomasz. 1997. Niemcy i Polacy w oczach Górnoślązaków [The Germans and the Poles as Perceived by the Upper Silesians] (pp. 149–158). *Kultura i Społeczeństwo.* No. 1.

Kamusella, Tomasz. 1998. Kreol górnośląski [The Upper Silesian Creole] (pp. 73–84). *Kultura i Społeczenstwo.* No. 1.

Kamusella, Tomasz. 1998a. The Dynamics of the Policies of Ethnic Cleansing in Silesia in the Nineteenth and Twentieth Centuries (pp. 21–23). *Research Support Scheme Network Chronicle.* No. 6.

Kamusella, Tomasz. 2001. Language as an Instrument of Nationalism in Central Europe (pp. 235–252). *Nations and Nationalism.* No. 2, Apr.

Kamusella, Tomasz. 2001a. Conference Report: Nations and Their Borders:

Changing Identities in Upper Silesia in the Modern Age (pp. 400–407). *German History*. No. 3.

Kamusella, Tomasz. 2003. The Deictic Aspect of the Ideology of Nationalism as a Factor Contributing to the Creation of the Other (pp. 55–80). In Mitrofanova, Anastasia, ed., *Religia v mezhdunarodnykh otnosheniakh: za peredelami 'mezhkonfesionalnogo dialoga'* [Religion in International Relations: Divisions and the Inter-Confessional Dialog]. Moscow: Diplomaticheskaia akademia MID Rosii Kafedra vneshnei politiki mezhdunarodnykh otnoshenii.

Kamusella, Tomasz. 2004. On the Similarity Between the Concepts of Nation and Language (pp. 107–112). *Canadian Review of Studies in Nationalism*. Nos. 1–2.

Kann, Robert A., and David, Zdeněk V. 1984. *The Peoples of the Eastern Habsburg Lands, 1526–1918*. Seattle: University of Washington Press.

Karski, Sigmund. 1996. *Albert (Wojciech) Korfanty*. Dülmen: Laumann.

Karwat, Krzysztof. 1997. Amerykańska droga Korfantych [The Road the Korfantys Followed to America] (p. 9). *Dziennik Zachodni*. No. 154, Jul. 4.

Kedourie, Elie. 1960. *Nationalism*. London: Hutchinson.

Kemilainen, Aira. 1964. *Nationalism: Problems Concerning the Word, Concept and Classification*. Jyväskylä: Kustantajat Publishers.

Kennedy, Paul. 1989. *The Rise and Fall of the Great Powers: Economic Change and Military Conflict from 1500 to 2000*. New York: Vintage Books.

Kinder, Hermann, and Hilgemann, Werner. 1978. *The Penguin Atlas of World History* [*dtv-Atlas zur Weltgeschichte*. 1964/1966. Munich: dtv] (2 vols.). Harmondsworth, Middlesex: Penguin Books.

King, Jeremy. 2002. *Budweisers into Czechs and Germans: A Local History of Bohemian Politics, 1848–1948*. Princeton, NJ: Princeton University Press.

Kinsky, Ferdinand. 1995. *Föderalismus: Ein gesamteuropäisches Modell* [Federalism: A Model for United Europe]. Bonn: Europa Union Verlag.

Kinsky, Ferdinand. 1995a. *Federalism: A Global Theory*. Nice: Presses d'Europe.

Klaußmann, Anton Oskar. 1996. *Górny Śląsk przed laty* [Upper Silesia of the Past] (Polish translation of *Oberschlesien vor 55 Jahren* [Upper Silesia 55 Years Ago]. 1911. Berlin). Katowice: Muzeum Historii Katowic.

Klein, Edmund. 1972. Problem antypolskiego ustawodastwa wyjątkowego na Górnym Śląsku w latach 1914–1919 [The Problem of the Special Anti-Polish Legislation in Upper Silesia in the Years 1914–1919] (pp. 11–51). *Studia Śląskie*. Vol. 22.

Klemmer, Clemens. 1993. 80 Jahre Jahrhunderthalle in Breslau (1913–1993) [80 Years of the Jahrhunderthalle in Breslau (1913–1993)] (pp. 1–5). *Schlesischer Kulturspiegel*. Nos. 2–3.

Kłoczkowski, Jerzy. 1998. *Młodsza Europa* [Younger Europe]. Warsaw: PIW.

Kłosek, Eugeniusz. 1994. *'Swoi' i 'obcy' na Górnym Śląsku od 1945 roku* ['Us' and 'Them' in Upper Silesia after 1945] (Ser.: Ethnologica, vol. 1). Wrocław: Wydawnictwo Uniwersytetu Wrocławskiego.

Kłoskowska, Antonina. 1996. *Kultury narodowe u korzeni* [National Cultures at the Grass-Roots Level]. Warsaw: PWN.

Knie, J. G. 1845. *Alphabetisch-statistisch-topographischer Übersicht der Dörfer, Flekken, Städte und andere Orte der Königliche Preußische Provinz Schlesien...* [The Alphabetic-Statistical-Topographic Overview of the Villages, Settlements, Towns and Other Localities in the Royal Prussian Province of Silesia...]. Breslau: Druck und Verlag von Graß, Barth und Comp.

Knop, Alois. 1967. *Dějiny českého jazyka ve Slezsku a na Ostravsku* [History of the Czech Language in Silesia and in the Ostrava Land]. Ostrava: Socialistická akademie.

Knop, Alois. 1992. K dějinám českého jazyka ve Slezsku [On History of the Czech Language in Silesia] (pp. 109–114). In Anon., ed., *Slezsko* [Silesia]. Opava: Matice Slezská.

Köhler, Joachim. 1996. *Bistum Breslau: Reformation und Katholische Reform* [The Breslau Diocese: Reformation and the Catholic Reform]. Kehl: Echo-Buchverlags.

Köhler, Joachim. 1997. *Bistum Breslau: Neuzeit 1740–1945* [The Breslau Diocese: The Modern Times 1740–1945] (Ser.: Bistum Breslau [The Breslau Diocese], vol. 3). Münster: Apostolischer Visitator der Priester und Gläubigen aus dem Erzbistum Breslau.

Kohn, Hans. 1944. *The Idea of Nationalism: A Study in Its Origins and Background.* New York: Macmillan.

Kohn, Hans. 1962. *The Age of Nationalism: The First Era of Global History.* New York: Harper and Row.

Kohn, Hans. 1965. *Nationalism: Its Meaning and History.* New York: Van Nostrand.

Kokot, Józef. 1973. *Problemy narodowościowe na Śląsku od 10 do 20 wieku* [National Problems in Silesia from the 10th to 20th Centuries]. Opole: Instytut Śląski.

Kolejka, J. 1956. Moravský pakt z roku 1905 [The Moravian Agreement of 1905] (pp. 590–615). *Československý časopis historycký.*

Kołłątaj, Hugo. 1990 [1808]. Musi być poddźwigniona na nowo Polska [Poland Has to Be Reestablished] (pp. 41–43). In Wrzesiński, Wojciech, ed., *W stronę Odry i Bałtyku. Wybór źródeł (1795–1950)* [Toward the Odra and the Baltic: A Choice of Sources (1795–1950)] (vol. 1: O ziemię Piastów i polski lud (1795–1918) [In the Struggle for the Piast Lands and the Polish People (1795–1918)], ed., Kułak, Teresa). Wrocław and Warsaw: Volumen.

Konrad, Gyorge. 1986. Is the Dream of Central Europe Still Alive? (pp. 109–122). *Cross Currents: A Yearbook of Central European Culture.* Vol. 5.

Kopaliński, Władysław. 1991. *Słownik mitów i tradycji kultury* [The Dictionary of Myths and Cultural Tradition]. Warsaw: PIW.

Kopeć, Eugeniusz. 1980. Z zagadnień integracji śląskich kresów Rzeczypospolitej [On the Problematic of the Integration of the Silesian Periphery of the Republic of Poland] (pp. 7–48). In Chlebowczyk, Józef, ed., *Z problemów integracji i uni-fikacji II Rzeczypospolitej* [On the Problematic of the Integration and Unification of the Second Republic of Poland]. Katowice: Uniwersytet Śląski.

Kopeć, Eugeniusz. 1981. *Południowo-zachodnie kresy Rzeczypospolitej 1918–1939. Społeczne warunki integracji* [The Southwestern Periphery of the Republic of Poland 1918–1939: The Social Conditions of Integration]. Katowice: Uniwersytet Śląski.

Kopiec, Jan. 1991. *Dzieje Kościoła katolickiego na Śląsku Opolskim* [A History of the Catholic Church in Opole Silesia] (Ser.: Encyklopedia wiedzy o Śląsku [The Encyclopedia of Knowledge on Silesia]). Opole: Instytut Śląski.

Kopiec, Jan, ed. 1997. *Biskupowi Józefowi Nathanowi w hołdzie* [Commemorating Bishop Józef Nathan]. Opole: Święty Krzyż.

Koprowski, Jan. 1995. Życie i twórczość Józefa Eichendorffa [The Life and Writings of Józef Eichendorff] (pp. 11–18). In Koprowski, Jan, ed., *Józef Eichendorff. Ostatni rycerz romantyzmu* [Józef Eichendorff: The Last Knight of Romanticism]. Warsaw: Elipsa.

Kořalka, Jiří. 1995. Tscheschen und Deutsche im Alten Reich und in der Habsbur-germonarchie [The Czechs and the Germans in the Holy Roman Empire and in the Habsburg Monarchy] (pp. 13–29). In Storch, Dietmar, ed., *Tschechen, Slowaken und Deutsche. Nachbarn in Europa* [The Czechs, the Slovaks and the Germans: Neighbors in Europe]. Hannover: Niedersächsiche Landeszentrale für politische Bildung.

Korfanty, Eugenia. 1999. Wspomnienie rodzinne o Wojciechu Korfantym [A Family Recollection on Wojciech Korfanty] (pp. 52–53). *Śląsk*. No. 3, Mar.

Körner, Günther. 1981. *Selbstschutz in Oberschlesien 1921: Bilddokumentation* [The Self-Defense Troops in Upper Silesia 1921: A Pictorial Documentation]. Dülmen: Laumann.

Kosler, Alois M. 1929. *Die preußische Volksschulpolitik in Oberschlesien 1742–1848* [The Prussian Elementary Education Policies 1742–1848]. Breslau: Priebatsch.

Kosman, Marceli. 1989. *Litwa pierwotna. Mity, legendy, Fakty* [Primordial Lithuania: Myths, Legends, Facts]. Warsaw: Iskry.

Kossakowska-Jarosz, Krystyna. 1994. *Polskie kalendarze górnośląskie* [Polish Calendars in Upper Silesia]. Opole: WSP.

Kotzian, Ortfried. 1991. *Die Sudetendeutschen. Eine Volksgruppe im Herzen Europas* [Sudeten Germans: An Ethnic Group in the Heart of Europe] (Ser. Kulturelle Arbeitshefte [Working Papers on Cultural Problematic], vol. 16). Bonn: Bund der Vertriebenen.

Koziarski, Stanisław M. 1993. *Sieć kolejowa Polski w latach 1842–1918* [The Polish Railway Network in the Years 1842–1918]. Opole: Instytut Śląski.

Kozłowski, Jerzy. 1994. Niemcy w Poznańskiem do 1918 r. [Germans in the Province of Poznań up to the Year 1918]. In Sakson, Andrzej, ed., *Polska-Niemcy-*

mniejszość niemiecka w Wielkopolsce. Przeszłość i teraźniejszość [Poland-Germany-the German Minority in Wielkopolska: The Past and the Present] Ser.: Studium Niemcoznawcze Instytutu Zachodniego [German Studies Center of the Instytut Zachodni], no. 67). Poznań: Instytut Zachodni.

Kracik, Jan. 1996. 'Plama na czole'. Mija 150 lat od rzezi galicyjskiej ['[Blood]stain on the Forehead': 150 Years Have Elapsed since the Galician Massacre] (p. 8). *Tygodnik Powszechny*. No. 2, Feb. 18.

Kraszewski, Józef Ignacy. 1990 [1869–1870]. Konstatacje o ludziach i ziemi polskiej pod panowaniem pruskim [Thoughts on the Polish People and Land under Prussian Rule] (pp. 80–87). In Wrzesiński, Wojciech, ed., *W stronę Odry i Bałtyku. Wybór źródeł (1795–1950)* [Toward the Odra and the Baltic: A Choice of Sources (1795–1950] (vol. 1: O ziemię Piastów i polski lud (1795–1918) [In the Struggle for the Piast Lands and the Polish People (1795–1918)], ed. Kulak, Teresa). Wrocław and Warsaw: Volumen.

Krause, Adolf. 1995. Beuthen (pp. 20–25). In Stoob, Heinz, and Johanek, Peter, eds., *Schlesisches Städtebuch* [Book of Silesian Towns] (Ser.: Deutsches Städtebuch. Handbuch städtischer Geschichte [Book of German Towns: A Handbook of Town History], vol. 1: Schlesien [Silesia]). Stuttgart: Kohlhammer.

Krejci, J., and Velimsky, V. 1981. *Ethnic and Political Nations in Europe*. London: Croom Helm.

Krige, Eileen J. 1975. Zulu (XI: 596–601). In Potgieter, W. D. J. et al., eds., *Standard Encyclopaedia of Southern Africa*. Cape Town: Nasou.

Kroutvor, Josef. 1998. *Europa Środkowa: Anegdota i historia* [Central Europe: Anecdote and History, a translation from the Czech original]. Izabelin: Świat Literacki.

Krzyżanowski, Lech. 1996. Kościół katolicki i inne związki wyznaniowe [The Catholic Church and the Churches of Other Confessions] (pp. 101–129). In Serafin, Franciszek, ed., *Województwo Śląskie (1922–1939). Zarys monograficzny* [The Silesian Voivodeship (1922–1939): A Monographic Outline]. Katowice: Wydawnictwo Uniwersytetu Śląskiego.

Kuhn, Walter. 1977. Skotschau (p. 508). In Weczerka, Hugo, ed., *Schlesien* [Silesia] (Ser.: Handbuch der Historischen Stätten [Handbook of Historical Places]. Stuttgart: Körner.

Kuhn, Walter. 1977a. Bielitz (pp. 27–30). In Weczerka, Hugo, ed., *Schlesien* [Silesia] (Ser.: Handbuch der Historischen Stätten [Handbook of Historical Places]. Stuttgart: Körner.

Kulak, Teresa, ed. 1990. *O ziemię Piastów i polski lud (1795–1918)* [In the Struggle for the Piast Lands and the Polish People (1795–1918)] (Ser.: Wrzesiński, Wojciech, ed. *W stronę Odry i Bałtyku. Wybór źródeł (1795–1950)* [Toward the Odra and the Baltic: A Choice of Sources (1795–1950)], vol. 1). Wrocław and Warsaw: Volumen.

Kulak, Teresa. 1993. Wizerunek Ślązaka w opisach etnograficznych i relacjach z podróży po Śląsku w 2 połowie 19 w. [The Picture of the Silesian in Ethnographic Descriptions and Travel Accounts from the Second Half of the Nineteenth Century.] (pp. 99–116). In Wrzesiński, Wojciech, ed., *Wokół stereotypów Niemców i Polaków* [On the Stereotypical Representations of the Germans and the Poles] (Ser.: Historia [History], vol. 114). Wrocław: Wydawnictwo Uniwersytetu Wrocławskiego.

Kundera, Milan. 1984. The Tragedy of Central Europe. *New York Review of Books.* Apr. 26.

Kuper, Adam. 1988. *The Invention of Primitive Society: Transformations of an Illusion.* London: Routledge.

Kwaśniewski, Krzysztof. 1997. Czy istnieje narodowość śląska? [Does the Silesian Nationality Exist?] (pp. 129–151). *Sprawy Narodowściowe.* Vol. 6, no. 1 (10).

Kwiatek, Aleksander. 1982. Korfanty, Wojciech (pp. 241–243). In Hawranek, Franciszek, et al., eds., *Encyklopedia Powstań Śląskich* [Encyclopedia of the Silesian Uprisings]. Opole: Instytut Śląski.

Kwiatek, Jolanta. 1991. *'Eleusis' na Górnym Śląsku w latach 1903–1914* [The Eleusis in Upper Silesia in the Years 1903–1914]. Opole: Instytut Śląski.

Kwiatek, Alesksander. 1991a. *Spór o kierunek działań narodowych na Górnym Śląsku (1918–1921)* [The Contestation Over the Direction of National Activities in Upper Silesia (1918–1921)]. Opole: Instytut Śląski.

Kwiatek, Jolanta. 1992. Księża misjonarze w Krakowie a Górny Śląsk na przełomie 19 i 20 wieku [Missionary Priests in Cracow and Their Relations with Upper Silesia at the Turn of the 19th and 20th Centuries] (pp. 80–99). *Kwartalnik Opolski.* Nos. 3–4.

Labocha, Janina. 1997. *Polsko-czeskie pogranicze na Śląsku Cieszyńskim. Zagadnienia językowe* [The Polish-Czech Borderland in Cieszyn Silesia: The Linguistic Problematic]. Cracow: Księgarnia Akademicka.

Lakoff, George, and Johnson, Mark. 1980. *Metaphors We Live By.* Chicago: University of Chicago Press.

Lang, Waldemar. 1989. Deutsche Polenbegeisterung im Vormärz [German Enthusiasm for the Polish Cause in the Period 1830–1848] (pp. 372–395). In Häring, Ludwig, Kühnel, Horst, and Hansel, Paul, eds., *Die Deutschen und ihre östlichen Nachbarn,* vol. 2: *Deutsche und Polen* [The Germans and Their Eastern Neighbors, vol. 2: The Germans and the Poles] (Ser.: Akademiebericht no. 141). Dillingen: Akademie für Lehrerfortbildung; and Munich: Haus des deutschen Ostens.

Latoszek, M., ed. 1990. *Kaszubi. Monografia socjologiczna* [The Kashubs: A Sociological Monograph]. Rzeszów: TNOiK.

Łęcki, K., et al. 1992. *Świat społeczny Ślązaków. Rekonstrukcja treści świadomości społecznej* [The Social World of the Silesians: A Reconstruction of the Contents of the Social Consciousness]. Katowice: Uniwersytet Śląski.

Lemberg, Hans. 1995. Tschechen, Slowaken und Deutsche in der Tschecho-slowakischen Republik 1918–1938 [The Czechs, the Slovaks, and the Germans in the Czechoslovak Republic] (pp. 30–49). In Storch, Dietmar, ed., *Tschechen, Slowaken und Deutsche. Nachbarn in Europa* [The Czechs, the Slovaks and the Germans: Neighbors in Europe]. Hannover: Niedersächsiche Landeszentrale für politische Bildung.

Łepkowski, Józef. 1990 [1849]. Wiadomości o Śląsku [Information on Silesia] (pp. 67–70). In Wrzesiński, Wojciech, ed., *W stronę Odry i Bałtyku. Wybór źródeł (1795–1950)* [Toward the Odra and the Baltic: A Choice of Sources (1795–1950] (vol. 1: O ziemię Piastów i polski lud (1795–1918) [In the Struggle for the Piast Lands and the Polish People (1795–1918)], ed. Kulak, Teresa). Wrocław and Warsaw: Volumen.

Lesiuk, Wiesław. 1973. *Rady robotnicze, żołnierskie, chłopskie i ludowe w Rejencji Opolskiej w latach 1918–1919* [The Workers', Soldiers', Peasants' and People's Councils in the Opole Regency in the Years 1918–1919]. Opole: Instytut Śląski.

Lesiuk, Wiesław. 1982. Rada Ludowa [The People's Council] (pp. 467–468). In Hawranek, Franciszek, et al., eds., *Encyklopedia Powstań Śląskich* [The Encyclopedia of the Silesian Uprisings]. Opole: Instytut Śląski.

Lewaszkiewicz, Tadeusz. 1995. Łużyczanie wobec idei wspólnego języka słowiańskiego [The Attitude of the Sorbs Toward the Notion of a Common Slavic Language] (pp. 101–110). In Jaworski, Tomasz, and Ostrowski, Mieczysław, eds., *Łużyce w nowożytnych i najnowszych dziejach Europy Środkowej* [Lusatia in Modern and the Latest History of Central Europe] (Ser.: Zielonogórskie Studia Łużyckie [Zielona Góra Lusatian Studies] no. 1)]. Zielona Góra: Verbum.

Lewis, Bernard. 1999. *The Multiple Identities of the Middle East*. New York: Schocken.

Liebermann, Philip. 1994. The Origins and Evolution of Language (pp. 108–132). In Ingold, Tim, ed., *Companion Encyclopedia of Anthropology*. London: Routledge.

Linek, Bernard. 1993. Oddźwięk polemik wokół sposobu rozwiązania problemu ludności śląskiej na Opolszczyźnie w latach 1955–1957 w ówczesnej prasie wojewódzkiej [The Disagreement on How to Solve the Problem of the Silesian Population in the Opole Land in the Years 1955–1957, as Reflected in the Contemporary Voivodeship Press] (pp. 287–302). *Studia Śląskie*. Vol. 52.

Linek, Bernard. 1997. '*Odniemczanie' województwa śląskiego w latach 1945–1950 (w świetle materiałów wojewódzkich)* ['De-Germanization' of the Silesian Voivodeship in the Years 1945–1950 (in the Light of the Voivodeship Archival Materials)]. Opole: Instytut Śląski.

Lis, Jerzy. 1988. *Henryk Sienkiewicz przeciw* Drang nach Osten [Henryk Sienkiewicz against the *Drang nach Osten*]. Katowice: Stowarzyszenia 'Wisła-Odra'.

Lis, Michał. 1993. *Górny Śląsk. Zarys dziejów do I wojny światowej* [Upper Silesia: An Outline of Its History until World War I]. Opole: Instytut Śląski.

Lompa, Józef. c. 1996. [Reprint of the 1821 ed.]. *Krótkie wyobrażenie historyi Szląska* [A Short Outline of the History of Silesia]. Zabrze: Wydawnictwo Muzeum Miejskiego w Zabrzu.

Lubos, Arno. 1974. *Geschichte der Literatur Schlesiens* [History of Silesian Literature] (vol. 3). Munich: Bergstadtverlag Wilhelm Gottlieb Korn.

Lüer, Jörg. 1995. Die Oberschlesier im preußisch-deutschen Denken/Górnoślązacy w myśli prusko-niemieckiej (pp. 79–87). In Bździach, Klaus et al., eds., *'Wach auf, mein Herz, und denke'. Zur Geschichte der Beziehungen zwischen Schlesien und Berlin-Brandenburg von 1740 bis heute/ 'Przebudź się, serce moje, i pomyśl'. Przyczynek do historii stosunków między Śląskiem a Berlinem-Brandenburgią od 1740 do dziś* ['Wake Up, My Heart, and Think': A Contribution to the History of the Relations Between Silesia and Berlin-Brandenburg from 1740 until Today]. Berlin: Gesellschaft für interregionalen Kulturaustausch; and Opole: Instytut Śląski.

Łukasiewicz, Juliusz. 1988. *Początki cywilizacji przemysłowej na ziemiach polskich* [The Beginning of the Industrial Civilization in the Polish Lands] (Ser.: Dzieje narodu i państwa polskiego [History of the Polish Nation and State], vol. 3, part 50). Warsaw: KAW.

Łysohorsky, Óndra [pen name of Ervín Goj]. 1934. *Spiwajuco piaść* [The Singing Fist]. Prague: Družstevní práce.

Łysohorsky, Óndra. 1998. *Dorf wo Karpaten an Sudeten rühren. Lachische Gedichte* [The Village where the Carpathians Meet the Sudeten Mountains: Lachian Poetry] (introduced by Gurlich, Rudolf) (Ser.: Poesis Ethnica, no. 11). Ulm: Gerhard Hesse Verlag.

Macartney, Carlie Aylmer, Barany, Georg, et al. 1992. Hungary (vol. 20: 693–714). In McHenry, Robert, et al., eds., *The New Encyclopaedia Britannica*. Chicago: Encyclopaedia Britannica, Inc.

McCrone, David. 1998. *The Sociology of Nationalism*. London: Routledge.

Machray, Robert. 1945. *The Problem of Upper Silesia*. London: George Allen and Unwin Ltd.

Madajczyk, Piotr. 1996. *Przyłączenie Śląska Opolskiego do Polski 1945–1948* [The Incorporation of Opole Silesia to Poland 1945–1948]. Warsaw: ISP PAN.

Magocsi, Paul Robert. 1978. *The Shaping of a National Identity: Subcarpathian Rus', 1848–1948* (Ser.: Harvard Ukrainian Series). Cambridge, MA: Harvard University Press.

Magocsi, Paul Robert. 1995. *Historical Atlas of East Central Europe* (Ser.: A History of East Central Europe, vol. 1). Seattle: University of Washington Press.

Majewicz, Alfred F. 1989. *Języki świata i ich klasyfikowanie* [The Languages of the World and Their Classification]. Warsaw: PWN.

Malicki, Jan. 1987. *Początki sporów o polskość i niemieckość Śląska* [The Origins of the Arguments on Polishness and Germanness of Silesia]. Katowice: Muzeum Śląskie.

Malinowski, Lucjan. 1990 [1872]. Listy z podróży etnograficznej po Śląsku [Letters from an Ethnographic Travel in Silesia] (pp. 90–94). In Wrzesiński, Wojciech, ed., *W stronę Odry i Bałtyku. Wybór źródeł (1795–1950)* [Toward the Odra and the Baltic: A Choice of Sources (1795–1950) (vol. 1: O ziemię Piastów i polski lud (1795–1918) [In the Struggle for the Piast Lands and the Polish People (1795–1918)], ed. Kulak, Teresa). Wrocław and Warsaw: Volumen.

Mandziuk, Józef. 1996. Bonczyk (Boncek, Bontzek), Norbert (pp. 42–44). In Pater, Mieczysław, ed., *Słownik biograficzny katolickiego duchowieństwa śląskiego 19 i 20 wieku* [The Biographical Dictionary of Silesia's Catholic Clergy of the 19th and 20th Centuries]. Katowice: Księgarnia Św. Jacka.

Martuszewski, Edward. 1974. *Polscy i nie polscy: szkice z historii Mazur i Warmii* [Polish and Not Polish: Sketches from the History of Mazury and Warmia]. Olsztyn: WSP.

Matern, Robert. 1998. Visitatoren sollen in Bischofkonferenz bleiben [The Visitators Should Remain in the Conference of the Bishops] (p. 7). *Deutscher Ostdienst*. No. 3, Jan. 16.

Mazrui, Ali A., and Tidy, M. 1984. *Nationalism and New States in Africa*. London: Heinemann.

Mendel, Edward. 1987. *Dzień powszedni na Śląsku Opolskim w czasie I wojny światowej* [The Workday in Opole Silesia during World War I] (Ser.: Encyklopedia wiedzy o Śląsku [The Encyclopedia of Knowledge on Silesia]). Opole: Instytut Śląski.

Miarka, Karol. 1984. [Reprint of the 1865 ed.]. *Głos wołającego na puszczy górnośląskij* [The Voice in the Silesian Wilderness] (introduction by Brożek, Andrzej). Katowice: Śląsk.

Michalkiewicz, Stanisław, ed. 1970. *Historia Śląska* [History of Silesia] (vol. 2: 1763–1850, part 2: 1807–1850). Wrocław, Warsaw and Cracow: Ossolineum.

Michalkiewicz, Stanisław, ed. 1976. *Historia Śląska* [History of Silesia] (vol. 3: 1850–1918, part 1: 1850–1890). Wrocław, Warsaw and Cracow: Ossolineum.

Michalkiewicz, Stanisław, ed. 1985. *Historia Śląska* [History of Silesia] (Vol. 3: 1850–1918, Part 2: 1890–1918). Wrocław, Warsaw and Cracow: Ossolineum.

Michna, Ewa. 1995. *Łemkowie - grupa etniczna czy naród?* [The Lemkos: An Ethnic Group or a Nation?]. Cracow: Nomos.

Migdał, Stefan. 1965. Niektóre właściwości antypolskiej polityki pruskiej na Górnym Śląsku w początkowym okresie imperializmu [Some of the Features of Prussia's anti-Polish Policies in the Initial Period of Imperialism] (pp. 61–75). *Kwartalnik Opolski*. No. 3.

Migdał, Stefan. 1967. Położenie mas pracujących rejencji opolskiej w latach 1914–1918 [The Situation of the Working Masses in the Opole Regency in the Years 1914–1918]. *Kwartalnik Opolski*. No. 3.

Miles, Robert. 1989. *Racism*. London: Routledge.

Miłosz, Czesław. 1989. Central European Attitudes. In Schöpflin, G., and Wood, N., eds., *In Search of Central Europe*. Totowa, NJ: Barnes and Noble.

Minahan, James. 2002. *Encyclopedia of the Stateless Nations: Ethnic and National Groups around the World* (4 vols.). Westport, CN: Greenwood Press.

Miś, Engelbert. 1969. Losy i rola siołkowiczan w Brazylii ze sczególnym uwzględnieniem działalności Sebastiana Edmunda Wosia-Saporskiego [Life and Role of the Inhabitants of Siołkowice in Brazil with the Special Focus on the Activities of Sebastian Woś-Saporski]. In Anon., ed., *100 lat Polonii brazylijskiej* [Centenary of Polish Settlement in Brazil]. Opole: Instytut Śląski.

Mołdawa, Taeusz. 1991. *Ludzie władzy 1944–1991* [The People Who Ruled 1944–1991]. Warsaw: PWN.

Molik, Witold. 1993. The Elites of the Polish National Movement in Prussian Poland in the Late 19th and Early 20th Centuries (pp. 61–80). *Polish Western Affairs*. No. 2.

Morby, John E. 1994. *The Wordsworth Handbook of Kings and Queens*. Ware, Hertfordshire: Wordsworth.

Morley, C. 1952. The European Significance of the November Uprising (pp. 407–416). *Journal of Central European Affairs*. No. 2.

Mosse, George L. 1975. *The Nationalization of the Masses: Political Symbolism and Mass Movements in Germany from the Napoleonic Wars through the Third Reich*. Ithaca: Cornell University Press.

Mrass, Peter. 1995. *Mapy Górnego Śląska/Landkarten Oberschlesiens* [The Maps of Upper Silesia]. Opole: Biblioteka Publiczna; and Ratingen-Hösel: Stiftung Haus Oberschlesien.

Mroczko, Marian. 1994. *Ziemie dzielnicy pruskiej w polskich koncepcjach i działalności politycznej 1864–1939* [The Lands of the Prussian Partition in the Polish Conceptions of and in Political Activity 1864–1939]. Gdańsk: Marpress.

Muirhead, Findlay. 1908. Prussia (8: 461–467). In *Chambers's Encyclopaedia: A Dictionary of Universal Knowledge*. London and Edinburgh: Chambers; and Philadelphia: Lippincott.

Mykita-Glensk, Czesława. 1988. *Polski teatr amatorski na Górnym Śląsku w 19 stuleciu* [The Polish Amateur Theater in Upper Silesia in the 19th Century] (Ser.: Wszechnica Muzeum Śląskiego [Academy of the Silesian Museum]). Katowice: Muzeum Śląskie.

Myška, Milan, Dokoupil, Lumír, and Barteček, Ivo, eds. 1993. *Biografický slovník Slezska a severní Moravy* [The Biographical Dictionary of Silesia and Northern Moravia] (vol. 1). Opava: OPTYS; and Ostrava: Ostravská univerzita.

Myška, Milan, and Dokoupil, Lumír, eds. 1994. *Biografický slovník Slezska a severní Moravy* [The Biographical Dictionary of Silesia and Northern Moravia] (vol. 2). Opava: OPTYS; and Ostrava: Ostravská univerzita.

Myśliński, Jerzy. 1986. Ludowy trybun [The Tribune of the People] (pp. 5–32). In

Daszyński, Ignacy, *Teksty* (Texts) (Ser.: Polska myśl polityczna [Polish Political Thought]). Warsaw: Czytelnik.

Myszor, Jerzy. 1996. Adamski, Stanisław (pp. 6–11). In Pater, Mieczysław, ed., *Słownik biograficzny katolickiego duchowieństwa śląskiego 19 i 20 wieku* [The Biographical Dictionary of Silesia's Catholic Clergy of the 19th and 20th Centuries]. Katowice: Księgarnia Św. Jacka.

Nabert, Heinrich. 1994 [1890]. *Die Verbreitung der Deutschen in Europa, 1844–1888, mit zwei Karten* [The Spread of the Germans in Europe, 1844–1888, with Two Maps] (Ser.: Schriftenreihe des Bundes für deutsche Schrift und Sprache [Series of the Association for the German Writing and Language], vol. 12). Ahlhorn: Bund für deutsche Schrift und Sprache.

Namier, Lewis. 1992 [1946]. *The Revolution of the Intellectuals*. Oxford: published for The British Academy by Oxford University Press.

Naumann, Friedrich. 1917. *Central Europe*. London: P. S. King and Son.

Neubach, Helmut. 1992. *Krótka historia Śląska* [A Short History of Silesia]. Bonn: Bund der Vertriebenen.

Neubach, Helmut. 1995. Vom Wiener Kongreß bis zur Reichsgründung (1815–1871) [From the Congress of Vienna to the Establishment of the German Empire (1815–1871)] (pp. 206–233). In Irgang, Winfried, Bein, Werner, and Neubach, Helmut, *Schlesien: Geschichte, Kultur und Wirtschaft* [Silesia: History, Culture and Economy] (Ser.: Historische Landeskunde: Deutsche Geschichte im Osten [Regional Studies: German History in the East], vol. 4]. Cologne: Verlag Wissenschaft und Politik.

Neubach, Helmut. 1995a. Im Kaiserreich (1871–1918) [In the German Empire (1871–1918)] (pp. 174–206). In Irgang, Winfried, Bein, Werner, and Neubach, Helmut, *Schlesien: Geschichte, Kultur und Wirtschaft* [Silesia: History, Culture and Economy] (Ser.: Historische Landeskunde: Deutsche Geschichte im Osten [Regional Studies: German History in the East], vol. 4]. Cologne: Verlag Wissenschaft und Politik.

Nicolai, Helmut. 1930. *Oberschlesien im Ringen der Völker* [Upper Silesia Struggled for by Various Peoples]. Oppeln: Kampfbundes für deutsche Kultur; and Breslau: Graß, Barth and Comp.

Niemcewicz, Julian Ursyn. 1990 [1858]. Relacja Jana Ursyna Niemcewicza z podróży na Śląsk i do Wielkopolski [Julian Ursyn Niemcewicz's Account on His Travels in Silesia and Wielkopolska] (pp. 49–51). In Wrzesiński, Wojciech, ed., *W stronę Odry i Bałtyku. Wybór źródeł (1795–1950)* [Toward the Odra and the Baltic: A Choice of Sources (1795–1950] (vol. 1: O ziemię Piastów i polski lud (1795–1918) [In the Struggle for the Piast Lands and the Polish People (1795–1918)], ed. Kulak, Teresa). Wrocław and Warsaw: Volumen.

Nietzsche, Friedrich. 1954. On Truth and Lie in an Extramoral Sense. In Kaufmann, W., ed., *The Portable Nietzsche*. New York: Viking.

Noël, Jean-François. 1998. *Święte Cesarstwo* [The Holy Empire, Polish translation from the French]. Warsaw: Volumen.

Nowak, Krzysztof. 1995. Ruch kożdoniowski na Śląsku Cieszyńskim [The Kożdoń Movement in Cieszyn Silesia] (pp. 26–45). In Wanatowicz, Maria Wanda, ed., *Regionalizm a separatyzm—historia i współczesność* [Regionalism and Separatism: History and the Presence] (Ser.: Prace Naukowe [Scholarly Studies], no. 1492). Katowice: Wydawnictwo Uniwersytetu Śląskiego.

Ociepka, Beata. 1997. *Związek Wypędzonych w systemie politycznym RFN i jego wpływ na stosunki polsko-niemieckie 1982–1992* [The Association of the Expellees in the Political System of the FRG and Its Influence on Polish-German Relations 1982–1992] (Ser.: Niemcoznastwo [German Studies], vol. 7). Wrocław: Wydawnictwo Uniwersytetu Wrocławskiego.

Olesch, Reinhold. 1958–1959. *Der Wortschatz der polnischen Mundart von Sankt Annaberg* [The Dictionary of the Polish Dialect of Sankt Annaberg] (2 vols.). Berlin: Freie Universität Berlin; and Wiesbaden: Otto Harrassowitz.

Onions, C. T. et al., eds. 1983. *The Shorter Oxford English Dictionary on Historical Principles*. London: Book Club Associates and Guild Publishing.

Oommen, T. K. 1997. *Citizenship, Nationality and Ethnicity: Reconciling Competing Identities*. Cambridge: Polity.

Orłowski, Hubert. 1998. *Polnische Wirtschaft. Nowoczesny niemiecki dyskurs o Polsce* [*Polnische Wirtschaft:* The Modern German Discourse on Poland] (Polish translation of '*Polnische Wirtschaft'. Zum deutschen Polendiskurs der Neuzeit*). Olsztyn: Borussia.

Orzechowski, Kazimierz. 1971. Terytorialne podziały na Śląsku [The Territorial Divisions of Silesia] (pp. 53–69). *Kwartalnik Opolski*. No. 2.

Orzechowski, Kazimierz. 1971a. Terytorialne podziały na Śląsku [The Territorial Divisions of Silesia] (pp. 74–91). *Kwartalnik Opolski*. No. 3.

Orzechowski, Kazimierz. 1971b. Terytorialne podziały na Śląsku [The Territorial Divisions of Silesia] (pp. 83–105). *Kwartalnik Opolski*. No. 4.

Orzechowski, Kazimierz. 1972. Terytorialne podziały na Śląsku [The Territorial Divisions of Silesia] (pp. 28–44). *Kwartalnik Opolski*. No. 2.

Orzechowski, Marian. 1975. *Wojciech Korfanty. Biografia polityczna* [Wojciech Korfanty: A Political Biography]. Wrocław: Ossolineum.

Osborne, Sidney. 1921. *The Upper Silesian Question and Germany's Coal Problem*. London: George Allen and Unwin Ltd.

Pallas, Ladislav. 1970. *Jazyková otázka a podmínky vytvaření národního vědomí ve Slezsku* [The Language Question and the Conditions Which Fostered the Emergence of National Consciousness in Silesia]. Ostrava: Profil.

Pałys, Piotr. 1995. Polsko-czechosłowacki spór o przynależność państwową ziemi kłodzkiej w latach 1945–1947 [The Polish-Czechoslovak Contestation on the Right to Ownership of the Kłodzko Land] (pp. 31–49). *Kwartalnik Opolski*. Nos. 3–4.

Pałys, Piotr. 1997. *Kłodzko, Racibórz i Głubczyce w stosunkach polsko-czechosłowackich w latach 1945–1947* [Kłodzko, Racibórz and Głubczyce in Polish-Czechoslovak Relations in the Years 1945–1947]. Opole: Published by the author.

Pándi, Lajos, ed. 1997. *Köztes-Európa 1763–1993* [In-Between Europe 1763–1993]. Budapest: Osiris.

Partsch, Joseph. 1904. *Mitteleuropa. Die Länder und Völker von den Westalpen und dem Balkan biz zum Kanal und das Kurische Haff* [Central Europe: The Lands and Peoples from the Western Alps and the Balkans to the Channel and the Courland Lagoon]. Gotha: J. Perthes.

Pater, Mieczysław. 1978. Język polski w gimnazjach wrocławskich 1840–1912 [Polish Language Teaching in the Wrocław Grammar Schools in the Years 1840–1912] (pp. 224–236). *Studia Śląskie.* Vol. 34.

Pater, Mieczysław. 1991. *Polskie postawy narodowe na Śląsku w 19 wieku* [Polish National Attitudes in Silesia in the 19th Century] (part 1: do 1870 [Up to 1870]). Wrocław and Warsaw: Volumen.

Pater, Mieczysław. 1992. Ksiądz znany i ksiądz zapomniany. Jan Nepomucyn Alojzy Ficek i Jan Słaniowski [The Renowned Priest and the Forgotten Priest: Jan Nepomucyn Alojzy Ficek and Jan Słaniowski] (pp. 61–68). In Matwijowski, Krystyn, ed., *Ludzie Kościoła katolickiego* [People of the Catholic Church]. Wrocław: Centrum Badań Śląskoznawczych i Bohemistycznych, Uniwersytet Wrocławski.

Pater, Mieczysław. 1993. *Polskie postawy narodowe na Śląsku w 19 wieku* [Polish National Attitudes in Silesia in the 19th Century] (part 2: 1871–1890). Wrocław: Sudety.

Pater, Mieczysław. 1996. Kopp Georg (Jerzy) (pp. 188–192). In Pater, Mieczysław, ed., *Słownik biograficzny katolickiego duchowieństwa śląskiego 19 i 20 wieku* [The Biographical Dictionary of Silesia's Catholic Clergy of the 19th and 20th Centuries]. Katowice: Księgarnia Św. Jacka.

Pater, Mieczysław. 1996a. Förster, Henryk Ernest Karol (pp. 102–104). In Pater, Mieczysław, ed., *Słownik biograficzny katolickiego duchowieństwa śląskiego 19 i 20 wieku* [The Biographical Dictionary of Silesia's Catholic Clergy of the 19th and 20th Centuries]. Katowice: Księgarnia Św. Jacka.

Pater, Mieczysław. 1996b. Przyniczyński, Franciszek Ksawery (pp. 333–334). In Pater, Mieczysław, ed., *Słownik biograficzny katolickiego duchowieństwa śląskiego 19 i 20 wieku* [The Biographical Dictionary of Silesia's Catholic Clergy of the 19th and 20th Centuries]. Katowice: Księgarnia Św. Jacka.

Pater, Mieczysław. 1996c. Świeży, Ignacy (pp. 433/437). In Pater, Mieczysław, ed., *Słownik biograficzny katolickiego duchowieństwa śląskiego 19 i 20 wieku* [The Biographical Dictionary of Silesia's Catholic Clergy of the 19th and 20th Centuries]. Katowice: Księgarnia Św. Jacka.

Pater, Mieczysław. 1996d. Bertram, Adolf (pp. 25–27). In Pater, Mieczysław, ed., *Słownik biograficzny katolickiego duchowieństwa śląskiego 19 i 20 wieku* [The

Biographical Dictionary of Silesia's Catholic Clergy of the 19th and 20th Centuries]. Katowice: Księgarnia Św. Jacka.

Patzelt, Herbert. 1986. Der Protestantismus in Teschner Schlesien in Vergangenheit und Gegenwart [Protestantism in Teschen Silesia in the Past and Today] (pp. 271–292). *Oberschlesisches Jahrbuch*. Vol. 2.

Pawlicki, Zbigniew. 1995. Eichendorff w muzyce i w... Polsce [Eichendorff in Music and in ... Poland] (pp. 19–25). In Koprowski, Jan, ed., *Józef Eichendorff. Ostatni rycerz romantyzmu* [Józef Eichendorff: The Last Knight of Romanticism]. Warsaw: Elipsa.

Pearson, Raymond. 1994. *The Longman Companion to European Nationalism 1789–1920*. London: Longman.

Peretz, Don. 1990. Israel (14: 297–311). In Bram, Leon L., and Dickey, Norma H., et al., eds., *Funk and Wagnalls New Encyclopedia*. Columbus, OH: Funk and Wagnalls L.P.

Petry, Ludwig. 1989. Zur Rolle der Universität Breslau in der Zeit des Nationalsozialismus [On the Role of the Breslau University in the Time of National Socialism] (pp. 79–104). In Schmielewski, Ulrich, ed., *Nationalsozialismus und Wiederstand in Schlesien* [National Socialism and Resistance in Silesia]. Sigmaringen: Thorbecke.

Peuckert, Will-Erich. 1995. *Sagen aus Schlesien* [Legends from Silesia]. Reinbek: Rowohlt.

Pfohl, Ernst. 1984 [1932]. *Ortslexikon Sudetenland* [The Lexicon of the Localities of the Sudetenland]. Nuremberg: Preußler.

Piątek, Tadeusz. 1993. *Rola i pozycja starokatolicyzmu na Śląsku* [The Role and Position of Old Catholicism in Silesia]. Opole: Instytut Śląski.

Piegsa, Joachim. 1989. *Weg zum Himmel. Katholisches Gebet- und Gesangbuch/ Droga do Nieba. Katolicki Modlitewnik i Śpiewnik* [The Way to Heaven: The Catholic Prayer- and Songbook]. Münster: Apostolischer Visitator der Priester und Gläubigen des Erzbistums Breslau.

Pierzchała, Jan. 1997 Myśląc o teatrze. W 100-lecie działalności Tetru Zagłębia [Thinking on the Theater: The Centenary of the Zagłębie Theater] (pp. 48–51). *Śląsk*. No. 2, Feb.

Pitronova, Blanka. 1992. Śląsk Cieszyński w latach 1653–1848 [Cieszyn Silesia in the Years 1653–1848] (pp. 44–59). In Anon., ed., *Zarys dziejów Śląska Cieszyńskiego* [An Outline of the History of Cieszyn Silesia]. Ostrava and Prague: Komitet Czeskiej Administracji Terenowej.

Plaček, Vilém. 1996. Hans Kudlich osvoboditel rakouských poddanch [Hans Kudlich: Liberator of the Austrian Subjects] (pp. 18–20). *Vlastivědne listy*. No. 1.

Plaček, Vilém. 1996a. Hlučínští Moravci v Pruskm Slezsku a jeich spajatost s Katolickou Církví do sjednocení Německa roku 1871 [The Hlučín Moravians in Prussian Silesia and Their Ties with the Catholic Church until the Unification of Germany in 1871] (pp. 5–8). *Vlastivědne listy*. No. 2.

Pogonowski, Iwo Cyprian. 1988. *Poland: A Historical Atlas*. New York: Barnes and Noble.

Pogonowski, Iwo Cyprian. 1993. *Jews in Poland: A Documentary History. The Rise of Jews as a Nation from Congressus Judaicus in Poland to the Knesset in Israel.* New York: Hippocrene Books.

Pokorný, Jiří. 1993. Léta 1867–1918 (pp. 102–147). In Bělina, Pavel, et al., eds., *Dějiny zemí Koruny české* [History of the Lands of the Czech Crown] (vol. 2). Prague and Litomyšl: Paseka.

Polak, Jerzy. 1993. Postawa wielkich właścicieli ziemskich na Górnym Śląsku wobec powstań śląskich na przykładzie księcia pszczyńskiego [The Attitude of Upper Silesia's Large Landowners Toward the Silesian Uprising as Exemplified by the Pszczyna Prince] (pp. 383–390). In Brożek, Andrzej, ed., *Powstania Śląskie i plebiscyt w procesie zrastania się Górnego Śląska z macierzą* [The Silesian Uprisings and the Plebiscite in the Process of the Integration of Upper Silesia with the Motherland]. Bytom: Muzeum Górnośląskie.

Polak, Jerzy. 1995. Jeden z 'baronów węglowych'. Z dziejów upadku rzekomego Piasta na Pszczynie [One of the 'Coal Barons': On the Fall of the Spurious Piast of Pszczyna] (pp. 200–206). In Wanatowicz, Maria Wanda, ed., *Rola i miejsce Górnego Śląska w Drugiej Rzeczypospolitej* [The Role and Place of Upper Silesia in the Second Polish Republic]. Bytom: Muzeum Górnośląskie; and Katowice: Muzeum Śląskie.

Polišenský, Josef Vincent. 1991 [1947]. *History of Czechoslovakia in Outline*. Prague: Bohemia International.

Ponczek, Mirosław. 1987. *Towarzystwo Gimnastyczne 'Sokół' na Górnym Śląsku. Zarys dziejów (1895–1939)* [The Sokół Gymnastic Society in Upper Silesia: An Outline of History (1895–1939)] (Ser.: Wszechnica Muzeum Śląskiego [Academy of the Silesian Museum]). Katowice: Muzeum Śląskie.

Popiołek, Kazimierz. 1972. *Historia Śląska od pradziejów do 1945 roku* [History of Silesia: From Pre-History to the Year 1945]. Katowice: Śląski Instytut Naukowy and "Śląsk".

Porter, Brian. 2000. *When Nationalism Began to Hate: Imagining Modern Politics in Nineteenth Century Poland*. New York: Oxford University Press.

Prinz, Friedrich. 1995. Auf dem Weg in die Moderne [On the Way to Modernity] (pp. 304–377). In Prinz, Friedrich, ed., *Böhmen und Mähren* [Bohemia and Moravia] (Ser.: Deutsche Geschichte im Osten Europas [German History in Eastern Europe]). Berlin: Siedler.

Prizel, Ilya. 1998. *National Identity and Foreign Policy: Nationalism and Leadership in Poland, Russia and Ukraine*. Cambridge: Cambridge University Press.

Pudelko, Alfred. 1993. *Schlesische Landeskunde* [The Description of the Region of Silesia]. Kiel: Arndt.

Pynsent, R. B., and Kanikova, S. I., eds. 1993. *The Everyman Companion to East European Literature*. London: J. M. Dent.

Pysiewicz-Jędrusik, Renata, et al. *Granice Śląska* [The Borders of Silesia]. Wrocław: Rzeka.

Quine, Maria Sophia. 1996. *Population Politics in Twentieth-Century Europe.* London: Routledge.

Rada, Ivan, et al. 1993. *Dějiny zemí Koruny české* [The History of the Lands of the Czech Crown] (vol. 1). Prague: Paseka.

Rajman, Jan. 1990. *Zawadzkie. Historia i współczesność* [Zawadzkie: The Past and the Present] (Ser.: Encyklopedia Wiedzy o Śląsku [Encyclopedia of Knowledge on Silesia]). Opole: Instytut Śląski.

Reader, John. 1997. *Africa: A Biography of the Continent.* London: Hamish Hamilton.

Reichling, Gerhard. 1977. Myslowitz (pp. 324–325). In Weczerka, Hugo, ed., *Schlesien* [Silesia] (Ser.: Handbuch der Historischen Stätten [Handbook of Historical Places]. Stuttgart: Körner.

Reichling, Gerhard. 1977a. Kattowitz (221–225). In Weczerka, Hugo, ed., *Schlesien* [Silesia] (Ser.: Handbuch der Historischen Stätten [Handbook of Historical Places]. Stuttgart: Körner.

Reiner, Bolesław. 1966. Stanowisko Kościoła katolickiego wobec spraw polskich na Górnym Śląsku (19 i 20 wiek) [The Attitude of the Catholic Church Towards Polish Matters in Upper Silesia (19th and 20th Centuries)] (pp. 105–123). *Kwartalnik Opolski.* No. 4.

Reiner, Bolesław. 1971. Zmiany organizacji administracji Kościoła Katolickiego na Górnym Śląsku w 19 i 20 wieku [The Changes in the Organization of the Administration of the Catholic Church in Upper Silesia in the 19th and 20th Centuries] (pp. 385–405). *Studia Śląskie.* Vol. 20.

Reiter, Jan. 1966. Dzieje strajku szkolnego na Śląsku [A History of the School Strike in Silesia] (pp. 41–54). *Kwartalnik Opolski.* No. 3.

Reiter, Norbert. 1960. *Die polnisch-deutsch Sprachbeziehungen in Oberschlesien* [Polish-German Language Relations in Upper Silesia] (Ser.: Slavistische Veröffentlichungen [Publications in Slavonic Studies], vol. 23). Berlin: Freie Universität Berlin; and Wiesbaden: Otto Harrassowitz.

Reiter, Norbert. 1989. Die soziale Funktion des Wasserpolnischen in Oberschlesien [The Social Function of *Wasserpolnisch* in Upper Silesia] (pp. 115–127). In Hecker, Hans, and Spieler, Silke, eds., *Deutsche, Slawen und Balten: Aspekte des Zusammenlebens im Osten des Deutschen Reiches und in Ostmitteleuropa* [Germans, Slavs and Balts: Aspects of Living Together in the East of the German Empire and in East Central Europe]. Bonn: Kulturstiftung der deutschen Vertriebenen.

Rider, Jacques Le. 1994. *Mitteleuropa: Auf dem Spuren eines Begriffes* [Central Europe: The Roots of the Concept]. Vienna: Deuticke.

Rogall, Joachim. 1993. *Die Deutschen im Posener Land und in Mittelpolen* [Germans in the Land of Posen and in Central Poland] (Ser.: Vertreibungsgebiete und vertriebene Deutsche [Expelled Germans and the Territories from Which They Were Expelled], vol. 3). Munich: Langen Müller.

Roger, Juliusz. 1991. *Pieśni Ludu Polskiego w Górnym Szląsku* [Songs of the Polish People in Upper Silesia] (facsimile ed., edited and introduction by Świerc, Piotr). Opole: Instytut Śląski.

Rösner-Kraus, Walter. 1989. Flucht und Vertreibung aus Ostdeutschland [The Flight and Expulsion from East Germany] (pp. 197–221). In Häring, Ludwig, Kühnel, Horst, and Hansel, Paul, eds., *Die Deutschen und ihre östlichen Nachbarn,* vol. 2: *Deutsche und Polen* [The Germans and Their Eastern Neighbors, vol. 2: The Germans and the Poles] (Ser.: Akademiebericht no. 141). Dillingen: Akademie für Lehrerfortbildung; and Munich: Haus des deutschen Ostens.

Rothschild, Joseph. 1992. *East Central Europe Between the Two World Wars* (Ser.: A History of East Central Europe, vol. 9). Seattle: University of Washington Press.

Roucek, Joseph S. 1945. Czechoslovakia and Her Minorities (pp. 171–192). In Kerner, Robert J., ed., *Czechoslovakia* (Ser.: The United Nations Series). Berkeley and Los Angeles: University of California Press.

Sabin, James T. 1990. Africa (1: 186–215). In Bram, Leon L., and Dickey, Norma H., et al., eds., *Funk and Wagnalls New Encyclopedia.* Columbus, OH: Funk and Wagnalls L.P.

Sack, John, 1993. *An Eye for an Eye: The Untold Story of Jewish Revenge against Germans in 1945.* New York: Basic Books.

Sakson, Andrzej. 1990. *Mazurzy—społeczność pogranicza* [The Mazurs: A Social Group of the Borderland]. Poznań: Instytut Zachodni.

Samsonowicz, Henryk. 1997. *O 'historii prawdziwej'* [On 'True History']. Gdańsk: Novus Orbis.

Šatava, Leoš. 1994. *Národní menšiny v Evropě* [The National Minorities in Europe]. Prague: Ivo Železný.

Sawczuk, Janusz. 1966. [Unpublished ms.]. *Stanowisko* Katolika *wobec spraw wewnętrznych w Prusach i wobec partii politycznych w latach 1912–1914* [The Stance of *Katolik* on the Domestic Questions in Prussia and on the Political Parties in the Years 1912–1914]. Wrocław: Archiwum Uniwersytetu Wrocławskiego.

Schenk, Hans. 1993. *Die Böhmischen Länder: Ihre Geschichte, Kultur und Wirtschaft* [The Czech Lands: Their History, Culture and Economy] (Ser.: Historische Landeskunde: Deutsche Geschichte im Osten [Regional Studies: German History in the East], vol. 4]. Cologne: Verlag Wissenschaft und Politik.

Scheuermann, Gerhard. 1994. *Das Breslau-Lexikon* [The Breslau Lexicon] (2 vols.). Dülmen: Laumann.

Schmidt-Rösler, Andrea. 1999. Autonomie- und Separatismusbestrebungen in Oberschlesien 1918–1922 [The Endeavors for Establishing Autonomy in Upper Silesia or Separating This Region from Germany 1918–1922] (pp. 1–49). *Zeitschrift für Ostmitteleuropa-Forschung.* No. 1.

Schofer, Lawrence. 1974. *The Formation of a Modern Labor Force: Upper Silesia, 1865–1914*. Berkeley: University of California Press.

Scholz, Franz. 1989. *Zwischen Staats-Räson und Evangelium. Kardinal Hlond und die Tragödie der ost-deutschen Diözesen* [Between Raison d'Etat and Gospel: Cardinal Hlond and the Tragedy of the East German Dioceses]. Frankfurt am Main: Knecht.

Schöpflin, G., and Wood, N., eds. *In Search of Central Europe*. Totowa, NJ: Barnes and Noble.

Schramm, Tomasz. 1989. *Wygrać Polskę, 1914–1918* [To Win a Poland, 1914–1918] (Ser.: Dzieje narodu i państwa polskiego [A History of the Polish Nation and State], section 3, vol. 57). Warsaw: KAW.

Schulz, Eberhard Günter. 1991. *Der kulturgeschichtliche Beitrag der Schlesier* [The Cultural and Historical Contributions of the Silesians]. Würzburg: Korn.

Schulze, Hagen. 1991. *The Course of German Nationalism: From Frederick the Great to Bismarck 1763–1869* [English translation of *Der Weg zum Nationalstaat*]. Cambridge: Cambridge University Press.

Schulze, Hagen. 1998. *Germany: A New History*. Cambridge, MA: Harvard University Press.

Scobel, A. 1909. *Andrees neuer allgemeiner und österreichisch-ungarischer Handatlas* [The Andrees New Atlas of the World and Austria-Hungary]. Vienna: Verlag von Moritz Perels.

Seidl, Elmar. 1996. *Das Troppauer Land zwischen den fünf Südgrenzen Schlesiens* [The Troppau Land as Located among the Five Southern Borders of Silesia]. Ulm: Gerhard Hess Verlag.

Serafin, Franciszek. 1996. Stosunki demograficzne i społeczne [The Demographic and Social Relations] (pp. 78–100). In Serafin, Franciszek, ed., *Województwo Śląskie (1922–1939). Zarys monograficzny* [The Silesian Voivodeship (1922–1939): A Monographic Outline]. Katowice: Wydawnictwo Uniwersytetu Śląskiego.

Seton-Watson, Hugh. 1977. *Nations and States: An Enquiry into the Origins and Politics of Nationalism*. London: Methuen.

Simpson, A. J., et al., eds. 1991. *The Compact Oxford English Dictionary*. Oxford: Clarendon Press.

Sitek, W. 1992. *Kultura i struktura. Problemy integracji i polaryzacji różnych grup społecznych na Śląsku* [Culture and Structure: The Problem of Integration and Polarization of the Various Social Groups in Silesia]. Wrocław: Instytut Socjologii Uniwersytetu Wrocławskiego.

Sitek, W. 1996. *Mniejszość w warunkach zagrożenia. Pamiętniki Łemków* [The Minority in the Conditions Endangering Its Existence: The Memoirs of the Lemkos]. Wrocław: Wydawnictwo Uniwersytetu Wrocławskiego.

Siwek, Tadeusz. 1994. Podział Czechosłowacji a mniejszość polska [The Division of Czechoslovakia and the Polish Minority] (pp. 77–90). *Sprawy Narodowościowe*. No. 1 (4).

Ślusarek, Krzysztof. 1996. Narodziny nowoczesnego nacjonalizmu polskiego i konflikty narodowościowe na ziemiach polskich na przełomie 19 i 20 w. [The Birth of Modern Polish Nationalism and National Conflicts in the Polish Lands at the Turn of the 19th and 20th Centuries]. Paper presented at The Phenomenon of Modern Nationalism in Central Europe, conference organized by the Friedrich-Ebert Stiftung and the Freie Universität Berlin, Gliwice, Poland, October 9–11.

Smith, Anthony D. 1986. *The Ethnic Origins of Nations*. Oxford: Blackwell.

Smith, Anthony D. 1991. *National Identity*. Harmondsworth: Penguin.

Smith, Anthony D. 1998. *Nationalism and Modernism: A Critical Survey of Recent Theories of Nations and Nationalism*. London: Routledge.

Smogorzewski, Kazimierz Maciej, et al. 1992. Poland (25: 930–956). In McHenry, Robert, et al., eds., *The New Encyclopaedia Britannica*. Chicago: Encyclopaedia Britannica, Inc.

Snoch, Bogdan. 1991. *Ilustrowany słownik dziejów Śląska* [An Illustrated Dictionary of Silesian History]. Katowice: Wydawnictwo "Śląsk".

Snyder, Louis L., ed. 1958. *Documents of German History*. New Brunswick, NJ: Rutgers University Press.

Snyder, Timothy. 2003. *The Reconstruction of Nations: Poland, Ukraine, Lithuania, Belarus, 1596–1999*. New Haven: Yale University Press.

Sosnowski, Kiryl, and Suchocki, Mieczysław, eds. 1948. *Dolny Śląsk* [Lower Silesia] (Ser.: Ziemie Staropolski [The Lands of Old Poland] ed. by Wojciechowski, Zygmunt; vol. 1, parts 1 and 2). Poznań and Wrocław: Instytut Zachodni.

Stalmach, Paweł. 1990 [1948]. Żądania Ślązaków według memoriału Pawła Stalmacha [The Demands of the Silesians as Presented in Paweł Stalmach's Memorial] (pp. 63–64). In Wrzesiński, Wojciech, ed., *W stronę Odry i Bałtyku. Wybór źródeł (1795–1950)* [Toward the Odra and the Baltic: A Choice of Sources (1795–1950] (vol. 1: O ziemię Piastów i polski lud (1795–1918) [In the Struggle for the Piast Lands and the Polish People (1795–1918)], ed. Kulak, Teresa). Wrocław and Warsaw: Volumen.

Staněk, Tomáš. 1991. *Odsun Němců z Československa 1945–1947* [The Expulsion of Germans from Czechoslovakia 1945–1947]. Prague: Academia and Naše vojsko.

Staszic, Stanisław. 1990 [1807]. Rozległość polskiej ziemi topograficznie rozważana [The Extent of the Polish Land from a Topographical Point of View] (p. 41). In Wrzesiński, Wojciech, ed., *W stronę Odry i Bałtyku. Wybór źródeł (1795–1950)* [Toward the Odra and the Baltic: A Choice of Sources (1795–1950] (vol. 1: O ziemię Piastów i polski lud (1795–1918) [In the Struggle for the Piast Lands and the Polish People (1795–1918)], ed. Kulak, Teresa). Wrocław and Warsaw: Volumen.

Stein, Volkmar. 1993. *Joseph von Eichendorff: Ein Lebensbild/Obraz życia* [Joseph von Eichendorff: A Biographical Sketch]. Würzburg: Stiftung Kulturwerk Schlesien.

Steiner, Waltraud. 1999. Die Arbeit der Kanonischen und Apostolischen Visitatoren ist keinwegs beendet [By No Means Has the Work of the Chapter and Apostolic Visitators Come to an End] (pp. 1–2). *Deutscher Ostdienst*. No. 5, Feb. 5.

Steiner, Waltraud. 1999a. Schwerpunkt ist Integration junger Aussiedler [The Most Important Thing is Integration of Young *Aussiedlers*] (p. 1). *Deutscher Ostdienst*. No. 6, Feb. 12.

Steinert, Alfred. 1995. Oppeln (pp. 317–323). In Stoob, Heinz, and Johanek, Peter, eds., *Schlesisches Städtebuch* [The Lexicon of Silesian Towns] (Ser.: Deutsches Städtebuch [The Lexicon of German Towns], vol. 1). Stuttgart: W. Kohlhammer.

Stoob, Heinz, and Johanek, Peter, eds. 1995. *Schlesisches Städtebuch* [The Book of the Silesian Towns] (Ser.: Deutsches Städtebuch [The Lexicon of German Towns], vol. 1). Stuttgart: Kohlhammer.

Struve, Kai. 1997. Państwo i naród w niemieckiej historii do powstania Rzeszy Niemieckiej (1871) [The State and Nation in German History until the Founding of the German Empire (1871)] (pp. 25–39). In Linek, Bernard, et al., eds., *Fenomen nowoczesnego nacjonalizmu w Europie Środkowej* [The Phenomenon of Modern Nationalism in Central Europe]. Opole: Instytut Śląski.

Stüttgen, Peter, Neubach, Helmut, and Hubatsch, Walther. 1976. *Grundriß zur deutschen Verwaltungsgeschichte 1815–1945* [An Outline of the History of German Administration] (Ser. A: Preußen [Prussia] ed. by Hubatsch, Walther; vol. 4: Schlesien [Silesia]). Marburg: Johann-Gottfried-Herder-Institut.

Sugar, Peter F., and Treadgold, Donald W., eds. 1974– . *A History of East Central Europe*. Seattle: University of Washington Press.

Surman, Zdzisław. 1992. Księża utrakwiści na Śląsku w drugiej połowie 19 wieku [The Bilingual Priests in Silesia in the Second Half of the 19th Century] (pp. 69–74). In Matwijowski, Krystyn, ed., *Ludzie Kościoła katolickiego* [People of the Catholic Church]. Wrocław: Centrum Badań Śląskoznawczych i Bohemistycznych, Uniwersytet Wrocławski.

Suleja, Włodzimierz. 1992. Śląsk w myśli politycznej polskiej irredenty na przełomie 19 i 20 wieku [Silesia in the Thought of the Polish Irredenta at the Turn of the 19th and 20th Centuries] (pp. 41–48). In Smołka, Leonard, ed., *Śląsk a czynniki zewnętrzne w 19–20 wieku* [Silesia and External Influences in the 19th–20th Centuries]. Wrocław: Sudety.

Świątkiewicz, W., ed. 1995. *Region and Regionalism: Culture and Social Order*. Katowice: Wydawnictwo Uniwersytetu Śląskiego.

Świerc, Piotr. 1964. [Review of] Stowarzyszenia akademickie polskiej młodzieży górnośląskiej we Wrocławiu 1863–1918 [Academic Societies of the Polish

Youth of Upper Silesia in Wrocław in 1863–1918] (pp. 122–124). *Kwartalnik Opolski*. No. 1.

Świerc, Piotr. 1990. *Ks. Bernard Bogedain (1810–1860)* [Rev. Bernard Bogedain (1810–1860)] (Ser.: Wszechnica Muzeum Śląskiego [Academy of the Silesian Museum]). Katowice: Muzeum Śląskie.

Synak, Brunon. 1998. *Kaszubska tożsamość. Ciągłość i zmiana* [The Kashubian Identity: Continuity and Change]. Gdańsk: Wydawnictwo Uniwersytetu Gdańskiego.

Szacki, Jerzy. 1997. O narodzie i nacjonalizmie [On Nation and Nationalism] (pp. 4–31). *Znak*. No. 3, Mar.

Szafranek, Józef. 1990 [1948]. Wniosek złożony w Sejmie Pruskim [The Petition Lodged with the Prussian National Assembly] (pp. 65–66). In Wrzesiński, Wojciech, ed., *W stronę Odry i Bałtyku. Wybór źródeł (1795–1950)* [Toward the Odra and the Baltic: A Choice of Sources (1795–1950)] (vol. 1: O ziemię Piastów i polski lud (1795–1918) [In the Struggle for the Piast Lands and the Polish People (1795–1918)], ed. Kulak, Teresa). Wrocław and Warsaw: Volumen.

Szczepankiewicz-Battek, Joanna. 1996. *Protestantyzm na Śląsku. Geografia, demografia, kultura* [Protestantism in Silesia: Geography, Demography and Culture]. Wrocław: Silesia.

Szczepański, M., ed. 1993. *Dilemmas of Regionalism and the Region of Dilemmas*. Katowice: Uniwersytet Śląski.

Sziling, Jan. 1970. *Polityka okupanta hitlerowskiego wobec Kościoła katolickiego 1939–1945. Tzw. okręgi Rzeszy: Gdańsk-Prusy Zachodnie, Kraj Warty i Regencja Katowicka* [The Policy of the Hitlerian Occupying Authorities toward the Catholic Church 1939–1945 in the So-Called Gaus of the Reich: Gdańsk-West Prussia, the Warta Land and the Katowice Regency]. Poznań: Instytut Zachodni.

Szmeja, Maria. 2000. *Niemcy? Polacy? Ślązacy! Rodzimi mieszkańcy Opolszczyzny w świetle analiz socjologicznych* [Germans? Poles? Szlonzoks! The Autochthonous Inhabitants of the Opole Land in Light of Sociological Analyses]. Cracow: Universitas.

Szołtysek, Marek. 1998. *Śląsk, takie miejsce na ziemi (opisanie Ojcowizny Górnoślązaków)* [Silesia, a Place on Earth (A Description of the Fatherland of the Upper Silesians)]. Rybnik: Śląskie ABC.

Szporluk, Roman. 1988. *Communism and Nationalism: Karl Marx versus Friedrich List*. New York and Oxford: Oxford University Press.

Szramek, Emil. 1934. Śląsk jako problem socjologiczny. Próba analizy [Silesia as a Sociological Problem: An Analysis]. *Roczniki Towarzystwa Przyjaciół Nauk na Śląsku*. Vol. 4.

Szűcs, Jenő. 1983. The Three Historical Regions of Europe (pp. 131–184). *Acta Historica Academiae Scientarum Hungariae*. No. 29.

Szyfer, A. 1996. *Warmiacy* [The Warmiaks]. Poznań: SAWW.

Szyjkowski, Marian. 1948. *Czeskie odrodzenie w 19 wieku* [Czech National Revival in the 19th Century] (Ser.: Literatura światowa w wieku 19 [World Literature in the 19th Century], vol. 16). Warsaw: Czytelnik and WP.

Ther, Philipp. 1998. *Deutsche und polnische Vertriebene: Gesellschaft und Vertriebenenpolitik in der SBZ/DDR und in Polen 1945–1956* [The German and Polish Expellees: Society and the Expellee Policies in the Soviet Occupation Zone/GDR and in Poland] (Ser.: Kritische Studien zur Geschichtswissenschaft [Critical Studies in Historiography], vol. 127). Göttingen: Vandenhoeck and Ruprecht.

Thorne, J.O., and Collocott, T.C., eds. 1975. *Chambers Bibliographical Dictionary* (two volume edition with continuous pagination). Edinburgh: Chambers.

Tims, Richard Wonser. 1996. [Reprint of the 1941 ed.). *Germanizing Prussian Poland: The H-K-T Society and the Struggle for the Eastern Marches in the German Empire, 1894–1919*. New York: A.M.S. Press, Inc.

Tismaneau, Vladimir, and Mihaies, Mircea. 1998. *Vecinii lui Franz Kafka—romanul unei nevroze/The Neighbors of Franz Kafka—the Story of a Neurosis*. Iaşi, Romania: Polirom.

Tobiasz, Mieczysław. 1947. *Wojciech Korfanty*. Katowice: 'Ognisko' Spółdzielnia Księgarska.

Tokarski, Jan, et al., eds. 1971. *Słownik wyrazów obcych PWN* [The PWN Dictionary of Foreign Words]. Warsaw: PWN.

Tomasiewicz, Jarosław. 1997. Współczesne ruchy regionalistyczne w Europie [The Present-Day Regionalist Movements in Europe] (pp. 295–318). *Sprawy Narodowościowe*. No. 2 (11).

Tomkowiak, Eligiusz. 1994. Zbrodnie niemieckie popełnione na Polakach w okresie Powstania Wielkopolskiego 1918–1919 [German Crimes against Poles Committed during the Wielkopolska Uprising 1918–1919]. In Polak, Bogusław, ed., *Niemcy a powstanie wielkopolskie 1918–1919* [The Germans and the Wielkopolska Uprising 1918–1919]. Koszalin: WSI.

Třeštík, Dušan. 1995. Moderne Nation, hochmittelalterliche politische Nation, frühmittelalterliche *Gens* und unsere genetische Software. Der Fall Mitteleuropa [The Modern Nation, the Medieval Nation, the Early Medieval *Gens* and Our Genetic Software] (pp. 161–182). In Bues, Altmut, and Rexheuser, Rex, eds., *Mittelalterliche Nationes—neuzeitliche Nationen. Probleme der Nationenbildung in Europa* [Medieval Nationes—Modern Nations: Problems of Nation-Building in Europe]. Wiesbaden: Harrassowitz.

Triest, Felix. 1984. (Reprint of the 1864 ed.). *Topographisches Handbuch von Oberschlesien* [The Topographic Handbook of Upper Silesia] (2 vols.) (Ser.: Beiträge zur Geschichte und Landeskunde Oberschlesiens [Contributions to History and Regional Studies Devoted to Upper Silesia], vol. 1). Sigmaringen: Jan Thorbecke.

Trzeciakowski, Lech. 1976. Ziemie polskie pod panowaniem państw zaborczych (1815–1918) [The Polish Lands Under Rule of the Partition States (1815–1918)] (pp. 446–611). In Topolski, Jerzy, ed., *Dzieje Polski* [Poland's Past]. Warsaw: PWN.

Turner, Henry Ashby, et al. 1992. Germany (pp. 39–132). In McHenry, Robert, et al., eds., *The New Encyclopaedia Britannica*. Chicago: Encyclopaedia Britannica, Inc.

Ujazdowski, Tomasz. 1990 [1830]. Opinia o Śląsku w dobie powstania listopadowego [An Opinion on Silesia in the Time of the November Uprising] (pp. 51–52). In Wrzesiński, Wojciech, ed., *W stronę Odry i Bałtyku. Wybór źródeł (1795–1950)* [Toward the Odra and the Baltic: A Choice of Sources (1795–1950] (vol. 1: O ziemię Piastów i polski lud (1795–1918) [In the Struggle for the Piast Lands and the Polish People (1795–1918)], ed. Kulak, Teresa). Wrocław and Warsaw: Volumen.

Ullmann, Klaus. 1985. *Schlesien-Lexikon für alle, die Schlesien lieben* [The Lexicon of Silesia, for Everybody Who Loves Silesia] (Ser.: Deutsche Landschaften im Lexikon [German Regions in Lexicons], vol. 2). Mannheim: Kraft.

Urban, Thomas. 1994. *Deutsche in Polen: Geschichte und Gegenwart einer Minderheit* [Germans in Poland: History and the Present Day of a Minority]. Munich: C. H. Beck.

Urbanec, Jiří. 1965. Introduction (pp. 5–6). In Bezruč, Petr, *Petr Bezruč 1867–1958*. Opava: Památník Petra Bezruče v Opavě.

Wagner, Helmut. 1991. Die innerdeutsche Grenzen [The Intra-German Borders]. In Demandt, Alexander, ed., *Deutschlands Grenzen in der Geschichte* [Germany's Borders in History]. Munich: C.H. Beck.

Walas, Teresa, ed. 1995. *Narody i stereotypy* [Nations and Stereotypes]. Cracow: Międzynarodowe Centrum Kultury.

Waldenberg, Marek. 1992. *Kwestie narodowe w Europie Środkowo-Wschodniej* [National Questions in East-Central Europe]. Warsaw: PWN.

Walker, W. Dundas. 1908. Austria (1: 595–605). In *Chambers's Encyclopaedia: A Dictionary of Universal Knowledge*. London and Edinburgh: Chambers; and Philadelphia: Lippincott.

Wanatowicz, Maria Wanda. 1982. *Ludność napływowa na Górnym Śląsku w latach 1922–1939* [The Internal Migrants in Upper Silesia in the Years 1922–1939]. Katowice: Uniwersytet Śląski.

Wanatowicz, Maria Wanda. 1986. Stereotyp Galicjanina w środowisku górnośląskim w Polsce niepodległej 1922–1939 [The Stereotype of the Galician in the Upper Silesian Milieu in Independent Poland 1922–1939]. *Studia Historyczne*. No. 29.

Wanatowicz, Maria Wanda. 1992. *Społeczeństwo polskie wobec Górnego Śląska (1795–1914)* [The Polish Society's Attitude Towards Upper Silesia (1795–1914). Katowice: Uniwersytet Śląski.

Wanatowicz, Maria Wanda. 1994. *Historia społeczno-polityczna Górnego Śląska i*

Śląska Cieszyńskiego w latach 1918–1945 [A Sociopolitical History of Upper Silesia and Cieszyn Silesia in the Years 1918–1945] (Ser.: Skrypty Uniwersytetu Śląskiego [Textbooks of the Uniwersytet Śląski], no. 497). Katowice: Wydawnictwo Uniwersytetu Śląskiego.

Wandycz, Piotr S. 1992. *The Price of Freedom: A History of East Central Europe from the Middle Ages to the Present.* London: Routledge.

Waters, Malcolm. 1998. *Globalization* (Ser.: Key Ideas). London: Routledge.

Wawryszyn, Ludwik. 1992. *Wojciech Korfanty—bojownik o powrót Śląska do Polski* [Wojciech Korfanty: An Advocate of the Return of Silesia to Poland]. Opole: Polski Związek Zachodni.

Weber, Eugen. 1976. *Peasants into Frenchmen: The Modernization of Rural France, 1870–1914.* Stanford, CA: Stanford University Press.

Weber, Paul. 1913. *Die Polen in Oberschlesien. Eine Statistische Untersuchung* [The Poles of Upper Silesia. A Statistical Enquiry]. Berlin: Julius Springer.

Weczerka, Hugo. 1977. Beuthen (pp. 20–25). In Weczerka, Hugo, ed., *Schlesien* [Silesia] (Ser.: Handbuch der Historischen Stätten [Handbook of Historical Places]. Stuttgart: Körner.

Weczerka, Hugo. 1977a. Hultschiner Ländchen [Hultschin Land] (pp. 198–200). In Weczerka, Hugo, ed., *Schlesien* [Silesia] (Ser.: Handbuch der Historischen Stätten [Handbook of Historical Places]. Stuttgart: Körner.

Weczerka, Hugo. 1977b. Vorwort [Introduction] (pp. 9–93). In Weczerka, Hugo, ed., *Schlesien* [Silesia] (Ser.: Handbuch der Historischen Stätten [Handbook of Historical Places]. Stuttgart: Körner.

Weczerka, Hugo. 1977c. Langenbielau (pp. 266–268). In Weczerka, Hugo, ed., *Schlesien* [Silesia] (Ser.: Handbuch der Historischen Stätten [Handbook of Historical Places]. Stuttgart: Körner.

Weger, Tobias. 1998. Anatomy of Immigrants (pp. 24–25). *Transitions.* No. 11, Nov.

Whorf, Benjamin Lee. 1956. Language, Mind, and Reality (pp. 246–270). In Whorf, Benjamin Lee, *Language, Thought, and Reality* (ed. Carroll, John B.). Cambridge, MA: The MIT Press.

Wilson, Kevin, and Dussen, Jan van der, eds. 1996. *The History of the Idea of Europe.* London: Routledge.

Wiskemann, Elizabeth. 1938. *Czechs and Germans: A Study of a Struggle in the Historic Provinces of Bohemia and Moravia.* London: Oxford University Press.

Wiskemann, Elizabeth. 1956. *Germany's Eastern Neighbors.* London: Oxford University Press.

Wisłocki, Seweryn. 1994. Alchemik z Janowa [The Alchemist of Janów] (pp. 188–200). *NaGłos.* Nos. 15–16, Oct.

Wódz, K., ed. 1995. *Regional Identity—Regional Consciousness: The Upper Silesian Experience.* Katowice: Wydawnictwo Uniwersytetu Śląskiego.

Wojciechowski, Sebastian. 1998. *Nacjonalizm w Europie Środkowo-Wschodniej* [Nationalism in East Central Europe]. Wrocław: atla 2.

Wolf, Adolf. 1996. *Der Status des Spätaussiedlers nach dem Kriegsgefolgenbereinigunsgesetz* [The Status of *Spätaussiedlers* After the Act on the Consolidation of War Consequences]. Wiesbaden: Kommunal- und Schul-Verlag.

Woolf, Stuart. 1996. Introduction (pp. 1–39). In Woolf, Stuart, ed., *Nationalism in Europe, 1815 to the Present: A Reader*. London and New York: Routledge.

Wotawa, A. 1919. *Das ostmährisch-schlesische Industriegebiet (M.-Ostrau-Teschen-Bielitz) eine selbständige, neutrale Republik!* [The East Moravian-Silesian Industrial Basin (M.-Ostrau, Teschen-Bielitz) Should Become an Independent, Neutral Republic!]. Vienna: Alfred Hölder, Universitätsbuchhändler.

Wronicz, Jadwiga, ed. 1995. *Słownik gwarowy Śląska Cieszynskiego* [The Dialectal Dictionary of Cieszyn Silesia]. Wisła: Towarzystwo Miłośników Wisły; and Ustroń: Towarzystwo Miłośników Ustronia.

Wrzesiński, Wojciech. 1995. Wychodźstwo ze Śląska [Emigration from Silesia] (pp. 180–189). In Bździach, Klaus et al., eds., *'Wach auf, mein Herz, und denke'. Zur Geschichte der Beziehungen zwischen Schlesien und Berlin-Brandenburg von 1740 bis heute/ 'Przebudź się, serce moje, i pomyśl'. Przyczynek do historii stosunków między Śląskiem a Berlinem-Brandenburgią od 1740 do dziś* ['Wake Up, My Heart, and Think': A Contribution to the History of the Relations Between Silesia and Berlin-Brandenburg from 1740 until Today]. Berlin: Gesellschaft für interregionalen Kulturaustausch; and Opole: Instytut Śląski.

Wurbs, Gerhard. 1982. *Die deutsche Sprachinsel Bielitz-Biala* [The German-speaking Region of Bielitz-Biala] (Ser.: Eckartschriften, vol. 79). Vienna: Österr. Landsmannschaft.

Wycisło, Janusz. 1996. Reginek, Tomasz (pp. 345–48). In Pater, Mieczysław, ed., *Słownik biograficzny katolickiego duchowieństwa śląskiego 19 i 20 wieku* [The Biographic Dictionary of Silesia's Catholic Clergy of the 19th and 20th Centuries]. Katowice: Księgarnia Św. Jacka.

Wyglenda, Ewa. 1982. Polskie rady ludowe [Polish People's Councils] (pp. 423–424). In Hawranek, Franciszek, et al., eds., *Encyklopedia Powstań Śląskich* [The Encyclopedia of the Silesian Uprisings]. Opole: Instytut Śląski.

Wyglenda, Ewa, and Lesiuk, Wiesław. 1982a. Naczelna Władza dla Górnego Śląska [The Supreme Authority for Upper Silesia] (p. 321). In Hawranek, Franciszek, et al., eds., *Encyklopedia Powstań Śląskich* [The Encyclopedia of the Silesian Uprisings]. Opole: Instytut Śląski.

Wyglenda, Ewa, and Lesiuk, Wiesław. 1982b. Podkomisariat Naczelnej Rady Ludowej w Bytomiu [The Subcommissariat of the Supreme People's Council in Bytom] (pp. 407–408). In Hawranek, Franciszek, et al., eds., *Encyklopedia Powstań Śląskich* [The Encyclopedia of the Silesian Uprisings]. Opole: Instytut Śląski.

Wyglenda, Ewa, and Lesiuk, Wiesław. 1982c. Związki Wojackie [Veterans' Associations] (p. 670). In Hawranek, Franciszek, et al., eds., *Encyklopedia Powstań Śląskich* [The Encyclopedia of the Silesian Uprisings]. Opole: Instytut Śląski.

Wyglenda, Ewa, and Lesiuk, Wiesław. 1982d. Akcja wyborcza do Sejmu Ustawodawczego Rzeczypospolitej Polskiej [The Election Campaign to the Constituent *Sejm* of the Polish Republic] (pp. 15–16). In Hawranek, Franciszek, et al., eds., *Encyklopedia Powstań Śląskich* [The Encyclopedia of the Silesian Uprisings]. Opole: Instytut Śląski.

Žáček, Rudolf. 1995. Z historii regionalizmu i separatyzmu morawskiego [From the History of Moravian Regionalism and Separatism] (pp. 149–157). In Wanatowicz, Maria Wanda, ed., *Regionalizm a separatyzm—historia i współczesność* [Regionalism and Separatism: History and the Presence] (Ser.: Prace Naukowe [Scholarly Studies], no. 1492). Katowice: Wydawnictwo Uniwersytetu Śląskiego.

Zaczyk, Eugeniusz, and Nyga, Roman. 1994. *Stworoki. Wizerunki stworoków śląskich/Abbilder schlesischer Wunderwesen* [Pictures of the Silesian Spirits]. Bieruń: Bieruński Ośrodek Kultury.

Zahradnik, Stanisław. 1989. *Czasopiśmiennictwo w języku polskim na terenach czechosłowackich* [The Polish-Language Press on the Czechoslovak Territories] (Ser.: Studia i Monografie [Studies and Monographs] no. 146). Opole: WSP.

Zahradnik, Stanisław, and Ryczkowski, Marek. 1992a. *Korzenie Zaolzia* [The Roots of Zaolzie]. Warsaw: PAI-Press.

Zakrzewski, Andrzej. 1988. *Od Stojałowskiego do Witosa* [From Stojałowski to Witos] (Ser.: Dzieje narodu i państwa polskiego [History of the Polish Nation and State], vol. 3, part 53). Warsaw: KAW.

Zieliński, Władysław. 1983. *Wojciech Korfanty, 1873—1939* (Ser.: Wszechnica Muzeum Śląskiego [Academy of the Silesian Museum]). Katowice: Muzeum Śląskie.

Zielonka, Zbigniew. 1994. *Geografia życia literackiego polskiego kręgu kulturowego na Śląsku* [Geography of the Literary Life of the Polish Cultural Circle in Silesia]. Słupsk: [Wyższa Szkoła Pedagogiczna].

Zientara, Benedykt. 1996. *Świt narodów europejskich. Powstawanie świadomości narodowej na obszarze Europy pokarolińskiej* [The Dawn of the European Nations: The Emergence of National Consciousness in Post-Carolignian Europe]. Warsaw: PWN.

Znaniecki, Florian. 1952. *Modern Nationalities*. Urbana, IL: University of Illinois Press.

Index